earning & caring

IN CANADIAN FAMILIES

earning & caring
IN CANADIAN FAMILIES

◆

RODERIC BEAUJOT

broadview press

CANADIAN CATALOGUING IN PUBLICATION DATA

Beaujot, Roderic P., 1946-
    Earning and caring in Canadian families

ISBN 1-55111-166-7

1. Work and Family – Canada.   I. Title.

HD4904.25.B42 1999   306.3'6'0971   C99-930710-X

BROADVIEW PRESS, LTD.
is an independent, international publishing house, incorporated in 1985.

North America
Post Office Box 1243, Peterborough, Ontario, Canada K9J 7H5
3576 California Road, Orchard Park, New York, USA 14127
TEL (705) 743-8990; FAX (705) 743-8353; E-MAIL customerservice@broadviewpress.com

United Kingdom and Europe
Turpin Distribution Services, Ltd., Blackhorse Rd.,
Letchworth, Hertfordshire, SG6 1HN
TEL (1462) 672555; FAX (1462) 480947; E-MAIL turpin@rsc.org

Australia
St. Clair Press, Post Office Box 287, Rozelle, NSW 2039
TEL (612) 818-1942; FAX (612) 418-1923

www.broadviewpress.com

Broadview Press gratefully acknowledges the support of the Ministry of Canadian Heritage through the Book Publishing Industry Development Program.

Cover design by Liz Broes, Black Eye Design.
Typeset by Liz Broes, Black Eye Design.

Printed in Canada

10 9 8 7 6 5 4 3 2 1

contents

list of tables

list of figures

list of boxes

preface

As a demographer I have concentrated on building a better understanding of reproduction, and one of the facts that drew my attention was the declining birthrate in Canada. In the 1970s the explanation for lower birthrates tended to be straightforward: fertility was going down because female labour-force participation was going up. Yet in the last 20 years labour-force participation has kept rising while fertility has been stable. Looking more closely, I found that child-bearing patterns had undergone another important transformation in the past two decades, as more women had been giving birth at more advanced ages. It became clear to me that understanding reproduction involved not only questions of labour-force participation, but also, and especially, the changing family context.

The most visible parts of the changing family are greater incidences of divorce and cohabitation or, more broadly, a greater fluidity of partners in their entry into and departure from relationships. For women, an increased involvement in paid work has provided greater flexibility for leaving unhappy relationships. Women's work outside the home has also introduced the need for men to make adjustments in their involvement in domestic work; the failure to do so can lead to further pressure on relationships. These changes, according to Beth Anne Shelton (1992: 159), have "created conflict between work and family for both women and men, even if the conflicts are felt more by women than men." This book is about the patterns and the changes in family relationships, about work inside and outside of the home, and the resulting conflicts and resolutions; it is about earning and caring.

Although the book comes out of my academic interests and work as a university professor, my personal life has also played a part in its formation. I was married in 1974, and when I began writing this book our three children were all teenagers. My publisher encouraged me to tell the story of how we came to better share in household tasks. Writing in a Christmas letter, my wife called it "the family testing the ideas of the book." My own title for this account would be "a man's perspective on things that women have always known."

The approach seemed so obvious when it was first suggested. Our household was about to become made up of two full-time workers and three full-time students, so why shouldn't we each take responsibility for one weekday supper? Of course the setting we chose for this discussion was well placed to encourage consensus: riding in the van with no work in sight. We all agreed that this endeavour would involve much planning, to be done on a weekly basis. We would have to determine who would cook what and when, so that the proper supplies could be purchased. There would also be the cleaning up, and we quickly agreed that the person preparing the meal would also clean up; let us get it over with once and for all. The remaining housework would be shared by specifying various Saturday jobs that family members could "choose" to do.

Our first experiences of this arrangement were positive. We all had the benefit of making choices regarding what we would eat. We shared, especially, the rewards typically passed to the cook, because positive comments on the meal itself are generally more forthcoming than comments on, say, properly setting the table or cleaning up. We also found from the beginning that young cooks — the children were then ages 10, 12, and 16 — needed mature assistants. Sometimes it can take more effort to help someone do it than to do it yourself. But the children learned to follow instructions that were typically rewritten each time, or they learned to get a bit of help with pre-cooking the night before. And the assistant could also get some credit. Over time, though, some of the excitement melts away, and the comments sometimes take on a less-than-positive flavour. The daughter says, "If he did such a good job on the windows, why do I see streaks?" Or "Why are you cleaning it again?" ... "Well, he did a good pre-cleaning." Someone will say, "Are we just having lasagna? Couldn't we have a salad?" Another says, "Dessert would be nice." Or "That's boring, we had that last week."

At first it was exciting to be deciding things together, but eventually the planning became just another job. The question "What would you like to cook?" typically draws a blank. Better for someone to plan out the meals, then the family members show more readiness to indicate which ones they choose to do. In a sense the planner is in control, but she (or he) can also take abuse, as in "There he goes, coordinating us all again." We hear both "Thank you, you're so good at it" and "You are taking over and not leaving me any space." We gain both the rewards of caring ("That was great steak") along with its potentials to generate dependency ("You are doing too much and making me feel incompetent"). But through it all we have learned about the tasks of the house, and especially that things do not happen by themselves.

I am convinced that the new models for the sharing of earning and caring are crucial to family well-being, reproduction, and gender equality. While the opportunities of women and men have become more equal in education and the labour force, it is the unlinking of gender and caring that will permit greater equality in daily life. To think about new models we need to know more about how earning and caring occur in Canadian families—and that is the purpose of this study.

acknowledgements

My first acknowledgement goes to the Social Science and Humanities Research Council, for two research grants: "Rationales used in the central decisions on marriage and child-bearing" and "Production and reproduction: economic, cultural and structural accommodations for children." I would also like to acknowledge the various graduate students who have been involved with this research: Cindy Cook, Zora Knezic, Beverly Matthews, Seth McFarlane, Edward Ng, Margaret Rylett, Godfrey St. Bernard, and Peter Smith. Some were dedicated interviewers and assistants; others also wrote their theses within the context of this research program.

Another major acknowledgement goes to Statistics Canada, the source of much of the data. I took advantage not only of Statistics Canada's quality and depth of information, but also of the civil service attitude to making the data available to researchers, and the bureau's own analyses provided in various publications.

Thanks also to the Demographic Unit at Stockholm University for having accommodated my visit in summer 1997. Members of the unit were most hospitable, and generous with their thoughts, helping me especially to understand the dynamics of their social policy. I found researchers in Sweden, and the society more broadly, much more involved with social policy, rather than seeing policy as something that comes down from above and to which one largely has a critical attitude. It struck me after the visit that to achieve its desired goals a society needs to take hold of its social policy, not simply leave it to politicians. I also learned that, while there are pressures for levelling of policy coming out of our globalizing world, we can also aspire to achieve higher standards rather than engage in a "race to the bottom."

Some parts of this book first saw the light of day in other contexts, although the pieces have since been much revised. The following journals and their editors are warmly acknowledged: *Canadian Review of Sociology and Anthropology, Canadian Journal of Sociology, Canadian Public Policy, Policy Options, Canadian Studies in Population, Journal of Comparative Family Studies.* A few items have also been taken from my previous books and chapters (Beaujot 1991, 1995, 1998). I also want to thank various colleagues who have reviewed or commented on my papers and presentations at the Canadian Population

Society, the American Sociological Association, the International Union for the Scientific Study of Population, the International Sociological Association, and the Demography Colloquium at Stockholm University.

Others helped me with the manuscript. Tony Haddad, Garnett Picot, Zenaida Ravanera, Zora Knezic, Ravi Verma, and Martin Cooke have derived tables from Statistics Canada data sets. I have benefited from collaboration with Peter Smith and Beverly Matthews (chapter 2), James Teevan, Ted Hewitt, Zenaida Ravanera, Fernando Rajulton, and Ellen Gee (chapter 3), Cindy Cook (chapter 4), Zora Knezic, Seth McFarlane, and Tony Haddad (chapter 5), and Edward Ng, Don Kerr, and Darcy Hango (chapter 7). Chapter 8 benefited from comments from Ken Battle and Livia Olah. Suzanne Shiel was always able to locate the needed references, and ever helpful in many ways. A very special note of thanks goes to Tony Haddad, who read the entire manuscript as it was being written. His comments were always encouraging, perceptive, and engaging. Several people were helpful in checking the galleys: Stephen Gyimah, Kimberley Hunt, Haider Mannan, Deborah Matthews, Sabrina Musilli, Toby Nash, Judy Lynn Richards, Oksana Shkurat, Reem Attieh Shultz, and Piotr Wilk. The comments from two anonymous reviewers for Broadview Press were also very helpful. Michael Harrison at Broadview provided vision and support when they were needed, while Robert Clarke honoured my work with the quality of his intrusive copy editing. Thanks to Barbara Conolly, Production Editor at Broadview and Liz Broes at Black Eye Design for their careful work.

introduction

On the level of the society, a demographer's main interest is in understanding the relationships between economic production and demographic reproduction, to use the terms of political economy. On the level of families, the central issues are earning and caring. These functions include the *instrumental* activities, especially making a living and maintaining a household, and the *expressive* activities of caring for each other, especially for children and other dependants. Thus the key question underlying this book is how to better understand the changing links between earning and caring.

To look at this meshing of earning and caring we need, then, to consider the activities of men and women both inside and outside of families. Changes are taking place in the broader society not only in labour-market participation but also in the opportunities for work and the kinds of work available. These changes, I believe, are undermining the basis of *complementarity* in the roles of women and men and promoting roles based more on *companionship*: that is, as jobs become more precarious and incomes slowly rise, it makes less sense for women and men to complement each other through specialized roles inside and outside of the household. Similarly, it makes more sense for relationships to be based on a companionship that maximizes the potential for the economic self-sufficiency of both partners.

Companionate relationships can provide better insurance against both the economic incapacity of a breadwinner and the instability of marriage bonds. In taking a close look at what is happening inside of families, for instance, we can focus on key questions: how do the activities of family and work accommodate themselves to two-income and lone-parent families? And what does this accommodation (or the lack of accommodation) mean for women, men, and children?

The concepts of earning and caring also help to place the activities of *both* women and men in their family context. The literature on families tends to ignore the male perspective. In their conclusion on research needs, Frances Goldscheider and Linda Waite (1991: 206) suggest, "The most critical omission in the study of the family in recent years is information, theorizing and even attention—to men." Once when I was returning from a conference on "Men in Families," a colleague quipped, "It must have been a short conference." For years I have been arguing that the census question on children "ever born," which is now asked of *all* women — not just those who are married or have been married — should be asked of men as well. That way analysts would be looking at child-bearing in the context of men's lives as well as women's lives. More important, children would then somehow "belong" to men as much as to women. Yet during professional discussions of census questions I hear statements like "Many men don't know the answer to that question" (followed by laughter). But surely most men know very well how many children they have brought into the world, and they can probably give a more reliable answer on the question than they can, say, to the census question of their income. Researchers also sometimes assume that men are more often removed from their families because men spend more time at work. This ignores the importance of earning the income necessary for buying food, which goes hand in hand with preparing meals and creating the associated family solidarity.

Books on the family do necessarily focus on women, mostly because much of the meshing between family and work has involved women. But these studies can give an incomplete picture, which may partly explain why so few men take college and university courses on family or gender. When researchers note, for instance, that women take the major responsibility for domestic tasks, they often do not sufficiently link this phenomenon to men's greater responsibility for the family income. More important, the insufficient attention paid to men may assume that men's family activities are not changing. While we must understandably pay attention to families with absent fathers, we should also study families in which fathers are present. Although it may be difficult to jointly analyze the family activities of women and men, the data on time-use can be a very useful aid, along with the consideration of both paid and unpaid work as productive activities.

Family literature also pays considerable attention to variations across families associated with socio-economic and socio-cultural considerations. While these are important areas of study, they are not the focus of this book. These studies tend to see family behaviour as an outcome of the surrounding socio-economic conditions. While there is much validity to this perspective, family behaviour also has tangible economic consequences. As Scott Coltrane (1995) observes, family type, and numbers of earners in particular, may become the most important basis of class standing. Solid middle-class standing may require two secure and well-paying jobs. That is, families that want to be successful somehow need to "get it together" in both work and family terms.

Although families do show considerable variation, we must not lose track of the commonalities. For instance, most adults at mid-life are in relationships, most are living with children, and most are working. The variation that I find most fruitful to study is the one associated with gender. Here we find that men are more likely to be in relationships while women are more likely to be living with children, and men's work is more continuous and full-time.

Given these pervasive gender considerations, perhaps I should indicate where I stand in this regard. Clearly, gender involves questions of differentiation and equality across individuals, both in relationships and in the broader society. But equality can take various forms. Alena Heitlinger (1993: 293) proposes that it can be based on *maternal feminism* (focus on enhancing the special needs of women), *assimilation* (women become like men), and *androgyny* (enlargement of the common ground between women and men). While feminists who consider the public area of life tend to see equality in terms of assimilation, this could mean that women would come to resemble men in the sense of paying little attention to the private side of life. Rather than seeking egalitarian roles through the abandonment of family-centred activities, could we instead work toward more equal combinations of work and family life? Given the biological differences, we do need to recognize the special needs of women, but maternal feminism exaggerates these differences and does not consider how structures might evolve that lead to men playing better caring roles. Androgyny has neither of these disadvantages, although even persons who push for androgyny have to account for the biological differences between women and men. But those differences do tend to be exaggerated. Take the concept of "opposite sex," for example. In most regards men and women are not opposites to each other, and we should not teach our children that "boys and girls" are opposites, like "up and down" or "black and white." In the coital act we could say that there is "something that goes inside and something outside," but even sexual expression shows much more commonality than oppositeness between women and men. Thus the policy orientation that I elaborate at the end of the book is based on enhancing the common ground between women and men, in terms of both earning and caring, at work and at home.

ORGANIZATION AND FOCUS OF THE STUDY

Too often, treatments of the family take a life cycle approach: home-leaving, forming relationships, having children, the empty nest, widowhood, death. This *micro* approach provides an easy organization, and it takes advantage of the insights of social psychology, but it assumes a normal developmental sequence. The not-so-normal stages—for instance, divorce and reconstituted families—are difficult to place in a developmental sequence, but they tend to represent an increased proportion of family experiences. Or, to take another example, the micro approach might introduce common-law unions as an additional stage in the developmental sequence, but without paying adequate attention to how cohabitation represents changes in the structure of relationships—changes that have altered not only premarital but also marital and postmarital relationships. The micro approach, then, is less able to incorporate broader social and structural factors that intersect with family behaviour.

My approach begins with the social demography and social organization of families, using this information as the basis for the study of family change and family issues. I view the crux of this *macro* question through the lenses of earning a living and caring for family—that is, the basic instrumental and expressive activities through which people maintain life and community both in families and in society. Although I don't ignore life-course and micro questions, I don't use them as the organizing principle. While I reflect, for instance, on the greater acceptability of sexual expression for young persons in the life-course stage of home-leaving and the formation of relationships, I place these decreased constraints on sexual activity in the context of the structure of the agreements and dependencies associated with those instrumental and expressive exchanges of earning and caring.

The tension between caring and earning provides a useful entry point for a study of contemporary family life and family policy. Earning and caring are the key activities of families, in effect the very basis for family. Families are made and maintained, after all, through the sharing of earning and caring. Conversely, any problems that arise with earning and caring become central to the family experience. For one thing, women's increased involvement in earning necessitates significant family adjustments. Both caring and earning take up much time and introduce conflicting priorities in the use of time. In addition, the relative value placed on these activities colours the accommodations made in individual families.

In particular, the models of earning and caring provide a clear picture of the family activities of women and men and especially reveal the extent to which symmetry is reached in the division of paid and unpaid work. The common denominator of time allows for a standard metric. In effect, the accommodations made in families in the division of paid and unpaid work can reveal the extent of gender asymmetry, both in families and in the broader society. As historian Gerda Lerner (1986: 217) observed, gender inequality and its structural manifestation as patriarchy can be an exchange of "submission for protection," or "unpaid labour for maintenance." Gender inequality can result from how family members make decisions, or accommodations, on the fundamental dimensions of earning a living and caring for others—in effect, the division of labour.

Much family literature focuses on the activities of women; there is often an underlying theme suggesting that men do not carry their weight in family matters, and consequently there is a tendency to blame men for family problems. Rather than having data mostly on women, researchers need to seek out data on both sexes if we are to determine what is unique to each, along with the extent of commonalities between men and women. This approach also permits us to conclude that family models based on complementary and specialized activities for women and men present significant difficulties. When the economic prospects of young men have deteriorated in relative terms, while the prospects for women have improved, family models based on a collaborative approach — of two earners who are co-providers and co-parents—provide a stronger insurance against the loss of the breadwinner's earning capacity and a possible unwillingness to share income with a (former) spouse.

Various authors have proposed that the greater flexibility in relationships can be read as a *de-institutionalization* of the family (Burgess, Locke, and Thomas 1963; Farber 1964). For instance, in his analysis of the long-term change in Britain, C.C. Harris (1983) observes that contemporary families are largely residential groups resulting from personal and private contracts between individuals. That is, families are no longer institutions in which relations between individuals arise from their membership in the family group or "the institutional is the pre-condition of the interpersonal." The perspective of earning and caring offers another way of interpreting this de-institutionalization. With less complementarity between women and men in relationships, and more instrumental independence, the continuation of family life is no longer contingent on the institution itself but rather on the continuance of the interpersonal relationships within families. Families are now based more on expressive than on instrumental interdependence (Scanzoni and Scanzoni 1976).

In taking up this vast and fascinating subject-matter I start by first introducing the study of families (chapter 1), drawing out the importance of gender (chapter 2), and then go on to concentrate on the main aspects of family change (chapter 3). What I think of as the core of the book is in chapters 4 and 5, which treat "Paid Work and Family Income" and "Unpaid Work and the Division of Productive Activities." Thereafter a specific treatment of child-bearing appears within the framework first of the structure of production and reproduction (chapter 6) and second of the family context of children and youth (chapter 7). The final chapter takes up the objective of discussing the policy dimensions associated with gender equality and changing family models.

ONE

Family and Work

Sociologists and other scholars have tended to study the private and public spheres of life separately. But we also need to analyze the interconnections of these spheres in order to look at the interrelations between what is happening both inside and outside of families. One way of doing this is to focus on what I call earning and caring. Another way is to consider the key life priorities attached to relationships, children, and work.

The classical theoretical approach, following Durkheim, Marx, Parsons, and Becker, has usually focused on the distinctions between the public and private spheres. Such studies have for the most part highlighted gender specialization as a means of handling the activities of earning and caring and viewed the family sphere as dependent on structures in the public sphere. Feminist scholars have focused on women's work as an important interconnection between production and reproduction, and they have considered family models based on companionship or collaboration rather than specialization and complementarity. This feminist approach, along with the use of common terms such as paid and unpaid work, earning and caring, or production and reproduction, has led to a deeper analysis of the relations between family and work. Crucial to this approach is the question of domestic work, along with discussions of the time spent in paid work and especially the total time spent in productive activities. In the end, as we shall see, the interplay of earning and caring has a major impact on the welfare of adults and children, gender dynamics, employment issues, population issues, and policy questions.

◆

A good deal of the writing on families emphasizes the distinction between the public world of work and the private world of families. We often believe that our family lives are private, and that they should be kept that way. Families are seen as a haven of retreat from the public world. It follows that sociologists should respect this privacy, and governments should not interfere. The outside world of paid work involves competitive struggles and rewards for achievement, but at home, in the enclosed circle of our families, we expect to be accepted and nourished for who we are, regardless of our achievements.

But the public world does intrude on our family lives. Television intervenes early in the lives of children, bringing outside values into the home. Parents often take their work home with them, or at least they bring home the frustrations of the outside world. In their book *New Families, No Families?* Frances Goldscheider and Linda Waite (1991: xiv) suggest that social priorities value the workplace over the home:

> These priorities lead many women to want to escape from a life built exclusively on family relationships and the tasks of maintaining them, since they see them as burdens and barriers to their accomplishments in the workplace, where their work is valued and appreciated. These priorities also lead many men to stay away from the home, and to acknowledge the importance of family and family tasks only when they are urging them on women. And these priorities are now leading a new generation of children to learn little or nothing about the home and its tasks. School work, friends, and even their favourite TV programs seem to be taking precedence over sharing domestic responsibilities with their parents.

Still, when people speak about what is important to them, they attach particular significance to the role of the family. People tend to be concerned about their homes and their other family members. They may say that their work outside of the home is simply a means of securing the well-being of their families. For instance, Evelyne Lapierre-Adamcyk (1990) concludes that most people place a high priority on three goals: to live in a rewarding and continuing relationship, to have and raise children, and to have secure and meaningful work. For most people, the issue is not to set aside one of these priorities but to somehow fit them together and to deal with the resulting conflicts.

But, in the first place, is it legitimate even to separate the public world of work from the private nature of families? While these two spheres of life may seem distinct, they are also closely interconnected; and in considering—and emphasizing—these interconnections here I mean to help point the way toward a rediscovery of the family itself, not as a haven of retreat from the world of work, but rather as a key link to the public sphere. Part of this also means rediscovering family work. Although it is unpaid and consequently not recognized in labour-force statistics, much very real, and constant, work occurs in families. Indeed, borrowing Meg Luxton's (1980) insightful title, I would suggest that we look at the work of the home as *More than a Labour of Love*.

CHANGING FAMILIES

In looking at the role of the family we can easily spot some areas of change in recent times: lower marriage rates, more cohabitation, later ages at the time of marriage, fewer children, more divorces, more lone-parent families, more people living alone, and a longer and more fluid period between the time of leaving home and of forming a new family. Life today seems to have greater biological predictability—in the form of higher life expectancy—but increased social uncertainty. The high life expectancy would seem to offer the potential of family stability through the increased possibility of the partners surviving together and consequently having fewer children orphaned or left with a single parent. But the observed reality is a marked fluidity across various forms of conjugal and parental relationships.

Conjugal relations vary between marriage and cohabitation, with various meanings and durations. In 1996 Statistics Canada even considered no longer gathering data on marriages and divorces, because these two categories were taking in a decreasing proportion of union formation and dissolution. Parental relations include various combinations of biological and social parenting: bi-parenting, single-parenting, and multi-parenting. While we have many statistics on lone-parent families, we do not know the extent to which this too may be a misnomer, because most children do have two existing parents. Less clear is the extent to which an absent parent remains relevant to the child's life.

This fluidity and diversity can be read as implying that something is wrong with families: that is, we are living at a time when families could be stable, yet they are anything but stable. The pessimistic view often looks inside families to see if something is missing, perhaps making comparisons to some ideal form of family life or to a past when families seem to have been more united and happier. William Goode (1963: 6) referred to this phenomenon as the "classical family of western nostalgia." It seems that some people concerned about the new independence of women and the effect of mother's employment on young children want to return to the 1950s—to a time when families were more stable and had more children, women were very dependent on male incomes, and men were dependent on their wives' services at home.

The concern about how families function means that people tend to have high standards for family life; they do not want to give up on the intimacy and commitment that only families can provide. In effect, marriage or at least continuing relationships are *in*, not only for heterosexuals, but also for lesbians and gays. Parenthood is *in*, not just in suburbia but also for middle-aged feminists (Skolnick 1991). Fathers too are a hot topic, with everything from the Promise Keepers movements to new-age fatherhood (Cherlin 1998). Simon Szreter (1996: 31) argues that much sexual behaviour, despite significant changes in attitudes regarding sexuality and child-bearing, can still be interpreted as a case of perpetuating "durable dyadic relationships and the rearing of children as two central sources of adult identity." People living alone also consider themselves as having families, and they resent it when the census counts them as "non-family persons."

While this kind of look inside of families can bring insights into family change and diversity, it is equally important to link family change to what is happening outside of families. Too often, reduced family harmony and stability is attributed to a single factor: women's greater involvement in the labour force. But other factors need to be considered. Among these are changes in the work environment itself, particularly the growth of the information and service economy, and less job security. To what extent do workplaces make accommodations for workers' family lives? Changes in the lives of children, especially their earlier entry into nursery schools and kindergartens and their longer periods of schooling, also play a part. So too does the availability of new gadgets, appliances, and services: automatic stoves and dishwashers, microwave ovens, or meals readily available outside of the home, even for those who are not away from home.

Other factors of life outside of families also demand better explanation. For instance, the average income of full-time women workers is almost 30 percent lower than the average income of full-time men workers. Why are the lives of men and women still so different in a public sphere seemingly committed to equal opportunity?

One analytical problem of connecting what is happening inside and outside of families is to find concepts or terms that are common to or usable in both the family and work domains. We speak of families in terms of privacy, commitment, intimacy, love, and dedication. We speak of work in terms of employment, contract, income, and benefits. Still, we do have terms that enable us to make more systematic connections: "production and reproduction," "paid and unpaid work," and "earning and caring," for instance. Arnlaug Leira (1992) suggests that sociological theorizing of the family tends to neglect the role of mothers as both providers and nurturers. Similarly, sociology often neglects the relationship between the providing and nurturing roles of fathers. Again, what sociological theory has most often done is to consider these work and family questions separately, whether defining them as production and reproduction, or earning and caring, or paid and unpaid work. Sociological theory needs, then, to address more closely the complex interrelationship between work and care.

The responses to survey questions about marriage and family life reveal the relationship between these areas of life. For instance, I was involved in a qualitative survey on family life in and around London, Ontario, asking if people preferred being at work or staying home (Beaujot 1992). Our question was, "Should a man/woman have to make career sacrifices to accommodate his/her family?" While some people could relate to the question, others saw dedication to a career as their way of benefiting the family. We also asked, "Now we would like to compare 'working at a job' to 'taking care of one's children.' Which do you think would be the most enjoyable activity?" Some respondents could address the question, but many found themselves unable to make a decision (they said, "both equal"). Some, again, felt that working at a job was a way of taking care of their children.

Other survey work on child-bearing and family questions suggests that, as Lapierre-Adamcyk (1990) found, most people in adult life want to live in a relationship, have children, and have a meaningful job. For some people, one or the other of these three is not a priority at all, and that too is an orientation to which we will want to pay attention. But for the majority, relationships, children, and work are all important and, indeed, difficult to prioritize. Most people face the challenge of ensuring that all three of these key areas of life turn out to their satisfaction. For instance, if at a given time one of the priorities needs to be sacrificed for the sake of the others, which will it be? In the abstract that may be an easy question to answer, but in reality it can be a fateful decision—a decision that engages one's future fate, and after which reshuffling or starting over becomes far from easy.

Research on one of these three core life priorities—marital satisfaction—finds that, counter to what might be expected, young children tend to detract from, rather than contribute to, the marital satisfaction of their parents (Larson, Goltz, and Hobart 1994: 278). Still, a small survey of professional women sought to determine what past decisions made them happiest. As professional women, they would probably not want to consider a life that sacrificed their careers. But the survey results showed that the happiest ones among them were living in marital relationships and had children, while the least happy were those who had never married (Larson, Goltz, and Hobart 1994).

THEORETICAL VIEWS ON FAMILY AND WORK

Classical perspectives

In part because they were living during a time of much change in the social organization of work, the pioneers of sociology tended to pay much more attention to questions of work than family. These pioneers—Durkheim, Marx, and Weber—were also men who were less interested in the sociology of family relationships. The subsequent studies in the sociology of the family tended to look inwards at families from perspectives of social psychology, socialization, and the life cycle. Conventional sociology has seen families as a locus of affection, as generators of shared values and consensus (Dickinson and Russell 1986: 3), once again tending to ignore the connections between the public and private spheres. For their part, women sociologists have added a new look at families and paid more sophisticated attention to the links between what is happening inside and outside of families. For instance, they have tended to understand the persistence of gender inequality as a function of the interplay between family and work.

As a 19th-century sociologist, *Emile Durkheim* (1858-1917) sought to understand the change in the modern world as a function of a move from mechanical to organic solidarity. That is, he believed that traditional societies had been held together by an almost mechanical sense of belonging and immediate common identity with the surrounding community. In contrast, modern societies were held together by a division of labour wherein individuals were interdependent through each other's specialized abilities. He even thought of the sexual division of labour as an example of organic solidarity. The sexual division of labour held families together: "Permit the sexual division of labour to recede below a certain level and conjugal society would eventually subsist in sexual relations preeminently ephemeral" (Durkheim 1960 [1893]: 60). If it were not for the interdependence between husband and wife, produced by a division of labour, sexual relations would only be of short duration.

Although Durkheim did not perceive families as being held together through caring, a common sense of identity, or in effect through mechanical solidarity, his interesting ideas about forms of solidarity could be extended into the realm of the family. As societies have been increasingly held together by organic interdependence, families are increasingly held together by mechanical solidarity. While we know little about the inner dynamics of families in premodern times, some historians have believed they were based on organic solidarity (Shorter 1975; Stone 1977; Ariès 1962): that is, families were not so much homes as places of work. We know that workplaces benefit from clear authority patterns and allocations of tasks. Could it be that the reduction of the sexual division of labour, which Durkheim feared, would enhance relationships based on common identity or emotional interdependence? Of course, emotional interdependence is not as strong a base as organic or instrumental interdependence, and in that sense Durkheim was right that relationships in this new world would be less durable.

Karl Marx (1818-83) sought to understand the change in societies by focusing on modes and relations of production (see Marx 1973 [1867]: ch. 25). In particular, the evolving and conflicting interests of different groups in society in the process of economic production were the basis for important class divisions. Marx also used the word "reproduction," but usually in its most inclusive sense, for instance in terms of the reproduction of the capitalist mode of production: that is, he sought to understand the process of reproduction of the social relations of production. While families had a role in this reproductive process, they were very much dependent on the more fundamental dynamics of economic production.

This approach can help us in understanding how the unpaid work of families, and of women in particular, is exploited for the benefit of economic production, generating a "surplus value" for the capitalist investment. For instance, the worker is regenerated, or fed, clothed, and housed, in the family and thus able to go back to work the next day. In addition, families guarantee the reproduction of workers from one generation to the next.

However, for Marx the sphere of economic production structured the totality of social relations, which meant that the reproductive or family sphere was subordinate. He tended to ignore this subordinate sphere, including the domestic or unpaid work that occurred in families (Kempeneers 1992: 64). Consequently, he did not pay much attention to the social relations that structured this unpaid work, including the gender relations in families; while he paid considerable attention to the general relations in society, he tended to downplay the reproductive role of families in the very continuation of the society. In downplaying this reproductive role, he also effectively downplayed the contributions of families, and women in particular, to the reproduction of the population, and in effect their contributions to the modes of production. In today's terms, he downplayed the contributions of unpaid work.

This intersection largely ignored by Marx—between modes of production and reproduction—involves an exchange of resources that manifests itself largely at the family level. Labour resources, or paid income, are exchanged for subsistence resources or unpaid regenerative activities (Ursel 1986: 153). For instance, early industrialization sometimes involved the employment of women and children in gruelling tasks. But the resulting states of exhaustion could undermine women's ability to reproduce, while the abuse of child labour could mean the depletion of a future labour resource. The exchange that subsequently took place at the family level, between men's paid work and women's unpaid work, brought a better balance of production and reproduction at the societal level. But it also meant that the women doing the unpaid work in the family did not have direct access to the means of their livelihood. Jane Ursel (1986: 153) concludes that women's access to subsistence was contingent on their entry into reproductive relations. Women and men thus became fully dependent on each other: women on men's paid work and income, and men on women's unpaid regenerative work.

Talcott Parsons (1902–1979) further emphasized the distinction between life inside and outside of families. Conceiving of society as a series of interdependent structures, Parsons (1949) argued that modern societies moved toward greater structural differentiation: increasingly separate structures performed distinct functions for the whole society and for the other structures in society. Given that one of these structures is the family, Parsons provides useful conceptual tools for linking the family to other structures. In particular, he argued that families came to perform fewer functions. In pre-industrial societies, the family was the main structure, taking care not only of the functions of reproduction of the population and childhood socialization, but also of economic production and care of the old and disabled. In modern societies families retained the roles of reproduction and part of childhood socialization, but workplaces, schools, hospitals, and nursing homes took over other functions.

In addition, other researchers argue that families came to play a larger role in another domain, the stabilization of adult personalities (Hutter 1988). Families became a place of nurture, removed from the competitive struggles of the workplace, which led in turn to the view of the private world of families versus the public world of work. This tendency also accentuated the functional importance of differential gender roles for social integration: women's role in the private sphere, and men's role in the public sphere. Parsons himself saw the segregation of gender roles as a functional necessity for marital stability and even for the well-being of society (Oppenheimer 1994: 295).

In some regards this functional perspective places considerable importance on families. But in other ways it relegates families to the private sphere, which is somehow less important than the public sphere, where families have lost their roles. The approach also disregards the agency of families, because it tends to see family change as a consequence of change in other social structures. While the Parsonian conception does start with the idea of interdependent structures, of which the family is one, its emphasis on the private side of family life tends to lose track of the link to the broader society. It also tends to focus on a family form based on a gender division of tasks, which is somehow seen as the only workable alternative.

In *A Treatise on the Family*, Gary S. Becker (1981) also conceptualizes a family form based on gender divisions. As an economist, Becker argues that families benefit from specialization in the roles of husbands and wives, and that this tendency also makes spouses interdependent. Spouses specialize because that is the most efficient productive strategy. The consequent gender-role specialization increases the interdependence of spouses. According to exchange theory, this means that both husbands and wives "gain from marriage" by taking advantage of the specialization of the other partner. Some have called this a "trading model" of marriage (Oppenheimer 1994).

This form of exchange is popularized in the idea that men and women should play *complementary* roles. Many people believe that it is "natural" for men and women to be different, and that their roles in marriages and families should somehow complement each other. This idea is often extended to the view that the relation of the family to the work world should involve specialization, with one partner chiefly responsible for the income side of family well-being, and the other partner more responsible for the nurturance side.

Becker fails to recognize the disadvantages inherent in this kind of specialization. As long as the marriage is durable and employment is secure, complementary roles can carry advantages. But if that is not the case, the partner who has specialized in the nurturing has a serious disadvantage in terms of economic self-sufficiency. In effect, the viability of this model depends on labour-market opportunities. If one sex has significantly lower opportunities, the model has its advantages. But when the opportunities are more even, the involvement of both partners in the outside work world gives the family a certain insurance against the loss of earning capacity of one of the spouses.

In addition, inequality in family roles can perpetuate gender inequalities in the world of work. Women in particular have less to gain from the complementary roles arrangement, and they are more vulnerable to the durability of the marriage. The model, then, appears limited because it builds on a narrow understanding of the relationship between families and the outside world. While that understanding includes the role of specialization, it does not consider questions of insurance and security, both for the family unit and for the individuals who have different roles within the family.

Feminist perspectives

The theoretical conceptions of Durkheim, Marx, Parsons, and Becker indicate the links between family and work, but they tend to focus on the differences between these two spheres. In *Le travail au féminin*, Marianne Kempeneers (1992) investigates both domains through the common concept of women's work. She argues that women ensure the connections necessary for the relative coherence of the overall social system; that is, they ensure the connections between the changing needs of production and reproduction. A key concept is work interruptions: the periods of time in which women and men move temporarily and voluntarily out of the paid workforce. Kempeneers proposes that women's *work interruptions* are an important way to study the interplay of the work and family spheres. Child-bearing and child-rearing are clearly factors in these interruptions, but they do not provide the total explanation. For instance, some women have interruptions but no children, while others have several children but minimal interruptions. Our understanding of interruptions clearly needs to recognize alternative models of work and alternate models of family arrangements.

Kempeneers proposes that family life and work life are closely tied, as indicated by the contemporary transformations occurring in both domains, and that a close analysis of women's work will indicate their necessary complementarity. For instance, a person's various individual decisions (to work, have children, work part-time, choose a given occupation) reflect a pattern of adjustment between the structures of production and reproduction. Kempeneers also explores the extent to which women's standard position of conciliator between the two domains is responsible for the persistence of significant gender inequalities. While the realm of women's rights and opportunities has shown considerable improvement in recent times, inequalities in work interruptions, income, part-time work, and occupations have persisted.

Kempeneers' approach, though, sidesteps some aspects of the links between family and work, including hours of work and variation across occupations. Are women more likely to find themselves in occupations that permit a better interface of family and work? Are these occupations the ones in which human capital and experience are less rewarded? Shouldn't men's work also be analyzed as contributing to family well-being? While Kempeneers calls for a redefinition of women's work, why not seek a redefinition of work itself? Looking at women's work as such has its advantages, as Kempeneers indicates, but considering women's work in relation to men's work can also be useful. We need to be open to the possibility that, as Carl Grindstaff (1991: 45) suggests, the next major change in familial life may revolve around a larger contribution on the part of men to the requirements of household maintenance and child care. The paid and domestic work of both women and men need to be analyzed, then, along with the social relations within which this work is accomplished.

Other theoretical perspectives

Other authors have argued for a different model of marriage and family solidarity. Claude Levi-Strauss (1971: 348) once observed, "The sexual division of labour is nothing else than a device to institute a reciprocal state of dependency between the sexes." While *reciprocal dependency* has the advantage of being a solid basis for continuity of the relationship, some authors have pointed out other ways of establishing durable relationships. Goldscheider and Waite (1991) use the concept of *companionate marriage*. By this they mean persons who are not only emotionally interdependent but also both involved in the instrumental activities of life (Rossi 1985). They are companions in holding life together. Children can provide some of the basis for this companionship, especially if the relationship involves shared parenthood.

In *New Families, No Families?* Goldscheider and Waite (1991) propose that unless new models of families become predominant, people will resolve to avoid marriage and parenthood and instead live alone or without families. They understand these "new families" as "women and men sharing family economic responsibilities as well as the domestic tasks that ensure that family members go to work or school clean, clothed, fed, and rested, and come home to a place where they provide each other care and comfort" (p. xiii). Instead of seeing people as achieving egalitarian roles through the abandonment of family-centred activities, Goldscheider and Waite consider the potential for a more egalitarian combination of work and family life. Valerie Oppenheimer (1994) uses the concept of a *collaborative model* in which people place a high value on the marriage relationship, but which also has a built-in instability due not only to the complexities of the collaborative endeavour associated with family and work, but also to the greater ability of each partner to seek alternatives. In effect, these conceptions argue that we need to interpret the changes observed in marriage, fertility, and divorce as a matter of the restructuring of gender relations, both at work and at home.

Counter to Becker's notion that marriages work best if they are based on a trading model involving specialization and exchange, Oppenheimer (1994) argues that the employment of wives does not represent a threat to the family as a social institution but is, rather, a highly adaptive family strategy. In particular, having more than one family member in the labour force provides an insurance mechanism against the economic incapacity of a single breadwinner. In contrast, extreme sex-role segregation increases the vulnerability of individuals and families. John Conway (1997) expresses a similar idea when he speaks of "a joyous funeral" for the patriarchal family.

These conceptions, though, seem to exaggerate the stakes in terms of "new families vs. no families." For some people, traditional models of distinct and complementary roles for women and men remain viable, while others adopt alternatives that are intermediate between complementarity and equality. Consequently, we will want to consider various models of families in terms of the involvement of men and women in work and domestic tasks. In addition, the new families based on companionship are not without their own problems, and there are always conflicts in the interface of work and family. While companionate marriages involve more gender equality in the work world, they probably also involve lower rates of marriage and child-bearing, along with more divorce (Bumpass 1993). Companionate marriages may mean, in the end, that more and more people are left out of important life priorities involving relationships and children. It could be that many families will attempt to build on both an exchange of specialization *à la* Becker and companionship *à la* "new families." We will return later to these inherent contradictions.

One final theoretical orientation concerning the link between family and work comes from A.F. Robertson in *Beyond the Family: The Social Organization of Human Reproduction* (1991). We are too prone to thinking of reproduction, Robertson says, as a narrow or even private question, but reproduction is something that goes beyond the family domain. He argues that organizing reproduction involves lifetime and complicated relationships among many people. Because it includes both child-bearing and child-rearing, it also involves not only socialization at home but also at school, through the media, and via other institutions. Similarly, the care of children includes the food and remedies provided not only at home, but also at the marketplace and in health clinics. Consequently, Robertson (1991: 4) states, "A wide variety of organizations—banks and schools, factories and clinics, mortgages and retirement communities, even governments and political parties—are all involved in various ways in the vital tasks of reproduction, producing new individuals, rearing them to adult maturity, caring for the aged, and replacing the dead."

In effect, the inherent nature of families has much to do with the matching, over the life cycle, of productive endowments and consumption needs (Arthur 1988). While productive endowments are stronger at certain parts of the life cycle, consumption needs are present throughout life. This lack of overlap between productive endowments and consumption needs over the life cycle is at the basis of many social institutions, including banks, mortgages, and even the monetary system.

The traditional perspectives that began with Durkheim, Marx, and Parsons tended to separate the sociology of work from the sociology of families. Durkheim and Marx were primarily interested in what was happening in the sphere of production, where they observed new forms of solidarity around the division of labour and new class formations within capitalism. Parsons argued that families had lost some of their functions to the public sphere. The feminist perspectives suggested alternative conceptions of families based on companionship or collaboration rather than interdependence. Feminists have also paid more attention to the links between the spheres of family and work. Consequently, in the study of families feminist perspectives have borrowed some terms from the sphere of work or production: "family work" and "unpaid work," for examples. Conversely we now also need to borrow terms from the family or reproduction sphere to look at work or production, and we need to appreciate that work activities serve reproductive or caring needs.

THE CRUCIAL QUESTION OF DOMESTIC WORK

In interpreting long-term family change, Goldscheider and Waite (1991) speak of two revolutions. The first revolution dates back to the industrial transformation of society, which produced separate public and private spheres, with home and family becoming more private. The second revolution is contemporary and involves social priorities that value the workplace over the home not only for men, but also for women and children. With this second revolution a major concern becomes "Who will look after the home?" This concern raises the issue of the appropriate sharing of domestic work by women, men, and children.

Given a situation in flux, and resulting difficulties of measurement, researchers have held strongly opposing views on how much or how little change is occurring on the domestic front (see chapter 5). Nevertheless, it is clear that the work that goes on in households, including the social realities of daily care, must be taken seriously (Fox 1997).

Given households made up of male and female couples with children, we might expect to find that wives' employment circumstances would alter their husbands' contributions to domestic work. In part because employed wives simply have less time, men would seemingly take up some of the slack and do more. This expectation of greater male involvement in domestic work would also follow from the wives' greater resources and power to influence outcomes at home, and from beliefs about how things *should* be shared in couples. But in a thorough review of "Gender in Families," Linda Thompson and Alexis Walker (1989) concluded that the imbalance in household work remained intact in the 1980s. Their literature review found that a wife's employment situation was not having a direct bearing on the amount of family work done by the husband. Wives do cut back, especially in child care, but husbands do not increase their contributions. While there are prevalent views that housework, and especially child care, should be shared equally, this goal is far from realized.

Work is a larger part of men's identity, while women are more likely to see work as a means of responding to family needs. Consequently, discontinuity is more the rule than the exception in women's work lives, and both men and women are ambivalent about women as co-providers. They conclude that "the struggle about whether or not wives should work outside the home is not over." Larry Bumpass (1991) also finds considerable disagreement within couples regarding the amount of work wives should do.

Considerations of a wife's employment, time availability, resources, conscious ideology, and power, then, do not account for the inequity in the division of family work. Thompson and Walker conclude that gender, more than any other factor, accounts for this inequality. At the same time they observe that less inequality exists in the division of domestic work if a wife's paid work is defined as a necessity for the family. In addition, women who define themselves as providers are more likely to see their husbands' family work as being inadequate.

Other studies have reached similar conclusions. Looking at *The Workings of the Household* in the United Kingdom and the United States, Lydia Morris (1990) concluded that despite changes outside of the household, no fundamental change had occurred in gender relations in the household. Considering studies in the 1960s and 1970s showing that women were doing a total of 15 hours more work per week than men, Arlie Hochschild (1989: 3) aptly entitles her book *The Second Shift*. These extra 15 hours per week make up a month of 24-hour days in one year, or a "thirteenth month" of women's extra work. A select sample of couples with young children showed that wives were much more likely to be concerned about the conflict between work and family, and that both wives and husbands felt the second shift to be the wives' problem. Then too, using data from the United States on sharing of tasks from the early 1980s, Goldscheider and Waite (1991) found that wives who are not in paid employment do 75 percent of domestic work, while those who do outside work for 50 hours a week do 56 percent of domestic work. While the findings show that employment alone does not make a significant difference in women's domestic burdens, full-time employment in better-paying jobs along with career commitment does have an impact.

Important debates about proper measurement surround these kinds of studies. One question is whether to measure absolute time or relative share. The reduction in a wife's relative share of domestic work appears to be less a function of the increase in her husband's total hours of housework than it is a decrease in the wife's total hours (Bumpass 1993). Husbands do not make up the slack. Rather, wives accommodate their own lack of time by doing less and lowering the standards or simply by buying services. Interestingly as well, when husbands do take on more domestic work, children do less.

Perhaps rather than comparing time spent on domestic work, we should compare the total work inside and outside the household, paid plus unpaid. The differences between wives and husbands reflected in total work time are typically found to be smaller (Feree 1991a). For example, in a sample of married couples with children, from the 1987-88 U.S. National Survey of Families and Households, Masoko Ishii-Kuntz and Scott Coltrane (1992) found that husbands were approaching half of the total work when wives were employed full-time. The data from the 1986 and 1992 Canadian time-use surveys indicate rough equality in the averages of total work for men and women. In 1986, averaged over a seven-day week, men aged 15 and over in Canada spent 7.5 hours of "productive time" on paid work, education, and unpaid work (domestic work, plus child care, shopping, and services). In comparison, women spent an average of 7.4 hours of productive time (Harvey, Marshall, and Frederick 1991: 31). Considering only those employed with a partner and children under five years of age, men did an average of 10.1 hours of work per day compared to 9.8 hours for women (Harvey, Marshall, and Frederick 1991: 117). The 1992 comparison for employed persons with a partner and young children shows 9.4 hours for men and 9.8 for women (Che-Alford, Allan, and Butlin 1994: 40).

These small differences in averages show considerable variation across various types of couples. In addition, measuring time-use, and especially incorporating any measure of the intensity of work, are difficult exercises. For instance, women's domestic work can involve doing more than one task at the same time, such as cooking while simultaneously looking after children. The most difficult task, and the one that may be the most difficult to share, is the task of organizing and planning the work. Besides, women overwhelmingly take the major responsibility for daily domestic tasks such as cooking, cleaning, and housekeeping (Le Bourdais and Sauriol 1998a).

In *Feeding the Family: The Sociology of Caring as Gendered Work*, Marjorie De Vault (1991) provides a good description of the various parts of meal preparation that are difficult to observe: remembering schedules and food preference, setting meals that are acceptable and pleasing to everyone, monitoring supplies, improvising, responding to wishes and moods, and creating a period of order and pleasant sociability that is the ideal of the family meal. Much of this planning and co-ordination cannot easily be shared, and time-use surveys may not even measure this work because it often occurs in the midst of other activities.

In addition to the actual division of tasks, researchers have also considered the perception of fairness. Women, but not men, see fairness in task allocation as relevant to marriage viability (Bumpass 1991). It may even be that a man's involvement in domestic work is an indicator of his commitment to the relational aspects of the marriage (Thompson 1991). At the same time, many women show a persistence of traditional expectations, and the preferred paid work hours of U.S. women are only three-quarters that of men (Bumpass 1993).

THE INTERPLAY OF FAMILY AND WORK: THE BROADER RELEVANCE

The interplay of earning and caring feeds into a number of important sociological questions. Sociology studies the organization of economic activity and the socialization of children as key considerations in the continuity, change, and differentiation of societies. In effect, both economic production and social reproduction are essential to the survival of any society. Here we will focus briefly on how this interplay connects to individual welfare, gender dynamics, employment issues, population issues, and policy questions.

Individual welfare

As we have seen, when it comes to major life goals, most people want to live in a relationship, have children, and have a meaningful job (Lapierre-Adamcyk 1990). In his 1995 national survey, Reginald Bibby (1995: 2-4) similarly found that over three-quarters of the respondents wanted "family life" and "being loved." These were higher priorities than "a comfortable life," "success," and "a rewarding career," although half to two-thirds of respondents nonetheless spontaneously mentioned these goals. At ages 18-34, 82 percent wanted family life and 59 percent wanted a rewarding career, and the gender differences were not significant across these goals. These findings clearly suggest that the interplay of family and work is important to the dynamics of individual welfare.

In her presidential address to the Population Association of America, Waite (1995) outlined a number of possible answers to the question "Does marriage matter?" Focusing on the benefits to individuals, she effectively thought of marriage as an "insurance policy." Marriage promotes healthy behaviours; married people take fewer risks, such as heavy drinking and reckless driving, and they are less prone to unhealthy behaviours, such as poor eating habits. Behaviours that promote greater life expectancy are particularly important to men in marriage. For their part, women can benefit from marriage in their material well-being, including income, assets, and wealth. In addition, marriage provides a ready network of help and support. For Waite, the review of the evidence suggests that the consequences of marriage for individuals are unambiguously positive: better health, longer life, more sex (and more satisfaction with it), higher earnings, and in general more wealth. Compared to living alone, marriage provides the opportunity for economies of scale. It encourages a sharing of economic and social resources, and it provides a way of connecting to others. For example, the family meal provides not only replenishment, but also sociability and a sense of close personal identification with loved ones (De Vault 1991).

The welfare of children clearly depends on the earning and caring activities of parents. Leira (1992) defines motherhood in terms of both earner and caregiver, with caregiving including socialization, nurturing, and rearing. Her focus is on mothers, but arguably the aspects she ascribes to motherhood could be generalized as parental roles. Clearly, children depend on both the provider and nurturing roles of parents, yet this dual dependence is a relatively neglected topic in the sociological theorizing on the family.

The consideration of earning and caring also provides a perspective on the relationships and families that do not enhance the welfare of specific individuals. While families can be a source of insurance against the hazards of life, sometimes too family life can produce its casualties, and individual welfare may depend on an escape from a family situation. Families can be areas of abuse, serious conflict, and neglect or inadequate economic provision. In *The Canadian Family in Crisis*, Conway (1997) focuses on the harm done to children, women, and men in families. Children can be hurt by abuse and neglect, women can suffer from double burdens, and men can suffer from the estrangement of their children. Conway argues that a shift from a patriarchal to an egalitarian model of the family would relieve these crises. But his conclusion ignores the possibility of the continuing points of conflict and cleavage between the worlds of work and family, and consequently between the provider and nurturing roles of parents. Despite its advantages, a more egalitarian family also means that spouses become more independent and therefore more prone to separation. While separation can be in the interest of at least one of the spouses, it is not always beneficial to children's welfare.

Other authors have highlighted further problems associated with the modern family, especially for women. In a provocative book, Pat Armstrong and Hugh Armstrong (1994) argue that the double ghetto of segregated work and isolation in families limits women's potential. Questions related to families presented some of the most difficult stumbling blocks at the United Nations Fourth World Conference on Women held in Beijing in 1995. In effect, sociology views family as an institution ranging from the highly oppressive and anti-egalitarian to immensely liberating (Popenoe 1988). In addition different family members will almost always view the realities of family life differently (Fox 1997). As in Longfellow's rhyme about the little girl, for the family too, "When it is good it is very, very good, but when it is bad it is horrid."

Gender dynamics

If you look at women's wages, Waite (1995) argues, you see no benefit resulting from marriage. While you might say that men receive wage premiums if they are married, women pay marriage penalties in the form of lower hourly wages. The paid work of men and women has its well-known differences, such as proportions working full-time and average income. Yet the most significant difference involves married women. This difference has sometimes been called the "marital status suppressor," in the sense that it is married women who suffer the disadvantage. For women, marriage and having children both enhance the likelihood of work interruptions; for men, these conditions reduce the likelihood of work interruptions (Cook and Beaujot 1996).

Family issues play a significant part in the persistence of gender inequality. While the public sphere has progressed in the direction of equal rights and opportunities, the private institution of the family has tended to retain the older gender differences in the form of the behavioural roles of wives and husbands, mothers and fathers, and in sex-typed socialization of children. Coltrane (1998b) observes that the uncoupling of gender and caring is key to enhancing equality.

The gender differentiation in families may even orient women and men toward preferring certain jobs over others. The choice of an occupation can be a coping strategy, and while these strategies may well be beneficial to the welfare of families and children, they can pose problems for women and children when marriages are not viable. The gender distribution of domestic roles is clearly linked to gender differences in the work sphere: in labour-force participation, type of work, extent of part-time work, and levels of pay.

Kempeneers (1992) articulates the gender issue by observing that women largely provide the "junction" between work and family, between the changing needs of production and reproduction. Women are at the centre of the transformations of the structures of family and work. In other words, women largely bear the costs of the inevitable conflict between these two areas of life. Kempeneers thus seeks to analyze women's oppression by way of their dual roles in work and family. Similarly, Carol Baines, Patricia Evans, and Sheila Neysmith (1991) highlight the importance of *women's caring* for the understanding of gender inequality.

Lest we think these dynamics are easily changed, Leira (1992: 3) proposes that the "gender differentiated family is a central character of welfare state design." The welfare state, she would argue, depends on women's unpaid domestic work as a basic form of welfare provision for young and elderly dependants. The welfare states that have evolved, especially in the second half of the twentieth century, are based on the premise that the state has a responsibility for the welfare of individuals. In particular, the state has a responsibility for providing for and nurturing persons unable to look after themselves. But the welfare state clearly depends on families to provide most of this support, especially for dependent children; the state supports these providing and nurturing activities by building its welfare provisions on the model of a gender-differentiated family. Consequently welfare states have reinforced women's caring activities (Baines, Evans, and Neysmith 1991). For instance, they assume that most nurturing involves mothers who become dependent on their husbands' incomes, and as a result the state provides family benefits to workers to help support family well-being.

Without focusing specifically on welfare states, Ursel (1986) also argues that the interplay of productive and reproductive roles provides a key to the subordination of women. The extent of women's access to the means of livelihood is contingent on entry into particular reproductive relations. Ursel shows how labour laws in Ontario over the period

1884-1913 sought to protect women from difficult work, but in so doing the same laws limited the hours women could work, the places of work, and the kind of work they could do.

Policies on pay equity and employment equity have since attempted to ensure equal access to employment, for women and men, but these gender-symmetric public regulations face gender-typed family behaviours. For instance, after reviewing various factors in the division of housework Thompson and Walker (1989: 857) conclude, "More than any other factor, gender accounts for the amount of and allocation of housework and child care." This condition continues despite survey results showing that over half of wives and husbands believe that housework should be shared equally and over 80 percent believe that child care should be shared equally.

Clearly, the interplay of family and work is a crucial question in gender dynamics. While a variety of considerations, from biology to culture, help to explain gender differences, the interplay of family and work provides the basic framework for an analysis of these questions (see chapter 2). In her treatment of *The Creation of Patriarchy*, Gerda Lerner (1986: 217) also attaches particular significance to a "paternalistic dominance" that exchanges "submission for protection" and "unpaid labour for maintenance."

The difference between models of families based on complementary vs. egalitarian roles is also a key to these gender issues. Goldscheider and Waite (1991: 1) see a restructuring of male-female relationships, both at work and at home, "in which men are increasingly expecting their wives to share in economic responsibilities, and women are increasingly expecting help with domestic tasks." (See chapters 4 and 5 for a discussion of the extent of this restructuring.)

Dynamics of work and employment

Focusing on work issues means paying attention to both labour-market organization and the restitution of labour. We often pay insufficient analytic attention to how homes and families, on a daily basis, regenerate the labour potential of workers. For instance, the family changes in the 1950s, which accentuated the domestic roles of women, came during a time when the schooling of children was being extended. Wives were not only enhancing the potential of their husbands as workers but also providing the home base for a longer period of childhood dependency, and consequently they were investing in children's future earning potential. This shift stood in contrast to the period of early industrialization, with its prospect of increased female and child employment that both presented difficulties with regard to women's reproductive prospects and depleted the future labour potential of children. In effect, an immediate "use" of labour undermines the potential for engendering future workers.

Especially when it is defined as a career, work can require such total dedication that matters of regeneration are left to others. The image of monks comes to mind—celibates able to devote themselves totally to intellectual tasks under the assumption that others will look after the cooking and cleaning. A career involves not only a long period of educational investment but also, to become properly launched, a period of hard work. Clearly, a person would need to keep dedication to children and family at a minimum to achieve these goals. Hochschild (1989) concludes that careers involve rules made up for the male half of the population.

Some work environments provide greater opportunities for an interface with family responsibilities. These opportunities relate not only to the hours of work, but also to a flexibility in work schedules and the extent of support for the worker's family roles. Kempeneers (1987) proposes that the characteristics of given sectors of the workforce can be described according to how they handle the family/work crunch. For instance, she explores how differences in work structures (jobs, professions, careers) partly explain the variations in women's work interruptions, after taking family life-cycle questions into consideration. These same structures could also help to account for variations in men's family involvement, particularly their involvement in domestic work.

Various other transformations of paid work are also worth exploring, particularly the growth of the service sector and increased employment insecurity. Services involve inherent flexibility, compared to the primary and secondary sectors of the economy. The increased insecurity comes with "non-standard" employment: part-time work, irregular hours, holding two jobs, studying and working at the same time, and especially the prospect that a given job will not last until retirement (Foot and Stoffman 1996). These conditions encourage a family strategy that moves away from depending on one breadwinner and seeks the additional insurance of more than one earner. More wives move into the paid workforce, as a means of security not only against the possible breakup of the marriage, but also against the fragility of the husband's paid work.

Population issues: child-bearing and child-rearing

Clearly, children are a key to understanding the structure and organization of families, although many analyses focus on the interests of adults and on how adults organize their lives. The biological and social fact of children's dependency, however temporary, brings a crucial importance to the earning and caring roles of parents. From the point of view of the society and the work that needs to be done to ensure its future, we must pay attention to the labour involved in reproducing the species in history, as well as to the distribution of associated costs assumed by mothers, fathers, other relatives, or the society more broadly. Alice Rossi (1977: 24) proposes that mothers' bonding with the newborn facilitates species survival. She argues that the male attachment to their offspring is a learned role.

Societies have an obvious interest in fertility, in questions of who is responsible for reproducing the species and how many children are being born. These matters are too important to be left to individuals alone. While it is often seen as a very private matter, reproduction is necessarily a public question, and the moral dilemmas of reproduction are as old as society itself. Reproductive behaviour is grounded in both self-interest and social appropriateness. As Robertson (1991: 2-4) explains, reproduction is a vital process that must be controlled and manipulated, and it is a basic determinant in a society's development. For instance, making parents, and mothers in particular, carry the costs of child care is a means of social control over excess fertility. More broadly, the issue of fertility presents a unique point of entry to the study of the evolution of societies, and especially the articulation of productive and reproductive roles.

Jean-Claude Chesnais (1987) suggests that accommodations made between production and reproduction have come largely at the expense of reproduction, and this optimization of production could endanger the future of societies. For instance, Nancy Folbre (1994) suggests that modern economies are well below the level of caring needed to reproduce future members of society. This lack of investment in the future shows itself as a greater interest in the concerns of the elderly than in the concerns of children (Beaujot 1991: 217-18). While people may work to a more advanced age when there are fewer young workers, and immigrants can become a substitute for births, these accommodations are not without their problems. For instance, the societies that have the longest life expectancies and the highest average ages are also those in which retirement occurs at the youngest ages.

The study of fertility also has the advantage of a large body of literature, at least in comparison to the sociology of the home. The availability of reliable data on child-bearing permits comparisons over time, across subgroups, and with other societies. For instance, the noted differences in child-bearing behaviours based on levels of education, plus people's strong tendency to find partners with similar levels of education, have significant implications for the creation of inequality for children and consequently for establishing the profile of social security needs.

Robertson (1991) further argues that reproduction is the driving force behind the organization of material production. Parents at least partly tend to dedicate their earnings to the well-being of their children. More broadly, various social units including families have demographic strategies, involving births, marriages, migration, and the inevitability of deaths, that enable them to face the evolving material conditions and which in turn shape these material conditions (Cordell et al. 1993).

Policy issues

States have evident interests in economic production for matters of economic growth, employment, and trade. The state's interest in family questions, or the caring role more broadly, may be less obvious, but it is equally important. In effect, the broad question is to ensure both achievement and community, or a balance between "achievement in work and intimate involvement with other human beings" (Rossi 1977: 25).

A welfare state is a system, by definition, that aims to protect the health and well-being of all its citizens. The state, then, takes an interest in the caring role. Private enterprise also takes an interest in the caring role, because it confers various benefits to the families of workers. Charities and non-governmental organizations also play caring roles. Still, families carry the largest burden in caregiving, especially when it comes to children. State policy therefore has an interest in supporting the caring roles of families, charities, private enterprise, and government agencies.

While states have an interest in both economic production and demographic reproduction, they attach rights and benefits more to earning than to caring. The provider roles are linked to rights and benefits such as health insurance, unemployment insurance, workers' compensation, and pensions. The nurturing roles are linked mostly to family benefits. In Canada these benefits do not apply universally; that is, they do not go to everyone based on the amount of caring done by a given family or person. For instance, the state does not provide universal family allowance or day care and clearly has no pensions specifically for parents. Instead, it bases family benefits on the earner roles: people become eligible for family benefits if the earner roles leave the family "in need."

A key issue to consider, then, is how caring and earning are integrated into the welfare state benefit and entitlement system (Leira 1992). What social rights do people gain access to based on their earning and caring roles? Given that more rights and entitlements appear to be associated with earning, and that earning and caring are divided by gender, what we have, according to Leira, is a gendering of citizenship.

In effect, considerable ambivalence surrounds the question of state support for the caring role of families. On the question of day care, for instance, the state's role is both welcomed and contested. Some argue that it is best to have families look after child care, and others argue for a state role. But while ensuring that parents carry the costs of child care can be a fertility-control mechanism, when fertility proves inadequate for necessary population growth the state will need to remove some of the burden from parents. This issue of the division of responsibility for child care between the public and private spheres is crucial, especially for welfare states. The provision of care by formal state mechanisms and informal family relations also provides an important example of the links between the public and private spheres.

Another related issue is the extent of state support for the dual roles of parents as providers and nurturers. State efforts, for instance, can choose to support complementary arrangements that have fathers as earners and mothers as carers, or they can support egalitarian arrangements of co-providing and co-parenting. We are sometimes caught between an acceptance of gender-typed family behaviour and increasingly gender-symmetric public regulations (Nasman 1997). For instance, workplace-oriented policies that provide specific benefits for mothers (sometimes defined as parents) often assume gender-typed family behaviour. When the tax system allocates tax advantages to men who have dependent wives, it promotes traditional complementary roles for husbands and wives. Similarly, states and employers also promote this same model when they provide family benefits to spouses of workers. But other policies, especially employment equity and pay equity, promote the egalitarian model. Policies can also promote both models, despite the inherent contradictions. For instance, in promoting women's employment without providing a universal day-care policy, the government encourages families to seek child care in the informal economy. Some families, then, can live by egalitarian models precisely because they can obtain cheap child care from other families who live by traditional models. In analyzing the situation in Norway, Leira (1992: 132) concludes that this is exactly the case. The dual-earner family is therefore dependent on the conservation of a more traditional family form; the two forms are interdependent.

Leira goes on to argue for the importance of analyzing the agency of mothers. For instance, women's deliberate entry into paid work, along with the various demands that arise from this role, led to a state response in terms of policies for child care, parental leaves, and part-time work. Again taking the example of Norway, Leira (1992: 97) considers the nature of women's agency: "Women born in the first decades after World War II came to introduce new models of behaviour in almost all fields of everyday life. The most dramatic changes were seen in new approaches to motherhood. The modernization of motherhood encompasses women's increased control over fertility and social reproduction, it is manifested in family and everyday life, and in economic and political participation."

CONCLUSION

While sociologists often study the family as a private domain, I propose here to study the links between the public and private spheres. Traditional sociology has separated off work from family, production from reproduction, paid from unpaid work, or earning from caring. But studying the links between these activities can provide a basis for a rediscovery of the essential role of the family in society and for an understanding of gender inequalities. These links are a key to the behaviours of adults, who give high priority to both family and work, and to children, who depend for their well-being on the earning and caring roles of parents. The links are also a key to both the material production of the economy and the demographic reproduction of the population. Finally, the links are a key to the social-security policies of welfare states that look to enhance self-sufficiency, promote families as a basic form of security, and ensure a societal safety net. Although the welfare state is under attack and was, perhaps, diminished in the 1990s, the state maintains an interest in collective and individual welfare.

The sociology of earning and caring is complex because of the co-existence of alternative models and associated value orientations. For instance, the pressure of traditional expectations can clash with the interests in equality. Or the view that having children is a personal decision for which parents should carry the responsibility can clash with the view that children are part of a larger society that needs to absorb more of the costs associated with them. When it comes to gender roles, some people support the model of complementary roles—that it is natural for men and women to take up distinct roles and thus complement each other in family and work—while others support a family model based on equality in the responsibility of spouses, especially in parenting. Consequently, many people believe in an equal sharing of tasks, especially for child care, yet their behaviour manifests distinct activities for women and men.

While both earning and caring, along with paid and unpaid work, are central to the well-being of children and families, inevitable conflicts arise between these two major adult activities. State policy can attempt to reduce the tension through a better recognition of both roles and encouraging specific improvements, such as supporting family-friendly work environments. Still, individuals and groups will undoubtedly seek to displace the costs of the conflict onto others. For instance, men may push these costs onto women, and richer people may push the costs onto domestic servants, or workplaces onto families, providing part of the dynamics of social inequality.

The Gender Context

The involvement of the sexes in production and reproduction is central both to the persistence and changing nature of gender relations. Here, to set the context for our study of family and work, we start with definitions of gender and the relevance of the concept to structural differentiation in society as related to questions of resources, autonomy, and power. Following a brief consideration of male/female differences in various domains, the core of the chapter focuses on explanations of persistence and change in gender differentiation. Are these differences a function of economic questions, in particular the involvement of the sexes in relations of production? Or are they a function of the barriers and opportunities that are represented in cultural or symbolic systems? In particular, what should be the relative priority of these two explanations?

We also explore various explanations related to the link between earning and caring, taking advantage of a definition of patriarchy that not only incorporates material and cultural questions but also focuses on the exchange between paid and unpaid work in households. The division of paid and unpaid work, I would argue, is a key means through which we "do gender" at the levels of couples and the society.

WHAT ABOUT GENDER?

Research in the area of male-female differences initially adopted the overriding concepts of *sex* and *sex roles*. But the word sex not only has a biological connotation but also draws excessive attention to sexuality at the expense of other human differences and interactions. The idea of sex roles gives the impression of relatively fixed categories, comparable to the roles of parent, student, or manager—roles learned and enacted in specific contexts. The focus on male and female roles also accentuates the differences rather than the similarities between women and men. Consequently, these concepts can bring us both to pay less attention to the diversities among women and among men and to downplay the similarities between women and men.

For its part, the concept of *gender* has been adopted to refer particularly to the social, rather than biological, construction of male/female relations. Thus we can define gender simply as what it means to be a male or female at a specific time and place. Gender is social in the sense that it refers to how we think someone should look, act, or feel. This usage allows us to move beyond *gender as difference* and to consider *gender as organizer* or a structure of society and *gender as interactive process* (Lucia Gilbert 1993). As an organizer, gender has an analytic status similar to social class or race. That is, it is an organizing principal of society as seen in the differential association of men and women with the structures of power and leadership, or the differential expectations that employers have for women and men, or the prevalent views on the relative abilities of men and women. We need, then, to recognize the gendered nature of social life. As an interactive process, gender is ever-present in social interactions. Instead of being fixed roles enacted in specific contexts, the relations between women and men occur continuously, and the categories are fluid. As Linda Thompson and Alexis Walker (1989: 865) put it, women and men "do gender" all the time, in all situations: "Rather than an individual property or role, gender is something evoked, created, and sustained day-by-day through interaction…. Women and men participate together to construct the meaning of gender and distinguish themselves from each other as women or as men."

BOX 2.1 | *Four examples of doing gender*

1. The rules of a game can be used to illustrate gender as an interactive process. A parent opens a game bought for the family as a whole and begins to read aloud the accompanying instructions. They go something like, "The first player does this, then he does that, then he does that." A daughter listening to this list says, "I don't want to play this game, it's for boys." Now, maybe the daughter simply needs to know that the word "he" can refer to both boys and girls. The problem is, if we teach our girls that the games of life are boys' games, the experience becomes more than just a matter of semantics.

2. A five-year-old boy is learning to hit a baseball, and his coach suddenly yells, "Don't hold your bat like a girl!" It is hard to know how to take this statement. We can be sure that this five-year-old has never analyzed how girls and boys hold bats, and so he may have trouble modelling his behaviour on that observation. Most likely, the statement simply means, to him and to others listening, "You are doing it wrong," and that "Girls always do it wrong." It could also mean that girls (or women) should be excluded from this game because they cannot even take the basic step of holding a bat properly.

3. During the examination of a graduate thesis on the topic of unpaid work, one of the (male) examiners says, "It seems we're hearing about this topic all the time." Perhaps the examiner

Whether we are aware of it or not, the first thing we want to know about someone is whether they are male or female, and it seems that any uncertainty in this regard leads to difficulty. We are, then, active participants in "creating gender," a tendency that helps to explain both the resistance to change and the occurrence of change. Gender is important not just because of differentiation, but also—and especially—because it frequently leads to hierarchies that rank the relative worth of men and women, which in turn also leads to the relative power of the sexes in various kinds of interactions.

Arlie Hochschild (1989: 15) uses the interesting concept of *gender strategy*. As social beings, we face the problems of both getting things done and relating to other people in the process of getting things done. A gender strategy is "a plan of action through which a person tries to solve problems at hand, given the cultural notions of gender at play." Focusing on matters within families, Marlene Mackie (1995: 58-61) lists a number of strategies in the arsenal: persuasion, exchange, joking, gift-giving, conning, hassling, playing dumb, disengagement, coalitions, intimidation, and violence. Not only do we learn most of these strategies as children, but also over time we become experts in the subtle, and sometimes not so subtle, ways of including gender in our everyday social interactions.

These concepts of "doing gender" and "gender strategies" help to explain how gender is constantly being created, affirmed, and altered in the course of social interaction

> **BOX 2.1** CONT'D

believes more sociological mileage is to be gained by studying *real* topics, like the division of paid work—after all, wasn't that what Durkheim meant by "The Division of Labour"? Or perhaps it is best for the discipline if established professors—and men in particular—define the topics of sociological relevance. Could this be another example of gender relations, this time in the definition of what social issues are appropriate to study? Or perhaps this comment was an example of "doing gender," in the sense of establishing a range of appropriate interests and just who has the right to define the questions to be analyzed.

4. In the early 1990s Mackie (1995) asked her students in a sociology of the family class to keep a gender notebook. On reading these diaries,

Mackie found that most of the young men and women shared expectations of employment, marriage, and parenthood, but had significant differences about how they would accomplish these goals. The men assumed their futures would revolve around both family and employment. The women were more likely to see problems arising in the combination of family and career. For instance, they worried about choosing jobs that would fit well with being a wife and mother, about finding a mate who would share domestic tasks, and about how they would schedule both childbearing and careers.

Perhaps the responses indicate that these questions are particularly important to students who choose to take a course on the sociology of the family. But they also indicate how gender plays a role in the life strategies of young adults.♦

(Mackie 1995). Another important example revolves around the care of dependants in society. Mackie observes two products in this process of determining strategies to care for the young and old in society: one is the care given; the other is the gender relations established in providing the care.

Rather than thinking of sex or sex roles as properties of individuals, we need to think of gender as an aspect of how social life is organized at both the micro and macro levels. As Susan McDaniel (1991: 304) and Mackie (1991: 2) put it, "pink and white threads" run through "the fabric of society." Not only is gender an important aspect of interpersonal interaction, but it is also an organizer at the societal level, giving access to rights and opportunities. Before it was changed in 1918, the Elections Act of Canada stated, "No criminal, lunatic or woman shall vote." In its time this statement clearly established the relative rights of citizenship for women and men. Today governments and corporations still often assume that women are responsible for the care of children and that this responsibility limits their work lives. Myra Marx Feree and Elaine J. Hall (1996) find that even introductory textbooks in sociology need to "rethink stratification from a feminist perspective." Given that the structural forces in society include interacting individuals (micro level), interacting groups (meso level), and interacting institutions (macro level), gender is both an individual trait and an "institutionalized system that constructs hierarchies among and within institutions" (Feree and Hall 1996: 932). Theorists of gender seek to determine the place of gender in the processes that establish inequality at these interpersonal, group, and institutional levels.

The institutional level includes policies that regulate both the interaction of individuals and organizations and the state. As Yvonne Hirdman (1994: 11) observes: "In modern democratic societies the gender conflict demands the creation of a new gender contract which not only involves men and women at the level of individuals within a paired relationship, but which also incorporates both society and the state as indispensable partners."

Resources, autonomy, and power

Feree and Hall (1996) propose that social stratification, a central problem in sociology, involves access to resources (*economic* questions), freedom to make life choices (*autonomy* questions), and participation in the decision-making of social groups (*power* questions). Consequently, when we include gender in those analyses we must also take up economic considerations of income inequality, autonomy questions concerning people's potential to enter the labour market in the first place, and power issues related to the rewarding of given skills in the workplace. Similarly, feminist objectives would include the economic opportunities to earn a living, the autonomy to control one's body, and the power to interact as equals.

When we consider gender in the context of income inequality, we might find that labour-market involvement and the rewarding of skills at work imply that women will only be equal to men when they model their lives along male lines. Questions of power would include looking at whether that model is ultimately the most desirable social arrangement, or whether men should be encouraged to model their lives in the direction of a greater meshing of family and work.

Paid and unpaid work

This consideration of desirable social arrangements applies especially to matters of paid and unpaid work. In effect, mainstream sociology has failed to theorize the division between paid and unpaid forms of labour as a stratification process. Most stratification research only analyzes the paid labour market. Marianne Kempeneers (1992: 78-80) divides the feminist approaches to paid and unpaid work into three perspectives: patriarchy, Marxist feminists, and feminist Marxists. The approach based on *patriarchy* considers men's authority over women and the consequences for the sexual allocation of labour. *Marxist feminists* theorize that women have a different relation to production than men, and that women's status follows from their greater involvement in domestic work or private production. *Feminist Marxists* do not give causal priority to either men's authority over women (patriarchy) or to women's greater involvement in domestic work (relations of production). They emphasize the need for paid and unpaid work to be analyzed in terms of the dialectic relation between the two systems, that is, between patriarchy and relations of production.

Gender and the meaning of love

How do questions of gender play into common experiences of heterosexual love—especially interpersonal differences in the very meaning of love, and styles of love? Based on research that involved asking people for examples of their experiences, Alice Rossi (1985) proposed that, for men, love tends to mean providing practical help in a relationship, doing things together, and sexual intimacy. For women it is more likely to mean emotional closeness and verbal expression in a relationship.

According to Rossi, the most commonly accepted meaning of heterosexual love is closer to that attributed by women, involving *expressive* questions, emotional closeness, companionship, and verbal self-disclosure, including the disclosure of personal weakness. A good love relationship means honest and open communication, and affection, but it is less likely to mean working well together and sharing physical activities. That is, the more *instrumental* side of love—including doing things together, helping one another, or caring for someone by providing resources—is less likely to be defined as love. For instance, in one study, when a husband was asked to show more love for his wife he decided to wash her car. That was a case of instrumental help, but his wife did not accept it as a sign of love, nor did the researchers.

Rossi concluded that the commonly accepted definition of love tends to exaggerate women's dependency on the male-female relationship while repressing men's dependency. The idea is that women need to express their vulnerability while men need to be strong and instrumentally helpful. The approach makes women seem dependent, and men independent. She proposed that a more *androgynous* definition of love, combining expressive and instrumental channels, would better acknowledge the interdependence of men and women in relationships.

MALE/FEMALE DIFFERENCES: PERSISTENCE AND CHANGE

The study of gender necessarily includes research into average differences between the sexes, despite the disadvantage this brings of focusing on those differences and of overlooking both the similarities across the sexes and the differences within the sexes. Indeed, most aspects of gender makeup show more similarities than differences between males and females. In statistical terms, the male and female *distributions* overlap with *means* that may be only slightly different. For instance, men are on average taller, but some women are taller than many men, and some men are shorter than many women.

Biology

In their comparisons of various societies, researchers have found that biological differences between men and women cannot explain the variations that occur across societies and over time (Goode 1981); and this variability in differences over time and across societies is itself evidence for the social construction of gender. Nonetheless, biology and social experience are intertwined: we exist as biological organisms in a social context, just as cultural processes are manifested through our biological existence (Rossi 1984, 1994).

The *physiological* differences between males and females are the most obvious. They involve chromosomes (XX or XY), oestrogen and testosterone hormones, ovaries and testes, along with genitals (clitoris/vagina and penis). Scientists largely agree that chromosomes are primarily responsible for the other physiological components that emerge in the development of the embryo and subsequent maturation. The absence of a Y chromosome may make males more biologically vulnerable to a variety of conditions, from speech defects to premature death. Maturation occurs more quickly for girls, who reach puberty at least a year sooner and the terminal point of growth some three years earlier than boys. Male and female bodies show other average differences in height and weight and in the relative amount of muscle and fat.

The differences in *life expectancy* appear to be partly related to physiological factors. Unless maternal mortality is particularly high, or the life chances of baby girls are strongly disadvantaged, life-expectancy rates favour women. In Canada, the recorded differences dating back to 1831 show a 1.5-year advantage for women at that time (Bourbeau and Légaré 1982: 77). This difference increased from 2.1 years in 1931 to 7.3 years in 1976, and it had declined to 5.8 years by 1996 (Bélanger and Dumas 1998: 81). A variety of factors are associated with this difference, including matters of lifestyle: men take more risks such as drinking and driving, and engage in less healthy dietary behaviour, while women tend to seek more assistance with health problems (Beaujot 1991: 57-59). The reduction of maternal mortality is also a significant factor, because men never did die of this cause. As Roberta Hamilton (1978) observes, in times past childbirth was a frequent, inevitable, and high-risk activity for women.

As much as half of the current difference in life expectancy is probably a function of biological factors (Keyfitz 1989). Statistically, males are more likely to die before birth and at young ages, which is clearly not a function of lifestyle or the stress associated with working and living conditions. In Canada the male rate of mortality in the first year of life has consistently represented 125 percent of the female rate. Females are the stronger sex from the point of view of survival.

Psychological traits

Marlene Mackie (1991) provides a summary of available literature on psychological differences as well as personality traits and social-psychological disparities by sex. In terms of intellectual abilities, females and males show no average differences on IQ or creativity. On verbal ability, females have an average advantage from early childhood. Boys, though, have an average advantage that begins in late childhood for mathematical abilities and in adolescence for spatial skills. But these areas of development show only slight differences, and according to Mackie (1991: 39), "Training can significantly improve the performance of both sexes in these verbal, spatial and mathematical skills."

The differences regarding these traits should not, then, be interpreted as biological determinism (a theory of limits) but as biology permitting a range of possibilities. Subtle influences can enhance an initial advantage. For instance, when two children finish first and second in a race, that result could have been a pure accident. But the winner could well be seen as a good racer and encouraged to develop running skill. Clearly, the influences of biology and environment interact to produce given observed results. An article on "The Trouble with Men" in *The Economist* (1996) observes that at ages five to eleven girls often do better than boys on average test scores. More importantly, in England and Wales boys are no longer catching up after puberty. The article attributes these findings to social environments that discourage boys' school achievements.

On the issue of *personality traits* and social-psychological disparities, Mackie (1991) points out that males tend to have a higher aggressiveness, both physical and verbal, especially as children. Women are more persuasible and more likely to conform to social pressure. Women are better at decoding non-verbal communication. John Brigham (1986: 336) concluded from a meta-analysis of various studies that the variance accounted for by sex alone on these various psychological traits ranges from 1 to 6 percent. This finding, however, does not account for the observation that men obtained 79 percent of bachelor degrees in engineering in 1995, while women obtained 75 percent of the degrees granted in health related fields.

Nonetheless, according to Rossi (1984), evidence exists of biological contributions to sex differences in four areas: (1) sensory sensitivity, with males more sensitive to sight and females more sensitive to touch, sound, and odour; (2) aggression or activity levels are higher in males; (3) cognitive skills in spatial visualizing and mathematical reasoning compared to verbal fluency; and (4) parenting behaviour, with stronger bonding of mothers to infants. As for male bonding with infants, cross-cultural comparisons suggest, Rossi (1984: 12) states, that "men take care of their infants if they are not needed as warriors and hunters, if mothers contribute to food resources, and if male parenting is encouraged by women." Conversely, Rossi (1977: 24) finds, "Species survival has been facilitated by physiological factors in the bonding of mothers and their newborn."

Learning environments and education

Janet Lever (1978) observed interesting differences in the complexity of *play*. Based on a sample of 181 children in Grade 5 who were both observed and interviewed, Lever found that boys' play was more complex in terms of the size of the group, team formation, role differentiation, and interdependence between players. This play atmosphere provided valuable learning about maintaining cohesiveness and working toward collective goals by using impersonal rules in the face of interpersonal competition and group diversity. Lever's findings showed that girls' play made them adept at interpersonal communications. Playing with best friends or in small groups, girls had experiences that encouraged conversational, verbal, and expressive development.

Along with labour-force participation, the most significant changes in sex differences may have come in education. With the generalization of secondary education in the 1950s and 1960s, boys and girls came to have similar average levels of primary and secondary education. At ages 15 and over in 1996, 67.3 percent of men and 67.8 percent of women had completed high school or obtained some further education (see Table 2.2).

Until 1960, women comprised less than a quarter of university enrolment (Hamilton 1996: 152; Bellamy and Guppy 1991), but the decades since have seen remarkable changes in the proportions of women obtaining various forms of postsecondary certification (see Table 2.1). For diplomas obtained at community colleges, women increased from 53.7 percent of the total in 1970-71 to 58.3 percent in 1994-95. At the undergraduate university level, women obtained 39.9 percent of degrees, diplomas, and certificates in 1970 and 58.9 percent in 1995. Among graduate degrees (masters and doctorates plus graduate diplomas) women obtained 20.6 percent of degrees in 1970 and 48.3 percent in 1995.

It is particularly interesting to look at the list of specialties and observe the year at which women began to obtain more degrees than men. At the undergraduate level, in education, fine/applied arts, and health studies, this time came before 1970. By 1975 women were obtaining more humanities degrees than men, and by 1985 they had moved ahead in the social sciences and agricultural/biological sciences. In the areas of engineering/applied sciences and mathematics/physical sciences, the proportion of women gaining degrees increased but remained significantly less than half, at 20.8 and 31.1 percent respectively, in 1995. Looking at specific disciplines, Cameron Stout (1992) observed that between 1975 and 1990, veterinary medicine and zoology changed from having more men than women obtaining degrees to having the balance shift in favour of women. In addition, law, medicine, and business/management/commerce were male-dominated in 1975 but had over 48.5 percent women graduates in 1995.

As for graduate degrees, women have outnumbered men in the humanities, health, and fine arts since 1980, and in education since 1985. Still, women obtain fewer graduate degrees than men in four areas of specialization: social sciences (46.0 percent), agriculture/biological sciences (46.5 percent), engineering/applied sciences (17.5 percent), and mathematics/physical sciences (24.4 percent). More women gain masters as opposed to doctorate degrees. For instance, in 1995 women obtained 50.4 percent of all masters degrees granted but 31.4 percent of doctorates.

Significant changes have thus occurred in postsecondary education since 1970, as Table 2.1 indicates. In particular, once women began to obtain more than half of the degrees granted, it seems there was no turning back at both undergraduate and graduate levels. Only in undergraduate mathematics/physical sciences can one say that women's progress appears to be stalled: less than a third of certifications there go to women.

The 1996 census confirms that, at ages 20-29, more women than men become university graduates (43.6 percent men) and trade and other non-university graduates (46.2 percent men). Among ten major fields of study, men aged 20-29 outnumber women in only two fields for university graduates and three fields for college graduates (Statistics Canada 1998e: 3): engineering and applied sciences (university), trades/technologies (college), mathematics and physical sciences (university and college), agricultural and biological sciences/technologies (college).

All levels of education show a greater variability for men in the sense that they have both higher proportions who do not finish high school and higher proportions who obtain doctorates. Over the period 1921-81, a higher proportion of men than of women aged 20-24 attended school, but subsequent censuses show a higher proportion of women at school at these ages (Normand 1995: 20). The ratio of female to male undergraduates at more advanced ages becomes even higher, as more women at those ages are returning to school, either part-time or full-time.

The average years of education for the population as a whole has been similar for women and men since 1976. For the population aged 15 and over, the median years of schooling were 11.3 for men and 11.4 for women in the 1976 census, while the 1991 census showed the same average of 12.5 years for both men and women (Statistics Canada 1996: 191)

DEGREES, DIPLOMAS, AND CERTIFICATES GRANTED,
BY FIELD OF STUDY AND SEX, CANADA, 1970-95

	UNDERGRADUATE			GRADUATE		
	M	F	% FEMALE	M	F	% FEMALE
TOTAL UNIVERSITY						
1970	39,514	26,224	39.9	8,604	2,236	20.6
1975	49,139	39,868	44.8	10,268	3,752	26.8
1980	49,076	49,572	50.3	10,144	5,647	35.8
1985	53,888	60,184	52.8	11,170	7,657	40.7
1990	56,365	74,264	56.9	11,956	10,207	46.1
1995	61,936	88,876	58.9	14,086	13,176	48.3
Education						
1970	6,439	7,517	53.9	1,327	527	28.4
1975	9,562	13,169	57.9	1,892	887	31.9
1980	7,011	14,714	67.7	1,804	1,581	46.7
1985	5,369	13,054	70.9	1,508	2,060	57.7
1990	6,563	15,905	70.8	1,428	2,687	65.3
1995	7,988	18,000	69.3	1,412	3,243	69.7
Fine/Applied Arts						
1970	413	836	67.0	29	49	62.8
1975	913	1,437	61.1	74	72	49.3
1980	1,024	1,924	65.3	103	105	50.5
1985	1,182	2,250	65.6	139	191	57.9
1990	1,350	2,703	66.7	168	259	60.7
1995	1,528	3,169	67.5	212	331	61.0
Humanities						
1970	5,253	4,747	47.5	1,229	654	34.7
1975	4,689	5,782	55.2	1,378	1,051	43.3
1980	4,056	6,285	60.8	1,000	1,111	52.6
1985	4,553	7,583	62.5	1,047	1,310	55.6
1990	5,915	10,579	64.1	1,249	1,514	54.8
1995	6,956	12,205	63.7	1,472	1,878	56.1
Agriculture/Biological Sciences						
1970	2,258	1,299	36.5	634	118	15.7
1975	3,038	2,356	43.7	554	175	24.0
1980	2,969	2,827	48.8	590	270	31.4
1985	2,636	2,981	53.1	637	340	34.8
1990	3,352	4,244	55.9	712	529	42.6
1995	3,598	5,405	60.0	801	697	46.5
Social Sciences						
1970	10,997	3,968	26.5	2,511	628	20.0
1975	15,483	8,390	35.1	3,642	1,113	23.4
1980	17,727	13,118	42.5	4,006	1,851	31.6
1985	20,705	21,066	50.4	4,321	2,634	37.9
1990	23,255	28,876	55.4	4,471	3,573	44.4
1995	24,521	34,501	58.5	5,220	4,446	46.0

TABLE 2.1

DEGREES, DIPLOMAS, AND CERTIFICATES GRANTED,
BY FIELD OF STUDY AND SEX, CANADA, 1970-95 (CONT'D)

	UNDERGRADUATE			GRADUATE		
	M	F	% FEMALE	M	F	% FEMALE
Engineering/Applied Sciences						
1970	4,214	66	1.5	1,198	19	1.6
1975	5,138	137	2.6	1,158	47	3.9
1980	7,348	609	7.7	1,231	85	6.5
1985	8,297	1,056	11.3	1,766	188	9.6
1990	7,190	1,110	13.4	1,753	252	12.6
1995	7,839	2,062	20.8	2,445	517	17.5
Health Professionals						
1970	1,780	2,888	61.9	424	155	26.8
1975	2,455	3,461	58.5	434	258	37.3
1980	2,485	4,515	64.5	423	461	52.1
1985	2,376	5,683	70.5	589	623	51.4
1990	2,504	6,530	72.3	710	964	57.6
1995	2,574	7,550	74.5	887	1,462	62.2
Mathematics/Physical Sciences						
1970	3,047	643	17.4	1,245	83	6.3
1975	3,237	897	21.7	1,098	137	11.1
1980	3,231	1,297	28.6	959	165	14.7
1985	5,818	2,464	29.8	1,142	300	20.8
1990	4,930	2,057	29.4	1,424	387	21.4
1995	5,386	2,436	31.1	1,555	502	24.4
COMMUNITY COLLEGE AND DIPLOMAS						
1970-71	5,929	6,873	53.7			
1974-75	12,100	13,100	52.0			
1979-80	19,903	27,684	58.2			
1984-85	26,303	32,345	55.2			
1989-90	23,416	33,858	59.1			
1994-95	30,288	42,260	58.3			

NOTES: Total includes unclassified classification. Undergraduate data by discipline are based on university data for bachelors and first professional degrees, as well as undergraduate diplomas and certificates. Graduate data by discipline are based on masters, earned doctorates, and graduate diplomas and certificates.

Source: Statistics Canada, no. 81-204, 1991: Table 16; Statistics Canada, no. 81-229, 1997: Tables 33, 35, 37, 39, 41.

TABLE 2.1

Because women's greater participation in higher education is a recent phenomenon, women are more disadvantaged in terms of the statistics on the educational attainment of the whole population aged 15 and over (Table 2.2). For instance, in 1996, 46.8 percent of women but 48.6 percent of men had at least some postsecondary education, while 12.2 percent of women and 14.7 percent of men had university degrees. Nonetheless, the differentials have declined significantly since 1961, when 4.0 percent of men and 1.7 percent of women had university degrees.

PERCENTAGE DISTRIBUTION BY EDUCATIONAL ATTAINMENT
AND SEX, 1961-96, AGE 15+

	1961	1976	1985	1996
Male				
0–8 years	47.0	26.1	19.7	12.3
Some secondary	29.8	46.0	48.6	20.5
Completed secondary	10.7	—	—	18.7
Some postsecondary	5.4	9.9	9.4	8.4
Postsecondary diploma	3.1	8.8	10.6	25.5
University degree	4.0	9.1	11.7	14.7
Female				
0–8 years	41.4	25.2	18.9	12.8
Some secondary	33.4	50.6	51.7	19.3
Completed secondary	14.0	—	—	21.0
Some postsecondary	4.6	8.1	8.8	8.8
Postsecondary diploma	5.0	11.4	12.4	25.8
University degree	1.7	4.8	8.2	12.2
TOTAL	100.0	100.0	100.0	100.0

NOTE: In 1976 and 1985 the categories for some secondary and secondary
      completed are combined, which means some or completed secondary but no postsecondary.

Source: Picot, 1980: 25; Statistics Canada, no. 71-001, July 1976, July 1985, June, 1996. Statistics Canada, Labour Force Survey.

TABLE 2.2

Income

A variety of measures show sex differences in income. Table 2.3 provides median levels
of after-tax income by sex and age in 1980 and 1996. On this measure, women's income
represented 46.5 percent of men's income in 1980 and 62.8 percent in 1994. Comparisons
within age groups show significant reductions in the differentials at younger ages, but the
differences remain significant at ages 25 and over. The differentials are now particularly
large at ages 55-64, the ages when women have had the most relative disadvantage in sustained employment experience.

Kempeneers (1992: 75) states, "All studies of women's labour-force participation arrive
at this following conclusion: the massive increase in labour-force participation has not
altered the specific character of this labour-force or reduced male/female inequality." It
will obviously take many years to significantly reduce these large gaps. For instance, the
average wages of all working women increased by 63 percent in real terms between 1967
and 1993, compared to a 18 percent increase for men (Crompton and Geran 1995: 29); and
still, by 1994, women's after-tax income came to only 63 percent of men's.

Considering only recent university graduates, the gender-earnings gap declined over
cohorts graduating between 1978 and 1992, but a gap of some 10 percent remains (Davies,

Mosher, and O'Grady 1996; Wannell and Caron 1994). Only a small part of the gap can be attributed to productivity-related measures such as age, field of study, and industrial sector. Scott Davies and his co-authors (1996) conclude that women graduates are guided into predominantly female jobs because of real and perceived family obligations. The occupations they move into typically have shorter career paths and fewer opportunities for promotion. Davies, Mosher, and O'Grady propose that research should pay particular attention to the differential involvement of men and women in specific fields of study and particular labour markets.

To get a clearer picture we need to supplement these measures of average income with measures of income distribution. Measures of *low-income status* or poverty provide a systematic way of looking at the lower end of the income distribution. Table 2.4 provides such figures over the period 1980-96. This indicator of low income is a relative measure that takes into account household size and the urban/rural nature of the area of residence. The figures show a degree of stability: an average of 18.8 percent of women and 15.0 percent of men have low-income status. The sex differences are also quite stable: the differential between the male and female figures drop only from 4.2 percentage points in 1980 to 3.9 points in 1996. Based on data for the period 1973-86, Martin Dooley (1994) finds no increase in the proportion of women among the poor, although he sees an increase in the proportion of poor persons who live in lone-parent families with a female head. Indeed, the increase in the fraction of all families headed by lone females was found to have the largest impact on the feminization of poverty. Reviewing the data for the period 1980-96, the National Council on Welfare (1998: 85) found that most of the income differentiation by sex could be explained by high poverty rates for female single parents and for women who are "unattached," that is, not living in a family. Nonetheless, women as a whole constituted 60 percent of the poor in 1980 and 58 percent in 1996.

The figures presented in Table 2.4 do not indicate a feminization of poverty for the total population. The gender gap for income levels has remained relatively stable for the young and the elderly, but it

MEDIAN AFTER-TAX INCOME, BY AGE AND SEX, CANADA, 1980 AND 1996

AGE	M	F	FEMALE AS % OF MALE
1980			
19 and under	1,955	1,694	86.6
20-24	8,342	6,467	77.5
25-34	15,246	8,471	55.6
35-44	17,872	7,972	44.6
45-54	17,147	7,789	45.4
55-64	15,341	5,062	33.0
65-69	9,060	4,751	52.4
70+	6,483	4,922	75.9
TOTAL	13,027	6,058	46.5
1996			
19 and under	3,052	2,681	87.8
20-24	10,979	9,076	82.7
25-34	22,467	16,516	73.5
35-44	28,631	18,657	65.2
45-54	29,576	18,210	61.6
55-59	26,083	13,306	51.0
60-64	22,619	10,271	45.4
65+	18,400	12,859	69.9
TOTAL	22,260	13,985	62.8

Source: Statistics Canada, no. 13-210, 1980: 59; 1996: 105. Survey of Consumer Finances.

TABLE 2.3

PERCENTAGE WITH LOW INCOME, BY AGE AND SEX, CANADA, 1980-96

	TOTAL		CHILDREN UNDER 18		ELDERLY 65+		ALL OTHERS 18-64	
	M	F	M	F	M	F	M	F
1980	13.9	18.1	15.5	16.1	26.6	39.8	11.6	15.5
1981	14.0	18.0	16.2	16.6	26.5	39.5	11.5	15.0
1982	15.4	19.1	18.6	19.6	20.0	36.0	13.5	16.1
1983	17.0	20.3	20.2	19.4	22.7	38.3	14.9	17.6
1984	17.0	20.7	21.0	21.0	22.0	35.1	14.6	18.1
1985	15.8	19.6	19.3	19.6	20.1	33.9	13.8	17.1
1986	14.8	18.3	17.7	17.5	19.3	32.0	13.0	16.1
1987	14.5	18.2	17.3	18.0	17.6	31.2	12.9	15.9
1988	13.1	17.6	15.7	16.5	16.6	32.7	11.6	15.2
1989	12.2	16.0	15.5	15.1	14.0	28.7	10.6	13.9
1990	13.4	17.4	17.3	18.2	13.7	27.1	11.8	15.2
1991	14.7	18.2	19.0	18.7	14.0	27.8	13.2	16.2
1992	15.2	18.8	19.1	19.3	12.7	26.8	14.1	17.0
1993	16.1	20.0	21.0	21.7	14.8	28.8	14.3	17.6
1994	15.0	19.1	18.9	20.1	10.7	25.8	14.2	17.5
1995	16.2	19.5	20.6	21.4	10.9	24.6	15.3	17.7
1996	16.0	19.9	20.9	21.4	12.8	27.0	14.6	17.8
AVERAGE (1980-96)	15.0	18.8	18.5	18.8	17.4	31.5	13.3	16.4

Source: Statistics Canada, no. 13-207, 1996: 30-33. Survey of Consumer Finances.

TABLE 2.4

has declined for persons aged 18-64. Although a growing concern has been raised about poverty for female lone parents and for elderly women living alone (see chapter 4), given the comparative figures for women and men it is more appropriate to speak of a continuing gap rather than a feminization of poverty.

Furthermore, figures for exits from low-income status and re-entry into low income indicate that low-income situations last for a relatively short time for some 60 percent of persons, with the remaining four in ten having a chronic low-income status (Laroche 1998). Age, sex, marital status, and number of children are all important factors in these transitions. For instance, of all people with low-income status, after one year 60 percent are able to exit that condition; but 75 percent of two-income families with two children exit—and only 36 percent of female lone parents and 50 percent of male lone parents with two children exit. While lone mothers clearly have the greatest disadvantages, fathers in similar circumstances also have reduced chances of exiting the low-income status.

Violence

While it might not seem an easy fit among the other issues considered here, *violence* is another factor that differentiates women and men (see Table 2.5). According to the 1993 Violence Against Women Survey, 29 percent of women who had ever been married or lived in common-law relationships had been physically or sexually assaulted by their partners at some point (Rodgers 1994). Over half of these assaults were classified as serious or potentially life-threatening. The same survey found that 19 percent of women had been sexually assaulted and 8 percent had been physically assaulted by a stranger at least once in their adult lives (Strike 1995). Men also experience assault—they are more likely than women to be victims of homicide—but those assaults come mostly from other men. Women are thus more likely to lack a basic sense of personal autonomy and security in many public and private places.

Of the homicides in Canada over the period 1977-96, in one-third of the cases the victims and assailants were related by marriage, common-law relationship, or kinship; about half involved other acquaintances; and only 17 percent involved strangers (Bunge and Levett 1998: 4). For every male killed by his spouse, three females were killed by their spouses. The year 1996 saw 22,000 reported incidents of assault on spouses, with 89 percent involving female victims. Violence is more prevalent in common-law relationships involving young male partners, especially if the partners are experiencing chronic unemployment. Taking other factors into consideration, researchers found that income, education, and the consumption of alcohol were not significant predictors of spousal assault. Girls and boys are equally likely to be physically assaulted by a family member, but girls are four times more likely to be sexually assaulted by a family member. These are significant numbers, given that children were victims in 60 percent of sexual assaults reported to police in 1996 (Bunge and Levett 1998: 3).

Both domestic and public forms of violence are related to the subordination of women, and they especially raise questions of autonomy. Violence becomes a means of controlling other people. In addition, harassment continues to

DATA ON VIOLENCE AGAINST WOMEN, CANADA, 1993

PERCENT OF WOMEN AGED 18 AND OVER WHO HAVE EXPERIENCED NON-SPOUSAL VIOLENCE

Sexual attack	20%
Sexual touching	25%
Total sexual assault	37%
Physical assault	17%
Total victimized	42%

NON-SPOUSAL VIOLENCE BY RELATIONSHIP TO ASSAILANT

Date/boyfriend	20%
Other known men	34%
Stranger	45%
Total	100%

PERCENT OF EVER-MARRIED WOMEN AGED 18 AND OVER WHO HAVE EXPERIENCED WIFE ASSAULT

By current marital partner	15%
By previous marital partner	48%
All partners	29%

PERCENT OF EVER-MARRIED WOMEN AGED 18 AND OVER WHO HAVE EXPERIENCED WIFE ASSAULT, BY MOST SERIOUS TYPE OF VIOLENCE

Being kicked, hit, beaten up or choked, or having a gun or knife used against them	16%
Being pushed, grabbed, shoved, or slapped	11%
Non-physical assaults	2%

Source: Statistics Canada, 1995a: 105, 106, 113, 114; Statistics Canada, Violence Against Women Survey, 1993.

TABLE 2.5

prevent women from gaining equal access to various opportunities. For instance, the 1993 Violence Against Women Survey found that in the 12 months before the survey some 6 percent of employed women had experienced at least one form of workplace sexual harassment, and that over their lifetimes 23 percent of Canadian women had done so (Johnson 1994). While it is insufficiently studied as a social problem, sexual harassment is a means for men to subordinate women (Sev'er 1996).

MATERIAL EXPLANATIONS: ECONOMIC QUESTIONS

Gaining a broad understanding of gender differences is a complex matter that includes raising questions of biology, socialization, family dynamics, social structures, and cultural norms. Taking a historical point of view, Hamilton (1978) identifies the key questions in the subtitle of her book *The Liberation of Women: A Study of Patriarchy and Capitalism*. As she indicates, the matters of change and stability in gender differences are mostly a function of economic questions—the place of the sexes in the material relations of production—and cultural questions—definitions of appropriate male and female behaviour.

Marxist literature, which pays particular attention to the material basis of social arrangements, provides a theory for the economic side of these issues. Marxist theorists see the ways and means of economic survival as the key to understanding the different eras of historical development, and they consider in particular how social groups relate to the process of economic production as well as the effect of these relationships on the groups. What they see, among other things, is that males and females have often related differently to the productive process. In *The Creation of Patriarchy* (1986) Gerda Lerner goes so far as to conclude that class differences were *first* experienced through patriarchal relations: that the enslavement of women, combining racism and sexism, preceded class formation. In addition, Lerner (1986: 215) observes that "class for men has been based on their relation to the means of production," but for women it has been "mediated through their sexual ties to men."

Looking at the role of gender in certain gathering and hunting societies, Eleanor Leacock (1977) finds considerable equality, which she attributes to their broadly equivalent role in production. In many cases the food gathered by women was more important for survival than the food hunted by men. For instance, among the Naskapi people of the Labrador Peninsula, the choice of plans, undertakings, journeys, and winterings was in nearly every instance in the hands of the women. In many other small-scale societies, the women looked after preserving and storing the food. In a very real sense, then, they controlled the public treasure. In other small-scale societies, especially if they were patrilocal, women did not control the products of their labour and consequently had lower status. In some cases, women appear to have been enslaved to a man's society. Colonial contact also gave men in some gathering and hunting societies an advantage because they could more readily interact with the early explorers and traders, who were invariably men.

Women in agricultural societies and rural communities were also strongly integrated in production. Besides taking care of child-bearing and household management, women performed other farming activities along with the men. For example, women were important in settling the frontier in North America (Demos 1977). Frontier life involved a high level of female participation in economic activity, as well as a relatively high status for women in the community. Significantly, in Canada women's right to vote was first established in the prairie provinces, and it was from Alberta that Judge Emily Murphy established women's right to a seat in the Canadian Senate.

Hamilton (1978) argues that the 17th-century transition from feudalism to capitalism entailed a decrease in women's status. In the feudal economy, women had been involved in all work, including work that involved great physical strength and endurance. Peasant women laboured long and hard, a characteristic they shared with peasant men. But the demise of the feudal economy led to the reduction of the family basis for economic activity. Removed from the land, women "lost the means to help provide a living for her family" (Hamilton 1978: 40). As economic production was removed from the household, women and children became economically dependent on the extrafamilial occupations of husbands and fathers, and their status decreased. Women's sphere essentially shrank to the household only, and men emerged as the major participants in economic production. This change gave rise to the breadwinner model of families, in which wives were dependent upon their husband's income and husbands were dependent upon wives for the care of home and children.

An analysis of labour acts in Ontario over the period 1884-1913 provides a good example of the process through which women became economically dependent (Ursel 1986). The changing laws increasingly limited the use of child and female labour in the paid workforce. The authorities' stated concern was to improve the conditions of children and women, but the laws also entrenched the distinctions between male and female labour, limiting the hours women could work, the places they could work, and the kind of work they could do. Thus girls and women found it almost impossible to earn a living wage as a factory worker. For the most part, then, women's access to subsistence became dependent on entry into reproductive (family) relations.

Only in recent years, with enhanced opportunities for women to become more self-sufficient within the paid labour force, has this state of dependency been reduced. By 1996, of those age 15 and over, 57.6 percent of women, compared to 70.7 percent of men, were in the labour force. Women profited especially from the expansion of the service sector, including the public services associated with health, education, and welfare. Since 1980 the two-income family has become the largest category in husband-wife families. In addition, data from 1993 showed that women were the main earners in one-quarter of dual-earner families (Crompton and Geran 1995). Especially in difficult economic times, wives' income has helped prevent the deterioration of family income. Nonetheless, as an average for all husband-wife families in 1990, women's earnings contributed 28.9 percent and men's 65.6 percent of the average family income (see Table 4.11). As we will see later (chapter 4), the work that many women do in the labour force often involves less skills, less security, less opportunities for training and advancement, less prestige, and less union-ization, and it pays lower wages, than men's work (Armstrong and Armstrong 1994: 67).

The explanations on the material front consequently propose that the economic com-ponents of men's and women's lives are the key to their relative status in society and their relative power in relationships. The subordination of women is thus a function of their lack of access to the means of livelihood. William Goode (1981: 164) turns this proposi-tion the other way around: "Women who are more in command of productive skills ... are more resistant to exploitation or domination." Women make essential economic con-tributions in all societies, but their status depends on how this contribution is structured and on the extent to which they control the products of their labour.

CULTURAL EXPLANATIONS:
OPPORTUNITIES AND BARRIERS IN SYMBOLIC SYSTEMS

The relative status of women and men is also determined by opportunities and barriers in the culture and society—although separating the economic and cultural explanations or deciding on a causal priority is ultimately difficult. While economic explanations have the advantage of focusing on measurable components associated with earning a living, cultural barriers can prevent access to the very opportunity of earning a living.

Culture can be defined as "negotiated symbolic understandings" associated with both inherited traditions and continuing experiences (Hammel 1990). Culture is thus present before the individual, because it involves inherited traditions in a society; but it also con-nects present-day experiences to traditions inherited from the past. E. A. Hammel (1990: 457) speaks of "*evaluative* conversations conducted by actors out of ... tradition and ongo-ing experience." In other words, the symbolic understanding involves "evaluation" or con-siderations of appropriate behaviour. Indeed, our everyday conversations include this kind of evaluation. We invariably punctuate stories with expressions like "that sucks," "one should not do that" or "that was the right thing to do," or "she (or he) knew how to handle the situation." Culture is also negotiated—actors are constantly establishing cultural understandings. Hammel (1990: 456) uses the idea of "culture-specific rationalities, in the building of which actors are important perceiving, interpreting and constructing agents."

Ideally, researchers would find out about culture by overhearing informants speaking to each other about important matters. However, that is rarely possible, and consequently researchers frequently rely on observing behaviour rather than conversations, and inter-preting it in the social context. Often, researchers rely on collecting people's attitudes, making the assumption that these indicate what is important to people and how they think about these important things. Cultural explanations therefore pay attention to social norms regarding appropriate behaviour or to expressed ideas about what one "should do."

For instance, in observing more and more diversity in families, Louis Roussel (1989) relates this tendency to "a new image of women" that is bringing massive reorganization of gender relations in families, of which we may have only seen the first effects. Similarly, Charles Jones, Lorna Marsden, and Lorne Tepperman (1990) speak of the "individuation" of women's lives—of women who have fewer constraints and consequently show more "variety" from person to person and more "fluidity" over the life course. Cultural understandings of appropriate behaviour, it seems, have become less rigid (Roussel 1989). However, other theorists bring different interpretations to this diversity. For instance, Céline Le Bourdais and Hélène Desrosiers (1988) propose that diversity for women represents "discontinuity of matrimonial and professional trajectories," which leads to disadvantages at work and at home.

Patriarchy

A key concept in the cultural study of gender relations, patriarchy means giving more value and preference to males: it refers to how attitudes and structures of a society, whether large or small, ensure male dominance. We could say that Western civilization has inherited a long history of patriarchy, going back to Hebrew, Greek, Roman, and Christian traditions.

For example, in the old Hebrew world, males dominated all major aspects of life. They could even sell their daughters as slaves. Strict rules called for the punishment of women caught in adultery, but no such rules existed for men. The status of women was also very low in the Greek tradition. Only the men were educated. When guests came, they were visitors to the men in the household. In the Roman culture, the oldest male had power of life or death over his wife and children. Consider the following statement written by Cato, a Roman patriot and interpreter of custom: "The husband is the judge of his wife. If she has committed a fault, he punishes her; if she has drunk wine, he condemns her; if she has been guilty of adultery, he kills her.... If you were to catch your wife in adultery, you would kill her with impunity without trial; but if she were to catch you, she would not dare to lay a finger upon you, and indeed she has no right" (Hoult, Henze, and Hudson 1978: 33).

The Christian tradition inherited many of the Hebrew, Greek, and Roman family values and customs. For example, note these words, sometimes read at Christian weddings, from St. Paul: "Wives, give way to your husbands as you should in the Lord. Husbands, love your wives and treat them with gentleness" (Colossians 3: 18–19).

In her analysis of the impact of cultural questions, Hamilton (1978: 73) observes that the medieval church counselled a celibate life so that its male initiates would avoid the twin evils of women and sexuality. Despite women's economic role in the peasant society, the official ideology promoted by the clergy seemed to be that women were a threat to men, and useless except for procreation. While Protestants subsequently dropped the ideas about the evil natures of women, they also idealized the home as something akin to heaven on earth, or at least a "little church" in which family members could forget about the cares of work and feel good about themselves and their relations with others. While

Hamilton speaks of this "idealization of the home" as one of Protestantism's "more remarkable bequests to posterity," she also concludes that the older patriarchal ideology was changed rather than set aside. Protestantism handed over the authority of the celibate priest to husbands and fathers. In preaching that the worldly life was to be lived in a godly fashion, the church counselled a loving and companionate relationship between husband and wife, but gave the husband the responsibility to govern, while the wife had to be obedient. Especially in Victorian times, the "cult of true womanhood" involved a state of isolation in the domestic sphere (Garfield 1990: 34). Any man who needed his wife's help in providing for family needs was "not worth his salt."

An emphasis on the virtue of women—which concentrated attention on homemaking and child care—was also prominent in the mid-20th century. Although women moved into the labour force in the 1940s to help with the war effort, there was a strong pressure to move them back into their homes with the close of World War II. Susan Prentice (1992) documents how child-care centres were quickly closed after the war. An article in *Maclean's* magazine in the early 1940s provides an example of the subtle pressures put on women to return to a more traditional family form: "What will they [women workers] demand of [postwar] society? Perhaps—and we can only hope—they'll be tired of it all [working outside the home] and yearn in the old womanly way for a home and a baby and a big brave man" (*Maclean's*, June 15, 1942: 10; quoted in Boutilier 1977: 23).

While patriarchy has a variety of meanings associated with men's higher cultural status, Lerner (1986) proposes that "paternalistic dominance" has constituted its main form for nearly 4,000 years. By this she means the exchange of "submission for protection" or "unpaid labour for maintenance." In effect, this definition pays particular attention to the division of earning and caring activities. Starting with the "manifestation and institutionalization of male dominance over women and children in the family," there follows an "extension of male dominance over women in the society in general" (Lerner 1986: 217, 239).

Referring to the cultural and religious manifestations of patriarchy, Mary Stewart Van Leeuwen (1998) notes that the original mandate granted to men and women in Genesis did not differentiate the sexes. The book made a call for the ancient Hebrews to unfold the potential of creation and to "be fruitful and multiply." It gave both mandates to both members of the primal pair; the biblical call did not indicate that women should look after reproduction while men dominated the earth. Van Leeuwen observes that the notion wherein men should be "captains of industry" and women "angels of the home" is not a feasible objective for most mortals, men or women.

The golden age of the family and complementary roles

The encouragement for women to focus on the home was particularly strong during the 1950s. Arlene Skolnick (1987) called the decade a "golden age of the family," a time when women were very much encouraged to fulfil themselves through their roles as wives and mothers. The surge of "familism" meant that life was oriented toward families, with considerable hostility for deviations from appropriate roles. Western society tended to see single adults as failures, working mothers as depriving their children of proper care and affection, and voluntarily childless couples as selfish.

During the 1960s, work outside the home again became acceptable for married women, but only as long as that employment did not interfere greatly with family responsibilities. Women could take jobs with little prestige or that made few demands on their time and conceded authority to men. Not until the 1970s and 1980s was it acceptable for women to pursue lifestyles in which they devoted themselves to careers as fully as men have traditionally done.

Despite these changes, Western society retains considerable ambivalence regarding the appropriate behaviour of men and women. For instance, many people believe that the roles of men and women should remain different. Many people see these differences as natural and proper, because they believe the roles of men and women should somehow be *complementary* to each other rather than identical.

Attitudinal surveys

In a 1988 Canadian poll, 28 percent of men and 23 percent of women agreed that "everyone would be better off if more women were satisfied to stay home and have families" (Table 2.6). These survey results indicate that 40 percent of Canadians favoured women having careers of their own. While the survey showed variations across characteristics of persons in the extent to which they answered "stay home and have families," the categories in which less than 10 percent picked this option only involved women who were either aged 18-21, were professionals, or had no children at home. In Europe, two-thirds of the people surveyed in one poll indicated that they thought it was better for the mother, than the father, to stay home (*The Economist* 1996). The same article observed that men were spurning even well-paid work that was dominated by women.

Still, attitudes have become much more open to women working outside of the home. For instance, only 26 percent of Edmonton respondents in 1980 approved of "a married woman working if she has pre-school age children," but this approval had increased to 63 percent of Alberta respondents by 1991 (Neale 1993). In 1985, 85 percent of Edmontonians agreed that "a wife should have the same opportunities as a husband to pursue a career outside of the home," and in 1980 some 95 percent felt that "a wife should receive the same pay as a husband for performing work of equal value." In national samples in 1975, 34 percent of survey respondents agreed that "married women should not be employed if their husbands are capable of supporting them," but by 1995 only 10 percent registered this same opinion (Bibby 1995: 95).

Changes in attitude are not as evident on matters relating to domestic work. In a 1977 Vancouver study of 17-18-year-olds with working-class backgrounds, Jane Gaskell (1983) found that all of the women assumed they would eventually have primary responsibility for domestic work. Although three-quarters of them saw such work as isolating and

ATTITUDES TO WOMEN WORKING, CANADA, 1988

EVERYONE WOULD BE BETTER OFF IF MORE WOMEN:	M (%)	F (%)
were satisfied to stay home and have families	28	23
were encouraged to have careers of their own	40	39
neither/undecided	32	38
TOTAL	100	100
SAMPLE SIZE	1099	993

PERCENT INDICATING THAT WOMEN STAYING HOME WOULD BE BETTER, BY VARIOUS CHARACTERISTICS OF THE RESPONDENTS	M (%)	F (%)
No children at home	19	9
3+ children at home	29	29
Age: 18-21	14	4
21-25	23	13
36-50	20	18
51-64	38	41
65+	65	41
Less than secondary education	63	43
Graduate/professional	17	2
Family income under $30,000	39	31
Family income $80,000+	26	12
Not religious	25	10
Religious	37	26

Source: Lenton 1992: 91, 92, 93, 94, 95, 96.
National Election Study, 1988.

TABLE 2.6

boring, and valued paid work over domestic work, they also saw men as incompetent or unwilling to do domestic work. Gaskell concluded, "Men remain outside of the whole process of negotiation." Largely, these young women also believed that young children needed to be cared for by their mothers in order to grow up well-adjusted. They registered negative opinions on day care and babysitting. It appeared that the women had correctly perceived the attitudes of the men in the sample, because those men treated paid work as their main focus of concern and tended to accept a traditional view of the division of labour in the home. In effect, these young men did not appear to have spent much time worrying about domestic work. One statement is rather telling: "The males and females don't share the work in our house. The females got nothing else to do. When mother was working, she did all the housework too, but that's because my sister wouldn't do it."

Although expressed differently, the attitudes of students from middle- and upper-income backgrounds at a U.S. liberal arts college in the early 1990s were not that different (Novack and Novack 1996). For instance, 52.6 percent of the women and 69 percent of the men strongly believed that a mother should stay home with a young child. Another 15 percent "somewhat" believed that she should stay home. Asked if they would select career over marriage if they had to choose, 67 percent of men and 49 percent of women chose the career. Conversely, 18 percent of men and 38 percent of women said they would select marriage over career if they had to choose.

Box 2.2 provides further examples of core attitudes that portray a difference in the understanding of appropriate opportunity structures of women and men. These examples are taken from the lives of steelworkers living in Hamilton, Ontario. However, barriers expressed through oral communication do not apply only to working-class settings. At a university meeting in the early 1990s, someone expressed the hope that a given committee "would have the balls" to do the right thing. This implied that, lacking the proper anatomy, women would not be able to accomplish the task. In his book *Women at Work: Discrimination and Response*, economist Stephen Peitchinis (1989) focuses on the perceptions about capabilities that supposedly place women in a disadvantaged position.

Hopeful signs?

We know from our everyday experience that many cultural expressions reinforce the differences and relative statuses of the sexes. For instance, most people would not think that men and women are opposites to each other in the way that "up" is opposite to "down." Nevertheless, "the opposite sex" is a commonly used term. The same applies to the excessive use of "he" (when talking about people in general) and "girl." In effect, in various ways our very language defines the statuses of the sexes and undermines women's claim to a mature and equal adult status.

If we could manage to use more gender-neutral language, we might find it possible to negotiate other forms of cultural understandings that involve greater equality. In *The Second Shift*, Hochschild (1989: 270) emphasizes the inequality in the distribution of housework in two-income families, but nonetheless ends with hopeful views on the potential for the emergence of a "new man":

> The happiest two-job marriages I saw were between men and women who did not load the former role of the housewife-mother onto the woman, and did not devalue it.... They shared that role between them. What couples called "good communication" often meant that they were good at saying thanks for one tiny form or another of taking care of the family. Making it to the school play, helping a child read, cooking dinner in good spirit, remembering the grocery list.... These were the silver and gold of the marital exchange. Up until now, the woman married to the "new man" has been one of the lucky few. But as the government and society shape a new gender strategy, as the young learn from example, many more women and men will be able to enjoy the leisurely bodily rhythms and freer laughter that arise when family life is family life and not a second shift.

A study of changing values in Canada, the United States, and ten European countries reaches similar conclusions. In *The Decline of Deference*, Neil Nevitte (1996) observes a general pattern between 1981 and 1990 as people became less deferential in their outlooks toward politics, the workplace, and family life. In particular, they became less confident in a whole range of government and non-government institutions. The family remained one of the most important priorities in people's lives, but Nevitte found more permissiveness and tolerance surrounding family questions. Especially in Canada, he found that both men and women wanted spousal relations and parent-child relations to be more egalitarian. Among the 24 value dimensions considered, he found that Canadians were most egalitarian when it comes to spousal relations and shared responsibilities.

This comparison of Canadian values also shows that "sharing household chores" was the only value, among nine factors measured, that increased as an attribute considered important for a successful marriage (Nevitte 1996: 247). The very fact that people aspire to fairly democratic family relations may partly explain the lack of respect for institutions that do not operate on the basis of openness and merit. While Nevitte's study considered attitudes rather than behaviour, the results do express hopefulness regarding the possibilities for more egalitarian gender relations.

In their 1994 study in Hamilton, Livingstone and Elizabeth Asner (1996: 95) find that some respondents expressed egalitarian orientations. They quoted, for instance, a dual-earner couple who both held "intermediate employee" positions:

BOX 2.2 | *Gender consciousness among steelworkers and their spouses*

In 1983-84, David Livingstone and Meg Luxton (1989, 1996) surveyed the gender attitudes of Hamilton steelworkers and their spouses. Although they found considerable support for the general principle of equal opportunity for women, a majority of the survey responses indicated a belief that men should have priorities for jobs. In effect, the researchers found considerable support for the breadwinner model. For instance, one homemaker wife says:

> I make sure he goes to work happy and in a good mood every day. So he is going into his workplace not thinking about things. He can go and put his mind into his job, not worry about what is worrying at home... I gave up my job when we got married, but that was a mutual agreement. I didn't do it for him. He didn't make me quit my job, you know. I could probably go back to work somehow.
> (Livingstone and Luxton 1996: 121)

In addition, masculine shop-floor culture made it difficult for women to enter these previously all-male terrains:

> Sexually antagonistic language pervades the steel mill. The employees characterize work itself—especially difficult work—as feminine and to be conquered: "It's a real bitch," "Give her hell." Similarly, to deal with malfunctioning machinery they use derogatory terms for women—bitch, slut—terms that often have explicit sexual connotations. They similarly describe disliked bosses by using terms that either cast aspersions on their masculinity and sexual ability—wimp, creampuff, dick—or identify them with negative female terms—bitch. They express specific anger by using terms for sexual intercourse, and they often describe their exploitation by management by using rape terms—"We're getting fucked" or "We're getting screwed around." (Livingstone and Luxton 1996: 115)

My husband has always been very helpful, very supportive. Right from the beginning before we had kids, everything has been shared. We have both taken our fair share of courses; we have just always managed to balance it off. Sometimes he took courses during the winter while I babysat and summers I took courses while he babysat. We both reached the top salary category. He did before I did but I wasn't far behind.

On the basis of economic considerations, Scott Coltrane (1998b: 176) also ends his synthesis with optimistic projections. Given similar levels of education, with more women employed, the need to have two earners to maintain middle-class standing, and with wages and work hours converging, he expects to see significantly more sharing of family work by men. In particular, he expects new ideals of shared spheres to develop, first in child care and grocery shopping, then in cooking and cleaning.

> **BOX 2.2 CONT'D**

When the same steelworkers and their spouses were interviewed again in 1994, most of the women had been in paid employment, and there was less support for the breadwinner model (Livingstone and Luxton 1996). Nonetheless, some women homemakers continue to prefer the older division of labour:

> I just believe men should be able to work; women should be home taking care of the families. I'm kind of old-fashioned, that kind of thinking. But I also see both sides. That's not the reality these days. It does take two people to go out to working. So I know I'll have to go out as soon as the baby's old enough. I'll have no choice. But I don't really look forward to that, you know? I do in one sense—the feeling of accomplishment, feeling like you've got something more to live for than the next day's laundry, you know? (Livingstone and Luxton 1996: 129)

Most women see considerable obstacles in the way of gender equality:

> Men are *starting* to realize that they can't just be the breadwinner and come home to a home-cooked meal and that's it. Women are working now and you can't do it that way. But there's still an awful lot of men that just don't want to change. Even my husband, he'll always say, "What is there to do?" And later on he'll say, "Why didn't you tell me you had all that stuff to do?" Well, you can hear me doing dishes, why don't you come in and help me. I hate to ask you to do everything. If I'm still working, you should still be working. (Ibid.)

Livingstone and Luxton (1996: 129) conclude that until this household side of the breadwinner model is transformed, "Gender equality will remain very partial indeed."◆

EXPLANATIONS RELATED TO
THE LINK BETWEEN EARNING AND CARING

Given these economic and cultural explanations of gender differentiation and inequality, questions remain about the causal priority of material and cultural considerations, and about the direct connections between the domestic and outside-the-home work processes. In *Theorizing Women's Work*, Pat Armstrong and Hugh Armstrong (1990: 141) observe that an adequate explanation of women's work must "connect the labour processes in domestic and wage work." This link between paid and unpaid work, or earning and caring, involves material and cultural questions. Material questions relate to the gender distribution of paid and unpaid work. Cultural questions relate to the rationalization and institutionalization, in families and in the broader society, of this differential distribution of earning and caring by men and women. For Feree (1990), families are one of the institutional settings in which gender becomes a lived experience. Families construct gender especially through the division of labour, both paid and unpaid.

In *Le travail au féminin*, Kempeneers (1992) proposes that women's position as "conciliators" between the work and family domains is a primary factor in explaining the persistence of significant gender inequalities. For the most part, women and men are both involved in both spheres, but women bear the brunt of the accommodation between the two spheres. Especially as family needs change over the life course, it is women who tend to make the corresponding adjustments. That is why Kempeneers notes that work interruptions are a "privileged indicator" of the necessary complementarity between family and work.

Couples make various accommodations between earning and caring over the family life course. A typical accommodation involves wives doing less paid work, and men doing more, particularly during the phase when children are most dependent. Correspondingly, this phase typically involves women taking more responsibility for child care and domestic work—a division of labour that given families may see as an appropriate accommodation. State policies also support this typical division by conferring taxation advantages and administering other benefits based on the assumption that the spouse who earns less will be economically dependent on the spouse who earns more. Consequently, this accommodation would seem to have considerable "logic." However, this logic assumes the continuation of the marital relationship. When spouses stay together, they may manage to maximize, through these adjustments, the family's economic well-being, as well as maximizing the kind of care they want to give to each other and their children. If the relationship does not continue, the spouse who has carried the brunt of the accommodation is left with a serious disadvantage on the labour market.

This disadvantage on the labour market takes various forms. The main problem is that a work history of interruptions and part-time work leads to a lower level of experience. People with the objective of having a "career" rather than just finding work face the further difficulty of losing some of the investment in their careers. Career goals can require a "workaholic" period in which the worker gets established. This stage can also require the help of others to look after the domestic aspects of life, leaving the partner free to focus only on building the career and all that involves. Most people find it very difficult to be both a caring parent of young children and a workaholic on the job.

Another difficulty can arise when, for one parent, the experience of earning is not evolving satisfactorily. In this case, for a woman, child-bearing can become a strategy for opting out of the labour force (Ni Bhrolchain 1993). When someone experiences frustrations with paid work, the options can be to keep trying or to give up. If caring or parenting seems to be a viable alternative, the option of giving up is more readily available. Once again, this choice may well maximize the earning and caring well-being of the couple, but the spouse who has given up on earning at a given time will be at a disadvantage if marital breakdown necessitates a sudden return to the labour market.

That is why the options for women can also be double-edged swords. In addition, not all of women's work interruptions are the result of the family life cycle—the presence and number of children—and they are sometimes a function of other gender factors in families and societies (Kempeneers 1992: 22). In *Part-time Paradox* (Duffy and Pupo 1992) and *Few Choices: Women, Work and Family* (Duffy, Mandell, and Pupo 1989), the writers observe that all three of what they see as the major alternatives present difficulties for women. Parents working *full-time* with children at home can experience life as a "rat race" in which the overwhelming presence of work makes for a family life that is not worth living. The alternative of having one parent as a *housekeeper* presents the disadvantage of isolation and low status. The intermediate alternative of *part-time* work leads to a lack of seniority, few work benefits, and continued economic dependence, which does little to challenge patriarchal arrangements in the home.

Consequently, individual decisions, if they can even be thought of as choices, to work, choose an occupation, have children, work part-time, or change employment are a reflection of what Kempeneers (1992) calls the global adjustment processes between the structures of production and reproduction. It is women, much more often than men, who are at the junction between the activities that correspond to the needs of reproduction (domestic work) and that correspond to the needs of direct production (salaried work). Simply put, Kempeneers (1992: 82) says that women are at the heart of a key "social fact": the adjustment between the productive and reproductive structures.

Home-leaving

The very process of leaving home can be related to the life alternatives that are a priority for given persons. One team (Bloss, Frickey, and Novi 1994) studied women in France who were born in 1947 and who, by age 40, had both married and been in the paid workforce. They found that the "mode of entry into adult life," whether it was to form a union upon leaving home or to first live on their own, had significant impact on subsequent life alternatives. Those women who formed a union upon leaving home were less likely to have been continuously employed. They also had more children and were more likely to have had work interruptions associated with children or the mobility of the spouse.

Occupational segregation

The issue of occupational segregation or the dual labour market illustrates another aspect of this articulation between family and work. Women are concentrated in occupations that undervalue the human-capital value of both education and experience (on this, see also chapter 4). The processes of this segregation involve a variety of factors at work, at home, and in the society. Looking at the role of the family, Sonalde Desai and Linda Waite (1991) test the hypothesis that traditional female occupations attract women because they are easier to combine with motherhood. They find that this contingency mostly operates for women who do not plan to work in the long term: that is, the recruitment of women into "convenient" occupations seems to operate only for women who plan not to work over the long run.

Besides this recruitment aspect, there are likely to be self-perpetuating mechanisms in terms of the flexibility of given occupations. The occupations that have recruited more women are likely to have been prompted to make further changes in order to accommodate family roles. Conversely, occupations dominated by men have had less need to introduce family-friendly features, because few of the workers are balancing family and work. If these interpretations are correct, there is potential for transformation. The pattern could change as more women consider full-time work over the long term as their preferred life alternative and as more persons with parental responsibilities introduce change to occupations that previously had no need for such flexibility.

Domestic work

William Goode (1981), the renown family scholar, in a frequently quoted article on men's resistance to women's emancipation, spoke of two areas in which he saw little change and strong resistance: occupational segregation and domestic tasks. It is also significant that Betty Friedan's (1963: 15) famous "problem that has no name" emerged from conversations with housewives: "Each suburban wife struggled with it alone. As she made the beds, shopped for groceries, matched slipcover material, ate peanut butter sandwiches with her children, chauffeured Cub Scouts and Brownies, lay beside her husband at night."

The traditional family division of labour has men taking more responsibility for earning, with women helping, and women taking more responsibility for caring, with men helping. The unpaid work in and around the home also tends to be specialized. Women are much more likely to take responsibility for the dominant ongoing tasks (such as meals), while men are more likely to perform duties that are more specific (occasional cleaning up) and to take responsibility for chores that involve more time flexibility (repairs). Unpaid work involves not only the accomplishment of a variety of specific tasks, but also the coordination of the work and taking overall responsibility for its accomplishment. Questions of coordination are difficult to measure but they are probably very unequally distributed by gender. There are also differences in multi-tasking: women are more likely to do more than one thing at a time, including being preoccupied with household tasks when they might otherwise appear to be simply "taking care of themselves."

Although the typical division of labour represents a certain symmetry, it has profound outcomes that are far from symmetrical. For one thing, if a change comes in the amount of paid work performed by a given partner, the shift can present difficulties for the corresponding accommodations in unpaid work. If, for instance, a wife re-enters paid work, it may become starkly clear that the husband is not doing an equivalent share of unpaid work. With the woman having previously taken responsibility for the overall accomplishment of the household's unpaid work, there may be a limited amount of small tasks that can be delegated to the husband—unless a major change occurs in the overall responsibility for domestic work. Just as it takes time for men to accept that family work does not undermine their masculine identity, it also takes time for women to separate their identity from family work. Until then, women may even resist men's involvement in domestic work. One researcher found that wives who have worked over a longer period of time and have higher earnings are more likely to do less housework (McDonald 1990).

The slowness of these adjustments, along with the reasonable symmetry in the overall distribution of work, helps explain why the majority of couples are not unhappy with their own arrangements for the distribution of work (see Box 2.3). U.S. studies suggest that most wives are satisfied with the small amount of housework that their husbands do, and only a minority of women feel that husbands should do more (Thompson and Walker 1989: 854-55).

Family and gender

It would appear, then, that couples often have a sense of equity about the division of work, but still the division is far from symmetrical, at least in terms of the kinds of work tasks performed. While this condition may be fine in terms of equity within couples, it clearly reinforces inequity by gender in the broader society. The family links between earning and caring are responsible for the perpetuation of gender inequality in a number of ways. For one thing, it is in the family more than the workplace where we insist that males and females are fundamentally different (Coltrane 1998a).

Thus *The Gender Factory* makes a good title for a book on the "apportionment of work in American households" (Berk 1985). Continued gender inequality is not only a function of structures in the broader society but also a function of what is happening inside of families. Mackie (1995: 49) states succinctly that "gender and familial norms are simultaneously forged." Similarly, Coltrane (1998b) makes the case that family lives and gender meanings are mutually forged and inseparably linked. Much gender differentiation

BOX 2.3 | *Satisfaction regarding division of work*

A radio call-in program in London, Ontario, began one day with a quote from a study cited in the *Reader's Digest* (Levine 1997): a U.S. study had found that working women were doing two-thirds of the housework, that nearly half of women were doing 20 hours or more of housework a week, while half of the men surveyed were doing 5 hours or less. The host of the call-in program asked his listeners to talk about how they divided tasks and how wives were getting husbands to do more of their share. Surprisingly, caller after caller referred to their own cases, in which these things were working out properly, as being exceptions. Then a man called who said that things were not equal in his home, and he felt guilty about it, but that he and his wife couldn't figure out how to change the situation. The host of the program decided, using words from the callers, that London that morning was apparently populated by "saints" and "honest people."

While a call-in program by no means provides a random sample, it is true that in many conversations about the division of household labour people imply that they have found appropriate solutions. Women will be heard to say that, compared to other women, "I am lucky," or "my husband is good," or "my husband is an exception." In *The Second Shift* Hochschild (1989: xvi) even says that about her own marriage.

But, clearly, in many marriages one or the other of the partners (and usually the woman) sees the division of work as being significantly unjust. Interestingly, the statistic for this dissatisfaction, which is difficult to estimate but probably around a quarter to a third of all couples, is about the same as the figure for the proportion of marriages that end in divorce (Thompson and Walker 1989: 858). It would appear that the inability of couples to work out acceptable arrangements on the sharing of work can represent a major element of incompatibility. It could also be that persons who are not willing to do their share have already indicated that they do not care about the relationship. Putting it in other, more positive, terms, persons who care about each other will seek to establish relationships based on a sense of overall equity.

Researching U.S. couples, Joan Huber and Glenna Spitze (1983) found that over a fifth of men and close to a third of women had seriously "thought of divorce." Earnings had no effect on the likelihood of these considerations, but it appears that the more housework the husband was seen to do, the less likely the wife was to think of divorce. Based on interviews with U.S. couples in the late 1970s, two other researchers observed: "Married men's aversion to housework is so intense, it can sour their relationship. The more housework they do, for whatever reason, the more they fight about it. If this pattern continues into the future, it will be a major barrier to the reorganization of husbands' and wives' roles" (Blumstein and Schwartz 1983: 146).

But sharing tasks can also be difficult. Since the effort raises the potential for mutual criticism and, for the men, of entering the wife's domain, Thompson and Walker (1989: 859) find that "sharing family work is associated with greater marital strain."◆

revolves around the specific tasks performed by women and men. For Heidi Hartmann (1981: 393), the creation of gender can be seen as the creation of a division of labour between the sexes, or of two classes of workers who depend on each other. Sarah Berk (1985: 3) suggests that the context of household labour is the basis on which "partners come to know whether their marriages are made in heaven, hell or somewhere in between." Clearly, the solution suggested by the Marlo Thomas song "Free to Be" is not as easily achieved as the refrain implies: "If there is housework to do, do it together."

Consequently, Hochschild (1989) speaks of a "stalled revolution." She envisages three stages of fatherhood, comparing them to historical economic periods. In the first stage, typified by family farms, fathers taught their sons many of the skills they needed. In the second stage, typified by blue-collar industry, fathers worked away from the family and mothers ensured the children's upbringing. In the third stage both spouses are working, typically in the service sector. But the corresponding third stage of fatherhood, involving the division of household labour, is rare. This is precisely the "stalled revolution." Over the 1980s Hochschild found that more couples wanted to share domestic labour, and some imagined that they did. Sometimes couples made elaborate efforts to maintain a family myth of equal division. The concept of the "supermom" kicked in to cover up spousal conflicts over the second shift and consequently to hide the difficult choice faced by some women "between having a stable marriage and an equal one" (Hochschild 1989: 32).

Focusing on parenting in particular, Nancy Folbre (1994) asks, *Who Pays for the Kids?* She concludes that both inside the money economy and outside of the labour market, women shoulder much of the costs. Data from the 1981 and 1991 Canadian censuses show that parenting has significant consequences for women (Grindstaff 1990a, 1996). No one would be surprised to hear that women who were married or had children early in life would suffer disadvantages in the labour force, but the same would appear to be true, admittedly to a lesser extent, for women who have children later in life. Considering women who were aged 30 at the time of the 1981 census, Grindstaff found that the largest differences in terms of completed education, labour-force activity, and personal income were between those women with and without children. Turning to women who were aged 33-38 in 1991, he compared those with no children and those who had children at about age 30. Those with children had lower labour-force participation, greater likelihood of working part-time, and lower incomes.

The gender system

This discussion of gender in the context of the link between earning and caring allows us to come back to the question of the causal priority of material and cultural considerations. While both elements of the explanation are essential, the material—economic or structural—considerations have causal priority. Karen Mason (1995: 2) finds that "gender system" is the best term to capture both economic and cultural considerations, "because it comprises the entire complex of roles, rights and statuses that surround being male versus female in a given society or culture." This system involves a division of labour, along with attendant rights and responsibilities, that creates inequalities in well-being, autonomy, and power.

Bonnie Fox (1988) makes this same case for the causal priority of economic questions by conceptualizing patriarchy as a structure or a system that involves the production of economic goods and the reproduction of people. This system is first observable in the family, and particularly in "the mother-child relation and the motherwork involved in raising a child" (Fox 1988: 176). But this division of labour entails agencies beyond the family, because other social structures, including the state itself, perpetuate the privatization of domestic responsibilities and the separation of public and private activities. As a consequence, Fox concludes, in today's society these patriarchal social structures handicap the sex that bears children.

CONCLUSION

Gender is a pervasive phenomenon that infuses all of life. By "doing gender" in a variety of contexts, we are actively involved in the redefinition and perpetuation of gender differences. For instance, it is often assumed that women want to reduce gender differentiation, but many women feel comfortable with such differences and "most women collaborate with men to maintain gender specialization" (Thompson and Walker 1989: 865). In his book *Gender and Families*, Coltrane (1998b) shows how various ideals and family practices not only allow members to care for one another but also create gender differences and perpetuate inequality. He proposes that "people have more control over defining gender than they usually assume" and that persons who can develop their own perspective on gender and families are able to feel in control of their lives (Coltrane 1998b: 7, 10).

The differentiation goes beyond specialization and involves hierarchies of access to *economic* resources, of *autonomy* over one's personal and physical destiny, and hierarchies of *power* in the decision-making of groups and societies. The continuity and change in these domains include both material or economic considerations and the barriers and opportunities provided by *cultures* and ideologies. Family questions play a large part in this differentiation. A key question relates to the exploitation that can occur through the exchange, at the family level, between *paid and unpaid work*, or between earning and caring (Lerner 1986).

Gender differentiation is therefore manifest in family patterns, with gender specialization appearing in a variety of family activities, from styles of love to parenting. A central consideration is the primacy of men's earning activities and of women's caring activities. This division has wide implications within and beyond families. For instance, Mackie (1995: 68) observes, "The majority of men still operate under considerable pressure to give their jobs priority over their families." While this can be interpreted as men giving priority to their jobs instead of their families, it could also be seen as men accepting greater responsibility for the earning side of family well-being. In addition, many of the jobs in which men are located have little flexibility to allow for the interface of work and family roles. As Eugen Lupri and Gladys Symons (1982: 183) conclude, "The persistence of segregation in the labour force and the privatized nuclear family remain two of the most pervasive structural barriers to gender equality."

In *Familiar Exploitation*, Christine Delphy and Diana Leonard (1992) make a stronger argument. They propose that contemporary families perpetuate a system of control over women's labour, in the material interests of men. In effect, this is a strong "patriarchy" stance that argues that men's authority over women determines the sexual allocation of labour. However, as Julie Brines (1995) observes, this labour system involves codes of behaviour that vary across cultures and are not simply reducible to male material interests. In addition, it is hard to see how marriage and family, as weakened institutions, "could retain such a lock on women's options." While family questions are central, then, explanations need to include both material and symbolic elements, along with the interpersonal dynamics that define gender in an ongoing way.

Our review of these issues would suggest, as Goode (1981) said in his analysis of "why men resist," that the system is "marching in the right direction." Among the indicators presented, the change in education will probably have the greatest consequences. Nonetheless, serious gender inequality remains in the three axes of economics, autonomy, and power. In the economic sphere, significant differences remain in levels of income, along with a persistent poverty gap. As for autonomy, women suffer more abuse and harassment than men in both public and private places. In the matter of power, the relative presence of men and women in positions of political and economic power indicates persistent differences in the ability to make or influence decisions.

Given the conflicts between child care and labour-force participation, and the frequent observation that the division of work lacks symmetry especially when children are young, it might seem that childlessness is the easiest route to equality. But most people want children and are prepared to make sacrifices for them. Some other relationships can establish equality based on differentiated or complementary roles that are taken to be appropriate for the life goals of spouses. Other relationships are trying to achieve equality as co-providers and co-parents, that is, through a more equal division of both work and family activities.

THREE

Changing Families

Understanding the changing links between earning and caring means looking at how families are changing as well as at family diversity. Our focus in this chapter is on the trends affecting family variability and change, as seen especially through *entry into* and *exit from* family relationships. After establishing an *interpretive framework* for family change, I consider variability in terms of *family relationships, family units,* and the *lives of adult women and men.*

Men, in particular it seems, are more likely to be living in relationships, while women are more likely to be living with children. This poses problems for the economic welfare of women and for the intergenerational connectivity of men. At the same time, some of the changes with the most profound impact on the restructuring of families are the ones that break down the distinction between the adult roles of men and women, especially their paid work activity. As other chapters will further demonstrate, this restructuring is evolving in the direction of a family model based less on specialization and complementarity and more on the insurance gains of symmetrical and companionate relationships.

◆

As seen in the previous chapter, there are strong links between gender and family questions. In many respects, family and gender roles are forged together. The family would appear to be the main environment in which we do gender, and consequently where gender is produced and sustained. It is probably in the family, more so than in schools and workplaces, that we insist on males and females being different. For many people, the ideology of the ideal family includes a complementarity of roles for husbands and wives, fathers and mothers. This can be seen in reactions to propositions for gender equality. Such propositions are sometimes seen as attacking the family in its very foundations.

In tandem with these questions of gender, family questions provide the most relevant ongoing social context for most people. Family time tends to predominate in the non-work time of individuals, and much of the paid work done is itself oriented toward producing the resources needed for the family. Indeed, popular culture indicates the central importance of families to people's lives, with one situation comedy after another playing out common family situations and the ubiquitous talk shows often delving into family relationships. In addition, the family provides an important social network for most people. Based on data from France, Catherine Bonvalet and Eva Lelièvre (1995) find that the average size of an adult's network of relatives is around 40 persons. Even persons living alone cite an average of three to four "close family members."

To understand the changing links between earning and caring, we clearly need to analyze how families are changing and how they vary. As we will see, the main elements in this change and diversity are related to the means of entry and exit from family relationships. In the area of entry, factors are the delay of marriage, the prevalence of cohabitation as a means of entry into relationships, and fewer and later births as a means of bringing children into families. In the area of exit, a main factor is the instability of relationships and, consequently, voluntary departures rather than death marking the end of a marriage. However, "exit" may be an excessively strong term. Especially if a relationship has produced children, separation and divorce can bring the relationship to a different phase rather than to its termination. From the point of view of children, both parents typically remain part of family life even if the parents are not in the same household. Consequently, marital instability can both expand a person's family network and bring greater uncertainty regarding family relationships.

These changing means of entry and exit from family clearly have consequences for diversity. The diversity can include families with or without children, relationships with or without marriage, and children with or without two parents living with them in the household. Depending on the biological and social bonds across parents and children, the diversity can include step-relationships and blended families. Consequently, from the point of view of children, there may be two parents, one parent, or multiple parents. Other forms of diversity include same-sex relationships, or relationships that are not based on an understanding of sexual exclusivity. Diversity can also be associated with the paid and unpaid work activities of spouses or partners, distinguishing in particular between single-earner and dual-earner couples.

With all this change and diversity, it can become difficult to see what families have in common, and consequently what the concept of *family* really means. I propose (see Box 3.1) to define families as units of people who share resources and care for each other: again, emphasizing earning and caring. This pooling of earning and caring may be imperfect. Our definitions must not blind us to the exploitation, abuse, or violence that occurs in families. In effect, earning and caring are variables that can be more or less present, and more or less pooled, in a given family. Scott Coltrane (1998b) further proposes that families be defined in terms not only of shared activities but also of shared knowledge and practices. Each family is unique in terms of its history, experiences, and rituals. These experiences and history, especially as recalled in family stories, re-create a sense of belonging and uniqueness. Consequently, individuals construct their experience of family through stories and rituals—that is, "through narratives in which people make sense of themselves and the world around them" (Knowles 1996: 37). Often, gender plays an important role in the narratives that define given families.

In studying family change and diversity, we need also to observe that, in certain regards, the family shows less variability than it did at earlier times. In particular, the decline in the premature death of parents means that very few children are exposed to orphanhood and its associated life-threatening uncertainties. Living arrangements today clearly see more lone-parent families and more people living alone or sharing accommodations with friends, but fewer multiple-family households, and fewer households that include persons beyond the immediate family, such as a live-in grandparent, relative, boarder, apprentice, or servant. The changing means of entry into relationships, and longer lifespans, bring considerable diversity across families that are in the earlier or later parts of the life course. The mid-life stage, though—say, between ages 30 and 55—shows strong commonalities of experience: most adults are living in relationships, most are parenting, and most are working.

UNDERSTANDING FAMILY CHANGE

The historical transformations of the family involved two key transitions: a long-term change (from about 1870 to 1950), which brought smaller families; and a more rapid change (from about 1960 to the present), which increased flexibility in marital relationships (Lesthaeghe 1995). (See Box 3.2).

The first transition involved a change in the economic costs and benefits of children, along with a cultural environment that made it more appropriate to control family size. In effect, this transition changed family dynamics surrounding fertility from an emphasis on child quantity to child quality (see chapter 6).

The second transition in Western countries, according to Ron Lesthaeghe (1995), had three stages. The *first stage*, from about 1960 to 1970, involved the end of the baby boom, the end of the trend toward younger ages at marriage, and the beginning of the rise in divorces. The *second stage*, from 1970 to 1985, involved the growth of common-law unions and eventually of children in cohabiting unions. The *third stage*, from 1985 to the present, involves a plateau in divorce, an increase in postmarital cohabitation (and consequently a decline in remarriage), and a plateau in fertility due in part to higher proportions of births after age 30.

Table 3.1 presents statistics that capture these trends for Canada. The average *births per woman*, as measured by the total fertility rate, had reached a peak of 3.9 in 1957 (the first stage), declined to 2.2 in 1971 (the second), and remained stable at about 1.6 to 1.7 births per woman over the period from 1980 to 1996 (into the third stage). The median *age at first marriage* declined over this half-century to reach a low of just over 21 years for brides and 23 years for grooms in the early 1970s, then increased to ages 26 and 28 for women and men respectively in 1996. The law permitting *divorces* on grounds other than

BOX 3.1 | *Defining families*

Defining "family" is so difficult that even some textbooks on the subject do not include a definition (for example, Broderick 1979: 394-96). In one of my own chapters I define family as "two or more people related by blood, marriage, or adoption and residing together" (Beaujot 1998: 241). Bonnie Fox and Meg Luxton (1991: 9) find that this definition is inadequate because it accepts "biology and law as determinants of social relations" and "equating family and household is more reflective of ideology than social reality." One text (Larson, Goltz, and Hobart 1994: 550) defines family as "a kinship group normatively defined to carry out the nutrient socialisation of dependent children." This definition also seems to be restrictive because it excludes families without children. In an article headlined "Defining the Family: The New Cold War," The *London Free Press* (1992: E1) cites an even narrower definition offered by a Member of Parliament: "Legislation should define a family as a male and a female, living together to raise children ... and that's the only kind of family that ought to be defined." Indeed, while some laws recognize same-sex couples as common-law couples with comparable rights to spousal benefits, and some churches bless same-sex unions, by the end of the 1990s no province had recognized same-sex unions as an official marriage (Binder 1998).

In their extensive discussion "Conceptualizing Family," Fox and Luxton (1991: 35) observe that the legal definition of family is based on rights and obligations for certain legally described people, principally parents and children, husbands and wives. Without giving a strict sociological definition, they propose that family can be thought of "as the relationships that bring people together daily to share resources for the sake of caring for children and each other." Robert Glossop (1994) suggests a similar concept for the family, revolving around "relationships ... of affection and obligation."

In effect, families can be defined as people sharing resources and caring for each other, or people pooling earning and caring. For purposes of an operational definition useable in the field, some writers have simply defined families as "people eating out of the same pot." This is an interesting concept, because "the same pot" represents the key life-maintaining resources that have been both obtained and prepared (sometimes through paid and unpaid work), and eating together is clearly a means of looking after each other or caring for each other. This pooling of earning and caring is more likely to occur when people are living in the same household, as evidenced by the significant levels of default on child support payments by absent fathers. The "family class" sponsorship of immigrants to Canada also emphasizes the importance of living in the same household. In effect, persons sponsored in the family class are less likely to become dependent on social assistance if they live in the same household as the sponsoring relative (Thomas 1996). The Fox and Luxton idea of people "coming together daily" would also seem to imply living, or at least connecting to each other, in the same dwelling.

For its data-gathering purposes Statistics Canada uses these definitions:

CENSUS FAMILY: a married or cohabitating couple, with or without never-married children, or a lone parent with at least one never-married child, living in the same dwelling.

ECONOMIC FAMILY: a group of two or more persons who live in the same dwelling and are related to each other by blood, marriage, common-law or adoption.

While the concept of economic family is broader, it retains the limitation of being based on dwelling units. However, data-gathering needs to start with something easily identifiable in the field. It is possible to go from there to consider other persons beyond the dwelling and to observe the extent of pooling of earning and caring that occurs beyond the census or economic family. In particular, we need to know more about the relationships of absent parents and their children. We also need to observe the lack of pooling of earning and caring—exploitation and abuse, perhaps—that can occur within residential families.

The definition of "family" presents difficulties not only for data-gathering, but also for arriving at a consensus on key aspects of the future of humanity. In the proceedings of the Cairo International Conference on Population and Development, the chapter on families is one of the weakest, partly because the countries of the world could not agree on the definition of something so close to daily life (United Nations 1994). Similarly, at the 1995 Beijing Fourth International Conference on Women, the language on families presented some of the most difficult stumbling blocks to consensus. One would think that a conference seeking to

enhance the status and well-being of women would want to say something about families. But, while families are dear to the lives of women, and men, they also represent barriers to gender equality, and sometimes they produce serious exploitation or block opportunities. Consequently, while official government policy often seeks to enhance individual well-being by supporting families, sometimes it also deems that this well-being will best be served by removing an individual from a given family. Given that child-protection agencies are empowered to remove children, Caroline Knowles (1996) makes interesting use of their activities, looking at their functions as a boundary that defines acceptable family conduct.

We can avoid some of these conceptual difficulties by choosing not to define family units and focusing instead only on family relationships. We can then speak of relationships between *partners*, who may be married, cohabitating, or formerly married, and relationships between *parents and children*, who may or may not be living together, and relationships with other *relatives*. These kinds of configurations can be particularly useful in considering how the lives of individuals are changed by family events. They also provide the possibility of a "dyadic approach," in which each pair of relationships can be examined on such questions as power, structure, and emotional ties (Trost 1996).

This focus on relationships allows us to observe that given sets of people have various associations that are sometimes coordinated and sometimes uncoordinated. The various activities of life are constantly pulling individuals apart, but then again some things are also constantly bringing people together as a family. Dorothy Smith

(1997) conceptualizes this as "coordinating the uncoordinated." She also observes that this fundamental coordinating task, which "produces an ordinary family day," is a very gendered activity (see chapter 5). In her study of *Feeding the Family*, Marjorie De Vault (1991: 14) also defines families through experiences, particularly the shared activities of daily life. Households are therefore sites of material interdependence. She observes that we tend to focus on the emotional character of family life and to downplay the economic interdependence.◆

adultery dates only from 1968. For every 100,000 married women, there were under 200 divorces in each year over the period 1951-66 compared to 1,000 in 1976 and 1,200 in 1996.

Cohabiting unions were not specifically enumerated in the 1976 census, although some 0.7 percent of couples indicated that they were living common-law. By 1986 most of the Statistics Canada data no longer distinguished between married and cohabiting couples. The 1996 census determined that 13.7 percent of couples were cohabiting. The 1995 General Social Survey found that among persons born between 1951 and 1970, two out of five have lived in a cohabiting union, and over half of first unions taking place since 1985 were cohabitations rather than marriages (Dumas and Bélanger 1997: 135, 139). The proportion of births occurring to women who were *not married*, and most of whom were cohabiting, increased from 9 in 1971 to 36 percent in 1996.

In the third stage, by 1990, half of divorced persons aged 30-39, and more than a third of those aged 40-49, were in *cohabiting* relationships (Dumas and Péron 1992: 50). In addition to the stable fertility rate for the period 1980-96, the proportion of births occurring to women aged 30 and over increased from 19.6 percent in 1976 to 43.7 percent in 1996.

These changes in the rates of births, marriage, cohabitation, and divorce have not only produced fewer children, but also led to a higher proportion of children living apart from both biological parents. In particular, lone-parent families as a proportion of all families with children increased from 11.4 in 1961 to 22.3 in 1996.

These data also confirm the uniqueness of the 1950s as a period between the two transitions. Various authors have observed that life was family-centred in the 1950s. The decade not only represented the peak of the *baby boom*, but was also a period of *marriage rush*, with marriage occurring at younger ages and higher proportions of persons married at least once in their lives. It was possibly a "golden age of the family," in which many families corresponded to the ideal of domesticity, especially in the suburbs, and the time consequently saw less variability (Skolnick 1987: 6-16).

Subsequent research indicates, though, that not all was ideal in this golden age. Isolated housewives in particular experienced the "problem with no name" (see chapter 2). With the task of maintaining the home's internal affairs assigned to women, men became less competent at the social skills needed to nourish and maintain relationships (Goldscheider and Waite 1991: 19). The idealism of the time also introduced blinders

SUMMARY STATISTICS ON FAMILY CHANGE, CANADA, 1941-96

	1941	1951	1961	1971	1976	1981	1986	1991	1996
Total fertility rate (average births per women)	2.8	3.5	3.8	2.1	1.8	1.7	1.6	1.7	1.6
Median age at first marriage									
Brides	23.0	22.0	21.1	21.3	21.6	22.5	23.9	25.1	26.3
Grooms	26.3	24.8	24.0	23.5	23.7	24.6	25.8	27.0	28.3
Divorces per 100,000 married couples	—	180	180	600	990	1180	1302	1235	1222
Common-law couples as a percent of all couples	—	—	—	—	0.7	6.4	8.2	11.2	13.7
Births to non-married women as a percent of all births	4.0	3.8	4.5	9.0	10.9	14.2	18.8	28.6	36.3
Births to women aged 30+ as a percent of all births	35.6	36.2	34.1	21.6	19.6	23.6	29.2	36.0	43.7
Lone-parent families as a percent of all families with children	9.8	9.8	11.4	13.2	14.0	16.6	18.8	20.0	22.3

NOTES: For 1941-71 births to non-married women are designated as illegitimate births.
    Data for 1995 are shown as 1996 for divorce and births to non-married.

Source: Statistics Canada, no. 82-553, 1992: Tables 10, 16, 3. Statistics Canada, no. 82-552, 1992: Table 14. Statistics Canada, no. 84-212, 1995. Statistics Canada, no. 91-209, 1996: 19. Statistics Canada, no. 84-204, 1971. Special tabulations, Statistics Canada. Gentleman and Park 1997: 55; Adams 1988: 19. 1941 Census, vol. V: Table 19. 1951 Census, vol. III: Table 136.

TABLE 3.1

regarding certain realities of family life, including violence and abuse. Given a general denial that such things could ever occur in families, the victims of violence had little recourse. The times also saw a lack of autonomy, especially for women, to pursue routes other than the accepted path (Veevers 1980). Childless couples were considered selfish, single persons were seen as deviants, working mothers were considered to be harming their children, and single women who became pregnant were required either to marry or to give up the child to preserve family integrity. For instance, in the 1950s four out of five Americans described persons who did not marry as neurotic, selfish, or immoral (Kersten and Kersten 1991; Wilson 1990: 99).

The restriction on alternative lifestyles did mean that there were few single-parent families, and consequently the pain associated with that kind of variability was limited. In hindsight, we can nonetheless observe the existence of pent up problems that were preparing the way for the second transition, starting in the 1960s.

Macro or structural explanations

The phenomenon of family change has been addressed through two broadly competing explanations. The macro or structural perspective considers the relations of families to other parts of society and tends to see a reduction in the role of families. The micro or cultural perspective looks within families and observes in particular the greater importance of the expressive dimension. Both perspectives effectively argue that the family is weaker, either because it plays fewer roles in society or because families easily fall short of satisfying the high expectations for personal fulfilment.

Some writers have argued that family and kin groups had a larger number of functions in *pre-industrial* societies (for example, Goode 1977; Wrigley 1977). In those societies, besides being the chief units of reproduction and socialization of the young, families were also the units of economic production, and sometimes of political action and religious observance. Family groups performed many of the essential activities of the society: production, distribution, consumption, reproduction, socialization, recreation, and protection. For the most part, living space, the workplace, and child-rearing space were the same. Individuals depended on their families to cope with problems of age, sickness, and incapacity. In particular, the overlap between family and economy meant that economic activities occurred in family relationships. For the most part, only through membership in a family did people have a claim on membership in the broader society.

Industrialization and modernization brought *structural differentiation*: increasingly separate structures in society came to play specific functions. A substantial increase occurred in the role of non-family institutions such as factories, schools, medical and public health organizations, police, and commercialized leisure. The family lost many of its roles in economic production, education, social security, and care of the aged.

Consequently, the long-term changes in the family are related to societal changes, especially changes in economic structures. Families have become less central to the organization of society and to the lives of individuals, and this reduced role allows for more flexibility in family arrangements. For instance, the growth of wage labour for the young undermined parental authority and removed the barriers to early marriage. More broadly, families have become weaker institutions, with less cohesion, fewer functions, decreased power over other institutions, reduced influence on behaviour and opinion, and consequently less importance in life (Popenoe 1988). This change amounts to a de-institutionalization of the family, in the sense that fewer constraints exist on family behaviour. For instance, families have less control of the sexual behaviour of adolescents and are less involved in the socializing of children. Significantly, in some other areas of life more constraints on behaviour have emerged: for instance, smoking in public places, throwing out garbage, or sexually abusive behaviour at work. Not all areas of life have seen diminished constraints on individual behaviour.

In looking at the more recent transformations, the structural explanation pays attention to the shift to a *service economy*, which increased the demand for women's involvement in paid work (Chafetz and Hagan 1996). Until the 1960s the division of labour encouraged a reciprocal state of dependency between the sexes. Economic and policy structures discouraged women from participation in the labour force, and the family was thus based on the breadwinner model (see chapter 2). The expansion of the labour market in the 1960s especially involved jobs that might be seen as extensions of women's unpaid work: clerical work, teaching, nursing, and other services. This labour situation put pressure on women to postpone marriage as they extended their period of education and invested in their work lives. For both young women and young men, marriage became less important as a means of structuring their relationships and understandings, and consequently cohabitation became an alternative.

In the early postwar period, economic prosperity removed the barriers to early marriage for men, while women could keep busy in the home by having several children. It was a time when women not only had more children but also pursued more education and increased their labour-force participation. But the subsequent possibility for some women to become self-sufficient broke the dependency patterns associated with the breadwinner model. When women became less dependent on marriage, divorce and cohabitation became more feasible alternatives for both sexes. Focusing on men, Steven Mintz (1998) observes the long-term disappearance of patriarchal families based on father-son bonds, as well as the demise of the family wage and, consequently, the decline in the material basis of male familial authority. At the same time, he observes that the public concern about men's peripheral family roles dates back over a century.

In the first transition period, 1870-1950, *children* lost their economic value to parents as economic activities came to depend less on work within the family, including the labour of children, and the economic role of children changed from that of producer to that of dependant. Social security replaced the family as the basic welfare net in the face of economic hardships and incapacity. Thus the economic rationales for having children were seriously undermined. In the second transition, post-1960, children became an opportunity cost to employed women.

Still, these economic explanations are not definitive. According to economic logic, people today should be having hardly any children, yet the most common family size is two offspring.

Micro or cultural explanations

Other authors have focused on change within families, proposing that expressive activities have become more important (for example, Shorter 1975; Hareven 1977). While in the past the family was held together because people needed each other for survival, family relations have become based on the need for emotional gratification. Families have become centres of nurture and affection; individuals seek emotional support from families as a retreat from the achievement-oriented struggles of the outside world. These needs place heavy demands on family relationships, which may not always fulfil expectations. People are more prone to abandon family ties when their emotional well-being is not satisfied.

BOX 3.2 | *The two transitions*

Lesthaeghe (1995) proposes that it is possible to identify two somewhat separable transformations in the family, intimate behaviour, and children. In doing this he cites the work of several authors. For instance, in *The Making of the Modern Family*, Edward Shorter (1975) identifies two *sexual revolutions*. The first revolution involved young people making their own personal choices for marriage partners, and consequently the removal of the barriers to marriage previously placed by parents and society. This first revolution was based on the idea of the "one true love" expected to last a lifetime. The second sexual revolution accentuated the sexual aspects of mate selection and introduced experimentation with eroticism along with the possibility of sex without love. Eventually, people came to see sexual gratification as being indispensable for unions.

There are also two *contraceptive revolutions*. The first transition occurred before modern methods of contraception, when there were only inefficient methods, including abstinence and non-coital sex. This first contraceptive revolution occurred quietly, amidst the privacy of individual couples who sought to stop child-bearing after they had the desired number of children. The second contraceptive revolution involved efficient methods, principally the pill and sterilization. This was far from a quiet revolution. In particular, it liberated the premarital sexual activities from the concerns of pregnancy and allowed people to enter relationships earlier. Efficient contraception also permitted the postponement of births and gave strong control over the timing of children. For couples, per-

haps nothing has changed as much since the early 1960s as the degree of control over child-bearing. For the non-married, there was a significant reduction in the risks of sexual expression. In both cases, the links between sexuality, marital life, and reproduction were broken.

Philippe Ariès (1980) also speaks of two transitions in the relative priority given to *children and adults*. The first transition centred on children, with strong parental investments in child quality. Earlier, children seemed to be present for the benefit of parents, but later parents came to spoil their children in the sense of giving them more than they could ever expect in return (Caldwell 1976). Similarly, while previously many tasks and activities had competed for a mother's attention, maternal love came to put children's well-being second to none, and motherhood even emerged as a full-time vocation (Shorter 1975; Stone 1977; Garfield 1990: 37). The second transition involves a move to adult-centred preoccupations involving self-fulfilment and the quality of the dyadic relation between partners. It includes a shift in values and norms from family or child-centred orientations toward more self-centred pursuits (Ariès 1980; Lesthaeghe 1983; Roussel 1987). In particular, the second transition involves a weakening of the normative consensus that marriage and child-bearing are integral parts of the adult role. Instead, adults largely come to view children as a means through which they can receive affective gratification and blossom as individuals (Romaniuc 1984: 64). Of course, some have concluded that children can also interfere with this affective individualism. While children remain important for most people, they are no longer so important as to be impediments to parental divorce and subsequent self-fulfilment in other relationships.

Canada lacks a tradition of social surveys that would make it possible to analyze these types of trends in social values. For the United States, Samuel Preston (1986: 184-88) shows that "marriage" and "children" bring to mind increasingly "restrictive" connotations. U.S. survey data also indicate that people justify their behaviour more in terms of its consequences for their personal development and less on the grounds of adhering to social values.

Lesthaeghe (1995) further identifies two transitions as matters of individual *autonomy and political control*. The period until 1950 involved enhanced institutional control, first by the church through the reform movements and then by the state through an extension of its power over individual lives. The attempts to control sexuality during Victorian times went to the point of covering piano legs. Secularization did permit a certain breathing space and made it legitimate for couples to control their family size, although in Quebec this change did not occur until the Quiet Revolution of the 1960s. As the study of prevalent values indicates, the more recent period involved a resistance to external institutional authority, including the student movements of the 1960s, the second wave of feminism in the 1970s, and the decline of deference of the 1980s. In 1980, Neil Nevitte (1996: 226) finds, some 53 percent of Canadians thought "tolerance and respect for other people" were important qualities that "children should be encouraged to learn at home." By 1990, 80 percent were choosing tolerance as a

key value for children to learn. Already in 1984, respondents in Quebec had become more liberal on family values and more supportive of egalitarian gender roles, in comparison to anglophones in other parts of the country (Wu and Baer 1996).

This description of change can be seen as a liberal or choice model, in which individuals become free to make contracts that they define and that they can abandon (Van Leeuwen 1998). Lesthaeghe does not see this departure as a crisis in commitment. He observes a lack of commitment in earlier times—for instance, in the abandonment of pregnant girls and children. He sees the change as a matter of people wanting more out of life, and out of their relations in particular. This tendency can be seen as existentialism, giving priority to one's own existence and fulfilment; it is sometimes called the "me generation." For women in particular, the approach would question asymmetric gender roles as limitations on both achievement and self-fulfilment. In the 12 countries surveyed in the 1980 and 1990 World Values Survey, the value placed on egalitarianism in both husband/wife and parent/child relationships increased over the period (Nevitte 1996: 280). Nonetheless, both sexes still value parenthood and stable relationships. The 1984 Canadian Fertility Survey found that 84 percent of women believed that marriage was essential to a happy personal life (Lapierre-Adamcyk 1989).◆

Based on a survey of people aged 18-30 in France, Louis Roussel (1979) observes a radical transformation in the concept of marriage. A few people see marriage in traditional terms, based on established roles, expectations, and mutual obligations; the continuation of the relationship is not dependent on the maintenance of love as initially experienced. But the majority believe that a continuation of strong emotional exchanges and communication is essential to the marriage. They refuse to abide by the institutionalized prerogatives; they believe in the need for continued personal fulfilment, and therefore they do not make a firm commitment to a given partner.

Roussel (1987, 1989) suggests that the decades of the 1970s and 1980s involved a cultural change wherein people became less interested in living up to external norms and more interested in living up to what they themselves wanted. Marriage changed from an institution to a *"projet de couple"* in which people can follow their own drummer. In many other areas of life, people find it impossible to increase their freedom from external norms. For instance, workplaces and bureaucracies must set limits on the variability of individual behaviour. On questions such as child abuse and environmental protection, we now accept a higher level of social restrictions on behaviour. But in the areas of family behaviour it has become possible to live with fewer social constraints. Here the freedom ostensibly promised by the Enlightenment, the French Revolution, and existentialism has become manifest. Legislative changes making divorces easier and equating cohabitation with marriage also signified a greater acceptability of alternate sexual and marital arrangements.

This is not to imply that family behaviour was in the past constrained by strict norms while people are now free to do as they please. In some regards, people may have had certain freedoms in the past, for instance, to choose celibacy instead of marriage, or for aristocratic men to have mistresses in addition to wives. Cultural norms continue to operate; all societies will constrain individual behaviour in such crucial areas as sex, family, and procreation. The greater acceptability of individualism and self-fulfilment has relaxed, but not removed, the normative context of these behaviours.

Other persons who have written about the long-term changes in the family speak of a movement from institution to companionship (Burgess, Locke, and Thomas 1963), from orderly replacement of generations to permanent availability (Farber 1964), from instrumental to expressive relationships (Scanzoni and Scanzoni 1976; Thadani 1978), while children were transformed from duty-bound workers to emotionally precious objects (Coltrane 1998b). When the family was basically a unit of production and survival, relationships were instrumental; as families became a "private sphere," nurture and affection became the basis for relationships (Hareven 1977). These perspectives all imply a loosening up of relationships and a greater priority for emotional gratification. To go back to Durkheim's terms (chapter 1), the family has changed from a unit of survival in which relationships were based on a "division of labour" to a unit of "mechanical solidarity" based on a sense of common identity. Sentiment, though, is a weaker basis for relationships, and the need for continuous gratification puts heavy, and sometimes contradictory, demands on relationships. Spouses are expected to give each other the autonomy necessary to develop their own potential, but at the same time to "be there" for

94

each other's needs. Likewise, even while developing her or his potential, a partner is to remain the same person who was initially married.

Other authors have used similar frameworks (see Box 3.2). Based on the work of Anthony Giddens, David Hall (1996) uses the concepts of "pure relationships" and "reproductive individualism," which refer respectively to relationships based on personal choice rather than normative considerations, and reproduction oriented to self-fulfilment (see also Jones, Tepperman, and Wilson 1995). Others call this a collaborative model of marriage; it is based on few children, places a high value on the quality of spousal relationships, and produces instability due to both the complexities of the collaborative endeavour and the greater ability of partners to seek alternatives (Goldscheider and Waite 1991; Oppenheimer 1994).

As a consequence of these economic and cultural transformations, family relationships have become less important on some levels and more important on others. Families have lost some of the economic, political, and religious functions they previously provided for the larger society, and they have become more important as a source of emotional gratification for individuals. Nonetheless, families still perform social functions, in particular those of reproduction and early socialization. One analyst, Andrew Cherlin (1992: 125), emphasizes family change in the United States, especially the greater prevalence of cohabitation and divorce, and argues that marriage has become less of an economic necessity or a cultural imperative, but he nonetheless concludes that marriage persists as a preferred form of union, especially when children are involved. Similarly, a number of surveys of U.S. attitudes show a decline in negative attitudes toward remaining single, a greater concern about the restrictions associated with marriage, and a greater acceptability of divorce, childlessness, and premarital and extramarital sex—though not a decline in the expectation to marry (Thornton 1989). Most people apparently still value marriage, parenthood, and family life. Most people express a tolerance for alternatives, but do not actively embrace the ideas of remaining single or of not having children. Following these attitudes in France, Roussel (1992) also concludes that the family is not disintegrating, but remains a precious value to most people. Nonetheless, marriage in particular, as contrasted with relationships, is "declining in significance" (Bumpass and Sweet 1995).

In the end, these macro and micro explanations for family change prove difficult to separate. The structural explanations have a certain theoretical priority, and they play a role in shaping the cultural explanations. For instance, in pushing for egalitarian relationships, the Ontario Family Law Reform Act begins: "Whereas it is desirable to encourage and strengthen the role of the family in society; and whereas for that purpose it is necessary to recognize the equal position of spouses as individuals within marriage and to recognize marriage as a form of partnership ..." Similarly, the state has taken deliberate actions in the direction of equality, ranging from the establishment of a Royal Commission on the Status of Women in the mid-1960s to the sponsorship of feminist groups in the "just society" moves of the 1970s (Pal 1993).

Structural factors reduced the institutional role of families, permitting both more flexibility and more focus on affective individualism. According to Veena Thadani (1978), the structural preconditions for this family change include the decline of the enforceability of kinship obligations, the increased economic independence of nuclear family units, and the development of alternative support systems, such as welfare states. These structural transformations introduce changes in the constraints associated with culturally acceptable behaviour. Nonetheless, cultural transformations have their own momentum, and actors can, and do, bring about changes in structural conditions.

RELATIONSHIPS OVER THE LIFE COURSE

Given the difficulty of defining family units, we will put our emphasis here on specific family relationships, in particular adult relationships and parent/child relationships. Traditionally, the study of families has adopted a life-cycle framework, moving from the premarital stage to the marital, children, empty-nest, and widowhood stages. This approach tends to ignore people who do not follow the typical pattern. Thus a looser concept of the life course is more satisfactory: referring simply to the various ages of life, from children to young adults to mid-life and later life. Each part of this life course shows various kinds of intimate and family behaviour, which in turn occur to various extents for various people (Beaujot et al. 1995).

Using data from the 1995 General Social Survey, Table 3.2 summarizes the median ages at which various family life-course events occur for birth cohorts 1916-20 to 1971-75. The patterns tend to be uniform. The birth cohorts 1916-20 to 1941-45 show a general downward trend in the age of home-leaving, first marriage, first birth, last birth, and home-leaving of the children. Conversely, the subsequent cohorts have experienced an upward trend. The cohorts of the 1920s to 1940s show a tendency not only to marry early, but also to marry over a relatively narrow range of ages (Ravanera and Rajulton 1996; Ravanera, Rajulton, and Burch 1998a, 1998b).

The proportion of first unions that involved cohabitation increased over the cohorts, to levels above 50 percent for those born after 1965. The separations within 25 years of marriage are also on a continuous upward trend, from 5 percent in the 1916-20 cohort to 36 percent in the 1951-55 cohort.

At the same time, over the period of mid-life, ages 30 to 54, the proportions of marriages that have ended have ranged between 18 and 20 percent over the cohorts born between 1911 to 1950 (Ravanera and Rajulton 1996: 174). In addition, the most common events between these mid-life ages are the birth of a last child or a child leaving home. Those ages thus show considerable continuity. The change involves a higher proportion of separations among marriages that have ended, and divorces occurring sooner in the life course, before children leave home. Zenaida Ravanera and Fernando Rajulton conclude that the life course between ages 30 and 54 is characterized by stability rather than crisis.

Change has also occurred in the extent to which typical patterns have been followed (Ravanera, Rajulton, and Burch 1994). For instance, the pattern of leaving home, getting

**AGES AT VARIOUS FAMILY LIFE TRANSITIONS,
BIRTH COHORTS 1916-20 TO 1971-75, CANADA, 1995**

MEDIAN AGE AT	1916-1920	1921-1925	1926-1930	1931-1935	1936-1940	1941-1945	1946-1950	1951-1955	1956-1960	1961-1965	1966-1970	1971-1975
Home-Leaving												
Men	22.9	22.0	21.9	21.2	21.8	22.0	21.8	21.5	21.8	22.7	23.2	23.6
Women	21.8	21.6	21.0	20.6	20.1	20.3	21.0	19.9	20.6	20.9	21.2	21.6
First Union												
Men	26.6	25.7	25.2	24.8	25.0	23.6	23.8	24.4	24.5	25.2	25.1	—
Women	23.4	22.9	22.0	21.9	21.7	21.4	22.0	21.5	21.8	22.7	22.7	22.9
First Marriage												
Men	26.6	25.7	25.2	25.0	25.1	23.6	24.0	25.6	26.4	28.7	—	—
Women	23.4	22.9	22.0	21.9	21.8	21.6	22.2	22.1	23.3	25.3	26.1	—
First Birth												
Men	29.6	28.8	28.6	27.3	27.7	26.5	27.5	29.3	29.9	31.2	—	—
Women	26.2	25.0	23.9	23.5	23.5	23.3	25.4	25.6	26.3	27.8	27.8	—
Last Birth												
Men	38.0	35.6	35.8	33.6	33.5	32.5	32.5	33.7	33.2	32.1	—	—
Women	35.6	34.5	33.7	31.8	30.1	29.8	30.6	30.3	31.0	30.6	—	—
First Child's Home-Leaving												
Men	49.4	47.5	48.1	47.0	48.4	47.9	49.3	—	—	—	—	—
Women	45.4	45.0	44.6	43.3	43.7	45.1	48.0	—	—	—	—	—
Last Child's Home-Leaving												
Men	57.6	56.8	59.2	57.1	57.2	—	—	—	—	—	—	—
Women	56.7	57.1	56.3	53.0	54.6	—	—	—	—	—	—	—
Mean Number of Births												
Men	2.9	3.1	2.6	2.9	2.5	1.9	1.9	1.5	1.5	—	—	—
Women	3.3	3.6	3.4	3.3	3.0	2.3	1.9	1.8	1.7	—	—	—
Cohabitations as Percentage of First Unions												
Men	1.9	3.2	1.8	4.4	6.3	9.3	16.1	30.3	39.3	49.9	67.1	—
Women	0.3	1.0	2.5	1.6	2.9	9.2	13.5	25.0	35.9	47.5	55.3	76.6
Proportions Separated within 25 years of First Marriage												
Men	0.03	0.05	0.09	0.09	0.17	0.24	0.27	0.39	—	—	—	—
Women	0.06	0.06	0.10	0.13	0.14	0.29	0.30	0.34	—	—	—	—

Source: Special tabulation from Statistics Canada, 1995 General Social Survey.

TABLE 3.2

married, and then having a first child reached a peak in the 1931-40 cohort, at 65.6 percent of men and 65.8 percent of women. In the 1961-70 cohort, only 26.3 percent of men and 23.2 percent of women followed this pattern. Ravanera, Rajulton, and Thomas Burch conclude that the younger cohorts have not yet established a path or sequence that can be called typical.

Home-leaving

After having declined decade by decade, the average age at home-leaving started to rise in the late 1970s, producing what has been called a "cluttered nest" (Ravanera, Rajulton, and Burch 1995; Boyd and Norris 1998). In addition, some children returned home after leaving for a period of time, a pattern rare in the past. For instance, at age 20-24, 50.4 percent of women and 64.3 percent of men were living with parent(s) in 1996, compared to 33.6 and 51.4 percent respectively in 1981 (Boyd and Norris 1998).

Clearly, *economic factors* are at stake here, such as the difficulty of "Generation X" or the "Generation on Hold" to establish itself in the labour market (Côté and Allahar 1994). Clearly, as well, the younger generation is spending a longer period at school. Students also now have a greater likelihood of finding appropriate postsecondary education near home. Economic factors play a part: children from higher income families are less likely to express satisfaction about living with parents, while children trying to get established through a first job are more likely to return home (Wister, Mitchell, and Gee 1997; Gee, Mitchell, and Wister 1995). Using multivariate analysis on the bases of birth cohorts 1921 to 1960, Evelyne Lapierre-Adamcyk, Céline Le Bourdais, and Karen Lehrhaupt (1995) found that economic factors played a larger role for men leaving home than for women.

Cultural factors have also helped to make parental homes more suitable to older children, as the generation gap has narrowed. Parents have developed more flexible and tolerant attitudes toward their adolescent children. For instance, in the United States in the 1960s the typical first sexual experience occurred in a car, while in the 1980s it was more likely to occur in the parental home, admittedly when the parents were away. Writing in the mid-1980s, R.W. Bibby and D.C. Posterski (1985: 82) found a surprising similarity in the basic attitudes of Canadian teenagers and parents on a range of factors, from the acceptability of sex before marriage for people in love to attitudes on abortion and the rights of homosexuals. The importance of cultural factors is apparent in the observation that children are less likely to be living at home when the parents are more religious, remarried, or from certain ethnic groups (Wister, Mitchell, and Gee 1997; Zhao 1994; Boyd and Norris 1995).

While these tendencies may create problems around a lack of independence, Monica Boyd and Doug Norris (1995) observe that the later departure of children presents various advantages for parental investment in children. Significantly, the average age at home-leaving is the highest in intact families. As in the case of an absent parent, a sharing across family members and consequently an investment in children are more likely to occur within households than across households. If parents separate, any children they have are most likely to live with their mother, except if she has established a new relationship. In effect, children tend to prefer living with a father who is not in a relationship over a mother who is in a new relationship.

Cohabitation

While some common-law unions have always existed, especially in the case of persons who for one reason or another were not allowed or able to marry, the modern phenomenon of cohabitation started with university students, especially in Scandinavia and North America, in the 1960s. The behaviour spread to professional classes in the 1970s and subsequently to other classes. Initially, couples took up cohabitation for a short pre-honeymoon period. Later it became a longer period that most often led to marriage but sometimes resulted in separation. Cohabitation has now become the normal form of entry into unions, not just for persons who are single, but especially for the previously married. In France, after a 30-year evolution, by the 1990s three-quarters of couples are initially formed without marriage, and one-quarter of births occur outside of marriage (Leridon and Villeneuve-Gokalp 1994: 2).

In Canada, only 2 percent of persons born in 1934-38 began their lives as couples through cohabitation, compared to 53 percent of persons born in 1959-63 (Lapierre-Adamcyk 1989). At the time of the 1996 census, 13.7 percent of all couples were cohabiting, compared to 6.4 percent in 1981 (Statistics Canada 1997a: 3). Of unions formed in 1970-74, 17 percent were cohabitations, compared to 57 percent of unions formed in 1990-95 (Turcotte and Bélanger 1997: 8). For the ages 30-39 in 1991, over a quarter of single persons and a third of divorced persons were cohabitating (Péron et al. 1999).

To a certain extent, less formal relationships are simply being substituted for marriage. Yet, in some respects, cohabitation is not a true replacement for formal marriages. By comparing various characteristics of cohabiting people with those of single and married people, Ronald Rindfuss and Audrey VandenHeuvel (1990) found that the cohabiting persons were more similar to the single people than to the married couples. Surveys show that people who are living together do not consider themselves as married, and that cohabitation is best viewed as an *alternative to being single* or as a *prelude to marriage*. However, increasing numbers of people do consider cohabitation as an *alternative to marriage*, and by 1996, 47 percent of common-law unions involved children, sometimes from a previous relationship. Céline Le Bourdais and Nicole Marcil-Gratton (1996) propose that cohabitation may well be on the way to losing its marginal status and acquiring more stability. It could be becoming more like marriage, with a similar long-term commitment, but without the same legality. Still, they suggest that it may also signal less commitment and a desire for a greater flexibility in relationships. In effect, attitudes on liberal and permissive orientations imply that common-law unions are more likely to be "pure

99

BOX 3.3 | *Cohabitation as an insurance against separation*

Contrary to the notion of cohabitation as representing an insurance value, various results indicate that marriages preceded by cohabitation have higher rates of dissolution. After ten years of legal marriage, the rate of dissolution, according to the 1990 General Social Survey, was 26 percent for those preceded by cohabitation and 16 percent for those not preceded by cohabitation (Le Bourdais and Marcil-Gratton 1996: 428). The 1984 Canadian Fertility Survey found that marriages preceded by cohabitation had a 33 percent higher risk of separation (Hall 1996). One might think that experimenting with marriage-like relationships before marriage would enable people to test their long-term prospects as a couple and to make better marital choices. However, persons willing to be in informal partnerships are probably also more willing to dissolve formal arrangements (Hall and Zhao 1995). It is mostly at the early stages of marriage that cohabitation predicts a greater likelihood of separation (Halli and Zimmer 1991). It may be that those who cohabit before marriage profit less from a honeymoon period *within* marriage, during which separation would be unlikely.

The lack of understanding associated with some common-law unions probably underlies the greater likelihood of violence. The probability of assault is 19 percent for young common-law couples compared to 5 percent for young married couples (Bunge and Levett 1998: 15). Part of the difference may come from the difficulties that men can experience with insecure relationships, especially if they also have insecurity associated with unemployment and income. ◆

relationships" that do not fit an institutional mode (Hall 1996). In particular, this tendency corresponds to a liberal or choice model that accepts contractual obligations but not necessarily lifelong commitments. Box 3.3 develops other comparisons between these alternative forms of relationships.

While cohabitation periods have become longer, those relationships that are not transformed to marriages have particularly high rates of dissolution. After ten years, close to 70 percent of these relationships have ended in separations. For those cohabitations that occurred in 1985-95, within ten years 15 percent of the couples were still cohabitating, 52 percent had separated, and 33 percent had married. Compared to the relationships that started in 1975-84, there are now fewer marriages and more separations. The greater propensity to separate is attributable to higher proportions of cohabitations, and of marriages preceded by cohabitation, while there is not much change in the stability of relationships that started as marriages (Bélanger and Dumas 1998: 42, 48, 49).

Given the difference in the meaning of cohabitation, Jean Dumas and Alain Bélanger (1997) developed an interesting typology (Table 3.3). The largest category, representing 36 percent of the total, are *stable unions without commitment*, defined as lasting three or more years but having no children. This category is more common for older persons. The

**PERCENTAGE OF COMMON-LAW UNIONS BY TYPE
AND PERIOD OF ENTERING THE UNION, CANADA, 1995**

PERIOD	PRELUDE TO MARRIAGE	TRIAL MARRIAGE	UNSTABLE UNION	STABLE UNION WITHOUT COMMIT-MENT	SUBSTITUTE FOR MARRIAGE	OTHER	TOTAL
Before 1977	18.3	17.9	12.6	33.3	14.7	3.3	100.0
1977-79	13.5	25.8	15.6	31.0	11.6	2.6	100.0
1980-82	11.5	13.6	17.8	40.0	15.1	2.0	100.0
1983-85	8.8	13.9	21.4	40.9	13.7	1.3	100.0
1986-88	9.3	17.5	19.4	33.8	15.7	4.4	100.0
1989-91	8.2	12.8	21.9	36.8	17.7	2.6	100.0
TOTAL	11.4	16.2	18.4	36.1	15.1	2.8	100.0

Source: Dumas and Bélanger, 1997: 150; Statistics Canada, General Social Survey 1995

TABLE 3.3

second-largest category, which has increased in importance and represents 18 percent of cohabitations, are *unstable unions*, defined as lasting less than three years with no marriage and no children. The categories of *prelude to marriage* (11 percent) and *trial marriage* (16 percent) are persons who marry within a year or three years respectively, but do not have children until marriage. Both of these categories have declined, so that the proportion of cohabitations converted to marriage within three years declined from 36 to 21 percent of the total. Finally, 15 percent are classified as *substitutes for marriage*, in the sense that children are born within three years and the couple remains unmarried for at least another six months following the birth. Based on these analyses, the authors conclude that common-law union is no longer a trial period of living together, but increasingly a substitute for marriage.

Economic factors may play a role in the trends toward cohabitation. In particular, the difficulties of finding good paid work, for men in particular, may make marriage difficult. For women, one analysis of various risk factors indicates that employed women are more likely than non-employed women to enter a cohabiting union (Turcotte and Bélanger 1997). The authors suggest that greater financial autonomy may give employed women increased flexibility in choosing their conjugal arrangement. Cohabitation, then, may express an exchange between two economically independent people. At the same time, women are more likely to enter a common-law union if they are already lone parents. In comparison, it may be easier for women who do not have children to form a marriage relationship with a man who wishes to raise his own children and has sufficient economic status to be ready for marriage.

In addition, *cultural factors* are central to the changing prevalence of cohabitation, and these factors have also influenced marriage itself, including its greater instability. The study of change in France suggests to Henri Leridon and Catherine Villeneuve-

Gokalp (1994) a denunciation of the hypocrisy of bourgeois marriage, a growth of hedonism, and attempts at personal growth without the constraints of marriage. For many, these tendencies influence not only those who cohabit but also marriage itself. These authors also relate these trends to the greater security of contraception and the rising status of women. Women who have access to status in other ways than through marriage can more easily enter "pure relationships." Another indicator of cultural factors is the higher propensity to cohabit for those who had not attended any religious services in the past year (Dumas and Bélanger 1997). Clearly, the devaluation of the institution of marriage has not involved a comparable devaluation of "la vie à deux." At the same time, the prevalence of cohabitation does not necessarily mean multiple relationships. The 1995 General Social Survey found that more than three-quarters of the persons who had cohabited did so only once, and less than 5 percent had three or more relationships (Dumas and Bélanger 1997).

Interestingly, the 1976 census did not even ask about cohabitation for fear of raising sensitive issues, while in 1996 Statistics Canada considered doing away with the publication of data on marriages and divorces, because these capture a decreasing proportion of union formation and dissolution. Statisticians are also finding a limited utility for publishing data on births to non-married women, because these data give the false impression that the births are occurring outside of relationships. In Quebec, the number of cases of "no declared father" on the birth registration is both low and stable, at about 5 percent of total births (Duchesne 1997: 1).

Consequently, Leridon and Villeneuve-Gokalp (1994) see the generalization of cohabitation as the most radical change that has occurred to families in the past 20 years. Cohabitation is displacing marriage as a form of first union, and its duration is increasing. While cohabitation could be interpreted as simply an alternative form of entry into unions, it has also transformed premarital, marital, and postmarital relationships. It signals a greater flexibility in unions, and this change has significant consequences for children (see chapter 7).

Marriage

Until the beginning of the 20th century, marriage patterns involved a relatively advanced age at marriage and reflected significant proportions of the population who did not marry (Gee 1986). Over the first six or seven decades of the century, except for a slight reversal in the 1930s, marriages occurred earlier in people's lives and higher proportions of people were getting married. Then, suddenly, these trends reversed. In 1972 the median age at first marriage was 21.2 for brides and 23.4 for grooms, but by 1996 it had risen to ages comparable to those at the turn of the century, at 26.3 for women and 28.3 for men. In 1965, 30.8 percent of first-time brides were under 20 years of age, compared to 4.7 percent in 1995. Within given cohorts, later marriage is also associated with higher socio-economic status (Ravanera, Rajulton, and Burch 1998a, 1998b).

MARITAL STATUS OF POPULATION BY SEX AND FIVE-YEAR AGE GROUP, CANADA, 1981 AND 1996 (IN PERCENTAGE)

| | NEVER MARRIED | | ALL UNIONS | | | | SEPARATED, WIDOWED, OR DIVORCED | |
| | | | Cohabiting | | Total | | | |
	M	F	M	F	M	F	M	F
1981								
15-19	98.4	93.3	0.7	2.9	1.4	6.5	0.1	0.2
20-24	71.9	51.1	7.1	9.4	26.9	45.9	1.2	3.0
25-29	32.0	20.0	8.1	7.1	63.7	73.0	4.3	7.0
30-34	15.0	10.5	6.0	4.7	79.1	80.2	6.0	9.4
35-39	9.3	7.3	4.7	3.6	83.8	81.7	6.8	11.0
40-44	7.8	6.1	3.6	2.8	84.8	82.0	7.4	11.9
45-49	7.5	5.8	2.8	2.1	84.6	80.9	7.9	13.3
50-54	7.8	6.0	2.1	1.7	83.7	78.1	8.4	15.8
55-59	7.8	6.3	1.6	1.2	86.2	76.8	5.9	16.9
60-64	7.6	7.1	1.2	0.9	85.5	68.7	7.0	24.2
1996								
15-19	98.9	96.4	0.7	2.6	0.9	3.4	0.1	0.2
20-24	84.7	70.8	9.1	14.6	14.8	27.8	0.6	1.4
25-29	51.7	35.5	16.5	17.3	45.6	59.4	2.6	5.1
30-34	29.2	19.2	14.5	13.7	65.2	72.0	5.5	8.8
35-39	18.7	13.1	11.7	10.8	73.0	74.9	8.3	12.0
40-44	12.9	9.6	9.4	8.5	76.4	75.2	10.7	15.2
45-49	9.1	7.5	7.9	6.7	79.0	75.1	11.9	17.5
50-54	7.1	6.1	6.9	5.3	80.7	74.5	12.2	19.4
55-59	6.4	5.4	5.3	3.5	81.7	72.9	11.9	21.6
60-64	6.3	5.3	3.9	2.1	81.6	68.2	12.1	26.5

NOTE: For 1981, sample estimates were derived for the separated category. "All Unions" includes married and cohabiting.

Source: Statistics Canada, no. 92-901, 1981: Table 5; no. 92-325: Table 6.11. Statistics Canada, no. 92-325, 1993: 28; Beaujot 1995: 41. Ravanera 1995: 10, 152; Gee 1995: 159-60; 1996 Census, no. 96-004, no. 96-005. Statistics Canada, Census of Canada.

TABLE 3.4

Not only is marriage occurring later in life, but it is also happening with less frequency. Using life-table techniques to combine the 1970-72 age-specific marriage rates implied that 90 percent of adults could be expected to marry at some point in their lives, compared to 75 percent in 1991 (Table 3.5). The changes at entry into first marriage are partly a function of an increased rate of cohabitation. However, especially under age 35, the combined proportion who were married or cohabiting declined appreciably over the 1981-96 censuses (Table 3.4). With achieved characteristics, particularly education and occupation, playing an increasing role in their lives, women are delaying the transition to marital relationships while they establish stable work careers. Women's greater economic independence allows them to search longer for the right person (Oppenheimer 1987). For both sexes, marriage has become less central to the transition to adulthood and to the set of roles defining adult status (Goldscheider and Waite 1986).

Still, the 1990 General Social Survey found that 80 percent of persons aged 18-29 expected to marry, and another 10 percent were uncertain about their prospects. The Survey showed that between the ages of 30 and 39, 90 percent of persons had been in a union at some point in their lives; the figure increased to 95 percent at ages 50-64. Only 28 percent of the divorced population intended to remarry (McDaniel 1994: 13, 26, 31).

Table 3.5 presents summary statistics on various states of life, from never-married to widowhood. These results are calculated for 1970-72 and 1991 using life-table techniques, which assume that events occurring over a given period can be summarized for a population over the entire life course. They show that individuals can expect to spend, on average, slightly less than half of their whole lives in the married state, with the average number of marriages per person being 1.3 for men and 1.2 for women. While the average duration of marriage had declined by the 1956-61 marriage cohort, it was still estimated to be above 30 years (Dumas and Péron 1992: 94).

Another important feature of marriage is the extent of *homogamy*, or people marrying others who are like themselves. In everyday conversations about mate selection, two contradictory principles often emerge: "opposites attract" and "like marries like." Clearly, most people do choose someone different from themselves in that they choose someone of the other sex. Beyond that, the idea that opposites attract receives little research support. On certain characteristics, such as religion, homogamy has declined, yet among marriages occurring in 1990, more than half of the people in each of the following groups married others of the same religion: Jewish, Mennonite, Pentecostal, Jehovah's Witness, Catholic, Eastern Orthodox, and other Christian and non-Christian. Even those whose religion was "unknown or not stated" were more likely to marry someone in the same category (Statistics Canada 1997b). U.S. data show that both education and social class remain important in mate selection, but that education has become more important than the social class of the parents (Kalmijn 1991). Homogamy by education, when both spouses are working outside the home, is connected to inequality across families: given couples who both have high education will have many combined advantages compared to other couples with less education.

It is probably in the age factor that marriage partners are most likely to be different. These differences are systematic, with women being on average younger than men. The difference in the age at first marriage is about two years—a figure that declined from a difference of about three years in the 1960s and four years in the early part of the century. The 1990 General Social Survey found that among the currently married population, in 51 percent of cases the man is two or more years older, and in 38 percent of cases he is three or more years older (McDaniel 1994: 21). In contrast, only 6 percent of women are two or more years older than their husbands. At the same time, 41 percent of couples are within two years in age.

Although a two-year gap may seem small, it can have considerable implications, at least for people marrying at young ages. A younger person is less likely to be experienced at taking responsibility and leadership, and more likely to have achieved less in life. Taken together, for most couples the *mating gradient*, or the differential status of the

SUMMARY STATISTICS ON THE NEVER-MARRIED, MARRIED, DIVORCED, AND WIDOWED STATES, BY SEX, CANADA, 1970-72 AND 1991

	MEN		WOMEN	
	1970–1972	1991	1970–1972	1991
Never-married state				
Average age at first marriage	25.0	30.2	22.8	27.7
Percentage of population never marrying	10.0	30.0	8.0	25.0
Percentage of lifetime spent single (for total population)	26.3	45.0	25.0	38.0
Married state				
Percentage of population marrying	90.0	70.0	92.0	75.0
Percentage of lifetime lived as married	58.0	45.0	52.0	43.0
Number of marriages per person marrying	1.3	1.3	1.3	1.2
Average age of the married population	49.2	52.6	46.3	50.2
Divorced state				
Percentage of divorced persons remarrying	85.0	64.0	79.0	52.0
Average length of divorce	4.9	14.8	10.0	21.5
Average age at divorce	41.5	41.8	38.6	39.0
Average age of divorced population	51.5	55.4	56.8	58.3
Average age at remarriage	42.8	47.1	40.6	42.4
Widowed state				
Percentage of lifetime spent widowed (for total population)	2.0	3.0	9.7	10.0
Average length of a widowhood	7.8	8.7	14.5	15.1
Average age at widowhood	68.6	74.1	67.0	71.2
Percentage of widowed persons remarrying	24.0	11.0	9.0	4.0
Average age of the widowed population	72.3	76.2	73.4	76.5
Average age at remarriage	60.5	65.6	56.5	58.7

Source: Adams and Nagnur 1988: 11, 14, 15; Nault and Bélanger 1996: 36, 42.

TABLE 3.5

spouses, means that the wife will have a somewhat lower achieved status than the husband. In the average marriage the husband will tend to earn more money, partly because he is older and more established. As a result, for the benefit of the total family income his job may have a higher priority in the family life. The family is more likely to move for the sake of his job than for hers, and the wife is more likely to withdraw from the labour force for the sake of the children. The wife's slight disadvantage at the beginning of the marriage—established just because she was younger—can become entrenched over the course of the marriage.

Frances Goldscheider and Linda Waite (1986) analyzed the *propensities to marry* in light of the relative costs and benefits of marriage for the sexes. They found that, for the United States before 1980, long-term employment increased the likelihood of marriage for men but not for women. It seemed that women were more likely to use a higher personal income to "buy out of marriage," and that greater options outside of marriage reduced their relative preferences for marriage. In terms of benefits, women tended to gain financially from marriage while men gained more in terms of non-economic benefits, including enhanced survivorship—both mental and physical health. Goldscheider and Waite proposed that, leaving out finances, "his" marriage was more desirable than "hers" on many dimensions. Having gained other options for financial support, women would be less prone to marry. Also for men, the greater "access to wifelike social and sexual services outside of marriage" was reducing the "incentive to make longer-term commitments of financing and support" (p.93). Still, Goldscheider and Waite expected these differential effects by sex to weaken with the transformation of the role of marriage as a factor in men's and women's transitions to adulthood.

Using longitudinal data from the United States, a later study by Goldscheider and Waite (1991: 60-84) further analyzed important aspects of the transition to marriage and its differential dynamics for women and men. Men who had experienced the dissolution of their parents' marriage were more likely to marry, they found, while women in that circumstance were less likely to marry, especially at older ages. Similarly, the experience of non-family living as an adult increased the probability of marriage for men but decreased the probability for women. It could be that men who have lived on their own are more attractive because they have become more adept at domestic work, while women who have lived on their own do not want to lose the associated independence. Higher parental education lowers the probability of marriage for both sexes, but higher parental income reduces women's marriage probability, having no effect on men. Having parents with higher prestige occupations increases men's probability of marriage and reduces women's probability. Once again, these results can be interpreted in terms of the relative extent to which women and men are interested in marriage or can avoid marriage.

At the same time, Goldscheider and Waite (1991) find that employment predicts marriage, especially for men, but also for women. Many people believe that a successful marriage these days calls for two jobs. The time needed to establish these two jobs may well be an important part of the delay of marriage. Analyzing the propensity to marry among U.S. cohorts marrying in the 1970s and 1980s, Megan Sweeney (1997) finds that economic prospects have become positively related to marriage for both men and women in the later cohort, suggesting, as Goldscheider and Waite (1986) had expected, that men and women have come to resemble one another in terms of the relationship between economic prospects and marriage.

On the basis of the 1991 Swedish Family Survey, Ann-Zofie Duvander (1998) analyzed the determinants of the transition from cohabitation to marriage. The life-course stage made a difference, with cohabiting women in their twenties being more likely to marry, along with men in their late twenties and early thirties. However, marriage propensity decreased in unions of long duration and was not always influenced by the presence of children or a pregnancy. Attitudinal questions were also important, with a higher propensity to marry among those who placed a high value on family and children, compared to their own leisure time. Women who agreed with a traditional division of labour were more likely to marry, but the opposite held for men. It may be that men with less traditional orientations are preferred as marriage partners. There was not a strong effect of economic activity, but cohabiting women with more education were more likely to marry.

Separation and divorce

Although the rates of separation and divorce have increased since the 1960s, the most common situation is still for people to be married only once. For instance, 1990 statistics indicated that at ages 30-54, some 10 percent had never been married, another 10 percent were formerly married, 67 percent were married or cohabiting with no previous marriage, and 12 percent were married or cohabiting after a previous marriage (Beaujot 1995: 42). In terms of family units, the 1995 General Social Survey found that 70 percent of families with children included both biological parents, while 22 percent had only one parent and 8 percent were stepfamilies with one biological parent and a step-parent (Statistics Canada 1997c).

According to one estimate, at least one-third of marriages taking place in the 1980s and 1990s would end in divorce within 25 years (Péron et al. 1999). This figure grew out of the observation that among persons who married in 1968-69, 29.3 percent had divorced within 25 years (Dumas and Bélanger 1996: 35). Subsequent cohorts show a higher propensity to divorce. For instance, within 10 years of marriage, the 1968-69 cohort had 11.4 percent divorces, while the 1983-84 marriage cohort had 18.4 percent divorces. The peak incidence of divorce occurs after five years of marriage (Gentleman and Park 1997).

Life-table techniques that extrapolate on the basis of the data from a given year suggest that between 1986 and 1991 the divorce rate stabilized at slightly more than 30 percent of marriages (Nault and Bélanger 1996: 18). The comparison of divorces by duration of marriage also suggests the beginnings of a decline in the propensity to divorce (Bélanger and Dumas 1998: 35). In part, this may be because marriages are becoming more selective, with more cohabitation and less marriage. Compared to other countries, Canadian divorce rates are higher than the rates in Japan, France, or Germany, roughly the same as those of Sweden and the United Kingdom, and considerably lower than in the United States.

Life-table techniques, on the basis of 1991 data, indicate an average age at divorce of 39 years for women and 42 for men, and an average of 21 and 15 years respectively spent in the divorced state (see Table 3.5). These statistics do not include the period of separation that often precedes an official divorce, nor do they include the period of cohabitation that sometimes follows divorce.

BOX 3.4 | *Orientations to marriage*

The following study is based on a 1989-90 survey of 444 persons aged 18 and over in the Ontario counties of Oxford and Middlesex, including the city of London. People were asked open questions concerning marriage and the ideal age to get married.

The most common responses to the questions "Why do people get married?" and "What are the advantages of being married?" referred to companionship, love, social support, or the emotional aspect of life. Respondents saw marriage as providing stability, as providing someone to come home to and share happiness and problems with, someone to lean on in good times and bad, and someone who is there for you, offering the experience of being needed, or of working together on common goals. People often saw it as "natural" to get married—they largely take it for granted, as providing a base for a family, to bring children into the world. Marriage is the norm: people are made to be together, to have a partner in life. Respondents also expressed family-related reasons: marriage is a good foundation for a family, it is better for children to be raised in a family. A few mentioned practical aspects such as tax breaks, security, or sharing finances or economic benefits. Others mentioned a healthy sexual relationship without fear of AIDS.

According to the respondents, the advantages of being single relate largely to the freedom to do what you want, when you want, as you want. Many seemed to ignore certain constraints on single people—for instance, constraints related to responsibilities at work. They spoke of single people being able to pick up and go as they please. Being single provides independence, no need to compromise with anyone. Being single allows one to make career and other decisions without having to take anyone else into account. A few, especially younger respondents, said that by being single you can keep your money or car, for yourself, without having to share it with anyone else. Others mentioned being able to date a number of partners. Some 4.9 percent of respondents said being single had no real advantage. Some older respondents could not see how anyone would possibly want to go through life single; they thought such people simply did not find the right partner.

Asked to compare the advantages of being married or single, the overwhelming majority (85.1 percent) said that marriage provides more advantages. Some said they were happy to be single now but preferred marriage for the life course. The few (5.1 percent) who said being single was preferable included persons who had separated from a marriage and had no intention of getting married again, or women who believed the workload was greater in marriage. Being single meant not having someone dominate your life; you don't have to answer to him.

When asked what they would guess a man or woman was like if all they knew about the person was that she or he did not want to get married, many found the question difficult to answer without knowing something about the circumstances. They thought people would know best what is best for themselves; it is their choice. Some thought such people might have strong goals, know what they want, be independent; others spoke of the people as being self-centred,

▶ BOX 3.4 CONT'D

not willing to take responsibility, fancy-free, or a partygoer. Such people might have made a conscious decision and were not interested in having children; women might be facing the difficulty of combining career pursuits and a family.

How is a man's life changed by being married? According to the respondents, he becomes more responsible. Marriage provides a stabilizing function, and he has more responsibilities. Even if the respondents mentioned negatives, such as limitations on what he can do, or having to compromise in making decisions, they typically saw the overall change as being positive for the man. He becomes more devoted to the family and the welfare of his family; it is good to have to take another person into account in making decisions. A man settles down, he is more oriented toward family and home, he goes out with the boys less. Most see this as a positive thing: getting to understand himself, a growing experience that may be more important for men who are less mature. A man, they said, also has more responsibilities, especially financial.

The respondents gave similar feedback on the changes in a woman's life. Marriage gives stability, and women become more responsible, devoted to the family, more secure. Some spoke of the extra domestic workload, especially if she had children. Some women said that a man's life was not much changed, but for women there was more work—there is no such a thing as an egalitarian marriage, women need to do the majority of the housework, put themselves second, make more compromises—although they still see marriage positively. Some men thought women's career prospects were more likely to be hindered by marriage, and they admitted that women did do more household

chores, even if the partners had the ideal of sharing chores 50-50. Interestingly, 72.3 percent of the men said these changes for women were positive compared to 65.3 percent of women.

The respondents believed the ideal age for a man to get married was in the mid- to late-twenties, after gaining a certain maturity and stability in life, having the freedom to do things as a single person first, and achieving a certain "state of mind" appropriate for marriage. Men should complete their education and have a sense of direction in life before they marry. Many said a man should live on his own first, be independent, learn to take care of himself. He should have had his opportunity to ride motorcycles or whatever he needed to do as a single person, to find himself, or had time "between families." They gave largely minimum ages for the time to get married, and considered marriage at older ages as acceptable. Some said that if they waited too long they might become too established, unwilling to make sacrifices; it gets hard to make compromises together.

The respondents gave similar feedback on the ideal marriage age for women, although the age could possibly be a year or two younger. Women also need a certain level of maturity, to be able to handle the responsibilities of marriage, to have the education necessary to get a job. Many said that women mature faster and are ready for marriage sooner. They can handle the responsibilities sooner, and men take longer to settle down. Still, most respondents did not support a large age gap at marriage.

Despite the common view that marriage and children may be "out of favour," the survey respondents spoke rather eloquently of the importance of these questions to their lives.

> BOX 3.4 CONT'D

Asked at the end of the interview about what contributed most to their sense of happiness in life, 76 percent specifically referred to marriage or family questions. While those who refused to take part in the survey may well have included a higher proportion of people who viewed marriage and children less favourably, the results correspond to those obtained in other surveys. While people indicated little active embracement of lifestyles that did not include marriage and children, they also expressed considerable tolerance toward those who might decide not to marry or not to have children. (See Box 6.1 in chapter 6 for further results concerning orientations toward having children.)

These responses, including the high degree of consensus expressed, could be seen as indicating ways in which the culture sets limits on the options available to individuals at a given point in time. The attitudes also express ambivalence in terms of gender roles in marriage. In particular, people seem to be subscribing to both the breadwinner and the dual-earner family.◆

Source: Beaujot 1992.

Given the prevalence of cohabitation—and its longer duration, sometimes as a substitute for marriage—it is useful to look at the *separation rates of unions of all types* (Figure 3.1). The separations in effect vary considerably according to the type of union. After 25 years, 20 percent of marriages not preceded by cohabitation end in separation, compared to 40 percent of unions that involved a marriage preceded by cohabitation, almost 65 percent of unions that started as cohabitations, and close to 85 percent of cohabitations that did not involve marriages. Even after five years the rates show significant differences, with half of unions having dissolved if they involved cohabitations not converted into a marriage, compared to only a 5 percent dissolution rate for unions that started as a marriage not preceded by cohabitation.

In their analysis of the *transition to divorce*, Goldscheider and Waite (1991: 104-6) found that the risk of divorce is greater when a partner's parents have separated, or when the parents of the partners have higher education. However, higher education for husbands reduces this risk, and higher earnings on the part of the husband both decrease divorce and hasten the transition to parenthood.

Canadian data show similar patterns (Balakrishnan, Lapierre-Adamcyk, and Krotki 1993). For instance, higher education is linked with higher divorce rates, but the presence of children reduces the rates. Higher men's incomes reduce divorce. Women with higher incomes have higher divorce prospects, but lower rates of dissolution of cohabitation. Divorce propensities are particularly high for those who married at a young age and had premarital births. Divorce is also higher for couples raising stepchildren, for those who have a larger age difference at marriage, and for persons whose parents had separated (Hall and Zhao 1995).

In analyzing "what holds marriage together," Jan Trost (1986) proposes that most of the standard bonds have declined. The state has redefined the legal bonds to permit divorce by mutual consent; and the trend to two-income families means less economic interdependency. The trend to fewer children means weaker bonds through parenthood. At the expressive and sexual levels, expectations are higher and consequently a higher likelihood exists that people fall short of their expectations.

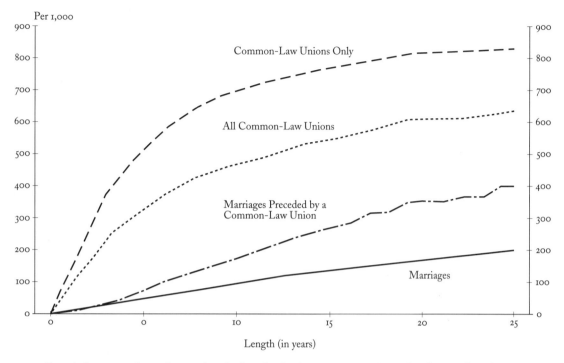

FIG 3.1 Cumulative proportions of separations by length of union, per 1,000 unions of each type, Canada, 1995.

Source: Bélanger and Dumas 1998; 41. Statistics Canada, 1995 General Social Survey.

Divorce trends: instrumental, expressive, and commitment factors

The understanding of divorce trends can be placed in the context of instrumental and expressive factors in marriage and the changing nature of the marriage commitment. With the decrease in the *instrumental* functions fulfilled by families, families have less holding them together. This is particularly true in the economic domain, where families now experience less economic interdependence. A wife in particular has a much easier time getting out of an unhappy marriage if she is employed and living in a two-income family. Moreover, if the marriage no longer determines her status, the prospect of moving out is less negative. The greater independence of women makes the divorce alternative more viable.

Instrumental questions also explain several other patterns about the incidence of divorce. Divorces are less likely to occur when a family has young, dependent children, because that is the time when the family is most economically interdependent. Indeed, both childless couples and those in the empty-nest stage have higher risks of divorce (Rowe 1989; Hoem 1995).

Divorce rates are also higher at the lower levels of socio-economic status. A lower income means that the instrumental exchanges in the marriage are less rewarding, and consequently the prospect of divorce is not as negative. In Sweden, the relationship between education and the propensity to divorce has changed (Hoem 1995). In cohorts born before 1940, those with more education were more likely to divorce, possibly because of more liberal attitudes toward divorce. However, in subsequent cohorts those with more education have lower divorce probabilities, possibly because of the more rewarding nature of their instrumental exchanges. On another instrumental dimension, only 19 percent of men and 14 percent of women in the 1995 General Social Survey thought that an unsatisfactory division of household tasks was a valid reason for marital dissolution (Frederick and Hamel 1998: 8).

The greater relevance of the *expressive* dimension is equally important in understanding the divorce trend. Given that marriage is now seen much more as an arrangement for the mutual gratification of participants, spouses expect more from families in terms of intimacy and interpersonal rewards, and they see individual well-being and self-fulfilment as significant values. Families are expected to serve individual needs, rather than individuals serving family needs. Divorce today, then, may be more prevalent because it represents a natural solution to marriages that do not serve the mutual gratification of the persons involved. In particular, 88 to 95 percent of respondents to the 1995 General Social Survey considered divorce to be justified if there was a "lack of love and respect from the partner," "unfaithful behaviour," or "abusive behaviour" (Frederick and Hamel 1998: 8). According to the survey, the most common grounds for divorce are abusive behaviour, infidelity, lack of love and respect, and excessive drinking by a partner—all factors at the expressive level. For Tamara Hareven (1983), high rates of divorce are proof that people care about marriage and about the quality of their relationships. Still, Anne-Marie Ambert and Maureen Baker (1988) found that significant numbers of people were regretting their decision to divorce. In a third of separations, the partners had no serious grounds for divorce. Some divorces happen because of circumstances that have little to do with the marriage, such as problems at work, mid-life crises, or continuing emotional problems. Other divorces are due to "taking a risk" with an affair that ultimately does not lead to a permanent relationship.

One of the most consistent findings in divorce research is that the probabilities of divorce are higher for those who get married at an early age. For women aged 35 to 49 in 1984, the probability of marital dissolution among those who married at 19 years of age or younger was almost twice as large (26 versus 14 percent) as for those who married at the age of 25 or older (Balakrishnan and Grindstaff 1988; Desrosiers and Le Bourdais 1991). The same applies to the risk of dissolution of common-law unions, which are higher for those entering unions at young ages or if there was a conception before the union (Turcotte and Bélanger 1997: 19-20). The higher divorce levels among those marrying young occur for several reasons, some of them related to instrumental questions.

The lower income associated with youth means that the instrumental exchanges may be less rewarding. Furthermore, those marrying young are more likely to be downwardly mobile, especially if the wife is pregnant at the time of marriage, which detracts from the possibility of pursuing further education. On the expressive level, as these young married persons mature they may find that their spouses were poor choices for them, and that they are not receiving the expected gratification. It may even be that, for persons marrying at younger ages, emotional gratification is particularly important. Early marriage may have been a way of escaping an unrewarding situation in their families of origin. If the expressive dimension is especially important to them, they will show less hesitation about separating when that dimension is not working.

The higher incidence of divorce for second marriages can also be seen in this light. The lowest dissolution rate is for marriages that begin with two single people, while those involving a divorced woman and a single man or two divorced persons have the highest rates (Dumas 1990: 28). Persons who have already divorced are more likely to see marriage in terms of mutual gratification and to leave an unrewarding marriage.

Obviously, divorce would be less common if everyone frowned on it and if the legal restrictions were formidable. But the attitudes toward divorce in Western societies have changed significantly. The social stigma attached to marital dissolution has lessened considerably, and people now accept that divorce occurs frequently for "normal" people. The definition of acceptable grounds for dissolving marital commitments has also changed. Until 1968 adultery was the only grounds for divorce in Canada. The 1968 Divorce Act extended the grounds for divorce to include both fault-related grounds and marriage-breakdown grounds. Fault-related grounds include adultery and other sexual offences, prolonged alcohol or drug addiction, and physical and mental cruelty. To obtain a divorce on these grounds there must be an injured party who brings the other spouse to trial, as well as a subsequent determination of guilt. As of 1986, divorce under marriage-breakdown grounds can occur after spouses have lived apart for one year, for whatever reason.

Interesting analyses have considered the economic outcomes of separation, for both men and women. Administrative data, especially from taxation files, have enabled a five-year follow-up for persons who separated between 1987 and 1993 (Galarneau and Sturrock 1997; Galarneau 1998). The study did distinct analyses for the 40 percent who did not have children under 18 living at home and for the 60 percent who did have children. For those without children, the adjusted family income (after tax and after adjustment for support payments and receipts) declined significantly for women in the first year (by 16 percent), but after five years it showed a 5 percent decline for women and a 2 percent gain for men. After five years, 51 percent of men and 47 percent of women had gained in adjusted family income, compared to the year of separation. Those who were once again living as part of a couple after five years were more likely to have made gains: 53 percent of men had gained, and 56 percent of women. But women were less likely to be living as part of a couple after five years.

EARNING AND CARING IN CANADIAN FAMILIES

For those with children under 18, even more significant declines in income came for women in the first year (23 percent), but after five years the decline was 5 percent for women compared to a 15 percent gain for men. Once again, those who went on to form couples made greater gains, with an average 18 percent gain for men and 14 percent for women. Also, women were less likely than men to be in a couple, especially if they were receiving support payments, but paying support reduced the proportions of men who were in couples. Men who made support payments (38 percent of the men after five years) had made more income gains, while the women who received support had suffered more losses. Similarly, the 10 percent of men without children who made support payments had more income gains in the subsequent five years.

Remarriage

Given the prevalence of divorce, more people are now marrying for the second time or living in postmarital consensual unions. Among persons getting married in 1990, 77 percent had never been married before, 20 percent had been divorced, and 3 percent were widowed. In a third of the marriages, at least one of the partners had previously been married. Under conditions implied in the 1991 life table of marriages, the average number of marriages per person marrying was 1.3. According to the 1984 Family History Survey, of all ever-married persons, 90 percent married only once and less than 1 percent married three or more times (Burch 1985: 31).

The propensity of divorced persons to remarry has declined significantly, especially for women. Under conditions of the 1991 life table of marriages, 64 percent of divorced men and 52 percent of divorced women could be expected to remarry (Table 3.5).

The lower proportions of remarriage, especially for women, probably relate to the changing costs and benefits. Given greater economic independence, people have less need to be married, and women who have been married may be more likely to conclude that the relative "costs of marriage" are not always to their benefit. Given age differences at marriage, and especially at remarriage, and the higher mortality of men, there are also less potentially available mates for older women.

Clearly, postmarital cohabitation has a bearing on these statistics. In 1990, half of divorced persons aged 30-39 and more than a third of those aged 40-49 were cohabitating (Dumas and Péron 1992: 50). Nonetheless, data from France indicate that the number of lifetime unions is not large on average. For instance, at ages 21-44, for persons who were cohabitating at the time of the survey, the never-married had been in an average of 1.2 unions and the divorced in 2.1 unions (Leridon and Villeneuve-Gokalp 1994: 52). The authors conclude that cohabitation, whether premarital or postmarital, does not imply extensive conjugal instability.

The changes in nuptiality and divorce overtook a number of generations at one time. Not only young people but also older ones suddenly became less likely to marry and more likely to divorce and to live in common-law unions. Not only were younger couples having fewer children, but also somewhat older couples were revising downward their family-size intentions. These changes are also clearly interrelated. Persons marrying for the second time are more likely to separate than those marrying for the first time (Dumas 1990: 28); and people who cohabit before marriage are more likely to separate (Burch and Madan 1986). Children of divorced parents are more likely to take up marriage by cohabitation (Thornton and Axia 1989). Both childless couples and those in the now-longer empty-nest stage have higher risks of divorce (Rowe 1989).

Common life trajectories at ages 30-54

Table 3.6 presents estimates of the more common trajectories experienced by men and women between ages 30 and 54—though to reduce the alternative life paths that need to be considered the table uses only the two states of "in union" and "not in union." The five trajectories can be compared among four cohorts born between 1911-20 and 1941-50.

The estimate of those who were *never in union* throughout the period of ages 30 to 54 is generally under 10 percent, reaching its lowest point of around 6 percent in the 1921-40 birth cohorts, and rising again for the most recent cohort.

The most common trajectory involves persons *in union* at age 30, with no further changes between age 30 and 54. About three-quarters of persons in each cohort have had this experience. For women, the estimates are remarkably constant over the cohorts, ranging from 71 to 73 percent. Men show a decline from 83 percent in the 1911-20 cohort to 73 percent in the 1941-50 cohort, who would be in union at age 30 and throughout the period of mid-life.

While the other trajectories are increasing, they clearly represent a minority of life experiences. The most common of these patterns involves marriage or cohabitation followed by a stage of being separated, divorced, or widowed (*postmarital single*). Those who were in union at age 30, and subsequently experienced a non-union state lasting until age 55, amount to some 4 to 8 percent of men and 10 to 15 percent of women.

The fourth pattern involves persons in a marital union at age 30, but who thereafter lived a segment of their lives outside of any union before *remarrying or cohabitating*. This history of union formation and dissolution involves a smaller proportion than the proportions who never married. Specifically, this trajectory represents the life experience of some 7.7 percent of men and 6.2 percent of women in the most recent cohort.

The proportion of people who were not in union at age 30, and *experienced a union* between ages 30 and 54, is remarkably low, reaching only 3 to 4 percent in the most recent cohort. Up to and including the 1941-50 birth cohort, persons not in unions at age 30 have tended not to marry or cohabit over the period of mid-life.

In summary, for the most recent cohort on which estimates are possible—persons born between 1941 and 1950—some 72 percent were in union at age 30 and can be expected to remain in union for the duration of mid-life. The second pattern also involves uniformity, that is, not being in union at age 30 and for the remainder of the mid-life period. The next

UNION STATUS CHANGES BETWEEN AGES 30 AND 54, BY SEX
AND BIRTH COHORT, CANADA, 1911-50

| | 1911-1920 | | 1921-1930 | | 1931-1940 | | 1941-1950* | |
	M	F	M	F	M	F	M	F
Not in union at 30: no further change between ages 30 and 54	8.2	10.8	6.1	5.7	6.1	5.0	9.1	8.2
In union at 30: no further change between ages 30 and 54	83.4	71.1	81.9	73.0	75.7	73.1	73.0	71.7
No union at 30: change to union between ages 30 and 54	1.6	0.6	0.7	1.6	1.6	3.2	3.4	4.0
In union at 30: change to union between ages 30 and 54	4.2	15.1	5.8	14.1	8.1	12.1	6.8	9.9
In union at 30; change to no union and to union between ages 30 and 54	2.6	2.5	5.5	5.4	8.5	6.7	7.7	6.2
TOTAL	100.0	100.0	100.0	100.0	100.0	100.0	100.0	100.0
SAMPLE SIZE	362	518	665	751	803	811	1,134	1,144

* These cohorts have not been exposed to the risks of change as long as the other cohorts.
NOTE: "Union" includes married and cohabiting; "No Union" includes never married, divorced, and widowed.

Source: Beaujot 1995: 45. Statistics Canada, General Social Survey, 1990.

TABLE 3.6

most common patterns involve persons who change from union to no union, or from union to no union to union. Together these two patterns amount to some 15 percent of experiences. The least predominant pattern involves persons who were not in union at age 30 and who experienced a union during the period of mid-life.

Widowhood

Widowhood affects men and women differently. Although we can, and should, feel sorry for all the widowed women, the fact is that men have to die to produce these widows. Projections for the generation of persons born in 1921–36 imply that 60 percent of men will be married at the time of their deaths, compared with 20 percent of women (Péron and Légaré 1988).

The average age at widowhood is 74.1 for men and 71.2 for women. The average length of time spent in this state is 8.7 and 15.1 years respectively. Widowed persons are not likely to remarry: according to 1991 statistics, only 1 in 25 widowed women remarry, which is partly a result of the number of available men of comparable age.

Not living in union and living alone

In 1991, 30 percent of women at ages 25–34 were neither married nor cohabiting, compared to 15 percent in 1971. For men at these ages and times, the proportion not in union has increased from 21 to 39 percent. That is, even when cohabitation is included, living in relationships is down compared to levels experienced over the last 50 years (Beaujot 1995: 40).

A larger proportion of people are now living alone. For the whole population aged 15 and over, 12 percent were living alone in 1996. By age group, the figures are 10 percent or lower until age 55, but they reach 48 percent at ages 85 and over (Statistics Canada 1997a: 7). Between 1991 and 1996, the rate of living in union decreased for all age groups (Bélanger and Dumas 1998). Among the reasons suggested for increased singlehood are that young people are postponing living together, common-law relationships are breaking up much more frequently than marriages, marriages of young people are breaking up earlier than those of previous generations, and the tendency to remarry after divorce or widowhood is declining.

Living alone is particularly predominant among older women, including 42 percent of those over 65. But these elderly women are not necessarily isolated (Stone 1988). Only some 7 to 10 percent of the elderly have no surviving children (Péron and Légaré 1988). Even elderly who have never married usually have family and friends they are involved with in exchanges (Strain 1990). The evidence indicates that while the co-residence of elderly persons with their children has declined, older people do remain in contact with their families. Contact between siblings in later life is also important, especially for women, those who are not married, and those without children (Connidis 1989).

While there has indeed been an increase in the numbers of persons living alone, it is possible to take issue with the basic premise of *New Families, No Families?* (Goldscheider and Waite 1991). While people are waiting until later to marry or form unions, there has not been a major increase in the numbers of persons living outside of families. Children are staying longer in their families of origin. The increase in widows living alone is a function of life expectancy rather than of a disaffection with family living. In addition, elderly persons living alone tend to remain in contact with their families.

Those of a younger age not only show a delay in leaving home, but also, in significant numbers, are in relationships. At ages 21-44 in France, between a quarter and a third of single persons indicated that they were in a stable love relationship (Leridon and Villeneuve-Gokalp 1994: 51). In Canada, the high rate of approval for premarital sex would also imply that many young people have established relationships. For instance, at ages 18-34, 90 percent approve of premarital sex (Bibby 1995: 69). According to the 1994-95 National Population Health Survey, 80 percent of persons aged 20-24 said they had at least one sex partner in the previous year (Galambos and Tilton-Weaver 1998: 12).

PARENTING

We turn now to relations across generations through parenting—including not only conjugal but also parental bonds, along with their relative importance. In terms of co-residence, children are part of the lives of parents for an average of some 30 years (Ravanera and Rajulton 1996).

In *Centuries of Childhood*, Ariès (1962) argues that children, once largely ignored, later became the centre of family preoccupations. Shorter (1975: 170-72) used similar themes in *The Making of the Modern Family*. Some two centuries ago many things competed for the mother's time. Doctors complained about how infants were left unattended for hours on end. In the region around Montpellier in France, where mothers were kept especially busy during the time of the silk harvest, there was even a saying: "*Le temps auquel on élève les vers à soie, est le temps auquel on peuple le plus le paradis*" ("In the time you see the silk worm rise, the most kids go to paradise"). But over the 20th century, attention was placed on children to the point that many people concluded that children needed full-time mothers. At the extreme, in the 1950s, a prevalent concern was that it would be harmful for children to have their mothers working outside of the home.

John Caldwell (1976) used these ideas as a basis for interpreting the demographic transition to lower fertility. As families became nucleated, a dramatic shift occurred in the intergenerational transfer; whereas parents had previously benefited from having children, children now came to be the net beneficiaries. Others have talked about this as representing a shift from child quantity—from ensuring that some children would survive to provide for their parents in old age—to child quality, with a parental emphasis on having a number appropriate to each of the *children* having the best possible life.

Other authors have proposed that the pendulum has somewhat swung back over the period since the 1960s. In his later writings, Ariès (1980) observed a second transition and maintained that the period of the "child king" had come to an end. The second transition involved a move to adult-centred preoccupations with self-fulfilment and attention to the quality of the dyadic relation between partners. John Kettle (1980) suggested that the parents of the baby boom had been a "dutiful generation," while their children were a "me generation." Given conflict between self-interest and the interests of other family members, a dutiful person would make sacrifices for groups beyond themselves—for instance, staying married for the sake of the spouse and children—whereas a "me generation" person with high expectations of success and personal gratification would find that empty marriages were not worth saving. In other words, the existentialism that influenced a few philosophers in the 1940s and 1950s became generalized as a key principle in intimate relations. What became important was not the preservation of an institution like marriage, but one's existence and experience in the here and now. This goes back to Giddens's idea of a "pure relationship," one based on the continuing fulfilment of both partners.

Having children was increasingly seen as a form of emotional gratification for adults, or *child-bearing as affective individualism*. Some people concluded that having children could well interfere with this kind of affective individualism, and some opted to be child-free; almost by definition, having children involves some commitment beyond the here and now. Others sought to have both children and relationships that were at least open to divorce. For instance, the proportion of persons who agree with the statement, "When there are children in the family, parents should stay together even if they don't get along," has continued to decrease. Lesthaeghe's (1995) article "The Second Demographic Transition in Western Countries" discusses this second transition in terms of an accentuation of existential needs and of gender-related egalitarian values, wherein children are no longer considered as impediments to parental divorce.

Parental vs. conjugal interests

Parents differ extensively as to the relative weight of self-interests versus interest in the welfare of the next generation. This variation is particularly visible in union formations and dissolutions in cases with existing children. Consider first the point of view of men involved in union formations that include previous children. If a man does not have children of his own, he may be contributing to the welfare of his new partner's children. Research by Hillard Kaplan, Jane Lancaster, and Kermyt Anderson (1998) suggests that he is doing this mostly as the payment necessary for access to the mother. For instance, if this second union is dissolved, the former male partner will then contribute very little to children for whom he is neither the biological nor, now, the social parent. If the man has children from a previous union, a new union may bring into play questions of "deadbeat dad," because he is having to divide his loyalties between an older and a younger family, and he may not have enough emotional and instrumental resources for both. If a woman with existing children establishes a new relationship, that new union may be a means of obtaining resources not only for herself, but also for her children, or it may endanger her children. That is, her dyadic interests may have superseded the children's interests. For the whole population, attitudes indicate that only 43 percent of persons in the 1995 General Social Survey would stay in a relationship for the sake of the children (Frederick and Hamel 1998: 8).

Clearly, all societies have both *conjugal and parental bonds*, and what comes into play is their relative importance. While conjugal bonds have become more important, most adults want to have children and consequently to establish parental relationships. Just as a relaxation of the social prescriptions surrounding the entering and leaving of relationships has occurred, so too a weakening of the normative imperative to have children as a necessary part of adult roles has come about (Thornton 1989). Despite a greater tolerance for alternatives, most people still value stable relationships, parenthood, and family life. Little evidence exists of an increased preference to remain outside of relationships or to not have children.

At the same time, the greater flexibility in conjugal relations adds complexity to parental relations, which range from bi-parenting to lone parenting and multi-parenting. Partly because researchers gather most of the data at the household level, the field suffers from a serious deficiency of information on the extent of parental involvement on the part of biological parents who are not members of the household.

In their study "The Changing Context of Fatherhood in Canada," Heather Juby and Le Bourdais (1998) observe that nine out of ten men experience fatherhood. While two-thirds of paternal roles are limited to a single, durable, and intact family, over a fifth (23 percent) are exposed to a "new" or "second" paternal role. On the one hand Juby and Le Bourdais observe that the reduction in male wages, higher unemployment, and greater opportunities for women to work put pressure on men to be more involved as parents. On the other, separations weaken the links between children and their fathers, who may no longer engage in either provider or carer roles. They conclude that

---

BOX 3.5 | *Costs for children*

Various authors conclude that the flexibility of marital relations comes at the expense of children's welfare. Basing his results especially on an analysis of trends in Sweden, David Popenoe (1988) argues that families have become incapable of adequately producing, nurturing, and socializing children. Considering *Marriage, Divorce, Remarriage* in the United States, Andrew Cherlin (1992) observes not only the gains for adults in autonomy, opportunities for women, and a greater emphasis on love and companionship, but also the costs, especially for children who may suffer from the "choices" of adults. Barbara Whitehead (1998) further argues that the *Divorce Culture* tends to produce blinders in regard to these negatives. Goldscheider and Waite (1991) observe that many poor marriages result in poor parenting, and the children may be better off "out of there." But they find that many persons with poor marriages are still able to parent effectively. Consequently, children are the least likely of all concerned to benefit from divorce and remarriage.

Mary Stewart Van Leeuwen (1998) summarizes, "Divorce is anything but a minor blip on the developmental trajectory of children." Even when there is proper alimony or a quickly reconstituted family, the average consequence for children is negative. It is true that parental conflict is a problem for children, even in intact marriages, but parental conflict also makes co-parenting difficult after divorce, especially once new relationships are formed. Van Leeuwen proposes that a two-parent family provides more time for child care, a constant presence, and day-to-day predictability, which allows children to concentrate on developmentally appropriate tasks. For instance, an intact family does not call on the children to play the role of a stable presence in the lives of adults or to understand the difficulties faced by the parent.

Still, these are average results, and cases exist in which separations enable children to rise to the challenge and "be their own persons." In the case of serious conflict or abuse, children are better off without one of the parents.♦

"paternal transitions are stressful, emotionally and economically, for all involved" and. that many of the problems within families are due to the "ambiguity surrounding non-traditional parental roles." Nonetheless, they expect a continued widening of the divide between conjugal and parental careers.

These patterns on the relative importance of parental and conjugal bonds also help explain the delay in child-bearing and the smaller numbers of births. Roussel (1992) observes that a key question is the compatibility between the decision to have a child and the other gratifications sought by a couple. Consequently, partners tend to feel that having a child should not be an obstacle for either of them, and they often delay having children in order to arrive at an optimum situation. While two children are often considered necessary to ensure the gratification of adults and the well-being of the children, having more than two can easily be seen as standing in the way of other goals.

With the rising importance of self-gratification in relationships, people are more likely to be committed to their relationships only to the extent that these remain satisfying. This tendency presents a problem for child-bearing, because having children involves a long-term commitment. The parent-child relationship, and at least to some extent the relationship to the other parent of one's child, remains in place for life. Thus people may be having fewer children to avoid the associated commitments to spousal relationships (Beaujot 1986). The 1984 National Fertility Survey provides evidence that less stable relationships lead to fewer children. For instance, among women married in the period 1966-81, those with no marital interruptions expected a total of 2.2 children, while those with interruptions expected 1.6, a difference of 25 percent (Lapierre-Adamcyk 1987).

COMPOSITION OF FAMILY AND HOUSEHOLD UNITS

The consequences of changes in relationships and parenting show up in the changing composition of Canadian families and households. The data in Table 3.7 are based on census definitions. A *household* is defined as one or more people living in a separate dwelling. A *separate dwelling* is one that people gain access to either from outside or from a common hallway without having to pass through another dwelling. A *family* is defined as a husband and wife with or without children who have never married, or one parent with at least one never-married child, living in the same residence. In 1996, 71 percent of all households involved families, and 84 percent of Canadians lived in families with an average size of 3.1 persons. At the same time, persons living alone made up 12 percent of the population aged 15 and over, or 24 percent of households.

Over the period 1981-96, the number of single-person households increased by 56 percent, while lone-parent families increased by 59 percent. In contrast, the number of husband-wife families with children at home increased by only 10 percent. In effect, the largest increases are for what might be called non-traditional family forms. Common-law families comprised 11.7 percent of the families in the 1996 census, while lone-parent

FAMILY AND HOUSEHOLD TYPES, CANADA, 1981 AND 1996

| | NUMBER (THOUSANDS) | | CHANGE (%) |
	1981	1996	1981-96
Total households (private)	*8,281.5*	*10,820.1*	*30.7*
Family households	6,231.5	7,685.5	23.3
Non-family households	2,050.0	3,134.6	52.9
One-person households	1,681.1	2,622.2	56.0
Total families	*6,325.3*	*7,837.9*	*23.9*
Husband-wife families*	5,611.5	6,700.4	19.4
Husband-wife families with children at home	3,599.1	3,970.6	10.3
Husband-wife families without children at home	2,011.4	2,729.8	35.7
Total married-couple families	*5,257.3*	*5,779.7*	*9.9*
Married with children	3,478.9	3,535.6	1.6
Married without children	1,777.4	2,244.1	26.3
Total common-law families	*354.2*	*920.6*	*160.0*
Common-law with children	120.2	435.0	261.9
Common-law without children	234.0	485.7	107.6
Single-parent families	*713.8*	*1,137.5*	*59.4*
Male led	124.4	192.3	54.5
Female led	589.4	945.2	60.4

* Includes common-law unions.

Source: *1981 Census, no. 92-325; Beaujot 1991: 244; The Daily, 14 Oct 1997: 3.*

TABLE 3.7

families comprised another 14.6 percent. Thus over a quarter of families were either lone-parent or common-law. By 1996, 47.2 percent of common-law families included children, compared to 61.2 of other husband-wife families.

In the review of change in families and households for the period 1971 to 1991, Yves Péron et al. (1999) emphasized that households with two or more people have maintained their "family" character. That is, the reduction in the relative predominance of family households is almost totally a function of the growth of single-person households. Consequently, living in non-family households especially occurs for the elderly who have previously lived in families, and for the young who are between families. While we often emphasize the increasing diversity, at this level there is considerable simplicity. Non-family households usually involve only one person, while family households usually include only one family and no additional persons. Consequently, in 1996, nine out of ten households were either one-family or one-person units.

Lone-parent families

The growth of lone-parent families has drawn considerable attention in recent years. Among families with children, 11.4 percent were lone-parent in 1961 but 22.3 percent in 1996. In 1971 the largest category was still the widowed parent, but in 1991 families made up of a separated or divorced parent constituted 60 percent of the total, with another 18 percent covering the never-married-parent category (Lindsay 1992: 17). The proportion of male-headed families among the lone-parent families has been stable, amounting to 16.9 percent in 1996.

Maureen Moore (1987, 1988, 1989a) has analyzed female lone-parenting with the help of the 1984 Family History Survey. Compared to currently married women of the same age, female lone parents are more likely to have lived common law and to have had their children earlier in life. Among women aged 18 to 64 in 1984 and who had had children, 26 percent had experienced lone parenthood. For about two-thirds of these, parenting alone had ended either through a new union or (for 16 percent of them) through the children leaving home. The average duration of lone-parent episodes was 5.5 years, with 10 percent of episodes lasting less than six months and 17 percent lasting more than ten years. Among those who experienced at least one episode, 12 percent experienced two or more episodes of parenting alone.

Families in later life

Families with husbands aged 65 or over comprised 15 percent of all family households in 1996. In addition, 28.7 percent of persons aged 65 and over were living alone (Statistics Canada 1998a, 1997a). In her examination of later-life families, Ellen Gee (1995) emphasizes the dimensions of continuity, change, and diversity. In terms of continuity with the past, a high percentage of today's aged people have married, had children (sometimes in large numbers), and stayed married until death or widowhood. In large part, factors outside of an individual's control, such as the early death of a spouse or involuntary childlessness, account for the variation from the normative pattern. In terms of change, the most dramatic element is the increase in the incidences of living alone, particularly among older women. However, other changes are beginning to surface, including divorce and cohabitation.

Gee (1995) further emphasizes the diversity among the older population in terms of family characteristics, including age, economic status, cultural background, and especially gender. Women are more likely to be widowed, men are more likely to remarry, and women have a higher incidence of living alone. In addition, the female population has more heterogeneity with regard to family life. This is especially visible at ages 85 and over, when over 50 percent of men are married, compared with less than 12 percent of women. We will return to the economic side of these questions in chapter 4.

WOMEN AND MEN IN FAMILIES

Another useful approach to the study of family and change is to consider how family events intersect with the lives of individuals over time. This allows us, for instance, to emphasize the differences in the family life patterns of women and men.

BOX 3.6 *Lifetime probability of various family events*

Péron et al. (1999) have performed interesting analyses using life-table techniques to estimate the lifetime probabilities of various family events, given the history of events by age observed in the 1990 Survey (Table 3.8). In this analysis, they focused on family episodes involving children. A total of 78 percent of both women and men could be expected to form bi-parental unions involving children. Some 12 percent of these involve a period of cohabitation, and the remaining 65 percent are "direct" marriages.

The probability of having an episode of single parenthood is 34 percent for women and 23 percent for men. These episodes are considerably shorter for men. The departure from these single-parenthood episodes for women occurs through forming a new cohabitation (39 percent), marriage (30 percent), or the departure of children (22 percent).

The probability of experiencing a reconstituted family is 16 to 17 percent for women and men. In both cases, these episodes are more likely to occur through cohabitation than through marriage, and they are more likely to end through the departure of children. Among reconstituted

families, 80 percent have children only from the wife, 8 percent from the husband, and 12 percent from both (Desrosiers and Le Bourdais 1995). This means that only 2 percent of families have children from three origins ("hers, his, theirs").

Despite considerable diversity, 89 percent of women and 88 percent of men will have at least one parental episode, and two-thirds will see the departure of the last child while they are in union with the other parent of the children. For persons aged 35-64 in 1990, 36.9 percent of women and 26.3 percent of men will have a lone-parent episode, but over 60 percent of these people will be part of a couple before the last child leaves.

The most significant changes occur from one generation to the next (Le Bourdais, Neill, and Turcotte 1998). For instance, among women aged 60-69 in 1995, 96 percent married directly, compared to 35 percent for women aged 20-29. For all women aged 40-69, 36 percent had at least one separation, and 28 percent had at least two unions. The constant factor is that some 95 percent of each cohort has at least one union.◆

Source: Adapted from Péron et al. 1999; Le Bourdais, Neill, and Turcotte 1998.

The 1990 and 1995 General Social Surveys, which obtained the history of the respondent's family life, are especially helpful to the analysis of these questions. At the time of the 1990 survey, 76 percent of women and 68 percent of men aged 18-64 were living in a conjugal or parental relationship (Péron et al. 1999). Among women living with children, 89 percent were living with the father of their children and 94 percent had not lived with any spouse other than the father of their children. In families that had been reconstituted, nine out of ten women had brought their own children into the new union. By the time they were aged 45 and over, 97 percent of women and 96 percent of men had lived in a union or raised children. However, at ages 35-44 close to half of the men surveyed either were not living with their biological children or had never had children of their own. At ages 18-34 10 percent of men were living with children who were not their biological children.

The general prevalence of union formation for the adult population is understandable given that married persons, both men and women, tend on average to be better off in terms of happiness, satisfaction, physical and mental health, and longevity (Glenn 1997; Waite 1995).

Research in the United States and Sweden indicates considerable differences across men in terms of the likelihood of being in various kinds of families (Goldscheider, Bernhardt, and Kaufman 1996). In particular, men with low incomes are most likely to be cohabiting with a partner who has children, while those with the highest incomes are most likely to be married and to be living with their own children. Men with more resources would tend to avoid entering situations with a high likelihood of the need to invest in someone else's children. The deteriorating economic situation of young men would be an important reason for a lower marriage rate. Pamela Smock and Wendy Manning (1997) further find that cohabiting men's economic circumstances carry far more weight than women's in predicting marriage formation.

The 1996 census shows comparable results for Canadian women (Statistics Canada 1998a: 10). For instance, among women aged 25-34 who have children under six years of age, the proportion with a post-secondary certificate or degree is highest for those who are married (55.2 percent), followed by those who are cohabiting (45.0 percent), and lowest for those previously married (43.5 percent) or never married (34.5

LIFETIME PROBABILITIES OF VARIOUS FAMILY EVENTS, 1990

CUMULATIVE PROBABILITY OF LIVING IN AN INTACT TWO-PARENT FAMILY BY AGE 65	F	M
Starting as a common-law union	5	5
Starting as a common-law union with marriage before childbirth	8	8
Direct marriage	66	65
TOTAL	79	78

FOR THOSE WHO HAVE LIVED AS INTACT TWO-PARENT FAMILY, PROBABILITY OF LEAVING THIS STATE WITHIN 40 YEARS		
Due to death	8	4
Due to separation	24	17
Due to departure of child	58	55
TOTAL	90	76

PROBABILITY OF LIVING A PERIOD OF SINGLE PARENTHOOD BY AGE 65		
Due to birth out of union	6	6
Due to widowhood	9	3
Due to separation	17	12
TOTAL	34	23

FOR THOSE WHO HAVE LIVED A LONE-PARENT EPISODE, PROBABILITY OF LEAVING THIS STATE WITHIN 20 YEARS		
Through departure of children	22	28
Through marriage	30	40
Through common-law union	39	26
TOTAL	90	94

PROBABILITY OF LIVING IN A RECONSTITUTED FAMILY BY AGE 65		
Through marriage	5	7
Through common-law union	10	9
TOTAL	16	17

FOR THOSE IN A RECONSTITUTED FAMILY, PROBABILITY OF LEAVING THIS STATUS WITHIN 20 YEARS		
Through death	2	1
Through separation	32	21
Through departure of children	53	53
TOTAL	87	75

Source: Péron et al. 1999: 124, 129, 147-152, 181, 186, 201-206 . Statistics Canada, General Social Survey, 1990.

TABLE 3.8

percent). For women with young children, those with higher status are more likely to be married.

Returning to men, there are certainly some bases on which we can observe reductions in their attachments to families. Steven Mintz (1998) sees masculine detachment from the family as a long-term trend, based both on the breadwinner model that involved their working outside of the family and the disappearance of the family wage, as well as, more recently, the relative deterioration of the wages that men can bring to families. Consequently, the material basis of male familial authority has declined. Nonetheless, the structural differences in most marriages mean that men are older and have a higher status at work, thus providing the greater share of family income (McQuillan and Feree 1998).

There is long-standing public concern about men's neglect of family roles (Mintz 1998). Whereas men previously had a status in their families based on lineage rights, they now have to work at these roles. Consequently, women have become the primary parent, and motherhood has less variability than fatherhood. Nonetheless, Steven Nock (1998) finds that men are looking for ways of being in families, and indeed they do provide more child care than anyone else besides mothers. That is, fathers provide more care than other categories of individuals or institutions that care for children (O'Connell 1993). For the most part, men need the element of common habitation as a factor in their investment in children (Draper 1998): in effect, men invest more in the non-biological children they live with than in the biological children with whom they are not living (Marsiglio 1998). At the same time, fathers do matter in two-parent families, and they can matter in father-absent families (Furstenberg 1998). Marriages are more stable if fathers are involved with the children (Nock 1998).

CONCLUSION

Several important differences, then, are apparent in men's and women's family experiences. Women enter relationships at slightly younger ages, and men are more likely to remarry. Once they have had children, women are likely to continue living with children, while formerly married men are more likely to be living in relationships with other women's rather than their own children. Compared to women, then, men are more in union but less with children. In terms of living with children, men are more likely to deviate from the normative sequencing, while in terms of living with a partner it is women who are more likely to deviate.

There is less reversibility to motherhood than to fatherhood, then, while re-establishing a partnership after a separation is more common for men. Both of these features effectively play against the economic well-being of women relative to men: women are less likely to have a partner who contributes to family earnings, and they are more likely to be living with children who are dependent on their care. In addition, men are more likely to end the life course married, while women are more likely to be widowed.

In their analysis of the transition to marriage in the United States, Goldscheider and Waite (1991: 84) found that women's likelihood of marriage is reduced if they have experienced non-family living or have parents with more education and income. They expect that, to the extent that marriages become less traditional, these pressures on women to delay or avoid marriage will be reduced. In effect, this is already the case with regard to employment, because employed women are more likely to marry.

Data from the 1992 Swedish family study indicate that both men and women with greater economic self-sufficiency are more likely to cohabit and to marry, but not necessarily to pass from cohabitation to marriage (Bracher and Santow 1998). The marriage propensities of more recent U.S. cohorts also indicate that economic status has become positively related to the marriage propensity of both men and women (Sweeney 1997). Persons with more education and more secure jobs would be more attractive as partners because they are not economically dependent. In their analysis of the transition to divorce and to parenting in the United States, Goldscheider and Waite (1991: 104-6) find that the husband's education reduces the risk of divorce, and the husband's higher earnings both decrease divorce and hasten the transition to parenthood. Therefore earning questions are important, and finding a well-educated spouse becomes an important form of protection against divorce. In addition, the researchers find, more educated men are more modern in their gender attitudes and consequently more willing to share in housework. Men's education, then, may be an attribute on both economic and gender grounds, or in terms of both earning and caring.

Goldscheider and Waite (1991: 61-6) conclude that important differences exist in the relative costs and benefits of marriage to women and men. In particular, while both partners benefit, women's benefits are more economic, and men's benefits are more in terms of health and longevity. Both gain in economic terms by having greater combined assets, but women's individual incomes suffer, especially in the long term. In non-economic terms, women suffer more of the restrictions associated with traditional marriages. Still, these authors propose, "The changes having the most powerful impact on restructuring the family are those that are breaking down the separation between male and female adult roles" (p. 8). In particular, as the next two chapters will also show, specialization and complementarity by gender produce fewer gains, while symmetrical and companionate relationships show emerging gains.

Marriage and family patterns have shifted toward more flexibility as manifested through divorce and cohabitation, along with later entry into relationships. While achieved status has always been important for men's entry into reproductive relations, it has now become equally important for women. For instance, among women with young children, those who are married or cohabitating have the most education, while those who are formerly married or never married have the least education. Men's part-time work has increased, along with more labour-market participation by women. Women's double day remains an important feature of some couples, and in most couples women have the major responsibility for domestic work. Once established, the division of domestic work appears to be difficult to renegotiate. However, some couples are establishing a better sharing of unpaid work, especially if the commitment to paid work remains continuously important for both spouses. This suggests a move away from the breadwinner model toward models of co-providing and co-parenting.

Paid Work and Family Income

The main changes in paid work include slow wage growth, high unemployment, and an increase in non-standard work, such as part-time and temporary work. By the mid-1990s one-third of workers were in non-standard jobs, with typically less security, and only half of employed persons were working full-year full-time. In effect, only one-third of workers have what might be considered to be a typical work pattern of one job, 35-48 hours per week, Monday to Friday during the day, working on a permanent basis for an employer at a place of work.

These changes have been explained in at least two ways. Sociologists who focus on work have emphasized an increased corporate concentration that is altering working conditions, often to the disadvantage of workers. These changing conditions clearly have an impact on the extent to which individuals and families have security in employment, and consequently they influence individual and family strategies.

The perspective of family change provides a complementary view on the dynamics of change in work. A higher proportion of women, and consequently of the population, in the labour force creates a higher supply of workers. The existence of dual-earning couples and a 24-hour economy results in considerable variation in the types of employment. In addition, the strongest variations in economic well-being are themselves associated with family contingencies, especially the greater predominance of lone-parent families and single-person households. While there are deteriorating relative labour-market outcomes for young men, the proportion of workers with stable jobs has not declined and per capita family income has been rising. That is, couples and families have come to position themselves differently vis-à-vis economic security and to focus on maximizing the participation of all the household's adults in the labour force. Family models may also come to be based less on specialization through complementary roles and more on companionship and equivalent roles.

This chapter, then, develops two major themes: variations in the work patterns of individuals by gender and family status; and family strategies for the organization of work and family.

The work patterns of women and men show rather systematic differences. While women's labour-force participation has increased, significant differences remain, especially lower proportions of women working full-year, full-time. Important income differences also remain in place, with incomes being most similar for men and women who are single with no children.

The explanations of gender differences in income relate to productivity, occupational segregation, and discrimination, but these factors must be placed in the broader context of the tensions between earning and caring. Consequently, work interruptions are a particularly sensitive measure of this earning/caring equation. Marital and parental status operate very differently for women and men, with marriage and parental status increasing women's interruptions but reducing men's work interruptions.

Strategies for the organization of work and family initially changed with the greater involvement of women in the labour force, and they have evolved to the consideration of alternative divisions of work within couples. These changes have been further prompted by the difficulties young persons face getting established in the labour market. Nowadays family and work must be considered together, and experiences in these two spheres are determined by family strategies and evolving socio-economic conditions. The most prevalent alternative, the dual-income strategy, is not without its own forms of stress, especially when a family has young children. The strategies taken up also relate to other family types, such as lone-parent families, young and elderly families, and persons not living in families. I conclude by reflecting on the implications of these strategies, and their associated earning/caring tensions, for gender inequality.

◆

Families, as we have seen, have changed extensively in the past 30 years. In particular, the phenomena of cohabitation and divorce have implied changing definitions of marital unions, and the decline in the numbers of children has been significant.

Work—which in this chapter means paid work—has also undergone change: a larger proportion of the total population is employed, but workers have also seen limited wage gains and higher unemployment, a continued growth of the service sector, and a greater predominance of part-time work and other forms of non-standard work. The Economic Council of Canada (1990) used the title *Good Jobs, Bad Jobs* to underline the growing inequality in employment. This report, along with others written in the early 1990s and stressing similar themes, such as *The New Face of Poverty* (Economic Council of Canada 1992), contributed to the political demise of the Council, which had been providing annual commentary and policy suggestions since 1964. Other aspects of the change in work include greater participation of women, earlier ages at retirement, longer periods of education and training, and the difficulties of young persons seeking to establish themselves in the labour force.

Clearly, some of the changes in paid work are closely related to family change. Higher female labour-force participation and the growth of two-earner families are the most obvious examples of change in both families and work, but other examples are the growth of flex-time and non-standard work. The uncertainty of many jobs may be a driving force behind new family strategies that focus less on *specialization* in terms of the division of paid and unpaid work and more on *insurance* against the potential unemployment of the main breadwinner. The relation between work and family may also be seen in evolving gender social contracts concerning the division of paid and unpaid work. In the extreme, it would seem that "contract work" contingent on the changing needs of the economy has to some degree supplanted the "family wage" that seeks to support a family.

Marie-Agnès Barrère-Maurisson (1995) proposes that researchers need to analyze family and work together, using a concept she calls "the family division of labour." She further suggests that socio-demographic change in most developed countries has altered both economic structures and family structures. Consequently, we need a concept to analyze these structures simultaneously. Emile Durkheim (1893) considered *The Division of Labour* to be the principal bond holding modern societies together, but he gave little attention to the family division of work. The quarterly publication from Statistics Canada, *Perspectives on Labour and Income*, does pay close attention to the interplay of family and work, with articles on gender, marital and family status, two-earner and single-earner families, and unpaid as well as paid work.

Here we will take up two approaches to the family division of work, in keeping with the major focus of this chapter. The first approach looks at the division of work as a function of the family status of *individuals*. Using this approach we can analyze the differentials in work, including work interruptions, in terms not only of gender but also of the marital and parental status of women and men. The division of work, in effect, entails individual adaptation between the demands of paid work and domestic work.

The second approach starts at the *family level* and stresses family accommodation to evolving socio-economic change through both family and work strategies. That is, instead of considering how a person's family status can influence their work, we look at how the broader concept of family strategy can determine both family and work. In statistical terms, we no longer consider family status as the independent variable influencing work, but both family status and work status are taken to be endogenous variables. Family strategy becomes the broader concept that determines both family status (union formation, union dissolution, and child-bearing) and work status (division of paid and unpaid work, kinds of work, and associated income and security). Clearly, family strategies are difficult to observe, and similar empirical observations are subject to alternative theoretical interpretations. It is also important to remember that individuals within a family can have strategies that may be different or even conflicting.

In effect, it is complex to disentangle the causal nexus between family and work questions. For instance, difficulties on the labour market may make it hard for people to start new families, and these difficulties are part of the reason for marital separations. Economic questions are thus influencing family questions ("*It's the economy, stupid!*"). But separations are also part of the reason for the lower incomes of the formerly married, and married persons have a division of labour that disadvantages the earned income of wives. In that way, family questions influence economic questions ("*It's the family, stupid!*"). My own sense is that both of these factors are operative. Scott Coltrane (1995) proposes that, for the most part, a couple needs two secure jobs to establish a solid middle-class standing. To achieve this kind of security, people have to "get it together" in both family and work.

CHANGING WORK PATTERNS

Work is a highly significant social process. In effect, Durkheim, Weber, and Marx, the modern pioneers of sociology, all concerned themselves with changing work relations. Work involves a relation with society and with other people. It is key to both macro questions of class divisions in society and to micro questions of individual well-being and alienation (see Box 4.1).

Harvey Krahn and Graham Lowe (1993: 2) define work as "activity that provides a socially valued product or service." They observe that this work may be paid or unpaid, legal or illegal, esteemed or despised. Nonetheless, for the most part their book on *Work, Industry and Canadian Society*, like this chapter, applies itself to work that is paid and legal.

In *The Making of Post-War Canada*, Peter Li (1996) interprets broad societal changes in terms of the impact of corporate ownership, first on industrial organization and then on the nature of work. In particular, the evolution of corporate capitalism, including the increasing concentration of ownership and control, brings with it the treatment of labour as a commodity. Directly or indirectly, the leading 100 enterprises in Canada controlled 55.9 percent of total assets in 1988, compared to 46.5 percent in 1975 (p.27). Paid workers, or wage-earners, increased from 68 percent of the labour force in 1945 to 90 percent in 1975 and remained at this level into the 1990s (p.150). Capitalist production and mass consumption have also included an expansion of the labour force, with especially more women and young persons, as well as immigrants from abroad.

James W. Rinehart (1996) makes a similar broad diagnosis in *The Tyranny of Work: Alienation and the Labour Process*. The logic of capitalist accumulation and competitiveness brings alienated labour, significant unemployment, and governments that lose the potential for autonomous actions. In particular, Rinehart considers three sources of alienated labour: concentration of the means of production, markets in land, labour, and commodities, and a complex division of labour. Consequently, workers are less in control; they become commodities; and they are fragmented into jobs that separate the conception from the performance of work.

Jeremy Rifkin (1995) indicates an even more serious diagnosis, *The End of Work*. He observes that the increased productivity of the industrial age was translated into reduced work hours. For instance, the typical workweek, which was close to 60 hours in 1901, and 50 hours in 1941, has been stable at some 37 to 40 hours since 1960 (Sheridan, Sunter, and Diverty 1996; Sunter and Morissette 1994). Rifkin argues that the increased productivity of the information age should be translated into a further reduction to 30-hour workweeks. In a broader context, the pre-industrial period involved a shortage of workers, to the point that slavery and indentured work were used to hold persons at work. Capitalism reduced the coercion associated with work (Russell 1993). In comparison to the pre-industrial period, industrialization has produced a surplus of workers, which has been further accentuated by automation and the information age.

The changes have also brought a greater prevalence of non-standard forms of work, including part-time, temporary, and contract. Gordon Betcherman and Lowe (1997)

BOX 4.1 | *Observations on changing work patterns*

The continued expansion of the service industries, a polarization of employment opportunities, further growth in women's labour force participation, rising levels of unemployment, more part-time and other forms of nonstandard work, increased automation, global economic restructuring, readjustments in union-management relations, and a "new wave" of management thinking.

(Krahn and Lowe 1993: 1)

An increase in social inequality is probably the most disturbing trend we have observed. After three decades of growth, family incomes are no longer increasing in real terms. Nonstandard jobs have become more common.... The overall picture of Canadian society that emerges, especially compared with the more affluent and expansionary 1960s and 1970s, is one of increased inequality, fewer opportunities for upward mobility, and greater employment insecurity.

(Krahn and Lowe 1993: 371)

Transformations in work are profoundly affecting individuals, families and communities. New technology, economic globalization, high unemployment, declining job security, stagnant incomes, polarized working time, and work-family tension define a new context of work for many Canadians.

(Betcherman and Lowe 1997: 1)

These have not been good years for working people. We have witnessed two free trade agreements; the dilution of social programs; a deep recession accompanied by double-digit unemployment; the disappearance of relatively secure working class jobs and the rapid growth of contingent (part-time, temporary) forms of employment; the erosion of real wages.

(Rinehart 1996: v)

Two out of three Canadians will never be poor in their working lives. For the other third, however, spells of joblessness and poverty are a reality. Within this group, there is a growing segment that is poor and/or unemployed for prolonged periods. It is the children of this group who are the most disadvantaged in preparing for their adult lives.

(Economic Council of Canada 1992: 54)

The implication of our research is that the labour market is offering economic security to fewer Canadians.

(Economic Council of Canada 1990: 17)

In the ebbing years of the twentieth century, work appears to be in a state of crisis, and, to some analysts, we appear to be approaching a societal precipice. The dramatic changes in employment patterns—the entrenchment of high rates of unemployment, moves to casualize more of the labour force, the growing gap

➤ BOX 4.1 CONT'D

between core workers with "good jobs" and peripheral workers with "bad jobs," the increasing insecurity of almost every form of employment, the dramatic increase in personal bankruptcies, and the absence of entry level jobs for the young—may presage a collapse into greater social inequalities and conflicts, intractable poverty and general personal and social dislocation.

(Duffy, Glenday, and Pupo 1997b: 1) ◆

speak of a move toward "work, not jobs" in the sense of a lack of continuing employment or career opportunities and their replacement with more fluid contractual arrangements.

With these changes in the nature of work, a number of key issues arise: the distribution of the remaining work in the population; the family adaptation to changing work conditions; and the extent to which various kinds of work are paid or unpaid.

The family context

Clearly these transformations of work have significant impacts on families. Li (1996) attaches particular attention to the conversion of previously unpaid female labour into wage labour. The occupational categories of service, clerical, and sales, which amounted to 23 percent of the labour force in 1941, have come to comprise 42 percent in 1991 (p.151). It is into these occupations, more similar to unpaid household service, that women have especially been absorbed. More recently, women have also moved into the managerial and professional occupations, which amounted to 13 percent of the labour force in 1941 and 27 percent in 1991. In contrast, the primary occupations, along with processing and crafts, declined from making up 64 to 31 percent of the labour force, and they have involved significantly smaller proportions of women workers.

The largest expansion of women's work has been into areas that have offered greater flexibility in the accommodation of family questions. This has probably been an iterative process. Not only did women join occupations that permitted more flexibility, but to accommodate other aspects of their lives they have also introduced more flexibility to these very occupations. In contrast, occupations in the secondary sector have not been pushed to make comparable adaptations. It may be partly for these reasons, rather than intrinsic differences in the feasibility of women actually doing the work, that women remain significantly outnumbered in the occupations of the secondary sector. These gender divisions in the workplace, seen especially as occupational segregation, have in turn reinforced gender divisions in the home.

As an example of this iterative process, in a small sample of women graduates from the University of Alberta, the proportion employed full-time declined over the period after graduation, while the proportion working part-time increased (Ranson 1995). For instance, 84 percent of the graduates were working full-time in 1986, compared to 69 percent in 1992. The sample showed substantial differences in the proportion of women who were raising children seven years after graduation, broken down by faculty of graduation. Women with degrees in education were much more likely to be raising children than women in business or engineering. The author attributes this difference to the shorter probation period in teaching and the greater accommodations that the profession has made for family responsibilities. These accommodations include the potential to have an interruption, or to work part-time, without loss of seniority.

Families have also become more dependent on the consumer market and the wage economy, with a resulting contradiction between the maintenance and renewal of labour at the family level (Li 1996: 59-75). The maintenance of labour involves the care of workers on a daily basis, while renewal involves the reproduction of workers into the next generation. Specifically, two full-time earners in the same family can find it particularly difficult to both care for each other and care for children. Li interprets the decline of fertility within this contradiction: the family response is to maximize earnings by increasing the number of wage-earners, but to reduce the costs of child-rearing by having fewer children.

Because capital requires both the maintenance and renewal of labour, Li expects to see changes that would reduce this contradiction such as subsidized day care, tax incentives for child-bearing, or extended paid maternity leaves. But a surplus of labour power could work against these possibilities. The immigration alternative, and the potential to move activities that are labour-intensive to off-shore locations, allowing capital accumulation to live with this particular contradiction, can also come into play. Analysts in Sweden, for example, tend to make a link between that country's low immigration and high female labour-force participation (Hoem and Hoem 1997). Without access to cheap immigrant labour, employers had to hire more women. Families nonetheless remain important to the economy as consumers of goods and services, and thus a minimum number of children are needed to continue the consumption into the next generation.

Employment and income trends

The long-term growth of the *demand for labour* is certainly confirmed in the labour-force trends (Table 4.1). For instance, the total number of employed persons in Canada doubled between 1961 and 1991. Particularly significant is the increase in the proportion of the population aged 15 and over who are in the labour force, which includes those either employed or looking for work. The labour-force participation rate had been around 55 per 100 in the period until 1961, and has since increased to 65 per 100, in spite of greater numbers of retired persons.

The last two columns of Table 4.1 present what may seem like contradictory results. The unemployment rate has been climbing from decade to decade, averaging 5 percent in the 1950s and 1960s, then 7 percent in the 1970s, and around 10 percent in the 1980s and 1990s. But the number of people who have employment—the employment to population ratio—has increased steadily from 50 per 100 persons aged 15 and over in 1961 to almost 60 in the 1980s and 1990s. Consequently, as the labour force has expanded, in part due to the participation rates of women, the country has seen both *more unemployment* and *more employed* persons per population aged 15 and over. Part of the reason for the

LABOUR-FORCE STATISTICS, 1901-96

| | LABOUR FORCE 1000S | EMPLOYED 1000S | PARTICIPATION RATE[a] | | | UNEMPLOYMENT RATE[b] | EMPLOYMENT POPULATION RATIO |
			TOTAL	F	M		
1901	—	1,782	53.0	16.1	87.8	—	—
1911	—	2,724	57.4	18.6	90.6	—	55.0
1921	—	3,164	56.2	19.9	89.8	—	53.4
1931	—	3,921	55.9	21.8	87.2	—	53.7
1941	—	4,511	55.2	22.9	85.6	—	52.9
1951	5,223	5,097	54.3	24.2	84.1	2.8	52.4
1961	6,521	6,055	55.1	29.1	80.8	5.0	50.2
1971	8,639	8,104	58.1	39.9	75.4	4.8	54.5
1981	12,332	11,398	64.8	51.8	78.3	7.0	60.4
1991	14,408	12,916	66.7	58.5	75.1	9.7	59.8
1996	15,145	13,676	64.9	57.6	72.4	10.4	58.6

a Per population aged 15+.
b Average of the previous decade or part of decade.

Source: Canadian Social Trends, *no. 40: 34, no. 44: 30; Krahn and Lowe 1993: 62; Statistics Canada, no. 11-516, 1983: D1-7. Statistics Canada, Labour Force Survey.*

TABLE 4.1

higher unemployment may be the increased *supply of workers* in the population, which also means that there are more employed persons who are able to support those who are not employed.

In the period 1991-96, the labour-force participation rate declined, but most of the change occurred for age groups under 25 and over 55 (Sunter and Bowlby 1998). For the young, the decline in labour-force participation is largely a function of the increased proportions who are at school full-time and an increase in the proportion of students not looking for work. For older persons, declining labour-force participation is associated with earlier retirement. The average age at retirement in 1996 was 62 years for men and 60.7 for women.

The *growth in wages* shows equally interesting trends (Table 4.2). Particularly significant is the growth in wages over the period 1940 to 1970, amounting to more than a 250 percent increase in average real wages over the 30-year period. This growth slowed down significantly in the subsequent period, amounting to only a 2 percent growth over the decade of the 1980s and a 2.6 percent decline over the period 1990-96. In the period 1980-96, men's average wages declined while women's increased.

Some analyses of *earnings inequality* indicate significant polarization, especially when considering market incomes (Yalnizyan 1998). Still, other analyses show no overall change in polarization in the period 1985-95 (Picot 1998; Zyblock 1996b; Statistics Canada 1998d: 16; Human Resources Development Canada 1996). Looking at certain categories of the population, some researchers see an increased inequality for men, and for young persons of both sexes, but a reduction of polarization for women, especially for those working full-time (see also Morissette, Myles, and Picot 1996; Beach and Slotsve 1996).

AVERAGE ANNUAL WAGES BY SEX IN CONSTANT (1995) DOLLARS, 1920-95

| | AVERAGE ANNUAL WAGE | | | PERCENT CHANGE IN PREVIOUS DECADE | | |
	BOTH SEXES	M	F	BOTH SEXES	M	F
1920	7,566	8,379	4,552			
1930	8,479	9,243	5,600	12.1	10.3	23.0
1940	9,351	10,701	5,280	10.3	15.8	-5.7
1950	12,567	14,348	8,237	34.4	34.1	56.0
1960	17,909	20,642	11,193	42.5	43.9	35.9
1970	24,497	29,265	15,273	36.8	41.8	36.4
1980	26,578	33,370	17,550	8.5	14.0	14.9
1990	27,170	33,333	19,824	2.0	-0.4	14.2
1995*	26,474	31,917	20,162	-2.6	-4.2	1.7

* Change over five years.

Source: *Statistics Canada 1998b: 5; Statistics Canada, no. 62-010; Rashid 1993: 13. Census Data.*

TABLE 4.2

The increased inequality for men applies especially to differences between younger and older persons. On the basis of the 1971-93 Survey of Consumer Finances, Paul Beaudry and David Green (1997) find that, in constant dollars, successive waves of men are earning less than their elders at every stage of their careers. The study, which follows men from age 25, finds that this pattern began in 1978 for those with high-school education and before 1964 for university graduates. For all male workers, the difference in wages between ages 25-35 and 45-54 increased by 18 percentage points in the period 1981-95 (Statistics Canada 1999: 19). While younger men are earning dramatically less than their predecessors at the same age, women are earning at least as much as their predecessors, at each level of education. Beaudry and Green conclude that the growing gap between the earnings of older and younger men cannot be explained by differences in education or experience. They suggest that the deteriorating labour-market outcomes of younger male workers may be a function of institutional factors like less unionization for the young, or supply effects like increased numbers of workers with higher education and greater female labour-force participation.

Part of the overall increase in inequality, then, is a function of a higher proportion of workers in the population, some of them being women workers with low wages. The greater supply of workers has also had an impact on the wages of young men. This has made it difficult for men to establish secure marital relationships (Oppenheimer 1994). It may also be that the increased labour-market prospects of women encourage a division of paid and unpaid work, in which men take less of the responsibility for earned income. The work and family trends may thus be influencing the labour-market prospects of both women and men. Women gain more paid work and experience increases in income over time, while young men make fewer income gains, which may translate into delayed marriages or changes in the division of paid and unpaid work.

Non-standard employment

Another important feature of the change in employment is the rise of part-time work and other forms of *non-standard employment*, such as temporary work, multiple jobs, and own-account self-employment. The 1989 and 1994 General Social Surveys and the 1990 and 1995 Survey of Work Arrangements noted these trends. For the most part, these types of employment have advantages for employers through increased flexibility and reduced costs (Krahn 1995). But from the point of view of employees, the trends can bring greater insecurity, fewer benefits, and lower pay. For workers between the ages of 15 and 64, a total of 28 percent of employment was in one or the other of these categories in 1989, and 33 percent in 1994 (Table 4.3). Given that this form of employment mostly involves lower pay, this change increases the amount of inequality in the labour force.

The Survey of Work Arrangements defines the category of *temporary work*: non-permanent jobs, including temporary, contract, and term, as well as seasonal and casual jobs. Altogether, 11 percent of employed persons in 1995 were in non-permanent work, with 74 percent of the usual weekly hours and 65 percent of the weekly earnings of permanent jobs (Grenon and Chun 1997: 25). Non-permanent jobs are common for women, for persons under 25 years of age, students, never-married persons, and university graduates.

Across industries, non-standard employment is most common in the service sector (social services, retail trade, and other consumer services), but it is spreading to the goods-producing sector (Krahn 1995). The increase over the years is especially apparent for ages 15-24 and 55-64, and the specific category of part-time work also shows important differences by gender. In 1994, 24 percent of women and 8 percent of men were working part-time (Table 4.3). The comparison over the five-year period nonetheless indicates that non-standard work is spreading to men. John Myles, G. Picot, and T. Wannell (1993) found that 44 percent of all new jobs added to the economy in the 1980s were in the low-wage consumer and retail services, many of which involved non-standard employment (see Swift 1997). For all persons who worked in 1995, 51 percent worked full-year full-time, another 8 percent worked full-year part-time, and 41 percent worked less than 49 weeks in the year (Statistics Canada 1998f).

Involuntary part-time work has also increased (Logan 1994). By 1995, slightly more than a third of all part-time workers were classified as involuntary part-time; the proportion was higher for men. More people also have *multiple jobs*: from some 2 percent of workers in 1977 to 4.9 percent of women and 5.3 percent of men in 1995.

In effect, *work hours* have become polarized, with a smaller proportion working the regular workweek of 35-40 hours, for both men and women (Betcherman and Lowe 1997: 28). Consequently, only one-third of workers have what might be considered to be a typical work pattern of one job, 35-48 hours per week, Monday to Friday during the day, working on a permanent basis for an employer at a place of work (Human Resources Development Canada 1997).

NON-STANDARD EMPLOYMENT BY AGE AND SEX, AS PERCENTAGE OF TOTAL EMPLOYMENT, CANADA, 1989 AND 1994

	PART-TIME		TEMPORARY		MULTIPLE JOBS		OWN ACCOUNT[a]		TOTAL NON-STANDARD[b]	
	1989	1994	1989	1994	1989	1994	1989	1994	1989	1994
Total	15	15	8	9	5	7	7	9	28	33
Women	25	24	8	8	5	8	6	8	35	40
15-24	40	46	13	17	6	13	3	–	49	64
25-34	20	17	7	8	6	8	5	8	30	33
35-44	23	21	8	6	6	8	8	9	35	37
45-54	21	18	6	7	3	6	8	13	31	35
55-64	24	29	—	—	—	7	8	11	35	41
Men	7	8	7	9	5	7	8	9	22	27
15-24	31	36	14	16	4	7	5	5	41	52
25-34	4	4	6	10	5	7	6	8	18	25
35-44	—	3	4	7	5	7	9	10	16	22
45-54	—	2	3	5	6	5	10	9	19	19
55-64	5	6	9	6	—	7	10	20	20	30

a Self-employed, works without paid employees; these are not counted within the temporary worker category.
b One or more of the four specific categories listed.

Source: Perspectives on Labour and Income, *vol. 7, no. 4: 37, 40. Statistics Canada, Work Accommodations Survey.*

TABLE 4.3

The 1995 Survey of Work Arrangements also provides information on the hours that employed persons would prefer to work, at current wage rates. While two-thirds prefer to keep their hours, for every worker who would like fewer hours there are five who would like more hours (Drolet and Morrissette 1997). Those preferring fewer hours (6 percent of workers) are more likely to be women with high family incomes. In the specific category of persons with preschool children, women are more likely to prefer fewer hours while men tend to work more hours. The remaining 28 percent of workers would prefer to work more hours for more pay (Akyeampong 1997).

Other aspects in the change of work involve increased flexibility: some 24 percent of workers had *flex-time arrangements* in 1995, compared to 16 percent in 1991 (Akyeampong 1997). Flexible schedules are more common for husband-wife workers, particularly those with children under six (Human Resources Development Canada 1997). In two-parent families, mothers with young children usually have the non-traditional work patterns (Marshall 1994). *Working at home* has also increased, climbing to 8 percent of the labour force according to the 1996 census (Statistics Canada 1998f; Pérusse 1998).

Looking at comparable data from the United States, Harriet Presser (1998) speaks of a "24-hour economy" that is pushing the trend to non-standard work. This demand-side explanation points especially to the growth of a service economy. It is also linked to women's greater participation in the labour force, which necessitates additional hours for retail services and encourages the purchase of homemaking services in the marketplace.

The higher incomes of dual-earner families also prompt an increased demand for recreation and entertainment. While non-standard work patterns make it harder for adults to schedule family activities, Presser (1998) observes potential benefits for children in more care by fathers and grandparents. She also finds that non-standard work increases men's share in household tasks. Consequently, the 24-hour economy, with the associated growth of non-standard employment, brings changes at work, in families, and in the relations between family and work.

Implications for earning and caring

In terms of the broader issues of earning and caring, we need to look not only at the labour force but also at the entire population. Krahn and Lowe (1993: 371) pay attention to higher unemployment, more part-time and non-standard work, more short-term jobs, greater employment insecurity, and consequently more inequality. The share of middle-level jobs has been declining, and polarization has taken place with the growth in both high-paying and low-paying jobs (Economic Council of Canada 1990). Still, these observations of increasing inequality take into account only inequality within the labour force. Taking the whole population into consideration, researchers have noted a reduction in the relative size of the component that is not in the labour force whatsoever and that consequently has no earned income.

Along similar lines, René Morissette, John Myles, and Garnett Picot (1996) found that the increase in earnings inequality in the 1980s was mostly due to shifts in the distribution of annual hours worked. Certain conditions—more women and young persons working, and consequently a larger proportion of workers having fewer hours of work—created higher earnings inequality within the labour force. The larger proportion of persons employed may be part of the reason for the slower growth of labour productivity since 1975. Diana Galarneau and Cécile Dumas (1993) found that productivity increased at an average rate of 3.3 percent per year over the period 1961-75, but at a rate of under 1.5 percent per year in the period 1976-91.

The period 1961 to 1996 involved, then, a considerable reduction in the proportion of the population aged 15 and over who were without employment, and the expansion of the labour force has also seen more part-time and non-standard forms of employment, and consequently more persons working at low wages. For instance, more people working part-time is a negative in the sense that significant numbers of people would like to work full-time, but it is also a positive in the sense that more people are working. While more people are working on a *temporary* basis, the proportion of employed persons who have been with the same employer for five or more years has also increased (Belkhodja 1992). The probability of being laid off has not increased, nor has the average duration of jobs decreased (Statistics Canada 1999: 22).

In part, greater inequality across jobs occurs because more women are counted as paid workers. If we include all adults in the measures of inequality and count unpaid work as

AVERAGE INCOME IN CONSTANT (1996) DOLLARS AND RELATED CHARACTERISTICS OF FAMILIES AND UNATTACHED INDIVIDUALS, 1971 TO 1996

| YEAR | FAMILIES | | | | | UNATTACHED INDIVIDUALS | ALL UNITS |
	AVERAGE INCOME ($)	AVERAGE INCOME PER CAPITA($)	AVERAGE FAMILY SIZE	AVERAGE # OF CHILDREN UNDER 16	AVERAGE # OF INCOME EARNERS	AVERAGE INCOME ($)	AVERAGE INCOME PER CAPITA ($)
1971	44,101	11,729	3.76	1.31	1.57	18,486	12,276
1976	54,250	15,544	3.49	1.09	1.64	21,748	16,155
1981	55,042	16,761	3.28	0.87	1.76	24,617	17,632
1986	55,294	17,447	3.17	0.80	1.72	24,034	18,238
1991	56,623	18,155	3.12	0.79	1.71	24,522	19,003
1996	56,629	18,400	3.08	0.75	1.64	24,433	19,205

Source: Statistics Canada, no. 13-207-XPB, 1996: 25. Survey of Consumer Finances.

TABLE 4.4

work with zero pay, the reduction in the numbers of unpaid workers both increases total earnings and reduces the inequality.

Consequently, despite stagnant levels of earned income and pressures toward inequality within the labour force, per capita income has increased by 8.9 percent in constant dollars from 1981 to 1996 (Table 4.4). With the reduction in the numbers of children per family, and fewer persons per family, families have experienced more gains in average income per capita than in average family income. Interestingly, with the larger proportion of dual-earner families and the larger number of lone-parent families, the average number of income-earners per family has remained remarkably constant (Table 4.4).

The changing nature of work participation, along with changes in family structure, helps explain trends in family income (Table 4.5). While average family income declined in the periods 1980-85 and 1990-95, it nonetheless increased from 1980 to 1995. Focusing on the period 1990-95, in which average family income dropped by 4.8 percent in real terms, the decline was the most severe in husband-wife families in which the wife had no earned income and in lone-parent families. The increased proportion of lone-parent families accounts for almost one-fifth of the overall decline in the average income of all families between 1990 and 1995 (Statistics Canada 1998b). In addition, the reduced proportion of families in which both husband and wife reported employment income and the increased proportion of husbands or wives without income account for close to half of the decline in the average income of husband-wife families over this period 1990-95.

As a result, a major source of inequality in family incomes is itself associated with family questions—with the contrast between the sole-earner and two-earner models, along with union dissolution and lone parenthood. Work and family are linked through the limited option of lone-parent families to have more than one person in the labour force. For instance, the 1994 cycle of the Survey of Labour and Income Dynamics shows a 25 percent turnover in the low-income group over a one-year period (Statistics Canada

NUMBER AND AVERAGE INCOME OF CENSUS FAMILIES IN CONSTANT (1995) DOLLARS, BY FAMILY STRUCTURE AND COMBINATION OF EARNERS, CANADA, 1980-95

	1980	1985	1990	1995
NUMBER OF CENSUS FAMILIES				
All families	6,325,315	6,733,845	7,355,730	7,837,870
Husband-wife families	5,611,495	5,880,550	6,402,090	6,700,355
No earner	585,080	748,300	854,760	1,067,430
Husband, wife and child	623,385	686,130	899,435	909,705
Husband and wife	2,323,150	2,552,005	3,063,005	3,048,555
Husband and child	428,405	352,695	257,160	227,845
Husband only	1,408,180	1,206,555	957,970	951,460
Wife and child	32,940	49,595	58,330	78,065
Wife only	121,900	177,080	200,745	282,775
Child only	88,455	108,185	110,685	134,515
Husband with earnings	4,783,120	4,797,385	5,177,570	5,137,565
Husband without earnings	828,375	1,083,165	1,224,520	1,562,790
Wife with earnings	3,101,370	3,464,810	4,221,510	4,319,105
Wife without earnings	2,510,125	2,415,740	2,180,575	2,381,255
All lone-parent families	713,815	853,300	953,645	1,137,505
Male lone-parent families	124,380	151,485	165,245	192,275
With earnings	112,850	133,150	147,075	162,840
Without earnings	11,530	18,335	18,170	29,430
Female lone-parent families	589,435	701,810	788,400	945,235
With earnings	437,540	506,750	595,795	667,005
Without earnings	151,895	195,065	192,600	278,230

Source: Statistics Canada, The Daily, *12 May 1998: 15. Census Data.*

TABLE 4.5

1998d: 19). The turnover was driven first by labour-market dynamics, but family changes such as marriage and separation also played a significant role. There are also examples of gains through intergenerational income mobility, which is judged to be relatively high in Canada (Lefebvre and Fortin 1997: 24). For instance, 20 percent of persons whose fathers were in the bottom quarter of income distribution have themselves ended up in the top quarter of this distribution in the next generation. In other words, prevailing economic structures are permitting positive economic mobility.

NUMBER AND AVERAGE INCOME OF CENSUS FAMILIES IN CONSTANT (1995) DOLLARS, BY FAMILY STRUCTURE AND COMBINATION OF EARNERS, CANADA, 1980-95 (CONT'D)

	1980	1985	1990	1995
AVERAGE FAMILY INCOME				
All families	53,089	52,625	57,339	54,583
Husband-wife families	55,945	55,957	61,053	58,763
No earner	24,890	27,140	30,896	30,399
Husband, wife and child	83,829	82,594	87,526	85,501
Husband and wife	60,484	61,650	65,968	65,561
Husband and child	71,174	68,485	72,508	68,733
Husband only	46,975	47,184	50,137	47,993
Wife and child	54,603	53,262	58,834	57,690
Wife only	33,698	34,738	39,122	39,211
Child only	45,800	45,003	51,579	49,939
Husband with earnings	60,507	61,510	67,109	65,979
Husband without earnings	29,604	31,364	35,448	35,041
Wife with earnings	64,061	64,302	69,186	67,894
Wife without earnings	45,916	43,988	45,307	42,200
All lone-parent families	30,640	29,661	32,408	29,962
Male lone parent families	46,133	43,478	45,557	40,974
With earnings	49,413	47,619	49,239	45,666
Without earnings	14,032	13,409	15,757	15,008
Female lone-parent families	27,370	26,679	29,652	27,721
With earnings	33,244	32,714	35,150	33,960
Without earnings	10,449	11,001	12,642	12,765

Source: Statistics Canada, The Daily, *12 May 1998: 15. Census Data.*

TABLE 4.5

GENDER DIFFERENTIALS IN WORK AND INCOME

In their article "Women, Work and Family in America," Suzanne Bianchi and Daphne Spain (1996) point to the progress achieved in several areas of their subject-matter: reduced gender gaps in labour-force participation, and in earnings and education, and more women in managerial jobs. In other areas they saw little change: workplace segregation is reduced but persistent, and the poverty gap continues. The areas that show increasing differentials relate especially to family questions: the growing gap between married couples and mother-only households, and the uneven economic toll of divorce on women and men.

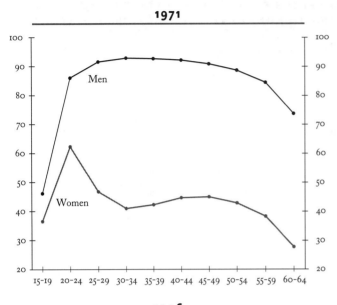

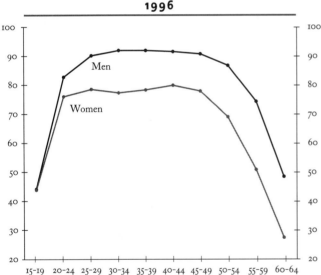

FIG 4.1 Labour-force participation rates by age and sex,
Canada, 1971 and 1996

*Source: 1971 Census, no. 94-704, Table 9; 1996 Census, no.
93F0027XDB96001.*

Labour-force participation and work hours

In Canada in 1901, as a proportion of the population aged 15 and over, 87.8 percent of men were in the labour force and 16.1 of women. The rates for women increased from decade to decade, but especially in the period 1961-81, reaching over half of women by 1981 and 58 percent by 1996. Men's rates remained close to 90 percent in the period 1901-31, and afterwards declined to 71 percent by 1996. (See Table 4.1.)

The age patterns for labour-force participation by gender have also become more similar (Figure 4.1). In 1971 women's rates still showed a bimodal distribution, or a pattern of two humps, with higher participation especially at ages 20-24 and again at 40-54, but rates not much above 40 percent in the whole period of mid-life (Gunderson 1998: 35-36). By 1996 the patterns were rather similar for women and men, showing an inverted U-pattern that involved relatively stable rates over the ages 25-49. Considering the initial life-course events of work or union formation for women and men over generations, Fernando Rajulton and Zenaida Ravanera (1998) find a rather constant proportion of some 80 percent of men who have first entered work, but an increase from 44 to 71 percent for women who have first entered work rather than unions over the birth cohorts 1916-25 to 1956-65.

Women's labour-force participation rates have increased not only from generation to generation, but also across time for given generations

(Galarneau 1994: 13). Besides the patterns of employment, the entrance to retirement has also become more similar for women and men (Duffy and Pupo 1992). Looking at the period 1990-92, Penny Basset (1994) sees, as her article title indicates, a "Declining Female Labour Force Participation." But the decline during the recession mostly involved young persons, and men more so than women. Indeed, as a long-term trend, the decline in labour-force participation is clearly more relevant to men than to women. Nonetheless, men's participation rates remain significantly higher, especially at ages 30 and over.

While participation differences have declined, important gender gaps do remain. For instance, at ages 25-44 in 1996, 15.2 percent of men compared to 28.8 percent of women were not in the employed labour force. Using life-table techniques, Alain Bélanger and Daniel Larrivée (1992) estimated that the total lifetime years in the labour force would be 39.4 for men and 31.0 for women under 1986-87 conditions, or 27 percent higher for men. Their estimates also indicated an average of 2.4 lifetime labour-force exits for men and 3.4 for women.

The differences are stronger when we take full-time employment into account. For instance, at ages 25-44 in the 1996 census, 74.9 percent of men and 51.6 percent of women were working more than 30 hours per week; and 9.9 percent of men and 19.7 percent of women were working part-time. In comparison, the June 1986 Labour Force Survey at ages 25-44 showed 86.3 percent of men and 52.2 percent of women working full-time. While the proportion of women working full-time was stable, men's proportions declined by over 10 percentage points.

Part-time employment has become more common, especially for younger workers (Table 4.6). In 1976, only 3.4 percent of employed men

PROPORTIONS WORKING FULL-TIME, PART-TIME, AND AVERAGE HOURS OF WORK, BY AGE AND SEX, 1976-96

MEN				
1996	*Total*	*15-24*	*25-44*	*45+*
Full-time	89.8	65.6	95.2	92.4
Part-time	10.2	34.4	4.8	7.6
Hours (Total)	41.9	32.9	43.5	43.4
Full-time	44.7	42.1	44.7	45.5
Part-time	17.0	15.3	19.7	18.1
1985	*Total*	*15-24*	*25+*	
Full-time	94.2	82.9	97.4	—
Part-time	5.8	17.1	2.6	—
Hours (Total)	42.4	37.7	43.7	—
Full-time	44.0	42.2	44.4	—
Part-time	15.9	15.7	16.2	—
1976	*Total*			
Full-time	96.6	—	—	—
Part-time	3.4	—	—	—

WOMEN				
1996	*Total*	*15-24*	*25-44*	*45+*
Full-time	72.3	51.0	77.8	74.2
Part-time	27.7	49.0	22.2	25.8
Hours (Total)	33.8	27.8	35.2	34.8
Full-time	40.0	38.9	39.8	40.6
Part-time	17.9	16.3	18.9	17.9
1985	*Total*	*15-24*	*25+*	
Full-time	77.2	73.8	78.5	—
Part-time	22.8	26.2	21.5	—
Hours (Total)	34.2	33.0	34.7	—
Full-time	39.4	39.0	39.6	—
Part-time	16.7	16.4	16.9	—
1976	*Total*			
Full-time	82.6	—	—	—
Part-time	17.4	—	—	—

Source: Statistics Canada, no. 71-001, June 1996: Tables 18, 23; July 1985: Tables 29, 27; July 1976: Table 21. Labour Force Survey.

TABLE 4.6

were working part-time, along with 17.4 percent of employed women. By 1996, these figures had risen to 10.2 of men and 27.7 of women. At ages 15-24 in 1996, close to half of all employed women were working part-time, along with over a third of employed men. At all ages, women had a greater likelihood of working full-year full-time in occupations not traditionally held by women, but still their rates remained lower than for the men in the same occupations (Hughes 1995).

Even among full-time workers, the usual hours of work differ by sex. For instance, at age group 25-44, the 1996 average was 39.8 hours for women and 44.7 for men—an average of 12.3 percent more hours for men. Between 1976 and 1995 the proportion of persons working standard hours (35 to 40 hours) decreased and the proportions working both less than 35 hours and more than 40 hours increased (Sheridan, Sunter, and Diverty 1996). This polarization in work hours applies to men in all age groups, and to women in age group 25-34. More women than men now hold multiple jobs, but the women on average work 40.2 hours per week compared to 51.6 for men (Sussman 1998: 29).

Analyzing the case of Sweden, Marianne Sundstrom (1991a; 1994) concluded that a relationship existed between labour-force participation and part-time work. In particular, the opportunity for part-time work increased women's labour-force participation. Part-time work in Sweden carried more benefits, and mostly involved 20 to 34 hours per week. Compared to Canada, a higher proportion of women in Sweden were working part-time, with higher average hours of work. Consequently, in Sweden in 1992 the average workweek for all employed women was basically the same, at 33.6 hours, Canada in 1996, at 33.8 hours. But 80 percent of women aged 16-64 are in the labour force in Sweden, compared to less than 60 percent of women aged 15 and over in Canada. These results lead Sundstrom (1991a) to conclude that part-time work in Sweden had increased the continuity of women's labour-force attachment, strengthened their position in the labour market, and contributed to gender equality by reducing their economic dependency. In addition, part-time work had facilitated the combination of work and child care, and the shift to full-time work once the children are older.

Occupational segregation

Differential distributions across occupations represent another important gender difference in work patterns. Gender segregation is substantial: in 1981, over 60 percent of men or women would have to change their occupational categories in order to have the same occupational distribution (Fox and Fox 1987: 390). Looking at the period 1931-81, Bonnie Fox and John Fox find that segregation remained very high, though there was some decline in the 1960s and 1970s. The chief reason for the decline involved the entry of women into occupations previously almost exclusively male. Other researchers cite the same reason for the reduction in sex segregation in the United States over the period 1970-88, compared to relatively stable patterns from 1900 to 1970 (Reskin and Padavic 1994: 63).

Considering the more recent period in Canada, Jo-Anne Parliament (1989) finds that the range of jobs being done by women had grown, but most of the jobs were still concentrated in a narrow range of traditional female occupations. In 1994, 70 percent of women, compared to 31 percent of men, were in clerical, sales, service, teaching, or health occupations (Allahar and Côté 1998: 108). The 1996 census finds that the three most common jobs for men are truck drivers, retail sales, and janitors, while for women they are retail sales, secretaries, and cashiers (Statistics Canada 1998f: 6)

Using 12 categories of skills profiles, Paul Bernard and his colleagues (1996) found that 60 percent of persons were in categories that were either 80 percent male or 80 percent female in composition. Similarly, Karen Hughes (1995) found that the proportion of women in traditionally female occupations had declined, though remaining at 78 percent in 1991 compared to 86 percent in 1971. Krahn and Lowe (1993: 70) concluded that job ghettos still existed, but women were entering a broader range of occupations. In the 1990s, in three industrial categories, men were more concentrated in goods-producing industries while women were more concentrated in the lower-tier services (retail trade and other consumer services).

The two categories of managerial/administrative and professional occupations (Table 4.7) are especially worth noting. The professional occupations include lawyers, doctors, accountants, teachers, nurses, engineers, mathematicians, social workers, artistic and literary jobs, librarians, journalists, performing artists, photographers, designers, athletes, and coaches. Together, these two categories of managers and professionals comprise the white-collar sector and about a third of jobs in 1996. In 1976, women comprised only 20 percent of managers and 48 percent of professionals, but by 1996 they made up over half of these combined categories of white-collar occupations. While this change indicates progress, it is far from indicating equality in these occupational categories. There are important differences both between the managers of small and larger enterprises and between health professionals, such as doctors in comparison to nurses. Occupational segregation is not only horizontal, but also vertical within given occupational categories, and women are more likely to occupy the lower tiers. Monica Boyd (1997) finds that the higher proportion of women in the labour force has been accompanied by continued gender segregation of occupations. Gender, she concludes, is ever present in power relations in the workplace.

MANAGERS AND PROFESSIONALS, BY SEX, 1976 AND 1996

	MALE	FEMALE	TOTAL
Managers			
1976	79.8	20.2	100
1996	55.0	45.0	100
Professionals			
1976	51.9	48.1	100
1996	43.9	56.1	100
Both			
1976	60.5	39.5	100
1996	48.5	51.5	100

Source: Statistics Canada, no. 71-001, June 1976: Table 8; June 1996: Table 14. Labour Force Survey.

TABLE 4.7

NUMBER AND AVERAGE EARNINGS OF INDIVIDUALS 15 YEARS AND OVER, IN CONSTANT (1995) DOLLARS, BY SEX AND WORK ACTIVITY, CANADA, 1980-95

	1980	1985	1990	1995
Number				
Both sexes	12,495,345	13,074,460	14,905,395	14,996,115
Worked full-year, full-time	6,212,125	6,580,875	7,718,780	7,513,790
All others	6,283,215	6,493,580	7,186,610	7,482,325
Males	7,309,330	7,386,820	8,105,020	8,051,900
Worked full-year, full-time	4,181,160	4,249,365	4,699,895	4,514,850
All others	3,128,175	3,137,455	3,405,125	3,537,050
Females	5,186,010	5,687,640	6,800,370	6,944,210
Worked full-year, full-time	2,030,965	2,331,515	3,018,885	2,998,940
All others	3,155,045	3,356,125	3,781,485	3,945,270
Average earnings				
Both sexes	26,784	26,062	27,170	26,474
Worked full-year, full-time	37,517	37,258	37,652	37,556
All others	16,172	14,715	15,912	15,345
Males	33,458	32,319	33,333	31,917
Worked full-year, full-time	42,556	42,438	43,162	42,488
All others	21,299	18,614	19,768	18,422
Females	17,377	17,935	19,824	20,162
Worked full-year, full-time	27,145	27,817	29,074	30,130
All others	11,089	11,069	12,440	12,586

NOTE: Full-year, full-time=49-52 weeks in the reference year, mostly full-time

Source: Statistics Canada, The Daily, *12 May 1998: 5. Census Data.*

TABLE 4.8

Income differences

Breaking down gender differences in income, Table 4.8 presents average incomes from censuses since 1981. The statistics show converging trends in the proportions of men and women with employment income, in the proportions working full-year full-time, and in the average income of people working full-year full-time.

The average income of persons working full-year full-time is a key statistic. Data from the labour-force survey on this question go back to 1967, when the average income for women represented 58.4 percent of men's incomes, compared to 63.7 in 1981 and 73.4 in 1996 (Statistics Canada 1998i: 18). Most of the change since 1980 has involved increases in women's incomes; men's incomes have been stable. This trend has helped to reduce differences, but the wage gap remains sizeable for the workforce as a whole (Coish and Hale 1995).

In a given age group the wage gap for full-year full-time workers has narrowed over time, although it also remains substantial (Galarneau 1994: 36). Comparisons over censuses for a given cohort show that the gap increases as the cohort ages. The gap is smallest at the youngest ages, and the reduction over the period 1980-90 for the age group 15-24 is largely a function of the deterioration of young men's wages (Kerr, Larrivée, and Greenhalgh 1994).

The gaps in the average earnings of persons working full-year full-time have also narrowed by marital status (Table 4.9). The largest relative change is for the formerly married. While declining, the gaps are most significant in the married category, where women's earnings represent 68.9 percent of men's earnings in 1996. The ratios are also declining by level of education: women with university degrees have the most relative advantages, but their earnings represent 76.3 percent of

FEMALE TO MALE EARNINGS RATIO FOR FULL-YEAR, FULL-TIME WORKERS, BY AGE, MARITAL STATUS, AND EDUCATION, 1981-96

	1981	1986	1991	1996
TOTAL	63.7	65.8	69.6	73.4
By age				
15-24	76.6	79.1	86.0	90.3
25-34	69.5	71.6	76.4	80.0
35-44	61.5	65.2	69.6	72.1
45-54	57.0	60.4	65.7	70.1
55+	65.8	65.4	62.7	71.2
By marital status				
Single	86.0	86.9	90.1	93.2
Married	59.2	61.0	65.1	68.9
Other	67.8	75.2	75.8	80.1
By education				
0-8 Years	60.5	56.3	66.7	71.1
Some secondary*	62.0*	64.5*	64.1	65.5
Graduated from high school	—	—	69.3	72.9
Some post-secondary	65.6	62.7	69.0	72.7
Post-secondary Certificate or diploma	65.0	69.8	70.9	71.0
University degree	68.3	67.3	72.5	76.3

* In 1981 and 1986, "Graduated from High School" is with "Some Secondary."

Source: Statistics Canada, no. 13-217, 1998: 20-21. Survey of Consumer Finances.

TABLE 4.9

men's earnings in 1996. According to another study, though, for recent university graduates, the wage gap for those working full-time has disappeared altogether (Wannell and Caron 1994).

FAMILY DIFFERENTIALS IN WORK AND INCOME

A U.S. survey asked pregnant employed women who planned to work within a year how soon they expected to return to work after giving birth (Scommenga 1996). The results showed that many of the women had not anticipated the competing demands of work and breastfeeding. Some 95 percent of them had expected to return to work within 20 weeks, but only 59 percent had actually returned by that time.

Using a long-term framework, Cynthia Rexroat (1985) looked at young women's expected work plans for mid-life and compared this to their actual work experiences. She found that, first, the very expectation to work had a significant impact on their likelihood of working at mid-life. Nonetheless, even those who had not planned to work ended up working more than expected. In addition, the presence of children reduced the employment experiences of those women who had anticipated to be working.

Work status

The sex differences in work patterns have certainly declined from the times when married women were essentially excluded from the paid labour force. For instance, in 1931, only 3.5 percent of married women were employed (Duffy, Mandell, and Pupo 1989: 10). Canadian feminist Dorothy Johnson wrote that in 1941 as a married woman she could not even get employment as a substitute teacher unless she could prove she was destitute (Schmid 1991). While married women had previously made money by taking in boarders or selling various products produced at home, and they had worked during wartime, it was only in the 1960s that regular paid employment for women became generally acceptable—although it still tended only to be as long as there were no young children at home.

Focusing on "Female Baby Boomers: A Generation at Work," Galarneau (1994) finds that the increases in labour-force participation over time are strongest for women with more children. Indeed, the only group that showed a decline in labour-force participation in 1991 was single women with no children. It would appear that having children reduces women's labour-force involvement in the short term, but it may also prompt greater involvement in the long term, in large part because the family's economic needs increase. For instance, mothers with older children are more likely to work full-time (Péron et al. 1999).

Table 4.10 presents the proportions of persons in various work statuses, by gender and marital status, for those aged 35-54 in 1971 to 1991. The proportions working full-time increased significantly for women in the married category (including cohabitation) as well as the formerly married (separated, widowed, divorced). Single women were more likely to be working full-time than single men, and this marital status category saw very little change over the period. Women in the formerly married category were somewhere in between the single and the married. The work status of men and women in the married category reflected the greatest difference, with 46 percent of women compared to 81 percent of men working full-time in 1991. Nonetheless, this difference has become smaller over time. In 1971, 22 percent of married women and 83 percent of married men were working full-time.

Marriage would seem to reduce the likelihood of women working full-time and increase the likelihood of men working full-time. The effect is strongest for persons currently married (or cohabiting), but also applies to persons formerly married (separated, widowed, divorced). Clearly, the causation may be partly in the other direction; for instance, men working full-time may be more likely to be married.

PROPORTION WORKING FULL-TIME, PART-TIME AND NOT EMPLOYED, BY SEX AND MARITAL STATUS, AGES 35-44 AND 45-54, CANADA, 1971-1991

	MALES			FEMALES		
	FULL-TIME	PART-TIME	NOT EMPLOYED	FULL-TIME	PART-TIME	NOT EMPLOYED
AGES 35-44						
1971 Total	81.0	14.9	4.0	25.4	23.6	51.0
Married or cohabiting	84.2	13.6	2.2	20.7	24.1	55.2
Single	60.7	22.1	17.2	64.4	16.9	18.7
Separated, widowed, or divorced	69.2	22.7	8.1	43.0	23.8	33.2
1981 Total	81.2	14.4	4.4	35.8	30.8	33.4
Married or cohabiting	84.2	13.2	2.6	31.7	32.6	35.5
Single	58.9	22.0	19.1	62.9	15.9	21.2
Separated, widowed, or divorced	72.9	19.3	7.8	48.8	25.5	25.8
1991 Total	77.8	16.4	5.8	50.3	30.5	19.2
Married or cohabiting	81.4	14.8	3.8	47.8	32.6	19.5
Single	58.9	23.6	17.5	64.0	19.2	16.8
Separated, widowed, or divorced	68.8	21.6	9.7	55.4	25.7	18.8
AGES 45-54						
1971 Total	78.9	15.5	5.6	28.4	21.0	50.6
Married or cohabiting	82.5	14.1	3.4	23.1	21.3	55.6
Single	56.3	22.0	21.7	61.1	14.3	24.6
Separated, widowed, or divorced	62.1	25.4	12.5	42.0	23.5	34.5
1981 Total	78.0	15.0	7.0	33.5	26.1	40.5
Married or cohabiting	81.5	13.9	4.6	29.3	27.6	43.1
Single	53.2	21.0	25.9	61.4	13.4	25.2
Separated, widowed, or divorced	64.7	20.7	14.6	44.5	22.8	32.8
1991 Total	76.9	15.1	8.0	47.1	26.7	26.2
Married or cohabiting	80.0	14.1	5.9	45.0	28.2	26.8
Single	54.2	20.7	25.2	60.9	16.0	23.1
Separated, widowed, or divorced	65.6	19.3	15.0	52.2	23.2	24.6

NOTE: Full-time means full-time for 40 or more weeks.

Source: Beaujot 1995: 60. Statistics Canada, Census Data.

TABLE 4.10

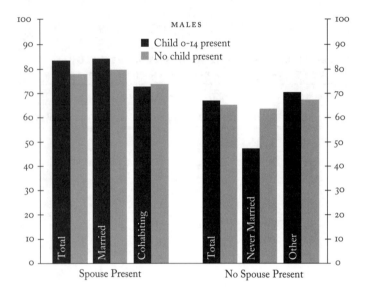

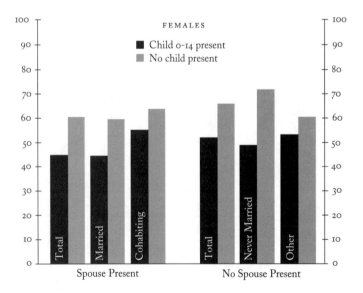

FIG 4.2 Proportion working full-time, by sex, presence of spouse, and presence of children aged 0-14, persons aged 40-44, Canada, 1991

Source: Beaujot 1995: 64. Statistics Canada, Census Data.

Men living with children are more likely to be working full-time, while women living with children are less likely to be working full-time (Beaujot 1995: 62). The differences are also systematic by age of children: the younger the children, the more likely it is that men will be working full-time, and the less likely it is that women will be working full-time. When there are no children present, work patterns are very similar for women and men, especially at the ages under 40.

Figure 4.2 compares the relative importance of the presence of a spouse and the presence of children, based on the proportions of men and women working full-time at ages 40-44. With its various breakdowns, the figure relates both the presence of children and the presence of spouse to the probability of men and women working full-time. For men, the presence of a spouse has a larger impact: it increases the proportions working full-time. But the presence of children also has an impact on men's work experience: in the age group 40-44, 83 percent of men living with a spouse and children under 15 are working full-time, compared to 65 percent of men living with no spouse and no children.

For women in this age group of 40-44, the presence of children has the larger impact, reducing the proportions working full-time. In addition, the presence of a spouse further reduces the proportions work-ing full-time. Consequently, 45 percent of women living with a spouse and children under 15 are working full-time, compared to 65 percent of women living with no spouse and no children.

With the presence of spouse and children apparently pushing men and women in opposite directions, the most similar cases involve people with neither spouse nor chil-dren: 65 percent of both men and women work full-time. In the subcategory of never-married with no children, women are more likely than men to be working full-time. As well, marriage rather than cohabitation enhances men's likelihood of working full-time and reduces women's likelihood of working full-time.

Individual income

Not only does marriage reduce the likelihood of women working full-time, but among all women working full-time, married women also have the lowest average income (Beaujot 1995: 65-69). As with work status, those who are formerly married have inter-mediate full-time incomes between the married and never-married. Over time married women show important changes both in work status and in relative income, but strong differences remain in comparison to married men.

In each age group, the presence of a spouse increases men's average incomes and decreases women's average incomes (Beaujot 1995: 67). Those who don't live with a spouse show more similar incomes. Figure 4.3 confirms that women have higher incomes when they have no children at home, while men have higher incomes when there are children at home.

The presence of a spouse tends to play a larger role than the presence of children, especially in men's average incomes (Beaujot 1995: 68-69). Once again, the smallest dif-ferences occur for the category of never-married with no children. For instance, in that category the average income of women aged 40-44 represents 101 percent of the average income of men. For persons working full-time in that category, women's average income represents 95 percent of men's. The difference between never-married women and men is not very large for those living with children: both of these categories have very low incomes. Also, the state of cohabitation does not appear to enhance men's incomes as much as marriage does, nor does it reduce women's incomes as much as marriage does. Once again, some of the causation may be in the other direction: men who have higher incomes are more likely to be married rather than cohabiting; and women with higher incomes are more likely to cohabit rather than marry.

While the work status of men and women has become more similar, and the two-income family is clearly the dominant category for persons at mid-life, family questions continue to influence the lives of women and men in different ways. Marriage and chil-dren reduce the labour-force involvement and incomes of women, but enhance the labour-force involvement and incomes of men. The groups that are most similar are the

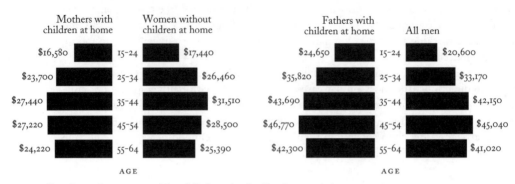

FIG 4.3 Earnings of persons working full-time, by family characteristics, 1990

NOTE: persons working full-time for 49 to 52 weeks.

Source: Logan and Belliveau 1995: 26–27. Statistics Canada Census Data.

never-married with no children, especially at younger ages. In effect, family questions play a large role in the income differences between women and men.

Other results confirm these observations. For instance, the ratios of women's to men's earnings are highest at youngest ages, which show the smallest differences in work experiences and family responsibilities (Gartley 1994). In addition, the largest earnings differences are for the married, where the gap increases with age. Women are more likely to cite personal or family responsibilities as the main reason for working part-time, leaving a job, not looking for work, having an irregular work schedule, or working at home (Stone 1994; Best 1995). In explaining income differences between women and men aged 45 and over, Julie Ann McMullin and Peri Ballantyne (1995) first identify questions of status attainment and factors associated with the segmented labour market; but they find that family variables also play a significant role. In particular, domestic responsibilities associated with marriage and parenthood play a critical role in women's incomes.

Nonetheless, cohort data from the United States suggest that household specialization associated with parenthood is declining. Using data from the 1980–92 Panel Study of Income Dynamics, Shelly Lundberg and Elaine Rose (1998) followed the effects of having a first child on hours worked and wage rates of new parents. Even before the birth of the first child, both fathers and mothers earned about 9 percent less than non-parents. For the whole sample, the birth of a first child did not influence the men's work hours, but it did increase their wage rate by 9 percent. For women, the first birth reduced hours worked by 45 percent, with the wage rate falling by 5 percent. Couples in which wives interrupted their careers for child-rearing showed increased task specialization associated with childbirth, including a reallocation of time by both husband and wife and declines in the mothers' wage rates. The authors found the patterns to be significantly different for couples in which the wife participated continuously in the labour market. In those cases, after the birth of the first child the mothers' wage rates did not decline, and the hours worked by

BOX 4.2 | *Explanations of gender differences in income*

The analyses that have attempted to account for income differences by gender have considered productivity-related factors, occupational segregation, and wage discrimination (Royal Commission on the Economic Union 1985, II: 624-30). Each of these factors can be placed within the earning/caring equation.

Productivity-related factors, or human capital—differences in education, training, and experience—probably account for more than half of the difference. Although education has become less differentiated by sex, it continues to play a role at older ages, and men are more likely to have advanced degrees. In this kind of analysis it is particularly difficult to account for past work history, because most surveys do not ask the extensive questions that would help account for differences in employment experience. Even though persons may be working full-time in the year under observation, they may have considerable differences in their past work histories. For instance, Céline Le Bourdais and Hélène Desrosiers (1988) conclude that job interruptions are costly to women in revenue and professional status. They note that women frequently experience interruptions or part-time work at ages 25-35, precisely when acquiring experience is crucial to a career.

Using the data from the 1973 Canada Mobility Survey, which does have information on employment history, John Goyder (1981) finds that sex differences in work histories are more important than education and occupation in explaining income inequalities between women and men. Based on data from the 1988 Current Population Survey in the United States, Tony Tam (1997) finds that human-capital variables and differences in specialized training across occupations and industries account for most of the lower average wages in female-dominated occupations. Consequently, there would not appear to be a devaluation of workers in occupations with large numbers of female workers.

Work experience is an important component of productivity differences. The 1993 Survey of Labour and Income Dynamics allows the measurement of work experience after a person's first full-time job (Lathe and Giles 1995). The proportion of persons aged 15-69 who had worked only full-year full-time after their first job was 46 percent for women and 69 percent for men. Adding fractional values for part-year and part-time experience, women had 10.1 years of experience and men 17.1 years, or 70 percent more than the women. For those aged 45 and over, men had 32.7 years, women with no children had 26.5 years, and women with children had 15.4 years of experience—less than half of that of men.

Occupational segregation is probably the second most important factor in employment-income differences. While more women have moved into professional and managerial categories, their concentration has also increased in lower-paying occupations, such as community, business, and personal services, and clerical, sales, and service (Connelly and MacDonald 1990: 22-23; Shea 1990). M. Patricia Connelly and Martha MacDonald (1990: 33) find that the occupations with the largest increase in numbers of women are those in which employment incomes are low. Judith Maxwell (1990) adds that women are overrepresented in what the Economic Council of Canada calls "bad jobs," with low wages, poor benefits, and much part-

EARNING AND CARING IN CANADIAN FAMILIES

➤ BOX 4.2 CONT'D

time or temporary employment. Krahn and Lowe (1993: 163) observe that three out of ten employed women, compared to two out of ten men, are in the lower tier of the service sector. An analysis of trends in Germany points to occupational segregation, rather than gender differences in education or wage discrimination by employers within the same job, as being primarily responsible for wage differences (Hannan, Schomann, and Blossfeld 1990).

The relative importance of discrimination in explaining gender-income inequalities depends on the breadth of definition given to this concept. In some definitions, occupational segregation is seen as part of discrimination in a broad sense: the structural divisions in society discriminate against the potential for equal opportunity. Even in a narrower sense, women clearly suffer discrimination just because they are women—for instance, as victims of harassment, rape, and spousal violence.

Partly because of these differences in definition, and partly because *wage discrimination* is generally measured as a residual when other factors have been taken into account, researchers show considerable disagreement about its relative importance. Reviewing the various studies, the Royal Commission on the Economic Union (1985, II: 626) observed that wage discrimination within given occupations and establishments was responsible for some 5 to 10 percent of income differences between women and men. Overt discrimination of the "door-slamming variety" has surely become rare, but more subtle hiring and job assignment practices can bar women from access to employment and promotion opportunities (Calzavara 1988). Especially when men make the personnel decisions, the possibility exists

for an uneven evaluation of women and men. The federal Employment Equity Act of 1986 is designed to encourage employers to remove such barriers. The organizations subject to the act are those under federal jurisdiction (Crown corporations, banking, communication, and transportation) with more than 100 employees. Looking at the period 1989-93, Joanne Leck, Sylvie St. Onge, and Isabelle Lalancette (1995) found that these organizations were closing the gap somewhat, at least for white women.

But after making careful controls for other characteristics, researchers see the wage differences to be typically rather small. For the same job in the same establishment, Morley Gunderson (1989) found that women's salaries were 90 to 95 percent of men's salaries. He concluded that work experience and the segregated labour market are the main factors in income differences by gender. Similarly, D.M. Shapiro and M. Stelcner (1987) suggested that wage discrimination was accounting for some 12.5 to 25 percent of the earnings gap in the 1970s. Using data on university faculty for 1986, Michael Ornstein and Perci Stewart (1996) found an overall gap of 16.8 percent in average salaries, which is still a 9.7 percent gap after controlling for age and level of highest degree. The gap is less at lower ranks, suggesting that the extent of gender discrimination is decreasing. However, analysts see discriminatory processes of promotion as accounting for much of the gender gap.

In their study of university graduates two years after graduation, Scott Davies, Clayton Mosher, and Bill O'Grady (1996) found a wage gap of 9 percent for the youngest cohort, whose members had graduated in 1986. They were able to explain 26 percent of this gap through a variety of productivity factors—though their controls for productivity proved inadequate. For instance, they use age as the measure of experience and broad categories for the area of the university degree, which does not allow for a differentiation between doctors and nurses, because they are all medical and health professions. For the 1982 graduates, they found that the income gap increased from 17 percent two years after graduation to 22 percent after five years. It is here that differences in full-time work experience, which cannot be measured by age, may be playing an important role. In effect, there was almost no gender gap among the 1990 BA graduates when they were interviewed in 1992 (Statistics Canada 1999: 19). However, after two years the gap increased, and this was mostly related to differences in hours worked.

A U.S. study found less differences for engineers, at least after introducing several controls. Using data from 1982 to 1989, Laurie Morgan (1998) found no differences for the youngest cohort. She also saw that for older cohorts the differences between men and women were stable over time, which suggests that the initial wage at work entry plays a large role and that there is not a "glass ceiling effect," in which women's wages would be constrained while men's increased. Morgan's study involved controls for human capital and family status (marital status and presence of children at home) in a longitudinal context. One of the controls allowed for an interaction term between sex and children at home, suggesting that children have a different effect for women and men. The overall effect of being female was a 1.3 percent wage penalty, while before controls the wage penalty was statistically significant at 17.9 percent.

Clearly, the explanation of earnings differentials is complex, involving both human-capital questions and barriers to equality. It is equally difficult to determine the extent to which differences are a function of choices made—for instance, when someone decides to devote attention to her or his human capital, or decides to accept the constraints associated with various life circumstances. It would appear, though, that family questions play a significant role in income matters, especially in producing barriers or constraints to equality. Questions of productivity, occupational segregation, and discrimination can be placed in the context of the tension between earning and caring.

Both differentials in experience and occupational segregation at work are related to the division of labour within households (Shapiro and Stelcner 1987). To accommodate their parental and household activities some women may take up jobs that are less demanding or permit part-time work, or jobs in which they do not suffer unduly from intermittent work patterns. This means that they are in jobs that give human capital less value. In addition, the basis for discrimination may be associated with the employers' expectation about the workers' felt tension between earning and caring.

Consequently, the nature of women's work in the home and in the labour force reinforces and perpetuates broader gender differences. For instance, S. J. Wilson (1991: 85) observes that women have responded to the fluctuating needs of the economy. They have also responded to the shifting needs of families in which each of the choices— to work full-time, to work part-time, or not to be on the labour force at all—presents problems (Duffy, Mandell, and Pupo 1989). ◆

fathers declined by more than 7 percent. In addition, the wage differentiation on the birth of a first child was significantly larger for older cohorts. That is, the greater specialization associated with childbirth was less applicable to younger cohorts, and it did not apply to the subsample of continuously participating wives. The authors see, then, converging time-use patterns for husbands and wives and a declining wage differentiation associated with parenthood. They suggest that the decline of household specialization "should contribute to a continued narrowing in the gender gap in earnings and other outcomes" (p.17).

Family income

With the employment income of men the highest when they are married, and women's the lowest, some of the income differences become less significant when families are used as the unit of analysis. What emerges as the basis of differences is the number of earners in the family, which places lone-parent families at a particular disadvantage. The increase in both two-earner families and lone-parent families has accentuated the income differences across families. Lone-parent families comprised 9.3 percent of families in 1970 compared to 13 percent in 1990 (Table 4.11). Among husband-wife families, the proportion with two or more earners increased from 50.3 percent in 1970 to 67.2 percent in 1990 (Rashid 1994: 27).

Family incomes increased over the period 1970-90, though at a lesser rate in the 1980s (Table 4.11). In the 1980-90 period, the average incomes of husbands and male lone parents did not increase, but the average income of wives increased by over 40 percent. Of the combined average of incomes of husbands and wives, wives contributed 16.2 percent in 1970, 23.6 percent in 1980, and 30.5 percent in 1990. In 1990, then, as an average in husband-wife families, the income of husbands remained close to 70 percent of the total of the two incomes. Even when wives worked full-year full-time, their average income only comprises 40 percent of average family income (Rashid 1994: 17).

AVERAGE FAMILY INCOME IN CONSTANT (1990) DOLLARS BY FAMILY STRUCTURE, CANADA, 1970, 1980, AND 1990

	1970	1980	1990
All families			
Number	5,054,630	6,325,315	7,355,730
Average income	37,036	47,565	51,342
Median income	32,815	42,490	44,891
Husband-wife families			
Number	4,585,215	5,611,495	6,402,090
Average income	38,479	50,124	54,667
Median income	34,135	44,858	48,091
Husband's average income	30,134	35,774	35,856
Wife's average income	5,827	11,063	15,772
Male lone-parent families			
Number	99,445	124,385	165,240
Average income	30,749	41,333	40,792
Median income	26,683	36,322	35,374
Female lone-parent families			
Number	369,970	589,440	788,395
Average income	20,838	24,523	26,550
Median income	16,446	19,263	21,364

Source: Rashid 1994: 9. Statistics Canada, Census Data.

TABLE 4.11

BOX 4.3 | *The specific case of work interruptions*

Work interruptions are a central factor in the tensions between earning and caring, and two conditions are particularly important in accounting for gender differences in those interruptions: the presence of children and marital status.

Marital status reflects on the spousal arrangements, either present or past, involving the division of paid and unpaid work. A person who has never married has typically not had the opportunity to make an arrangement with another adult in the division of work. Consequently, never-married men and women, especially if they have no children, should be rather similar in the extent of paid work and associated discontinuities. In comparison, married persons, under the assumption that the relationship will continue, can more easily make decisions on the division of work based on an optimization of the couple's welfare. Formerly married persons too, may well suffer from assumptions made with regard to the continuity of the relationship. In particular, if one of the spouses has done more of the unpaid work, after the termination of the relationship that person will be in a disadvantaged position with respect to paid work.

Clearly, the *presence of children* influences these accommodations. Their presence increases the amount of unpaid work as well as the need for income obtained from paid work. In the 1992 Canadian General Social Survey on time-use, persons with young children had the largest average hours of paid and unpaid work over the week (Che-Alford, Allan, and Butlin 1994: 40). One government estimate found that, compared to families without children, a family with one child needed some 20 percent more income to maintain the same standard of living (Federal, Provincial, and Territorial Family Law Committee 1995: 10).

As Ann Duffy, Nancy Mandell, and Norene Pupo (1989) have established, a family has "few choices" in the decisions around work. The choice of maintaining two full-time jobs presents considerable pressures for accommodating family life. The alternative of one person working part-time presents the disadvantages, for that person, of acquiring a lack of seniority and minimal benefits. A third alternative of one person staying at home combines the disadvantages of no pay with low career status. The viability of these alternatives is clearly affected by inequities in the division of household labour, the extent of state support for social parenting, the kinds of jobs available, and the wages offered (see Calzavara 1988). Given that each alternative has its benefits and costs, it follows that people will be pushed from one situation to another—a condition that manifests itself as work interruptions.

The 1984 Canadian Family History Survey paid attention to work interruptions of one year or more during people's work history. The findings showed that 49 percent of women and 18 percent of men had experienced one or more work interruptions (Burch 1985: 25). An even larger gender differential resulted when two or more such interruptions were considered: 2.1 percent of men and 13.7 percent of women had experienced this level of discontinuity.

Looking at various cohorts, the Family History Survey found that the gender differentials were smaller in the younger cohorts. Still, differences remained substantial, with women twice as likely as men to have had one or more interruptions. For women, the highest proportions with no interruptions are for those cohabitating with no children or those who have had no union and no children (Le Bourdais and Desrosiers 1988: 139, 122). Women aged 18-34 at the time of the 1984 survey had more continuous work histories than older cohorts had experienced at that stage of their lives (Le Bourdais 1989). While labour-market behaviour is changing for recent generations, it is still influenced by marital and reproductive history. To some extent, interruptions may also be delayed, along with the delay of marriage and child-bearing.

The differences in reasons given for interruptions were particularly noteworthy in the Family History Survey. The major reasons for men were lay-off, school attendance, and illness, while for women they were child care, marriage, and lay-off. In particular, less than 1 percent of men cited marriage, pregnancy or child care, or relocating in order to be with a partner as the reason for an interruption. For women, almost two-thirds cited one of these reasons (Burch 1985: 26). Thomas Burch concludes, "The exigencies of marriage, pregnancy and childcare had a major impact on the continuity of work for a large majority of women, but almost no impact for men."

On the basis of multivariate analysis of data from the 1984 Family History Survey, Garnett Picot (1989: 326) found that having young children did not radically alter the probability of changes to employment status. Women with newborns understandably were more likely to leave the labour force, but not mothers of children over one year of age. Marital status played a larger role, with married women being more likely to leave employment and less likely to re-enter the labour force. While the effect was less for men, it was in the opposite direction, with married men more likely to enter the labour force. Analyzing these same data, Patricia Robinson (1989) also found that marriage was associated with a higher risk of work interruption for women, but that having children at home could reduce the likelihood of interruptions.

On the basis of the U.S. National Longitudinal Survey of Youth, Sonalde Desai and Linda Waite (1991) found that women who indicated a strong preference to be working at age 35 had less work interruptions surrounding the childbirth period. A French study also found significant differences between women who first left their parental homes for marriage compared to those who left home to be independent. Those who left home for marriage had more work discontinuity and presented a greater likelihood of this discontinuity being associated with family issues (Bloss, Frickey, and Novi 1994). In Sweden the mean duration of career breaks associated with childbirth tended to be long, 16.2 months on average, but people eligible for paid leave returned to work faster than people without this benefit (Ronsen and Sundstrom 1997). Another Swedish study found that parental leave had a negative effect on men's subsequent wages, but not on women's wages (Albrecht et al. 1997). This result may be because most women take a leave and thus the practice does not signal lower work commitment. Still, the researchers found that women's leaves not associated with childbirth do have negative consequences for their subsequent wages.

➤ BOX 4.3 CONT'D

Using the 1984 Canadian Fertility Survey, Marianne Kempeneers (1991) analyzed the changing work interruptions over generations of women born between 1934 and 1953. By age 30 some 90 percent of women had held paying jobs. Nonetheless, the average years of interruption by age 30 declined only from 4.7 to 3.6 years between the older and younger cohorts. The presence of children played an important role in this discontinuity, yet in the younger cohort one-third of the women had no children at the time of a first interruption (Kempeneers 1991: 26). The survey respondents were more likely to refer to factors associated with children than to those of "husband or home" in accounting for interruptions, working part-time, or not being in the labour force (Kempeneers 1992: 142). Kempeneers concluded that children had an impact but it was relative and declining. The different potential for work flexibility in given occupations and industries, she said, needed further study.

Most studies have focused on women and have not explored the possibility that marriage and children, while decreasing women's work stability, might increase men's. Data from the 1988-90 Labour Market Activity Survey, based on interruptions of six months or longer indicate important gender differences (Cook and Beaujot 1996). In particular, marital status and parental status operate differently for women and men. Using logistic regression to establish the interactions and control for the effects of age and other socio-economic and socio-cultural variables, Figure 4.4 shows the adjusted probabilities of work interruptions, within categories of gender, marital, and parental status. Marital status has more impact on interruptions for men, and

parental status for women. Consequently, nearly twice as many married women with young children experienced a work interruption in comparison to childless women of the same age.

Single men and women show the most similar tendencies in this regard, while married men and women are the most different. Married women are three times more likely than married men to experience work interruptions. Similarly, when it comes to parental status, men and women without children show relatively similar tendencies. Women with young children are four times more likely to experience interruptions than are men with young children.

The 1995 General Social Survey indicates that women continue to undergo interruptions, but these are becoming shorter and more concentrated at childbirth (Fast and Da Pont 1997). Some 62 percent of women experienced work interruptions of six months or more, compared to 27 percent of men who had ever worked. For both sexes, the rates were higher for younger persons. While family-related reasons were still cited as the cause of close to half of women's interruptions in the 1990-94 period, that figure was down from over 70 percent in the period before 1980. Another interesting trend is reflected in the increasing proportion of new mothers who had paid employment at some time before the birth of their first child: from 75 percent in the period 1970-84 to 84 percent in the period 1985-94.

Despite the increasing equality in labour-force participation by gender, significant differences persist in certain areas. Although statistics on unemployment, defined as looking for work, do not show large gender differences, work interruptions reveal significant variations.

> ➤ BOX 4.3 CONT'D

Gender inequities in family life still clearly have an impact on employment activities. Women and men adjust their paid work activities to their responsibilities as spouses and parents, and these adjustments are far from symmetric. They enhance the continuity of men's work but reduce the continuity in women's work. Eva Bernhardt (1993) even argues that work and motherhood are incompatible precisely because work and fatherhood are compatible.◆

Both the average incomes and the changes in income vary extensively over family types (Table 4.12). Family incomes are highest with more income earners and lowest for persons living alone or in lone-parent families. Between 1991 and 1996, the average incomes were stable, but there were increases in income for two-parent families with children, especially if two or more persons had incomes. In the case of a family with one person working, the average income declined. While low, family incomes also increased for women lone parents who had earned incomes.

THE ORGANIZATION OF WORK AND INCOME IN FAMILIES

The influence of marriage and parenthood on work patterns may be placed within a broader conceptual framework of *family strategies*, to consider how families organize themselves for work and income generation. Basically, families have a firm interest in maximizing income through the paid work activities of their members, but this investment brings various forms of stress that have to be resolved through accommodations, especially when families also have high needs for unpaid work.

In their book *Few Choices: Women, Work and Family*, Duffy, Mandell, and Pupo (1989) observe that women's decisions about work and family are intermingled—that they reflect the interpenetration of domestic and wage labour. This intermingling can also be interpreted as being based on the interests of families in the benefits of both paid and unpaid work—that is, work and parenting decisions are reflections of broader family strategies for the organization of earning and caring. For instance, Desai and Waite (1991: 564) observe that women sometimes choose occupations that are easier to combine with parenting. It would appear that the "convenience" of combining work and parenting is particularly pertinent for women who do not plan to work over the long run. This is an example of how work and parenting decisions may be determined together as family strategies. In statistical terms, work and parenting are endogenous or determined by the broader family strategy. This strategy may be seen as a choice, but it may also be interpreted as an outcome of the structural constraints that impinge on families.

Looking at the 1988-90 British General Household Survey, Sara Arber and Jay Ginn (1995) find that, despite the progress made toward equality in occupational achievement, persistent income inequalities between marital partners remain a fact of life. For all couples, wives earned 23 percent of family income, increasing to 30 percent for dual-income families. At ages 20-59, 13 percent of husbands and 32 percent of wives were not employed. If wives were employed full-time, they had a higher occupational status than the husband in 22.7 percent of cases, but they had a higher income in only 11.1 percent of cases. Arber and Ginn conclude that despite the gains in education and occupational standings, "Economic equality is proving more intractable, both in the labour market and in the family" (p. 40). They suggest a reciprocal relationship: women's economic disadvantages at work influence their domestic roles in the family; and the domestic roles reduce their potential for full economic participation in the labour market. The income differences between marital partners are a persistent source of inequality, both in families and in the broader society.

The dual-income alternative

Reflecting the shift in family strategy to dual incomes, among husband-wife families with children under 16, over 62 percent involved dual-earners in 1997, compared to 36 percent in 1961 (Marshall 1998a: 10). Nonetheless, the presence of children influences the extent to which couples

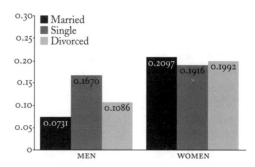

PROBABILITY OF A WORK INTERRUPTION: GENDER BY MARITAL STATUS

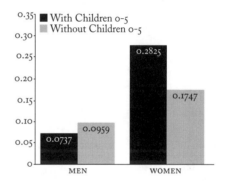

PROBABILITY OF A WORK INTERRUPTION: GENDER BY PARENTAL STATUS

FIG 4.4 Probabilities of work interruptions by sex, marital status, and parental status, Canada, 1988-90

Source: Cook and Beaujot 1996: 36. Statistics Canada, 1988-90 Labour Market Activity Survey.

are dual-earners. In 1991, for women aged 25-44 in husband-wife families, 68 percent of them were in the labour force when the families had children under five, compared to 90 percent when there were no children (Marshall 1994: 28). Among those working, 69 percent were working full-time when there were children under five, compared to 91 percent when there were no children.

As Table 4.11 shows, in 1990 husbands contributed 65.6 percent of the average family income, compared to 78.3 percent in 1970. In addition, when husbands have incomes over

AVERAGE INCOME IN CONSTANT (1996) DOLLARS FOR SELECTED FAMILY UNIT TYPES, 1981-96

	1981	1986	1991	1996
ECONOMIC FAMILIES, TWO PERSONS OR MORE	*55,042*	*55,294*	*56,623*	*56,629*
Elderly families[a]	*37,225*	*39,627*	*42,708*	*42,759*
Married couples only	32,838	36,339	38,328	39,588
All other elderly families	45,970	47,652	53,205	51,745
Non-elderly families[b]	*57,618*	*57,807*	*59,017*	*59,032*
Married couples only, total	55,141	54,075	56,990	56,674
One earner	43,548	44,456	43,806	47,026
Two earners	61,978	60,682	64,590	64,369
Two-parent families with children[c]	*59,892*	*61,476*	*63,121*	*63,981*
One earner	46,708	46,950	46,029	45,322
Two earners	60,651	62,816	64,027	66,241
Three or more earners	78,018	78,679	80,325	82,762
Married couples with other relatives[d]	*79,156*	*79,156*	*78,718*	*81,183*
Lone-parent families[c]	*28,266*	*26,100*	*25,801*	*26,147*
Male lone-parent families	45,702	39,829	39,673	39,428
Female lone-parent families, total	25,257	23,657	23,761	24,044
No earner	11,330	13,633	14,156	13,726
One earner	26,209	25,767	25,993	27,706
All other families	*46,169*	*46,184*	*46,954*	*48,814*
UNATTACHED INDIVIDUALS	*24,617*	*24,034*	*24,552*	*24,433*
Elderly	*17,167*	*17,550*	*19,572*	*20,023*
Male	19,892	18,901	21,990	25,020
Female	16,173	17,133	18,771	18,139
Non-elderly	*27,397*	*26,295*	*26,341*	*26,217*
Male	31,089	28,637	28,270	28,158
Female	22,990	23,212	23,764	23,432

NOTES: a Head 65 years of age and over.
b Head less than 65 years of age.
c With single children less than 18 years of age. Children 18 years of age and over and/or other relatives may also be present.
d Children less than 18 years of age are not present, but may include children 18 years of age and over.

Source: Statistics Canada, no. 13-207, 1996: 26-27. Survey of Consumer Finances.

TABLE 4.12

$30,000, the likelihood of the wife working no longer drops off as the husband's income increases (Rashid 1994: 16, 17). While this shift represents considerable change, the average contribution of wives who were working full-year and full-time increased only from 36.9 to 39.9 percent of average family income in this 20-year period.

Another indicator of change involves the greater predominance of wives earning more than husbands (Crompton and Geran 1995). As a proportion of husband-wife families with employment income, 11 percent fell into this category in 1967 compared to 25 percent in 1993. In a third of these cases, wives were the sole wage-earners, partly because of the age differences in couples and the retirement patterns of men. In the other two-thirds, wives were the primary wage-earners, either because of their own high-paying employment or because their husbands were unemployed for part of the year. Susan Crompton and Leslie Geran (1995) also observed that the average earnings of working men and women increased by 25 and 60 percent respectively between 1967 and 1989. During the recessionary period 1989-93, the average earnings of men actually declined by 6 percent, while that of women increased a further 2 percent.

Among dual-earner couples working full-time, a significant

BOX 4.4 | *Work–family tensions*

According to one survey of Canadian employees, 40 percent of mothers and 25 percent of fathers experienced a high degree of work-family conflict (Higgins, Duxbury, and Lee 1993). In the 1992 General Social Survey, for persons working full-time, 16 percent of men and 24 percent of women indicated that they were "highly time stressed" (Fast and Frederick 1996: 17). Although dual-career marriages would appear to have "the good life" associated with a high family income, Rosanna Hertz (1986) also sees complex struggles wherein women worry more about children and couples become trapped in a system that needs two incomes. Nonetheless, Lois Verbrugge (1993: 191) finds that women with multiple roles are happier and healthier than those who are less active. In particular, having both a job and children appears to be beneficial to married women's well-being.

A question from the 1988 Child Care Survey provides a good indicator of work-family tensions. Persons who had primary responsibility for the care of children under 12 years of age were asked, "When considering your own needs and those of your family, would you most prefer to work full-time, to work part-time or not to work at a job or business?" Among the employed respondents, over half said they would prefer to work part-time, and another 13 percent indicated they would prefer not to work at all (Lero et al. 1993: 48). Many more persons, then, beyond those currently working reduced hours preferred to work part-time, and some of the persons working would have preferred not to work. In addition, the kinds of benefits that interested parents the most were parental

leaves and the opportunity to work part-time.

The work-family conflicts introduced by children also involve lower total family earnings (see also chapter 7). A comparison of the economic status of families with and without children shows that children have a significant downward effect on the standard of living of families, and they increase the probability of having low-income status (Brouillette et al. 1990, 1991). Having more and younger children increases the risk of low-income status (National Council on Welfare 1998: 43). Researchers attribute the high costs of children not only to direct costs, but also to the more frequent work interruptions and the increased burdens that may reduce the possibilities of professional advance.

Table 4.13 illustrates the gender differentials in the resolution of job-family tensions. For instance, women are more likely to cite personal or family responsibilities as the main reason for working part-time. Nonetheless, at ages 45-54, the few men working part-time also frequently indicate family reasons for working reduced hours. In addition, women are more likely to cite family-related reasons for leaving a job or for having an irregular work schedule.

Absenteeism at work, though amounting to an average of only 7.4 days in the year, is higher for women and averages 11.7 days for women with preschool children (Akyeampong 1998). In 1997 the average time lost for personal or family responsibilities was 1.2 days for the total labour force, but 1.8 for men and 4.2 for women with preschool children. In families with preschool children, men are less likely than other men to have days lost due to illness or disability, while women are more likely than other women to have work absences due to personal or family responsibilities.

The rate of working *paid overtime* is higher for men (Cohen 1993). The Work Arrangements Survey found that 10 percent of men and 6 percent of women worked overtime in November 1991. Significantly, overtime rates are higher for both men and women when they are the only wage-earners in a given family; overtime is also higher for men in dual-earner families with children under six.

Flextime work involved an estimated 24 percent of workers in 1995 (Akyeampong 1997). Though slightly higher for women, the rates do not vary extensively by gender, age, and marital status. Nonetheless, flextime is more common for both men and women in dual-earner families than in single-earner families, and it is still higher if the family has children under age six.

According to the 1992 General Social Survey, women with children are more likely to have *family-friendly work arrangements*, such as working part-time, self-employment, and flexible work schedules. While flextime and especially part-time work reduce time stress, other forms of flexibility, such as compressed workweeks and working on-call, increase stress, especially for women (Fast and Frederick 1996).

Dan Charette (1995) concludes that the presence of children no longer has much influence on whether a family has one or two earners, but it does play a role in determining hours worked. He highlights the impact on the hours worked by wives, and Table 4.14 shows as well the impact on men's hours. In dual-earner families, with a child under 16, wives are more likely to

work part-time and husbands are more likely to work more than 40 hours per week. As a consequence, the combined hours of work do not vary much based on the age of the youngest child. It is the distribution of these hours between husband and wife that is changed rather than the combined hours. For instance, with a child under 6, the average is 76.5 combined hours, compared to 78.5 when the youngest child is 6-15 and 79.2 hours with no child under 16.

While the presence of preschool children now has less effect on wives working, the presence of children nonetheless alters the work patterns of dual-earner couples (Chaula 1992; Marshall 1994). In particular, husbands and wives are more likely to have different schedules when the family has young children, and wives are more likely to be working part-time. For instance, in dual-income families with wives aged 25-44, some 31 percent of those wives are working part-time if they have a child under six, compared to 9 percent if there are no children. As Figure 4.3 shows, the income of mothers is lower when they have children, and the income of fathers is higher on average. The family strategy of balancing the paid work of spouses becomes more difficult when there are children, and couples are more likely to opt for maximizing the income of one spouse while temporarily sacrificing the income of the other spouse. These outcomes are far from being gender-neutral.◆

number are working shifts other than the regular "9 to 5" schedule. According to the 1995 Survey of Work Arrangements, nearly four out of ten such couples have shift work, including 10 percent in which partners worked at completely different times of the day (Marshall 1998b). The number of children at home does not significantly alter the likelihood of shift work for these full-time dual-earner couples.

Women's employment patterns relate to the deteriorating relative economic status of young men and to family strategies that seek insurance against the loss of a primary wage-earner (Oppenheimer 1994). When both men and women have employment prospects, the family strategy is no longer that of specific members specializing in paid and unpaid work, but of optimizing the paid work of both spouses. The viability of specialization as a family strategy depends on the labour-market opportunities of men and women. If women's prospects are limited, specialization makes sense, but the complementary roles are not as attractive when women's prospects have increased relative to that of men.

In the United States, Valerie Oppenheimer's work has documented how both the employment and income prospects of young men have declined, especially in the 1980s.

DIMENSIONS OF JOB-FAMILY TENSION, 1991

		AGES				
		15-24	25-34	35-44	45-54	55-64
Percentage of part-time workers who gave personal or	M	1	2	12	25	8
family responsibilities as main reason for working part-time	F	3	29	25	10	5
Percentage of persons not working who gave personal or	M	1	4	1	2	1
family responsibilities as main reason for leaving last job	F	8	23	9	5	4
Percentage of persons who gave illness or personal	M	4	7	13	8	—
responsibilities as the main reason for not looking for work in the past four weeks	F	9	35	22	20	—
Percentage of paid employees with irregular work	M	0	0	2	0	0
schedule who reported child care as main reason for irregular schedule	F	1	13	10	3	0
Percentage of paid employees who work at	M	0	2	0	4	1
home who reported child care as the main reason	F	0	15	13	0	0
Percentage of paid employees with irregular work	M	0	0	0	0	0
schedule who reported care of other family members as the main reason	F	0	0	4	4	9
Percentage of paid employees who worked at home who	M	0	4	2	2	0
reported care of other family members as the main reason	F	5	5	2	6	2

Source: Stone 1994: 65-74. Statistics Canada, Work Arrangements Survey.

TABLE 4.13

USUAL WEEKLY WORK HOURS OF DUAL-EARNER HUSBANDS AND WIVES, 1994

USUAL WEEKLY HOURS	HUSBAND	WIFE
Couples with no children under 16		
1-29*	5	21
30-39	17	35
40	43	29
41-49	10	6
50+	25	9
TOTAL	100	100
Couples with children under 16		
1-29*	3	30
30-39	16	35
40	45	25
41-49	11	4
50+	26	6
TOTAL	100	100

* defined as part-time

Source: Charette 1995: 11. Statistics Canada, Labour Force Survey.

TABLE 4.14

Canada has seen similar trends: a greater proportion of young men are not in permanent positions, and the real hourly wages of full-time male workers under 35 years of age declined in the period 1981-93 (Morissette 1997, 1998). Consequently, Oppenheimer speaks of wives' employment, be it intermittent or regular, part-time or full-time, as an adaptive family strategy in a modern society. The contribution of women to family income is therefore related to the evolution of both relative human capital and gender social contracts (Grindstaff and Trovato 1990).

One-earner families

In 1976, 57 percent of husband-wife families with children under 16 involved only the father as earner, and another 2 percent had only the mother earning (Marshall 1998a: 10). By 1997, the number of families with the father as the only earner had declined to 26 percent, while those with the mother as the only earner had increased to 6 percent. Even in the case of "traditional earner families," the wives had typically worked at some earlier point, and they would probably work again at a later time (Oderkirk, Silver, and Prud'homme 1994). In traditional earner families with wives under 35 years of age, 64 percent of the wives had worked in the previous five years.

In addition, families with husbands as sole earners had lower incomes and were more likely to have low income status. Significantly, when husbands are under 40 years of age, the incomes of the husbands are lower in dual-earner than traditional earning families (Oderkirk, Silver, and Prud'homme 1994). Possibly husbands are pressed to work more when they are sole earners.

Lone-parent families

For the most part, lone-parent families do not have the option of having more than one earner, and they often find it difficult to have even one full-time earner (McQuillan 1990). The very forming of lone-parent families—which increasingly comes through a separation of parents into two households rather than through the death of a parent—also puts stress on their income (Dooley 1988). Consequently, the incomes of lone-parent families have not kept pace with other families, producing a widening gap. There is also an increased concentration of female lone-parent families in the lower income groups (Rashid 1994: 13). Terrance Hunsley (1997) observed that although the overall poverty rates had eased downward over two decades, that was not the case for lone parents. In addition, the period 1976-91 saw a 66 percent increase in the numbers of mothers raising children alone. Observing the distribution of family income by deciles, Abdul Rashid (1999: 13) finds that lone-parent families comprised 37 percent of the lowest decile in 1970, but 44 percent in 1995. In contrast, two-income families comprised 50 percent of the highest decile in 1970 and 81 percent in 1995.

These figures are particularly important with regard to the well-being of children. (See also chapter 7.) As a proportion of all families with children, lone-parent families doubled from 11.4 percent in 1961 to 22.3 percent in 1996 (Statistics Canada 1992: 15; Statistics Canada 1997a: 3). In their overview of the situation, Donna Lero and Lois Brockman (1993: 91) observe, "These families comprise a large and growing segment of adults and children whose present and future well-being is frequently at risk."

Until 1982 women were more likely to be employed if they were single parents than if they were wives in two-parent families (Devereau and Linsay 1993), but that is no longer the case. Over the period 1976-93, the employment/population ratio of mothers with children under six doubled for married mothers but remained stagnant for single-parent mothers (Crompton 1994). On average, married mothers also have more education. A comparison of various categories of family composition by presence of one or more adults and by age of the youngest child shows that labour-force participation declined between 1986 and 1991 only in the one category of single-parent families with children under six (Che-Alford, Allan, and Butlin 1994: 35). The prospects do improve for lone mothers as the children get older, but the overall proportions below the low-income cut-off are close to 60 percent (Table 8.3; Devereau and Linsay 1993). Male lone parents also have above average proportions with low income, but the rate is closer to 30 percent (Oderkirk and Lockhead 1992). They are also older on average, have more education, and are more likely to be employed.

Lone parenthood is clearly the most significant negative element of the increased marital flexibility. The labour-force participation of lone parents is particularly affected by the age of the youngest child, and they are less likely to work part-time than when there are two parents (Lero and Brockman 1993). The 1988 Child Care Survey found that 36 percent of those who were not employed wanted to have a job. Of those who wanted a job, 30 percent said they could not take a job because they wanted to stay home to look after children, and another 10 percent said they had difficulty finding or paying for suitable child-care arrangements. For the working parents of children under six, day care was the primary form of child care for 35.7 percent of lone parents, compared to 17.3 percent for two-parent families. When the person primarily responsible for child care was working, close to a third of the children in two-parent families were still in the care of the parent(s), but this form of care was basically non-existent for one-parent families (Lero and Brockman 1993: 110).

Close to 60 percent of divorces involve children. In his analysis of the disadvantaged economic situation of women following divorce, Ross Finnie (1993) proposes that couples who have shared the benefits of specialization in paid and unpaid work during the marriage should better share in the costs of this specialization after the marriage. Other studies document the difficulties of lone mothers, especially in the period after separation. For instance, marital disruption contributes to significantly increased levels of distress, while remarriage reduces distress (Avison and Wade 1995). At the same time, both married and non-married mothers decrease their distress through social supports (Rietschlin and Thorpe 1997). As well, lone mothers living with their own parents have the best prospects for continuing their education (Sorenson and Grindstaff 1995).

Young families

Families with the husband or lone parent aged less than 35 comprise a quarter of all families (Rashid 1989: 15). Among the various family types, these young families are the only group whose real family income declined between 1970 and 1995 (Rashid 1998). The proportion of families with low-income status was 42.1 percent for families with the husband or lone parent under 25 years, compared to an average of 14.5 for all families in 1996 (Table 8.3).

Various analyses point to the difficulties of young persons in the labour force (Gauthier 1990; Côté and Allahar 1994; Morissette 1997). While the labour-force participation rate of persons aged 15-24 increased until 1989, it then went into decline. The proportion of persons aged 15-24 with no labour-force experience consequently increased from 9.7 percent in 1989 to 19.9 percent in 1996 (Statistics Canada 1997c). An analysis of specific age groups under 35 in the period 1981-91 shows an increase in proportions at school, declines in labour-force participation, increases in unemployment, increases in part-time employment, and declines in real incomes (Ravanera 1995: 29-33).

Consequently, Richard Marcoux, Richard Morin, and Demarais Rose (1990) attribute the relative deterioration of incomes of families with parents under age 35 to the difficulties in the labour market. The same difficulties would also be responsible for the lower formation of households in the young population. Families without children are found to have done even more poorly, which is possibly why they did not have children. Alternatively, for these young couples working less and not having children may be at least a temporary family strategy.

Elderly families

The average family incomes of the elderly are lower than the average for all age groups except the youngest families. Still, over the period 1973-86, elderly couples did experience the highest income growth rate of any type of family (Dooley 1988).

For persons aged 65 and over, the rates of low income have declined systematically, reaching levels below that of other population groups (Picot, Myles, and Pyper 1998; Cheal 1997). This is a function of transfer payments, as well as public and private

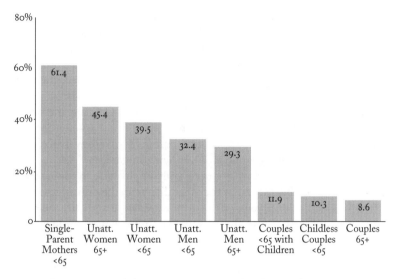

FIG 4.5 Proportions with low-income status, by family type, Canada, 1996

Source: National Council of Welfare 1998: 34. Statistics Canada, Survey of Consumer Finances.

pensions, rather than direct labour-market considerations. In effect, the proportions of persons aged 65 and over living in households with no earners increased from 58 percent in 1973 to 74.4 percent in 1994. At the same time, the proportions in households with no one receiving payments from the Canada/Quebec Pension Plan declined from 70.5 to 11.3 percent, and those with no private pension declined from 71.1 to 46.0 percent (Picot, Myles, and Pyper 1998).

Labour-force participation also declined for men aged 55-64, from 76 percent in 1975 to 61 percent in 1990. At ages 60-65, 40 percent of men were retired in 1994 compared to 25 percent in 1984 (Gower 1995). Krahn and Lowe (1993: 65) attribute these changes to both greater income security and loss of employment. According to the 1994 General Social Survey, personal choice also plays a role, because plans to retire early increase with household income. While a quarter of the workers retire as a personal choice, another quarter retire for health reasons. Clearly, elderly families remain vulnerable. When older people have insufficient assets and pension plans, they usually do not have access to the strategy of working as a means of achieving a desired standard of income.

Persons not in families

Low-income status is much more prevalent among persons not living in families. The rates are second only to that of lone-parent families (Figure 4.5). In 1996, 40 percent of persons not living in families were classified as having low income, compared to 15 percent of persons living in families (Table 8.3). Among all low income units, 54 percent were unattached individuals (National Council of Welfare 1998: 34). Both for persons living in families and for the unattached, the proportions with low-income are highest for those under 25 and those aged 60-65. However, for the unattached, the proportions with low income remain high in the retirement years.

Women over age 65 have significant levels of low income, especially if their marriages have ended through separation or divorce (Gee 1995: 113). The 1995 proportions with low-income status are 28.7 percent for men and 50.6 percent for women living alone, compared to 7.8 percent for persons aged 65 and over living in families.

Clearly, not living in a family does not necessarily imply more freedom to earn more income. In effect, the causality may be in the other direction: the difficulties in the labour market may make it difficult for young persons to leave home and start their own families, and those same difficulties may also prompt certain marital separations.

CONCLUSION

This chapter has considered two alternative explanations of changing work patterns. Is it the economy or is it the family? These explanations are not incompatible. To some extent, families are adapting to changing economic conditions, but it is also the economy that is adapting to changing families. Family and work therefore need to be considered concurrently. One way to consider both of these activities is to conclude that families are more efficient if one person specializes in paid work and the other in unpaid work (Becker 1981) or that nuclear family structures and wage labour are incompatible (Luxton 1997a). Others have argued that work has evolved in ways that are even less family friendly, with slow wage growth, increased insecurity, and high unemployment (Duffy, Glenday, and Pupo 1997b).

However, it is important to go "beyond the separate spheres" of family and work, and to recognize that they need to be analyzed together. In particular, the economy has evolved in ways that have influenced families, but families have also evolved in ways that have influenced the economy. The economy has evolved in particular toward the service sector, with higher demand for labour and a greater monetarization of work. This has brought families to supply more workers, women in particular, and to shift toward a model that has all able adults in the labour force. The economy has also adjusted to family change. The new family models have promoted a 24-hour economy with more part-time and non-standard work to accommodate the caring needs of families. Much of this accommodation has involved women. Nonetheless, men's work has also changed. For instance, between 1986 and 1996 the proportion of women aged 25-44 working full-time did not change, remaining at 52 percent. However, the proportion of men at these ages working full-time declined from 86 to 75 percent. As another example, U.S. polls find that more than 80 percent of women, but also 70 percent of men, are torn between the demands of their jobs and a desire to spend more time with their families (Coltrane 1998b: 68).

These observations help explain other things about economic change. For instance, slow wage growth occurs in part because fewer persons are working full-time and persons who are employed are working fewer hours. More non-standard work occurs in part to accommodate the needs of families. There is more unemployment and lack of job security, but also a higher proportion of the population employed. There is polarization in certain directions and convergence in others. There is polarization across men's incomes, in particular between younger and older men who are living according to different family models, with younger men less likely to be breadwinners. Polarization also occurs across younger persons, contrasting those who are employed with those who are staying longer at school and at home, delaying their labour-force entry. But there is convergence between women and men, especially at younger ages, when women's incomes have continued to increase while men's are stagnant. For those employed, there are pressures for divergence with a higher proportion of persons working part-time and in non-standard jobs. However, the convergence is especially evident when we consider the total population, because more people are employed.

The greatest polarization is across family types, in particular between lone-parent and two-earner families (Zyblock 1996c). In effect, according to the Survey of Labour and Income Dynamics, entering or exiting low income is just as frequently determined by changes in family status as by gaining or losing a job (Statistics Canada 1999: 19). The two-parent families have evolved in ways that allow both parents to be employed for a large part of the adult life course. In contrast, lone-parent families have typically had their children at younger ages and the caring needs of young children clearly present difficulties for the parent's labour-force activity.

Duffy and Pupo (1992: 260) conclude that we need to rethink the meaning of work and its place in our lives. Husband-wife families are experiencing stress associated with the interface of family and work, but there are also significant constraints on the organization of family and work in the cases of lone-parent, young, and elderly families, and of persons not in families.

These constraints between family and work are manifested differently across gender and marital status. For persons at ages 30-55, the gender differences among the never-married without children are minimal (Beaujot 1995: 72). For those who are married and living with children, the gender differences are substantial, because marriage and parenthood increase the labour-force participation of men while decreasing that of women. Among the formerly married, the main gender difference is that women are more likely to be living with children, which presents problems for both work and income generation.

For the married, gender differences are largely a function of the division of paid and unpaid work within couples. Many couples accommodate the needs of families by sharing rather unequally the paid work in the labour force and the unpaid family work. While couples may establish a division of labour that is appropriate for them, they often do this, as we have seen, at the expense of the continuity in women's employment. In one sense, withdrawals from the labour force, or working part-time, can be seen as signs of flexibility that permit people to achieve a variety of objectives (Jones, Marsden, and Tepperman 1990), including the chance to look after the needs of children and the family in general. The 1988 Child Care Survey suggested that, while parents would have liked further public support through day care, they were also interested in gaining flexibility around work that would permit them to look after their own children (Beaujot 1997). In other regards, work interruptions present significant problems, particularly in the form of lower average incomes for women.

Work interruptions pose the most serious problems for the formerly married, who lose the potential to share paid and non-paid work with a spouse. Low-income status is particularly predominant for female lone-parent families. While the greater possibility of moving out of unsatisfactory relationships gives adults more autonomy, it is at the cost of more poverty for women and more insecurity for children (Cherlin 1992: 139).

Marriage, and especially children, then, establish more gender differences between the family and work parts of people's lives. For the most part, they bring more family responsibilities for women and more paid work responsibilities for men. For instance, Carl Grindstaff (1989) compared various cases of women aged 30 at the time of the 1981 census, finding that women who had married early or had children early were disadvantaged in terms of education, occupation, and income. Those with the most achievements were women who were either not married or had no children by age 30.

Conversely, women who give priority to paid work are those most likely to have children later in life or not to have children. For instance, Bali Ram and Abdur Rahim (1993) show that women who have an early employment experience tend to space out childbearing and in the end have fewer births. It may be that childlessness is the easiest route to equality. Still, there has not been a significant increase in childlessness, which would imply that avoiding children is not a favoured solution to the work-family conflict.

Women's increased involvement in paid work has provided a greater potential for them to leave unhappy relationships. It has also introduced the need for men to adjust their involvement in unpaid work. If these adjustments are not forthcoming, there is further pressure on relationships, which may be particularly costly to women.

Unpaid Work and the Division of Productive Activities

Domestic work carries many implications, or meanings. For some, it is a necessary daily grind, sometimes paid (poorly), more often unpaid. For some it is an expression of love or caring, and it may also be used as a form of discipline or as a tool for learning to take care of oneself. It could be an unwelcome task ("We have to do something about this house!") that comes before the reward (a movie, TV program, a visit to a friend's, a game).

Domestic work also lends itself to various measurements, from determinations of who is most responsible for given activities to detailed time-use information on household work activities over a 24-hour period. According to estimates, in monetary value unpaid domestic work is worth about a third of Canada's Gross National Product. Clearly, domestic work is central to family well-being.

Before looking at theory and data, we start with an overview of observations concerning unpaid work. Many of the generalizations found in Canadian textbooks on families propose that working women carry a double burden: they work all day and then come home for a second shift of housework. Generalizations from other sources suggest that over time a change has occurred, especially in the relative share of domestic work performed by men, but that the case is still overwhelmingly that women do more unpaid work than men. The sex differences are even larger in who takes responsibility for given domestic tasks. At the same time, research shows that most couples do not consider the distribution of work as unfair.

Although no systematic national measurements of domestic work were done until the mid-1980s, we are able to consider a number of Canadian studies based in a city or region. Despite the difficulties of generalizing across these different studies, they do tend to reveal a move toward a greater openness around sharing domestic work. The greatest equality in this regard occurs in dual-earner couples with both spouses at an intermediate position in the class structure—that is, professionals and administrators. The studies also show that once a couple has established a pattern for the division of work, the two tend to have difficulties changing that pattern—a finding that points to the importance of a continuous paid work commitment on the part of both spouses, which prompts a greater symmetry in unpaid work.

The theoretical perspectives that attempt to explain the distribution of unpaid work tend to focus on economic questions (relative resources and the time-availability of spouses) and cultural questions (ideology and conceptions of gender). While all of these factors do come into play, it would appear that gender itself plays a key role, with unpaid work being one of the important bases on which we "do gender in our daily interactions." This perspective would also suggest that gender is produced differently in different types of households. Remarriage, cohabitation, and childlessness may involve different forms of negotiation around the gender division of household labour. The centrality of the spouses' work commitments, measured especially in terms of continuity, also alters the material conditions under which couples do gender. This gender perspective may be considered within an exchange framework, in which the exchange need not involve doing less unpaid work because one does more paid work. That is, the exchange can take various forms that are conditioned by understandings about gender. These gender understandings and processes are in turn determined by the relative opportunity structures of males and females in families and in the broader society.

Canadian data, especially from the 1992 time-use survey, show considerable similarity between women and men when considering total time-use in productive activities, that is, paid plus unpaid work. In particular, for both men and women, total productive time is highest for those who are employed, are in relationships, and have young children. For employed persons, men are less likely to participate in unpaid work on a given day; they show more flexibility in their time-use associated with unpaid work. The greatest differences occur when it comes to taking responsibility for given tasks: women mostly take responsibility for cooking, cleaning, and washing, and men for household and property maintenance.

Women also take more responsibility for child care, although those men who do participate in child care also devote considerable time. After mothers, fathers are the most important source of child care. The differences on elder care are not as great, with men actually more likely to participate in that care, and the average time-use being similar for men and women.

The last section of the chapter considers alternate models for the division of paid and unpaid work. Certainly, studies show considerable diversity across couples. While the most common case is women doing more unpaid work and men doing more paid work, couples are spread out across the spectrum in the division of work. In about 5 percent of cases, spouses are doing about the same amount of both paid and unpaid work. But the second-largest category, amounting to about 15 percent of couples, is the case of the double burden, in which partners do the same amount of paid work but the wife does more unpaid work. Nonetheless, in some cases the opposite is true, and there are also cases in which men do more of both paid and unpaid work. A variety of family models do co-exist, but studies show a move toward more symmetrical models in which spouses are co-providers and co-parents.

◆

Earning and caring represent two major family activities, but they do not always receive equivalent recognition, nor is their interaction properly appreciated. In *Gender Relations in Canada*, Marlene Mackie (1991: 221) suggests that one of the great achievements of the women's movement has been the "elevation to visibility of unpaid domestic activities, and their definition as productive work." In effect, while censuses have always included several measures of paid work, the 1996 Canadian census was the first to obtain measures of unpaid work. Paid and unpaid work, then, both represent time spent in productive activities, in contrast with the down-time associated with personal care and leisure.

While the two types of productive activities clearly complement each other, they can also be in conflict: earning can encroach on caring, just as caring can encroach on earning. Partly because earning is assigned a dollar value, paid work and the activities associated with employment tend to be seen as more valuable. The word "work" has come to mean paid work, and other activities are often considered to be non-productive. For instance, Frances Goldscheider and Linda Waite (1991: xiv) observe that social priorities have come to value the workplace over the home. They suggest that this emphasis makes women want to escape the home, which is viewed as a burden and barrier to paid work accomplishments. The tendency also leads men to give little priority to the home and to offer little acknowledgement of the importance of family tasks. Children also learn little about the home and its tasks, seeking to avoid domestic responsibilities in favour of more pleasurable activities.

With the increased presence of women in the workplace, the administration of work in the home presents a significant challenge. In their analysis of what is happening to families, Goldscheider and Waite (1991) argue that society is undergoing a revolution associated with non-paid work. In particular, wives are resisting the double day of employment and housework, while husbands are resisting the demands to share in family tasks. Depending on the outcome of this struggle, either new families with more symmetrical roles will emerge, or many women will give up on families. The equalization of the allocation of household tasks, then, would seem to be essential for the very preservation of the family. In their text *Families in Canada*, Lyle Larson, J. Walter Goltz, and Charles Hobart (1994: 302) also give high stakes to this question: "Women's labour force participation rates and incomes levels will probably continue to increase significantly, with a parallel increase in women's power. It seems reasonable to predict that one result of this will be continuing high levels of marital conflict and break-up, until Canadian husbands learn to share domestic work in the home and family decision-making as willingly as they have shared paid employment with their wives." Through her detailed study of two-income couples, Arlie Hochschild (1989) also sees the difficulties around the division of domestic work as a major element in the "stalled revolution" of gender equality.

In a subsequent study of 130 persons working at a large U.S. plant, Hochschild (1997) found that work was absorbing much of people's lives, and as a result they had little time left over for children and family life. Either because they liked their work and identified with their work lives, or because they felt pressured not to lose their employment, many persons worked more hours than the job demanded, and few took advantages of opportunities for part-time work or job-sharing. In the "contest between work and home, working parents are voting with their feet, and the workplace is winning" (p. 198).

Clearly, just as labour-force participation plays a crucial role in gender questions, so too does unpaid work. Jean-Claude Chesnais (1987) sees three stages in the improvement in women's status. First came the opportunity to participate in education, second the opportunities in the labour force and associated financial independence, a stage that remains incomplete. The third stage, which is just beginning, involves equal opportunities in daily life. The gendered character of daily life is especially visible in the light of time-use (Ornstein and Haddad 1993). Not only is there strong sex-segregation into various kinds of non-paid work activities, more pronounced than for paid work activities, but on a given day a much higher proportion of men than women report no participation in non-paid work. The second and third stages in the changes of women's status are of course linked, and transformations for both women and men are essential to the maintenance of family life, as they are to the sustenance and reproduction of the labour force.

In her book *Women, Men and Time*, Beth Anne Shelton (1992: 158) observes that both women and men are now hurt by the conflict between family and work: "Change in women's roles has created conflict between work and family for both women and men, even if the conflicts are felt more by women than men." Nonetheless, we can also see the interplay of family and work as a family strategy rather than a conflict. For instance, in an article on basic human needs, Denise Beaulieu (1998) observes that to look after the basic needs of the family women and men need to form a partnership. She proposes that in dealing with the basic issue of human needs, men should not be divided from women.

THE MEANING OF UNPAID WORK

The concept of unpaid work involves a diversity of meanings. Caring for someone can be experienced as a form of love or a form of drudgery. The work that goes into creating special family occasions can be valued as the material that "makes family" or it can be seen as having no value because it comes with no monetary reward. Domestic work is often taken for granted, seen as an activity that requires no special skills or abilities. This denigration of homemaking skills, though, would appear to be a 20th-century urban phenomenon (Goldscheider and Waite 1991: 20). Being a homemaker once meant household management and home production; now it has come to largely mean the management of child care and household consumption (Wilson 1991: 53).

Despite this denigration of domestic work, Marjorie De Vault (1991) gives a compelling account of some of the various activities involved in *Feeding the Family*. Producing family solidarity while making each family member feel cared for and loved involves various invisible but important components: for instance, remembering the schedules and food preferences of family members, planning meals acceptable or even pleasing to everyone, monitoring supplies, improvising to meet daily contingencies, and responding to individual wishes and moods—all the while trying to create the period of order and pleasant sociability that is the ideal of the family meal. Indeed, much of this work of planning and coordination cannot be easily shared with other household members or replaced by purchased services or products.

Modes of caring

In "Toward a Feminist Theory of Caring," Berenice Fisher and Joan Tronto (1990) observe that care involves a mixture of physical and emotional aspects. One aspect is *caring about*, which means being concerned and attentive. Caring about someone means showing love and affection, and it can include making money to provide for someone's needs. *Taking care of* someone means assuming a responsibility toward another person's needs. It includes appraising someone's needs, deciding what needs are not being met, and arranging and organizing caring activities. Finally, *caregiving* or caring for someone is the direct meeting of needs through concrete tasks that take time. For the most part, time-use surveys specifically measure only the caregiving activities.

Clearly, for both the species and the society, care is essential. Fisher and Tronto (1990: 40) define caring as "a species activity that includes everything that we do to maintain, continue and repair our world so that we can live in it as well as possible." They observe that households, markets, and bureaucracies are all involved in caring, but that these various spheres also entail different modes with their associated benefits and limits. The *household and community* mode has typically involved women at the centre of support networks. This mode is in many regards the least expensive and most direct, but it can be deficient when family systems are not working or are insufficient to meet the needs. When caring occurs through the *marketplace*, the men with higher incomes often have power over the caring process itself, and women are often displaced as "solo caregivers" for individual households. When caring occurs through the bureaucracy or *public sector*, it is often directed to those who are particularly disadvantaged. Through a division of labour, the public sector tends to distort and fragment the caring process, just as the marketplace involves distortions associated with profit motives. Consequently, while caring is a basic practical activity, Fisher and Tronto argue that it raises real questions about justice and equality, by class, by population groups, and by gender.

Varieties of meaning associated with unpaid work

Louise Vandelac (1985) entitles her critical study of domestic life *Du travail et de l'amour*. She finds that the domestic world envelops us to the point that we do not see it. Just as families are at the crossroads of our fears and ideals, both supportive and repressive, so too does our understanding of domestic work have its contradictions. Meg Luxton (1980) used the same idea in entitling her study of domestic work over three generations in Flin Flon, Manitoba, *More Than a Labour of Love*. While caring involves both love and labour, Carol Baines, Patricia Evans, and Sheila Neysmith (1991: 14) observe that the love is expected and the labour is often rendered invisible.

Children may experience domestic work as a form of punishment or part of a system of rewards. Parents may see it as a means of teaching children to look after themselves. When it comes to encouraging husbands to share in domestic work, these meanings of disciplining and learning may interfere with attempts to work toward a new meaning of sharing and paying attention to someone else's needs.

U.S. surveys of married life indicate that women see fairness in task allocation as relevant to the viability of a marriage (Bumpass 1991). Lack of participation in domestic work may be an expression of not caring. Linda Thompson (1991) in effect finds that a man's involvement in household work is an indicator of his commitment to the relational aspects of the marriage. At the same time, the very discussion of the division of household tasks may interfere with their meaning as a form of interpersonal care and support. Is it still love when you have to discuss and argue how tasks might be better divided, and whether each partner is doing their fair share?

Family members may therefore see housework as routine and tiring, or an expression of love and care. The phenomenon is a strange mixture of labour and love, though most treatments emphasize the negative aspects. For instance, Ann Oakley (1974) qualifies housework as repetitive and dull, a labour often performed in isolation and without control over the timing of the activities. Besides being unpaid with no benefits, housework offers few entitlements such as tax advantages or pensions and little recognition for superior performance. In their book *Women's Caring*, Baines, Evans, and Neysmith (1991) also emphasize the negative consequences of gendered caring, including its connections to women's poverty, vulnerability, and disadvantage.

As exemplified by its use as a form of parental discipline in families, housework also carries the meaning of dominance. In imposing undesirable activities on selected persons, household labour involves power, authority, and submission. In *Familiar Exploitation*, Christine Delphy and Diana Leonard (1992) argue that marriage and family structures support male material interests by perpetuating a system of control over the labour of family members. Women's subordination includes the exploitation of their unpaid labour within families and households. Julie Brines (1995) proposes that the Delphy-Leonard model is excessively deterministic. Especially given the weakness of the institution of marriage, Brines asks how marriage could "retain such a lock on women's options."

Nonetheless, the power and submission aspects of unpaid labour remain real. Candace West and Don Zimmerman (1987) showed how interactions around domestic work were establishing and reinforcing gender expectations in the society at large. In *The Gender Factory*, Sarah Fenstermaker Berk (1985) found that the total work expected or demanded by the household is the most important factor influencing the wife's contribution of domestic labour, but it does not influence the husband's contribution. Consequently, the division of domestic labour not only provides the various goods and services (meals, washed children, for instance) that the household needs, but it also simultaneously produces gender. Men and women *do gender* as they do, or do not do, housework and child care. Gender is produced through everyday enactments and behaviour, many of which surround domestic work. More broadly, just as couples need to find ways to express their collectivity, individuals also need to express their individuality. This singularity may be expressed in the uniqueness of the tasks performed by a given person, or in a person's unwillingness to perform certain tasks.

Just as paid work shapes the daily activities of families, so too does household work shape the material life of family members (Berk 1985). Shiva Halli (1991) is even fearful that men's involvement in domestic work may come to introduce new patriarchal control over women. Fisher and Tronto (1990: 36) also express concern that the integration of men's and women's work may well produce new patterns of male dominance. However, Gale Cassidy (1997) finds that carrying one's weight in performing household chores can be a source of mastery for both women and men, and that men's mastery scores are highest when they do an equal share of child care.

Measuring unpaid work

Given its variety of meanings, unpaid work is clearly difficult to measure. Still, measure it we do, most commonly using three kinds of measurements. One method entails detailed time-use to measure the various activities of the 24-hour day. The advantage of this approach is that it forces an accounting of all parts of the day, and numerous activities can be coded. For instance, in the 1992 Canadian General Social Survey, the researchers coded over 150 activities (see Box 5.2). The problem was, the measurement did not include activities occurring simultaneously. Because the approach captured only the primary activity of a given time, it did not cover multitasking. In addition, the method does not take into account the differences in the intensity of a person's involvement with an activity at a given time, or the difference between helping with an activity and being responsible for its accomplishment. For instance, a person can care for children and at the same time watch television, just as paid work includes socializing with workmates while on the job.

The 1990 General Social survey asked respondents, for each of four common specific domestic duties, to indicate who is mostly responsible for the activity. The problem with this second approach is that it does not measure the time spent on the specific tasks in question, and it focuses on a limited number of activities, ignoring other relevant tasks. In addition, various family members, when asked, tend to consistently exaggerate their own roles and downplay or underestimate the roles of others.

A third approach simply asks for respondents to indicate the total amount of time spent on household work over a week or the proportion of total work done by given

---

BOX 5.1 | *Unpaid work and family rituals*

In *Gender and Families*, Scott Coltrane (1998b) observes that family rituals are one of the means through which we create, usually unconsciously, a sense of ourselves as gendered beings: as mothers or fathers, wives or husbands, daughters or sons, women or men, boys or girls. On special occasions like Thanksgiving, it is largely women who orchestrate the ritual event. They usually plan the meal, buy the food, prepare and serve the meal, and clean up afterward. Often the whole occasion is planned around the family meal, and it is the women who make it happen. If the dinner includes a turkey, a man is usually expected to carve the meat, even if he is not particularly competent at this task. ◆

Source: Adapted from Coltrane 1998b: 13–22.

BOX 5.2 | *What is unpaid work?*

DOMESTIC WORK	EXAMPLES
Meal preparation	making a pot of tea, setting the table, cooking, baking, cleaning up after meals or baking, washing/drying dishes
Cleaning	mopping floors, dusting, vacuuming, making beds, taking out the garbage
Clothing care	washing laundry, hanging it out to dry, folding clothes and linen, mending clothes, sewing on buttons, shining shoes, hemming
Repairs and maintenance	painting, plastering a wall, plumbing, fixing or washing the car, renovations, mowing and watering grass, weeding, composting, raking leaves, watering house plants
Other domestic work	packing for a move or vacation, rearranging furniture, putting groceries away, feeding and grooming pets

HELP AND CARE	
Child care	feeding, changing and bathing babies and other children, putting them to bed, teaching them to learn, helping with school work, reprimanding, reading and talking to children, administering first aid, medicines, or shots, taking temperature, playing games with children, walking or biking with them, unpaid babysitting by household members (not parents or guardians), visiting children in hospital
Adult care	washing and cutting hair, running a bath, providing help to disabled and elderly members of the household, administering first aid, preparing and administering medicines, taking temperature

OTHER UNPAID WORK	
Management and shopping	paying bills, balancing chequebooks, making shopping lists, preparing tax returns, shopping for groceries, clothing, hardware, gasoline, looking for a house or apartment, getting appliances repaired
Transportation and travel	travel related to management and shopping for goods and services, taking family members to day care, work, school, hospital, and other places, other travel related to domestic work
Volunteer work	fundraising, answering a crisis line, delivering meals
Transport	other unpaid work travel related to volunteer work and other help and care ◆

Source: Jackson 1996:27

family members. While this approach has the advantage of using a simple question to measure total time or its division, the estimated responses can be highly inaccurate, with the same problem of subjectivity depending on who happens to be the respondent. Box 5.3 gives a further example of the difficulties associated with the meaning and measurement of domestic work.

UNPAID WORK: DISTRIBUTION AND CHANGE

On the whole, unpaid work, it seems, usually takes up slightly more time than paid work. One study showed that in the early 1990s Canadians aged 15 and over were spending 13 percent of their time on paid work and 14 percent on unpaid work (Jackson 1996). With women spending more time in paid work, they have less time for domestic work (Bumpass 1993); but this increased paid work on the part of women has not greatly changed men's domestic work time, at least in absolute hours. Still, with women doing less, men's relative hours spent on domestic work have increased. Their share of unpaid work has thus increased (Bumpass 1993), which means that some movement has occurred toward a more equal division by sex. Nonetheless, the differences remain strong, with women doing considerably more than men.

A number of U.S. analysts of domestic work conclude that women do about two-thirds of the total, or that women do twice as much as men (Thompson and Walker 1989: 850; Ishii-Kuntz and Coltrane 1992). A study based on Canadian data from 1983 also showed men doing a third of housework, which rose to 37.5 percent when wives were working full-time (Nakhaie 1995). These generalizations depend on whether the researchers are counting all kinds of domestic work or only the main regular indoor tasks of cooking, cleaning, and washing. Studies vary in the extent to which they include child care, elder care, maintenance, and voluntary work. Nonetheless, it seems reasonable to conclude that women still do about two-thirds of the domestic work.

Once the analysts consider paid and unpaid work together, though, they see much less gender difference. In effect, many studies do not explicitly relate unpaid work to paid work. They justify this in the interest of focusing on specific activities, especially the routine daily activities of cooking and cleaning, and on the extent of men's involvement in these activities, though this approach tends to exaggerate the gender imbalance. As we will see, several observers of the North American scene have concluded that men and women do about the same amount of total productive work (Feree 1991a; Thompson and Walker 1989). As an average for 13 industrialized countries, women do 51 percent of total work (Riley 1997: 30). In addition, a certain symmetry exists in the sense that men are responsible for about two-thirds of family income while women do two-thirds of unpaid work. Behind this apparent symmetry, though, lies large gender differences not only in the distributions of paid and unpaid work, but also in the specific types of paid and unpaid work performed (Blair and Lichter 1991; McQuillan and Belle 1997). In addition, for specific categories of population—say, for employed persons, employed married persons, or employed married parents—the average total work tends to be slightly higher for women than for men.

The finding that on any one given day a rather small proportion of women but a significant proportion of men do no unpaid work implies considerably more flexibility in men's unpaid work activities. The gender difference is particularly strong in terms of the responsibility for the main ongoing domestic tasks. Women largely "make family" in the sense of being responsible for coordinating schedules and activities. Regardless of their paid work status, mothers manage a long list of family-related responsibilities: "In addition to continuing to care for infants (and stay home from work when their school-aged children are ill), women keep social calendars for their children and spouses, plan the graduations and weddings of their children and the anniversary parties for their parents, and generally do the social, emotional, and physical work associated with maintaining the family" (Goldscheider and Waite 1991: 9).

These coordinating and planning activities are particularly difficult to share or delegate, and women are thus more likely to be doing two or multiple tasks at once, such as cooking one meal while planning another, or doing both child care and cleaning up. Consequently, studies invariably find women to have higher average levels of stress

---

BOX 5.3 | *Problems associated with the meaning and measurement of domestic work: a personal example*

With the birthday of one of my daughters approaching, my spouse offered to pick up the cake on her way home from work. Then we realized that we could do the business together, because we were both going to the mall to shop in the evening. Once there, since I had less to do, we decided I would go to see the available cakes. While this was a seemingly easy task that could be measured in very few minutes of time-use, it posed various problems for me. Was I cutting off my wife, who might want to make this choice, or at least have a say in it? And there were many possible choices and various possibilities for error. I found myself thinking of the reactions my choice might bring. "You paid that much for a cake?" Or "this is a birthday, surely not just any cheap cake will do?" So, in addition to the job that had to be done, I was facing questions around the quality of the decision and the tensions—including getting credit—surrounding a task with a significant symbolic component. Only on reporting back—with these questions, and without a cake—did I realize that the broader issues I was pondering were not relevant. My spouse just wanted me to do the job and make my own decisions so that we had a cake and could get out of there as soon as possible. The activity simply represented a time-use question and there I was, wasting time. ◆

associated with family and work activities. Looking at Canadian fathers' participation in family life, including work and leisure, Jarmila Horna and Eugene Lupri (1987) observed that men find the parental role less taxing and confining. With lower expectations and less sense of obligation, men experience child care and household tasks like cooking to be more like leisure. At the same time fathers view their paid work as their primary family obligation, and they place it above other kinds of activities, including domestic work. In a study of 60 married couples, Susan Shaw (1988) also found that men were more likely to define household activities as leisure, and that women were more likely to define these activities as constraints.

Although few studies of children's involvement in domestic work exist, it would appear that the participation of the young has declined significantly. According to Goldscheider and Waite (1991: 143-52), girls do about twice as much as boys, and both do more when they are living with a lone parent. While children do more domestic work when their mothers have more egalitarian gender attitudes, they do less when mothers are younger or have more education, and children's involvement is not much influenced by the mother's employment status. It could be that children have little left to do once men begin to take up household tasks. It could also be that parents are not at home enough to supervise the children's tasks. In any case, Goldscheider and Waite conclude that few families are reacting to the changing family/work context in ways that include children, and that parents are not sharing domestic tasks in ways that might prepare children for the possibly egalitarian homes of the future. To a large extent, they argue, neither boys nor girls are being taught the skills associated with domestic tasks.

International comparisons show that men do about twice as many hours per week as women on paid work. The differences are smallest in the Scandinavian countries, where the average earnings of wives are also highest compared to husbands (Spain and Bianchi 1996: 189). It is also in Sweden that men do the most unpaid work, at 20 hours per week, compared to 33 hours for women. The Canadian average is 16 hours of unpaid work for men and 29 hours for women, making a similar difference of 13 hours per week (Table 5.1).

The United Nations (1995: 133) tabulated time-use data for 14 European countries, plus Australia, Canada, and the United States, in the 1980s and 1990s. The percentage share of unpaid housework done by men varies from a low of 18 to 23 percent in Spain, Poland, and Austria to a high of 39 to 43 percent in Lithuania, Sweden, and Russia. The Canadian proportion of 35 percent in 1992 is in the middle of this distribution.

The historical context

As a long-term trend, the gender difference in domestic work seems to have increased as the breadwinner-homemaker model became more dominant and then to have gone into decline in the 1970s. In pre-industrial times, for which we have no detailed data, men and women often had segregated tasks, but they worked together for the instrumental well-being of the family. The subsequent physical separation of work and family came to

BOX 5.4 | *Canadian summaries of unpaid work*

Most Canadian summaries conclude that women do face a double burden. Vandelac (1985: 368) speaks of growing inequality by sex in both total work time and income. She concludes that "sharing" is an inappropriate concept to use in relation to domestic work. Mackie (1991: 231) argues that for most working women, "Being in the paid labour force is simply added to family work." Similarly, Harvey Krahn and Graham Lowe (1993: 151) state, "Most married women spend their days in paying jobs, yet still assume most of the responsibilities of child care and domestic tasks when they get home." Lyle Larson, J. Walter Goltz, and Charles Hobart (1994: 302) observe that the slight movement toward greater equity in the division of household chores has not kept pace with the increased hours of paid work of wives. Maureen Baker and Shelley Phipps (1997: 127) speak of a double workday and the associated strains, because "changes in the paid work patterns of women have not resulted in corresponding changes in the organization of domestic work." Observing that women's work-

loads have increased, Norene Pupo (1997) uses the title "Always Working, Never Done: The Expansion of the Double Day."

These conclusions are largely based on studies that preceded the 1986 and 1992 time-use surveys. In effect, summarizing earlier surveys and applying associated time-use rates to census data from 1911 to 1976, Martin Meissner (1985) finds that while the hours of domestic work are unchanged for men and women, the hours of paid work have declined for men and increased for women. He concludes that the leisure society is carried on the backs of women. However, Luxton's (1980) account of the domestic work of the generation of women born in 1927-39 suggests that women's domestic work involved more hours in earlier times than it does in more recent generations. In addition, most authors find that women's domestic work time declines when they are in the paid labour force. They simply spend less time in the home and consequently less time doing domestic work. ◆

mean that men had very little place in domestic work. Media messages about domestic activities came to be addressed largely to women. Especially if the family had few young children, and with the introduction of modern appliances, housewives had fewer hours of work than their husbands, and consequently men remained largely removed from routine domestic work.

Married women's "double burden" or "second shift" began when they started to work outside of the home, because most men did not adjust to the greater involvement of wives in paid work. Hochschild (1997) even speaks of a third shift, which represents the struggle to cope with the emotional consequences of a compressed second shift. As Luxton (1990) demonstrated, altering responsibilities for domestic work is a complex task for couples. Consequently, the difficulties Hochschild (1989: 3) observed may have been unique to generations in which women re-entered the labour force, sometimes on a part-time basis, after a child-bearing period. When couples start their lives together with equal commitment to paid work, the unpaid work can also be more equally divided.

Evidence of change

In their study of the late 1980s, Goldscheider and Waite (1991: 109) indicated that although women working outside the home had added a second shift to their daily lives, "We feel that this adjustment is likely to be only temporary." Indeed, evidence of change has come to the fore. Bianchi and Spain (1996: 32) determined that while in 1965 women did 85 percent of the housework (30 hours for women, 5 for men), in 1985 they did two-thirds (20 hours for women, 10 for men).

However, on the basis of detailed data from some 200 families in Utah in 1977-78 and 1987-88, Cathleen Zeck and Jane McCullough (1991) found that in two-parent, two-child households, both men and women increased their total weekly hours of productive work. In the non-paid category, women had reduced and men had increased by about 3.5 hours per week. In addition, women had increased their average paid work by 11 hours. Consequently, women had increased their total hours by over 7 hours and men by 3.5 hours per week.

Using data from the United States and the United Kingdom in the 1960s and 1980s, Jonathan Gershuny and John Robinson (1988) concluded that in the 1980s women were doing substantially less housework while men were doing a little more than in the 1960s. Shelton (1992) also found that men's proportion of household labour, and women's proportion of paid work, had increased in the United States between 1975 and 1987. Using data from 1984 and 1993 in Sweden, Lennart Flood and Urban Grasjo (1995) found that the gender difference had declined for both paid and unpaid work, and as a consequence the two-hour difference per week in total work in 1984 had been reduced to identical averages for women and men in 1993. These studies therefore suggest a decline in the gender differential in domestic work.

Monetary value and time spent in unpaid work

Another useful way of understanding the nature of total unpaid work is through attempts to estimate its monetary value. One approach for doing this, the opportunity-cost approach, is based on the person's wage rate applied to the time spent doing unpaid work. This method places a higher value on the unpaid work performed by highly paid persons. A second approach, the replacement-rate approach, is based on the rate that someone would be paid to perform a given task. While this method produces a lower total value, it can still lead to an exaggeration of the value, because the average person would probably take more time to do the work than someone hired to do the job. Nonetheless, the

BOX 5.5 | *Fairness*

While the division of work is clearly by no means fair in hours spent, many women still indicate that they are satisfied with the state of affairs (Berk 1985: 188). Linda Thompson and Alexis Walker (1989: 855) observe that only a minority of women feel their husbands should do more domestic work. Myra Marx Feree (1991b) finds it striking how little explicit conflict exists over housework in many families. The 1984 Canadian Fertility Survey found that 78 percent of women thought that household chores should be shared equally, but only 8.2 percent indicated that they often had a problem with sharing housework, even though some 70 percent did given tasks "always or mostly" themselves (Balakrishnan, Lapierre-Adamcyk, and Krotki 1993: 170-73).

Nonetheless, the division of work is a source of conflict in some marriages, especially when employed women work significantly more total hours than their husbands (Gershuny and Robinson 1988). The perception of fairness is more important to the personal well-being of wives than of husbands (Davies and McAlpine 1998), and employed wives are less satisfied with their marriages if their husbands fail to share in housework (Yogev and Brett 1985). Well-being is lowest and depression highest among wives whose husbands do little housework (Ross, Mirowsky, and Huber 1983). Among wives employed full-time, those who report an unfair division of household labour are significantly more likely to report having trouble in their marriages (Bumpass 1991). Still, the sharing of family work has also been associated with greater marital strain, possibly because it too can lead to more potential areas of disagreement, negotiation, and mutual criticism (Thompson and Walker 1989: 859).

Daphne Spain and Suzanne Bianchi (1996b: 171) conclude, "Academic researchers are more troubled by the division of household labor than the women they interview, many of whom think their household arrangement is equitable." This

attempts to estimate the value of unpaid work conclude that it is worth about a third of the GNP (Statistics Canada 1995b; Jackson 1996). Measured in constant 1992 dollars, and per person aged 15 and over, the value of unpaid work would have been $11,300 in 1961 and $10,900 in 1992.

Table 5.1 displays some of the data used in calculating the value of unpaid work, expressed as hours per week. For instance, in 1992 employed wives spent an average of 27.3 hours per week, compared to 17.2 for men. This difference of 10 hours a week is certainly significant, but it is less than the 15 hours a week estimated by Hochschild (1989: 3). It also does not take into account the tendency for wives to be working part-time, giving them more space to find the extra 10 hours per week.

While these differences do not in themselves indicate a second shift, it is nonetheless significant that, in each category under comparison, women do more unpaid work then

may be because cognitive dissonance brings couples to reconcile their expectations with reality. The assessment of fairness may also be a function of the comparison to others, or of perceptions of what is appropriate. But it is probably also a function of exchange and dependency, with the person who is more economically dependent considering it fair to be doing more of the housework. Indeed, Mary Clare Lennon and Sarah Rosenfield (1994) find that women who have few alternatives to marriage and who have less economic resources are more likely to see the distribution of tasks as being fair.

When a partner does perceive the division of labour as being unfair, some couples engage in destructive or constructive conflict, while others avoid the problem. A survey of 494 Dutch couples (Kluwer, Heesink, and Van de Vliert 1996, 1997) found that wives with traditional gender role ideologies, and those with traditional husbands, were more inclined to avoid conflict, despite their discontent about the division of labour. Although traditional relationships may seem to be more peaceful, this condition may

partly result from the avoidance of conflict. When the Dutch couples did show high levels of discontent, the most common pattern was *destructive conflict*, largely manifested as the wife making demands and the husband withdrawing. This pattern of pressures and demands impeded the resolution of conflict over the division of labour. The *constructive conflict* of mutually integrative interaction was more likely to occur when the couples had lower levels of discontent. The observation that mutually integrative interactions rarely occur when there is high discontent might imply that conflicts over the division of labour can only be positively faced by couples who already have a reasonably equitable division of labour and are able to engage in positive interactions surrounding conflict. This indicates the centrality of the division of labour in marital interactions. While women have a "growing sense of entitlement," clear difficulties exist in putting these goals into practice in relationships that are not based on considerable mutuality (Kluwer, Heesink, and Van de Vliert 1997).◆

men. For instance, persons living alone who are not employed show a difference of 4.9 hours per week. The gender differences are largest for persons with children, at 12.4 hours for employed spouses and 8 hours for employed single parents. As we saw in chapter 4, it is precisely in the case of employed spouses with children that men do the most paid work compared to women.

A study based on data from the early 1970s in Halifax found that not-employed married men did less housework than not-employed single men (Clark and Harvey 1976). Heidi Hartmann (1981: 383) even suggested that married men may be a net drain on domestic work in the sense that they require more housework than they contribute. But the Canadian data in both 1986 and 1992 showed that married men who were not employed did more unpaid work than not-employed men living alone (Table 5.1).

AVERAGE WEEKLY HOURS OF UNPAID WORK BY DEMOGRAPHIC GROUPS, CANADA, 1986 AND 1992

	1986		1992	
	F	M	F	M
All Persons 15+	28.3	14.0	28.5	16.0
Employed	23.2	13.0	21.6	14.7
Not employed	33.3	16.3	33.9	18.5
Wives and husbands	34.5	16.3	33.9	19.3
Employed	27.0	14.4	27.3	17.2
with children	31.9	16.0	32.5	20.1
Not employed	42.3	22.6	42.4	24.7
with children	49.2	25.5	52.3	26.9
Lone Parents	30.9	19.2	34.0	19.5
Employed	25.1	18.6	26.8	18.8
Not employed	36.5	20.6	41.3	20.9
Children 15+ with parents	12.8	7.3	13.0	7.6
Employed	14.5	7.2	13.4	7.4
Not employed	11.2	7.4	12.6	7.8
Persons living alone	22.2	14.1	22.4	16.0
Employed	17.7	12.5	17.8	12.9
Not employed	25.0	16.7	25.2	20.3
Other persons	16.9	11.1	19.1	10.0
Employed	14.0	11.4	13.8	8.6
Not employed	19.6	10.5	24.4	12.2

Source: Statistics Canada, no. 13-603, 3: 67. General Social Survey, 1986, 1992.

TABLE 5.1

Between 1986 and 1992 the gender difference declined for the total population, for husbands and wives, and for persons living alone, mostly because men were doing more unpaid work (Table 5.1). For instance, in the case of employed husbands and wives with children, the gender difference declined from 15.9 to 12.4 hours per week. Still, the gender difference increased for lone parents, for children aged 15 and over who were living with their parents, and for "other persons."

In 1992, among employed persons, for both men and women, lone parents and husbands or wives did the most unpaid work. Conversely, employed persons who were living as "children" in their parents' household, or living alone, did the least (Table 5.1). Among those not employed with children, the gender differences were particularly large: wives did 25.4 hours more work than husbands, and lone mothers did 20.4 more than lone fathers. Husbands who were not employed might have been resisting unpaid work as a remaining source of marital power. Still, they did more unpaid work than employed husbands. Significantly, in proportionate terms the gender differences were largest for children living with their parents (girls did 81 percent more unpaid work than boys) and in husband-wife families (wives did 59 percent more than husbands). It would appear to be in the family situations involving husbands and wives, and especially for older children living at home, that "doing gender" means women doing the most unpaid work compared to men.

SUMMARY OF CANADIAN STUDIES INVOLVING LOCAL SAMPLES

A number of specific studies, then, have focused on the dynamics of the division of domestic work. While these studies largely involved limited samples for given cities or regions, they do represent important observations on the central question of time-use.

Meissner et al. (1975) entitled their 1971 study of 411 couples in Vancouver "No Exit for Wives." When wives did more paid work, they did less domestic work. Husbands did little domestic work, though it increased slightly when wives were employed. When the wife was employed full-time she did 46 hours of paid work and 18 hours of unpaid work, while the husband did 50 hours of paid work and 4 hours of unpaid work. Consequently, the gap in total work was 10 hours. This gap, though, was largely eliminated when wives were working part-time. In selected interviews men showed considerable reluctance to accept working wives as co-providers (see Box 5.6).

Obtaining data from 2,141 respondents in Halifax in the early 1970s, S. Clark and A. Harvey (1976) focused on the differences associated with paid work, marital status, and the presence of young children. The children, they found, had an impact on the hours of paid work of women, but not of men. Married men who were not employed spent less time in housework than non-employed single men. They concluded that for the most part wives did the adaptation in family housework.

In the late 1970s, William Michelson (1985) obtained detailed time-budget data from 538 families in Toronto. Focusing on the impact of wives working, he concluded that there was a cultural lag in accommodating for women's employment. In families in which the wife was working full-time, women worked an average of 1.25 daily hours (paid plus unpaid) more than their husbands. When the wife was not employed, she did an average of 1.75 hours less work than her husband. The time spent was most equal when she worked part-time; then the wife's total work was 0.9 hours more than the husband (pp.65-67). When wives were working full-time, they still did 70 percent of the housework and childcare.

Eugene Lupri and Donald Mills (1987) analyzed the time budgets of 562 married couples in Calgary, surveyed in 1981. Fathers increased their rate of domestic participation somewhat when the families had young children and the mothers were working (Horna and Lupri 1987). But the study's main conclusion was that the husbands' conduct regarding household responsibilities did not change much to accommodate wives' employment. Childless couples, with both partners working, had divided their labour, including both paid work and housework, in a way that approached symmetry, but dual-earner couples with children had far from symmetrical patterns. For cases in which both partners were employed and the family had children, the wife did an average of 38 percent more total work over the week. It would appear that children tend to introduce a more traditional division of labour, even in marriages that started out on a relatively equal footing. Single-earner couples with no children also had a significant gender gap in total work, with housewives working some 30 hours less than their employed husbands. For men, housework was relatively uniform over the life cycle, but for women it expanded with children, producing a gender gap of 22 weekly hours of total work in dual-earner couples with children under six (Lupri 1991: 246). Only 26 fathers were in the category of doing 45 percent or more of the family's domestic work. In these cases at least one parent had a professional job or flexible work schedule.

BOX 5.6 | *Views of Vancouver men on wives as co-providers, 1971*

Out of the over 400 couples in the 1971 Vancouver study, Meissner and his co-authors (1975) interviewed 10 to explore in more depth their feelings and conceptions of the division of paid and domestic work. The selected quotes here include representatives from various social classes.

A forklift driver in his mid-fifties, whose wife worked two days a week as a switchboard operator (they had three children, aged 13 to 22), talked about sharing housework:

> "If a woman *has* to work, then the husband and wife should share the housework, but if it isn't necessary for her to work then she should consider looking after the house first. It isn't necessary for her to work in the first place. She's doing this for herself and to satisfy herself, where the man has to work to keep the house going."

A skilled repairman in his early forties whose wife had been upgrading her education and was contemplating further training was asked how he felt about his wife taking a job (four children, aged 5 to 16):

> "I'd want her home when the kids come home from school or at least when I get home from work. I'm sure as hell not cooking my own supper, I didn't get married for that."

A policeman in his early forties whose wife worked a few hours a week as a salesperson in a store (two children, aged 9 and 13) said about his wife's income:

In 1986 a team of researchers (Le Bourdais, Hamel, and Bernard 1987) obtained summary data on paid and unpaid work time from 1,300 Quebec couples. When both partners were employed, the total work per week was four hours more for women than for men. The authors concluded that the workweek of men and women was similar in numbers of hours, but different in all other regards. In particular, domestic work was marginal for men but comprised a significant component of women's time. In dual-earner couples, women did an average of two-thirds of the domestic work. For the total sample the average increased to three-quarters.

On the basis of 1988 interviews in 250 households in the Great Northern Peninsula of Newfoundland, Peter Sinclair and Lawrence Felt (1992) found that neither the presence of children in the home nor the employment of wives led to significant changes in men's responsibilities for domestic tasks.

Based on a 1984 sample of 796 married persons in Hamilton, D.W. Livingstone and Elizabeth Asner (1996) found that women's average contribution to household income was 17 percent, rising to 27 percent in dual-earning couples. While women's greater involvement in the labour force was bringing a decline in the breadwinner model, male economic power was prevailing across the class structure. The average time per week spent doing housework was 12 hours for men and 27 hours for women. Women's time in

> BOX 5.6 CONT'D

"It doesn't mean anything because it's so little. I told her to put it away into a little account, do whatever you want with it."

He gave his reaction to two recent weeks when his wife's job was full-time:

"To stand back and say there's no way she's going to work steady if this is what it's going to do. It wasn't the money, it was just getting a break from housework to cut the boredom down a little bit and having fun at it and no stress or strain or nothing. Once a job starts to develop the stresses and strains it's not worth it any more. You've lost your sense of direction."

A manager in his mid-thirties whose wife was a full-time housewife (three children, aged 7 to 14) pondered the hypothetical question of his wife taking a job:

"I wouldn't stand in her way, if that's what she wanted to do, but fortunately for me she doesn't want to do that. My wife's first priority should be the family and the home as long as I am able to provide for the family."

A lawyer in his late forties whose wife had just quit a part-time professional job because the double burden was too much (three children, aged 15 to 19) talked about getting housework done:

"If the guy comes home completely beat because he's got a job of much more pressure and his wife has a job because she's bored with the housework, this gives her a lift and she's more up to doing the housework." ◆

Source: Meissner et al. 1975: 438-39.

housework varied from over 30 hours for full-time homemakers to around 20 hours for those employed full-time. There was less variation for men, but they did more if the wife was employed full-time. However, even if the man was not employed and the family was dependent on the wife's income, she did five hours more on average. Livingstone and Asner divided the respondents by social class: the capitalist class consisted of business owners employing two or more persons plus higher level managers; the proletarian class included persons with manual jobs and no supervisory duties; and the intermediate class was made up of professionals and lower-level managers. The most equality came in the "intermediate" category. In dual-earner couples in which both spouses were in the intermediate category, the average domestic work time over the week was 15.1 hours for women and 13.1 for men, while women contributed 30 percent of average family income. The total domestic work was lowest in this intermediate category, possibly because there were fewer dependent children. However, the category also had large differences in terms of partners taking responsibility for domestic tasks; in the total sample women were responsible for 85 percent of the tasks.

Other studies, based on smaller samples, have used more qualitative approaches. Luxton (1980) analyzed the differential situations of three generations of women in Flin Flon, Manitoba, based on data collected in 1976-77. Her findings clearly demonstrated the longer and harder housework day earlier in the century. For women of the first generation, who had set up households in the 1920s and 1930s, tasks such as washing and ironing took whole days, starting with heating the water on a wood stove, then drying clothes outdoors, and finally ironing most items. The women also frequently participated in the domestic production of food through preserving garden vegetables or meat obtained from hunting.

Luxton (1990) returned to Flin Flon in 1981 and this time focused on women from the third generation, who had set up households in the 1960s and 1970s. While in 1976 half of these women had worked outside the home for some period after marriage, none had worked when the children were at preschool ages. By 1981, 44 of the 49 women surveyed were working full-time, even though half of them had preschool children. Luxton focused on their changing identification with the housewife role, and especially on their attempt to reorganize their domestic labour. Men had increased the amount of time spent on domestic labour from 10.8 hours per week in 1976 to 19.1 in 1981. But the domestic work hours of working women had only been reduced from 35.7 to 31.4 hours. Thus

---

BOX 5.7 | *Reallocating domestic work*

In 1981 Luxton interviewed 49 working women in Flin Flon, Manitoba, asking them about how they organized their housework. The women were divided into three categories. A small number did not believe that men, as the main breadwinners, should be involved in housework. These women did a full double day of work, sometimes even working harder than ever at domestic labour to prove they were continuing to do their household duty. A larger group of women felt that women's real work was in the home, but they should be helping to earn money when necessary. These women tended to compromise by doing most of the domestic labour but easing up on their standards. The women in the third category, representing half of the sample, were trying to get their husbands to share the domestic work, but were having much difficulty achieving this change. They used various tactics, ranging from gentle appeals for fairness to militant demands. They

faced difficulty in part because the husbands had higher incomes and were inexperienced at domestic work. When men did help they often did so halfheartedly, doing one small task at a time, while women took overall responsibility and often did multiple tasks at a time.

A recurring theme was that men preferred jobs that involved working with machinery. A number of men were willing to do the vacuuming because they enjoyed playing with the vacuum cleaner. Some men were afraid, though, that they would be subjected to teasing and ridicule if it were publicly known that they did "women's work." One man, for example, did the vacuuming on his knees so that no one would see him from the street.

Furthermore, men "babysat" their own children—something women never did. The implication of this typical reference was that the children were the responsibility of the mother and the father "helped out." Children also

---

the employed wives, all but four of whom were working full-time, were doing 62 percent of the domestic work. Box 5.7 demonstrates some of the power struggles involved in the redistribution of domestic labour, and the consequent tensions between spouses.

Melody Hessing (1993) obtained detailed data from 51 married women in clerical and technical positions at a postsecondary college in 1987-89. Compared to the wife's current position, the husband's job had generally been a more stable element in the organization of the family. The typically higher status of the husbands' jobs was used as a tool for "insulating themselves from work within the home," and the men made few accommodations. While husbands participated in some domestic activities, women retained responsibility for orchestrating this performance. Women sought to accommodate office employment to meet household needs, and they sought various forms of support at home, especially from extended family members and other caregivers. In effect, they were "continuously involved in directing and negotiating the time, people and activities." Clearly, in these two-earner couples, the wives had the continuing responsibility to "make family."

> BOX 5.7 CONT'D

learned from experience that their mothers were more likely to be helpful, and so they would turn to the mother rather than the father for assistance, thus actively perpetuating the traditional division of labour.

Because most couples were unable to openly negotiate a redistribution of labour, they often got locked into tension-producing manipulations. When she started working full-time, one woman first talked to her husband about the sharing of domestic work. He agreed in principle, but would not do specific jobs, even when he had agreed to do them. She decided to get him to do the laundry. First she left the laundry basket of sorted clothes sitting at the top of the basement stairs. As he was going down to his workroom she asked him to take the laundry down and put it on top of the machine. She repeated this several times until he automatically took the basket down without being asked. Next she asked him, as he went down with the basket, to put the laundry into the machine. Later she asked him to put

in the soap and turn the machine on. Finally she began getting him to pick up the dirty clothes. Eventually, after more than six months of careful, though unstated, strategizing on her part, the man was doing all the work involved in laundry. The woman was bitter about the whole experience: "I fooled him and now he does it; but the whole thing's really stupid."

Luxton concluded that these women were having difficulty because they were challenging traditional notions of masculinity and femininity. Moreover, they were doing this on their own, in individual households. In other parts of society where gender assumptions have been challenged, change has occurred with the help of status of women committees, employment equity legislation, and the equality provisions of the Charter of Rights and Freedoms. Generally speaking, however, efforts to challenge gender assumptions around housework do not have access to such policy levers. ◆

Source: Adapted from Luxton 1990: 39-54.

In a sample of 117 immigrant men in Toronto, Tony Haddad and Lawrence Lam (1988) found that the men's participation in domestic work was increased after coming to Canada, but it was mostly in the "helping out" category. Only a small minority of the wives had worked outside the home before coming to Canada, but most held jobs at the time of the interview. The majority category for men was called "adapters," in the sense that they were somewhat forced to do more domestic work in the circumstances. However, their involvement in family work was often "rationalized as temporary and situational, as imposed by their life circumstances."

Based on a sample of 179 couples in Sudbury in 1993-94, Christiane Bernier, Simon Laflamme, and Run-Min Zhou (1996) concluded that while women were continuing to do more domestic work, the differences were reduced in comparison to previous studies. When they took child care into account, the division was less equal. While both women and men do more work when they have children, women are more affected by the presence of children. Based on an analysis of age, education, occupation, and the relative income of spouses, the researchers found that women's paid work was a "trump card" against their exploitation through domestic work. If the woman worked outside the home, the man participated more at home. Occupational prestige, income, and education played much smaller roles than work status and the relative income of spouses.

Looking toward the future, Bernier and her co-authors (1996) noted that greater labour-force participation, along with fewer children, should further reduce the gender differences in housework, although the persistent income inequality both in the society and in families perpetuates the inequality. While more equality exists when incomes are relatively equal, the reduction in the gender differentiation in domestic work time is not limited to such couples, nor is this reduction concentrated in younger, educated, or affluent couples. Based on their observation that reduced inequality in the time spent on domestic work was occurring in various types of couples, though to varying degrees, the authors concluded that a change was happening in the structure of society, though it was still far from feminist ideals.

While it is impossible to generalize on the basis of a series of specific studies in different locations, it would appear that the change over time is at least toward a greater openness to sharing domestic work. The 1971 study by Meissner et al. (1975) and the 1994 study by Bernier, Laflamme, and Zhou (1996), both published in *Canadian Review of Sociology and Anthropology*, display a sharp contrast. The distinction is strongest in the qualitative parts of these studies: the earlier study speaks of "no exit for wives" and the second notes a reduction in the inequality in the sharing of domestic work across various types of couples. The differences between men and women are also greater when the responsibility for domestic tasks is compared rather than the time-use in these tasks. It would appear that the most symmetry in time-use occurs in dual-earner couples, when both partners are intermediate in the class structure, that is, professionals or managers but not the higher level managers. Difficulties also occur for given couples in changing established patterns of division of work, which points to the importance of a continuous paid work commitment on the part of both spouses as a factor in achieving greater symmetry in non-paid work.

EXPLANATIONS OF THE DISTRIBUTION OF UNPAID WORK

In his study of the sexual division of household labour, Haddad (1996) uses the subtitle "pragmatic strategies or patriarchal dynamics." In effect, the broader understandings of the distribution of unpaid work can be usefully divided into these two perspectives. Julie Brines (1994) makes a similar division by comparing economic and cultural considerations. The economic perspective, or pragmatic strategies approach, pays particular attention to the relative amount of available time, income, and other resources that spouses exchange for unpaid work. The cultural perspective, or patriarchal dynamics approach, sees housework as a form of doing gender; it finds that there is something about gender itself that maintains an inequality in unpaid work.

The pragmatic strategies approach is based on liberal-functionalist conceptions of society. Talcott Parsons and Robert Bales (1955) argued that a role differentiation between expressive and instrumental activities permitted a functional allocation of tasks. Similarly, Robert Blood and Donald Wolfe (1960) argued that the amount of unpaid work was a function of the relative resources of spouses. The person with more resources would do less domestic work. Gary Becker (1965, 1981) bases his understanding of families on the efficiency obtained by spousal specialization in income generation and unpaid work respectively. In effect, these conceptions are based on the view that the key issue is not gender, but rather a pragmatic allocation of tasks. As Haddad (1996) indicates, this approach assumes that it is individual abilities that count, rather than differences in the opportunity structures of women and men.

The *patriarchal dynamics* approach challenges the notion that sexual inequality is founded on individual differences in abilities. For instance, Frederick Engels (1975) argued that families are the primary site of the subordination and oppression of women. Delphy and Leonard (1992) interpret domestic work in terms of husbands exploiting the products of women's labour. Similarly, Hartmann (1981: 372) proposes that the family is the primary arena in which men experience their patriarchal power over women's labour. In this framework, women's greater involvement in domestic labour is a key element in sexual inequality (Haddad 1996: 89). It is around household work that gender relations are produced and reproduced on a daily basis (Berk 1985).

Both of these broad theoretical conceptions are useful for interpreting specific empirical observations. In particular, the residual that remains unexplained after we take into account a variety of individual differences is support for the role of gender. In addition, the stronger sex differences in unpaid work within married couples, compared to men and women living alone, indicates that married persons have a further arena in which they "do gender." Still, the cases in which couples are relatively egalitarian in their division of labour would indicate that gender does not necessarily involve patriarchal exploitation. Researchers have even pointed out cases in which individual abilities, circumstances, and interests lead men to perform a disproportionate share of domestic work (Coltrane 1996).

These broad theoretical views can also be related to more immediate factors. The economic or practical perspective pays particular attention to *relative resources* and *time avail-*

ability, while the cultural or patriarchal perspective focuses on questions of *ideology* and *gender*. When appropriate measures are available on a large sample, research has found the variables related to each of these factors to be statistically significant (Kano 1988). Brines (1994), also finding support for both economic and cultural considerations, concludes that matters of relative resources apply especially to women who typically do more unpaid work if they do less paid work. Cultural questions especially apply to men, who sometimes even seek to avoid housework if they are economically dependent. Avoiding housework is a form of doing gender, and it may be particularly relevant to those men who do not have access to other forms of status.

Relative resources

The basic idea of this perspective is that households seek efficiency by allocating their resources to achieve the greatest possible family well-being. In terms of unpaid work, the person who brings more resources into the relationship can exchange this for doing less onerous work around the house. Relative resources may be seen as a measure of the differential power of spouses, and negotiations regarding domestic work are based on this relative power.

Spain and Bianchi (1996: 169) observed in U.S. surveys that husbands were performing a greater share of domestic tasks and child care in families in which wives worked outside of the home, and the higher the wife's contribution to the family's income, the more equitable the division of labour in the home. Berk (1985) found that a wife's contribution to domestic work was influenced both by her employment income and the husband's income. Similarly, Yoshinori Kano (1988) found that the husband's share of domestic work was negatively related to his earnings and positively related to his wife's earnings. In addition, power was the strongest variable in the analysis: persons with more power did less domestic work. Harriet Presser (1994) found that a wife's earnings relative to her husband's was a particularly important variable in increasing the husband's share in household tasks. In an Alberta sample, the greater the wife's income relative to the husband, the greater his involvement in cooking and cleaning (Harrell 1995). In their Hamilton sample, Livingstone and Asner (1996) found that the bargaining power coming from a partner's own income and share in the family income played the largest role in explaining time-use in domestic activity. A study of a national Canadian sample also found relative income and personal resources to be significant factors associated with the amount of housework of women and men (Nakhaie 1995).

A difficulty of the resource model is the absence of considerations for the normative and institutional constraints on people's behaviour—which may be why other tests based on Canadian data have found little support (Haddad 1996; McFarlane 1997). Using 1986 and 1992 time-use data respectively, the analyses by Haddad and Seth McFarlane attribute little predictive value to relative income—that is, to a person's income relative to total family income. In addition, the 1986 data show that income and education are positively related to men's domestic work, contrary to the predictions of the resource model. The differential applicability of the exchange model to women and men leads Brines (1994) to question the gender-neutral paradigm on which it is based. Men who are dependent because they have lost their job were in fact found to be doing less domestic work. The model would appear to apply more adequately to women, who tend to do more domestic work when they are economically dependent.

Questions of relative resources are based on a model in which spouses specialize because that is the most efficient productive strategy. However, as Valerie Oppenheimer (1994) argues, this "trading model" makes more sense when one sex has limited opportunities in the paid labour market. Specialization in domestic work has always presented problems in terms of the well-being of women following marital separation. With the deteriorating relative economic status of young men, specialization presents further problems for young couples. Especially in its extreme form, sex-role segregation increases vulnerability. The two-earner model thus becomes an adaptive strategy. In particular, it provides an insurance against the loss of the breadwinner's earning capacity and against his unwillingness to share income with a (former) spouse. Oppenheimer (1994: 333) concludes, "If the basis for marriage is specialization and exchange, then marriage seems an increasingly anachronistic social form." The alternative of a collaborative model has a stronger basis in a low fertility society in which the opportunity structure involves less gender difference and consequently women's economic well-being is not contingent on entry into reproductive relations.

Time availability

Time availability includes both the extent to which people are available to do domestic work, given their paid work, and the family demands on their time, given in particular the number and ages of children. In effect, this factor considers questions of immediate practicality with regard to doing unpaid work. Kano (1988) found that a husband reduced his share of domestic work if he worked full-time and increased if he worked part-time; in addition, he increased his share if his wife worked full-time and reduced it if she worked part-time. Presser (1994) found that having more children increased the hours of domestic work for both spouses but also reduced the husband's share in household tasks.

Based on a 1981 Canadian time-budget survey, Robin Douthitt (1989) found that, when wives were employed, the husbands with no children did 9.2 hours of weekly domestic work, but they did an average of 19.2 hours if there were young children in the family. Within couples with children under five, husbands did 19.2 hours of domestic work when the wife was employed compared to 17.3 when she was not employed. While these variations for men were in the expected directions, women's domestic work was clearly higher, and the study showed stronger variations by presence and ages of children as well as by their own work status. In another study based on Canadian data, M. Rela Nakhaie (1995) found that paid hours of work were particularly important in explaining gender differences in unpaid work. In effect, the author observes of the total sample, "Females do more housework because gender stands as a proxi of a relatively fewer paid hours of work by women compared to men" (p.419).

In the analyses based on the 1986 and 1992 Canadian data, both men and women did less domestic work if they did more paid work (Haddad 1996; McFarlane 1997). Also, as would be expected, the presence of young children increased the amount of time spent in domestic work and child care—although this increase applied more to women than to men. An analysis based on the 1982 Canadian survey of Class Structure and Class Consciousness also found that women who did more hours of paid work did less domestic work but not less child care (Carrier 1995). In addition, the researchers found that men's paid work influenced women's housework, more so than women's paid work influenced men's housework.

Based on U.S. data from the early 1980s, Goldscheider and Waite (1991: 189) found that wives who were not employed did 75 percent of domestic work, while those doing 50 hours of paid work in a week did 56 percent of the family's domestic work. Employment alone is not found to make much difference for women's domestic work, but full-time employment in better paying jobs, as well as career commitment, does make a difference.

Employment schedules are significant determinants of men's domestic work in dual-earner families (Presser 1994). In particular, when men are at home without their spouses, especially during the day, they do more domestic work. Shelley Coverman (1985) also found that variables relating to available time were the most powerful predictors of the husband's hours of domestic work.

Similarly, Sampson Lee Blair and Daniel Lichter (1991) found that female employment was positively related to men's absolute and proportionate contribution to housework. They interpreted the employment of wives as a power variable: that is, matters of relative resources and time availability make the same prediction, that more paid work on the part of wives increases their resources in negotiating domestic work and reduces their time available for unpaid work. Blair and Lichter analyze especially the segregation of household tasks. When tasks are highly segregated, this differentiation is reduced when men are working less than 20 hours or women are working more than 40 hours. Lorraine Davies and Donna McAlpine (1998) found that the amount of domestic work done by spouses is most similar when the man is not employed—when he has more time on his hands. Nonetheless, this Canadian sample found that women who were not employed were doing three-quarters of the domestic work, while men who were not employed were doing less than half.

Ideology

In the context of unpaid work, ideology refers to the behaviour expected of women and men, and especially the extent to which women and men endorse the principle of gender equity. In this regard too, contrary to their treatment as factors that would increase a person's resources, we would treat higher educational and occupational status as factors that promote more equality in domestic work by increasing men's and reducing women's involvement.

Based on data from the 1995 General Social Survey, Nancy Zukenwick Ghalam (1997) found that Canadian attitudes were contradictory, characterized by both traditional and contemporary views on the division of labour by sex. For instance, 73 percent of women and 68 percent of men believed that both spouses should contribute to household income, but 51 percent of women and 59 percent of men said a preschool child was likely to suffer if both parents were employed.

Presser (1994) found that when both spouses had professional or managerial occupations, husbands did a larger share of the total domestic work. This may be because those couples buy more services that reduce the wife's share, or because the men are more egalitarian. However, ideological considerations are probably the explanation for another finding from this study: a higher education on the part of the husband increases his domestic work and reduces the wife's. In the specific measure of gender ideology, the wife's ideology was particularly relevant. Presser concluded that men appeared to be more responsive to their wives' role expectations than to their own gender ideology. Based on data from the same 1987-88 U.S. National Survey of Families and Households, Theodore Greenstein (1996) found that the husband's ideology was not a significant predictor unless the wife was also egalitarian. Husbands did relatively little domestic work unless both spouses were relatively egalitarian in their beliefs about gender and marital roles.

A small Dutch sample (Van Dongen 1995) also provides evidence regarding the importance of ideology. In it men indicated, contrary to what one might expect from negotiations associated with relative resources, that they wanted to be *more* involved in child care. An older analysis of domestic role-sharing in Sweden suggested that although that model was on the increase, it faced two obstacles (Haas 1981): children, who decreased the chances for equality, at least in the short term; and attitudes toward men's roles as breadwinners. Presser (1994) observed that questions of gender ideology might also be involved in standards of household maintenance. In particular, it seems that greater equity within the home can be achieved through reductions in women's standards as well as by enhancing men's participation.

The causal mechanisms associated with ideology or gender-role attitudes do not easily lend themselves to interpretation. A willingness to consider alternatives to traditional roles, although important, can also be a rationalization for a behavioural change that has already occurred. While persons who have sought to change attitudes in an egalitarian direction might like to take credit for changes in behaviour, studies of innovative behaviour in the family area do not point to ideological questions as the key element of change. For instance, in a study of two-career marriages in Chicago, Rosanna Hertz (1986) did not find that spouses were particularly concerned about feminist or egalitarian issues. Instead they were both career- and achievement-oriented, rather than conscientiously seeking a new relationship called a dual-career marriage. Similarly, Ann Duffy, Nancy Mandell, and Noreen Pupo (1989) found that full-time housewives were no more traditional in ideology than employed mothers. Among fathers who shared extensively in child care, Coltrane (1996) found traditional attitudes, such as not wanting to leave the children with strangers. Patricia Jane Carrier's (1995) analysis based on 1982 Canadian data found that men in female-dominated occupations did more domestic work. It could be that men in such occupations are more feminist in their gender-role attitudes. But it could also be that female-dominated occupations have established more family-friendly practices that increase the potential for family time of both female and male workers.

The analysis of ideology involves a further complexity; there are often contradictions. Hochschild (1989: 190) demonstrated that people's ideas about gender are often fractured and incoherent. For instance, there may be differences between what people say they believe, what they seem to feel, and what their actual behaviour implies. A man may speak an egalitarian language but hold deep sexist views, just as he may espouse traditional gender concepts and still do female household tasks. Indeed, a study of married men in Toronto found that their sex-role orientation did not influence the amount of housework they did, but the work hours of their wives did make a difference (Lam and Haddad 1992).

Gender

The focus here is on the material and cultural basis on which social relations between men and women are realized. Berk (1985) finds that the allocation of time and tasks in household production not only produces goods and services, but also produces gender. In particular, the total work to be done influences the wife's but not the husband's domestic work tasks and time. She concludes, "The division of household labour represents a process whereby both gender and work shape and are shaped by each other" (p.185). Feree (1990) argues that the symbolic and structural division of labour, both paid and unpaid, is one of the key ways in which families construct gender. Stated differently, gender itself has meanings associated with housework. For Hartmann (1981: 393), the creation of gender can be thought of as the creation of a division of labour between the sexes, of two categories of workers who depend on each other.

Based on data from Halifax, Shaw (1988) analyzed the different meanings attributed to housework by women and men. These differences could be attributed to "the fact that household labour is closely associated with the female gender role and as such is thought of as women's work." In particular, men perceived more freedom of choice in their participation in housework activities, while women more often evaluated their own performance in these activities.

In making a case for a cultural perspective on domestic work, Brines (1994: 661) observes, "Marriage provides a setting for childbearing, the division of labor... and a stage for the enactment of claims... particularly those attached to the deepest sense of what one is—one's gender identity." Consequently, when wives are the main providers couples may resort to traditional divisions of housework for reasons of doing gender. In effect, wives tend to do more housework if they are more dependent, as the relative resources model predicts. But husbands, according to this study, did less housework when they depended on their wives for income. Haddad (1996) also found that women who earned more than half of the family income did more domestic work. Brines concludes that this gender asymmetry may be partly understood through the cultural framing of manhood as an accomplishment and masculinity as "not feminine," that is, as someone who does not do domestic work. In effect, her analysis found that men did least housework if they were complete providers or completely supported. Haddad (1996) found that the men who were equal earners did the most housework, possibly because their masculinity was less dependent on avoiding domestic work.

Several authors have concluded that gender is a crucial variable, based on the observation that the variation in women's and men's participation in domestic work remains largely unexplained, even by the theoretically important variables of relative resources, time availability, and gender ideology. While these variables explain some of the difference, there is need for a further explanation of the remaining uniformity wherein women do more domestic work than men (Shelton 1990; Calastanti and Bailey 1991; Leslie, Anderson, and Branson 1991). Especially for specific household tasks, role-sharing is limited, and spheres of domestic activity are highly segregated by sex (Blair and Lichter 1991).

Further support for the importance of gender itself emerges from the frequent observation that models apply differently to women and men. While, for instance, women's time at work reduces their time available for domestic work and thus increases the husband's relative share in domestic work, men's time at work does not have such an influence (Peterson and Gerson 1992). Seth McFarlane (1997) also finds important asymmetry between women and men in terms of the variables affecting domestic work. In particular, for couples where both are working full-time, men's time in domestic work does not respond to the number and ages of children, or to the wife's hours of paid work. Women's domestic work does respond to the spouse's time in paid work. More broadly, authors have concluded that the relative stability in the division of domestic labour points to the importance of gender roles (see, for instance, Shelton 1990).

Nonetheless, the examples that depart from the typical patterns can help us understand the possibilities for change in these gendered processes. From his analysis of select parents who said they shared at least some aspects of parenting, Coltrane (1996) predicts an increase in future sharing, because sharing is more likely to occur in certain conditions: when wives are employed more hours and more attached to their jobs; when women earn more of the total household income and, especially, become co-providers; when wives negotiate for change and relinquish control over managing the home and children; when there is more ideological support for gender equality; when husbands are employed fewer hours; when fathers are involved in the care of infants; and when families are smaller. In addition, women who delay parenting and women who remarry are more likely to be able to negotiate a more equitable arrangement.

The life course and the exchange and gender perspectives

The various stages of the life course also have a bearing on the division of domestic labour, as we've already seen. For instance, when there are children, mothers do a larger share of total household labour (Presser 1994). Other interesting observations can be related to marital status and work history. For instance, in the analysis of the segregation of household tasks, Blair and Lichter (1991) found somewhat less segregation for persons who had been married for fewer than five years, and for those cohabiting rather than married. Using the 1987-88 U.S. National Survey of Families and Households, Scott South and Glenna Spitze (1994) found that the gender gap in weekly hours of housework exists for all marital status groups, but it is largest for married persons. Masoko Ishii-Kuntz and Coltrane (1992) observe from this same data set that remarried husbands participate more in housework. In step-parent families, children do more, which in turn encourages fathers to do more. The highest contributions by husbands occur for remarried biological parents. Nonetheless, these husbands are still doing less than a quarter of total housework.

The gender perspective would suggest that gender is produced differently in different types of households. Remarriage, cohabitation, and childlessness may involve different forms of negotiation around the gender division of household labour. Possibly, women with previous marriages may be selecting subsequent partners who are more willing to share in domestic work (Sullivan 1997; Presser 1994).

Again using the National Survey of Families and Households for 1987-88, Joe Pittman and David Blanchard (1996) demonstrate the importance of the wife's employment history. First of all they note a strong sex differential, with men having worked 79 percent and women 53 percent of the time since age 18. Even using a crude measure that does not separate full-time and part-time work history, a more extensive employment history leads to doing less housework oneself, and to a spouse doing more. Pittman and Blanchard conclude that for both spouses, when men's contribution to housework is being negotiated, employment continuity is a more important bargaining chip than income or occupational status. They suggest, "Couples may not perceive an imbalanced allocation of housework as inequitable, even when wives are currently employed, unless the wives have made a long-term commitment to employment and breadwinning, evidenced by continuity of work history." These results are less easily interpreted within a gender perspective. One might say that work history provides a material condition that determines the dynamics under which couples do gender. Alternatively, work history may help set up some of the boundaries for the accommodations that couples make concerning paid and unpaid work.

The culture perspective suggests that "doing gender" would be different in different contexts as defined by marital status and household arrangements. In particular, persons who are single, cohabiting, remarried, or without children may negotiate gender differently—which supports the observations made in chapter 3 that the tendencies to cohabitation and divorce are transforming relationships before, during, and after marriage. Part of this transformation may be associated with the division of domestic work.

The exchange perspective suggests that people may do different kinds of exchanges, but exchanges themselves remain important to relationships. In a breadwinner-homemaker arrangement, it might be concluded that instrumental activities are exchanged for expressive ones. However, it is more useful to observe the exchanges occurring at each of the instrumental and expressive levels. The exchanges at the expressive level involve empathy, companionship, and sexuality. At the instrumental level they involve earning a living and maintaining a household. It would appear that work history, and the scheduling of the jobs of spouses, are connected to the forms of exchange that take place. Thus the exchange need not be, "I will earn the income if you look after the house and children." It may instead be, "I'll start supper if you pick up the birthday cake on the way home."

The theoretical perspectives that attempt to explain the distribution of unpaid work have therefore focused on economic (relative resources and time availability of spouses) and cultural questions (ideology and conceptions of gender). While all of these factors are pertinent, it would appear that gender itself plays a key role, with unpaid work being one of the important bases on which we "do gender." This perspective would also suggest that gender is produced differently not only in different types of households, but also over the life course. The centrality of the spouses' work commitments, measured especially in terms of continuity, also alters the material conditions under which couples do gender. This gender perspective may be brought into an exchange framework. In other words, the exchanges between spouses, whether they are traditional or egalitarian, are conditioned by understandings concerning gender. These gender understandings and processes are in turn determined by the relative opportunity structures of males and females in families and in the broader society.

TIME-USE AND PARTICIPATION IN DOMESTIC ACTIVITIES: SURVEY DATA

Time-use was the content area of one of the five cycles of the General Social Survey, a telephone survey with 9,744 and 9,815 respondents in 1986 and 1992 respectively (Harvey, Marshall, and Frederick 1991; Frederick 1995). These findings provided the first nationally representative data on time-use. Following conventions established in a number of countries, the survey first contacted the respondents and asked them if they would be willing to take note of the timing of their activities on a given day. The interviewer and respondent then went over the 24-hour day under investigation, starting at four o'clock in the morning. The survey obtained only information on the main activity of a given time, which was subsequently coded into 95 and 166 categories in 1986 and 1992 respectively. The fact that only the main activity of a given time was coded especially affects the time spent in child care. Judith Frederick (1995: 30) estimates that three-quarters of child care is carried out as a secondary activity.

For our purposes, these activities can be collapsed into four components. *Paid work* involves actual work time, plus driving and other activities associated with the work, and time spent in education. *Unpaid* work involves household work (cooking and washing up, housekeeping, maintenance and repair, other household work), shopping for goods and services, and child care. It also takes in civic and voluntary activity, which includes assisting persons outside of the household and assisting adults in the household (for example, personal care, elder care, medical care, coaching). These two types of work—paid and unpaid—are called productive activities. The other two components are *personal time* (sleep, meals, religious services) and *leisure activities* (socializing, passive leisure, such as television, entertainment events, and active leisure).

For instance, in 1992 the average day involved 4.2 hours (17 percent of the total time) of paid work, 3.6 hours (15 percent) of unpaid work, 10.5 hours (44 percent) of personal time, and 5.7 hours (24 percent) of leisure (Frederick 1995: 7-8). The productive activities amounted to an average of just under eight hours or a third of people's time (Table 5.2). For the total population aged 15 and over, the sex differences in total productive time were very small, amounting to 0.1 more hours for men in 1986 and 0.1 more hours for women in 1992. The change from 1986 to 1992 involved an increase in unpaid work for both sexes, but more so for men. In addition, paid work declined for men.

In part, the similarity between the overall averages for women and men resulted from the greater variation for women: employed wives do the most total work, while non-employed wives do the least (Haddad 1996: 107). Among employed persons, women consistently have slightly more total productive work time than men, amounting to an average of 18 minutes per day or 2.1 hours per week in 1986. For couples in which the respondent and spouse were both employed full-time, the total work time of women in 1992 was once again 2.2 hours more per week than men (McFarlane 1997).

As an average for the whole population, the total productive time of women and men shows little difference (see also Che-Alford, Allan, and Butlin 1994: 39-40). But the two components of this time show important differences (Figure 5.1). In 1992 men spent an average of 1.8 more hours per day than women on paid work, and women spent 1.9 more hours on unpaid work. For every hour that men spent on unpaid work, then, women spent 1.73 hours; for every hour that women spent on paid work, men spent 1.55 hours. The inclusion of a broader spectrum of paid and unpaid work, including education, travelling associated with work, child care, elder care, and volunteer activities, reduced the gender difference. We can no longer say that women do twice as much unpaid work while men do twice as much paid work (Thompson and Walker 1989).

Similarly, the "down time" associated with personal care and leisure shows little difference for women and men. Men do, however, spend 0.5 hours more per day in leisure time, and women spend 0.5 hours more in personal care time.

**TIME USE (AVERAGE HOURS PER DAY) OF TOTAL
POPULATION AND EMPLOYED PERSONS, 1986 AND 1992**

| | POPULATION 15+ | | | | EMPLOYED PERSONS | | | |
| | 1986 | | 1992 | | 1986 | | 1992 | |
	M	F	M	F	M	F	M	F
Total productive activity	7.5	7.4	7.7	7.8	9.0	9.2	9.1	9.4
Paid work and education	5.6	3.3	5.1	3.3	7.2	6.0	6.8	5.9
Unpaid work	1.9	4.1	2.6	4.5	1.8	3.2	2.3	3.5
Personal care	10.8	11.2	10.3	10.8	10.2	10.6	9.9	10.3
Leisure/free time	5.7	5.3	6.0	5.5	4.8	4.2	5.1	4.3
TOTAL	24.0	24.0	24.0	24.0	24.0	24.0	24.0	24.0

Source: Ghalam 1993: 53; Devereau 1993: 13-16; Harvey, Marshall, and Frederick 1991: 31. Statistics Canada, General Social Survey, 1986, 1992.

TABLE 5.2

Marital status and the life course

Time-use varies considerably over the life course, and across the marital status categories. Figure 5.2 illustrates a progression in amounts of productive time from those who are single to those who are married or cohabitating and then a decline for the formerly married who are not living alone and for the formerly married living alone.

In the age group 25-44, for women, paid work increases with marriage and increases even further for the formerly married, especially if they are living alone. Women's unpaid work decreases a little with marriage, but declines significantly for the formerly married, especially if they are living alone. Consequently, women's total work varies less by marital status, but it is highest for married women. For men, paid work is highest for the married and for the formerly married who are living alone. Men's unpaid work is also highest for the married category, and consequently their total work is highest in this group. There are clear gender differences in paid and unpaid work, especially for the married persons in this age group, but, equally important, the married are identical in average total work. Women's total work is higher than men's for the formerly married who are not living alone, while men's total work is higher than women's for the formerly married who are living alone.

At age groups 45-65, and especially at 15-24, married men's average total work is higher than that of married women. The gender differences remain for those aged 65 and over, especially for those who are formerly married and not living alone. Still, single persons aged 65 and over have similar total work, mostly unpaid, at about four hours per day.

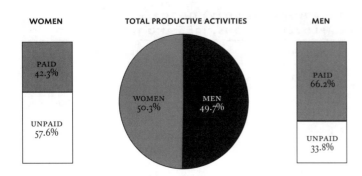

FIG 5.1 Relative share of time in productive activities, women and men
aged 15 and over, Canada, 1992

NOTE: Based on averages per capita.

Source: See Table 5.2. Statistics Canada, General Social Survey, 1992.

Marital and parental status

In *As Time Goes By: Time Use of Canadians*, Frederick (1995) observed that the main factors affecting the distribution of activities were a person's labour-force activity, along with sex, marital status, and parental status. Those doing the most work were married parents with both partners working full-time. The most equal by gender in total productive time were persons aged 65 and over along with younger non-parents. Frederick found that the baby boom generation—persons aged 25-44 in 1992—was the group facing the biggest challenges in balancing job, family, career-building, child-bearing, and child-rearing, along with community responsibilities. But that generation also had the highest family income, because there were more two-earner families.

Table 5.3 illustrates the main results from this baby boom generation. In parental status, the gender gap in total work is smallest for those married with no children, and the gap is largest for married parents. Those who are not married and have no children work about 8.5 hours per day, the average being just slightly higher for women than men. Compared to the single group, marriage without children brings more paid work for both spouses, less unpaid work for women, and more unpaid work for men. However, these persons without children remain quite similar, with an average of 7 hours of paid and 2 hours of unpaid work.

Compared to the unmarried with no children, both marriage and children therefore increase the total productive activity of men and women aged 25-44. However, as long as there are no children, marriage actually reduces the gender gap, both in paid and in unpaid work. It is for married parents that the gender gap increases in total productive time, and especially affected is the distribution by paid and unpaid categories.

For the most part, the gender gap in total hours is not large. Nonetheless, Frederick (1995: 32) observed that it amounted to 3 hours per week for married parents working full-time in this baby boom generation. What is more significant is the reduction in women's paid work when there are children. This may "jeopardize their economic future, and that of their children, especially in the event of marital dissolution" (Frederick 1995: 32).

The leisure hours are in many respects the converse of the productive work hours. In each category, men have more leisure hours, but marriage and children bring more similarities. In each of the categories shown in Table 5.3, women have more personal time,

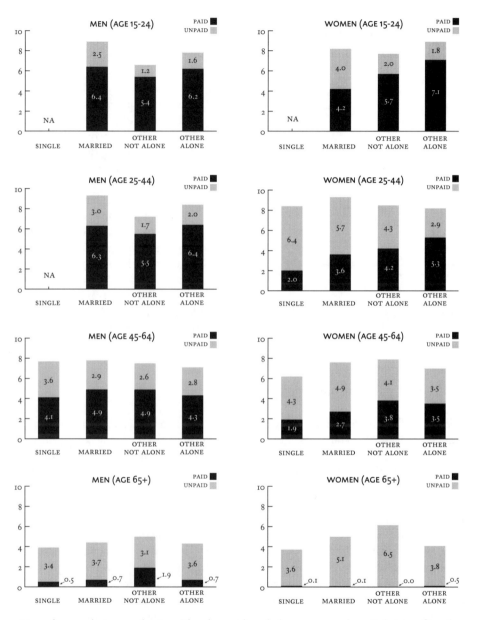

FIG 5.2 Average hours per day in paid and unpaid work, by sex, age and marital status, Canada, 1992

Source: Special tabulations from Statistics Canada, 1992 General Social Survey.

TIME USE (HOURS PER DAY) OF POPULATION AGED 25-44 BY MARITAL AND PARENTAL STATUS, 1992

	UNMARRIED NO CHILDREN		MARRIED NO CHILDREN		MARRIED PARENTS	
	M	F	M	F	M	F
Total productive activity	8.4	8.7	9.3	9.4	9.9	10.3
Paid work and education	7.0	6.0	7.3	7.0	6.7	5.5
Unpaid work	1.5	2.6	2.0	2.4	3.2	4.8
Personal care	9.7	10.4	9.8	10.5	9.7	10.1
Leisure/free time	5.9	4.9	4.9	4.0	4.4	3.6
TOTAL	24.0	24.0	24.0	24.0	24.0	24.0

NOTE: Married includes cohabitating.

Source: Frederick 1995: 21, 22, 26. Statistics Canada, 1992 General Social Survey.

TABLE 5.3

though the differences are smallest for married parents.

The 1992 U.S. National Study of the Changing Workforce (Yu and Moen 1997) shows similar results. In particular, both working wives and husbands do the most domestic work when children are young and the least when they do not have children at home. In addition, wives who work part-time, have shift jobs, or are self-employed do more domestic work. In effect, working wives often seek these alternative work arrangements as a means of dealing with the shifting domestic demands over the life course. The non-professional husbands married to professional spouses spend the most time caring for preschool children. Men generally do not adopt strategies like part-time work to allow them to do more housework.

Marital, parental, and employment status

Table 5.4 further differentiates productive activities by various characteristics of households and individuals. The table breaks down two categories of living arrangements: people living in husband-wife families and people not in such families. The parental status is based on the presence and ages of children. For husband-wife families, the table shows three categories of employment status: both employed full-time, two employed but not both full-time, and one employed. For those who are not in husband-wife families, the table distinguishes those employed full-time from those who are either working part-time or not employed. These results are based on the age group 30-54.

The average total productive work time is essentially identical for this population of persons at mid-life. The difference comes to 0.005 hour per day or under two hours per year.

In total productive time, for both women and men the figures are highest when either both spouses or a lone parent are working full-time. Total time is also higher when there are children under 19, and especially if the children are under 6 years of age. Consequently, the most total work, an average of 10.6 hours per day, is done by women where both are working full-time and there are children under six years of age. The total productive time is similarly high for men in this category, amounting to 10.2 hours per day.

The husband-wife families show the most similarity between men and women in total work when both are employed but are not both working full-time. For instance, women have 0.7 of an hour more per day when they are both working full-time, and men have 1 more hour per day if only one is employed. In the intermediate category, in which both are employed but not both full-time, men have 0.3 more total work time per day. The observation is even more pronounced with children aged 0-5, where the intermediate category (both employed) involves the same figure of 9.8 hours for men and women. When there are no children under 19, women do about an hour more work if both are employed full-time, while men do about an hour more in categories of husband-wife families where they are not both working full-time.

When both partners are working full-time, men's average paid work amounts to 6.5 hours, while women's amounts to 6 hours. Conversely, men's unpaid work

TIME USE (HOURS PER DAY) IN PAID AND UNPAID WORK BY SEX, FAMILY STATUS, EMPLOYMENT STATUS, AND PRESENCE OF CHILDREN, PERSONS AGED 30-54, CANADA, 1992

	MEN			WOMEN		
	PAID	UNPAID	TOTAL	PAID	UNPAID	TOTAL
H-W FAMILIES						
Both FT	6.5	2.9	9.4	6.0	4.1	10.1
Child 0-5	6.4	3.7	10.2	4.9	5.8	10.6
Child 6-18	6.4	2.9	9.3	5.5	4.4	9.9
No child	6.8	2.3	9.2	7.3	2.9	10.2
Two employed	6.6	2.8	9.4	3.0	6.1	9.1
Child 0-5	6.3	3.5	9.8	1.9	7.9	9.8
Child 6-18	6.5	2.8	9.3	3.5	5.9	9.4
No child	7.1	2.1	9.2	3.0	5.1	8.1
One employed	6.1	3.0	9.0	1.2	6.8	8.0
Child 0-5	6.3	3.7	9.9	0.5	8.9	9.4
Child 6-18	5.8	3.0	8.7	1.4	6.4	7.8
No child	6.2	2.2	8.4	1.4	5.8	7.1
NOT IN H-W FAMILIES						
Employed FT	7.0	1.7	8.7	5.7	3.2	8.9
Child 0-5	—	—	—	5.2	4.7	9.9
Child 6-18	6.0	3.2	9.2	5.3	3.9	9.2
No child	7.1	1.6	8.7	5.9	2.9	8.7
Employed PT or not employed	2.3	2.9	5.2	1.6	5.2	6.7
Child 0-5	—	—	—	0.5	7.6	8.2
Child 6-18	0.0	3.7	3.7	1.5	6.3	7.8
No child	2.5	2.8	5.2	1.8	4.0	5.8
TOTAL	6.1	2.8	8.9	3.7	5.2	8.9

NOTE: — =fewer than 5 cases; FT=full-time; PT=part-time; H-W=husband-wife; two employed- excludes cases where both are working full-time; child 6-18 excludes cases where there are children 0-5; no child=no children under 19; total includes cases of husband-wife families where neither are employed, and cases of marital status not stated. The total sample is 4,163 cases.

Source: Special tabulations from the Statistics Canada, 1992 General Social Survey.

TABLE 5.4

amounts to 2.9 hours while women's comes to 4.1 hours. These differences are even stronger when there are children aged 0-5 present.

In her analysis of persons aged 25-44, Frederick (1995: 27-28) found that the wife's labour-force status did not greatly change the unpaid work hours of husbands. In effect, in this age group, a husband with a spouse who is not employed spends more hours (3.1) in unpaid work than a husband whose spouse is employed part-time (2.8 hours) or full-time (2.8 hours). As Frederick observes, "Contrary to strong anecdotal evidence, the difference in the amount of unpaid work done by dual-earner husbands is not significantly different from other husbands." But Frederick's analysis failed to control for the presence of children, and it focused on only one type of work. The observation that men whose spouses are not employed are doing the most unpaid work appears surprising until one realizes that these are the households with more children and consequently with more unpaid work. In Table 5.4, within categories of presence and age of children, all comparisons show both men and women doing the most total work if both spouses are working full-time, followed by cases in which one spouse is working part-time, and finally by cases in which only one spouse is employed.

For persons not in husband-wife families, the presence and ages of children also significantly alter the amount of total and unpaid work. Indeed, researchers have found that the time-use of lone parents, whether employed or homemakers, resembles that of their counterparts with partners (Ornstein and Haddad 1993: 24). However, for persons working full-time, the lone mothers do slightly less total work than mothers in husband-wife families with both working full-time (Table 5.4). Total hours also vary considerably between male and female lone parents, with men doing less total work (Statistics Canada 1992: 33). Although the data on men lone parents are based on small numbers, the findings for men and women are similar when they are working full-time, while men do less work when they are either working part-time or not employed.

For persons with no children under 19 years, the gender differences in total work show women doing more when both parents are working full-time or for persons not in husband-wife families who are not working full-time. Conversely, men do more when two are employed but not both full-time, or if only one is employed. Interestingly, the small category of persons working full-time, who neither are in husband-wife families nor have children under 19, shows the same average of 8.7 hours per day for men and women. Even here there are differences, with men doing more paid work and women doing more unpaid work.

The comparison of the categories associated with children suggests that children have two effects: they increase the unpaid work of both women and men, and they bring more gender differentiation in the distribution of paid and unpaid work. It is when a family has young children that the gendered division of work into its two components is most unequal. As children get older, women do more paid and less unpaid work, bringing less gender differences (Marshall 1994). Based on the 1986 time-use data, Ghalam (1993: 54-55) also observed that employed women with a partner and children were devoting relatively large amounts of time to unpaid work, amounting to about half of their total productive activity. These women allocated at least twice as much time as comparable fathers to unpaid work.

Consequently, both marital status and parental status influence work patterns, but the presence of young children has more impact on the gender gap in unpaid work, producing more total work for women. In fact, as we have seen, when there are no children under 19, some comparisons show men doing more total work than women.

Participation in paid and unpaid work

The surveys also show important differences in terms of the participation in paid and unpaid work on a given day. In 1986, 85 percent of women and 52 percent of men participated in domestic activities (excluding child care and shopping). Conversely, 54 and 34 percent of men and women participated in paid work activities on a given day (Harvey, Marshall, and Frederick 1991: 43, 50; Marshall 1990). Among married employed parents in 1986, the participation rate in housework was 63 percent for men and 95.3 percent for women (Haddad 1996: 153).

In 1992, for parents with children under 19, with both spouses employed full-time, 95.9 percent of women and 77.4 percent of men participated in housework on a given day. In addition, for those who had children under 19, 63.7 percent of women and 43.9 percent of men participated in child care (McFarlane 1997: 73-77). Not only do employed men spend slightly less time in total productive activity than employed women, but men's participation in unpaid work shows greater flexibility; they can more easily work around their paid work. This is probably a key factor underlying the higher stress experienced by women. It is especially for married parents working full-time that women experience the most stress (Frederick 1995: 28-30). The presence of children contributes to feelings of "time crunch" for women and not for men (Frederick 1993; Fast and Frederick 1996). Based on data from Sweden, Klas Rydenstan (1997) finds that caring work is much more fragmented, because it is dependent on the needs of other people. While men can do their jobs and be done, women's productive time is much more fragmented, with more interruptions of one activity by the next.

The 1996 Canadian census asked about the extent to which people aged 15 and over had participated in unpaid work over the previous week (Statistics Canada 1998f). Overall, 90 percent of Canadians reported some unpaid work, including 89 percent for housework or home maintenance, 38 percent for child care, and 17 percent for elder care. In each category, women did more: for instance 92.3 percent of women, compared to 84.6 percent of men, had done housework or home maintenance in the previous week.

Responsibility for domestic work

Another measure of participation is available from the 1990 General Social Survey, which considered four specific domestic activities: meal preparation, meal cleanup, house cleaning, and laundry, along with house maintenance and outside work. In each case, the survey determined who was primarily responsible. In addition, for each member of the household, the survey determined whether the person did none, less than a quarter, less than half, half or more, or all of the activity. Table 5.5 gives the basic results, expressed in terms of men's relative contribution. Men, it seems, rarely take the major responsibility for cooking, cleaning, and washing, and in some 35 to 45 percent of families with children they do not contribute to a given activity. Still, in these same families close to 80 percent of men take the major responsibility for maintenance, and in 55 percent of cases women do not contribute to maintenance.

The analysis of the first three activities among parents shows that women clearly do more of the domestic work (Marshall 1993a, 1993b). For given activities, husbands are more involved when both work full-time than if the wife is either working part-time or not employed. Nonetheless, the involvement of husbands is limited. Even in the case of dual-earning couples in which both partners work full-time, 52 percent of wives have all the responsibility, and another 28 percent have most of the responsibility. In 10 percent of cases the responsibility is shared equally between spouses, and another 10 percent involves mostly or only the husband.

Men's participation is higher if they work fewer hours, if the wife works more hours, if his schedule is flexible, and if there is a smaller age difference between spouses. It is also higher for men who are in cohabiting couples, along with those who have more education (Le Bourdais and Sauriol 1998a, 1998b). Nonetheless, it is surprising that men are less involved when there are more young children. It could be that men spend more time in child care, which was not included as a task, or that couples with young children have mothers who are doing less paid work and who thus take more responsibility for these domestic tasks. Further analysis confirms that the most important consideration in the sharing of domestic work is the employment status of the wife and whether she is working part-time or full-time (Le Bourdais and Sauriol 1994). Mothers are also more likely to have full responsibility if they are older, have less education, or have lower income (Marshall 1993b). More sharing appears to take place among families with fewer children and in cohabiting couples.

The data from the 1990 survey clearly indicate more gender differences than those from the 1992 time-use survey. This may be partly a function of the nature of the questions that cover only part of unpaid work. However, these 1990 data demonstrate how little sharing occurs in domestic activities, and how much women take responsibility for these tasks. April Brayfield (1992) also found that men's involvement in domestic work was increasing, especially for the younger among them, but this change had not altered the distribution of responsibility for housework. While they observed a tendency to more equality, Le Bourdais and Sauriol (1998b) concluded that housework and child care were essentially female activities. When women are stuck for help with children, they often depend on other women, such as mothers, sisters, female friends, or domestic servants. These 1990 data do not allow us to determine the extent to which men take the main responsibility for the earning activities of families.

Women's satisfaction with the allocation of housework was lower if they did all of the housework (Marshall 1993a). Nonetheless, 75 percent of these wives were satisfied. In addition, 80 percent of respondents were satisfied with the balance between work and family.

RELATIVE CONTRIBUTIONS OF MEN TO DOMESTIC WORK, AND RESPONSIBILITY FOR DOMESTIC WORK, FOR COUPLES LIVING WITH CHILDREN AGED 0-17, CANADA, 1990

	ALL FAMILIES				TWO-EARNER FAMILIES			
	ALL	1/2 OR MORE	LESS THAN 1/2	NONE	ALL	1/2 OR MORE	LESS THAN 1/2	NONE
Relative contribution of men towards:								
Meals	2.1	19.5	42.9	35.5	2.7	24.9	44.1	28.3
Dishes	3.2	24.1	38.6	34.1	3.9	28.2	38.8	29.1
Washing and cleaning	1.6	16.4	35.5	46.5	1.9	20.0	38.9	39.2
Maintenance	45.3	37.8	5.4	11.5	48.3	36.9	4.3	10.5
	MAN	BOTH	WOMAN	OTHER	MAN	BOTH	WOMAN	OTHER
Person principally responsible for task:								
Meals	10.3	10.1	77.7	1.9	13.0	13.6	70.8	2.6
Dishes	12.8	13.3	66.9	7.0	16.1	15.7	59.3	8.9
Washing and cleaning	6.3	11.1	79.5	3.1	7.7	14.0	74.2	4.1
Maintenance	78.5	4.6	8.0	8.9	80.5	4.2	6.6	8.7

Source: Le Bourdais and Sauriol 1998a: 19. Statistics Canada, General Social Survey, 1990.

TABLE 5.5

The results, then, depend to some extent on whether the analyses focus on participation in domestic work, responsibility for given tasks, or time-use in productive activities. The greatest inequality occurs in the matter of taking responsibility for given tasks, with men rarely taking the major responsibility for cooking, cleaning, and washing; and in significant numbers of families they do not contribute to these activities at all. Men do largely take the major responsibility for maintenance and outside work. As for participation in domestic work and child care, men are less likely to have participated on a given day, which translates into more flexibility in their time-use for unpaid work. The greatest similarities between women and men come in total time-use in productive activities: for both men and women, total productive time is highest for those who are employed, in relationships, and with young children.

CHILD CARE

For parents, a large part of unpaid work involves the care of children. Among parents with at least one child under 19 living at home in 1986, 67 percent of mothers and 36 percent of fathers contributed some time to child care (Harvey, Marshall, and Frederick 1991: 61). For those who did child care, the average involvement in activities called "primary child care" was 2.1 hours for mothers and 1.6 hours for fathers. These primary child-care activities included physical care, helping, teaching, reading, talking to and playing with children, as well as travel for children. As a broader measure, 94 percent of mothers and 84 percent of fathers spent time interacting with their children each day, for an average of 5.9 and 4.4 hours respectively. For both men and women, the time spent in child care was higher if they were not employed and if the children were younger.

In the 1992 survey, as an average for persons aged 15 and over, men spent 16.6 minutes per day and women 43 minutes caring for their own children or caring for other people's children without pay (Table 5.6). This represents some 11 percent of men's and 16 percent of women's total time in unpaid work. This counts only child care as a primary activity, and it includes the 83 percent of men and 76 percent of women who spent no time in child care on the day under observation. For those who did child care on a given day, the average time is 1.6 hours for men and 2.2 hours for women. For both men and women, time spent in child care is significantly higher at ages 25-44.

Because the time-use surveys did not focus on child care, we also need to review other results. Based on data from the U.S. 1991 Survey of Income and Program Participation, Martin O'Connell (1993) estimated that fathers were the single most important source of family-provided child care during times when mothers worked. The percentage of preschool children cared for by fathers increased from 15 in 1988 to 20 in 1991. The work schedules of parents and employment of fathers influenced their participation. Fathers participated more if they worked part-time, had non-day shifts, or had not worked in the past four months.

Further data from the United States indicated that fathers were not only spending less time than mothers, but also, and especially, that they were taking less responsibility, in terms of availability on short notice or the selection and management of child care (Lamb 1995). When mothers are not employed, fathers' caregiving is about 25 percent of mothers', and it rises to some 33 to 65 percent when the mother is employed. In both cases, the responsibility of fathers is negligible. In Sweden, where policy promotes the involvement of fathers, there is no large difference in the average time spent talking or playing with children, but mothers remain more involved in helping and supervising children (Rydenstan 1997).

Using data from the Labour Force Survey, Katherine Marshall (1998a) defines stay-at-home parents as those who have children under 16, are not employed, not looking for work, not attending school, or permanently unable to work. The numbers of families with a stay-at-home parent declined by 40 percent between 1976 and 1997, coming to represent 20 percent of these two-parent families with children under 16. While the numbers of stay-at-home mothers have declined, that of fathers has increased. Thus the proportion of men increased from 1 percent in 1976 to 6 percent in 1997. The lower average occupational and educational attainment of stay-at-home parents suggests that reduced employment options may be part of the context.

The 1988 Child Care Survey focused on the care arrangements for children under 13 years of age when the respondent worked or studied. The respondent of the survey was to be the parent most responsible for child care; in the cases where parents were equally responsible, the mother was the respondent. These survey procedures meant that 95 per-

TIME USE (MINUTES PER DAY) IN CHILD CARE
AND ELDER CARE, BY SEX AND AGE, CANADA, 1992

AGE	SAMPLE SIZE	CHILD CARE			ELDER CARE		
		MINUTES FOR TOTAL	PARTICI-PANTS %	MINUTES FOR PARTICIPANTS	MINUTES FOR TOTAL	PARTICI-PANTS %	MINUTES FOR PARTICIPANTS
Male							
15-24	698	4.1	4.2	97.6	6.8	9.4	72.9
25-44	1945	29.5	29.7	99.3	8.6	11.3	76.4
45-64	887	6.5	7.3	89.3	6.7	9.2	72.2
65+	472	1.0	1.5	69.1	9.5	11.2	84.4
TOTAL	4002	16.6	17.0	98.0	8.0	10.5	76.0
Female							
15-24	786	30.7	19.7	155.6	6.4	10.1	63.9
25-44	2214	78.1	54.1	144.5	6.5	8.9	73.6
45-64	1084	13.6	10.8	126.2	9.2	10.6	86.8
65+	910	2.9	2.1	137.2	5.0	6.7	75.2
TOTAL	4994	43.0	29.8	144.2	6.8	9.1	75.5
Both sexes							
TOTAL	8996	31.2	24.1	129.7	7.3	9.6	75.7

NOTE: Child care includes baby and child care of household child, helping children, reading/conversation, playing, medical child care, and travel for household child plus unpaid babysitting. Elder care includes housework, cooking assistance, house maintenance/repair assistance, transportation assistance, care for disabled or ill adult, correspondence assistance, personal or medical care of household adult, and travel for household adult.

Source: Special tabulations from Statistics Canada, General Social Survey, 1992.

TABLE 5.6

cent of respondents were women. The survey found that, in the case of dual-earner families, 40 percent of fathers provided child care at least part of the time while the mother was working (Lero et al. 1992a: 100).

Table 5.7 gives the main child-care arrangement used during periods when respondents were working or studying. Besides school, 19.6 percent of the care of children under 12 involved the spouse or partner of the respondent, and another 8.6 percent involved the respondent while working. In comparison, organized care (day care, kindergarten and nursery school, before-school and after-school programs, and licensed family day care) amounted to 10.6 percent of the main method of child care. For the majority of children, informal arrangements, especially care by relatives and unrelated caregivers, are the major source of child-care support.

Clearly, parents manage work, child care, and family responsibilities in a number of ways. Among all families in the 1988 Child Care Survey, 43.1 percent involved either two parents working (or studying) full-time or a lone parent working full-time (Lero et al. 1992a: 51). In another 17.8 percent of families, one parent was working part-time. Consequently, 39 percent of families with children under 12 could organize at least part of child care through the parent who was not employed or studying. Besides one parent working part-time, many families make a number of arrangements to care for children themselves. In effect, only 32.7 percent of dual-earner families involved two parents who each worked a standard week (Lero et al. 1992a: 78).

The preference to work part-time is also strong among mothers of young children. Almost two-thirds of employed respondents in the 1988 survey indicated that they would prefer either to work part-time or not to be working (Logan and Belliveau 1995: 28).

Nonetheless, licensed day-care spaces are not keeping up to the demand, and many Canadians would prefer this type of care if it was available and less costly (Lero et al. 1992a). For instance, for children under six years of age, day care is the actual care for 12.2 percent but the preferred care for 22.4 percent of children (Beaujot 1997). Only 43 percent of persons who prefer day care or nursery school are using such care, mostly because of lack of availability and costs.

Child-care arrangements therefore involve considerable diversity across families and across the life course of children. The diversity includes the extent of parental work, the extent to which care involves parents and non-parental situations, and the type of non-parental care that children receive. In effect, there is no clear boundary between the state and the family, or the private and social sides of child care (Leira 1992; Luxton 1997a). In addition, there is no standard or agreement on what constitutes proper parenting (LeMasters and DeFrain 1983). In the circumstance, Luxton (1997a: 172) found that the choice of care is based on a combination of convenience, economics, and the quality of care. But it is difficult for parents to know what is best. They may consider that they can do

MAIN METHOD OF CHILD CARE USED OTHER THAN SCHOOL, BY AGE OF CHILD, 1988

	LESS THAN 3 YEARS	3-5 YEARS	TOTAL LESS THAN 6 YEARS	6-12 YEARS	TOTAL LESS THAN 13 YEARS
Parents	26.6	26.7	26.6	29.4	28.3
While working	10.1	10.2	10.1	7.6	8.6
By spouse/partner	16.5	16.5	16.5	21.8	19.6
Relatives	23.9	16.1	19.7	10.7	14.4
Unrelated caregivers	37.0	30.7	33.6	15.8	23.1
Regulated/ organized care[a]	12.3	24.2	18.7	5.1	10.6
Self or sibling	—	—	—	23.4	14.1
No arrangement[b]	—	—	—	15.6	9.5
TOTAL	100.0	100.0	100.0	100.0	100.0
TOTAL CHILDREN (000s)	496	577	1,073	1,561	2,633

a Includes kindergarten and nursery schools, day-care centres, before- and after-school care, and licensed family day care.
b Includes children who, during the reference week, were in school all the time the parent worked or studied, as well as children whose non-school hours were spent in transit to and from school, in the hospital, or in sports, music lessons, or activities not included as child care.
NOTE: Refers to main care arrangement used while the parent most responsible for child care worked or studied.

Source: Ghalam 1993: 52. Statistics Canada, Child Care Survey, 1988.

TABLE 5.7

best by taking care of the children themselves. At least, that way, they will have tried to do their best by giving child care their full attention. Consequently, there is lack of experience with community-based care.

ELDER CARE

Before the advent of pensions and other benefits for seniors, the care of the surviving elderly was the responsibility of families and charities. Indeed, when they are asked why people have children, many persons in countries without these social benefits say that having children is important to help ensure support for themselves in their old age (Beaujot 1988).

The Canadian welfare state may well be in its most complete form for the elderly. During and after the Second World War, the government first established provisions for returning soldiers, including disability and pensions, as well as education, training, start-up grants, and land grants for veterans. While the first payments for the elderly date back to 1927, they involved only $20 per month and were limited to persons over 70 years of age who were in need. This approach became a universal program in 1951, amounting to $40 per month (Beaujot 1991: 219). Especially through Old Age Security, Guaranteed Income Supplements, the Canada Pension Plan, and socialized medicine, the welfare state now benefits the elderly more than any other group. In particular, for the elderly a social wage has replaced a market wage. John Myles (1981) argues that the principle of retirement gave the welfare state its characteristic form: a welfare state for the elderly. The largest component of federal social spending is on the elderly, with elderly benefits constituting the biggest transfer program in the country (Prince 1985).

Consequently, families are far from being the only source of support for the elderly, and the lives of the elderly are not greatly affected by their number of surviving children (Marcil-Gratton and Légaré 1987). Given that the elderly are generally no longer dependent on their children for economic and instrumental support, relationships with elderly parents tend to be liberated from these considerations and based more on expressive and interpersonal support.

Nonetheless, the 1996 General Social Survey found that 14 percent of women and 10 percent of men are involved in looking after someone with a chronic illness or disability (Cranswick 1997). Among these informal care providers, some two-thirds were employed, more than a quarter reported altered sleeping patterns, almost half had adjusted their social activity, and in 12 percent of cases either the provider or recipient of care had moved to be closer together. For those who were employed, about half reported repercussions at work, especially in terms of time off or absences.

Based on data from the 1986 Health and Activity Limitations Survey, Eric Jenkins and Jacques Légaré (1995) found that spouses and relatives were the chief source of help in daily activities for persons aged 60 and over who were in need of such help.

Consequently, persons living as a couple or with a relative are better off in comparison to those living alone or with non-relatives. More generally, living as a couple provides insulation against the harmful effects of stressful conditions, both by preventing negative behaviours and by providing support when problems arise. Consequently, those living as a couple are in a better state of health in comparison to people who are single or formerly married. The married have lower mortality, morbidity, and disability, and better mental health. But, while those living as a couple are better off, the authors found that they might use external help less efficiently.

In certain circumstances, adult children remain an important form of support for their aging parents. The time-use surveys of 1986 and 1992 captured some of these activities. In 1986, three activities showed up: help and personal care of adults, adult medical and dental care (outside home), and adult medical care (at home). But for the whole population the total of these activities involved only five minutes per day, or a fifth of the time spent on primary child care (Ornstein and Haddad 1993: 38, 39).

The 1992 survey defined elder care as including these activities: housework, cooking assistance, house maintenance/repair assistance, transportation assistance, care for disabled or ill adults, correspondence assistance, personal or medical care of household adults, and travel for household adults (Table 5.6). The survey used these categories in an effort to capture all care for dependent adults who are living inside or outside of the household. The average total elder care for the whole population amounted to 6.8 minutes per day for women and 8 minutes for men. However, only 9.1 percent of women and 10.5 percent of men participated in this activity on a given day. For the participants the average was 1.25 hours on a given day. Participation did not vary extensively over ages, although it was highest for men aged 25-44 and women aged 45-64. The average time for participants also did not vary extensively over ages, with averages always above one hour per day. Just as with child care, some elder care, such as shopping for both oneself and one's parent, or driving to visit an institutionalized parent, would undoubtedly occur as a secondary activity.

The 1990 General Social Survey obtained information on giving and receiving unpaid help from persons outside of the household. The types of help included transportation, child care, housework, house maintenance, and financial support. Altogether 75 percent of persons had provided such help at least once in the previous year, and 56 percent had received such help (McDaniel 1994: 82, 83). This finding includes 15 percent of persons providing help to parents. While there are gender differences when it comes to more frequent provisions of help, and specific types of activities, it is interesting that 13 percent of men and 16 percent of women provided help to parents. In addition, 4 percent of all persons aged 15 and over had received help from sons and 4 percent from daughters.

Table 5.8 tabulates the information from this survey for persons receiving help from non-coresident children and giving help to adult children. Leroy Stone, Carolyn Rosenthal, and Ingrid Connidis (1998) also estimated the intensity of help based on frequency and types of help provided or received. Significantly, only for age group 75 and over did people receive more from children than they were giving to children. Clearly, even into retirement years, parents continue to give to their children more than they receive. For instance, parents often provide child care for their grandchildren, which partly explains the larger amounts of help provided by women when they are aged 45 to 64. Stone, Rosenthal, and Connidis observe that these private forms of intergenerational support, which heavily favour children, offset the government supports that disproportionately favour the parental generation, and the resulting dependency is a foundation of social cohesion.

A survey of persons in eight organizations found that 8 percent of men and 14 percent of women provided assistance to relatives in at least one of five basic living activities (bathing, dressing, eating, taking medications, and toileting), for an average of nine hours per week (CARNET 1993). In addition, 34 percent of employees provided other forms of assistance, from helping with shopping to dealing with memory and mood difficulties, for an average of three hours per week. Persons who cared for both children and elderly had the highest levels of work-family conflict. For instance, 5.7 percent of respondents in these organizations had children under 19 at home and also provided assistance to the elderly in basic living activities.

Given the needs of elderly and children, there has been talk of a "sandwich genera-tion" that may have to care for both young children and elderly parents at the same time. For instance, at age 35-64, one-third of Canadians in the early 1990s had both children at home and parents who were of retirement age (Smith and Dumas 1994: 122). However, less than a quarter of those people were providing help to parents. Most parents have little need, but those who have needs receive more than half of this from family members, with women helping more than men. The time-use data do not provide much support for the concept of a sandwiched generation (Table 5.6). Nonetheless, in some specific circumstances, enormous personal costs are borne by women who "turn down promotions, change jobs and work part time in order to meet the needs of their immediate and extended families" (Myles 1991: 82). Consequently, concerns have been raised about a

GIVING INSTRUMENTAL HELP TO, AND RECEIVING INSTRUMENTAL HELP FROM, NON-CORESIDENT CHILDREN, BY SEX AND AGE, CANADA, 1990

	25-44	45-54	55-64	65-74	75+	25+
Percent giving any help						
TOTAL	30.7	42.3	47.1	35.2	17.8	37.9
M	33.3	36.4	42.2	32.3	22.9	35.5
F	27.6	46.9	51.7	37.5	14.2	39.9
Percent receiving any help						
TOTAL	3.1	13.2	19.0	26.3	36.0	18.9
M	1.7	7.5	14.6	18.5	22.5	12.5
F	4.8	17.8	23.1	32.4	45.5	24.5
Percent giving significant levels of help						
M	29.6	26.6	29.6	20.5	12.7	25.3
F	18.3	36.1	40.2	25.2	6.8	29.1
Percent receiving significant levels of help						
M	1.6	5.4	6.8	12.5	17.2	7.9
F	3.8	10.6	16.3	23.6	35.4	17.4

Source: Stone, Rosenthal, and Connidis 1998: 40, 47.
Statistics Canada, General Social Survey, 1990.

TABLE 5.8

"caregiving crisis," because the organization of caregiving is based on a model of family and work that is increasingly rare.

MODELS FOR ACCOMMODATING PAID AND UNPAID WORK

The literature on the division of labour within families points to a variety of models that families employ to meet the demands of paid and domestic work. Husband-wife families can follow the breadwinner and two-earner models. Single-parent families vary in their approach, depending primarily on the employment status of the parent, but also on the economic and child-care contributions of the absent parent.

Based on the instrumental and expressive aspects of marriage, Letha Scanzoni and John Scanzoni (1976) identified one historical and three contemporary models of marriage structures. In the historical *owner-property marriage* model the husband is legally the owner of his wife: "The two are one but the one is the husband." This marriage type is based primarily on the instrumental exchanges associated with earning a living and maintaining a household, rather than the expressive exchanges of empathy and companionship. In the *head-complement* model, the wife is "the other half," expected to find meaning in life largely through her husband and family. On the instrumental level, this is the breadwinner arrangement, although expressive matters are also important and spouses are expected to "be friends and lovers," enjoying each other's company and supporting each other. In the *senior partner-junior partner* marriage, the wife—the junior partner—has more independence, perhaps, but the main instrumental responsibilities remain the same. The husband contributes the larger share to the family income and the wife takes care of the family and household. The *equal partner-equal partner* model has spouses equally committed to their jobs and sharing equally in household and family tasks. While all marriages have instrumental and expressive elements, these models, in progression, show a decrease in instrumental interdependence and an increase in expressive exchanges. The first three types involve complementary roles for the partners, and the fourth type is symmetrical.

Goldscheider and Waite (1991) suggest that the future will bring either "new families" or "no families." *New families* will consist of symmetrical and companionate formations, while *no families* mean, as you might guess, people living outside of the conventional arrangements altogether. Most likely other forms of *old families* will continue as well, including the single-earner or breadwinner model and other models in which employed wives do most of the domestic work, possibly by working part-time when the children are young. In addition, *single-parent* and *shared-custody* alternatives will co-exist. Each of these models involves accommodations in earning and caring.

While many analysts have concluded that the two-earner model has largely replaced the breadwinner model, many variations remain. In looking at trends in the United States over two centuries, Donald Hernandez (1993: 103) separates off the two-parent farm family from the breadwinner model. The *farm family*, which represented 70 percent of families two centuries ago, became less important than the breadwinner family before the turn of the 20th century and now represents less than 5 percent of families. Besides this long-term trend, Hernandez notes the rise in dual-earner non-farm families after 1940 and the rise in one-parent families after 1960. According to this classification, the father breadwinner and mother homemaker non-farm family represented more than 50 percent of all families only during the period 1920-70, and it never exceeded 57 percent of families. While the largest category has since shifted from one-earner to dual-earner, neither of these categories has ever represented more than 60 percent of families.

As well, based on the division of housework, Feree (1991a) points to four categories of two-earner families. In the *semi-housewife* category, the wife does most of the housework and contributes little time to earning. The *drudge-wife* model has the wife still doing most of the housework, but also working full-time. In the *cash-paying* case, the couple largely pays others to do the housework. Finally, in the *two-housekeeper* model, the wife does less than 60 percent and the husband more than 40 percent of the housework.

When it comes to earning, two-earner families can be divided into those in which both partners work full-time and those in which one partner works part-time. It would appear that few families with children fit the model of having two full-time earners over the whole period of child-raising. Focusing on married women with children under 16 years of age, Duffy, Mandell, and Pupo (1989) found important differences for those working full-time, part-time, and as housewives. Their sample of the lives of women from the Toronto area indicates that those working *part-time* had the most "contentment with their present circumstances." The women said they felt able to accommodate family and work, including gaining a sense of satisfaction from part-time work and of accomplishment in balancing home and work. At the same time, many of them did not see part-time work as a continuing circumstance, and they were making changes at home in order to be able to work full-time. The women working *full-time* reported that doing so took a tremendous effort, and many of them expressed astonishment at being able to perform a dual role. While they clearly saw the benefits of two incomes, and expressed a sense of efficacy about the situation, they also acknowledged that they had primary responsibility for the domestic work. The marriages remained gender-segregated, with the men largely working longer hours outside the home and earning higher incomes. The women experienced a greater conflict between family and work. It was not in terms of gender-role ideologies that the *housewives* were different, but they tended to "experience life as something happening to them." For instance, at age 18, they reported, they had been vague about their career plans. Although they experienced a lack of economic independence and low status, they felt happy to "be there for the children." Given the mixture of benefits and stresses associated with these three types, Duffy, Mandell, and Pupo concluded that women were left with "few choices."

When the partners in two-income families are in professional or managerial occupations, we can speak of *dual-career couples*. Here again there are different models. Based on research in the United States, Sid Gilbert (1993) suggests that three categories of heterosexual dual-career couples are more or less equally important. In the *traditional/conven-*

tional case, the male partner is more professionally ambitious, with a "more important" career, and only "helps out" with housework and child care. The *participant/modern* case has less extensive gender-based role specialization and has shared parenting, and the father is "active" while the wife does most of the other housework. In the *role-sharing/egalitarian* case, both partners are actively involved in career pursuits as well as in housework and family life. This last category also applies to the majority of lesbian and gay partners, although they would be less likely to have children. Gilbert suggests three requisites for egalitarian career families: economic equality between the sexes, in both the society and specific families; compatibility of occupational and family systems, contrary to a world in which careers often involve the assumption that occupants are "family-free"; and the partners themselves need to seek role-sharing and mutuality based on an "interdependency free of the constraints of gender." Basing her work on a study of 18 shared-parenting couples, Anna Dienhart (1998) shows that they have deliberately co-created alternatives to traditional parenting roles.

Models based on doing more, less, or the same amount of work

Clearly, the elaboration of family models needs to go "beyond separate spheres" with their opposite and exclusive sex roles (Feree 1990). Instead, men and women make a variety of accommodations that achieve earning and caring objectives while also linking individuals and families to other social institutions.

The data we have looked at so far have mostly been averages, for women and men, based on given life conditions associated with marital, parental, and work statuses. Available Canadian data do not permit extensive elaboration of models at the family level. Nonetheless, Table 5.9 illustrates certain alternatives based on the 1992 time-use survey, which in turn is based on the simple idea that a given spouse could do "more," "less," or "about the same" paid or unpaid work as the other spouse. The category of "about the same" is measured as being within four hours' difference in a week—four hours is about 15 percent of either paid or unpaid work. The table is based on husband-wife couples with respondents aged 30 to 54 and spouses less than 65 years.

These time-use measures are therefore different from those in the earlier tables, which were based on the timing of the respondent's various activities over a 24-hour day. Table 5.9 is based on broad questions that asked respondents to estimate, both for themselves and their spouse or partner, the total weekly time spent in paid work, plus the time spent in domestic work, household maintenance, and child care. While the daily time-use involved only the main activity at any one time, this weekly measure may have included given activities as secondary activities. The top and bottom panels of the table comprise the male and female respondents respectively. These results also confirm other studies indicating the tendency to underestimate a partner's time, especially in unpaid work.

The main observation is that a variety of models co-exist; each of the categories across the top of the table show some respondents. While over half of the respondents fall into the one category, in which the man does more paid work and the woman more unpaid work, for about 10 percent of the respondents the woman does more paid work, and in 14 percent women and men do the same amount of domestic work (taking an average of the distributions for men and women). In both distributions, the second-largest category,

MODELS OF HUSBAND-WIFE FAMILIES BY RELATIVE PARTICIPATION IN PAID AND UNPAID WORK, FOR RESPONDENTS AGED 30-54

| | COMPARED TO RESPONDENT, SPOUSE DOES | | | | | | | | |
| | MORE PAID | | | SAME PAID | | | LESS PAID | | |
	MD	SD	LD	MD	SD	LD	MD	SD	LD
Men respondents									
DISTRIBUTION (%)	4.0	1.9	2.8	12.4	4.6	4.1	55.8	8.7	5.5
Household income ($1,000s)	44.7	47.6	50.6	51.4	62.7	51.7	53.1	60.6	57.7
Children under 12 (#)	0.8	0.4	1.1	0.8	0.4	1.1	1.1	0.5	1.0
Two or more under 12 (%)	23.4	10.9	43.8	28.9	15.6	31.1	36.2	16.5	33.0
Three or more under 12 (%)	3.5	3.5	5.9	7.8	2.1	11.2	8.7	1.7	4.7
Child under 6 (%)	22.9	15.1	26.2	23.1	3.5	26.2	29.4	15.8	29.1
No child under 19 (%)	26.1	71.0	35.5	33.6	54.7	19.5	25.8	58.7	24.0
Hours per week									
Paid self	20.0	17.4	9.1	32.1	37.2	30.1	48.8	51.6	46.3
Paid spouse	40.4	40.8	41.0	31.7	37.0	29.8	14.1	27.1	27.5
Domestic self	23.7	18.5	57.3	22.4	18.3	49.1	20.7	21.8	41.9
Domestic spouse	50.5	18.2	32.8	49.7	18.6	31.9	63.2	21.6	26.6
Total household	134.6	94.9	140.2	135.9	111.1	130.9	146.8	121.1	142.3
Women respondents									
DISTRIBUTION (%)	2.1	4.4	54.0	2.0	5.3	19.7	3.8	2.6	6.0
Household income ($1,000s)	52.2	63.3	50.2	54.9	57.6	45.6	46.6	55.2	52.3
Children under 12 (#)	1.0	0.2	1.1	0.7	0.3	0.8	0.6	0.2	0.9
Two or more under 12 (%)	29.4	8.3	38.8	21.3	7.8	23.1	16.2	0.9	29.3
Three or more under 12 (%)	6.6	3.8	11.0	0.0	1.8	4.5	0.5	0.0	9.8
Child under 6 (%)	14.7	5.2	25.8	12.2	4.4	16.8	4.5	0.0	20.5
No child under 19 (%)	37.8	69.2	24.3	39.1	67.7	35.4	49.6	62.7	28.1
Hours per week									
Paid self	22.7	30.0	14.3	31.1	31.2	27.1	42.4	43.3	40.7
Paid spouse	42.4	46.3	48.0	31.8	31.2	27.6	11.8	19.7	20.5
Domestic self	25.3	12.4	68.0	23.6	18.3	48.4	24.7	13.5	52.7
Domestic spouse	39.7	11.4	14.2	35.1	16.8	16.2	40.8	12.5	18.6
Total household	130.1	100.1	154.5	111.6	97.5	119.3	119.7	89.0	132.5

NOTE: MD=more domestic; SD=same domestic; LD=less domestic. Cases in which spouse is 65 or over are excluded. Total sample is 2,346.

Source: Special tabulations from Statistics Canada, 1992 General Social Survey.

TABLE 5.9

amounting to 19.7 percent of the women's responses and 12.4 percent of the men's responses, is when they do the same amount of paid work but the husband does less domestic work. The concept of a double day or second shift is most relevant to this category, because the amount of time in paid work is very similar but the women do an average of two to three times as much unpaid work. Nonetheless, in 2.1 percent of couples the man does more paid and more domestic work (according to the women's responses), and in 4 percent the woman does more paid and more domestic work (according to the men's responses).

The table shows the average hours of paid and unpaid work in each of the nine categories. For instance, in the category of same paid and same domestic, with "same" defined as within four hours, the average paid work is 31 hours for both self and spouse according to the women's responses and 37 hours according to the men's responses. Similarly, the domestic or unpaid work in this 5 percent of the sample amounts to 18.3 hours for self and 18.6 for spouse (according to the men's responses) and 18.3 and 16.8 for self and spouse (according to the women's responses). In contrast, the traditional category involves women doing 14.2 hours of paid and 65.6 hours of domestic work, with men doing 48.4 hours of paid and 17.5 hours of domestic work (taking the average of men's and women's responses). This is also the category in which the total work is highest, at 150 hours per week, or an average of 10.8 hours per person per day. In contrast, the total work is least in the 2 percent of the sample in which the wife is doing more paid and the same domestic, with the average 92 hours per week or 6.6 hours per day. The next lowest total work is for "same paid, same domestic," involving some 5 percent of the sample. Significantly, in the category opposite to traditional, in which the woman does more paid and the man more domestic, involving some 3 percent of the sample, the man does very little paid work, an average of 9.1 hours per week (men's responses).

The average household incomes are not extensively different in the different categories of couples. Average income is highest when women do less paid work and the spouses do the same amount of domestic work, or when they are the same in both categories. Incomes are lowest when women do more paid and more domestic work (men's responses) or men do less paid and more domestic (women's responses). The models are especially differentiated by the ages and numbers of children. In particular, the category of "same domestic" involves the fewest children. In contrast, the traditional category, in which women also do the most total work, registers the most children, at least for women's responses. This finding confirms that equal divisions of work are easier to achieve given few children and that children push families into more traditional divisions of work. Equal divisions of domestic work are also more common when families do less total work.

CONCLUSION

Time-use indicates important variations between women and men in their relative involvement in work and family, or paid and unpaid work. Both marriage and children reduce the likelihood of women working full-time, while they increase this likelihood for men. Time-use data indicate that the total work of women and men is especially altered by the presence of young children, and it is in families with children that the gender gap in the division of work is strongest. Total work is most equally divided when one spouse is employed part-time. Models based on spouses doing more, less, or the same amount of paid and unpaid work suggest that a variety of situations co-exist. While about half of the cases involve men doing more paid work and women more unpaid work, the second-largest category (about 15 percent of couples at mid-life) involves the same amount of paid work but the wife doing two to three times as much unpaid work. At the same time, other patterns include situations in which men do more total work, as well as symmetrical arrangements of more equal involvement in economic and domestic activities.

Clearly, several areas of *stress* exist between family and work, especially when the family includes young children. In *The Family in Crisis*, John Conway (1997) observes various difficulties in the ability of families to support children, women, and men. In particular, various contradictions appear between the move toward gender equality and the assumptions of the traditional patriarchal family based on complementary roles for husbands and wives. Consequently, children are subject to the insecurity of family breakdown and absent fathers, as well as vulnerable to abuse and poverty. Women in particular are also caught in various contradictions, because they most often bear the brunt of the work-family interphase. Some women decide to move out of a marriage to resolve the conflict, but that brings the additional problems of single parenthood. Men are also suffering from the contradictions between the traditional and egalitarian assumptions. In some ways, men can also become subject to the pressures of work and family life, expected to devote themselves to their jobs but also to do more at home. In addition, many men are separated from their children and miss the basic human interactions with children that many people consider to be an important part of family life.

Besides these conflicts, family and work models also involve *interdependence*. Family members depend on each other's paid and unpaid work. Clearly, their economic well-being depends on paid work, while the unpaid work provides the nurturance essential to the lives of both children and adults. Unpaid work also provides an economic contribution by sustaining the worker and making it possible to perform paid work.

Given that the models of earning and caring entail both interdependence and stress, the potential is there for both conflict and cohesion among family members. The family can be viewed as a locus of struggle among members rather than an active agent with a unified interest (Hartmann 1984). In particular, it is the space in which people with different activities and interests in the productive processes are not only interdependent but can also come into conflict. Conversely, a more equitable involvement in the productive processes can carry with it new forms of family cohesion.

In "Beyond Separate Spheres," Feree (1990) proposes that analysts should see both women and men simultaneously as family members and workers, in order to "recognize the gendered meaning and structural conditions of paid and unpaid work." As part of this exploration, she adds, "The feminist perspective redefines families as arenas of gender and generational struggles, crucibles of caring and conflict, where claims for an identity are rooted, and separateness and solidarity are continuously created and contested" (p. 880).These issues have not been sufficiently central to the sociology of families, given the traditional focus on marriage, divorce, marital interaction, child-bearing, and the family life cycle.

Paying attention to the issues of paid and unpaid work also enhances the understanding of how families construct gender through the division of labour and control over the products of labour. If gender is a hierarchical structure of opportunity and oppression, as Feree (1990:870) says, "Families are one of the institutional settings in which these structures become lived experience." Although it is a shared experience of most women, housework in particular has lacked public and academic recognition (Wilson 1991). Women have especially felt the strains associated with the meshing of family and work. Patricia Evans (1991) notes a particular contradiction between a family ethic that delegates caring responsibilities to women and a work ethic that rewards self-sufficiency rather than economic dependency.

Consequently, the extent to which men make or do not make adjustments for women's paid work is a crucial matter for gender equality and family well-being. Spain and Bianchi (1996: 171) observe, "As long as men have fewer family responsibilities and women have many more, the potential exists for women to choose or accept lower occupational status and earnings, which in turn affects their bargaining position within the marriage." It is precisely in jobs that offer more flexibility in terms of departure, re-entry, and the potential to work part-time that workers have the least status and autonomy. In the conclusion of *The Gender Factory*, Berk (1985) suggests that the impetus for change in gender relations is not likely to come from within the "work-gender production process" and that a reorganization of household tasks is more likely to find its origins in forces outside of the household. In looking at the 10 percent of "outlier" husbands who do as much in the home as the average woman, she notices especially the importance of small family size and wives working full-time. Change within families is therefore interdependent with the achievement of equal opportunities in the broader society.

In effect, gender can be said to operate on three levels: on the basis of individual orientations, the structure of couples, and structures in society (Matthews 1994). When couples and society are organized along traditional lines, childlessness might seem to be the easiest route to equality for women with egalitarian gender orientations. As one qualitative survey (Matthews and Beaujot 1997) shows, the family strategies of women oriented toward egalitarian principles do not differ extensively from the strategies of traditional women on questions such as the desirability of marriage, children, and family. But egalitarian women are oriented to later marriage and child-bearing.

Focusing on men, Hochschild (1995) observes that while men are more involved with child care when mothers are working, less stable marital bonds also mean that men are more often separated from their children. Nonetheless, she remains optimistic, partly because of the factors that bring men to invest more in their children, and partly because of the one-fifth of the cases studied in *The Second Shift*, in which "new men" were fully sharing in the care of children and the home. Mirjam Van Dongen (1995) argues that men want to be more involved with child care. She even suggests that the fathers who lose touch with their children after divorce may be the men who were once particularly attached to their children—people who could find no other way of coping once they are separated.

In *Women at Work*, Stephen Peitchinis (1989) is similarly optimistic, based on the trend toward a lower amount of labour being needed within households. Just as the microwave and processed foods have reduced the labour associated with producing meals, Peitchinis expects changes associated with computers and telecommunications to reduce the work associated with planning, scheduling, and managing the household. He sees a greater overlap between the formal market economy and the informal household economy. For instance, by doing more of the paid work at home, men would come to share more in the unpaid work. Goldscheider and Waite (1991: 197) derive hope from the case of women with career-level jobs—the category in which domestic activities most respond to gender changes in the workplace and in which husbands and wives are starting to become co-providers and co-parents. As we have seen, the more equivalent prospects for employment also bring reduced gains from specialization and complementarity in gender activities.

Returning to questions of family models, Goldscheider and Waite (1991) find that "old families" pose various problems, especially in terms of women's dependence on men's employment, which brings insecurity to women and heavy pressures on men. The alternative of "no families" also presents problems, because adults then do not profit from the various benefits of relationships, to say nothing of population replacement. Thus, along with Conway (1997), these authors see a potential for "new families" that are more egalitarian in their marital relationships and in their mode of sharing in the parenting pleasures and responsibilities.

An interesting analysis by Phyllis Moen and Yan Yu (1997) finds that "success at work does not compete with success at home." Based on the 1992 U.S. National Study of the Changing Workforce, despite concerns regarding work overload, the analysis shows a tendency toward a positive relationship, for both men and women, between perceptions of success at work and at home. Nonetheless, men feel slightly less successful than do women in balancing work and personal obligations, and a negative relationship persists between perceptions of these two kinds of success for working women in the "launching stage" with young children. Women at this stage, around ages 25-39, feel less success in their family and personal lives than do men at the same stage. At the "anticipatory stage" of the early twenties, both men and women feel the least successful in both areas, while persons in the "shifting gears" stage of ages 50-64 feel the most successful in their jobs, in their personal lives, and in balancing work and family.

Many family models are likely to continue to co-exist. Frank Furstenberg (1995), for instance, observes that the symmetrical family, in which both partners contribute more or less equally to economic and domestic activities, is "more prevalent as an ideal type than as an actual arrangement." Despite the dual-earner model as the seeming norm, most families could be described as "neo-traditional" because paid and unpaid work remains divided along traditional lines. The idea of fatherhood includes not only the ideal of a more involved father, which is seen as an opportunity for men to express their nurturing feelings, to take an equal role in parenting, and to be there for their children, but also a remaining expectation that men participate fully in the economic sphere, acting as providers and constructing their identities as men through their work roles (Lupton and Barklay 1997).

The practice of new families would not necessarily reduce the conflicts between family and work, nor would it make for more stable relationships. While new families may involve new forms of cohesion, they will also lack the solidarity associated with instrumental interdependence. While work can be more family friendly, the potential for conflict between family and work will always remain, if only because time does not permit people to be at two places at once. That is why, besides "new families" and "no families," other models of families will surely continue, particularly the single-parent alternative, along with various family forms involving complementary roles, as well as various other "alternatives," including temporary partnerships and gay and lesbian unions.

Fertility

For most families, child-bearing and child-rearing are central aspects of life. Sometimes the birth of a child brings a family into existence. In addition, the day-to-day earning and caring activities of families are more often than not associated with the needs of children.

The objective of this chapter is to summarize the wealth of existing information and data on fertility and to interpret the trends and dynamics of fertility in the context of earning and caring. The first part of the chapter considers the basic patterns and broad determinants of child-bearing. In Canada fertility trends have seen both a long-term decline and, in the past two decades, considerable stability. In the period 1976-96 the total fertility rate was between 1.8 and 1.6 births per woman, with family size about 1.85 children among cohorts who had completed their child-bearing years. Intended child-bearing nonetheless remains above the replacement level of two births per women. What has changed is the timing of child-bearing: higher proportions of births occur after age 30. Consequently, the main pattern for persons at mid-life, especially ages 30-49, is not only to be in relationships and working but also to be living with children. Men who are not in relationships or who are in new relationships are less likely to be living with children.

What researchers call the demographic transition, which includes economic and cultural considerations, helps to explain long-term population trends. Economic questions relate to the reduced instrumental utility of children, which have made adults ready to have fewer children. Cultural attitudes have increased the acceptability of people taking personal control over family size and of having smaller families in particular. The norms have made adults willing to have fewer children.

Fertility in itself can be determined by three sets of factors: the proximate factors (especially union formation and contraceptive usage); the intermediate factors (value and cost of children); and the societal-level factors (particularly the organization of paid and unpaid work).

While fertility has become less strictly tied to marital unions, most child-bearing occurs in relationships. Survey data also find that persons who intend to marry expect to have more children, while persons who are cohabiting have fewer births. Thus the lower proportions of persons living in unions, along with the greater flexibility in their definition and reduced union stability, are important as a proximate factor of fertility. The uncertainty of unions is probably one of the reasons why people have fewer children than initially intended. Another proximate factor is the greater use of secure contraception, especially for people who are married or cohabitating. Sterilization has become the method of choice once couples have achieved their desired family size. Men are also taking more responsibility for contraception than they did in earlier days.

The intermediate factors of the value and cost of children refer to both economic and cultural considerations. Children represent considerable costs, which respondents can readily identify. In effect, there is no longer an economic rationale for having children. The fact that people still have children must be explained in terms of cultural values. But respondents to surveys are not entirely forthcoming in identifying these values, and sometimes they simply say that it is "natural" to have children. Children can represent a unique experience in life or an important source of personal fulfilment. They can also be a means of reducing uncertainty; when other relationships are less stable, children represent stable family members. People sometimes also see children as social capital, or as a means of having access to other members of the community and society.

While surveys document largely positive orientations toward children and families, other responses indicate the difficulties sometimes experienced by people in fitting children into their lives. For instance, people often seem to believe that it is best to have had a degree of independence before starting a relationship, and that a relationship should mature and solidify before they have children. Many also consider it best to establish secure employment before having children. Yet many prefer to start having children before age 30, so they will be relatively young with their children and have the necessary energy. Thus, around age 30 there seems to be a narrow window of opportunity that is best for having a first child, with the second one coming some two years later. All of this assumes that other things in life are in place as expected, particularly the security in a relationship and in employment. Perhaps because of difficulties in these areas, a certain number of people do not have the children initially anticipated.

These values and costs of children, and the complexities around having the anticipated births, relate as well to considerations of the structure of paid and unpaid work, or the interface of production and reproduction. Especially in the period 1960-75, higher labour-force participation was often associated with lower fertility. Children were seen as an important opportunity cost for employed women. In the two subsequent decades labour-force participation continued to increase, while fertility was stable. In effect, women who have completed their education and have secured employment are now more likely to have a first or second birth, but less likely to have a third child. One accommodation has been to have children later in life, after establishing a place in the world of paid employment. Part of the conflict between children and work, it seems, has also been absorbed by men's greater participation in unpaid work. There is also some improvement in the societal interface between child-rearing and work, along with a greater supply of family services on the market. All of this makes it possible for most people to have two children, if they want. Some analysts had feared that an egalitarian society would not reproduce itself. It appears that we can set these fears aside, especially given the continued expressed interests of most people to have children.

◆

Child-bearing and child-rearing are clearly of central importance for most families. While families do not have to include children, the organization of family life takes as a central facet the connections across generations. Consequently, the study of fertility is an important avenue through which to study families. In addition, a substantial body of research on fertility does exist, and much of this research pays attention to the family role in child-bearing. Demography in particular focuses on the births, deaths, and movement of people as the means through which populations change.

Whether to have children, and the number of children to have, are immensely personal questions, but they are also questions of great social importance. As a consequence, to promote general well-being, societies, families, or human groups try to influence people's decisions on having children. Child-bearing is, then, not only a matter of personal satisfaction, but also a link to the broader society and its future.

The dynamics of fertility operate at both the micro and macro levels and are connected to both individual and collective considerations. On the individual level, the value and cost of children to parents come into play. For instance, the 19th-century economist Thomas Malthus viewed child-bearing as a natural "urge to reproduce" that was balanced against the moral considerations of "responsible parenthood." As for the *social context* of reproduction, Karl Marx, for instance, believed that each stage of human history had unique dynamics of population, of production and reproduction, and that in particular the structures of production and reproduction, and their interrelationship, needed to be considered together.

The historical, long-term trends in the dynamics of fertility show a substantial change from an average of seven births per woman in the mid-19th century to under two births in the last decades of the 20th century. John Gillis, Louise Tilly, and David Levine (1992) have termed this a "quiet revolution," a turnaround just as consequential for society as the other great transformations of this period, urbanization and industrialization. This modern reproductive pattern, or "culture of contraception," then, is just as significant a mark of our times as the urbanized life patterns and higher average standards of living in industrialized economies, and the dynamics of this historical change are a key to the prevalent reproductive pattern. The change hinges not only on the concrete number of children, but also on child-bearing as an important symbolic activity. Child-bearing contributes to how people "think about themselves, communicate with one another, and construct their gender, class and communal identities" (p. 8).

On the family level, the last third of the 20th century saw dramatic changes (Goldscheider, Webster, and Kaufman, 1995). The previous hundred years had brought a declining fertility within marriages but little change in the demographics of marital behaviour except a slow increase in divorce. In contrast, the period after about 1970 saw a sharp rise in divorce, the growth of non-marital cohabitation, including child-bearing in cohabitation, and persistent below-replacement fertility. These changes inevitably led to a variation in parental experiences. Women's parental role became increasingly separated from marital relationships, and men's parental role became even more dependent on marital relationships, because men became less likely to be living with their own children and more likely to be parenting the children of their spouses. The higher levels of divorce represent costs for men in their parental roles. In time, as men become more aware of this tendency, as Frances Goldscheider, Pamela Webster, and Gayle Kaufman (1995) suggest, they may become more interested in avoiding divorce by becoming more flexible and willing to participate in housework and child care.

On the societal level, the decline in mortality ultimately required the re-establishment of a demographic equilibrium. The making of this new equilibrium took in both structural and cultural questions; that is, it involved "the structural conditions that motivate behaviour and the spread of ideas and information that reinforce behavioural change" (Hirshman 1994). A central part of these structural conditions is the very social organization of paid and unpaid work. For instance, Ronald Rindfuss and Karin Brewster (1996: 264) propose that agricultural or pre-industrial societies have a "greater compatibility of household responsibilities and economically productive work." In industrial societies, the degree of incompatibility experienced by working parents is an important aspect of fertility dynamics. It may be argued that this incompatibility between paid and unpaid work has become less accentuated, permitting a stable fertility at somewhat under two births per woman.

FERTILITY TRENDS

Figure 6.1 shows the long-term changes in fertility. These data are based on the *total fertility rate*, which is called a period rate because it takes the rates of child-bearing of women at various ages in a given year and sums them to get a measure of what would be the average births per woman if the rates for this one year represented the lifetime experiences of women. The trend is not uniform, but the overall pattern is a decline from about seven to under two births per woman. The period from about 1946 to 1966 represents an exception to the long-term trend. This period measure of fertility tends to exaggerate the "baby boom," because it was partly a function of an earlier onset of child-bearing and the closer spacing of children. The measure also exaggerates the subsequent decline, because it was partly a function of the delay of child-bearing. Significantly, the period 1976-96 saw a fairly constant level of between 1.8 and 1.6 births.

Because it excludes the question of timing, the *cohort completed fertility* better represents the underlying reality, but is less current. This measure gives the average number of children ever born, for women from given birth cohorts. Figure 6.2 shows that the cohorts born in the early 1930s had levels as high as 3.4 births on average. The subsequent decline shows an estimated 1.9 births for the cohorts of the early 1950s and 1.8 for those born in the late 1950s.

Using data from the 1995 General Social Survey, we can also take a cohort measure of children ever born until the time of the survey (Table 6.1). The youngest women represented here are those born in 1952-56, who had 1.85 children on average. It is useful to

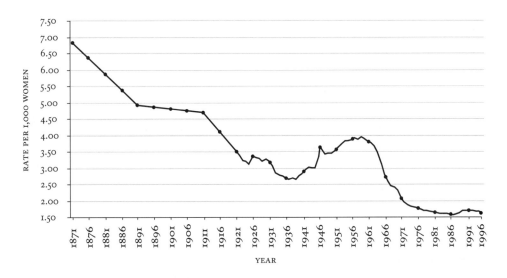

FIG 6.1 Period total fertility rate, Canada, 1871-1996

Source: Romaniuc 1984: 121-122; Statistics Canada, no. 82-553, no.84-210; Beaujot and McQuillan 1982: 54; and special tabulations.

consider the various family sizes separately, because the most prevalent sizes are now two, three, zero, one, and "four or more."

In the 1927-31 cohort, 46 percent of women had four or more children, and consequently three-quarters of all children were in families of this size (Dumas and Bélanger 1997: 41). In the 1952-56 cohort, 8 percent had four or more children, representing a fifth of children.

In the 1942-46 and subsequent cohorts, 42 percent have two children, and the next largest category is three children. In the younger cohorts, larger numbers of women stop at two children, with less than half of those with two children proceeding to a third birth (Dumas and Bélanger 1997: 44) The fertility decline over cohorts has mostly involved lower proportions of third or higher order births and a greater concentration at the level of two births (Péron, Lapierre-Adamcyk, and Morissette 1987). Consequently, three-quarters of children are in families of size two or three.

In the mid-1990s some 15 percent of fertility is a function of third births (Bélanger and Dumas 1998: 51-65). According to the 1995 General Social Survey, having a third child was more common for women born before 1946, for those who had their first child before age 25, and those who had a short interval between the first two births. A third birth is much less likely for women who are not in relationships. Socio-economic variables are also important, with higher probabilities of third births for women without a secondary school certificate or who are not employed. According to socio-cultural variables, women born outside of Canada, the United States, and Europe, as well as those who attend religious services on a weekly basis, have higher propensities for third births.

235

WOMEN BY FIVE-YEAR BIRTH COHORTS, 1927-56, AND NUMBER OF CHILDREN EVER BORN, 1995

	1952-56	1947-51	1942-46	1937-41	1932-36	1927-31
no children	19.1	12.8	12.1	10.7	13.0	10.5
1 child	14.6	13.7	9.5	11.1	12.0	7.4
2 children	38.3	42.1	41.5	26.1	15.9	24.8
3 children	19.6	23.0	21.1	27.4	16.7	10.9
4 children	7.1	6.8	6.8	8.0	16.1	13.3
5+ children	1.3	1.4	8.9	16.8	26.4	33.1
per woman	1.85	2.03	2.33	2.77	3.12	3.41

Source: Dumas and Bélanger 1997:41. Statistics Canada, General Social Survey, 1995.

TABLE 6.1

The proportion of women with one child increased slightly in the last two cohorts, but remained under 15 percent. While research suggests that children in one-child families have various advantages, people tend not to prefer this option. For instance, only 5 to 6 percent of persons aged 15-29 indicated in 1990 that they intended to have only one child (Ravanera 1995: 19). It is also noteworthy that the proportion with no children did not change as sig-nificantly as the average number of children. While 19 percent of the youngest cohort had no children, some of these women aged 39 to 43 may still have had a child after the survey date. This would suggest a cohort fertility of about 1.8 to 1.9 and a level of childlessness not too much above 15 percent.

Table 6.2 shows the total intended births for women and men. The lowest average expected family size was 1.9 for women aged 35-39 in 1990; younger persons expected an average of 2.3 children. According to these intentions the level of childlessness would not exceed 16 percent. The 1995 General Social Survey also showed that persons under 30 expected to have an average of 2.3 children. The lowest intended size was 2 for persons aged 40-49 in 1995, and fewer than 10 percent of persons under age 40 expected to have no children (Dupuis 1998: 3). The analysis of intended births indicates that some of those births might not materialize, in part because respondents may be assuming stable relationships when the time comes to have children. They may also not antic-ipate other complications associated with child-bearing, or even the difficulties of conceiving a child.

INTENDED NUMBER OF CHILDREN BY AGE AND SEX, CANADA, 1990

	0	1	2	3	4+	AVERAGE
Males						
15-29	6.0	4.9	52.2	26.3	10.6	2.31
30-34	8.5	9.8	49.4	23.3	9.1	2.19
35-39	10.5	10.2	52.6	17.0	9.7	2.10
40-44	13.0	13.0	42.7	21.9	9.1	2.03
Females						
15-29	6.8	6.0	47.9	28.4	10.7	2.30
30-34	7.7	11.5	51.1	21.7	8.0	2.12
35-39	15.7	11.3	47.0	18.3	7.7	1.93
40-44	15.1	12.3	42.8	21.1	8.7	2.00

Source: Beaujot 1995: 19, 54. Statistics Canada, General Social Survey, 1990.

TABLE 6.2

Age patterns of child-bearing

In addition to the larger numbers of women who stop at two children, the other major trend is the increasing delay in having a first child. While the level of fertility changed extensively from 1966 to 1976, bringing the total fertility rate from 2.8 to 1.8 births per women, the age patterns remained remarkably constant (Table 6.3). Between 1976 and 1996, the number of births per women only changed from 1.8 to 1.6, but the age patterns changed so that 37 percent of births were occurring to women in their thirties, compared to 24 percent in 1976. Similarly, the births occurring to women before age 25 declined from 39 to 28 percent of births. As well, only 6.7 percent of first births were occurring to women over 30 in 1971, compared to 26.7 percent in 1993 (Dumas and Bélanger 1996: 40).

This changing age pattern is also visible in the trends in birth rates by age groups (Figure 6.3). The downward trend at ages 15-29, especially at 20-24, is in contrast to an upward trend at ages 30-39. In 1970, age group 25-29 replaced age 20-24 as the age of highest fertility (Grindstaff 1995: 13). By 1990, age group 30-34 had come to occupy second place among these rankings.

The decline is less substantial at age group 15-19, but nonetheless it shows a change from 34.0 births per 1,000 women in 1976 to 22.1 births per 1,000 in 1996. This is not because of the postponement of first intercourse, which is occurring at earlier ages on average. The estimates from the 1990 Health Promotion Survey suggest that slightly more than half of the teenage respondents had intercourse by age 16 and over 80 percent by age 20 (Odynak 1994).

Marital status

The proportions of younger women who have had at least one child vary significantly by marital status (Table 6.4). The category most likely to have had a child is the formerly married, followed by the married and cohabitating. For the total ages 15-29, over two-thirds of the formerly married have children. Zenaida Ravanera (1995: 18) observes that some of these marriages may have occurred at younger ages, but that this nonetheless represents a significant burden for women under 30 who are no longer married.

DISTRIBUTION OF AGE-SPECIFIC FERTILITY, CANADA, 1966-96

	1966	1976	1986	1996
15-19	8.5	9.4	7.3	6.8
20-24	30.1	29.8	24.9	21.1
25-29	29.1	35.6	37.3	33.6
30-34	18.4	17.9	22.6	26.8
35-39	10.2	5.9	6.9	10.0
40-44	3.4	1.2	1.0	1.6
45-49	0.3	0.1	0.0	0.1
TOTAL	100.0	100.0	100.0	100.0
Total Fertility Rate	2.8	1.8	1.6	1.6

Source: Statistics Canada, no. 82-553, 1993; special tabulations.

TABLE 6.3

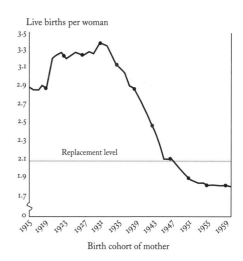

FIG 6.2 Completed fertility by women's birth cohorts, 1915 to 1960, Canada
Source: Ford and Nault 1996: 44.

237

PERCENTAGE WITH AT LEAST ONE CHILD AMONG WOMEN AGED 15-29, BY FIVE-YEAR AGE GROUP AND MARITAL STATUS, CANADA, 1991

	15-19	20-24	25-29	TOTAL 15-29
Never married	2.4	8.9	16.0	7.2
Cohabiting	26.6	28.3	41.1	34.6
Married	39.5	48.4	67.0	54.2
Separated, widowed or divorced	43.5	66.8	70.2	68.8
Ever-married	31.3	41.2	62.0	55.2
All women	3.7	20.3	48.4	26.2

Source: Ravanera 1995: 18. Statistics Canada, Census Data.

TABLE 6.4

Some of the births to women who had never been legally married would have occurred in cohabiting relationships that had since moved into the separated category. In effect, by 1996 a third of births occurred to women who were not married or who did not declare their marital status, up from 9 percent in 1971 (Belle and McQuillan 1994). The majority of these births are occurring in cohabiting relationships.

Living with children at mid-life

Table 6.5 presents data on children ever born and children (natural, adopted, step) currently in residence with a given parent. At ages 30-34, the experience of men and women is relatively different. Some 58 percent of men have children, but only 52 percent of men have children living with them. In comparison, 73 percent of women in this age group have children, and 71 percent are living with children. Men also show more marital status differences than do women, especially those who are not married. For the separated, widowed, and divorced, 8 percent of men compared to 77 percent of women are living with children. Living with children is also more common for remarried women than men: 73 percent compared to 39 percent. That is, at ages 30-34, the majority of men in a first union are living with children, but that does not apply to men in subsequent unions or men who are not in a union status. For women at this same age group, the majority of all groups except the never-married are living with children.

Similar variations occur at ages 40-44, though the differences are not as marked. Men in this age group have an average of 1.9 children ever born and 1.5 children in residence, compared to women's 2 children ever born and 1.6 children in residence. The experiences of married or cohabiting men and women are similar, but other marital status categories show considerable differences. For instance, the proportions living with children are 51 percent of remarried men and 36 percent of separated, widowed, and divorced men, compared to 60 percent of remarried women and 62 percent of separated, widowed, and divorced women.

At the oldest of the mid-life age groups, half of the men and 53 percent of the women are not living with children. While they have had an average of 2.7 children for women and 2.4 for men, the average numbers living with parents are reduced to 0.7 and 0.9 for women and men respectively. The major differences are in the married or cohabiting and remarried categories, in which a higher proportion of men than women are living with children.

**CHILDREN EVER BORN AND PERCENTAGE LIVING WITH CHILDREN, WOMEN AND MEN
AGED 30-54, BY FIVE-YEAR AGE GROUPS AND MARITAL STATUS, CANADA, 1990**

	MEN				WOMEN			
	30-34	40-44	50-54	30-54	30-34	40-44	50-54	30-54
Percent with zero children ever born								
Single	93.4	92.9	—	91.9	79.0	79.3	74.9	82.7
Married or cohabiting	27.7	9.4	5.3	14.2	19.4	—	3.9	12.3
Remarried	18.2	11.2	5.0	13.7	19.0	15.5	3.0	13.6
Separated, widowed, or divorced	—	22.1	—	22.1	15.3	19.3	8.2	14.5
TOTAL	41.8	18.2	12.2	24.3	26.7	15.6	7.8	18.5
Average children ever born								
Single	0.09	0.20	0.12	0.16	0.41	0.23	0.39	0.29
Married or cohabiting	1.34	2.09	2.71	1.95	1.67	2.21	2.89	2.14
Remarried	1.58	1.96	2.55	1.96	1.67	1.87	2.61	2.01
Separated, widowed, or divorced	1.39	1.58	2.25	1.64	1.63	1.69	2.52	2.02
TOTAL	1.07	1.85	2.45	1.71	1.50	1.98	2.69	1.96
Percent living with children								
Single	2.5	1.0	0.0	2.7	19.5	20.7	14.3	14.5
Married or cohabiting	71.8	88.4	64.0	79.2	79.8	—	51.9	77.8
Remarried	39.5	50.6	34.9	48.1	73.3	60.2	21.0	58.7
Separated, widowed, or divorced	—	36.3	—	21.9	77.4	61.9	49.8	62.6
TOTAL	51.9	70.3	50.4	61.6	71.3	76.9	47.2	68.5

Source: Beaujot 1995: 52. Statistics Canada, General Social Survey, 1990.

TABLE 6.5

Considering the total over all marital status categories, living with children is more common for women in the early years of mid-life, but for both men and women it is also the dominant experience for at least half of each age group. About half of the men aged 30-34 are living with children, reaching a peak of 70 percent at ages 40-44, and down to half once again at ages 50-54. For women, 70 percent are living with children at ages 30-34, reaching a peak of 75 percent at ages 35-44, and down to slightly less than half by age 50-54.

This table does not permit us to measure change over time, which would clearly be in the direction of lower proportions living with children. For instance, Thomas Burch (1990: 39) found that at ages 40-59, some 29 percent of persons were living with children under 15 years of age in 1986, compared to 33 percent in 1981.

Part of the change over time is a function of the greater predominance of marital status categories other than married or cohabitating. As Table 6.5 shows, persons, especially men, who are single, separated, widowed or divorced, and even those who are remarried, are less likely to be living with children. But at mid-life over three-quarters of men and women are living in relationships. For all of them, the most common experience is not only to have children, but also to be living with children at least until ages 45-49.

INTERPRETING THE LONG-TERM TREND

In interpreting the long-term trend, demographers often make reference to the theory of demographic transition. In the history of the more developed countries, and more recently in what is called the Third World, mortality and fertility have moved from high to low levels over periods of economic and industrial transformation. Researchers often disagree, though, about the relative role of economic and cultural factors in accounting for this transformation. Economic explanations highlight people's adaptation to evolving opportunities, while cultural explanations concentrate on the social construction of preferences and the evaluation of opportunities. In analyzing fertility decline, economic explanations consider the advantages of smaller families, while cultural explanations consider the "think ability" of control over family size (Coale 1973). One study (Lesthaeghe and Vanderhoeft 1997) speaks both of the economic conditions that make people "ready" and the cultural conditions that make them "willing" to have fewer children.

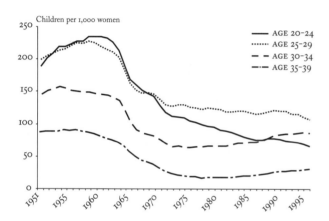

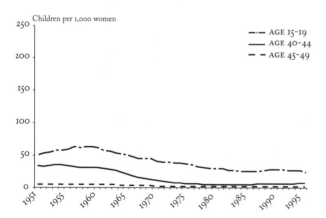

FIG 6.3 Fertility rates by age groups, Canada, 1951–96

Source: Statistics Canada, no. 82-553; and special tabulations.

In the pre-transition stage, say, before 1850 for Canada, fertility tended to be uniformly high, in the order of seven births per woman. An economic explanation for this would focus on the role of the family in pre-industrial societies. The family, as the basic economic unit in society, was responsible for not only consumption, but also production and security. From a fairly young age, children were important as labour in family production and sustenance. A cultural explanation would suggest that the very idea of planning family size was probably foreign to most people's mentalities (Van de Walle and Knodel 1980). Although some forms of contraception were known, especially coitus interruptus/withdrawal and abstinence, the spacing of births was not greatly changed by the number of previous births or surviving children. Etienne Van de Walle and John Knodel (1980) suggest that a considerable number of unwanted births occurred. They refer, for instance, to sayings such as "Smallpox is the poor man's friend" (eliminating unwanted children) and to the high level of infant mortality, which would have partly been a function of the neglect of children who were not wanted in the first place (Boswell 1988). Thus, even if they were ready and willing to have fewer children, couples would have needed to find the "ability" to control family size through contraception (Lesthaeghe and Vanderhoeft 1997).

Demographic transition

The transition in fertility, which started in Canada in the 1870s, also had both economic and cultural facets. With the industrial and economic transformations of society, most economic production became organized outside of families, and the role of the family changed. Children became less valuable in family production, and the costs of children increased as they needed to be in school for a longer period; the economic role of children changed from that of producer to that of dependant. The movement of economic production out of the household thus ruptured the close link between economic production and demographic reproduction (Dickinson and Russell 1986; Boily 1987). In addition, in the face of economic hardship, incapacity, and old age, social security replaced the family as the basic welfare net. The economic rationale for having children was reduced with the extension of state power; family and kin groups became less important as a guarantee of security. Looking at more recent trends, Anatole Romaniuc (1991) largely focuses on economic explanations related to issues such as the deteriorating relative income of young adults and the pressure for higher standards of living in an individualistic society. These factors all influence the extent to which people are "ready" to have children.

The cultural explanation suggests that the idea of limiting births within marriage and the use of contraception were innovations whose legitimacy spread over time, that fertility changed as new models of the family and appropriate behaviour became prevalent. The deliberate regulation of births within marriage represented a new model of behaviour, which was diffused across societies that were in cultural contact, first in Europe and eventually around the world. For instance, in his interpretation of the higher fertility rate in Quebec until the 1950s, Jacques Henripin (1957) saw an "acceptance of nature" as a "cultural attitude toward life" or an "approach to existence" that contrasted with a modern model, which he called a "contraceptive control civilization."

Cultural explanations notice that fertility transitions, rather than involving slow adaptations to economic change, have sometimes been "sudden, sharp and discontinuous" (Pollak and Watkins 1993: 468). In addition, cultural barriers have sometimes impeded the spread of new models of behaviour. In Belgium, for example, fertility rates declined sooner in the French-speaking population than in the Flemish population. Similarly, French-Canadian fertility rates for a long time stayed above those of English Canada. Family limitation had just scarcely started before 1925 among French-Canadians in Montreal, while it had begun in the last quarter of the 19th century in Europe. Minorities, such as Native peoples, could resist the "penetration" of different forms of behaviour, including the adoption of changed modes of fertility. Looking at the European fertility transitions, Susan Cotts Watkins (1990) observed that there had once been a strong association between linguistic diversity and demographic diversity and that reductions in demographic differentials went hand in hand with reductions in linguistic diversity. Once the change starts in groups that have been isolated, it tends to be very rapid. In support of this cultural explanation, Van de Walle and Knodel (1980) noted that the beginning of the fertility decline had occurred in a variety of different socio-economic conditions, and once the decline started the process appeared to be irreversible, as if people had simply adapted to a new form of behaviour. In their analysis of the 1984 Canadian Fertility Survey, T.R. Balakrishnan, Evelyne Lapierre-Adamcyk, and K.J. Krotki (1993: 103) found that economic factors were far less important than socio-cultural considerations.

Nonetheless, both economic and cultural factors are key to understanding fertility trends. In his discussion of a "unifying theory" for the global fertility transition, John Caldwell (1997) observes that these economic and cultural elements are an integral part of the transition in Western and Third World countries. The economic elements involve couples making spontaneous adjustments to changed life conditions. The cultural elements include ideological debates, like those introduced by Malthus, as well as activist interventions, like those associated with the birth control movement or the United Nations conferences on population and development. Once fertility decline starts, it tends to spread rapidly, especially in societies that are linguistically homogeneous or that started the decline at a later time in history. The "willingness" to control fertility can spread rapidly.

Earlier versions of the demographic transition theory had expected fertility in the post-transition phase to fluctuate around replacement levels as a function of changing socio-economic climates, but given the persistent below-replacement fertility certain authors have to come to question this aspect of the theory. The period since the mid-1960s has seen changes in a series of family-related behaviour. Compared to the earlier period, with its slow rise in divorce rates and long-term decline in birthrates, the recent period has seen higher divorce rates, greater propensities to cohabit, lower marriage rates, older ages at first marriage, lower levels of child-bearing, and more births in cohabitating unions. These changes, which are highly interrelated, have occurred throughout the countries of European-based civilization, both in the market economies and in the former state economies of Eastern Europe (Roussel 1989). Dirk Van de Kaa (1987) has gone so far as to call it a second demographic transition. Like the earlier transition, which brought markedly lower levels of mortality and fertility to this same cultural region, these more recent demographic changes are deeply rooted in the institutional and cultural makeups of these countries, and they have had profound effects on entire societies.

Baby boom and baby bust

These explanations remain inadequate for interpreting the baby boom phase in Canadian fertility. Although a number of countries had higher fertility rates after the Second World War, this pattern persisted only in Canada, the United States, and Australia. Looking at the trends until the mid-1970s, some researchers suggested that the fertility patterns were cyclical (Easterlin 1980). But the subsequent trends indicated that there was only one cycle, or that the baby boom was best seen as an exception to the trend (Wright and Maxim 1987). This exception can be interpreted in both economic and cultural terms. The 1950s were a period of sustained economic growth with much confidence in the future. In addition the decade was a time, sometimes called the "golden age of the family," in which life was family-centred and there was strong reinforcement for an ideal of three or four children, with mother at home. People who did not follow these trends, including those who did not marry or had no children, were seen as deviants, and it was considered inappropriate for women to work while their children were young (Veevers 1980; Boyd 1984).

In effect, with children going to school longer, mothers who stayed at home were devoting themselves to their children's education and future earning potential. Children were doing less paid work, and also probably less unpaid work, so that they could devote themselves to their own education, as an investment in their future earnings.

At the same time, in some regards the baby boom fits into long-term trends. The baby boom accentuated the long-term trend toward more universal marriage, at an earlier age, and less childlessness (Gee 1986). While marriage rates subsequently declined, the universality of entry into relationships and the ages of these entries did not change extensively, especially if we include all intimate relationships. In addition, the long-term trends, including those of the baby boom period, have involved a greater compression of child-bearing and a certain standardization both in entry into relationships and the focus on two or three children (Gee 1986).

PROXIMATE FACTORS OF FERTILITY

Studies of fertility find it useful to consider the specific factors involved in any birth. Except in cases of artificial reproduction, what is needed is the ability to conceive (fecundity), along with sexual intercourse without contraception or abortion. For instance, Balakrishnan (1989: 235) calculated that under 1984 Canadian health conditions, the "maximum" fecundity would be an average of some 16.4 births per woman. Of these, some 11.5 births are eliminated through contraceptive usage, 0.6 though induced abortions, 1.9 through non-marriage, and 0.8 through lactation, which can delay ovulation, resulting in an actual fertility rate (excluding births outside of marriage) of 1.6 births per woman. At least in an "accounting" framework, the level of child-bearing is a function of

243

these proximate factors of exposure to the risk of conception and successful parturition. In effect, these factors largely involve union formation and dissolution, along with contraception and abortion. To understand fertility rates, then, researchers need to consider people's age at entry into and exit from unions as well as the proportions of people in unions.

These immediate factors go beyond the pure mechanics of fertility. For instance, secure and efficient contraception can change attitudes and norms toward sex, marriage, and children, as people become accustomed to the idea of sex without marriage and relationships without children (Preston 1986). Also, with union dissolution more common, women have to be more concerned about their own independence and self-sufficiency (Davis 1986).

Union formation and dissolution

The links between marriage and fertility have become attenuated to the point that Susan McDaniel (1989, 1996) suggests the need for a reconceptualization of the nuptiality/fertility relationship. In 1996 over a third of births occurred outside of marriage, compared to 13 percent in 1980 (Dumas and Bélanger 1997: 155). The births outside of marriage are largely occurring in common-law unions. For instance, in Quebec the proportion of births involving no declared father was stable at about 5 percent of births over the period 1975-94 (Duchesne 1997: 1)

Despite this weaker connection, marriage and fertility retain significant links. At each age group, the fertility rate is higher in married couples than in cohabiting relationships (Beaujot 1995: 50; Dumas and Bélanger 1997: 159). The formerly married also have more children than do couples in cohabiting unions. In addition, the lowest fertility rate is among the never-married, and fewer couples in cohabiting unions express the intention of having babies, especially if they do not plan to marry (Dupuis 1998: 3).

The 1995 General Social Survey showed other links between marriage and fertility. For instance, single people who planned to marry expected to have more children than those who did not expect to marry. The survey also found that a higher proportion of married than common-law persons indicated that "having at least one child is very important to be happy in life" (Dumas and Bélanger 1997: 156). At ages 35 and over the proportions with no children varied extensively by marital status: 27.5 percent of persons living common-law and 81.9 percent of never-married persons had no children, compared to 9.1 percent of married persons and 12.2 percent of formerly married persons. As well, Zheng Wu (1997) found that remarried persons were more likely to consider having a third child than were formerly married persons in new common-law unions.

Thus the lower prevalence of marriage, along with the greater prevalence of cohabitation, tend to reduce rates of fertility. The later entry into unions and the greater prevalence of union dissolution have less effect on child-bearing, because births tend to be compressed into a short part of the life cycle. Nonetheless, it would seem reasonable to speculate that the greater instability of relationships makes some persons reluctant to go for third or subsequent births.

Based on data from the 1984 Canadian Fertility Survey, Fernando Rajulton and T.R. Balakrishnan (1990) found that cohabitation was having little effect on the first birth, but subsequent births were rare in such unions. Conversely, third births were mostly restricted to women who had not cohabitated. Using the same survey, Lapierre-Adamcyk (1987) found that the average expected family size of women aged 18-34 who "choose only cohabitation" was 1.4 compared to 2.3 for those who "choose only marriage." Among women who chose cohabitation but not marriage, 30 percent expected to have no children. While the differences have since declined, data for 1985-94 indicated an average total fertility rate of 2.87 for married persons and 1.44 for common-law partners (Dumas and Bélanger 1997: 163).

Studies also show an association between a later age at first birth and lower completed family size (Rao and Balakrishnan 1988)—although people who start having children later still have time to reach the smaller average family size of two or three children. The difference in completed family size between those who start early and those who start later was reduced to about 0.5 children (Balakrishnan et al. 1988). Women who start having children later are more likely to have more education, higher incomes, and married later (Grindstaff, Balakrishnan, and Maxim, 1989).

Contraception

The main proximate factor is contraception. In *The Bedroom and the State*, Angus McLaren and Arlene Tiger McLaren (1986) observe that in the period 1880 to 1945 access to birth control and abortion in Canada was limited by relatively deliberate state action. According to the 1984 National Fertility Survey (Balakrishnan, Krotki, and Lapierre-Adamcyk 1985), among all women aged 18-49, some 68.4 percent were using contraception at the time of the survey. Contraceptive usage was highest among cohabiting never-married couples (83.1 percent), but it was still 50.8 percent among never-married women who were not cohabiting. For single women using contraception, 71.2 percent were using the pill. Among currently married persons using contraception, 59.4 percent were using sterilization. For all women aged 30-49, 52 percent had either been sterilized or their husband had been sterilized (Balakrishnan et al. 1988). Once they had reached their desired family size, partners showed a high propensity to turn to an irreversible method of contraception, making for less unplanned births in marriage. According to the 1995 General Social Survey, a quarter of couples aged 30-34 and half of couples aged 35-39 chose the option of sterilization for one of the partners (Bélanger and Dumas 1998: 68-69). While only 14 percent of couples chose sterilization after they had one child, the figure increased to 47 percent with two children.

For people using contraception, by far the most common method is sterilization, followed by the pill for 26 percent of couples (Bélanger and Dumas 1998: 79). The continued importance of the pill was partly anticipated by the findings of the 1984 survey, which indicated that 10 percent of women had regrets about sterilization. They said, "If they were to make the decision now they would not elect to become sterilized" (Balakrishnan, Lapierre-Adamcyk, and Krotki 1993: 226). In addition, as a method of contraception, male sterilization has become more common than female sterilization among younger couples (Boroditsky, Fisher, and Sand 1996; Bélanger and Dumas 1998). This finding reflects a significant change from the 1984 survey, which had found that the rate of female sterilization was twice as high as the male rate (Balakrishnan, Lapierre-Adamcyk, and Krotki 1993: 198). Given that condoms have also increased in relative usage, and are much more important than female barrier methods or the IUD, it would appear that men have increased their responsibility for contraception.

Abortions increased from 3 per 100 live births in 1970 to 27.4 in 1994 (Balakrishnan 1987; Wadhera 1990; Dumas and Bélanger 1997: 48). Data collection has become more difficult because abortions occur both in hospitals and clinics, but it would appear that more efficient contraception methods do not preclude significant numbers of abortions. The 1994 age-specific abortion rates imply a sum of 0.48 abortions per woman over the reproductive years.

Both the Ansley Coale (1973) and Richard Easterlin and Eileen Crimmins (1985) explanations of the demographic transition highlight the importance of contraception. For Coale, a fertility decline requires not only that a smaller family size will bring advantages for the family members, but also that it becomes "thinkable" to control family size and that the means of fertility regulation are available. To place these concepts into a broader framework, we could say that people have to be ready for a change that represents advantages, willing to make a change that is seen as legitimate, and able to gain access to the circumstances that make the change possible (Lesthaeghe and Vanderhoeft 1997). For Easterlin, mortality reduction brings an increased supply of children, which may be larger than the demand for children. People will act on this imbalance between supply and demand depending on the cost of fertility limitation. Economic and cultural factors are relevant both to the demand for children and to the effective availability of contraception (Alder 1992). The demand for children is a function of both the economic value they represent for parents and the symbolic values that adults place on children. Similarly, contraception depends not only on its availability but also on its cultural acceptability.

Clearly, this cultural acceptability has changed from the times when Malthus was concerned about the "vice" represented by forms of contraception other than abstinence and coitus interruptus. Today we not only value "responsible parenthood," as Malthus proposed, but also see the deliberate promotion of family planning. For instance, the 1994 International Conference on Population and Development argued for "reproductive health and reproductive rights." There has been an increased acceptance of the view that individuals should have the right to decide their own child-bearing patterns and have access to the facilities that would permit them to exercise that right.

Fecundity

Fecundity, or the ability to conceive, is another basic proximate factor. Estimates indicate that while 91 percent of women can become pregnant at age 30, the numbers are reduced to 77 percent by age 35 and 53 percent by age 40 (Rajulton, Balakrishnan, and Ravanera 1990). With infertility defined as a length of time—one year—in which someone tries without success to achieve a pregnancy, estimates indicate that as many as 15 percent of couples have problems in this area (Achilles 1986). The Royal Commission on New Reproductive Technologies (1993) suggested that we "proceed with care" in this area. Given the moral issues and financial costs, the Commission proposed that various constraints be placed on the use of new technologies. For instance, it recommended in vitro fertilization only for women with blocked fallopian tubes, which represents about half of current users. The Commission suggested a ban on couples choosing the sex of their child through artificial insemination or abortion. Still, research is proceeding, including methods of injecting sperms into eggs and of permitting fertilized eggs to better emerge from their coating.

These considerations of fecundity, contraception, and unions are not just the proximate factors of fertility. They also shape our identities and our relationships. By removing the link between sex and reproduction, and permitting relationships without children, effective contraception has had a profound effect on relationships and marriages. Few aspects of family behaviour have changed so fundamentally as the extent and effectiveness of control over marital fertility. Nonetheless, unintended pregnancies remain frequent. U.S. estimates indicate that almost 40 percent of pregnancies taken to term were unintended at the time of conception (Montgomery 1996: 100).

THE VALUE AND COST OF CHILDREN

In his extensive analysis of *Fertility, Class and Gender in Britain, 1860-1940*, Simon Szreter (1995) employs the concept of "perceived, relative childrearing costs" as the underlying thesis that he uses to make sense of the trends and differentials. By relative costs he is referring to the costs relative to the benefits or value of children. He includes not only the economic but also the social, cultural, and emotional costs and benefits. Of all of these, the economic costs are the easiest to identify, and economic development brings a rise in the "normatively sanctioned cost of childrearing" (p. 443). He calls these "normatively sanctioned costs" because many of them are a function of cultural understandings. For instance, the value of children's labour in comparison to the needs for their education can help explain why fertility in 1911 was highest for coal miners and lowest for professionals as well as clerical and commercial agents (p. 312).

While difficult to measure, the desire for children, or the demand for children, is a function of the values and costs associated with children. When asked about the advantages and

BOX 6.1 | *Orientations to having children*

Among other questions, the 1989-90 Oxford-Middlesex survey (see Box 3.4) asked people open questions concerning various aspects of child-bearing. The responses tell us much about the normative context of child-bearing.

Asked, "Why do you think people have children?" and about the advantages of having children, most respondents referred to love, companionship, and the joy of watching them grow and achieve things in life. Many spoke of the joy of teaching children in a fundamental way, watching them develop into responsible human beings. Some spoke of a deeply personal experience or referred to intangible things, the little smiles of the babies, the enduring love of children, feelings that are hard to put into words, "the true joys in life" so that the hard parts do not mean that much. Some spoke simply of enjoying children, that parenting is a learning experience, you get to know yourself, or the joy of doing things as a family and the comfort of having people around when you are older, of being part of an extended family. Some spoke of carrying on the family name or of regeneration in the broad sense: reproducing yourself, seeing yourself in the children, having someone to pass things along to. Others mentioned creating a bond within the family, or children being healthy for a marriage, or simply the need for families to have children.

A number of people found it difficult to say why people have children. It was not something consciously figured out: people want children, it is the natural thing to do, tradition, they had not thought much about it. Many, especially older respondents, did not know why people have children. Having had children, they enjoyed raising them; older people also mentioned friendships with children, which was not the reason for having children initially.

The disadvantages of having children relate especially to financial and emotional costs: children involve personal costs, you have to give a lot of yourself, they represent constraints on your time and on the decisions you can make. Some spoke of the worry when children are sick or in trouble or about how they will turn out (given the condition the world is in). The worry focuses especially on the teenage years. Others spoke of the workload. In effect, some see lots of disadvantages: children are so expensive, they are at home for a longer time through school and college, they are so much work, you have to make so many sacrifices for them, from being up in the night to steering them through all the stress and worry of the teenage years. But they note that all this disappears once the children are adults. Many said they would not consider these things to be disadvantages; you have to expect these problems. Sometimes children can be a real disappointment, especially if they do not turn out to meet your expectations.

Asked if having children produced more benefits or disadvantages, most respondents (86.2 percent) said there were more advantages. Those who said there were more disadvantages (4.8 percent) simply did not care too much for children. A few were single mothers who were referring to the disadvantages at the stage of life in which children were dependent. Some 15.2 percent specifically said there were no real disadvantages.

Regarding the best age for women to start

having children, most thought it was around the mid-twenties to late twenties. Women should first get their lives in order, but not wait until it is too late to have the children they want. Those who said it was best to wait until after age 30 referred to having careers in order and then taking time out for children and going back to the career. Persons who suggested younger ages, say, the early twenties, referred to being more flexible at that age, and that having children was more difficult later. Some suggested a gap of some two years after marriage. Women should be mature enough to handle the responsibility, physically ready, and have some financial security. They should first develop themselves, be married a few years, be secure in their jobs or careers. Some referred to the difficulty of doing so many things by a given age: education, be on your own, career, marriage, children. In effect, the ideal age varied considerably, between 20 and 35.

Asked why they think there is an increase in the number of women having their first child after age 30, most referred to career questions, higher education, and financial stability. Some saw this very positively, for instance, in terms of careers for women, or orienting family and marriage questions in terms of women's interests. Slightly less than half of the respondents were basically positive about the change to later childbearing. Others saw negative aspects: it could be too late, it may be hazardous to wait too long, there are health questions, it is not fair to children to have older parents, or you might be physically too tired by that time. Some referred to making choices, not following the set patterns in terms of marriage and the time to marry and have children. Older respondents were more likely to see the negative side, possibly consider-

ing it more appropriate for women to stay home and raise a family. Younger women sometimes spoke of it being safe to have children later, when you are more financially secure and can give the children the things they need.

The majority (73.7 percent) of respondents said the ideal number of children was two or three. When they were asked why not have more, most referred to the costs, that it was hard to afford more, hard to manage, there were time and emotional costs, there was a need to give a certain amount of time to each child each day. Respondents said the world was built for smaller families given the number of bedrooms in houses or seats in cars, for example. Some also noted the population and environmental problems with larger families. When asked why not fewer than two or three, most said a child should have at least one sibling or that one child did not make for a real family.

Asked what they thought of couples who deliberately choose not to have children, most said that was acceptable if it was what the couple wants: fine, their decision, their choice. Some, especially older people, wondered why people bothered to get married if they did not want to have children. Some referred to the couple being selfish, but acknowledged that if they did not want the responsibility they should not have children. Having no children can be justified for health or career reasons. A few said that if people married they should have children.

When asked, "What do you think of couples who only have one child?" most respondents were somewhat negative: having one child is not good for the child, they need sibling interaction to really develop as individuals. One child is lonely, selfish, and spoilt, gets too much

► BOX 6.1 CONT'D

attention, does not have to share, lacks the companionship of other children. Having one child was acceptable if it was due to medical reasons or if the couple could not afford to have more (mentally or financially). Some said it was fine to have one child, it was their choice, better to take care of one properly, yet it is not that great. If some people realize they are not suited to take care of children, then it is best to stop at one.

The respondents generally saw having large families, say, five or more children, as unrealistic. Quite a few respondents said they would value a large family, but constraints made it difficult if not impossible. Some said they preferred two or three but people could have as many as they want if they like children, are happy with more, and have the resources. Large families can mean having more fun at Christmas, birthdays, and family gatherings, it is a joy, and as you get older the joy of the large extended family grows. While a few said it was great if the couple could manage, most said a large family was very hard in this day and age, or that it was not a possibility in their own life. Some said people were crazy to have a large family, they cannot understand someone doing this, there is simply no need, you have to struggle more, why do it? Some said they knew some large families, especially from olden days, and things were great,

but most said it was not practical today.

Considering the hypothetical situation in which a husband wants more children than his wife, most said that these things should be discussed, negotiated, a compromise reached, or they should make a joint decision, make these decisions before they marry, have equal say. Pressed further, most said that the wife should have the last word or that a couple should not have an extra child unless both wanted it, that they should settle for the lower number. If there was disagreement, they should not have the child because one of them would resent the child and it would cause tension in the family. Some said that if the man really wanted the extra child he should do more around the house, or coach a hockey team to get it out of his system. The wife should have more say, because the pain of childbirth and much of the responsibility falls on her. It is the woman's decision, her body.

As for cases in which the wife wants more children than the husband, the responses are largely the same: ultimately not to have a child that only one wants, both should want it. The partners should discuss the reasons why he does not want more children, find out how strong his opinions are. Some said the wife should have the final word because it will impinge more on her life. ◆

disadvantages of having children, respondents fairly readily identify the costs. Eventually respondents can also identify the benefits, or they may say that the values of children are obvious (see Box 6.1). In reference to women's and men's life strategies, Maire Ni Bhrolchain (1993) makes the important observation that there is no a priori reason for assuming that having children is an end in itself. She observes that having children can serve other purposes, such as old age security or maintaining the stability of a marriage, or it can also be a strategy for women to opt out of the labour force. Children, then, can represent various benefits in the life strategies of women and men.

Economic values and costs of children

On the economic level children are very costly because they are largely dependent on their parents and do not contribute to family income. The costs vary with the age of the child, from the relatively inexpensive preschool years to more expensive adolescence. Using data from the 1982 Family Expenditure Survey, Henripin and Lapierre-Adamcyk (1986) as well as Anne Hélène Gauthier (1987) attempted to estimate these costs. The exercise is difficult, because the survey does not directly identify most of the expenditures for children. In effect, these authors compared families at the same standard of living (for example, considering the proportion of income spent on food and necessities) to see how much more income it takes with more children to achieve the same standard of living. The two studies placed the average annual direct costs of the first child at slightly more than $8,000 per year in 1996 dollars. The costs varied by age of the child, with two children of preschool ages costing a total of $3,200, but two children aged 11 and 13 costing almost $16,000.

Using similar approaches, Gauthier (1991) calculated the direct costs to age 18 of a first child, excluding child care, at $165,000 for a higher income family and $68,000 for a lower income family (in 1996 dollars). The average costs for three children to age 18 would be $250,000. When child care and indirect costs are added, the figure rises to $500,000. Claude Dionne (1989) calculated that three children aged 17, 12, and 10 would reduce a family's standard of living by 33 percent, compared to a family with no children. Using data from the Survey of Consumer Finances, other researchers (Lefebvre, Brouillette, and Felteau 1994) found that even small government transfers to parents make a difference in defraying some of these costs.

Explanations focusing on economic questions consider not only the costs of children, but also the levels of income. For instance, analysts have suggested that the baby boom was a function of sustained economic growth while the baby bust occurred in a period of greater economic restraint, but fertility trends do not relate closely to any simple economic indicator. The sharpest fertility decline was over the period 1961-66, which was not a period of recession. The periods 1982-84 and 1990-93 involved the strongest recessions since the 1930s, yet the total fertility rate during those times was basically stable.

Nonetheless, the economic costs of children, along with levels of income, clearly play a role. Romaniuc (1984: 72) observed that the income of family heads under 25 had deteriorated relative to average family income, making a less secure environment for having children. James Stafford (1987) argued that the changing levels of economic well-being provided the context for the making of family fertility decisions.

Attempts to analyze fertility differences through these economic factors have shown mixed results. For instance, Natalie Kyriazis (1982) found that a husband's income had a positive effect on the likelihood of a first or second birth but a negative effect at higher parities. Once couples have one or two children, there is a decreased marginal utility of children relative to other goods. Robert Wright (1988) found that the relationship between income and fertility was U-shaped, with higher births at both the lower and

BOX 6.2 | *Value of children*

Psychologists have provided long lists of the values that children might satisfy.... One such list ... includes *expansion of the self*—in response to the evanescent quality of life, many people feel the need to anchor themselves beyond their own lifetime; *primary group ties and affiliation*—children have value as a bulwark against the impersonalization of modern society; *stimulation, novelty, and fun*—children introduce an element of unpredictability and excitement into life; *creativity, accomplishment, competence*—needs for creative expression emerge when society advances beyond the subsistence level and when large numbers of people are assured the basic necessities of life, and rearing children provides an outlet for such needs; *power over others*—children afford unique opportunities to guide, teach, control, and generally exert influence over another human being; and, finally, parents may value children for their *vicarious achievement possibilities*. ◆

Source: Friedman, Hechter, and Kanazawa 1994: 380.

higher levels of income. However, the point of inflection in the curve is rather high: only 2.3 percent of couples are in the upper-income range in which fertility is positively related to income. Based on data from the 1991 census, Edward Ng and François Nault (1996) also observed U-shaped relationships between income and fertility. Women have the highest fertility rates when their own incomes are in the middle range. But the highest fertility occurs when the partner's income is either below average or above average.

In effect, the values and costs attributed to children depend on the relative priority given to various possible life pursuits. Indeed, careful economic analysis of those values and costs would seem to suggest that one should not have any children at all (David 1986). At the macro level, Enid Charles (1936) long ago pointed out the "paradox" of economic interpretations of fertility. When real incomes rise, fertility declines. At the same time, people everywhere cite inadequate economic means as the most potent motive for limiting the family. Charles (1936: 189) stated it simply: "Hence arises the paradox that people limit their families for one of two reasons, because they are prosperous or because they are not." It may be that economic rationales explain why people do not have more children, but those rationales are less helpful in explaining why people want children in the first place.

Cultural values and costs of children

The non-economic costs and values of children are more difficult to determine. Children are costly in the sense that parents have less time and energy for themselves. Children are sometimes emotional and psychological burdens; parents worry about them and have to put up with various inconveniences ranging from a messy place at the dinner table to a dented car fender. In addition to the economic costs, respondents especially refer to children as a heavy responsibility in other ways. Presented with various alternative considerations, 94 percent of respondents to the Canadian fertility survey said that having children "means taking on heavy responsibilities" (Balakrishnan, Lapierre-Adamcyk, and

Krotki 1993: 159). Taking a small sample of Australian women who had made transitions to motherhood, Mirn Crouch and Lenore Manderson (1993: 136) found that motherhood was "laden with responsibilities and, in most cases, socially isolating.... Thus many women feel vulnerable, lonely and confused most of the time and all women feel some or all of these things some of the time." Most studies find a drop in marital satisfaction, especially for women, when spouses become parents (for example, Lupri and Frideres 1981; Waite and Lillard 1991). Linda Thompson and Alexis Walker (1989: 863) suggest that the increased gender differentiation and specialization that comes with parenting may be responsible for this reduced satisfaction. They state: "Many mothers experience their husbands' new devotion to providing as pulling away from home at a time when they are needed most." Children may also be a cost in the sense of keeping a person in a relationship that they no longer find fulfilling.

On the positive side, children do offer certain advantages: people's status as adults can be more firmly established when they are parents; having children can provide a sense of achievement and even of continuity beyond death (see Box 6.2). Respondents often refer to the enjoyment of being with children—it is nice to see them grow and learn things, and they bring fun, excitement, and laughter into the home. In the Canadian fertility survey, 84 percent said that children "provide an irreplaceable source of affection" and 72 percent said children "provide an irreplaceable goal in life" (Balakrishnan, Lapierre-Adamcyk, and Krotki 1993: 159). According to Thompson and Walker (1989: 861), mothering is a complex and contradictory experience: it is "frustrating, irritating and overwhelming, but also pleasing and fulfilling" (see Box 6.3).

Children also provide a stable interpersonal relationship, which can be especially fulfilling when other relationships are less stable. One team of researchers (Friedman, Hechter, and Kanazawa 1994) propose that parenthood is a strategy for reducing uncertainty, especially when people lack the opportunities for stable marriages and careers. In effect, Wu (1995) finds that, among cohabiting persons, those who would have more uncertainty in their lives are more likely to have children. That is, children provide a certain insurance against unstable relationships. In addition, while marital satisfaction is lower when there are children at home, marital stability is higher. Couples with young children are less likely to separate, and marriages with no children are the most prone to divorce (Waite and Lillard 1991). Swedish data (Andersson 1996) confirm that divorce risks are lowest when the family has two or more children, especially if these children are young, and highest with no children.

Children enhance social integration, not only in terms of family ties but also at the community level. Children provide contact with others in the neighbourhood, at school, and in the community—what James Coleman (1988) calls *social capital*. As a "social resource," children help establish new relationships among persons, along with the support that these relationships can provide.

In the article "Why Do Americans Want Children?" Robert Schoen and his co-authors (1997) observe that the parents of adult children are more likely to provide support when their own children become parents. Using data from the 1987-88 National

Survey of Families and Households, the team found that people are more likely to intend to have another child when they attach importance to the social relationships created by children. In addition, "the social capital effect is found to be strong across parity, union status, gender and race" (p. 349). Respondents also tend to emphasize primary group ties, along with affection, stimulation, and fun, as intrinsic values of children. In studying other societies, anthropologists have long recognized the kinship ties and other relationships that come with children. In some African societies, child placement establishes a special bond between families. Schoen et al. (1997: 350) conclude by observing, "Childbearing is purposive behavior that creates and reinforces the most important and most enduring social bonds. We find that children are not seen as consumer durables; they are seen as the threads from which the tapestry of life is woven."

BOX 6.3 | *Motherhood and the muse*

Interviewing Canadian women authors, journalist Margie Rutledge (1998) found them committed to having children while also acutely appreciating the difficulties associated with the combination of parenting and writing.

It helps to establish yourself as a writer before having children. Judith Thompson won a Governor-General's Award when her first child was five months old, and she says she's very glad to have been on her way before having children. She insists, "It is not possible to be a full-time mother and a full-time artist, it is not possible." She continues, "I still feel sick when I turn my back on my four-year-old and my baby, especially because, in order to write creatively, I must turn entirely away, I must leave this world and enter another."

Alice Munro, winner of the 1998 Giller Prize, observed, "The hardest thing when I'm writing is that I feel very self-indulgent." When asked whether the situation would be different if she were a man, she laughs. "It would be worse if I were a man. I'd be considered a sissy."

Is there a good side to all of this? Are writing and mothering compatible in any way? Children, says Thompson, "reveal to us our deepest secret selves—the dreadful weaknesses that might have remained dormant for a lifetime without children to draw them out, and of course the great, previously unknown strengths."

Carol Shields, winner of the 1994 Pulitzer Prize, says, "Having children made me grow up. I was more focused." Says Alice Munro, "I've never for a moment regretted having children, I could never have done without the experience." Both speak of children providing a deep connection to the continuity of life. Shields says that continuity itself is heartening. "Having children for a writer and mother allows a person to witness the development of character, it puts it in perspective," she says. "I feel my children have given me a breadth of understanding and a window on the world." ◆

Source: Adapted from Rutledge 1998: D1-D2.

Most likely, most people want children because children represent more values than costs. The proportion of survey respondents who indicate that they do not want children is lowest among the youngest in the available samples. For instance, in 1995, only 4 percent of women and 6 percent of men aged 20-29 indicated that they intended not to have children (Dupuis 1998: 3). For all married persons in the 1990 survey, only 5 percent indicated an intention not to have children (McDaniel 1994: 45). In a 1988 survey of postsecondary students, Charles Hobart (1991) found an average desired family size of some 2.5 children for both male and female students. When answering these questions, respondents probably assume that they will be in stable relationships and be able to have the births when they want them. In the end, unfortunately, some of the respondents may be frustrated in achieving these goals.

When asked about the things that are important for being generally happy in life, respondents indicate, as among the most salient factors, relationships, children, and jobs. Among respondents to the Canadian Fertility Survey, 96 percent said that "having a lasting relationship" was important for being generally happy in life. In addition, 72 percent identified "having at least one child," and another 72 percent identified "being able to take a job outside the home" (Balakrishnan, Lapierre-Adamcyk, and Krotki 1993: 174).

Based on data from Quebec, Jacques Marleau and Jean-François Saucier (1993) found considerable symmetry in the desire for having either boys or girls. For those who had no children and were expecting a child, 62 percent of women say they did not care about the sex of the child, while 22 percent preferred a boy and 16 percent preferred a girl. For those who had one child, about half said they would want the other sex and the other half said they didn't care. Among those who had two boys, 79 percent preferred their next to be a girl, but only 47 percent of those who had two girls preferred a boy.

Data from Sweden would also imply considerable symmetry in the role of women and men with regard to intended births (Thomson and Hoem 1998). Births are most likely to occur if both partners express definite plans to have a child. As would be expected, few couples had children if they both indicated that they did not plan to have a child. However, the likelihood of having a child was equally low when the couple disagreed. That is, both men and women appeared to exercise veto power over the birth of a child. On the other hand, a study of the fertility rate of remarried men in France indicated that the number of children the male partner brought from a previous relationship made little difference to the possibility of having a child in the new relationship, but whether or not the wife brought children made a decisive difference (Anderson 1997: 12; see also Marsiglio 1998).

Several authors have considered that *religiosity* can influence the value placed on children. Balakrishnan and Jiajian Chen (1990) find that categories of church attendance (religiosity) involve significantly different fertility levels. These differences, in the order of 0.4 children after adjusting for other factors, are larger than differences by other factors such as income and education. More religious people are also less likely to have lived common-law and are more likely to have stayed in their first marriages. The same applies to intended fertility, with persons who cited no religion reporting the lowest expected average fertility, and those who attended religious services every week expecting an average of 0.5 more children than those who never attended (Dupuis 1998: 5).

In a culture that promotes individualism, children necessarily compete with other forms of gratification. Romaniuc (1984: 64) observes that children are largely viewed as a means through which adults can receive affective gratification and blossom as individuals. But children can also interfere with this affective individualism. Based on the childbearing intentions of postsecondary students, Charles Hobart (1991) finds that those who hold more individualistic values expect fewer children. In their conclusion to *Family and Childbearing in Canada*, Balakrishnan, Lapierre-Adamcyk, and Krotki (1993: 243) suggest that the tendency for greater individualism in postmodern societies is evident in both attitudes and behaviour. The tendency has brought an erosion of "norms favouring a strong family that includes children as a prerequisite for a happy fulfilling life."

Nonetheless, for many people children are a very special form of personal fulfilment. Carl Grindstaff (1990b) argues that Canada is a pro-natalist society in the sense that both women and men highly value having children. Consequently, most people do have them, even if it runs counter to the logic of economic rationality, and families with two children are the most popular outcome. Having more than one child allows parents to experience not only children but also relationships among their children.

CHILD-BEARING AND THE STRUCTURE OF PAID AND UNPAID WORK

The value and cost of children are considerations for the micro or individual level. On the macro level, we need to look especially at the social organization of paid and unpaid work: at how the value and cost of children to parents partly reflects the organization of paid and unpaid work. As we've seen, this organization has evolved toward a lower involvement of children in both paid and unpaid work, with family strategies focusing on investing in the future earning potential of children; and with the greater involvement of women as well as men in paid work, adults have become less available for unpaid work.

These family strategies can be related to the broader political economy or, in Marxist terms, to the mode of production and the relations of production. Paid and unpaid work depend on the form of economic production and on the relations of various categories of people to the production process. Marx believed as well that different relations of production would involve different dynamics of population. In particular, the relations of women, men, and children to the production process is a key to understanding demographic reproduction in the society. At the same time, the vital tasks of reproduction of the species in history have helped organize production. As A.F. Robertson (1991) observes, in the process of modernization many of the costs and burdens of reproduction were absorbed by institutions such as schools, clinics, and even banks and retirement communities.

For instance, Jane Ursel (1986) pointed out that labour acts in Ontario over the period 1884-1913 increasingly limited the use of child and female labour in the productive system. The manifest concern was to improve the conditions of children and women, but the laws also entrenched the distinctions between male and female labour. By putting limitations on the hours women could work, the places they could work, and the kind of work they could do, the state made it almost impossible for a female factory worker to make a living wage. Because women were in an economically dependent position, their livelihood was contingent on entry into reproductive relations. The resultant division of labour, the "breadwinner model," produced a reciprocal state of dependency between the sexes.

Especially since the 1960s, our economies have changed in ways that have produced increased demands for workers in the service areas of the economy, traditionally dominated by women (McQuillan 1989). The consequent change in the integration of women in the paid labour force has altered the relations between women and men and raised the opportunity costs of children. Women have become less dependent on marriage, making divorce, cohabitation, and childlessness more feasible alternatives. Charles Westoff (1986) argues that the most important force underlying the weakening of marriage is the growing economic independence of women. Nathan Keyfitz (1986) maintains that low fertility is the ultimate natural outcome of gender equality, brought about by the economic roles of women. He concludes that societies that do not constrain women will contract. Kingsley Davis (1984) even questions the extent to which societies based on an egalitarian gender role system can survive—that is, reproduce themselves. Other views suggest that, if there is gender equality both at the level of the couple and in the broader society, women may absorb less of the costs of children and are more likely to have the number of children they desire (Matthews and Beaujot 1997).

These broad structural factors are useful for understanding changes in the family, gender roles, and child-bearing. With the industrial revolution, the family lost much of its function in economic production, and children became economic dependants. Since women became excluded from the economic production that moved outside of the household, they also became more dependent on the extrafamilial occupations of their husbands. Only more recently did women regain their roles in the labour force. Fertility went down first when children lost their economic value to parents, and again when child-bearing became an opportunity cost to employed women. According to this perspective, we might expect further reductions in fertility as the labour-force participation of women continues to increase. In 1996, 51.6 percent of women and 74.9 percent of men at ages 25-44 were employed full-time (30 or more hours per week). Room still exists, then, for further labour-force involvement on the part of women.

Traditionally there have been important fertility differences across groups, as defined by ascriptive factors such as ethnicity, language, and religion. Now these differences have all but disappeared, and the differences that do remain are a function of achieved characteristics, such as education and labour-force participation (Ravanera 1995: 20; Beaujot 1995: 55). In other words, a woman's economic roles rather than her social origins are now the crucial factor affecting her fertility. For instance, women with more education have fewer children and have them later on average (Ng and Nault 1996). By occupation, there is broad similarity across professionals, semi-professionals, semi-skilled, and unskilled women, and the differences that remain are the higher fertility rates for women who are farmers or not in the labour force. As another example, in 1991, women aged 30-34 who were not employed had an average of 0.8 more children than those employed full-time (Beaujot 1995: 57).

These trends help explain why children represent considerable costs, especially for women. No one would be surprised to hear that women who were married or had children early in life would suffer disadvantages, but the same would appear to be true (admittedly to a lesser extent) for women who have children later. Looking at women aged 30-44 at the time of the 1981 census, Grindstaff (1986) found that those faring best in terms of completed education, labour-force activity, and personal income were the ones without children or who had never married.

In another analysis of women aged 30 at the time of the 1981 census, Grindstaff (1989) observed that never-married women without children had a substantive economic advantage over women with children. Children, it seemed, reduced the probability of women's economic roles outside the home. Women without children were nearly twice as likely to be in professional occupations, and they earned nearly twice as much as their child-bearing counterparts. Similarly, women aged 33-38 in 1991 who had a child aged 2-5 were less likely to be in the labour force, and, if they were, more likely to work part-time and have lower personal incomes (Grindstaff 1996).

Labour-force participation

Various analyses of fertility trends suggest that the strongest predictor of fertility changes in the period 1965 to 1975 was the changing labour-force participation of women. Romaniuc (1984: 75) presents a graph showing the close relation between increasing labour-force participation and decreasing fertility in the period since the early 1960s. Observing that "fertility behaviour is by and large determined by female work outside the home," and taking into account the increasing labour-force participation of women, the analysts of the 1984 Canadian Fertility Survey expressed considerable uncertainty toward the future of fertility (Balakrishnan, Lapierre-Adamcyk, and Krotki 1993: 91, 244).

Various researchers have noted that women now have high labour-force involvement, but also many interruptions associated with children and family (Kempeneers and Saint-Pierre 1993; Robinson 1989; Cook and Beaujot 1996). In contrast, compared to non-married men, married men have less work interruptions.

However, the period since 1975 has seen rather stable fertility and increases in women's labour-force participation (Figure 6.4). The same applies in the United States, where since 1975 the labour-force participation of mothers with children under six continues to rise but fertility is stable (Rindfuss, Brewster, and Kovce 1996).

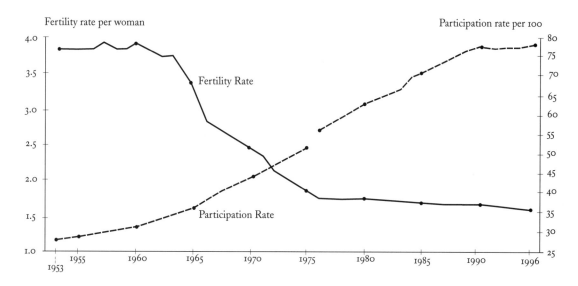

FIG 6.4 Total fertility rate and labour-force participation rate of women aged 25-44, Canada, 1953-96

Source: Romaniuc 1991: 69; Statistics Canada, no. 84-204 and no. 71-001.

The differentials in labour-force participation by marital status involve a "marital status suppressor," in the sense that it is married women who have lagged behind in participation. While labour-force participation is still highest among married men, married women now have a level of participation comparable to never-married and formerly married women (Table 6.6). Nonetheless, what remains significant is the lower proportions working full-time for married women and for mothers in particular (see Table 4.10).

These differentials have often been interpreted in terms of role incompatibility or alternatives to motherhood. But paid work and parenting need not be seen as incompatible. Since they both involve time, and often a different place, paid and unpaid work do have their built-in incompatibility, but some flexibility remains in how parents arrange their total work.

In looking at the discontinuity in women's employment, Kempeneers (1991) noted that questions of incompatibility between work and child care represent only one part of the question. For instance, based on data from the 1984 Canadian Fertility Survey, she finds that, among women born in 1934-48 who had not had children, close to half had significant labour-force interruptions (one year or longer). Conversely, in this same cohort of women with three or more children, close to a quarter had had no interruptions of this length.

Comparisons of various countries at a particular point in time also question the incompatibility between child-bearing and labour-force participation. Using data from

20 countries of the Organization for Economic Co-operation and Development (OECD), Marianne Sundstrom and Frank Stafford (1992) found a positive relationship between labour-force participation and the total fertility rates. They expected fertility to rise if policies were used to ease the worker-mother conflict. Rindfuss and Brewster (1996) suggest that the degree of such conflict would partly explain the diversity of fertility in advanced industrial countries. Especially in terms of attitudes, the degree of conflict between work and child-rearing has declined significantly, as fewer people consider it to be problematic for mothers to be employed in paid work when children are young. Rindfuss, Brewster, and Andrew Kovce (1996) even propose that this reduced conflict has played a role in stabilizing U.S. fertility levels. Besides the changing norms regarding the effects of mothers working, the extent of incompatibility would also be a function of work conditions themselves, along with the structure of child care.

In Sweden the state has specifically addressed the potential for combining child-bearing and gainful employment (Hoem and Hoem 1997). The approach includes the potential for people to work part-time and take maternity leaves, which in turn necessitated the greater flexibility in jobs associated with the growth of the welfare state—a flexibility that later spread to other jobs. In effect, some of the work previously done at home was replaced by new professional occupations in health, personal services, and child care. Consequently, child care also changed, with public care becoming much more available. With childbirth leaves paid out of employment benefits, a positive link has been formed between work and child-bearing. People who want to take a paid leave need to first establish their credits through work, much as happens with unemployment insurance.

On the basis of data from the Canadian Fertility Survey, Wei-Jun Jean Yeung (1991) also found that employment status in a given birth interval affects this status at a subsequent stage. On the basis of data from the 1995 General Social Survey, Margaret De Wit and Zenaida Ravanera (1998) found that women who had completed their education and established regular full-time work were more likely to proceed to having a first or second child. In other words, secured employment would seem no longer to be an impediment to child-bearing, but is instead making it more feasible to have children. At the same time, the likelihood of having a third child is higher for women who had their first child early and who are not employed (Bélanger and Dumas 1998: 57).

Gillian Ranson (1998) observes that women's employment security, at least in those occupations that allow for flexibility, can provide the basis for starting a family. She cites an elementary school teacher who described the part her permanent contract played in her decision to have children: "I have it [a permanent contract], yeah. And I am so thankful for that. I think I knew I wanted that before I even considered having kids. I needed that. That was my security blanket in a sense. And I know now, I think you can take up to a two-year leave with your permanent, then they have to place you. Not necessarily at the school that you left but they do have to place you" (p. 525).

In addition, the seeming increase in men's involvement in unpaid work may also play a part in fertility rates. But change is slow in given relationships that started with an unequal distribution of paid and unpaid work, or that involved an extensive period of unequal division during child-rearing. Change is also slow because women are much more likely to have worked part-time and thus to have had the flexibility necessary for accommodating unpaid work. It would seem that women's increased education and labour-force participation should have pushed fertility rates down further in the period 1976-96. If fertility remained relatively stable in that period, it could be because men's involvement in unpaid work has somewhat reduced the incompatibility of paid and unpaid work for women.

An alternative explanation is that the incompatibility is manageable with an average family size under two children. Goldscheider and Waite (1991) have proposed that new families with more equitable divisions of unpaid and paid work are necessary to avoid the "no family" alternative. While it is not totally a "new family," the slow change in unpaid work may be making it less necessary to opt for "no family."

LABOUR-FORCE PARTICIPATION RATE AND EMPLOYMENT/POPULATION RATIO, AGES 35-44, BY SEX AND MARITAL STATUS, CANADA, 1951-96

		1951	1961	1971	1981	1991	1996
Labour Force Participation Rate							
M	TOTAL	96.7	94.2	92.8	95.2	94.5	91.8
	Single	—	82.3	79.8	84.8	84.6	82.2
	Married	—	95.9	94.4	96.4	96.2	94.3
	Widowed and Divorced	—	86.7	88.9	91.6	90.4	88.1
F	TOTAL	21.8	31.0	43.9	64.3	79.6	79.0
	Single	—	77.5	75.3	81.7	83.3	79.8
	Married	—	25.1	40.4	62.2	79.0	78.9
	Widowed and Divorced	—	60.1	63.0	73.1	81.6	78.9
Employment/Population Ratio							
M	TOTAL	—	—	88.8	91.6	87.0	84.2
	Single	—	—	72.2	77.3	72.1	68.9
	Married	—	—	90.9	93.3	89.8	88.2
	Widowed and Divorced	—	—	80.3	84.5	77.6	76.5
F	TOTAL	—	—	41.4	60.2	72.9	72.5
	Single	—	—	72.4	78.3	76.2	71.8
	Married	10.5	21.0	38.1	58.1	72.5	73.3
	Widowed and Divorced	—	—	58.7	68.0	73.1	68.7

Source: Beaujot 1995: 59; Statistics Canada, 1996 Census Data: 93F0027XDB96001.

TABLE 6.6

Some demographic literature suggests that the movement from a breadwinner model to a more egalitarian model will imply below-replacement fertility (Keyfitz 1986; Davis 1986). Conversely, patriarchal family systems have both constrained women and maintained high fertility. However, another study (Matthews and Beaujot 1997) found, using qualitative interviews (see Box 6.1), that change toward greater equality in the division of gender roles would not necessarily undermine child-bearing, and it might allow women to have the children they desire without the high personal costs of a less equal division of roles.

For instance, women may be more disposed to have children if they know that the burden of child care will be somewhat divided. As an example, Oystein Kravdal (1992) found that Norwegian women with more education have become *more* likely to progress from a second to a third birth. The author speculates that a higher level of participation in unpaid work on the part of well-educated fathers may have produced this positive effect for education. Among Canadian women aged 20-29 in 1995, those with more education intended to have more children, which was also the case for men (Dupuis 1998: 4). In Sweden, women are more likely to proceed to a subsequent birth if the husband has taken some leave-time during the previous birth or if there is more sharing of child care and household work between partners (Olah 1996). Eva Bernhardt (1989) too observes that the incompatibility between employment and motherhood has been undermined through the growth of part-time work and the increased availability of child care.

As Valerie Oppenheimer (1994) observes, a more egalitarian opportunity structure may prompt new family strategies. In particular, these strategies may well involve moving away from the efficiency associated with gender-role specialization and complementarity. Already, the economic roles of both men and women are becoming an important form of insurance against uncertainty in employment and in relationships. The economy has also evolved in the direction of greater potential to use market mechanisms as substitutes for domestic production. As Peter Li (1996) observes, the family has become ever more dependent on goods and services available in the market. Consequently, the dynamic has involved maximizing earnings through having more wage-earners and economizing on the cost of children by having smaller families.

CONCLUSION

Structures of paid and unpaid work, including the associated gender structures, influence the values and costs of children, and consequently child-bearing dynamics in society. To understand fertility and its variation, then, we need consider not only the structure of paid and unpaid work as a macro factor at the level of the society, but also the values and costs of children as micro factor at the individual level, along with the proximate factors of union formation and contraception. People tend both to see children as costly and to value them. The accommodations to the structures of paid and unpaid work remain difficult, especially for persons having three or more children, and the uncertainty in unions also reduce child-bearing from the births initially intended.

While the decline in fertility from the early 1960s to the mid-1970s—"the baby bust"—was clearly associated with greater labour-force participation, the subsequent increases in women's paid work had little further impact on fertility levels. Also, across developed societies, a relationship between women's labour-force participation and the level of child-bearing was no longer apparent (Sundstrom and Stafford 1992). It would appear that certain accommodations in both paid and unpaid work have taken place, ensuring a level of reproduction somewhat below replacement levels and older ages at child-bearing. Paid work now has more family-friendly elements, and pregnancy and child-bearing no longer necessitate a systematic termination of women's paid work. The trend in unpaid work has been toward somewhat greater participation on the part of men, with more domestic services either purchased on the market or obtained from the public sector. Women's accommodations to paid work roles are reflected in their later ages at child-bearing. In particular, mothers with more security and seniority in paid employment may be better placed to pressure the workplace, and fathers, to take up more of the work associated with young children.

In an article on the potential for pro-natalist policies, Paul Demeny (1986) highlights the importance of structural questions associated with paid work and security in old age. In particular, he argues, an "incorporated nuclear family" would give more economic security to women, making them less vulnerable in having children. In addition, he suggests mechanisms through which parents would receive additional old age security benefits if they had children in the labour force. In Sweden, for example, the dilemmas of employed parents are a public rather than a private issue (Moen 1989), and the state's attempts to ensure that working women can also be parents have weakened the incompatibility between home and paid workplace (Bernhardt 1991). Nonetheless, for the most part the onus is still on women to juggle the two roles and to limit their child-bearing in order to be able to work in jobs similar to men. Bernhardt (1991) stresses that men need to become more involved in parenting, but she also observes that the idea of "women becoming more like men" is a self-defeating strategy for population replacement.

In the end the changes in the structure of paid and unpaid work have altered the values and costs attached to having children. The costs of children have increased— from the transformation of children as producers to dependants and the "opportunity costs" that children represent to employed women. Children have always competed with other demands on adults' time, but changes in paid work have systematically heightened this competition.

But the economic value and cost of children clearly do not fully explain fertility trends. The non-economic, or cultural, values and costs are equally important, though quite difficult to pin down. Clearly, most people want to have children. Most people value children, or simply consider it natural to have children (see Box 6.1).

In a survey from Tunisia, I found two principal answers to a question asking, "Why do people have children?" According to the respondents, children are valued "for support in old age" and because "children are the joy of life" (Beaujot 1988). In some regards, the Canadian answers are similar. Now that we have extensive pension plans and other benefits for the elderly, people are not exactly looking for support in old age but they are looking for "someone who will be there." The interest in having children is typically not expressed in terms of continuing the family name, but in somehow reproducing oneself. Especially given insecure marital relationships, people seem interested in having someone in life who represents a close and enduring relationship. Similarly, they express the joy of children in a variety of ways, such as the pleasure of seeing children smile, take their first steps, learn new things, develop, and eventually become mature adults who provide their own kind of special relationship. In a variety of ways, respondents indicate that they are able to experience life more fully with children, including experiencing the unique relationships among children, as well as in the broader family.

Having children also involves non-economic costs. Parents can experience children as a heavy responsibility, especially when the offspring are young and completely dependent, but sometimes too when they are older. Sometimes parents experience children who do not "turn out" as expected and become a source of fundamental frustration and loss. Sometimes they have a basic ambivalence regarding the net value or cost of children, and some parents can regret their decision to have children. The move to have a child is a "fateful decision" in the sense that it cannot be reconsidered. Having a child also creates a permanent link to the other parent of the child, and sometimes it is that link that a former partner would prefer to forget.

The increased social hold of individualism or the ascendency of the "me generation" can mean that children represent yet another cost: they interfere with other pursuits that adults want to follow. This issue includes an uncertainty with regard to how much one generation keeps for itself, and how much it gives to the next generation. The constraints that children represent are clearly most significant for working parents.

That is why, when asked about the optimum number of children to have, many persons, in both Tunisia and Canada, say something like, "Not too many and not too few." Not too many because there are significant costs, but not too few to miss out on the experience of children in one's life. In Tunisia the numerical answer to the question, when it was asked in 1982, was typically "four." That way each boy ideally had a brother and each girl a sister. How unfortunate it is to go through life without a brother or a sister! In Canada the typical answer is "two," because two children can be accommodated in our complex lives, and the number still represents the makings of a real family. Another important factor for couples is that both husband and wife need to want to have the child.

Clearly, children not only represent an end in themselves, but are also part of the life strategies of adults. They may, for instance, be a strategy for maintaining the stability of a marriage. For women as well as men children can be a source of variety in life, a contrast to the daily grind of continuous full-time work.

As for the proximate factors, contraception has become a more standard factor as women and men plan the meshing of their earning and caring activities. Probably nothing in recent decades has changed so much for couples as the security and effectiveness of contraception—although significant numbers of unplanned pregnancies do still occur, especially for younger persons. But the questions of union formation and dissolution also bring differences between intended and actual child-bearing. With most young adults apparently wanting to have children at some time or other, and usually in the order of two to three births each, the assumption is that other things in life will evolve according to intended plans: finding the right partner, with similar intentions, at the right time, and achieving work ambitions. These things do not always work out, which is probably the main reason why actual cohort fertility is closer to 1.85 births per woman.

The questions surrounding fertility also inevitably lead back to issues of gender, and especially the evolution of gender. Based on interviews with 59 mothers in Toronto, Martha McMahon (1995) argues that becoming a mother is an engendered and engendering process. She finds that the effect of women embracing motherhood reproduces gender inequality. Through their interactions, couples construct gendered parenting (Thompson and Walker 1989: 864). For instance, it is mothers who are more likely to provide the "continuous coverage" that babies require, while it is much more legitimate for a father to say that work keeps him away from his children, that he is impatient with children, or incompetent in child care. Parenting tends to push couples toward a more traditional division of labour, which is probably responsible for some of the lowered marital satisfaction, especially for women who are at home with young children. Child-bearing does often differentially influence the opportunity structures for women and men. As we have seen, for the most part the incompatibility of paid work and parenthood applies only to one parent. Still, as Larry Bumpass (1993) observes, many men are also stretched by the competing demands of family and work. Summarizing the situation in Sweden, Britta Hoem (1997) explains that most couples do not see the mother doing most of the child-rearing as a problem; it is their way of adapting to a difficult situation. A part-time job, even if it is not particularly exciting, can ensure a continuation of outside social contacts while reducing the total stress associated with the double day.

According to one study, motherhood and fatherhood are intrinsically different: motherhood represents a direct link between mother and child, while fatherhood is defined by the link between a man and the child's mother (Touleman and Lapierre-Adamcyk 1995). Alternatively, men may be becoming more aware of the costs of marital disruption to their parenting bonds. If men do come to accept the principle of a more equal participation in housework and child care—that is, if women are not called upon to absorb most if not all of the costs—the resulting egalitarian gender structures can support rather than undermine child-bearing.

Children and Youth

Even though children are the very basis for families, analysts of family change have focused most of their attention on the interests of adults. Nonetheless, the earning and caring activities of families are closely associated with children and youth, and we need to look closely at the conditions that affect their welfare. Several family changes over recent decades have benefited children. The smaller family sizes mean that parents can devote more energy to a given child. The tendency to later child-bearing and the greater proportions of families with two incomes enhance the resources that parents can offer. Other changes are less beneficial. Smaller families and the close spacing of children mean that children are less likely to have the advantages an older sibling can bring, and mothers working outside the home can mean less parental time. But perhaps the greatest change is the increased likelihood of parental separation, which has especially altered the interactions between fathers and children and consequently the amount of financial, human, and social capital that comes to children through their fathers. What is more, the increased propensity for cohabitation also has an impact on children, because the children of cohabitating parents are much more likely to experience separation.

Consequently, family patterns bring considerable diversity to the world of children: from children who experience intact parental relationships to those who experience episodes of lone parenthood, reconstituted relationships, and step-parenting. While many bad marriages undoubtedly create poor situations for raising children, the threshold of disorder is different for adults and children. Many parents with marital problems can still parent effectively. Consequently, children are less likely than parents to benefit from divorce and remarriage.

A specific manifestation of the juncture of earning and caring activities is the question of *child care.* Just as there is a variety of family models, there is also a diversity of views on child care, both in public opinion and in public policy. Many parents say they would prefer to do less paid work outside the home so they could look after the children themselves, especially when children are young. At the same time family change trends and the interests of gender equality are pushing for more public child-care services.

We need also to look at various aspects of the *welfare of children and youth*—from their economic and family situations to education, home-leaving, work, and the stage of starting their own families.

Again, the marital separation of parents represents a distinct disadvantage for the well-being of children. While some of the disadvantage results from the dysfunctional nature of the two-parent family in which the child once lived, and children can profit from associated reductions in marital conflict and from the subsequent relationships of parents, on average marital break-down presents a more significant disadvantage for children than for parents. At the same time, income inequality is highest in lone-parent families, which means that considerable variation exists around the average. That is, the impact is not rigid or deterministic, and most children in lone-parent families flourish. Those most likely to be disadvantaged are with parents who have limited economic prospects and poor parenting skills, or in situations when the absent parent is not involved with the children.

Youth have also undergone a delay in *home-leaving* and *starting relationships,* which can be interpreted as a prolonged period of dependent adolescence or as a means of building the investment in their human capital and job prospects given a difficult labour market. The delay has meant a juggling of school and work, with reduced demarcation between the two activities. It has also meant lower labour-force participation and declining incomes, especially for men under 25. Still, it would seem that those who put off home-leaving, intimate relationships, and full-time work also become best situated for the future. The youth who are particularly disadvantaged are the women who have children early, especially if they then become lone mothers of young children. Youths living with two biological parents are most likely to delay home-leaving and to pursue higher education, while young persons who are neither employed nor at school are most often also mothers with young children.

Clearly, the earning and caring activities both of the parents and the children themselves are crucial to the well-being of young persons.

◆

As Maureen Baker (1991: 37) states, "Most sociological research on family life has focused on the problems and points of view of adults, especially wives and mothers." Researchers may be overlooking children because many families today do not include children living at home: the proportion of families with children at home declined from over 70 percent in 1961 to under 60 percent in 1991 (Kerr, Larrivée, and Greenhalgh 1994: 11). Nonetheless, children and parent-child relationships remain central to most families. In effect, the arrival of a child changes a family, just as children are shaped by their family context. This chapter considers the family experiences of children and youth, with a focus on the conditions that help determine their welfare.

In its statement on *The Progress of Canada's Children*, the Canadian Council on Social Development (1996) noted some encouraging and discouraging trends. By the 1990s, infant mortality had dropped significantly, and very few children were living with teen mothers. Most children were growing up healthy, well-adjusted, and progressing well in school (Statistics Canada 1998k). But the Council also noted some discouraging trends: the difficulties of managing family time for working parents, the fact that some 8 percent of children lived in dysfunctional families, and the problems families faced with employment and economic security.

In effect, the quality of children's experiences is closely related to family earning and caring—and children are central to these activities. In particular, children prompt earning and caring, because they are dependent on the adults in the family and because parents feel the need to give their children the best life possible. Especially when they are young, children encroach on earning, and on mothers in particular. The time spent with children can also affect the time and care that spouses have for each other.

The interests of adults and children do not always overlap. Marlene Mackie (1995: 56) observes, "Children need their parents more than their parents need them, and they know it." Harriet Presser (1995) asks, "Are the interests of women inherently at odds with the interests of children?" While she observes that the key issue is time—a factor that tends to make paid work incompatible with caregiving—she also notes that the conflict emerges out of the double standard of parenthood that expects more caregiving time from women than from men. At issue, then, according to Jean-Claude Chesnais (1987), is a third stage of gender equality. If the first stage brought equal opportunities in education, and the second stressed financial independence through labour-force participation, the third aims at equal opportunities in daily life. This third stage can carry the most conflict between the interests of men and women, especially when children are involved.

This particular consideration of "gendered time" indicates that the interests of women and children are not at odds, but rather the interests of men and women. Presser concludes that the conflict is not inherent, but actual. Nonetheless, the interests of mothers, fathers, and children in two-parent families can diverge, and divorce can exacerbate that divergence (Seltzer 1994).

The involvement of mothers and fathers with children shows two conflicting trends. On the one hand, the gender gap in parental time with children is narrowing (Presser 1995: 305). On the other hand, larger proportions of fathers are not living with their children and are consequently less involved with daily child care. An-Magritt Jensen (1995) speaks of a similar "paradox," wherein some fathers are becoming more emotionally attached to children while others—an increasing share—are physically detached from them. In general Jensen sees a widening of the gender gap in relationships with children—that is, a widening gap between men and children—and consequently a "feminization of childhood." Similarly, Judith Seltzer (1994) says that the economic, emotional, and social needs of children of divorced parents are most often met through women's efforts. Women orchestrate the relationships of absent fathers and stepfathers with children.

Men, it seems, largely relate to children through living with their mothers, though according to Jensen they do have the potential for being more involved. Since mothers are less economically dependent, fathers have been "freed from" their responsibility as breadwinners. This can mean that new fathers are "freed to" take more child-care responsibility. Paul Amato (1998) concludes that fathers do matter in two-parent families and they can matter in father-absent families. In particular, fathers can provide financial, human, and social capital. Frank Furstenberg (1998) finds that fathers who are more involved with children get higher approval ratings from wives, resulting in higher marital stability. They are also more likely to continue their relationships with their children beyond divorce.

The family changes of recent decades—including later marriage, more cohabitation, fewer births, more births occurring in cohabitating relationships, more marital instability, and more reconstitution of adult relationships—influence children in a variety of ways. The greater variety in the family lives of adults means that their life trajectories are less likely to be followed by their children. For instance, the standard family life stages of beginning relationships, child-bearing, empty nest, and widowhood do not necessarily correspond to children's experiences. Consequently, we need to pay close attention to the family lives of children themselves.

In addition, we will want to ask if society, which has profoundly transformed families, is properly organized to take care of children (Lapierre-Adamcyk and Marcil-Gratton 1995). How are children affected by marital instability and reconstituted relationships? To what extent are children paying the price for the transformations in the lives of adults? For instance, Constance Shehan and Karen Seccombe (1996) conclude that the change in the family situation following divorce has profound effects on children's lives, a considerable proportion of it being negative. Similarly, Nicole Marcil-Gratton (1993) observes that while flexibility may well present benefits for adults, "For children it may take the less appealing shape of instability." Consequently children face inequalities in conditions and treatment based on their parental situation, along with other differences associated with available resources.

FAMILY CHANGE AND CHILDREN

In his sweeping consideration of *America's Children*, Donald Hernandez (1993) considers two long-term transformations in the family economy and the work of parents. The first transformation, brought by industrialization, changed families from settings in which parents and children lived and worked together to places in which fathers were mostly employed at workplaces outside of the family and children over six were away at school most of the day. The second transformation, after the 1940s, involved mothers stepping out of the home and larger amounts of non-parental care of children at preschool ages. By considering the amounts of child care received from parents and the broader society, Hernandez proposes that this second transformation is about half completed.

In addition to those long-term changes important differences in the current living arrangements of children also took form, as seen in the data from the National Longitudinal Survey of Children and Youth (Table 7.1). In the mid-1990s, while 84.2 percent of children under 12 were living in two-parent families, only 78.7 percent were with both biological or adoptive parents. Besides the 15.7 percent of children living with a lone parent, 5.5 percent were living with two-parent families that did not include two biological parents. However, only 0.1 percent were living with no custodial parent. In addition to the 78.7 percent living with both parents, another 18 percent were living with their mothers and 1.8 percent with their fathers. Given these figures—which make no distinction between adoptive parents and biological parents—96.7 percent of children under 12 were living with their mothers and 80.5 percent with their fathers, leaving 1.5 percent with neither parent: foster parents, two step-parents, or no custodial parent.

By obtaining the relationships among all persons in the family, this survey was able to determine that 8.6 percent of children were in stepfamilies, in which one of the parents was not the biological or adoptive parent of all of the children (Cheal 1996: 95). The proportion in blended families, in which at least one child did not have the same biological or adoptive parents as the other child(ren), amounted to 6.1 percent of children under 12 years of age. This means that, at a given point in time, 24.3 percent of children under 12 were already living with either a lone parent (15.7 percent) or in a stepfamily (8.6 percent).

Timing and numbers of children

Given the delay in marriage and child-bearing, the family units into which children are born have changed. For instance, the proportion of children and youth with no brothers or sisters at home increased from 11.8 percent in 1971 to 20.7 percent in 1991 (Kerr, Larrivée, and Greenhalgh 1994: 13). Another 44.8 percent had one brother or sister at home in 1991. For children under 12 in 1994-95, some 19.4 percent were only children, and the average was 1.3 siblings (Ross, Scott, and Kelly 1996: 30). In any one year a few children were placed in adoptive homes; the number amounted to 2,840 children in 1990, representing 1.4 percent of births or half of the number ten years earlier (Daly and Sobol 1994).

In the early 1960s, 25 percent of births were to first-time mothers, compared with 44 percent in the early 1980s (Marcil-Gratton 1988). Consequently, greater proportions of babies were being born to "inexperienced" parents. With fewer brothers and sisters, children also had fewer older siblings. For instance, half of the generation born in the early 1960s had two older brothers or sisters, compared with one-fifth of those born 20 years later; and one in five in the early 1960s had a brother or sister ten or more years older,

DISTRIBUTION OF CHILDREN AGED 0-11 BY FAMILY TYPE AND PARENTING ARRANGEMENT, CANADA, 1994-95

FAMILY TYPE	%
Children with two parents	84.2
Both biological parents	78.7
One biological and one step-parent	4.3
Foster parents or two step-parents	1.2
Children with a single parent	*15.7*
Female single parent	14.6
Male single parent	1.1
No custodial parent	0.1

PARENTING ARRANGEMENT	%
Two biological parents	78.7
Biological mother and no father	14.4
Biological mother and stepfather	3.6
Biological father and no mother	1.1
Biological father and stepmother	0.7
Other parenting	1.4
No custodial parent	0.1

NOTE: Biological includes adoptive.

Source: Ross, Scott, and Kelly 1996: 29; Cheal 1996: 95. Statistics Canada, National Longitudinal Survey of Children and Youth, 1994-95.

TABLE 7.1

compared with one in twenty for the later generation. Fewer births, and their concentration over a shorter time in the lives of adults, not only imply more potential parental resources per child, but also mean that children have less opportunity to interact with and learn from siblings.

Cohabitation, marriage, and divorce of parents

In the early 1960s, 95 percent of children were born in marriages, compared with 64 percent in the mid-1990s (see Table 3.1). What has changed is not the births to single mothers, but births to cohabiting couples (Festy 1994). In effect, for children under 12 in the National Longitudinal Survey of Children and Youth, 7.4 were born to lone mothers, but only 40 percent of these mothers had never lived with the father and 56 percent had the father's name on the birth certificate (Marcil-Gratton 1998).

Among children born in the early 1960s, 8 percent were either born to a lone parent or experienced the separation of their parents by age six. By the mid-1980s this figure had climbed to 22 percent (Table 7.2). By age 16, more than a quarter (27 percent) of the 1971-73 birth cohort had experienced similar conditions. In the 1990s the experience of lone parenthood was occurring earlier and earlier in the lives of children, to the point where it applied to more than a fifth of children by age six (Marcil-Gratton 1998).

Of children born into two-parent families, 20.5 percent experienced lone parenthood by age ten, and 60 percent of those had also experienced a stepfamily as a second major family change, all by age ten. Marcil-Gratton (1998) concluded that children were being born into increasingly diversified families, even over the birth cohorts 1983-84 to 1993-94 as followed by the National Longitudinal Survey of Children and Youth.

Children also experience strong differences depending on whether or not the parents had ever cohabitated. For instance, by age six in the 1987-88 cohort, among children born to two-parent families, only 8 percent had experienced

CUMULATIVE PERCENTAGE OF CANADIAN CHILDREN EXPERIENCING FAMILY DISRUPTION, BY COHORT

	BY AGE		
	6	16	20
Proportion born to a lone-parent or experiencing separation of parents			
1961-63 birth cohort	7.8	19.8	24.2
1971-73 birth cohort	13.0	27.3	—
1981-83 birth cohort	18.1	—	—
1987-88 birth cohort	22.6	—	—
Of children born to two-parent family, proportion experiencing separation of parents			
Parent never cohabitated			
1971-73 cohort	6.0	19.5	—
1981-83 cohort	8.0	—	—
1987-88 cohort	8.1	—	—
Parent ever cohabitated			
1971-73 cohort	18.0	53.2	—
1981-83 cohort	23.1	—	—
1987-88 cohort	24.6	—	—

Source: *Péron et al. 1999: 232; Marcil-Gratton 1993: 80, 81, 82; Marcil-Gratton and Lapierre-Adamcyk 1992: Tables 4, 5, 6; Marcil-Gratton 1998: 14, 18. Statistics Canada, General Social Survey, 1985, 1990, 1995. National Longitudinal Survey of Children and Youth, 1994-95.*

TABLE 7.2

their parents' separation if respondents had never cohabitated, but 25 percent if they had cohabitated (Table 7.2). The proportion experiencing the separation of parents by age six reached 43 percent if the parents had cohabitated and never married (Marcil-Gratton 1998: 18). For children born in 1971-73, only 9 percent involved parents who had cohabitated, compared to 63 percent for children born in 1993-94 (Marcil-Gratton 1993, 1998: 8). While cohabitation implied unusual behaviour in the earlier cohorts, its more common occurrence later on does not seem to mean that it is any less deviant with respect to the likelihood of parents separating after the birth of a child. Consequently, the family life of children born to parents who had cohabitated at one point or another involves more change and is particularly unstable (Marcil-Gratton 1993).

Many children therefore live through a diversity of family trajectories, which Table 7.3 illustrates for children aged 6-8 in 1991. Among 1,000 children, 858 were in two-parent families, but only 656 were in intact first marriages and just 12 in intact cohabitations. For 57 of these 1,000 children, the couple was in a subsequent union but there were no children from a previous union. Another 133 were in reconstituted families with at least one child born from a previous union. In effect, 4 out of 1,000 children were in a second reconstituted family, all by the age of 6-8 years. In addition, a third of the children in reconstituted families had parents who were cohabiting rather than married. The 142 children in single-parent families included 27 who were in their second episode of single parenthood.

By age 16, only 72.7 percent of the 1971-73 birth cohort were living with both parents; another 17.5 percent were living with their mothers and 9.8 percent with their fathers (Table 7.4). Among those living with their mothers, 40 percent involved a step-parent; the same is true for 60 percent of those living with their fathers. Already by the age of six to seven, 25.8 percent of the 1986-87 cohort were not living with both parents. As Nathan Keyfitz (1994:7) observes, the presence of children, once the main reason not to divorce, no longer plays that role—and has not done so since the 1960s. Based on data from the U.S. Panel Study of Income Dynamics for 1968-85, Linda Waite and Lee Lillard (1991) estimate that, over the long run, children add only slightly to marital stability. In these data, children mostly delay marital disruption, especially when they are young. But, with separations occurring earlier in the lives of children, even this delaying factor is eroding.

What has also changed in the period since the 1960s has been the rate of births to cohabiting couples. For children aged 0-14 in the 1991 Canadian census, 7 percent were with parents who were cohabiting, more than double the proportion from ten years earlier (Kerr, Larrivée, and Greenhalgh 1994: 17). Marriage is no longer the basis either for couple formation or for births (Festy 1994).

DISTRIBUTION OF 1,000 CHILDREN AGED 6-8 IN 1991 BY FAMILY ENVIRONMENT AND FAMILY TRAJECTORY

TWO-PARENT FAMILY	858
Married parents	*796*
Intact family	656
Reconstituted couple	52
Reconstituted family	88
Cohabiting parents	*62*
Intact family	12
Reconstituted couple	5
Reconstituted family	45
SINGLE-PARENT FAMILY	142
Mother-only	*123*
First episode	98
Second episode	25
Father-only	*19*
First episode	17
Second episode	2
TOTAL	1000

Source: Péron et al. 1999: 225. Statistics Canada, 1991 Census, 1990 General Social Survey.

TABLE 7.3

DISTRIBUTION OF CHILDREN AGES 6 AND 16 BY RESIDENCE WITH PARENTS

| | 1971-73 COHORT | | 1981-83 COHORT | 1986-87 COHORT |
	AGE 6	AGE 16	AGE 6	AGE 6-7
With both parents	87.0	72.7	81.9	74.2
With one parent	13.0	27.3	18.1	25.8
Mother alone	4.6	10.3	8.2	16.1
Mother and another partner	3.7	7.2	5.6	—
Father alone	1.3	3.7	1.8	0.9
Father and another partner	3.5	6.1	2.6	—

Source: Marcil-Gratton and Lapierre-Adamcyk 1992: Table 8; Marcil-Gratton 1998: 5.
General Social Survey 1990, National Longitudinal Survey of Children and Youth, 1994-95.

TABLE 7.4

All of these trends—cohabitation, births outside of marriage, increased divorce, children no longer being seen as an obstacle to divorce, and family reconstitution either through cohabitation or marriage—represent changing attitudes to families and reduced family stability for children. While family reconstitution often provides children with multiple parents, it does not lessen the instability. Stepfathers can be important to the lives of children, and men appear to invest more in the non-biological children who are present than in the biological children who are absent (Marsiglio 1998). However, Evelyne Sullerot (1992: 181) observes that the father is replaced by a man who has no common genealogy and no common durable status. Step-fathers largely remove themselves from the lives of stepchildren once they are no longer living with the child's mother (Kaplan, Lancaster, and Anderson 1998).

In most cases the parents who decide to separate see the separation and possible remarriage as a beneficial step in their lives. Frances Goldscheider and Linda Waite (1991) observe that many bad marriages result in poor parenting, and consequently divorce can be a benefit to children. However, they also note that many other parents with marital problems can parent effectively. In general, children are less likely than parents to benefit from divorce and remarriage.

Consequently, Goldscheider and Gayle Kaufman (1996) propose that the level of commitment between men and women is the key variable missing in the study of childbearing. The lower commitment represented by cohabitation has especially eroded the male role in families. At the same time, men who are more involved with their children are less likely to divorce. Given that men are more likely to be absent, these authors see the centrality of parenthood declining more in men's than in women's lives. A non-resident father can have a positive influence if he is involved with his children, but the tenuous relationship with the mother on issues of parenting can also bring conflict into the children's lives.

BOX 7.1 | *Lone-parenthood episodes*

Comparing single parenthood in the 17th and 20th centuries, Hubert Denis (1994) finds that, because of reduced parental mortality, the rate of lone parenthood was lower in 1960-75 than in Quebec of the 17th century. However, by the early 1980s, it was even higher than three centuries ago. The change over the recent period was rapid, especially for young children. For instance, 8 percent of children aged 0-7 were with a lone parent in 1975, compared to 16 percent in 1994-95 (Leblanc, Lefebvre, and Merrigan 1996; Marcil-Gratton 1998: 5). Nonetheless, these rates of single parenthood experience in Canada are lower than in the United States, where half of all children spend part of their lives with single parents (Bumpass 1994).

Marcil-Gratton (1993: 85) illustrates the diversity of family experiences associated with episodes of lone parenthood:

Among the 27 percent of children born in 1971-73 whose parents parted, only thirty-nine out of a hundred were still within a first-time single parent family at age sixteen; sixty-one had known life within a family reconstituted with their guardian parent's new partner, twenty-two had seen this second two-parent family disintegrate propelling them a second time into single parenthood, twelve had experienced a second reconstitution, and five had experienced a third episode of single parenthood [all by age 16].

Maureen Moore (1987, 1988, 1989a) analyzed female lone parenting from the point of view of mothers, using the 1984 Family History Survey. Compared to currently married women of the same age, female lone-parents, she found, were more likely to have lived common law, to have had their children earlier, and to have less education, but they were also more likely to be in the labour force. In effect, they were raising children while facing a double disadvantage of lack of support from a spouse and fewer job skills.

In 1980 mothers in lone-parent families were more likely to be in the labour force than were mothers in two-parent families, but by 1990 the opposite was the case (Lindsay 1992). In addition, by the early 1990s the total number of women receiving alimony or child support payments represented only a third of the number of female lone-parent families (Galarneau 1993).

The average lone-parenthood situation involves considerable disadvantages. James Coleman (1988) analyzed the situation of children in terms of financial, human, and social capital. The financial capital available to families relates to the income of parents. The human capital is the parents' education and training, experience, and skills and aptitudes in general. Social capital is the social relationships and social support within and beyond the family, including the co-parental relationships that children may experience. Children in lone-parent families are more likely to have relative deficiencies on all three fronts. For instance, in terms of financial capital, among families with children under 18 in 1990, the proportion with low-income status amounted to 9.6 percent of two-parent families, 27.1 percent of male lone-parent families, and 60.6 percent of female lone-parent families (Lindsay 1992: 35). The disparity in family income had grown over the previous decade, probably because two-parent families increasingly involved two incomes.

The reduced human capital involves fewer adults and consequently less total available education and experience from parents. Social capital refers to relationships both with other family members and with other members of the community. The children of single parents probably form fewer such relationships. Data from the United States indicate that male single parents are more likely to be living with other adults who provide social, human, and possibly also financial capital for their children (Eggebeen, Snyder, and Manning 1996). Canadian data also indicate that lone mothers have less disadvantages if they are living in the household of their parents, where they would have access to more social capital (Sorenson and Grindstaff 1995). ◆

CHILD CARE

The long-term trends in work and the family economy show an increased need for child care outside the home. In the United States until 1840 at least two-thirds of children lived in two-parent families with both parents and children living and working together. With the transformation to breadwinners working away from the home and children over six largely at school, by 1920 half of U.S. families were of the breadwinner-homemaker type, which remained the case until 1970.

In 1870 only half of children aged 5-19 were at school, and the average school year took up only 21 percent of the full year (Hernandez 1993: 186). By 1940, four-fifths of the children of those ages were at school, and the school year had expanded to 42 percent of the year. Because the average work year makes up only 65 percent of the full year, school attendance had released mothers of children aged six and over from some two-thirds of a full-time adult work year. Over the next 50 years, from 1940 to 1990, the proportion of children aged 6-18 who had no parent at home full-time increased from 20 to 66 percent; for children aged 0-5 the proportion increased from 13 to 53 percent. By the 1990s, Hernandez suggests, this second transformation, to the two-earner model and non-parental care of preschool children, was about half completed. Nonetheless, the transformation had been rapid, taking 30 years to become the dominant arrangement for the majority of children, while the first transformation had taken 90 years. With more adolescents now working while they are at school, the family economy of children is once again similar to that of 150 years ago, with both parents and children working. But, as Hernandez observes, the work now involves different jobs and locations, and it produces much more affluence.

Diversity of views on child care

With the transformation in family models comes considerable disagreement about the relative advantages and disadvantages of home-based in comparison to centre-based child care. Based on a review of the literature and interviews with key informants in four countries, June Pollard (1991) outlines four prevalent ideologies: the conservative position is that home-based care is best because it promotes family values; the socialist position prefers centre-based care because of its advantage for socializing children to values of social co-operation and equality; the liberal position is that parents should be able to choose; the social-reproduction position proposes a mixture of both kinds of care, because children need both individual attention and social experiences.

Just as there are no typical families, so also do child-care arrangements vary extensively. The diversity includes the extent of parental work, the extent to which care involves parents and non-parental situations, and the type of non-parental care that children receive. Policy orientations toward child care are equally diverse and ambivalent. The context has changed considerably since the immediate postwar period, when child care was only provided in cases of severe neglect or abuse.

Still, a significant tension remains, in both policy and public opinion, regarding the extent of state involvement in child care and in family matters more broadly. The involvement of the state has been controversial, both welcomed and contested (Leira 1992:2). For instance, an Ontario Royal Commission on Learning argued in 1994 for bringing three-year-old children into the school system, but a year later the provincial government eliminated education funding for four-year-old children. One line of thought might insist that with more than two-thirds of the women with children at home participating in the paid labour force, Canada has a clear need for a national child-care program (Tougas 1993). Another would argue for a variety of policies reflecting the diversity of families and their associated child-care needs (Wente 1994).

The results of public opinion polls seem to be strongly related to the formulation of the question. A 1991 Health and Welfare poll found two-thirds of respondents indicating that the best place for preschool children was in the home, with 16 percent saying day-care centres (Vienneau 1991, as reported in Heitlinger 1991). In contrast, a 1993 poll for the Ontario Coalition for Better Child Care found the 30 percent were "strongly in favour" and 34 percent were "somewhat in favour" of a "national childcare program, including various kinds of regulated childcare services, planned at the local level and supported through a combination of parent fees and government funds" (Insight Canada Research 1993). Both of these polls showed rather limited approaches. For instance, asking about the "best place for children," as the first poll did, does not allow respondents to consider possible constraints that might prompt a second preference. In the second poll, some respondents may have been focusing on planning at the local level or on the sharing of costs by government and users, rather than on the preference for the day-care facilities themselves.

A qualitative survey of orientations to marriage and family questions (Beaujot 1992) found day care to be one of the most contentious issues. While respondents tended to agree on central life questions such as marriage, children, and state support of families through health and education, they provided a diversity of responses to open questions on day care. Over half of the respondents were in favour of government subsidies for day care, but a significant minority were opposed either on grounds of costs or because they believe day cares were an inappropriate environment for children. It appears that opposing models of state intervention in families are most manifest on the question of formal child care. Some people want more state support for day care as a basic means of family support, and more specifically as a means of enhancing the labour-market participation of mothers. Others want the state to support parents looking after their own children, or they may be open to day care only as a means of enabling one-parent families to be more self-supporting.

In theorizing on the question of *Welfare States and Working Mothers*, Arnlaug Leira (1992) elaborates some of the broader complexities underpinning the ambivalence in both public opinion and public policy. She starts with the basic idea, used throughout this book, that both economic activity (or production in a wider sense) and child care (or social reproduction more broadly) are essential to society. Given the variety of relationships between carer and earner roles, ranging from breadwinner to two-earner arrangements, the situations exhibit considerable complexity at both individual and collective levels. The collective level includes, on the one hand, the encouragement of women's labour-force participation and the provision of child-care facilities. But, on the other hand, the services may be too expensive or insufficient to permit the full and equal participation of mothers in the labour market. On the individual level, the everyday coping strategies for child care and economic provision typically consist of joining together components of family-based care and formal and/or informal services. This implies that the dual-earner family is actually dependent on the conservation of more traditional family forms, in which informal child-care services are obtained at a cheaper price. Given its juncture with regard to earning and caring activities, child care understandably becomes a crucial question both for families and for the society.

The work situation of parents

The 1988 Child Care survey provided extensive information on the family and care situation of children under 12 years of age in Canada. Given our subject, our focus here is on children under six years. While child-care needs clearly do not end after children enter school full-time, the needs then are rather different because they are limited to the hours before and after the school day. Nonetheless, this 1988 survey saw 47 percent of children aged 6-12 receiving some supplemental care beyond school and their parents, including 18 percent in paid child-care arrangements (Goelman et al. 1993: 35, 37).

WORK STATUS OF RESPONDENT (AND SPOUSE/PARTNER)
BY AGE OF CHILDREN, FOR CHILDREN 0-5 YEARS

	0-17 MO.		18-35 MO.		3-5 YR.		0-5 YR.	
	000s	%	000s	%	000s	%	000s	%
Two-parent families	*509.5*	*100.0*	*476.6*	*100.0*	*939.9*	*100.0*	*1926*	*100.0*
Both FT	172.1	33.8	150.8	31.6	310.3	33.0	633.2	32.9
One PT	79.2	15.5	85.3	17.9	187.6	20.0	352.1	18.3
One NE	258.1	50.7	240.5	50.5	441.9	47.0	940.5	48.8
One-parent families	*49.6*	*100.0*	*55.3*	*100.0*	*133.9*	*100.0*	*238.8*	*100.0*
FT	7.9	15.9	18.3	33.1	49.4	36.9	75.6	31.7
PT	3.1	6.3	4.4	8.0	10.8	8.1	18.8	7.7
NE	38.6	77.8	32.6	59.0	73.7	55.0	144.9	60.7

NOTES: FT: full-time. PT: at least one parent working part-time. NE: at least one parent not employed.
The sample has been weighted to the corresponding population sizes.

Source: *Special tabulations from 1988 National Child Care Survey, Statistics Canada.*

TABLE 7.5

Given the interaction of the earner and carer roles, researchers often see the need for child care as a consequence of mothers' work patterns. Table 7.5 presents data on children under six by work patterns of parents. For children under six, 11 percent are living with one parent. In these one-parent families, the dominant case (60.7 percent) is where the parent is not employed; this rises to 77.8 percent at children's ages 0-17 months. For a third (31.7 percent) of the children in single-parent families, that parent is employed full-time. The children in two-parent families also apparently gain access to much of their care through situations of one parent working part-time (18.3 percent) or being not employed (48.8 percent). Considering all these children together, half (50.1 percent) are living with a parent who is not employed, and another 17.1 percent are with at least one parent who is working part-time. That leaves a third (32.7 percent) who are with parents(s) working full-time. The other two-thirds have access to parental time associated with the parents either not working or working less than full-time. The 1994-95 National Longitudinal Survey of Children and Youth also found that about a third (35.3 percent) of children aged 0-11 were living with parent(s) working full-time, while 42.2 percent were with a parent who was not employed (Ross, Scott, and Kelly 1996: 36).

With the majority of mothers now employed outside the home, the number of preschool children with both parents working increased from 38 percent in 1981 to 56 percent in 1996. At children's ages 0-2, the proportion of mothers in the labour force increased from 32 percent in 1976 to 62 percent in 1991. At ages 3-5, the increase was from 41 percent to 68 percent (Lero et al. 1993). For children born in the early 1960s, 90 percent of mothers stopped working at the birth of their first child. For children born in the early 1980s, 50 percent of mothers did so (Marcil-Gratton 1988). The proportion of mothers working right after their child's birth in the early 1980s was comparable to the

PREFERRED WORK STATUS, BY CURRENT WORK STATUS AND FAMILY STATUS, FOR EMPLOYED RESPONDENTS WITH CHILDREN AGED 0-5 YEARS

| | PREFERENCE | | | | | |
	WORK FULL-TIME	WORK PART-TIME	NOT WORK	NOT STATED	TOTAL	POPULATION (1,000s)
Current work and family status of DA						
Total	25.0	50.8	13.0	11.3	100.0	671.5
Employed part-time	7.4	69.6	11.8	11.9	100.0	190.5
Employed full-time	32.0	43.6	13.4	11.0	100.0	481.0
Two-parent	22.5	52.9	13.1	11.6	100.0	597.5
Employed part-time	5.8	70.3	11.7	12.2	100.0	177.4
Employed full-time	29.5	45.5	13.6	11.4	100.0	420.1
Single-parent	45.3	34.0	12.1	8.6	100.0	74.0
Employed part-time	28.9	51.0	12.4	7.7	100.0	13.0
Employed full-time	48.8	30.4	12.0	8.8	100.0	61.0

NOTES: DA: designated adult most responsible for child care.
This question was asked only of respondents who used child care beyond that provided by spouse.

Source: Special tabulations from the 1988 National Child Care Survey, Statistics Canada.

TABLE 7.6

proportion working when children were 12 years old, some 20 years earlier. Nonetheless, part-time work and other interruptions in the work patterns of one of the parents still make for a considerable amount of parental time for child care.

International comparisons from the late 1980s indicated that the proportion of women not working when they had children under five years of age was higher in Canada, at 48 percent, than in Sweden, at 16 percent (Jensen and Sapariti 1992). However, mothers in Canada seem to have been just as busy working full-time. With children aged 0-16, 37.9 percent of women in Canada, compared to 40.8 percent in Sweden, were working full-time in 1988.

To determine the extent to which parents would like to be working, the 1988 Child Care Survey asked respondents who were employed and who had someone other than themselves or their spouse looking after any of their children while working: "When considering your own needs and those of your family, would you most prefer to work full-time, to work part-time, or not work at a job or business?"

For all respondents with children aged 0-5, 25 percent answered "work full-time," 50.8 percent said "work part-time," and 13 percent said "not work" (Table 7.6). Clearly, those desiring to work part-time outnumber those actually working part-time, which represents 28.4 percent of the work status of these employed respondents. Significant as well are the 13 percent of employed respondents who said they would prefer not to work. Donna Lero and her co-authors (1993: 47-49) concluded, "The majority of employed

CHILDREN AND YOUTH

parents with primary childcare responsibilities expressed a clear preference that differs considerably from their daily experience."

In surveys of life satisfaction, people tend to say that they are satisfied (Atkinson 1980: 284). But these responses on work preferences indicate considerable preferences for alternative arrangements. Among respondents working full-time, only 32 percent said they would prefer to work full-time, 43.6 percent preferred part-time, and an additional 13.4 percent said they would prefer not to work. The responses for male respondents were different, showing five times as much preference for full-time as compared to part-time work. Single parents also showed a preference for working full-time.

This difference between current activity and preferences is apparently not at all as common for people working part-time. For every person in this category who would prefer to work full-time, over nine would prefer part-time work. Those preferring not to work are more numerous than those preferring to work full-time. Once again, the people most likely to desire full-time work are the single parents. The survey specifically asked this question in terms of the family context: "when considering your own needs and those of your family."

The survey also asked employed respondents who depended on someone other than the spouse to look after children while working if they would prefer to change the schedule of hours they were currently working. Over a third expressed an interest in changing their work schedules. Almost 10 percent said they preferred to "work only during school hours." Among persons employed, then, especially among those working full-time, there is a considerable preference to either work part-time or to change the work schedule to accommodate for children. In effect, only a third of dual-earner couples included persons who both worked a standard week (Lero et al. 1992a: 78).

The 1988 Child Care Survey also found that in 31.4 percent of cases, the main reason for working less than 30 hours per week was "family or personal responsibilities," with another 41.7 percent stating that they did not want full-time work (Lero et al. 1992a: 46). Based on the 1991 Survey of Work Arrangements, Katherine Marshall (1994) confirmed that, for dual-earner couples, almost a third of mothers of preschool children were working part-time to "balance work and family responsibilities."

Part-time work is therefore a common outcome of the joint considerations of employment and child care. The disadvantages of part-time employment may be balanced by the advantages of providing child care within the family (Folk and Beller 1993; Hofferth and Brayfield 1991). In discussing the "part-time paradox," Ann Duffy and Norene Pupo (1992) also focused on family considerations, including the child-care advantages of part-time work in the absence of affordable and accessible day care.

Besides these structural considerations, predominant cultural values also play a role. Reflecting on results from a U.S. Survey of child-care choices, K.F. Folk and A.H. Beller (1993: 156) speak of "the continuing strength of traditional values emphasizing the importance of care of young children by family members or close relatives." Duffy and Pupo (1992: 120) speak of part-time employment as partly a function of mothers who reject day care "as an unacceptable option" or of mothers who seek to "be there" for other family members or to "preserve the home front."

Clearly, these attitudes are themselves influenced by structural considerations, including questions of the organization of work and the availability of child-care facilities. Evelyn Lapierre-Adamcyk and Marcil-Gratton (1995) ask if the society is properly organized to take care of the children affected by family change, which includes fewer children living with both parents and more parents working. Based on the 1990 General Social Survey, they observe that when children are more numerous and younger, they are less likely to have a mother working, but children who are not all from the same union, or children whose parents are cohabitating, are more likely to have mothers working. While parents can see part-time work as a way of combining work aspirations and parental obligations, that tendency does lead to the ghettoization and vulnerability of women workers. Children who have no siblings, regardless of age, and children in families in which the youngest child is of school age, are more likely to have both parents working full-time. This same condition also applies to children in single-parent families once one child is over two years or once two children are at school ages. However, when two of their children are under five, 56.6 percent of lone parents are not employed. Clearly, parents do adjust the intensity and timing of their work in relation to the exigencies of family life. Still, Lapierre-Adamcyk and Marcil-Gratton suggest that better social intervention in child care would reduce parental juggling around work and family, reduce the number of parents who are not employed, and consequently reduce the vulnerability of women and children facing marital separation. They argue for enhanced collective support both for child care and for the family-work interface more broadly.

In effect, policy in Sweden has encouraged this interface of work and parenthood. For instance, most women there take parental leave and then also take the opportunity to return to work on a part-time basis (Nasman 1990). Most couples do not see it as a problem for mothers to be doing most of the child-rearing; this is the way they want to solve the situation (Hoem 1997). Besides, they say that many jobs are boring, and part-time work ensures a continued social contact. At the age of eight months, 95 percent of children are receiving only parental care, but by 16 months only 50 percent do (Nasman 1993: 33). Men with very young children also work the shortest hours, and they have the highest rates of absenteeism from work, while men with teenage children work the longest hours (Nasman 1990). Although they are far from equal, according to Elisabeth Nasman (1995), gendered parental roles are converging in Sweden. Mothering includes earning, while fathering includes caring for young children. In addition, Nasman expects that the effects of caring fathers could lead to further changes in the gender identity of children.

In contrast, a qualitative U.S. study of 130 people in a large plant found that workers were very busy and giving priority to their work (Hochschild 1997). Parents expressed regret at leaving their children so long in day care, yet they were not taking advantage of opportunities to work fewer hours or to do some of their work at home. While working longer hours could be a means of manifesting commitment to work, Arlie Hochschild

CHILD-CARE ARRANGEMENTS FOR CHILDREN AGED 0-12, CANADA, 1988

| | EXCLUSIVE PARENTAL CARE | NON-PARENTAL ARRANGEMENTS | | | | | |
		AT LEAST ONE	ONE	TWO	3+	AT LEAST ONE PAID	AVERAGE HOURS IN PAID CARE
Age							
0-17 months	45.0	55.0	46.5	7.3	1.2	31.9	26.0
18-35 months	36.5	63.5	48.7	12.0	2.7	44.6	27.4
3-5 years	20.6	79.4	45.4	27.0	7.1	47.9	22.5
6-9 years	51.9	48.1	38.3	8.2	1.6	24.5	11.7
10-12 years	53.8	46.2	37.3	7.8	1.1	9.1	11.8
TOTAL	42.5	57.5	41.9	12.8	2.8	29.6	20.3

Source: Goelman et al. 1993: 35, 36, 37. Statistics Canada, National Child Care Survey, 1988.

TABLE 7.7

also found a stronger identification with work than with parenthood. For many people, the principal social exchanges of life occur at work.

Child care of preschool children

Most Canadian children receive some care in addition to parental care. In 1988, for all children under 12 years of age, and excluding school as a child-care arrangement, 57.5 percent had some arrangement besides the parents themselves, including 29.6 percent who had some paid arrangement (Table 7.7). Arrangements beyond parents were most common at ages 3-5, when 79.4 percent of children had at least one arrangement, and 34.1 percent had two or more arrangements. However, for the half of these children who spent time in paid arrangements, the average time was 22.5 hours, or about two-thirds of an average workweek. The 1994-95 survey did not capture as many child-care situations, finding that 32.4 percent of children aged 0-11 were in some form of non-parental child care and another 26.8 percent in child care at some point in the past (Ross, Scott, and Kelly 1996: 25). On average, children spent 21.1 weekly hours in their primary care arrangement. This is similar to the data from the 1990 General Social Survey, which found 34.2 percent of children aged 0-12 receiving non-parental child care (Lapierre-Adamcyk and Marcil-Gratton 1995: 139).

The 1988 Child Care Survey also determined the main form of child care for each child, other than care by the respondent when not working or studying (Table 5.7). Given the variety of care situations, it is useful to consider three subtotals: group care, care by non-relatives, and care by relatives (child's other parent, sibling, other relatives, and care by respondent while working). The two other categories involve "child in school" and "no arrangement" beyond the care by respondent. All children 0-5 are considered here, regardless of the employment status of parents. For all the children 0-5, group care (day

PREFERRED CARE BY MAIN CARE FOR CHILDREN OF EMPLOYED RESPONDENTS, FOR CHILDREN AGED 0-5

PREFERRED CARE / MAIN CARE	GROUP (000S)		NON-RELATIVE (000S)		RELATIVE (000S)		DA (000S)	TOTAL (000S)	%
	DAY	NURSERY	CHILD'S HOME	OTHER'S HOME	SPOUSE	OTHER			
Group care									
Day care	91.8	6.0	13.3	7.5	3.0	4.8	1.5	121.3	12.2
Nursery school	6.3	13.6	4.7	3.4	2.2	3.2	3.1	37.7	3.8
Non-relative									
Child's home	9.2	2.7	67.5	9.1	6.0	4.1	0.6	93.9	9.5
Other's home	49.3	10.9	51.3	129.0	13.1	16.2	4.4	264.2	26.7
Relative									
Spouse	20.8	4.2	15.1	17.9	103.8	14.3	2.6	165.6	16.7
Other	33.9	7.8	15.0	14.9	13.8	118.3	3.7	201.0	20.3
DA	10.8	3.6	8.2	6.4	6.1	10.1	71.0	107.5	10.8
TOTAL	222.2	49.5	175.6	188.4	148.5	171.1	88.0	991.3	100.0
%	22.4	5.0	17.7	19.0	15.0	17.3	8.9	100.0	

NOTES: Data based on target child of employed respondents, and excludes cases in which the child is at school during all the hours the respondent is working. Five percent of respondents gave more than one preferred choice; DA=the designated adult or respondent of the survey, who is the person most responsible for child care in the family; Nursery school include before- and after-school programs; Non-relatives other than in the child's home include licensed and non-licensed care. Other relatives include siblings.

Source: Special tabulations from the Statistics Canada National Child Care Survey, 1988.

TABLE 7.8

care, nursery school, kindergarten, school, and before-school and after-school programs) represent 25.6 percent of main care arrangements. Non-relatives do another 20.5 percent of the care, relatives do 29.8 percent, and no care arrangements beyond the care provided by the respondent are made for 24.1 percent (Beaujot 1997: 282).

Group care and other forms of licensed care take in a relatively small proportion of children. In Ontario in 1988, N. Park (1991: 53-54) estimated, 9 percent of children aged ten and under were enrolled either full-time or part-time in some form of licensed child care. The proportion rose from 2 percent at ages 0-18 months to 24 percent at ages 5-6 years. Considering the numbers of working mothers, Park concluded that the system was "meeting more than 10% but less than 18% of the need." The data from the National Child Care Survey gave somewhat higher figures: 23.5 percent of children 0-5 were in group care or licensed care (Beaujot 1997: 282). Another study (Burke and Crompton 1991) estimated that 4 percent of children with mothers working were in licensed spaces in 1981, and 18 percent in 1990. Based on the 1994-95 National Longitudinal Survey of Children and Youth, only 40 percent of children aged 4-5 were in care situations, including 12.2 percent in registered day care and 20.6 percent in unregulated care either at the child's home or in another home (Kohn and Hertzman 1998). Parents who had children in unregulated care tended to be more educated than those with children in day care or in the care of relatives.

To determine the preferred care, the National Child Care Survey asked respondents, "Given your current work schedule and your present income, which type of arrangement would you most prefer to use for [your child] while you are working?" It asked this question only of employed respondents, and not if the child was at school during all the hours the respondent was working.

As with work status, substantial differences show up between actual and preferred circumstances (Table 7.8). Although 5 percent gave more than one preference, the cases along the diagonal in which actual and preferred care match involve only 60 percent of the sample. For instance, among the 12.2 percent of children for whom day care was the main care, 75.7 percent preferred day care but another 11 percent said they would prefer care by a non-relative in the child's home. Across the categories that can be matched on actual and preferred care, two had 70 percent or more preferring their actual main care: day care and non-relative in the child's home. Three categories had some 60 to 65 percent preferring their actual care: designated adult while working, spouse, and other relative. The other two categories had less than half preferring their actual main care: non-relatives who are not in the child's home and nursery school.

The results, then, showed considerable divergence between actual and preferred care. Another way to look at the data is to consider actual care within categories of preferences (that is, within columns of Table 7.8). When the preference was group care, or care by a non-relative in the child's home, more than half were using other forms of care. But when the preference was care by non-relatives outside of the child's home or care by relatives, some 70 percent were using that care. The most frequent reason offered for not using a preferred care was that it was not available, followed by questions of cost or other circumstances. On the basis of these data from the National

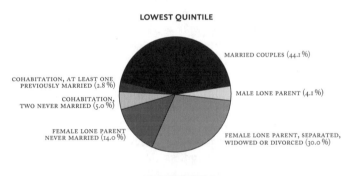

LOWEST QUINTILE

MARRIED COUPLES (44.1 %)

COHABITATION, AT LEAST ONE PREVIOUSLY MARRIED (2.8 %)

MALE LONE PARENT (4.1 %)

COHABITATION, TWO NEVER MARRIED (5.0 %)

FEMALE LONE PARENT NEVER MARRIED (14.0 %)

FEMALE LONE PARENT, SEPARATED, WIDOWED OR DIVORCED (30.0 %)

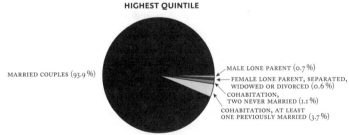

HIGHEST QUINTILE

MARRIED COUPLES (93.9 %)

MALE LONE PARENT (0.7 %)

FEMALE LONE PARENT, SEPARATED, WIDOWED OR DIVORCED (0.6 %)

COHABITATION, TWO NEVER MARRIED (1.1 %)

COHABITATION, AT LEAST ONE PREVIOUSLY MARRIED (3.7 %)

FIG 7.1 Distribution of children aged 0-17, by family status, for lowest and highest income quintiles, 1990

Source: Péron et al. 1999: 248. Statistics Canada, Census Data.

Child Care Survey, Gordon Cleveland and Douglas Huyat (1991, 1996) found that child-care costs influence demand and can push mothers, especially lone mothers, out of labour-force participation.

Other research looking at specific ages showed that the largest difference showed up with regard to day care at 0-17 months, when 3.8 percent of the children of employed respondents were using that care and 14.1 percent expressed a preference for it (Beaujot and Beaujot 1991: 39, 42, 43). Preference for group care was higher at ages 3-5 years, for children of parents working full-time (32.7 percent), and especially for single parents employed full-time (47.0 percent).

BOX 7.2 | *Implications of diversity in child-care situations*

Both policy and public opinion are divided on the extent to which child care should be seen as a private responsibility. In the book *Children First*, Penelope Leach (1994) argues for long parental leaves or part-time work as a means of having parents look after their own children. Based on U.S. data, Rachel Connelly (1992) finds that women with young children are more likely to choose self-employment or to be a child-care provider. She proposes that this is because mothers with young children value the ability to care for their own children while engaged in market work. In contrast, Martha Friendly (1994) argues that child-care policy should involve largely publicly available care. In this regard, she points out that the Canadian situation is more similar to that in the United States and United Kingdom and different from that in France, Sweden, and Denmark, which provide a more public system. Europe shows a general trend toward a publicly funded system for children aged 3-6, but more variability and lower coverage at younger ages (Moss 1997). Alena Heitlinger (1993)

argues for a combination of measures to fund both services and parents.

In theory child-care policy can support formal child-care systems, care by the parents themselves, and/or informal care including relatives and non-relatives. Indeed, the diversity of child-care situations across families, and the diversity of preferences for work and child-care arrangements, would seem to call for a diversity of approaches. The need is there not only to enhance the subsidization of child-care services but also to subsidize the ability of parents to look after their own children—or to allow them to use the various informal means they consider appropriate for child-care support.

Still, while parental preferences on child care are clearly important, other considerations, such as children's development needs, matters of gender equality, and public service to the collectivity, need to be taken into account (Friendly 1977). As Lapierre-Adamcyk and Marcil-Gratton (1995) point out, family change is clearly moving in a direction that places a stronger priority on public child care. ◆

The row and column totals of Table 7.8 show that preferences exceed actual care in the categories of day care, care by non-relatives in the child's home, and nursery school. In all other categories, preferences are less common than actual main care. Significantly, 40 percent of preferred care would be by relatives or the respondent, 35 percent by non-relatives, and 25 percent by group care.

Questions on the child-related benefits that respondents would like to have from their employers showed not only a clear interest in workplace day care, but also an equivalent interest in benefits that would allow parents more flexibility, especially in work hours, parental leave, and the opportunity to work part-time. Lero et al. (1992a: 100-2) concluded that parents "manage work, childcare and family responsibilities in a variety of ways." In the case of dual-earner couples, 40 percent of the partners provided care at least part of the time while the respondent was working. At the same time, 32 percent of children under six are in families of the breadwinner-homemaker type (Lero et al. 1993: 17).

THE WELFARE OF CHILDREN AND YOUTH

Having considered family change from the perspective of the experiences of children, and child care as a specific manifestation of the juncture between earning and caring activities, the chapter will now highlight various aspects of the welfare of children and youth, from their economic and family situations to education, home-leaving, work, and starting families.

Children can and undoubtedly do have a significant effect on the family standard of living. Compared to couples without children, families with children have an increased risk of poverty and reduced chances of affluence (Brouillette et al. 1991). Besides the direct costs, children can be the cause of work interruptions and leave less time available for parents to advance professional careers. Adjusting for numbers of persons in the household, Liliane Brouillette and her co-authors estimate that couples with two children have 16 percent less average income than those with no children. Conversely, 37 percent of couples with no children were 150 percent above the median income in 1987, compared to 12 percent of those with three children. Looking at data from 1973 to 1986, Martin Dooley (1991) also found that the presence of children under age 18 raised the incidence of low income for families.

Economic situation of children

While the period 1971-81 saw improvements in the real income of families with children, the years 1981-96 saw slower growth, fewer improvements in low income, and increasing inequality across families with children (Brouillette et al. 1990; Rashid 1998).

The more recent period also showed strong variations by family type, with markedly lower income for single-parent families, especially in comparison with two-income families. Income inequality was also highest across lone-parent families (Rashid 1998: 15). Consequently, the divergence of family types accentuated the economic inequality across children—a development that can be illustrated by comparing children in the top and bottom income quintiles (Figure 7.1). For children under 18 who are in the top quintile, 93.9 percent are in families with married parents, 4.8 percent are with cohabiting parents, and 1.3 percent are with a lone parent. In contrast, the children under 18 in the bottom quintile include 44.1 percent with married parents, 7.8 percent with cohabiting parents, and 48.1 percent with a lone parent. Other data confirm that increasing proportions of poor children

---

BOX 7.3 | *Effect of children on parents*

By their very presence, children are active agents in family change. In her book *The Effect of Children on Parents*, Anne-Marie Ambert (1992) highlights how children can change families, including the various members. Some of the following quotes from Ambert's book come from autobiographies written by students in a university class on the family.

> What has been the happiest moment since I've turned twenty-five is bound to be the birth of my son. I cannot describe how much joy and how much life he has added to our lives. An added bonus was that he is the first male grandchild my parents have and this has contributed a lot to my parents' respect for me, something that had been lacking in my life up to this point.
>
> (Married male student, in his autobiography)

Children can be victims of abusive parents, of disturbed, immoral, or simply uncaring and even ignorant parents. But, if one accepts the reality of the child as a social actor (rather than an idealistic tabula rasa that is, at the core, good or even angelic), one also has to accept the fact that the actor can impact negatively as well as positively on other actors, including parents.

As a specific observation, it is found that even neonates initiated four out of five of the mother-infant interactions.

> Since my mother was divorced at the age of twenty-six, and left to raise three children on her own, I feel I have had a great impact on her life at all stages.... I am sure that my mother's opportunity to remarry would have been far greater if she had had no children ... between eleven and fourteen ... she would often ask my opinion concerning someone she was dating.
>
> (Student's autobiography)

> I also think that I had a positive impact on my parents' lives when I was six to ten years old. This is because I made them delay the idea of separation. My dad told me that he would have separated from my mother earlier had it not been for me and my youngest brother.
>
> (Student's autobiography)

Source: Adapted from Ambert 1992: 1, 14, 18, 138, 144.

are in lone-parent families. For instance, those living with one parent comprised 21 percent of poor children in 1971 but 50 percent in 1996 (Table 8.3 and Conway 1997).

Several analyses have looked at the dynamics of change in the economic situation of children. Considering children aged 0-5 in the period 1971-86, Don Kerr (1992) found that children had benefited from various changes, including the higher labour-force participation of mothers, the fewer children per family, and the later age of mothers at childbearing. These factors were indeed more important than improvements in parental education and occupational status for improving the economic situation of preschool children. The big negative, though, was the higher proportions of children in lone-parent families. Altogether, the economic situation of children improved over the period, and there was also more inequality, especially in comparing the children in dual-earner families to those in lone-parent families.

Summarizing the situation in industrialized countries, Jensen (1995) observed that family dissolution and single-parent families, including the decline in support from fathers who are more likely to be absent, were the main factors contributing to increased poverty among children. For the United States, Daniel Lichter (1994) estimated that 60 percent of the difference in the incidence of poverty between white and black children could be explained by the differences in single-parenthood. But poor economic performance was also part of the reasons for separation. In effect, poverty is both a cause and consequence of marital instability (Furstenberg 1995).

Other analyses of Canadian data show a variety of factors at stake in children's economic well-being but indicate that single parenthood is a key negative element. Looking at the period 1973-88, Dooley (1991, 1993) found improvements in both the incidence and severity of child poverty for most types of families, and still poverty levels remained high, especially in the case of lone mothers and very young couples. The modest economic progress of children was largely a function of compensating factors, in particular smaller families but more lone parenthood. The role of government transfers and wive's earnings was critical in sustaining the economic welfare of children in two-parent families (Dooley 1988). In spite of the positive role of government transfers, the widening gap with lone-parent families occurred because the earnings of married women increased more than those of lone mothers, which is related to other factors, such as differences in age and education.

For the period 1973-95, Garnett Picot, John Myles, and Wendy Pyper (1998) found that the change in family composition had benefited the economic situation of children under 15 years of age. The positive factors were the later age at parenthood, the higher education of parents, the smaller family sizes, and a greater number of earners per family. The main negative factor was the proportion of families with single parents. Still, the period 1988-95 did not see an upswing in the education levels of parents or in the proportions of dual-earners, while single-parenthood continued to increase and declines occurred in the real earnings of men under 35. In that period the transfer system played a larger role in maintaining family incomes, compensating for the declining real wages of young adults (Picot and Myles 1996a). For children under 15 with low-income status,

**LOW-INCOME STATUS OF CHILDREN,
BY FAMILY TYPE, 1975 AND 1992**

	CHILDREN UNDER 18		CHILDREN UNDER 7	
	1975	1992	1975	1992
*Poverty rate**				
All family types	18.1	18.0	18.8	20.9
Lone-parent families	65.8	57.6	83.1	76.0
Two-parent families	13.5	11.2	14.8	12.9
Proportion of children in lone-parent families	*8.7*	*14.7*	*5.8*	*12.6*
Proportion of poor children in lone-parent families	*31.8*	*47.1*	*36.0*	*57.8*
For poor families: proportion of income from government transfers				
Lone-parent	59.7	71.3	63.3	78.9
Two-parent	26.7	42.9	24.6	47.7

* Based on 1986 low-income cut-offs.

Source: Zyblock 1996a: 23, 14,16. Statistics Canada, Survey of Consumer Finances.

TABLE 7.9

transfers became more important than earnings after 1983. By 1991, two-thirds of the after-tax income of poor families with children under 15 came from transfers, compared to one-third in 1973 (Picot and Myles 1996b).

The economic situation of children relates, then, to three factors: employment earnings of parents, family structure, and transfer payments. The employment earnings benefit by having two parents in the workplace. At ages 0–14, 38 percent of children had two working parents in 1973 compared to 62 percent in 1991 (Picot and Myles 1996b). However, since the late 1970s, the earnings of young men have declined in real terms. The changing family structure also has beneficial effects through smaller family sizes and later ages at parenthood, but this has to be balanced against the greater proportions of single parents, which has a negative effect. The proportion of children living with one adult more than doubled from 5 percent in 1973 to 11 percent in 1991. The transfer system has played a larger role over time, especially for children from poor families. The net result has been little long-term change in the proportions of children with low-income status.

Table 7.9 illustrates these trends. For all children under 18, the proportion classified as having low income was 18.1 percent in 1975 and 18 percent in 1992. But these figures mask improvements for both two-parent and one-parent families. The proportion of children in lone-parent families has increased, and they represent an increased proportion of poor children, in spite of the greater role of government transfers in the income of their families. As Myles Zyblock (1996a) observes, the growth in the proportion of lone-parent families has offset the benefits of economic growth for child poverty and brought an increased dependence on government transfers. Using a broad definition of transfers, including family benefits, unemployment insurance, tax credits, and social assistance, the period 1980 to 1994 saw the average transfer to families with children increase from $2,700 to $5,900, or by close to 70 percent in real terms (Crompton 1996). These transfers represented 8 percent of the 1994 family income of two-parent families and 31 percent of that of one-parent families.

BOX 7.4 | *Children and intergenerational transfer*

Several analyses have considered the intergenerational transfer from parents to children. Miles Corak and Andrew Heisz (1998) considered persons aged 28-31 in 1994 in relation to the situation of their parents in 1982, when the children were aged 16 to 19. The children's income was affected by the income of both fathers and mothers, with income from assets playing a more significant positive role and income from unemployment insurance playing a negative role. Children who had been in a two-parent family had a $4,000 income advantage, while those who had moved three or more times had $3,800 less income than those who had not moved (p. 69).

The likelihood of earning postsecondary educational credentials is almost three times as high for persons whose parents had such credentials (De Brouker and Lavallée 1998)—though about half of the children in the sample obtained higher education than their parents. Nicole Fortin and Sophie Lefebvre (1998) found intergenerational mobility to be higher in Canada than in the United States and the United Kingdom. M. Rela Nakhaie and James Curtis (1998) also found that the class position of parents especially influences that of children through the parents' own education. Comparisons over time show that parental education and class have decreased in importance; that is, the educational system has become more open. In their assessment of the school component of the National Longitudinal Survey of Children and Youth, Garth Lipps and Jeffrey Frank (1997) also found differences by socio-economic status,

but they determined as well that children's outcomes are by no means predetermined and that, with a few exceptions, children and their schools are functioning well.

Thus, in the transfers across generations, it would appear that human capital plays the largest role, but that financial capital and social capital are also important, while social transfers have a levelling effect. That is, the intergenerational influence is especially visible in terms of education, but financial capital, including its form, also plays a role. Although social capital is hardest to measure, it is manifested through the impact of family structure and residential moves (Hango 1998). For instance, Dooley et al. (1998) found that lone-mother status is more important than the income and education of parents in predicting poor outcomes for children. The second wave of the National Longitudinal Survey of Children and Youth also found that the movement of children into and out of low income between 1994 and 1996 could be attributed primarily to family breakdown and family formation (Statistics Canada 1998k). Some factors, especially the increased openness of education, have a levelling influence, but other social transfers to lone-parent families are only partly reducing the gap. ◆

LOW-INCOME STATISTICS OF
CHILDREN AGED 0-17, 1973-93

	1973-81	1982-87	1988-93
Two-parent families			
Percent poor before transfers	15.6	17.2	17.0
Percent receiving transfers	36.9	74.9	76.7
OF POOR FAMILIES BEFORE TRANSFERS			
Percent who receive transfers	59.1	97.0	99.0
Percent who stay poor	80.3	73.6	66.2
Percent poor after taxes and transfers	13.2	12.9	11.5
One-parent families			
Percent poor before transfers	67.3	66.3	66.9
Percent receiving transfers	63.0	94.0	96.2
OF POOR FAMILIES BEFORE TRANSFERS			
Percent who receive transfers	75.4	98.4	99.8
Percent who stay poor	90.0	90.8	86.3
Percent poor after taxes and transfers	60.8	60.3	57.9
All families			
Percent poor before transfers	20.2	22.6	23.2
Percent receiving transfers	39.2	77.0	79.1
OF POOR FAMILIES BEFORE TRANSFERS			
Percent who receive transfers	63.8	97.5	99.3
Percent who stay poor	83.2	79.4	73.4
Percent poor after taxes and transfers	17.4	18.2	17.2

NOTES: Excludes male-headed single-parent families. Poverty based on income less than half of the median family income. Transfers include social assistance, unemployment income, refundable tax credits, but not family allowance.

Source: Lefebvre, Merrigan, and Gascon 1996: 356-57.
Statistics Canada, Survey of Consumer Finances.

TABLE 7.10

As an average for the period 1988-93, 23.2 percent of children under 18 had low income before taxes and transfers, compared to 17.2 percent after taxes and transfers (Table 7.10). For two-parent families, the tax and transfer system reduced the number of poor children by 44 percent; for lone-parent families, the reduction amounted only to 14 percent. Although improvements were made to the depth of poverty, less improvement came in the extent of poverty, measured as incomes below half of the median family income.

Social situation of children

The 1994-95 National Longitudinal Survey of Children and Youth found that the majority of Canadian children live in families that function well (Scott 1996). On the whole, these data show that Canadian children are physically, emotionally, and socially healthy (Canadian Social Trends 1996). Still, disparities do exist, as we've seen, and the main threats are poverty and economic insecurity.

Even after controlling for family income, researchers find that the children of lone parents have an increased risk of emotional and behavioural problems. For instance, one study showed that among low-income children the proportion who were hyperactive was 9.6 percent in two-parent and 16.7 percent in one-parent families. Among children above the low-income line, 13.7 percent of children with one parent were hyperactive (Lipman, Offord, and Dooley 1996: 8). One study (Ross, Roberts, and Scott 1998a) found lower levels of well-being in children from lone-parent families. Another study (Haddad 1998) of two-parent and one-parent families also found significant differences in the likelihood of emotional or behavioural problems, though no significant difference based on whether the mother or father has custody, or whether custody is shared.

Considering children in lone-parent families, David Ross, Paul Roberts, and Katherine Scott (1998b) found that they are less vulnerable if the family has higher

BOX 7.5 | *Children suffering from neglect and abuse*

For obvious reasons, the National Longitudinal Survey of Children and Youth was not able to identify the proportion of children suffering from abuse of one kind or another. But there are significant indicators.

Among children under two at the time of the survey, a quarter of the mothers had smoked during pregnancy (Canadian Social Trends 1996). Children of women who smoked had a higher likelihood of being born with a low birth-weight (Connor and McIntyre 1998). Children represent 22 percent of the victims of all incidents of violent crime reported to police, and 60 percent of reported sexual assaults, with a third of the sexual assaults being committed by family members (Bunge and Levett 1998: 21). The numbers of children killed by a family member number some 50 per year, or 7.2 per million children (p.29). Most of these children are killed by parents—two-thirds by fathers and a quarter by mothers. The highest incidence of child homicide occurs for children under two years of age. John Conway (1997) proposes that a good deal of child victimization can be traced to the institutional failure of families.

The specific story of a toddler found walking alone in the middle of the night in downtown Toronto illustrates how some families face difficulties in providing basic care and supervision.

In interviews with *The Globe and Mail*, neighbours, relatives, and police pieced together some of the events that led up to the girl's accidental journey onto the street. The girl's father said the incident was isolated and should not be viewed as evidence of greater neglect. "I should be charged with stupidity," he said. "I made a stupid freakin' mistake. I've learned my lesson. I never want to let her out of my sight again, because it only takes a second."

On the night of July 30, 1998, he and his wife had a fight. The couple had previously agreed to separate and had divided custody of the two children. The husband would take the baby, and his wife would have custody of her six-year-old boy, a child from another relationship.

He said his wife left the apartment with the boy some time around midnight, leaving him with the girl, who was asleep in her stroller on the ground floor. When he awoke early to be at work for 7 a.m. and saw the girl was gone, he assumed his wife had taken her.

He said he and his wife have had difficult lives, but they are good parents. He said he is hard-working and loves his children. He has raised his wife's six-year-old son since birth. "I love him like my own. I changed his diapers and was a father to him."

A neighbour who lives next to the family said the adults were friendly when sober but rude and violent when they drank. She said the father frequently yelled at his children, and the boy in particular displayed aggressive behaviour.

That same night the police had been called to the apartment because of a domestic dispute. At the woman's request, no charges were laid. But police took the woman and her son to a shelter. The father said the incident had brought him and his wife closer together. ◆

Adapted with permission from Jane Armstrong, The Globe and Mail *10 August 1998, p. A5.*

income, parenting is consistent, and the parent has social support. Children in lone-parent families are more likely to be disadvantaged if the parent is hostile, ineffective, or depressed, and if the family is performing poorly. Tony Haddad (1998) also makes the important observation that most children in the survey were doing well, both behaviourally and emotionally, whether they lived in intact families or with one parent.

Children are also benefiting from the greater work participation of mothers. Considering children aged 4 to 11 years, Pierre Lefebvre and Philip Merrigan (1998) found that the mother's paid-work status did not increase the likelihood of behavioural problems, and it had a positive consequence on children's language skills.

Parental influence can start before birth. Based on persons born in Detroit in 1961, one team of researchers (Axinn, Barber, and Thornton 1998) found that 23 years later the 9 percent who were unwanted at the time of conception had significantly lower self-esteem. There was a much smaller but still negative effect for the 27 percent who were wanted but born earlier than had been planned.

Children in stepfamilies are also more likely to have less positive interactions with their parents (Cheal 1996). Children aged 10 and 11 filled in their own questionnaire in the National Longitudinal Survey of Children and Youth, providing data on difficulties with family relationships, level of emotional support, and levels of erratic punishment. A comparison of three family types showed more frequent difficulties with family relationships in single-parent families, while a lack of emotional support and erratic punishment were more common in families involving a stepfather. Although there was much variation, and in each family type the majority of children do not have problems, the averages were always better when children were living with two biological parents. While finding that both low-income families and single-parenthood made children more prone to behavioural problems, Ivan Fellegi (1998) concluded that having an ineffective or hostile parent was even more detrimental.

Another report from the same survey confirmed that children in the lowest socio-economic quintile (based on family income as well as the occupation and education of parents) were more likely to be receiving remedial education, less likely to be in programs for gifted children, more likely to have repeated a grade, and less likely to be among the top students in a given subject (Human Resources Development Canada and Statistics Canada 1997). Statistical controls indicate that both lone parenthood and low-income status are important risk indicators of childhood problems, but that lone parenthood has a stronger influence. For instance, both mother's education and single parenthood were found to be important factors in the development of mathematical abilities (Willms 1996). In grade 2 mathematics, having a single parent had an effect comparable to having a mother with 4.4 fewer years of education. Clearly, schools are not able to compensate for the potential disadvantages of children's backgrounds.

While the majority of children in poor families, single-parent families, and step-families are functioning at reasonable levels, it is also clear that poverty, single-parenthood, and step-parenthood are significant risk factors for children. In her review of the consequences of marital dissolution for children, Seltzer (1994: 261) concludes that children suffer the social and emotional difficulties of separation from a parent and the economic disadvantages of single-parenthood: "Although children are parents' most precious resource, the decision to separate is sometimes against the children's best interest. Because children depend on adults for physical and emotional care, divorce threatens children's well-being. They experience the loss of a parent's income, disruption of their daily routines, conflict between their parents, and reduced contact with a parent."

The problems that children suffer as a result of marital dissolution result mostly from the move to a lower level of living and the conflicts that precede and surround divorce, as well as the lack of stability in authority structure following divorce. This means that children are less hurt if they experience good financial support, an "amicable divorce," and the non-custodial parent remains involved and supportive of the custodial parent. In a small sample of lone mothers from Toronto who had "made it," Aysan Tuzlak and David Hillock (1991) found that the mothers were highly educated and the majority were able to retain their standard of living after separation. In other circumstances those requisites for stable parenting through divorce prove difficult for couples who are ending their marriages.

Longitudinal research is confirming that children who undergo their parents' separation continue to suffer consequences into adult years. Ellen Gee (1993) summarizes the adult outcomes as including less education, less income, fewer relationships, and lower life satisfaction. A team of British researchers provided an example of this by following a 1958 birth cohort until the members reached age 33. While they attributed some of the problems they saw to the dysfunctional nature of the original two-parent families, they found that parental divorce during childhood or adolescence continued to have a negative effect when the subjects were in their twenties and early thirties (Cherlin, Chase-Landale, and McRae 1997). For instance, controlling for economic status at age seven, they noted that both predisruption differences, along with divorce and its aftermaths, were continuing to present negative consequences for mental health at age 33. The adults who had the best mental health were those whose parents did not divorce, followed by those who divorced when the child was aged 23 to 33.

In *A Generation at Risk: Growing up in an Era of Family Upheaval*, Paul Amato and Alan Booth (1997) presented the results of interviews with adults aged 19 to 40 in 1995. Data had been collected from the time these subjects were children in 1980, and the most consistent finding was the link between parental marital quality and children's well-being. For instance, it seemed that both fathers and mothers had played key roles in their children's lives through relationships with the other parent. Divorce is advantageous to children under some circumstances, and especially when children are in highly conflictual families (p.237). However, Amato and Booth propose that only a quarter to a third of the marriages that dissolve are in this category. Consequently, when couples dissolve their relationships at "relatively low thresholds of unhappiness," many children undergo adverse effects that last into adulthood: "The worse situation for children to be in is either a high-conflict marriage that does not end in divorce or a low-conflict marriage that does end in divorce" (p.238). These influences are not rigid and deterministic, but on average they affect most aspects of the lives of young adults: standard of living, size of support network, whether they cohabit, quality of the marriage, whether the marriage ends in divorce, self-esteem, and general happiness with life (p.222). A divorce occurring early in a child's life carries more consequences for the child's economic attainment and psychological well-being, and weakens relations with both parents. A divorce occurring in adolescence weakens only the cross-sex parental relationship.

Still, despite these problems, in many respects children are better off now than they have ever been. Lefebvre and Merrigan (1998) argue that children tend to be more the result of planning on the part of parents; that children have better health, education, fewer siblings, and parents with more education. The parents spend more time in paid work and have their children later in life. These authors see two sources of problems, one relating to family change and the other to economic context. The children most at risk are those who are in lone-parent families, those at the lower end of the income scale, with parents who have low levels of education or poor parenting skills. But these at-risk cases

BOX 7.6 | *Paternal influences, step–parents, and absent parents*

Michael Lamb (1995) summarizes the research related to paternal influences on child development. Although living with a lone mother is not a problem in terms of the absence of a male role model, it does bring economic, social, and emotional disadvantages. Consequently, children do better if they are able to maintain meaningful relationships with both parents. Children of divorced parents can be harmed in several ways: the conflict that often precedes separation, the reduced economic circumstances, the isolation and distress of lone parents, and the withdrawal of the other parent. When fathers are closely involved in two-parent families—spending almost as much time with children as the mothers—the children gain various positive benefits, including better cognitive development, more empathy, and more internal locus of control. Lamb concludes that children benefit from varying parental styles. What counts is the relation-

ships with children rather than the sex of the parent, although the interaction of cultural context and gender makes a difference. In the 1950s, for instance, a typical father's influence produced a more masculine boy. In the 1990s fathers' involvement results in less sex-stereotypical sex-role attitudes in both boys and girls.

This might suggest that the problems of single-parenthood might be overcome through the introduction of a step-parent. While having a step-parent usually means living with two parents, and often two earners, it also means multiple family influences though less significant kinship bonds, and it may represent cumulative life-course stress (Bumpass 1994). It also can bring greater complexity to daily relationships. From their review of the evidence, Andrew Cherlin and Frank Furstenberg (1994) found that the well-being of children in stepfamily households is no better than it is in single-

are far from the dominant categories, and there is "less damage than commonly assumed." The Canadian Council on Social Development (1997) also observes that children with lone parents are at a greater risk of having problems, but that still most of them are doing well.

Youth finishing school

On average, young persons are staying at school longer. At ages 15-17 in 1981, 78.5 percent were full-time students compared to 88.3 percent in 1991 (Kerr, Larrivée, and Greenhalgh 1994: 30). At ages 22-24, this proportion increased from 13.2 to 24 percent. For youth aged 15-24, only 6 percent were neither at school nor in the labour force in 1992 (Sunter 1994: 34). Half of these youth neither in school nor in paid work were mothers with children.

➤ BOX 7.6 CONT'D

parent households. Elisabeth Cooksey and Michelle Fondell (1996) found, based on data from the U.S. National Survey of Families and Households, that of all fathers living with children, the ones who spend the least time with their children are step-parents. Children with the lowest school grades tended to have fathers who were single parents or stepfathers, rather than biological fathers. In general, U. S. research finds that children raised either by single mothers or in stepfamilies are disadvantaged compared with those raised by both original parents (Demo and Acock 1988).

Based on data from the United States and Sweden, Goldscheider, Bernhardt, and Kaufman (1996) found that men who are *informal parents,*" either as step-parents or in a cohabiting relationship with a mother, are quite different from men living with their biological children. For instance, the men with lowest incomes are likely to have neither a spouse nor children, and the men with highest incomes are most likely to have both a spouse and their own children. It is men with intermediate income who are most likely to be married and living with their partner's children. Men who are cohabiting with a partner and her children tend to have less education and lower incomes, and to be younger. The authors propose that, in the marriage market, men with more resources seek to avoid entering situations in which they would have to invest in other men's children. Persons with more resources also appear to be more desirable as partners and more ready to commit themselves to family roles. This interpretation may help to explain the findings indicating that children in stepfamilies are not advantaged compared to children in lone-parent families. Men, it seems, can more easily become partners at a particularly young age by entering cohabiting relationships with women who already have children, and on average these are men with low socio-economic status, in effect similar to the status of men with no spouse and no children.

At ages 20-24 in 1991, 23.8 percent of youth had not graduated from high school (Kerr, Larrivée, and Greenhalgh 1994: 31). However, the School Leavers Survey found that by age 24 in 1995, only 15 percent had not obtained a high-school diploma (Clark 1997). Persons who do not complete high school are much less likely to pursue other education and training. At age 22-24 in 1995, 24 percent of leavers compared to 80 percent of graduates had pursued further education.

Unemployment rates are also significantly higher among youth who do not complete high school (Table 7.11). For youth with both high-school graduation and further education, the labour-force participation rates are high, and unemployment rates are not very different from the national average. In addition, work participation and unemployment are equivalent for men and women in their early twenties who have both high-school graduation and further education. However, participation rates are lower for women who

➤ BOX 7.6 CONT'D

As for the absent parent, research in the United States finds that fathers tend to have limited contact with their children after divorce (Stephens 1996). Contact is especially curtailed if the father becomes remarried. For Canada, among children under 12 who were not living with a given parent in 1994-95, a third saw this parent each week, 23 percent once per month, and 44 percent saw the parent less than once per month (Canadian Council on Social Development 1998: 14). Children who had been born in a cohabiting relationship saw their father less regularly and were more likely never to see the father. According to a survey in France, among children separated from their father for more than three years, only a quarter were seeing their father several times per month (Leridon and Villeneuve-Gokalp 1994: 230). Some parents are able to co-parent even if they are not spouses, but on average mothers also spend less time with their children after a divorce, and children tend to leave home more quickly when their parents' marriage has broken up.

Research on the well-being of children by vari-

ous family types confirms the importance of financial, human, and social capital. While fathers can undoubtedly be important at each of these levels, non-resident fathers can also play a role, though the conditions are often less than favourable. Children benefit less from the father's human capital because they receive a lower investment in parental time (Bumpass 1994). Non-resident fathers have particular difficulty generating co-parenting social capital. Step-parents have a similar problem, possibly because the child does not "buy into" the co-parenting social capital (Amato 1998).

While the average well-being of children is higher in intact families, most children in lone-parent as well as two-parent and step-parent families are flourishing. Research would suggest that the problems with lone-parenting and step-parenting are a function of financial, human, and social capital, rather than parenthood per se. We need to know more about the conditions that allow children to flourish in lone-parent and reconstituted families. ◆

have only high-school education, and especially if they are high-school leavers. This factor is related to family responsibilities. In fact, at age 20 in 1991, 27 percent of female leavers had children, compared to 4 percent of graduates (Clark 1997).

School leavers in 1991 were more likely to be unemployed, especially men, or on social assistance, especially women (S. Gilbert 1993; see also Crysdale and MacKay 1994). There were also marked differences in the family context of youth aged 18-20 in 1991 between school leavers and those who had completed high school. Of those who had completed high school, 83 percent were living with both parents, 12 percent with one parent, and 3 percent with neither parent. Of those who had not completed high school, 61 percent were living with both parents, 25 percent with one parent, and 13 percent with neither parent (Sunter 1993: 46). It would appear that

LABOUR-FORCE STATISTICS ON YOUTH AGED 22-24 IN 1995

	HIGH-SCHOOL LEAVERS	HIGH-SCHOOL GRADUATES FURTHER EDUCATION OR TRAINING	
		NO	YES
Labour-force participation rates[a]			
Total	81	85	84
Men	91	92	84
Women	63	77	84
Unemployment rates[b]			
Total	21	13	11
Men	17	14	11
Women	30	11	10

a Percentage of people who were either working or unemployed and actively looking for work and available for work.
b Percentage of labour-force participants who were unemployed and actively looking for work and available for work.

Source: Clark 1997: 12. Statistics Canada, Labour Force Survey.

TABLE 7.11

parental investment in children, especially in providing a place to live, is related to the completion of secondary education. In addition, the investment of two parents makes a significant difference. Students who had no father at home were just as likely to drop out of school as those who failed a grade in elementary school.

Based on the 1994 General Social Survey, among persons aged 20-44, the likelihood of having completed high school was 82 percent if at age 15 they were living with two biological parents, compared to 71 percent with a lone parent, and 69 percent if they were living in a blended family or stepfamily (Frederick and Boyd 1998: 13). Commenting on the similarity between the context of lone and step-parents, Judith Frederick and Monica Boyd suggest that the economic advantages of having a step-parent may be offset by the stress created by another change in family structure.

In Sweden, Jan Jansson and Michael Gahler (1997) found that both the dissolution and reconstruction of families were associated with depressed educational attainment. Their analysis suggests that the downward social mobility associated with the departure of a parent plays the largest role. The factors include a loss of social and educational resources, the loss of a source of aspiration, and the stresses associated with family change. When a parent finds a new partner, this can present an advantage for the child, but it can also disrupt the investment of parental time and produce a net loss for the child. These conditions can play a particularly crucial role if they occur when the child is making an important educational choice. In the case of Sweden, the authors did not find the income deprivation associated with lone parenthood to be a particularly significant factor in educational attainment.

Home-leaving

As we've already seen (chapter 3), the delay in leaving home presents another important change for youth. The age at home-leaving was in decline until the late 1970s, when it suddenly started to increase. For instance, at age 20, 62.1 percent of never-married persons were at home in 1981 compared to 68.8 percent in 1991. At age 24, the percentage of youth at home increased from 20.5 to 31.5 percent (Kerr, Larrivée, and Greenhalgh 1994: 19).

A variety of factors come into play, including the longer period of education and the difficulties in obtaining secure employment. Other factors may include the lessened generation gap between parents and children, and smaller families making for more space in the parents' home. Youth are also more likely to return home, especially at times of economic difficulty or when relationships are not successful (Ward and Spitze 1996). Young persons who live at home would appear to be motivated by their need for assistance and support, along with the potential and willingness of parents to provide this support.

Analyses of the probabilities of home-leaving indicate that single-parenthood and step-parenthood are significant predictors of an earlier departure from the parental home (Zhao 1994; Zhao, Rajulton, and Ravanera 1995). Young persons are less likely to be living with parents who are separated or remarried (Boyd and Norris 1995). While children are most likely to live with their mother, that does not apply if the mother is remarried but the father has not; in these cases, children are more likely to live with the father. Monica Boyd and Doug Norris (1995) interpret children living with parents as an investment in children, which is most likely to occur if the parents are living together. Other researchers (Meunier, Bernard, and Boisjoly 1998) also conclude that families still play a major role as a haven for young people. Youth with strong family support can live at home longer, and they can concentrate on education and getting established rather than on earning their own incomes.

Using data from the United States, Frances Goldscheider and Calvin Goldscheider (1994) found that family disruption is linked with leaving

BOX 7.7 | *Frequent residential mobility*

Early home-leaving seems to have effects similar to frequent residential mobility when children are young. The National Longitudinal Survey of Children and Youth showed a two to threefold increase in childhood behaviour problems for children who had moved three or more times (De Wit, Offord, and Braun 1998). When parents move they probably do so to accommodate their own interests, and the change may play against the social capital available to children. The effects of frequent moves—often associated with low family socio-economic status and family disruption—can be countered by a high amount of parental monitoring of their children's situation. ◆

BOX 7.8 | *Initiation of sexual activity*

While 25 percent of youth in Grade 9 have had sexual intercourse, the figure reaches 50 percent somewhere between Grades 11 and 12 (Wadhera and Millar 1997:15). Based on the 1994-95 National Population Health Survey, 44 percent of persons aged 15-19 and 80 percent of those aged 20-24 had at least one sex partner in the previous year. Of those who were sexually active, about a third had two or more partners, and some 40 percent had used a condom "never or sometimes." Smoking and binge drinking are other forms of risk behaviour for youth. About a third of the youth in the survey said they had smoked and half said they had experienced binge drinking in the previous year.

The one-third who had not experienced any risk behaviour were more likely to be students, living at home, or married (Galambos and Tilton-Weaver 1998).

Pregnancy rates for persons under 20 years declined in the period 1974-87 and after that began to increase, though in the 1990s they remained below the figures for the mid-1970s (Wadhera and Millar 1997). By 1994 half of teenage pregnancies involved live births, and the other half were aborted. Consequently, the total births to teenage women decreased sharply from 1974 to the late 1980s before levelling off in the time since. ◆

---

home via all routes except college attendance. Its effect closely resembles that of low parental social class. They conclude that youth who are in a stable two-parent home or in a favourable social milieu have a higher chance of succeeding in the passage to adult life, thanks to greater parental support. Both family characteristics and social class, then, determine the extent to which the parental home provides the basis for the proper launching of youth into the world beyond.

In past centuries children who stayed at home participated extensively in household work. In effect, parents had an interest in delaying their children's marriages and departures in order to profit from their continued labour. Today, youth living at home appear to do a limited amount of unpaid work (Frederick 1995: 56). Goldscheider and Waite (1991) explain the low levels of children's share in household tasks by stressing the parents' interest in promoting their children's independence. If they want children to do housework, parents would need to exercise a certain degree of authority over them, which would militate against the promotion of independence. Children, it seems, do less housework if they are in two-parent families, or if the mother has more education, is younger, or lived away from home before marriage; and the mother's labour-force status is not a significant factor in this. But children do more housework when they are in lone-mother families and when mothers are more egalitarian. Noting that girls do twice as much work around the home as boys, Goldscheider and Waite conclude, like Berk (1985), that the home remains a "gender factory" and that children's part in this means they are not being prepared for egalitarian family settings. According to Goldscheider and Waite (1991: 171), parents probably want "their daughters to marry liberated men, who will share in the housework so that these daughters can be successful." But at the same time parents "are preparing their sons to marry traditional women, who will carry the household burden themselves to further their son's career. They are not yet ready to prepare their sons for someone else's ambitious daughter."

Youth at work

After 1966 youth labour-force participation began a long-term increase (Sunter 1994), ending in the late 1980s. Of the total age group 15-24, 70.6 percent were in the labour force in 1989 compared to 61.5 percent in 1996 (Jennings 1997). Half of the lower participation rates is a function of a higher proportion of full-time students, especially at ages 20-24. A second factor is the lower participation rates for students, especially at ages 15-19. The reduced participation of non-students accounts for only a minor part of the decline (Jennings 1998; Sunter and Bowlby 1998).

The period after 1981 also saw an increase in the proportion of youth working part-time (Kerr, Larrivée, and Greenhalgh 1994: 41). In effect, the increase in part-time work has only involved persons aged 15-24. For the total population aged 25 and over, part-time work did not increase between 1981 and 1991. Unemployment rates are also higher for youth, at 15.5 percent for the total age group 15-24. The difference between the unemployment rate of youth and of the population aged 25 and over declined slightly in the 1980s and increased slightly in the 1990s (Kerr, Larrivée, and Greenhalgh 1994: 44; Statistics Canada 1997c). Youth are also much more likely to be minimum-wage workers (Statistics Canada 1998h). Of the minimum-wage workers at ages 15-24, though, some 60 percent were students who lived with their parents. In effect, these comprised a third of all minimum-wage workers.

Compared to the average of the other countries of the Organization for Economic Co-operation and Development, Canadian youth at age 18 in the 1990s had a higher labour-force activity rate, a higher school participation rate, and a slightly lower unemployment rate (Blanchflower and Freeman 1998). What is particularly unique about youth in Canada is the high proportions who are blending school and work.

The incomes of young persons have consequently declined between 1980 and 1990 (Kerr, Larrivée, and Greenhalgh 1994: 58). In effect, the average earnings of men under 35 began to decline in the late 1970s (Picot and Myles 1996b: 17; Betcherman and Morissette 1994). For instance, at age group 25-29, between 1979 and 1993 the full-year full-time earnings of men with high-school education declined by 17.7 percent and of women by 13.1 percent (Table 7.12). For those with university degrees the decline was 18.3 percent for men, but women had a 3.1 percent increase. In addition, the proportions working full-year full-time declined in this period, except for women with university degrees. Consequently, young people starting their careers in the 1980s and

LABOUR-MARKET SUCCESS OF PERSONS AGED 25-29
AND 35-39, SELECTED YEARS

	EMPLOYMENT RATE (%)			AVERAGE EARNINGS (1993 $)	
	ALL WORKERS	FULL-TIME WORKERS*	UNEMPLOYED	ALL WORKERS	FULL-TIME WORKERS*
High-school graduates, ages 25-29					
MEN					
Cohort 1 (1979)	91	75	6.5	32,000	35,250
Cohort 2 (1984)	83	63	12.6	27,250	33,000
Cohort 3 (1989)	87	69	8.5	27,500	31,750
Cohort 4 (1993)	79	59	15.0	23,250	29,000
WOMEN					
Cohort 1 (1979)	58	52	9.4	18,250	24,750
Cohort 2 (1984)	60	46	12.6	17,000	23,500
Cohort 3 (1989)	68	56	10.3	17,000	21,750
Cohort 4 (1993)	64	46	13.9	16,000	21,500
One decade later ages 35-39					
MEN					
Cohort 1 (1989)	89	82	6.4	35,250	38,500
Cohort 2 (1993)	84	73	10.9	32,500	37,250
WOMEN					
Cohort 1 (1989)	72	55	7.5	20,500	26,000
Cohort 2 (1993)	70	50	10.5	18,500	24,500
University graduates ages 25-29					
MEN					
Cohort 1 (1979)	90	71	4.1	37,750	45,000
Cohort 2 (1984)	88	65	6.1	32,000	40,500
Cohort 3 (1989)	90	69	4.1	30,250	36,750
Cohort 4 (1993)	85	68	6.8	29,250	36,750
WOMEN					
Cohort 1 (1979)	76	56	5.7	25,000	32,000
Cohort 2 (1984)	79	58	7.5	25,500	32,750
Cohort 3 (1989)	84	59	5.1	25,000	32,250
Cohort 4 (1993)	82	57	7.1	24,750	33,000
One decade later ages 35-39					
MEN					
Cohort 1 (1989)	95	88	3.0	53,500	57,000
Cohort 2 (1993)	92	81	5.5	46,500	52,000
WOMEN					
Cohort 1 (1989)	82	64	4.3	35,500	42,000
Cohort 2 (1993)	82	65	6.2	32,250	41,250

* Full-year employment

Source: Crompton 1995: 10,11,12. Statistics Canada, Survey of Consumer Finances and Labour Force Survey.

TABLE 7.12

1990s are earning about 20 percent less than their counterparts in the 1970s, and the changes have hit young men particularly hard (Morissette 1998). In their study of inequality, Anton Allahar and James Côté (1998: 122) conclude that young men and women increasingly have more in common with their age-mates than with older persons of the same sex.

It was also mostly for the young that a polarization in incomes occurred between 1984 and 1993 (Human Resources Development Canada 1996). During that time income polarization declined for all women, especially if they were working full-time, but both male and female youth experienced an increase in income variation.

Although they have increased over the long term, the labour-force participation rates of young persons are strongly affected by recessions. In the 1990-92 recession, the decline in youth employment rates began earlier and lasted longer than similar declines for older age groups (Sunter 1994). Many youth continued to enrol at school while "waiting it out." The School Leavers Follow-up Survey found no clear point of transition between school and work (Human Resources Development Canada 1998). Young persons often start work before finishing school, and they often begin paid employment with non-standard jobs. In the 1990s some four out of ten employed youth were working in a part-time, temporary, or self-employed capacity. At ages 20-24, half of the people working part-time were going to school, and the rate of involuntary part-time was lower for those under age 25 than for the older ages (Statistics Canada 1998g).

Not surprisingly, then, the relative economic position of young households declined in the 1980s and 1990s. This decline came in spite of higher education rates and more earners per family, although it did follow the higher proportions of young households led by a lone parent (Sharif and Phipps 1994). For persons born between 1931 and 1961, family income rose over their lifetimes, but this was not the case for those born after the early 1960s. Their family incomes did not increase in the period 1988-92 (Leblanc, Lefebvre, and Merrigan 1996: 17).

The demographic factors would seem to have suggested an advantage for persons born during the "baby bust" of 1967-79 (Foot and Stoffman 1996). But after analyzing data from Quebec, Hervé Gauthier et al. (1997: 135) found that, at both ages 20-24 and 25-29, the generation born in 1964-69 was worse off than the one born in 1954-59, while the generation born in 1969-74 had the greatest disadvantages of all. The generation with the most economic success until their late thirties was the one born in 1944-49. If the baby boom has had any influence at all on generational economic prospects, it would appear to have disadvantaged all but the earliest members of the baby boom generation as well as the subsequent generations—or at least the ones for which we have data. David Foot and Daniel Stoffman (1996) describe an "echo generation" born since 1980, but the demographic size of generations has been stable since 1970. The economic prospects of given generations are influenced less by demographic factors and more by economic factors, especially the employment prospects at the time members of the generation are ready to join the labour force.

Starting families

Along with spending longer periods at school, the delay in leaving home, and declining relative earnings, young persons have also put off their marriages. For instance, at age group 20-24, some 32 percent of men were married in 1971 but only 18.2 percent in 1991. For women, the decline was from 55.7 to 34.8 percent (Ravanera 1995: 152). Even when we include cohabitation, the persons living in union still show a decline between 1981 and 1991. At age 24, the proportions of women either married or cohabitating declined from 62.2 to 48.7 percent between 1981 and 1991. For men, the decline was from 45.7 to 40.8 percent (Kerr, Larrivée, and Greenhalgh 1994: 24).

Among ever-married women, between 1971 and 1991 the proportions with children declined from 58 to 41.2 percent at ages 20-24 (Kerr, Larrivée, and Greenhalgh 1994: 155). Consequently, the proportions of young adults living as a couple with children declined significantly. For instance, in the age group 23-27, 30 percent of persons were heads of bi-parental families in 1975 compared to 15 percent in 1992 (Leblanc, Lefebvre, and Merrigan 1996: 9).

The delay in home-leaving, forming unions, and child-bearing may well be a prolonged period of adolescence, but it may also be a means of getting established before starting a family. Significantly, children from intact families, and with more highly educated parents, are most likely to delay forming their own families (Le Bourdais and Marcil-Gratton 1998). When their parents had separated, young persons were more likely to be cohabiting by age 25, to have children out of marriage, to have children before age 20, and to undergo a marital breakup.

In the age group 20-24, the proportions of women with children are highest for separated, widowed, and divorced women: more than two-thirds of them have children, compared to fewer than half of married women and a quarter of those who are cohabitating (Ravanera 1995: 18). It would appear that these formerly married persons had started their families early. There are also strong gender differences. For instance, at age group 24-26, only 0.2 percent of men but 9.1 percent of women are lone parents (p.23). Among the formerly married in this age group in 1991, 9.2 percent of men and 61.2 percent of women were lone parents.

CONCLUSION

At the end of his census monograph on *Families in Canada*, Thomas Burch (1990: 38) comments on the situation of children:

> Only a child is absolutely dependent on its family for survival and well-being. Adults can typically support themselves, and can seek to meet their social and emotional needs in many ways. They do not have to be married or to have children. But

children, especially infants and young children, have to live in a family or family substitute. Moreover, in most of the family changes discussed in this report, some elements of individual choice are involved—people choose to divorce, to live alone, to have a child, always, of course, in the face of constraints, including choices of others. But the young child has no choice. He or she must simply live with what society and his or her parents offer.

The profound transformation of the lives of children calls for a discussion of needs for alternative social and family accommodations that would maximize their potential in the evolving world. Lapierre-Adamcyk and Marcil-Gratton (1995) ask if society itself—the site of this transformation—is properly organized to take care of children.

In considering this transformation from the viewpoint of the welfare of children, we can see that they have benefited from the evolution of parental characteristics, in particular parents' higher levels of education and later ages at parenting, as well as smaller family sizes. Economically they have particularly benefited from the work status of mothers and increased social transfers. The main negative is that children are more likely to be born

---

BOX 7.9 | *Children and family well-being*

Most couples want to have children, and most often parents take the child-rearing role seriously. But the parenting role has its inherent difficulties (LeMasters and DeFrain 1983). There is, for instance, no margin of error; society expects parents to succeed with every child. In addition, parents cannot easily quit the endeavour. They can escape from an unhappy marriage, but not from parenthood. Another problem is that parenthood involves being totally responsible for other human beings, yet without full authority, because other agencies or institutions also have an influence on what happens to the children. Finally, despite the high standards called for in the performance of parenthood, no established model exists for the role, and little training is available. For the most part, raising children remains the preserve of the amateur. It may be

because of the high expectations combined with a lack of clear standards that parents show such a high interest in looking after young children themselves. That way, at least they will have given their full attention to fulfilling the prescribed role.

We also know that couples with young children at home are more likely to be dissatisfied with their marriages than are childless couples or those whose children have left home (Lupri and Frideres 1981). Margrit Eichler (1988: 181) proposes that the strain involved in raising children may have increased in recent years because children are dependent longer, while at the same time households have fewer adults and fewer children who can keep each other busy. Yet, while marital satisfaction is lower with children at home, marital stability is somewhat

---

into unstable relationships, including cohabiting relationships, and that is where the interests of adults and children are most likely to be in conflict. While adults benefit from marital transformations that permit flexibility in the pursuit of stronger satisfaction in relationships, children are more likely to experience the outcome as instability.

In some cases, the greater ease of dissolving a dysfunctional family permits children to escape from an environment that is working against their welfare. In other cases children do not experience the absence of a parent from the household, and often the addition of a step-parent, as positive changes. Thus from the point of view of children the decline of bi-parental families and the quicker move to single parenthood are more likely to be negatives than they are for adults. The problems are compounded by the lower labour-force participation rates of lone mothers. Even in two-parent families, average incomes have hardly kept pace with the cost of living, presenting various frustrations and hardships that can also harm children.

The economic welfare of children relates, then, to three factors: characteristics of families, economic conditions, and government transfers. While the characteristics of families have evolved in positive directions in terms of the age and education of parents, they

> ➤ BOX 7.9 CONT'D

higher. Couples with young children are less likely to separate, and marriages with no children are the most prone to divorce (Waite and Lillard 1991).

Given the difficulties, many parents understandably get frustrated when things do not go well, and some parents transfer this frustration onto the children in the form of child abuse. The factors of child abuse include parental immaturity, unrealistic expectations, lack of parental knowledge, social isolation, unmet emotional needs, and the parents' own abuse as children. A precipitating crisis typically sets the abuse in motion. Moreover, there is in effect a general propensity to abuse springing from the power that adults have over children, including the use of physical strength to impose their authority. Since most parents have high expectations for their children, abuse can occur when those expectations are somehow frustrated—

and especially when violence is seen as an acceptable form of family interaction (Propper 1984).

Society, then, faces a crucial dilemma in its interventions within the family structure. While society should support families as a means of supporting the welfare of individuals within those families, sometimes individual welfare depends on an escape from the family. In the case of abuse, the issue becomes one of trying to help the abusing parent or removing the child from the situation. Given the dependency of children, the resolution of this difficult issue should be based on the rights and well-being of the children rather than on the rights and well-being of adults and the family itself. Just as some children are better off without one of their parents, a few are better off with neither parent. ◆

307

have moved in a negative direction because of the existence of more lone-parent families. The income of families has benefited from the greater labour-force participation of mothers, but has suffered from the declining incomes of young persons, especially men. Parents with low human capital, and lone mothers in particular, have suffered greater disadvantages over time in terms of employment and security. Transfer payments have reduced levels of poverty—and they have become more effective over time in reducing child poverty—but they have also become more targeted toward the most disadvantaged families (Lefebvre, Merrigan, and Gascon 1995). Significantly, the tax and transfer systems of some European countries manage a much stronger reduction of child poverty. For instance, in 1987, 18.7 percent of Canadian children were poor before transfers and 12.6 percent after taxes and transfers, while in Sweden the similar reduction rate went from 13.1 to 3.7 percent of children (Leblanc, Lefebvre, and Merrigan 1996: 35).

Possible policy approaches for enhancing the economic welfare of children are to target the more disadvantaged, support the work of parents, possibly through subsidizing the incomes of the working poor, and make human capital investments benefiting parents and prospective parents. While existing policies on all of these levels could be improved, Zyblock (1996a: 21) makes a good case for giving priority to earnings supplementation, which would produce more attachment to the labour market and reduce the opportunity costs of working.

Another key to the puzzle is child care inside and outside the home. Lapierre-Adamcyk and Marcil-Gratton (1995) observe that collective support for child care remains deficient, given the family/work crunch. Consequently, child care depends on the willingness of women to mesh their family and work responsibilities. While fathering is undergoing certain transformations, domestic work is not shared equally and co-parenting is rare. At the same time, the labour market is based on efficiency and productivity, and so family conditions are not a strong priority.

If we assume that mothers need to work, both for the economic good of the family and for their own status and welfare, and that children need care, society then has a need for stronger social interventions around the care of children. Stronger interventions would help parents perform their earning roles and would reduce the complexities that parents face in coordinating work and child care. Parents have, though, also shown a strong interest in looking after their own children, especially when the children are young, by reducing hours of paid work.

While children would also benefit from more stable adult relationships, it is hard to envisage how the trends in union dissolution could be reversed. Consequently, families need to be supported as they are now, rather than attempting to make them correspond to some ideal. Given the co-existence of various models of families, policies should especially seek to enhance the welfare of children, regardless of the family setting.

In effect, it would appear that some societies are better able than others to insulate children against the negative consequences of family change. For instance, Sharon Houseknecht and Jaya Sastry (1996) compared four countries by looking at indicators of "family decline" and child well-being. They found that Sweden ranked highest on most of the indicators of family decline, and that the well-being of children was lowest in the United States. They concluded that although children are better off in societies with more traditional patterns, societies that lack those patterns can still mitigate the negative consequences for children. The social-democratic approaches in Sweden have involved both egalitarian policies and generous support to families and individuals. This approach also speaks to the importance of universal programs that seek to socialize some of the costs of reproduction rather than targeting children in disadvantaged situations.

Children could also benefit from stronger understandings regarding the obligations of parents. Paul Demeny (1986) proposed that the marriage, once children are involved, should entail greater contractual obligations. In effect, family law does identify the responsibilities of parents toward children, and governments have introduced various provisions, for instance, to increase the compliance with child-support obligations. While we still need better definition and enforcement of such obligations, they cannot be expected to solve all of the problems. In particular, they do not resolve the inherent problem that two households are more expensive than one and many parents do not have the economic means to meet their obligations. Also, the legalities themselves will not reduce the extent of separations. As Furstenberg (1995: 254) argues, the "effective enforcement of child-support laws ... is as likely to permit women to leave unsatisfactory relationships as it is to deter men from changing partners."

While clear limits exist on the extent to which societies can expect to change adult relationships, we should not hide the problems that flexible relationships represent for children. As adults justify the decisions made in their own lives, they should not be able to ignore the problems that "parent deficiency" represents for children. The National Longitudinal Survey of Children and Youth confirmed that single-parenthood and step-parenthood led to disadvantages for some children, even beyond the specific economic disadvantages. Given that parents have high standards for child-rearing, and often push schools to do the best for their children, they need also to be aware of the consequences of changes in their own lives on the welfare of the children. Their responsibilities may include the facilitation of co-parenting after separation rather than using children as pawns in their joint recriminations.

We also need to know more about the circumstances that lead to successful adaptations for children. For instance, we know very little about the family relationships that apply when a parent is living in a different household. In many circumstances, it would appear that those relationships can play a positive role. For instance, David Green (1991) argues that sole custody exacerbates family conflicts. In some circumstances, though, joint custody may be impossible, and some children might well be better off without one or even both parents. We also know little about the dynamics that distance non-custodial parents and their children. For instance, to what extent is alleviating the problem of this distance the responsibility of the absent parent, and to what extent does the lone parent promote this estrangement? While it is possible to better define the economic support obligations of absent parents, it is more difficult to build the optimum circumstances for their proper involvement in the lives of their children.

Policy Dimensions

Although the state deliberately sets up few policies specifically for families, a good deal of social policy discussion necessarily considers not only individuals but also the family context, including its change and diversity. In effect, many of the areas of disadvantage for family members relate to family structure and particular life-course stages. Although constraints do exist on its policies, the welfare state has become more generous over time, with difficult choices to make on forms of support and potential dependencies.

After establishing the policy context, the chapter elaborates on alternate models of family policy and looks at the approaches in given domains associated with earning and caring, the division of labour, the well-being of children, and lone parents.

States essentially base models of family policy on conceptions of the appropriate division of labour between women and men in their earning and caring activities, with the main differentiation being between models based on complementary roles and on equivalent roles. The approach of complementary roles promotes the division of earning and caring activities and has a preference for parents looking after their own children rather than public child care. It also includes a period of withdrawal from the labour force for one parent, pension splitting and spousal alimony in the case of divorce, and taxation based on family income. In a model based on equivalent roles, both parents are responsible for earning and caring activities, family income is supported by encouraging both spouses to be in the labour force, and parental leaves are associated with births. Child care becomes a public responsibility. The state provides security in the case of divorce by promoting the economic independence of adults, stressing joint custody, and using taxation at the individual level.

Partly because family policies are not explicit, the policies in many countries, including Canada, involve elements of both of these models. Using Sweden as an example, the chapter discusses these alternatives, along with the existing ambivalence in Canadian public opinion, and considers the various suggestions made with regard to income generation, parental leave, part-time work, family-friendly work, child benefits, child care, and the well-being of children, focusing as well on the specific case of lone parents.

Taking seriously the possibilities of a model that would increase the overlap in the earning and caring activities of men and women, the chapter ends with a suggestion based on shared parental leave and part-time work and the early entry of children to nursery schools and kindergartens. Provisions for low-income families would include an increase in the child tax benefit and, for lone parents, joint custody and advance maintenance payments.

These provisions would help establish parents as co-providers and co-parents. State support for child benefits, other basic social benefits, parental leaves, and education as of age three would undermine gender differences in families and consequently in the broader society. In particular, this approach would undermine the potential for the exploitation of one spouse by another based on inequality in the earning capacities generated by their family responsibilities.

◆

The study of families inevitably involves units, partnerships, and bonds across individuals, which in turn imply a need to resolve differences and to come together in common identities and destinies. But individuals also need to be different and to maintain their own identities. This search may be seen in the sharing of paid and unpaid work, which includes both a push to reduce the differences between women and men in the distribution of work activities and an interest in maintaining differences. While we can legitimately blame men for being unwilling to undertake caring activities, women too can show a certain resistance to giving up their position as the main persons responsible for the caring activities that "make family." In the world of paid work, some men may resist the incursion of women, and some women may be unwilling to enter that world under conditions established by and for men. In effect, wives and husbands may find disadvantages in competing in given domains; participation in a common pursuit can produce togetherness, but it can also become a source of friction and competitiveness rather than co-operation.

We often prefer to ignore these trade-offs and contradictions because they are too hard to face. We tend to like both nuclear families of parent(s) and children, and extended families that include grandparents and other relatives. But here again there can be tensions, especially surrounding which type of family has ascendency in cases of conflict. For instance, people tend to show an interest both in continuing the family traditions that they have inherited and in establishing the unique orientation of a given family unit. Then too there are the difficulties of melding the traditions that can arise from different family origins. People express an interest in establishing their independence, rather than being dependent on the care of others, along with an interest in providing care as a loving activity and in receiving the care of others. Many of these contradictions can loosen, or tighten, the bonds and partnerships between men and women; their interests in a given family can be different, and yet families are built on a commonality of interests.

These dialectics can also be visible across a family's siblings, who also have both a common interest and a need to be different. If one sibling is successful at school, will the other seek to excel at sports? If one is good at saving money, will the other try to excel as a consumer? If one is the Mary who focuses on strong emotional support, will the other seek to be the Martha who loves to provide good, practical care? These dynamics can especially differentiate siblings of different sexes.

The contradiction that we may be most unwilling to face is the one that separates the interests of adults and children. Families are largely organized around the interests of children, and their caring needs in particular. While parents gain considerable satisfaction from the presence of children in their lives, they are also interested in obtaining satisfaction from their relationships with marital partners and other friends. Similarly, children gain much from parents, but they also want to establish their own independence and relationships. Consequently, the interests of children may be undermined by the interests of adults, or children may be abused by adults frustrated by the strong caring needs of children or by a lack of fulfilment in their relationships with children. Similarly, parents can be exploited by their children, especially in later life, once the parents lack independence or are in need of care. The extent to which parents seek their own satisfaction, in comparison to the interests of children, can vary greatly. This question continues well beyond the time the children leave home: how much do I spend for myself, and how much do I invest in the reproductive inheritance passed to the next generation?

The contradiction between the interests of adults and children is most manifest in the dissolution of relationships and the formation of other partnerships. Some people maintain their marriages for the sake of the children, but in the context of an abusive relationship that loyalty can entail a loss of independence and identity. More often, the interests of adults in achieving fulfilling marital relationships come at the expense of the financial, human, and social capital they provide to their children.

People living in the same household are more likely to share resources. This tendency is most clearly manifested in the lesser transfer of absent fathers to children who are living with their mothers, which follows in part because of divided loyalties. Needless to say, spouses who have separated show less sharing. Children receive more when they are living at home than after they have left home. Consequently a longer period of home residence typically represents a larger investment in children. Lone parents, too, are less disadvantaged if they live with their own parents. The importance of co-residence is apparent in immigration policies that emphasize family sponsorship: sponsored immigrants are less likely to become dependent on social assistance if they live in the same household as the sponsoring relatives.

The changes toward more divorce and cohabitation have sometimes been interpreted as undermining families, and some critics have called for a return to family values. These conclusions, though, are based on a specific model of families that pays insufficient attention to converging gender trends that have produced greater adult independence. The converging gender trends are most clearly manifested in education and at work, but they also are seen in unpaid work, in the manifestation of interest in relationships with children, and even in responsibility for contraception. The call for a return to family values typically implies a return to traditional complementary roles for women and men, and it does not recognize the potential for family models based on companionship or a collaborative approach.

With all its difficulties, the distribution of the family activities of women and men contains the potential for greater symmetry. Besides the advantages of reducing dependencies, the new models provide more insurance against the loss of a partner or the inability of a given partner to provide income and other resources (Oppenheimer 1994). While many marriages remain based on a neo-traditional division of labour, in which the male partner takes more responsibility for earning activities and the female for caring activities, the general move toward more symmetry has changed the understandings of women and men. In particular, both partners show a much stronger interest in sharing responsibilities for both earning and caring. Instead of a clear-cut division, they have a greater understanding of a need for a partnership in meeting the basic needs of families.

While families are dependent on the opportunity structure offered by the society, and poverty presents various disadvantages, it is also true that *family strategies* are important to economic well-being. For instance, the largest factor in increased market income inequality across families is the rise in lone parenthood (Zyblock 1996c). Increasingly, two substantial incomes are needed to achieve stable middle-class standing. Those who are able to maintain two-income families are best able to invest in the well-being of their children, and in their own retirement. That is, not only unemployment, but also premature reproduction, or separation into two households, present various disadvantages for the accumulation of family resources. Consequently, as a society we should look for ways to encourage young people to attain more education, and for married couples to share work and family roles.

THE CONTEXT OF FAMILY POLICY

Canada does not have an explicit set of family policies. At the same time, the policies that have an impact on families are myriad. They are implicit, for instance, in many social and economic programs, including those dealing with income security, the labour market, and tax provisions. In her extensive review of Canadian family policies, Maureen Baker (1995a: 5) considers three areas: (1) laws relating to marriage, divorce, reproduction, adoption, custody, and child support; (2) support of family income through tax provisions, child benefits, and leave benefits; and (3) direct services such as child care, child protection, home-care health services, and subsidized housing. In a summary of policy concerning family and work in Canada, Berna Skrypnek and Janet Fast (1996) include family-related leave, child care, adult dependent care, and alternative work arrangements. It should be noted that since the mid-1980s Quebec has been the exception to the lack of direct policy attention to families. In that province various provisions have evolved in areas from housing to the labour market and social services, out of deliberate efforts "to think and act family" (Le Bourdais and Marcil-Gratton 1994).

In one sense, families are considered to be private domains, and efforts have been made to "remove the state from the bedrooms of the nation," as Pierre Trudeau put it in the 1960s when, as justice minister, he was introducing changes to the criminal code regarding penalties for adultery, conditions for divorce, and availability of contraception. In another sense, though, many policies and programs of the state have consequences for families.

A key domain is the sharing between families and the state in the care of people dependent because of age, disability, or health. In part, the state seeks to encourage family support of dependants and to encourage self-sufficiency. This approach has its contradictions, because the persons who look after dependents within families will have less ability to be themselves self-sufficient in the labour market. Thus the discouragement of dependency and the encouragement of the caring activities of families carry a continued need for balance. In addition, the needs of persons who are not self-sufficient and who also do not have access to family support networks have to be considered. In effect, three bases exist for support: individual, family, and society. The state needs to support individuals and families in ways that also encourage self-sufficiency.

A concrete example of thorny questions in the broad domain of family policy has occurred recently around the discussions of benefits for same-sex partners. In one sense, the state should have no concern at all as to whether or not people are living with same-sex partners, and it has in effect decriminalized homosexual behaviour. In addition, in only relatively few family units are the partners of the same sex, and consequently the matter of equivalent benefits for them would not significantly expand the costs of state benefits as a whole. The discussion, though, is partly about the basis for obtaining benefits. For instance, if there can be benefits for same-sex partners, what about no sex partners? As a person in the labour force, could I confer my benefits on a brother, or on any other individual living with me? In this light, benefits involving entitlements based on work are reminiscent of a "family wage" that sought to support a worker and his dependent family. The specific case of spousal support payments may not be as important for former same-sex partners, because they are not subject to the gender dynamics that can produce inequality in heterosexual marriages.

While these benefit structures are a means of encouraging family support for dependents, they also encourage dependency. Given that the family wage model no longer applies, it would seem that benefits should no longer be allocated in that manner. Perhaps, instead of having entitlements based on family ties with someone who is employed, they could be based on citizenship in the society. Indeed, what should be the interplay of individual, family, and social responsibility for benefits ranging from dental care to health and pensions? The outcomes of policy decisions around these discussions have consequences on the kinds of families and societies we live in.

Taxation is another example of a general policy with extensive consequences on families. One issue is whether the taxation should be at the individual or family level, and the extent to which the family context should be taken into consideration in tax calculations. Taxation at the family level tends to promote a one-earner model, because two earners will pay less tax if the state considers them separately. Although Canada uses taxation at the individual level, it uses the family income in calculations of child tax benefits, some elderly benefits, and the GST rebate. While these provisions are aimed at helping poorer families, they also encourage spousal dependency, because a family gains a tax benefit if it has no second income. As Shelley Phipps and Peter Burton (1996) argue, "Denying individuals the right to benefits on the basis of the higher incomes of other household members can generate extreme vulnerability in cases where resources are not shared." For instance, elderly women who have had minimal earned income may achieve a certain economic independence in retirement by receiving their own Old Age Security and Guaranteed Income Supplements. But if they find this benefit denied because of a high family income, then they lose access to the associated independence. Phipps and Burton conclude that a move toward not taking family income into consideration would mean that men with higher incomes would pay relatively more taxes while lower-income women would receive more transfer income. On the family level this would mean that one person would pay more taxes while the other would receive more transfer income from government. On the societal level, this proposition means more taxes and more transfers. While these transfers would benefit women living in richer households, it is not clear that there would be an overall net gain for poorer families. Optimizing on one consideration, then, can lead to difficulties on other levels.

ECONOMIC INDICATORS FOR TEN COUNTRIES OF THE ORGANIZATION FOR ECONOMIC CO-OPERATION AND DEVELOPMENT, 1985-93

	GNP PER CAPITA 1991[a]	HDI RANKING 1993[b]	AVG. ANNUAL WAGE 1993[c]	WOMEN'S WAGES AS % OF MEN'S 1990-91	UNEMPLOY-MENT RATE 1990-91	% OF TOTAL INCOME BY LOWER 40%[d]
Australia	22195	7	25197	—	9.5	15.5
Canada	25582	2	34109	63	10.2	17.5
Denmark	30234	13	25405	82	10.6	17.4
France	26227	8	16107	88	9.4	18.4
Germany	26445	12	27253	74	4.3	19.5
Netherlands	24166	9	27353	78	7.0	20.1
Norway	31155	3	27104	85	5.5	19.0
Sweden	32845	5	25241	89	2.7	21.2
United Kingdom	21222	10	26547	67	8.9	17.3
United States	28928	6	30783	59	6.6	15.7

a Canadian dollars at 1991 Purchasing Power Parities.
b HDI: United Nations Human Development Index.
c In manufacturing sector, using 1993 Canadian dollars.
d Percent of total wages received by lowest 40% of households; years vary between 1985 and 1989.

TABLE 8.1

The changing welfare state

The Canadian welfare state was mostly established in the 1950s and 1960s, at a time when the economic, family, and demographic contexts were rather different than in more recent years. For one thing, it was a period of rapid economic growth, filled with the expectation that the country could afford an expanding public domain. The breadwinner model of the family was still dominant. It was a peak period for husband-wife families: widowhood at young ages had declined, and separation and divorce had not yet gone on the rise. Demographically, there were large numbers of children and few elderly.

A main thrust of the changes toward a welfare state was an increased social responsibility for the elderly, through Old Age Security, the Guaranteed Income Supplement, the Canada Pension Plan, and associated benefits. Since then, not only have the numbers of elderly increased, but the programs themselves have aged. The Canada Pension Plan in particular was inexpensive when first instituted, because all employed persons were paying into the plan and relatively few were receiving benefits. There were few beneficiaries because there were fewer elderly—as well as because only those who had previously contributed could receive benefits. With a larger number of beneficiaries has come a higher cost and the need for significant restructuring (Beaujot and Richards 1997). This restructuring has occurred for the Canada Pension Plan, but not for the elderly benefits received through Old Age Security and the Guaranteed Income Supplement.

ECONOMIC INDICATORS FOR TEN COUNTRIES OF THE ORGANIZATION FOR ECONOMIC CO-OPERATION AND DEVELOPMENT, 1985-93 (CONT'D)

	PERCENT OF GDP				
TAXATION 1993[e]	GOV'T SPENDING 1993[f]	EDUCATION 1988	HEALTH CARE SERVICES 1990	SOCIAL SECURITY 1985-89	
34.0	37.7	4.8	8.2	8.0	Australia
42.6	49.7	7.2	9.3	17.3	Canada
58.7	63.1	6.9	6.6	27.8	Denmark
49.0	54.8	5.7	8.8	18.6	France
46.0	49.4	6.2	8.6	23.0	Germany
52.6	55.8	6.6	8.6	27.7	Netherlands
54.4	57.1	6.6	8.0	17.6	Norway
58.3	71.8	5.7	8.6	33.7	Sweden
35.8	43.5	4.7	6.1	17.0	United Kingdom
31.1	34.5	5.7	12.2	12.6	United States

e   Government total current receipts.
f   Total government outlays.

Source: Hunsley 1997: 30, 31, 34, 35, 36, 37.

TABLE 8.1

TOTAL SOCIAL SPENDING, CANADA, 1951-96

	SOCIAL SPENDING WITHOUT HEALTH		SOCIAL SPENDING INCLUDING HEALTH	
	% OF GDP	PER CAPITA (1996$)	% OF GDP	PER CAPITA (1996$)
1951	3.5	328	5.5	551
1956	4.3	492	6.1	748
1961	5.7	664	8.7	1,095
1966	4.6	695	8.2	1,310
1971	6.0	1,030	11.8	2,148
1976	7.8	1,757	14.0	3,152
1981	7.7	1,920	14.7	3,465
1986	9.7	2,500	17.3	4,411
1991	12.0	3,131	20.3	5,251
1996*	11.5	3,217	18.5	5,079

* Data for 1995 shown for social spending including health.
NOTE: Social spending includes federal, provincial, and local government
   expenditures, as well as costs of social insurance supported through
   employer and employee contributions. This includes income security
   programs, employment programs, and social services.

Source: Calculations by author based on special tabulations from Bruce Little,
The Globe and Mail, and Ken Battle, Caledon Institute of Social Policy;
Statistics Canada, no. 91-210.

TABLE 8.2

Focusing on women, and analyzing the Scandinavian experience with the welfare state, Arnlaug Leira (1992) highlights other contrasts and contradictions. In particular, state interventions in the realm of families have been highly controversial, both welcomed and contested. In one sense, state intervention has increased women's independence and reduced women's dependency on marriage. Women have not only increased their control over fertility, but also seen changes in the possibilities of everyday life and economic and political participation. Still, the welfare state remains tied to a gender-differentiated family in which women hold the first line of responsibility for caring and the social rights gained through those caring roles are second-class compared to the entitlements gained through earning roles. For instance, people have access to child tax benefits based on their caring activities, but the amount received depends on family income. The benefits gained through earning activities, including unemployment and disability insurance, pensions, and even parental leave, are considerably more extensive. The assumption that families will be the first line of support for dependants effectively promotes separate spheres for women and men. The noteworthy exception is health care, in which there is universal access to a public system, regardless of family membership. An equivalent system in the economic sphere would be some kind of guaranteed annual income that would not depend on the individual's earning role but would be a universal and basic right of citizenship (Royal Commission on the Economic Union and Development Prospects for Canada 1985).

Focusing on postwar Britain, Jane Lewis and Kathleen Kiernam (1996) observe that the changing boundaries between marriage, non-marriage, and parenthood have introduced concerns regarding lone motherhood. First came the separation of sex and marriage, a change often seen as liberating, and many people went through periods of marriage, divorce, and cohabitation. The state was not particularly concerned about these changing definitions of relationships. In Canada the state saw the relationships of consenting adults as private matters and applied some of the provisions of marriage to cohabitation. With the subsequent separation of marriage and parenthood, the state recast family law, placing a greater emphasis on the responsibilities of parenthood rather than marriage. The state became concerned, for the most part, with relationships in which children were present; the focus became the responsibilities of mothers and fathers, rather than husbands and wives. Lone parenthood thus came to pose a special problem due both to its greater frequency and to the issue of the proper definition of parental responsibilities. For instance, the 1978 Ontario Family Law Reform Act seeks to achieve "the equitable sharing by parents of responsibility for their children." However, instead of transfers from absent fathers to women and children, the men could simply pay more taxes so that the state could support mothers and children. However, this approach would also eliminate the benefit that children receive through economic and social transfers from their own fathers (Kaplan, Lancaster, and Anderson 1998). Consequently, John Richards (1997a) argues that social policy should clearly encourage child-rearing in the context of two-parent families.

Consequently, in Canada and elsewhere the welfare state comes under various pressures. An overriding consideration is the extent of social expenditures and associated taxation. A comparison of broadly similar countries indicates that Canada is toward the middle in this regard, with higher expenditures than in the United States, Australia, and the United Kingdom, but lower than many European countries (Brooks 1993). In the ten countries shown on Table 8.1, Canada ranks seventh in terms of GNP per capita, and sixth in terms of government spending as a percent of GNP.

Canadian spending on all social programs including health increased from 5.5 percent of GDP in 1951 to 20.3 percent in 1991, and then declined to 18.5 percent of GDP in 1995 (Table 8.2). While this has been the steepest fall in postwar history, the level remains higher than it was in the 1980s. Spending has increased because of more programs, improvements in programs, and greater demand associated with factors such as aging and higher unemployment (Little 1997; Battle and Torjman 1994; Ng 1992).

Exaggerated arguments are heard on both sides of the issue of government expenditures. The expenditure is not particularly high compared to that of European countries, nor have budget cuts substantially reduced social expenditure compared to previous levels. For instance, in per capita terms the reduction between 1991 and 1995 amounts to 3.3 percent. The main problem of the late 1980s and early 1990s was one of government deficits and mounting debts, in which interest payments comprised a significant proportion of

1986 PRICES

FIG 8.1 Index of social health and Gross Domestic Product per capita, Canada, 1970-95

NOTE: The Index of Social Health involves the following components: children (infant mortality, child abuse, children in poverty), youth (teen suicide, drug abuse, high school drop outs), adults (unemployment, average weekly earnings), elderly (elder poverty, out-of-pocket health costs), all ages (homicides, alcohol-related traffic fatalities, social assistance beneficiaries, access to affordable housing, gap between rich and poor).

Source: Human Resources Development Canada, Applied Research Bulletin, *vol. 3, no. 2: 7.*

budgets and consequently a risk that control over social programs would move into the hands of financial markets (Crowley 1998). Governments have clearly learned a lesson in terms of accountability in spending. However, as Richards (1997a) argues, the very existence of the welfare state in health, education, and welfare is a great feat of generosity and civilization. Public concerns around the protection of health care indicate much support

LOW-INCOME STATISTICS, SHOWING INCIDENCE AND DISTRIBUTION, BY FAMILY CHARACTERISTICS, CANADA, 1980 AND 1996

	DISTRIBUTION OF LOW INCOME		INCIDENCE OF OF LOW INCOME	
	1980	1996	1980	1996
Total persons	100.0	100.0	16.0	17.9
Children under 18	27.4	28.3	15.8	21.1
Elderly 65+	19.2	13.6	34.0	20.8
Others	53.4	58.1	13.6	16.2
Persons in families	70.2	70.0	12.7	14.5
Unattached individuals	29.8	30.0	43.5	40.2
Men	43.2	44.1	13.9	16.0
Women	56.8	55.9	18.1	19.9
Economic families (two or more persons)				
Elderly families	100.0	100.0	19.2	8.7
Non-elderly*	100.0	100.0	12.4	15.5
Married couples				
without children	7.8	11.1	6.7	10.0
Two parents with children	55.3	44.7	9.7	11.8
Lone-parent families	26.3	33.0	52.9	56.8
Male-headed	1.5	2.3	25.4	31.3
Female-headed	24.9	30.7	57.3	60.8
Other families	10.6	11.1	25.2	17.8
By age of family head	100.0	100.0	13.2	14.5
Under 25	9.3	9.3	20.4	42.1
25 – 34	27.7	27.4	12.1	20.9
35 – 44	22.4	27.9	12.0	14.8
45 – 54	16.3	15.2	10.9	10.1
55 – 64	13.6	11.4	12.2	12.0
65+	10.8	8.8	19.2	8.7
Children (under 18)	100.00	100.00	15.8	17.9
Two parents	62.0	49.0	9.7	11.8
Lone-mother parent	33.0	45.0	57.3	60.8
Lone-father parent	5.0	5.0	25.4	31.3

* For non-elderly families, distributions are shown for persons in given family types.

Source: Statistics Canada, no. 13-207, 1996: 28-35, 41, 180-181, 188. Statistics Canada, no. 13-207, 1980: 108. National Council of Welfare 1998: 79.

TABLE 8.3

for state intervention. Nonetheless, many open questions remain, especially regarding the relative participation of private and public agencies in delivering benefits. For instance, social programs have come to involve various interest groups that can both protect the programs and become obstacles to reform.

Indicators of well-being and pressures for policy

As an indicator of average well-being, Canada's GDP per capita indicates considerable progress since 1970 (Figure 8.1). Average incomes after taxes increased by 8 percent between 1985 and 1989, but in 1997 they were only 2 percent above the 1985 level (Statistics Canada 1998f). However, less progress has been made on an index of social health based on 15 indicators dealing with health, mortality, inequality, and access to services. This indicator reached a peak in the late 1970s and afterwards declined to its 1970 level.

In the 1998 Human Development Index, Canada ranked highest among the countries of the world (United Nations 1998), particularly because of its universal education programs, but also because of high life expectancy and average income per capita. However, on an index of inequality, Canada ranked tenth, especially in terms of the proportion who were poor as defined by incomes below 50 percent of the median.

While the UN statistics present a picture of both average well-being and disadvantage, the data on low-income status indicate the dispersion around the mean, and the persistent needs (Table 8.3). Particularly noteworthy is the differentiation of disadvantage by family and life cycle characteristics. While 15 percent of children live with a lone parent, half of the children living below the low-income line are living with one parent (Table 8.3). Over ages, the proportions of people with low incomes have declined significantly for the elderly, but persisted for children (Ng 1992). The disadvantaged elderly are mostly women who are not living within families.

Young adults have higher rates of poverty than any other adults (Table 8.4). In addition, change in family status is associated with young adult poverty, as is not living in a couple for young women (Cheal 1997). For the total population, taxes and transfers reduce the numbers of persons who are below 0.5 of median income by more than half (Table 8.5). The smallest reduction comes for children aged 0-14, and by far the greatest reduction is for persons aged 65 and over.

In *The New Face of Poverty*, the Economic Council of Canada (1992: 21-27) also observed that family questions had considerable consequence for income security needs. For instance, the Council found separation and divorce to be associated with higher rates of transition into poverty, especially if children are involved. Living in poverty for more than one year is more common for lone parents and single persons under 25, while there are high transition rates into poverty for single persons with children. Thus, in addition to the gender element of poverty (noted in chapter 2), significant differentials are associated with the factors of life-cycle stage, not living in families, and family type. In her summary of the new kinds of demands on family policies, Suzanne Peters (1995) also

POVERTY BY LIFE-CYCLE STAGE, 1993

	TOTAL	M	F
Incidence of poverty (%)			
Youth, 16-18	16.4	15.9	17.1
Young adult, 19-23	14.1	11.7	16.4
Prime adult, 24-38	12.6	10.7	14.4
Middle age 39-53	8.8	8.9	8.8
Senior citizen 54-63	10.1	8.9	11.4
Old age 64+	2.4	2.5	2.3
Median depth of poverty ($)			
Youth, 16-18	5,620	4,997	6,108
Young adult, 19-23	4,297	4,746	4,297
Prime adult, 24-38	4,697	4,291	4,949
Middle age 39-53	3,884	4,455	3,745
Senior citizen 54-63	3,096	3,096	3,215
Old age 64+	2,629	3,003	2,471

NOTE: Poverty line is calculated differently than other authors. It is based on after-tax income, adjusted for family composition (reflecting the number and types of persons supported by family income). Adjusted family size is based on a factor of 1.0 for a first person, 0.7 for other persons aged 16+, and 0.6 for persons 0-15. Median depth of poverty is calculated from the low-income line.

Source: Cheal 1997: 11, 12, 13, 15, 16.

TABLE 8.4

highlights many elements of family change: more diversity, the struggles of sole-support parents, the challenges of dual-earner families balancing jobs and sharing tasks at home, and the complexities of intergenerational family responsibilities. Other factors are the changing conditions associated with family membership, difficult labour markets, and constraints on public spending.

The various countries of the world have taken different approaches in dealing with family issues. In *The State and the Family*, Anne Hélène Gauthier (1996: 206) observes that many countries are under pressure to introduce more family policy, because of persistent low fertility, high female labour-force participation, and the large numbers of children living in poverty, especially in the context of lone parenthood. At the same time governments face pressure for less policy as well, because of budget constraints, a social agenda focusing on the concerns of aging, and ideologies that favour non-intervention and self-support.

Thus across countries there is a high profile of family issues, but also large disparities in the approaches taken and in the extent of benefits and services for families (O'Hara 1998). In France, for instance, the focus is on pro-natalist interventions, while in the Nordic countries it is on equality and labour-force participation (Gauthier 1993). In Great Britain and the United States the political agenda is dominated by questions of poverty, lone parenthood, and welfare dependency. Some countries have programs that are more universal, while others target benefits to the disadvantaged. Across Europe, the proportion of GNP devoted to family policies varies from over 4 percent in Sweden, Denmark, and Finland to under 1 percent in Greece and Portugal (Lévy 1998). The Canadian level is toward the bottom of this distribution.

Sometimes states provide funds directly to families, and in other cases they offer payments in kind through services. There are also variations in the extent to which policies follow a breadwinner model, as in Germany, or a two-earner model, as in Sweden. In Scandinavian countries the focus is on individuals, with children having specified rights, but in most countries the focus is on nuclear families, especially mothers and children—although in Southern Europe the states bring the extended family into consideration.

MODELS OF FAMILY POLICY

The resources necessary to achieve a population's general well-being are located in various spheres: domestic, informal, social, market, and state. The models of family policy can be differentiated in accordance with the division of responsibility between individuals, families, and society for obtaining and providing these resources. A key consideration is the extent to which the state acknowledges social responsibility for children, in contrast to seeing children as the private responsibility of their parents (Phipps 1996).

If models of family policy take questions of gender as a focal point, the main differentiation is between models based on complementary roles and on equivalent roles for women and men. The *complementary roles* model, which promotes the division of earning and caring activities, shows a preference for parents to look after their own children rather than placing them in public child care, and consequently one parent has to withdraw at least temporarily from the labour force. To provide security for that spouse, especially in case of divorce, the state introduces pension splitting and spousal alimony. The state applies taxation at the family level or implements tax deductions for spouses with low income levels.

In a model based on *equivalent roles*, with both parents responsible for earning and caring activities, the state supports family income by encouraging both spouses to be in the labour force, with parental leaves associated with births and child care seen as a public responsibility. The state provides security in the case of divorce by promoting the economic independence of adults. While the state recognizes the importance of child support and preferably joint custody in the case of divorce, it discourages pension splitting and alimony because they promote dependency. For similar reasons, it administers taxation at the individual level, without deductions for a spouse who is not employed.

Partly because family policies are not explicit, the policies in many countries, including Canada, involve some elements of both of these models. Policies in Sweden are closer to the equivalent roles model, while Canada retains many elements that encourage complementarity in gender roles. Until the 1970s and 1980s, policy in Canada largely considered marital roles to be complementary (Baker and Phipps 1997). While society has seen major shifts in gender roles and the configuration of families, Phyllis Moen (1992: 9) observes that we remain uncertain, if not divided, as to what men's and women's roles should be. She suggests, "The challenge is not for women to become exactly like men in

PROPORTION OF INDIVIDUALS BELOW 0.5 OF MEDIAN INCOME, PRE- AND POST-TAX/TRANSFERS, 1973-95

AGE	1973	1986	1995
Pre-tax/transfers			
0-14	22.3	23.0	26.4
15-19	21.8	22.0	23.7
20-24	14.9	22.3	26.8
25-34	11.8	17.8	18.6
35-44	14.8	15.1	18.3
45-54	14.3	14.2	15.8
55-64	22.9	23.5	24.1
65+	58.1	54.9	45.3
TOTAL	21.3	23.2	24.2
Post-tax/transfers			
0-14	17.3	15.0	15.7
15-19	16.0	14.2	15.0
20-24	10.2	15.4	18.9
25-34	8.7	11.7	11.1
35-44	11.0	8.7	10.5
45-54	10.1	9.0	9.3
55-64	16.1	12.7	13.1
65+	25.3	9.7	3.6
TOTAL	14.3	12.1	11.8

Source: Special tabulations provided by Garnet Picot of Statistics Canada, based on data from Survey of Consumer Finances.

TABLE 8.5

their work lives, or to return to the domestic hearth, but for us as a nation to restructure both family and work roles, for both men and women."

Both of these models involve individual, family, and social responsibility for well-being, but social responsibility is stronger in the equivalent roles model. In the complementary roles model, which Margrit Eichler (1997) calls a patriarchal model, the society becomes involved only when one parent is absent or when the family is unable to fulfil the earning and caring activities. Otherwise, families are responsible for the well-being of individuals. For Gauthier (1996), this "pro-traditional" model is most developed in Germany; it seeks to preserve a specific type of family, providing a low level of child care and encouraging a parent to stay home with young children.

The equivalent roles model shows more social responsibility, both for child care and for adults who are not self-sufficient. The state becomes involved in encouraging simultaneous participation in paid work and family roles and in minimizing the frictions between the two spheres (Skrypnek and Fast 1996). Gauthier calls this a "pro-egalitarian model," which is most developed in Sweden and Denmark, where gender equality is the main objective and the governments take a major responsibility for supporting families and working parents. The model pays particular attention to policies for parental leave, sick leave associated with children, and public child care. Clearly these models have important consequences for the structuring not only of women's employment, but also of the education, social security, and welfare systems (Crompton and Harris 1998: 132).

Eichler (1997) describes a third model positioned somewhere between the "patriarchal" and the "social responsibility" models, which she calls an "individual responsibility model." Still, clearly times exist when individuals cannot be self-sufficient and when the care of family members further reduces self-sufficiency. While there is always an interest in maximizing individual responsibility, the periods of dependency in the human life cycle mean that there will also always be a dependence on family, society, or both.

Gauthier (1996) defines a third model as a "pro-family but non-interventionist model." This approach is based on a belief in the self-sufficiency of families and the merits of a non-regulated market. The interventions are limited and targeted only to families in need. The United States and Britain are examples of this approach, because they have limited parental leave and low public support for child care.

Looking at the Canadian case, Jane Ursel (1992) found that the social reform movement at the turn of the century became the "architect of social patriarchy." These social reforms sought to reduce the conflicts between earning and caring that had resulted from the wage-labour system. Especially in difficult working environments, women's wage activities were seen as undermining their reproductive abilities. Agencies such as the National Council on Women, the Young Women's Christian Association, and the Women's Temperance Union sought to strengthen the family and protect women's caring roles. The activities of the Temperance Union also sought to ensure that men's wages would not be dissipated in non-family activities. This first wave of feminism, sometimes called maternal feminism, sought women's equal involvement in society not only through the vote, but also through encouraging distinct roles for men and women.

Various authors have argued that these complementary roles provide an efficient and ideal setting for the exchanges associated with marriage and family life (Parsons 1949; Becker 1981). In effect, the closing of nurseries and day-care centres in the period 1946-51 can be seen within this perspective: it was believed that women should return to the home once the war effort was over (Prentice 1992).

Ursel (1992: 284) uses the 1970 Royal Commission on the Status of Women as the benchmark for the *second wave of feminism*, which opposed the patriarchal assumptions associated with distinct roles, "giving clear warning that the consequences of women's new role would be far reaching and fundamental to the structures of our families, our work and our society." The shift included pressure to socialize the costs of reproduction in order to establish the possibility of equal opportunity for women and men. While the specialization and complementary roles may have their efficiencies, they also promote dependency and do not provide insurance in case of divorce or the economic incapacity of the principal wage-earner (Oppenheimer 1997).

The case of Sweden

Various authors have used Sweden as an example of family policies based on equivalent roles for women and men. From the 1930s, when other countries were focusing on the family wage model, Sweden sought to support family well-being by supporting women's economic activity and enabling working women to have children (Hoem and Hoem 1997). Thus the government systematically developed new models to combine working and parenting and to mesh child-rearing and employment. As Moen (1989: 136) pointed out: "Nowhere have the legal and societal norms regarding gender equality been more deliberately shaped than in Sweden. Nowhere is more assistance given to working parents ... in the form of parental leaves, reduced working hours, and other social supports. Nowhere in the western world has a larger proportion of mothers of young children entered and remained in the labor force."

Although initially unpaid, maternity leaves were introduced in 1931, and by 1962 they covered a period of six months at 65 percent of previous earnings (Hobson 1993). In 1939 it had already become illegal to dismiss a woman worker on grounds of marriage or pregnancy. In 1974 the leave became a parental leave of six months, which could be shared by parents, at 90 percent of earnings (Hoem and Hoem 1997). By 1989 the leave had become one year, and in 1995 it became a requirement that at least one of the twelve months be taken by each parent (Sundstrom 1991a).

By 1997 the replacement rate had been reduced to 75 percent of earnings, but the leave retained the flexibility wherein it could be taken any time before the child was eight years of age. The government had also introduced leaves associated with children's sickness and ten specific "daddy days" to be taken around the time of the child's birth. The social-security system pays for these benefits. In addition, family allowance from the state amounted to some $1,400 (Canadian) per year per child in 1996, and child care is heavily subsidized by municipalities.

Another important element is the right of one parent to work part-time, that is, 30 hours instead of the regular 40 hours per week, with a corresponding reduction in salary, until the child is aged eight. This part-time work comes with full social benefits, though proportionate to the hours worked. Workers have the right to return to full-time status with three months' notice. The system includes considerable flexibility, allowing parents to mix vacation, sickness periods, and full-time and part-time parental leave. Parental leave can be taken out at full-time or part-time levels, and it can be saved and used any time before the child is eight years old.

While Sweden's various benefits apply equally to women and men, it is overwhelmingly women who take the longer leaves and work part-time. Consequently, gender differences remain strong, and occupational segregation is probably higher than in Canada. Women are more likely to take jobs that allow for greater flexibility, and their lives are more varied in terms of full-time and part-time work and parental leaves. Consequently, women's lives are strongly affected by their family situations. Men's lives are also affected when they become parents, but during those periods their lives tend to be less, rather than more, varied (Hoem and Hoem 1997). Moen (1989: 147) concludes that equality remains as much an ideal as a reality: "The discrepancy between ideology and reality is due far less to employment options and occupational choices than to the still unequal responsibilities for home and family shouldered by men and women."

In United States, as Arlie Russell Hochschild (1997) documents, jobs have a strong pull for individuals and time at work has a high priority. But in Sweden it would be unacceptable for both parents to work full-time without taking time off to meet child-care needs. Moen (1989: 146) suggests simply that Swedes value home and family more than Americans do. Most Swedish parents prefer to have the children at home until age two or three and after that have them in a nursery school setting for some five to six hours per day, which is less than the regular eight-hour work day (Nasman 1997). Partly for these reasons, 24 percent of workers were part-time in Sweden in 1988, compared to a 12 percent average for the comparable OECD countries (Bélanger 1992: 25).

In Sweden, then, in addition to the employment benefits for working parents, the achievement of equality would require a marked redistribution of parenting responsibilities between men and women. While the country has policies in place for gender symmetry, and there is movement in this direction, the earning and caring activities of Swedish men and women still show marked differences.

Conflicting attitudes in Canada

While it seems fair to say that most Canadians would prefer a model of family policy that promotes gender symmetry, they still show considerable ambivalence on this question,

POLICY DIMENSIONS

with some apprehensions concerning equivalent roles and some remaining preferences for complementary roles.

The 1995 General Social Survey documented this ambivalence. For instance, when asked if "being able to take a paying job is important to happiness," some 86 percent of men agreed, but only 64 percent of women (Ghalam 1997). Younger women were more likely to say that a paying job was important to happiness, but nonetheless, at ages 25-44, only 70 percent said it was "important" or "very important." A majority of persons—68 percent of men and 73 percent of women—believed that "both spouses should contribute to household income." In addition, a slightly smaller majority of respondents—59 percent of men and 67 percent of women—said an "employed mother can establish just as warm and secure a relationship with her children as a mother who does not work for pay." But a majority—59 percent of men and 51 percent of women—also agreed that "a pre-school child is likely to suffer if both parents are employed." Reporting on these findings, Nancy Ghalam (1997) concluded that the attitudes were contradictory, characterized by both traditional and contemporary views on the division of labour by sex. The results of a small survey taken at the beginning of my second-year university course on "Canadian population and social policy" also showed this mix of views. The survey asked what the students thought best for children aged 0-4: for both parents to work full-time, for one parent to work part-time, or for one parent not to work? Taking the responses for 1997 and 1998 together, close to half of the students thought it was best to have one parent non-working, and almost as many thought it best to have one parent working part-time; but less than 5 percent preferred having both parents working full-time.

Reflecting on the results from the 1995 General Social Survey, a *Globe and Mail* (1997) editorial suggested that parental unpaid leaves should be extended to as much as 18 months per parent and that stay-at-home parents should get tax breaks. An organization called Kids First argues that the tax system penalizes parents who stay home. They propose taxation based on family income and conversion of the child-care deduction into an income-based benefit for all families (Brook 1997). This is rather different from the suggestions made by Stephen Peitchinis (1989: 12), who proposes, "As long as women are perceived to have different capabilities than men, and the perceived differences are not challenged with demonstrated evidence, women will remain typecast and disadvantaged in the market."

Conflicting attitudes, and the persistence of traditional views, are also found in other survey results. In a 1994 survey, among parents who worked 20 hours or less per week, 70 percent believed that they had achieved a good balance between job and time with family, but this experience of balance was only expressed by 36 percent of persons who worked 49 or more hours per week (Baker and Phipps 1997: 124). Nonetheless, in 1960 some 93 percent of respondents thought that women with young children should stay at home, compared to only 35 percent who responded this way in 1994 (p.124). In a survey taken in 1987, 74 percent of respondents thought day-care services should be available to anyone who wanted them, but 59 percent of those people also thought parents should pay most

327

of the costs (p.124). That result implies that only 30 percent of the respondents favoured a largely publicly funded system.

Feminism and family policy

Equality between women and men can take various forms. Alena Heitlinger (1993: 293) suggests three forms of equality: assimilation, androgyny, and maternal feminism. Assimilation means women becoming like men. Androgyny seeks to enlarge the common ground on which women and men share their lives. Maternal feminism sees the sexes as equal but complementary and focuses on the special needs of women. In some regards all three forms are needed, but as Heitlinger convincingly argues, in the consideration of family and work questions androgyny presents the greatest possibilities for effective equality. For one thing, if women were to simply become more like men this

---

BOX 8.1 | *Policy attitudes expressed in an Ontario survey*

The ambivalence regarding family models was also observed in a 1989-90 qualitative survey of 444 persons aged 18 and over in London, Ontario, and the surrounding area (Beaujot 1992). While people's priorities showed a high regard for marriage and children, the main difficulty experienced may be in finding room for everything that people want to achieve in life. According to the survey, people see it as important for both men and women to pursue education, to have a period of independence before marriage, to get established and to be married at least a short while before having children. At the same time, they generally expressed a preference to begin child-bearing before age 30. That is a lot to fit into a decade of life, and it assumes that all will happen as planned—and things don't always work out that way. While 38 percent of the respondents expressed a preference for three or more children, real-life situations may make it difficult even to have two children.

In addition, the survey revealed a basic ambivalence about the appropriateness of day care, and respondents often expressed a preference for having one parent at home or working only part-time while the children are young. This confronts people's general interest in maintaining employment prospects and preventing an entrenchment of gender-based divisions of labour. The contradictions in the expectations around marriage, gender roles, child-bearing, and child-rearing seem to follow from ascribing to two different models of the family. People appear to relate, to varying extents, to both the breadwinner and the dual-earner family.

The section of the survey dealing with programs and services started with an open question: "Are you in favour of programs and services for families with children, or are you not in favour ... if yes, what kinds of things do you think society should do to help support families with children?" Many respondents did not know what was meant by programs and

would leave little room for family, children, and caring activities more generally. The concept of equal but different may seem appropriate as an ideal, but differentiated activities will always involve differential evaluations and consequently effective inequality.

Questions of equal opportunity by gender—the core questions of feminism—are at the heart of alternative conceptions of family policy. Nonetheless, Meg Luxton (1997b) warns that feminist politics do not sufficiently take up explicit debates about families. The public debates about family values have been promoted by a conservative agenda, which claims that feminists themselves are destroying the family.

The feminist agenda is also based on the idea of a strong role for the state. For Heitlinger (1993: 293), "state feminism" is based on the "premise that family and work responsibilities should be shared by both women and men, and that workers with dependents should not be disadvantaged." This approach includes bans on discrimination by sex (especially pay equity), positive action (employment equity), and state intervention in the labour market and in the interface between work and family (child care

> BOX 8.1 CONT'D

services for families with children. Many said it was important to ensure that the disadvantaged be cared for. Sometimes anti-abuse programs and the needs of single parents were mentioned. Others spoke of the abuse of the welfare system, or that parents should be responsible for their own children.

When the survey suggested specific programs, respondents tended to be more positive, especially regarding education and health care (98 percent favourable), programs for those in need (80 percent favourable), and policies to enhance flexibility in work roles (82 percent favourable). Subsidized day care presented problems for some. They asked, "Why should the person who does not have children be responsible for paying taxes to subsidize those who do?" Some objected more to the inappropriate environment that day care provides for children. Day care proved a divisive issue, since others (56 percent) were clearly in favour of day-care subsidies. Regarding fiscal policies (family allowance and tax provisions for children),

some 60 to 80 percent were favourable. Others were against those measures because they implied increased government spending and higher taxes. Some noted that our list had not included programs to help one parent stay home with the children.

Given the responses, it would seem that space for reproduction may be best achieved by making changes in social organization that would focus on work leaves and/or part-time employment for one parent for a reasonable period following births. This would appear to be a higher priority than fiscal policies directly supporting the costs of children. While people do show an interest in increasing the availability of day care, it may be more important to enhance the choices for parents regarding the type of care provided in the first few years of a child's life—whether that be parental care, care obtained in the informal sector, or day-care settings. ◆

and family-friendly work environments). Luxton (1997b) sees the important feminist issues as those that reduce women's economic dependence on men: employment and pay equity, more equitable divorce and child support settlements, and access to social benefits on the basis of individual rather than family income.

Far from destroying the family, the thrust of these feminist orientations would bring about "new families" based on companionship and equality rather than duty and author-ity. For instance, Rosella Pamomba (1995: 195) proposes that the state must stop seeing men and women as having different family roles and particularly "try to encourage men to find a new identity as males and fathers based on companionship rather than author-ity." Some men's movements argue that feminism is bad for families, and they push for authoritarian marriage and parenting styles (Booth and Crouter 1998). However, what counts for children is not specifically the presence of fathers, which these movements promote, but *how* fathers are involved in their children's lives: frequency of conversations, knowing what the child is doing, having hopes for the child's future, for instance (Amato 1998). In effect, feminism encourages these kinds of changes, which are positive for chil-dren and families—changes such as increasing the social legitimacy of competitiveness and aggression in women, and the legitimacy of men accepting influence and leadership from women (McQuillan and Feree 1998).

POLICIES SUPPORTING INCOME GENERATION

Many policy areas relate to income generation, and these have implications for the earn-ing activities of families. For instance, the realm of employment raises issues of training, job creation, and support of the unemployed; issues of work incentives and of social wel-fare for those who are unable to work; and, finally, issues of workplace benefits and the basis for entitlement to various benefits.

Employment

Arguments for promoting more employment range from job creation to training; that is, policy can seek to increase available jobs or to train people and make them more employ-able. Matters of training and education clearly relate to families, because they are about finding ways for some family members to pursue further education. The state supports these efforts by providing subsidies for education, or by educational savings plans, but it undermines them through other policies that increase tuition and thus the individual costs of education. Besides contributing to the direct costs, families support education in a vari-ety of ways. For instance, the increasing numbers of students taking high-school educa-tion in the 1950s and 1960s were made possible, in part, by the large numbers of mothers who looked after the unpaid work in the home, with minimal support from their children.

In the 1980s and 1990s, the delayed departure of children from their parent's homes can also be seen as another form of family investment in the eventual earning potential of older children (Wister, Mitchell, and Gee 1997; Boyd and Norris 1998).

In terms of support for the unemployed, there are measures such as unemployment insurance and social assistance, along with more active measures such as training, subsidized employment, and mobility assistance. In an article on "Poor Families with Kids," Richards (1997b) observes that Canada spends proportionately less than Germany or Sweden do on active measures. He thus suggests earning supplements for the working poor, rather than child tax benefits. At the same time, these active measures are more feasible in the context of full employment. In addition, the child tax benefits are being restructured in ways that seek to encourage labour-force participation by providing equivalent benefits to the working poor and those on social assistance.

In Sweden, lone mothers with young children are considered to be employable, and they are more likely to work full-time than mothers in two-parent families, but more than half of lone mothers work part-time (Sainsbury 1996). Much of the part-time work in Canada comes without security and social benefits (Schellenberg 1997; Duffy 1997)— unlike Sweden, where part-time employment carries considerable security and benefits and is typically around 30 hours per week. The situation in Canada has some similarities with the United States, because policies have focused on employability and work incentives even for mothers of young children (Baker and Phipps 1997: 105).

Work incentives

Questions of work incentives are also relevant to the earning activities of families. Critics often suggest that social assistance and welfare payments for children reduce the incentive of the beneficiaries, including parents, to work. However, the case of Sweden indicates that generous social benefits can co-exist with strong labour-force involvement. An interesting experiment among 1,000 Manitoba families in the late 1970s found that administering social benefits in the form of a guaranteed annual income close to the low-income line did reduce the work that people did, but only by 1 percent for men and by 3 to 4 percent for women (Hum and Simpson 1991). People who have low standards of living always show an interest in earning additional income, and consequently the concern about work disincentives is typically exaggerated.

In the case of welfare benefits for children, the allocation of benefits through the tax system would have the advantage of making them available to all low-income families, regardless of whether the recipients are on social assistance or among the working poor or unemployed poor (Battle 1997b). The child tax benefit would seek to change a situation in which welfare families obtained about double the child benefits of working poor families. Administered through the tax system, and at equivalent levels for all low-income families, assistance to children would no longer be a work disincentive.

331

More problematic are social assistance provisions that involve marginal effective tax rates of 100 percent or more once people are earning income. For instance, persons on social assistance may have access to dental and drug plans that are discontinued once they are earning income. If these kinds of benefits were administered universally, that is, outside of social assistance, the benefit could also be retained not only for those on social assistance but also for the working poor.

Workplace benefits and the basis for entitlement

The issue of the basis for allocating social benefits goes beyond the matter of children and social assistance. An important consideration is the extent to which benefits are acquired through insurance associated with work, and associated payroll taxes, or acquired independently of work through general tax revenue. Programs like employment insurance, workers' compensation, and pensions are tied to work. While this may increase the incentive to work, it provides no benefits for those who are not working and who consequently are most in need. Some of these benefits, such as employment insurance and especially the employee benefits from specific employers such as supplemental health, dental, or drug benefits, have a family component. While this is a means of extending benefits to dependants of the worker, the approach is based on a family wage model and consequently can encourage dependency.

This allocation of benefits based on work also means that the other benefits not associated with work tend to become a second tier with lower provisions: social assistance, child benefits, and Guaranteed Income Supplements for the elderly. These are tied to family income and tend to be significantly reduced as this income moves above a certain floor.

Other workplace benefits are specifically tied to children. The 1988 Child Care Survey indicated that 32 percent of employed parents had access to flex-time and 23 percent to family sick leaves; 12 percent had parental leave benefits beyond those covered by employment insurance; and 6 percent had workplace child care (Lero et al. 1993: 32). These benefits clearly support the family-work interface. Significantly, flex-time does not necessarily reduce the stress associated with family and work. The 1992 General Social Survey found that male workers with access to flex-time had lower job stress, but female workers with such provisions actually experienced more stress (Fast and Frederick 1996). The 1988 Child Care Survey also asked respondents what workplace benefits they would like to have in addition to those currently in place. For parents with children aged 0-12, the most frequent suggestion was workplace day care (23 percent), followed by flexible work hours (19 percent), part-time work (9 percent), longer parental leave time (8 percent), and other leaves such as those for a child's sickness (5 percent), but 30 percent of these parents responded that they were not interested in further benefits (Lero et al. 1993: 52). Clearly, room exists for government incentives to employers that would encourage the extension of workplace benefits in a family-friendly direction (Duxbury and Higgins 1994).

POLICIES SUPPORTING CARING ACTIVITIES

While caring activities are important to families and the society, they receive little policy support. The entitlement to universal family allowance was based on numbers of children, but most programs and services that might now be tied to caring activities are in effect programs for persons in economic need: child benefits, welfare provisions for children, and some elderly benefits.

Parents arguably make huge investments in children and receive almost nothing in return (Burggaf 1997). In effect, through building human capital, the family is a primary engine of economic growth, but few benefits are attached to these caring activities. Even the tax provisions for dependent spouses apply on the basis of the spouse's low income and not on the basis of caring activities associated with young children.

Yves Péron et al. (1999) contrast the British and French approaches to the distribution of family benefits. They observe that states redistribute resources between economic classes, taking somewhat into account the family circumstances, but mostly taking into account the capacity of families to provide for their own income. The French approach to redistribution considers the costs associated with family composition, and it is better able to recognize the contribution of the caring activities of families to the health and development of the society. Gérard Calot (1990) proposes an extension of this idea in terms of taxation. He suggests that we should tax not on the basis of income but on the basis of standard of living: at equal standards of living, families should pay the same tax. Since, at a given level of income a family with children has a lower standard of living than a family without children, the family with children should pay proportionately less tax. This would be a major change, but it would ensure that people are not penalized for having children. Similarly, Jacques Henripin (1989) proposes that the family allowance should seek to equalize the levels of living between those with and without children, at given levels of earned income.

The British approach considers family composition as a private matter and bases redistribution only on family income, seeking to assist those in economic difficulty. While the French approach seeks to support all families with young children regardless of income, the British system only supports families at low incomes. The British approach effectively supports caring activities only for those at lower income levels.

By not supporting caring activities, the welfare state in effect pushes these activities onto families and consequently onto women in particular (Baines, Evans, and Neysmith 1991). For instance, the cuts to hospital services mean that families, and women in particular, absorb more of the care associated with medical conditions. More generally, it is estimated that the value of unpaid work would amount to some 32 to 54 percent of the Gross Domestic Product (Pupo 1997: 144). The analysis of caring helps to uncover the ambiguities of women's relationships to the welfare state, and it shows the implications of this invisible work for women's poverty, vulnerability, and disadvantage (Baines, Evans, and Neysmith 1991). Similarly, as Leira (1992: 3) observes, a "gender differentiated family is a central characteristic of welfare state design." In effect, she argues that the welfare state is based on three assumptions: the primacy of wage work over other forms of work, private responsibility for child care, and a gender division of labour. Consequently, when caring by the state is enhanced it reduces women's dependence on individual men but strengthens the mutual dependence of women and the state.

As another approach in addition to the entitlements that could be attached to caring activities, others have proposed wages for housework (Luxton 1997b), recognition for the economic value of caregiving (Evans 1991), or the collective provision of given services (Neysmith 1991). Such changes would involve a considerable shift from the assumption that individual families are responsible for these activities. In effect, they would imply a society organized more around the dynamics of caring and less around those of earning. A "socialist feminist" framework would "redesign laws, programs and practices to focus more on childbearing, consensus, cooperation, human needs, and environmental protection, and less on hierarchy, competition and profit making" (Baker 1997: 53).

EMPLOYMENT-RELATED POLICIES: PARENTAL LEAVE AND PART-TIME WORK

Although being a parent increasingly entails finding ways of meshing parenthood and employment, jobs are still mostly structured for individuals rather than for family members, and as a result someone, most often women but sometimes men, has to make career sacrifices. In the field of policy, a goal would seem to be to minimize the conflicts associated with parenthood and employment. For instance, in her article "Parental Benefit Policies and the Gendered Division of Labour," Baker (1997) observes that some countries have specifically "accommodated or encouraged two-earner families by modifying their economic or social programs," while others "expect parents to make their own personal adjustments with little public support."

Parental leave

While the opportunities to work part-time, as well as take up job-sharing and flex-time, are important to meshing parenting and employment, the most specific provisions have been introduced in the area of parental leaves. The Canadian government introduced maternity benefits in 1971, following recommendations of the Royal Commission on the Status of Women. Before that time most employed women had to resign from their jobs during pregnancy, with no guarantee of re-employment and no income provision while away from work (Heitlinger 1993: 209). The Labour Code was amended to prohibit dismissal on the grounds of pregnancy. The maternity benefits were paid out of unemployment insurance and made available to women who had worked for at least one year with the same employer. The provision was for 15 weeks of benefits, after a two-week waiting period. As with other unemployment benefits, the amount was set at 60 percent of regular salary, up to an established maximum.

In 1990 the government began to provide an additional ten weeks of parental benefits, which could be taken by either parent. Other provisions have changed along with alterations in unemployment insurance, now called employment insurance. In particular, the applicant must have done 700 hours of work in the previous year, and the replacement rate became 55 percent of wages, with a maximum payment of $413 per week in 1997. Besides being subject to taxation, the payments were also subject to clawback provisions for higher income families. Consequently, the average after-tax benefit in 1992 was only $273 per week (Baker and Phipps 1997: 132-34). Also, those receiving benefits represented only 44.3 percent of 1991 births. While either parent could take advantage of the parental benefits, only 4.8 percent of the leave beneficiaries in 1998 were men (Philip 1998). Clearly, those who did not work before the child was born, or the self-employed who did not pay employment insurance, or those who returned to work within the benefit period received no benefits or reduced benefits.

Quebec began seeking to administer its own parental leave, if it could arrange opting-out provisions with the federal government. A proposal made in November 1998 would have 18 weeks of leave for the mother, 3 for the father, and 7 for either parent, for a total of 28 weeks. Based on 70 percent replacement, it would start at the threshold income of $2,000 and reach a maximum when earned income is $51,000 (Fraser 1998). In contrast, the federal plan starts at the threshold income of $4,830 and reaches a maximum when income is $39,000.

Given provinces have provisions for longer leave periods with a guarantee of job security, but without funding the period beyond 25 weeks. The longest leave is in Quebec, at a full 52 weeks. In addition, given employers have provisions to either top up the employment insurance payments or to pay for a longer period. However, in 1987 only 20 percent of women on maternity leave received additional benefits (Baker and Phipps 1997: 134).

Part of the problem with Canadian parental leave is that the funding is administered through the employment insurance system. Parental leaves are notably different from unemployment, and it would make more sense to fund them through general tax revenue than through an insurance structured around the loss of a job. Another critique is that the rates are low in comparison to other countries. Among the 22 countries listed in Table 8.6, Canada is about in the middle in terms of the generosity of parental leave. Phipps (1996) has provided various useful suggestions, starting with fairly inexpensive changes to the parental leave policies, to introduce more flexibility for parents (see Box 8.2).

In Sweden, the parental leave of 12 months may also be taken at any time until the child is eight years old, and the replacement rate is at 75 percent of wages. Another three months are available at a low "basic rate." These benefits may be taken by either parent, except that in two-parent families at least one month must be taken by each parent. In effect, the proportion of men who have taken a parental leave has increased from 4.1 percent of men with children under age seven in 1968 to 6.1 percent in 1981 (Moen 1989: 66). Still, the proportions are much higher for women, at 16.2 percent in 1968 and 30.3 percent in 1981. Another

Swedish provision introduced in 1980 provided for the potential to have another child at the same level of benefits, as long as the births were within 24 months. In 1986 this period was extended to 30 months (Hoem 1993). That is, if a parent changes from full-time to part-time work after returning to work, the benefit rates would correspond to the full-time wages, as long as a subsequent child was born within 30 months of the previous birth.

INDICATORS OF STATE SUPPORT FOR FAMILIES, 22 COUNTRIES, 1990

	FAMILY ALLOWANCE			MATERNITY LEAVE BENEFITS, 1990			PUBLIC CHILD CARE AS PERCENT OF AGE GROUP	
	AS % OF MALE WAGES IN MANU-FACTURING[a]	IN $U.S.[b]	TOTAL TRANSFERS TO TWO-CHILD FAMILY[c]	DURATION IN WEEKS	PERCENT OF PAY	INDEX[d]	UNDER 3 YEARS[e]	3 YEARS TO SCHOOL AGE[e]
Australia	3.4	55	10.7	0	—	0.0	NA	5
Austria	11.3	185	23.6	16	100	16.0	NA	NA
Belgium	10.4	165	39.1	14	80	11.2	20	95
Canada	2.4	50	15.0	25	60	15.0	5	15
Denmark	5.2	95	26.3	28	90	25.2	50	85
Finland	6.2	85	20.8	53	80	42.4	20	50
France	7.1	90	19.2	16	84	13.4	20	95
Germany	4.9	85	21.2	14	100	14.0	5	65
Greece	3.2	30	23.2	15	50	7.5	5	65
Ireland	3.0	45	17.1	14	70	9.8	NA	NA
Italy	0.0	0	14.5	20	80	16.0	5	85
Japan	0.6	15	7.3	14	60	8.4	NA	20
Luxembourg	8.3	145	34.1	16	100	16.0	5	55
Netherlands	7.4	115	12.3	16	100	16.0	5	50
New Zealand	2.1	30	2.5	0	—	0.0	NA	NA
Norway	9.1	150	25.7	35	80	28.0	10.0	50
Portugal	4.9	30	11.9	13	100	13.0	5	35
Spain	0.3	5	6.5	16	75	12.0	NA	65
Sweden	7.2	115	15.0	52	75	39.0	30	80
Switzerland	4.7	85	14.1	8	100	8.0	NA	NA
United Kingdom	6.3	100	12.7	18	45	8.1	5	35
United States	0.0	0	9.7	0	—	0.0	NA	NA

NOTES: a   For a family with two children, 1990.
     b   Monthly amounts for a two-child family, 1990.
     c   Index of after-tax/transfer income available to a two-child family (with one income) as compared to a single worker, at earnings equal to average male wages in manufacturing, 1990.
     d   Equivalent weeks at 100 percent of pay. Data for Sweden and Canada based on other sources.
     e   Data for 1986-89 depending on the country. Figures include both part-time and full-time care, as well as subsidized family home care, and pre-primary school institutions.
    NA   Data not available. Often zero or little public child care.

Source: Gauthier 1996: 166, 167, 170, 174, 181.

TABLE 8.6

The accommodation of parenting and work consequently requires a restructuring of both family and work roles, for both men and women. In effect, women who have the right to paid leave are the most likely to resume employment (Ronsen and Sundstrom 1997). Moen (1992: 9) proposes periods of reduced work hours or sabbaticals for fathers and/or mothers while their children are infants and toddlers, with no loss of seniority or job security.

Part-time work

The meshing of employment and parenting in Sweden also occurs through the encouragement of part-time work. One parent has the option of working part-time, typically 30 hours per week, until the child is eight years old, with the right to return to full-time work at any point. It is mostly women who work part-time, but the rates have also increased for men. For instance, in 1968 some 2.6 percent of fathers with children under seven worked part-time, increasing to 6.4 percent in 1981 (Moen 1989: 66-67). For mothers the rates are much higher, and they also increased from 62.2 percent in 1968 to 66.8 percent in 1981. It is also interesting that very few parents would prefer to work more hours, but 12.1 percent of fathers and 19.7 percent of mothers in 1981 would prefer to work fewer hours.

Comparing these data with the United States, Moen (1989: 74-76) observes significant contrasts. In the United States a smaller proportion of mothers with young children are in the labour force, but among those working a higher proportion than in Sweden are working full-time. The situation in Canada would be more similar to that in the United States—with mothers with young children more likely to be either full-time at home or full-time at work—while Sweden adopts what Eva Bernhardt (1987: 9) calls a "combination strategy," with "one foot in the home and one in the labour market." Part-time work is viewed much more positively in Sweden, in part because it comes with the full range of social benefits, as long as it involves at least 20 hours per week. In particular, it is seen as being much better for women than not being in the labour force (Sundstrom 1997). Instead of seeing part-time work as a form of marginalization, Marianne Sundstrom (1991b) finds that it increases the regularity of women's labour-force attachment along with their position in the labour market, and it reduces their economic dependency.

Although Sweden is a prime example of a country that has sought to establish gender equality, nonetheless men and women have quite different jobs, and occupational segregation is probably higher than in Canada. This is partly because certain jobs, including those in public service, have the flexibility to permit part-time work. For instance, men take more leaves when they work at female-dominated workplaces or in the public sector (Nasman 1992). In addition, mothers who take longer leaves and work part-time pay a price in terms of income and advancement at work (Sundstrom 1994; Nasman 1992). The "combination strategy" thus reinforces gender differences. Equity remains as much an ideal as a reality, and the work patterns cannot be seen as representing the achievement of gender equality (Moen 1989: 147).

At the same time, the gender differences are declining. Over time men's paid work hours in Sweden are going down while women's are increasing. Consequently, in 1990, men with preschoolers at home averaged 44.2 hours of work per week, while women averaged 29.5 hours (Nasman 1992). In addition, men with young children work the least hours and have the most absenteeism, compared to other men. When fathers take a parental leave, there also appears to be a higher chance of a subsequent birth (Olah 1996). This may be because women in a more gender-equal relationship can expect to absorb less of the costs of children. By taking leaves, men are indicating not only their interest in children, but also their willingness to absorb some of the costs.

Although Canadian surveys show less support for part-time work, a significant proportion of mothers with younger children still move in that direction (chapter 4). Maureen Baker and Shelley Phipps (1997: 125) state, "Most wives and mothers work full-time outside the home." However, their data indicated that women working full-time were still less than half of mothers with children under 16 (p.130). For instance, in two-parent families, 64.6 percent of women were employed in 1991, but 29.1 percent of them were employed part-time, which means that 45.6 percent of all those mothers were working full-time. For lone parents the comparable figure is 42.1 percent of mothers with children under 16 working full-time.

Ann Duffy (1997) observes that good part-time jobs are clearly a possibility in Canada; in addition to liberating women from a double day, they can be helpful to students, and even to seniors. However, she concludes that they are more likely to represent "entrapment" than "empowerment," and they mean more social inequality. For instance, the benefits of pensions and medical, dental, or paid sick leave are available to less than a fifth of part-time workers, compared to about two-thirds of full-time workers (Schellenberg 1997). In 1995, 37.2 percent of part-time jobs were held by persons aged 15-24, with little differentiation by sex, while 48.3 percent were held by women aged 25 or more, and 14.5 percent by men aged 25 or more (Duffy 1997: 172).

Parenting and employment

The case of Sweden is particularly relevant, because it is probably the society that has most deliberately sought to address this meshing of child-rearing and employment (Moen 1989: 5). This initiative has involved a concerted effort by government and organized labour to both distribute the burden of parenting between women and men and to facilitate the employment of all adults.

In effect, the thrust of Swedish policy has focused on facilitating workers to have children, rather than on facilitating parents to work (Hoem and Hoem 1997). That is, the policy considers that adults are workers and makes provisions for their having children through benefits that are tied to employment. Moen (1989: 76) concludes, "Swedish public policies permit working parents to maintain an uninterrupted attachment to the labor force that assures them job seniority and benefit protection, while also allowing them to care for their children during the critical early years."

In Sweden as elsewhere, further moves to gender equality would require a significant redistribution of parenting responsibilities between women and men. For instance, on the one hand, it could be argued, the encouragement of part-time work represents a continuation of gender differences. On the other hand, it does represent a greater tendency toward the meshing of family and work. It also makes the lives of employed mothers easier and clearly improves their economic situations—it's better than being not employed. There is also the theoretical possibility that both parents will take up the option of working part-time, thus sharing that approach. For Elisabeth Nasman (1997) the important question is "how workplace cultures mediate between gender-symmetric public regulations and gender-typed family behaviour." That is, there is a push from the public side for symmetry but family behaviour promotes gender differences, and consequently workplace cultures could play a significant role in facilitating the equal involvement of women and men in the family-work interface.

While recognizing the importance of a "family responsive workplace," Jennifer Glass and Sarah Estes (1997: 306-7) also observe that "the economic motivations to institute family responsive policies remain unclear at best" and "solid research evidence showing economic benefits has been difficult to document," while "on-site child care appears to have little effect on either family or organizational functioning." Nonetheless, they find that informal social support, provided by sympathetic supervisors, does have positive effects on employees. While the demand for these family-friendly policies is increasing, most workers need this accommodation only for a short period of time. Consequently, many employers are not particularly interested in making extensive provisions for family-friendly work environments, and many employees are at life stages in which the policies are not relevant. Beth Anne Shelton (1992: 158) is also concerned that employer-sponsored policies are more likely to be used by women, which will only go to reinforce the gender differences.

CHILD BENEFITS AND CHILD CARE

In their focus on children's rights, R. Brian Howe and Katherine Covell (1997) propose that the policy changes needed to improve the well-being of children include especially the expansion of the child benefits program, more day care, and expanded school programs for children in need. The policies and services for children must be placed in the context of the general economic well-being of children, and the specific undertaking of the Canadian Parliament to seek to eliminate child poverty (see Box 8.2).

Child benefits

All welfare states help parents through financial allocations and subsidies of various kinds, but just how they make these provisions differs extensively (Bradshaw 1997; Gauthier 1996). Canada, unfortunately, is among the less successful countries in reducing child poverty (Baker 1995b).

Family allowance, introduced by the Canadian government in 1945, was the country's first universal social program. The benefit rates, although tripled in 1974, remained low compared to other countries. Among 22 comparable countries, only five countries had lower rates than Canada, and in total after-tax transfers to two-child families (in comparison to a worker with no family) 11 of the countries do better than Canada (see Table 8.6). Taking a total of tax allowances and credits, as well as universal and employment-based benefits for children, a comparison of 18 OECD countries shows that the situation in Canada compared favourably to other countries in 1950, while in 1985 the Canadian situation was better than that in the United States, Australia, Japan, Denmark, Germany, and Ireland, but worse than Finland, Sweden, Norway, Holland, Belgium, France, Switzerland, Austria, Italy, Britain, and New Zealand (Wannemo 1994).

In 1993 the Canadian government removed the universal family allowance in favour of a child benefit package that administered federal contributions through the tax system and was aimed at lower-income families. After that a major policy thrust was to enrich those benefits. In 2000 the benefits would amount to a maximum of $1,975 per year for the first child and $1,775 for each additional child, augmented by $213 for children under seven for whom child-care expenses were not claimed. The federal and provincial governments began looking to combine their programs for poor families—to make equivalent provisions for the working poor and people on social assistance. But combining the benefits would require a child tax benefit of $2,500 per child (Battle 1997c).

As of 2000, a family would obtain maximum benefits when its income was below $29,590, with a subsequent gradient so that families with two children would have no benefits at incomes above $70,400. For low-income families, the inflation-adjusted payments in 1998 were about $500 per child higher than in 1984, but families with incomes over $30,000 were receiving more in 1984 than in 1998 (Battle and Mendelson 1997: 10). While the government targeted the benefits to families with less income, its de-indexation of taxes has disproportionately increased the taxes of these same poorer families (Battle 1998).

Given that the cost of raising a child is conservatively estimated at falling between $4,000 and $6,500 per year, not counting child-care expenses, a family with net income under $26,000 would be receiving some 50 to 75 percent of this amount. However, at the average net family income of $30,000 (about half of average family income), a four-person family with two children would receive $1,000 per child or 15 to 25 percent of the cost (Battle 1997a: 9). Once family income is $60,000 the amount received would be under $300 per child, or 4 to 7 percent of the costs.

In his critique of this policy, Ken Battle (1997b) suggested that benefits be improved, especially for families with incomes below $35,000. He noted that payments are particularly low for the working poor with one child. Battle proposed that we first move to the figure of $2,500 per child for all low-income children, permitting all welfare-related child benefits to be replaced (Battle and Mendelson 1997: 18-22).

A critique of the move from family allowance to child benefits (Woolley, Vermaeten, and Madill 1996) emphasized that the change had left some parents without benefits and consequently without a social recognition of their contribution to society as parents. The

---

BOX 8.2 | *Policy options to enhance the economic security of Canadian families*

After studying the situation in France, Germany, Sweden, and Finland, Phipps (1996: 112-14) makes a number of suggestions for Canada. Her call for universal family allowance may limit the potential to redistribute toward poorer families.

First, to recognize the difficulties faced by most Canadian families in balancing home and workplace responsibilities, we should offer more flexible maternity and parental leaves and benefits. For example, we could allow parental leaves to be taken half-time (for twice as long), with parents returning to work half-time. Similarly, allowing parents even a small number of paid days off for the care of children each year would make their lives much easier. Canadian coverage of parental benefits shrinks as unemployment increases or non-standard employment grows. We should consider reducing entrance requirements to match those for regular EI benefits. We should think about extending coverage to workers with low wages or low hours, perhaps with a flat-rate floor on benefits. In addition to these changes that enhance flexibility, we should also offer higher rates of benefits for longer periods.

Second, we should reinstate family allowances paid monthly to all families with children. This measure would reduce child poverty. The value of these allowances should be at least equal to the benefits currently received by low-income families.

Third, we should design a system of advance maintenance payments for single-parents who are not receiving child-support payments (or receiving only infrequent or inadequate payments). With advance maintenance payments in place, all of society would share in the cost of non-payment by a defaulting non-custodial parent.

Many other family benefits beyond these few suggestions are available in each of the European countries Phipps studied. For example, Finland, France, Sweden, and to a lesser extent Germany offer much more comprehensive systems of public child care than we do in Canada. All four countries also make housing allowances available. In Sweden, while income-tested, these benefits are nonetheless received by 80 percent of single-parent families and 30 percent of two-parent families. All four countries offer a second tier of EI benefits to unemployed individuals without past labour-force attachment. They offer these benefits for an unlimited duration, although at a lower level of compensation, as long as people are looking for work. ◆

Source: Adapted from Phipps 1996: 112-14.

change had also eliminated the tax deductions for dependent children, and consequently richer families received no direct benefits associated with children. Canada thus became one of the few countries not to have universal child benefits or tax deductions for children (Woolley 1998). Still, the benefits for poorer families were enriched. In addition, richer families could profit from a higher limit on tax deductions for child-care expenses, which in 1998 was set at a maximum of $7,000 for children under seven and provided $3,000 for someone in the highest tax bracket.

Child care

Countries also vary considerably in the extent to which they provide support for child care (Kamerman and Kahn 1991). Peter Moss (1997) observed a widespread trend in the European Union toward publicly funded systems for ages three to six, though these are not necessarily full-time day-care programs. The aim of European programs is more in the direction of supporting child development than meeting the needs of working parents. Countries provide much less coverage for children under age three, and show greater variability. For children under three, the programs that exist tend to focus on the needs of working parents and the welfare needs of children at risk. Once again, Canada comes out low in comparison to other richer countries. Some 13 countries have more provisions than Canada (see also Table 8.6).

In Canada federal funding for child care has come from the Canada Assistance Plan, which in 1996 became part of the Canada Health and Social Transfer. This block funding supports the provincial costs of health, postsecondary education, and social welfare. These funds typically help pay the capital costs associated with day care, and they subsidize the fees of parents with lower incomes. In the 1980s the federal government had plans for a national child-care program, but it was never established. The orientation in the 1990s was to increase funds for child benefits and deductions for child-care expenses rather than to establish a child-care program with national standards.

Canadians appear to have mixed values in the area of child care, with some favouring a universal system and others proposing that the care should largely be a parental responsibility. When an opinion poll asked, "Do you favour a national child care program, including various kinds of regulated child care services, planned at the local level and supported through a combination of parent fees and government funds?" some 65 percent indicated agreement (Insight Canada Research 1993). But the question was in essence double-edged and did not indicate how much parents would have to pay. *Globe and Mail* columnist Margaret Wente (1993) suggested that while child care is indeed a big problem, most parents do not want a national system but prefer to have more options, including support for staying at home with children (see Box 8.3).

Support for child care can have at least two objectives, which adds to the complexity of the issue. If the objective is to support the labour-force participation of parents, the subsidy should be tied to working but not to a particular mode of care (Powell 1997).

However, if the objective is the well-being of children, the subsidy should be for modes of care that enhance child development.

Laura Johnson and Julie Mathien (1998) propose a system of early childhood education for four- to five-year-olds that would be integrated with the school system, in which parents would pay only for the time spent before or after regular school hours. Tom Kent (1999) suggests converting the $7,000 deduction for child-care expenses into a progressive refundable tax credit that would be paid to a child-care centre. In the longer term, he suggests some $8 billion as the federal contribution to a universal system of child centres. This would represent a major change from current arrangements, in which most child-care providers are "unregulated," which includes care in the child's home and informal care outside of the child's home. In 1994-95, only 17 percent of caregivers were "regulated" centres or family child-care providers (Child Care Human Resources Steering Committee 1998).

BOX 8.3 | *Options for child care*

In her newspaper column, Wente (1993) argued that parents want more options rather than a national day-care system. While she makes a rather strong case for parental choice, the economic circumstances of poorer families may limit the effective choice, especially if there is lack of public funding for child care.

Who gets to be a feminist?

Here's a short, simple question for all you women in the audience: Are you a feminist? If you're like most women I know, your answer will be not so short and not so simple. You might say something like this: "Well, it all depends on what you mean by the word 'feminist.'" I'm definitely not radical or militant. I guess I've been pretty much able to do what I want with my life. Maybe I'm just lucky. I don't feel like a victim and I think most men are pretty decent....

In the National Action Committee on the Status of Women's version of feminism, the leading orthodoxies go something like this: Violence against women is soaring; the recession and free trade have hurt women most; national day care is an urgent social priority; millions of single mothers live in poverty; and sexual harassment in the workplace is endemic.

It is certainly true that violence against women and sexual harassment are intolerable; that the recession has been vicious; that many young families are strained to the breaking point, and that single mums have it tougher than just about anyone else.

The rest of the facts are a letdown. Here they are. Women report many more minor sexual assaults than they did a decade ago because we now have a law against leering, groping and flashing, and because the police and the justice system enforce it. As for the rate of violent sex assaults, it's gone down slightly....

Child care is a big problem. But most parents want more options, not a government day-care centre on every corner. They'd much rather have a bigger tax break and make more of their own choices, including staying at home. ◆

Source: Wente 1993, reprinted with permission from The Globe and Mail.

Quebec has introduced a universal system. Parents using the program pay only $5 per day, reduced to $2 for parents on social assistance. In 1998-99 the program was available to three- to five-year-olds, and the province intended to have all preschool children eligible by the year 2001. Funding was arranged by putting aside the baby bonuses that had paid parents subsidies of $500 for a first child, $1,000 for a second, and $8,000 for a third and subsequent children. Still, critics say the funding is insufficient to maintain quality programs, a problem that would be even more serious after younger children became eligible.

In the 1989-90 survey in London and the surrounding area, a majority of respondents favoured day care, but some parents believed that day care was not the best setting for children and others simply preferred to look after children themselves or have them stay with a sitter (Beaujot 1992). In part, some parents may be apprehensive because they have insufficient experience with day care, which in turn is partly a function of lack of availability. But, according to various studies, some of these apprehensions are not well-founded. For instance, based on samples from 1986-88 in the United States, Toby Parcel and Elizabeth Menaghan (1994) found no evidence suggesting that non-maternal child care was damaging to children. They did find that longer parental work hours do entail some risks. In addition, children from impoverished environments can receive a "head-start" advantage from quality child-care settings.

Focusing on the needs of women, Duffy and Noreen Pupo (1996: 21) argue that, for many families, the provision of appropriate care for children is a key to women's equal opportunity and participation. By "lifting some of the family work from the shoulders of women" society would provide "greater opportunities for equality in the workplace and in the home." They propose community-based child-care centres that would draw on the resources of existing facilities, including schools and volunteer and social service organizations. In effect, this would build on school and after-school programs, provide a meeting place for families, and help create a societal responsibility for children.

Well-being of children

The long-term trend of the 1980s and 1990s—a slight increase in the proportions of children with low-income status—contrasts with a unanimous resolution passed in the House of Commons in 1989 to "seek to achieve the goal of eliminating poverty among children by the year 2000" (Battle and Muszynski 1995: 1). Child poverty is higher in Canada than in most other rich countries. In a comparison of 14 richer countries, only the United States has higher child poverty than Canada (Figure 8.2). Also, only in the United States, Canada, and the Netherlands are poverty rates higher for children than for the total population.

Comparing seven countries in the mid-1980s, Baker (1995b: 82) observes that Canada did better than the United States in terms of the proportions of poor families lifted out of poverty by government transfers, but France, Netherlands, Sweden, and the United Kingdom had done significantly better than Canada. She concludes that eliminating child poverty is a daunting task requiring a comprehensive overhaul of policies in several areas: taxes and transfers, parental leaves and employment strategies, social assistance, and child care.

Social transfers significantly reduce child poverty. In effect, since 1983, families with children aged 0-14 and with incomes that are less than half of the median income receive more of their income from transfers than from earnings (Picot and Myles 1996a: 248). That is, the relative stability of child poverty results from the decline in market income and increased transfers. In 1991 poor families received about 28 percent of their incomes from social assistance, 18 percent from child benefits, 15 percent from other transfers, and only 39 percent from earnings. For all families, total transfers of all kinds represented 22 percent of family income in 1975 and 26 percent in 1991 (Baker and Phipps 1997: 142). The federal cash benefits for children totalled over $5 billion in 1989-90, nearly double the amount from ten years before (Baker and Phipps 1997: 199). Still, while these figures represent extensive transfers, significant numbers of children remain below the poverty line.

In addition to the benefits of social transfers for poorer families, children have benefited from a number of other trends: more earners per family, more educated parents, fewer children per family, and the later age of mothers at childbirth. However, they have suffered from the stable or declining real annual earnings, especially for men under 35 years of age (Picot and Myles 1996a: 246). In addition, increasing proportions of children live in lone-parent families. The increased transfers, then, have not been sufficient to compensate for the detrimental trends in real wages and lone parenthood.

While the links are difficult to establish, the level of transfers may also be connected to low fertility rates. For instance, in Sweden the extensive set of family policies and services helped to increase fertility over the period 1983-90, bringing average births to above two per woman in 1989-93 (Hoem and Hoem 1997). However, partly as a function of a reduction

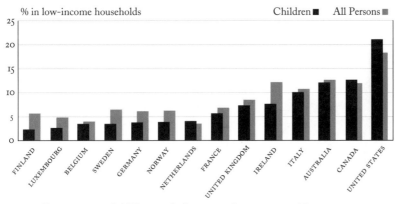

FIG 8.2 Poverty rate of children and all persons, by country, mid-1980s

Source: Battle and Muszynski 1995: 6.

in the income-replacement rate for parental leave, and with other economic concerns associated with rising unemployment, the subsequent patterns have seen a return to below replacement fertility. Much of the effect of transfers and other trends has been on the timing of births, since cohort fertility has been rather stable in Sweden at close to two births per woman (Walker 1995). While the fertility effect of Canadian transfers must be small, simulations based on data from the Survey of Consumer Finances for 1976-88 suggest that transfers can nonetheless have a marginal impact (Lefebvre, Brouillette, and Felteau 1994), which may have been undermined by the virtual elimination of transfers for families above median income. Possibly, prospective parents could interpret this lack of social support as a signal that society does not particularly value child-bearing.

THE CASE OF LONE-PARENT FAMILIES

While overall poverty rates have eased downward in the past two decades, this has not been the case among lone parents (Hunsley 1997: 1). Lone parents have also come to occupy a lower strata of the poor, compared to other groups such as elderly women and two-parent poor families. For instance, among ten countries in 1987, only the United States and Australia were doing worse than Canada in terms of the median net disposable income of lone mothers compared to two-parent families (Hunsley 1997: 43). While the median net disposable income of lone-mother families was 52.6 percent of that of two-parent families in Canada, it was 74 to 87 percent of the income of two-parent families in France, Germany, Norway, and Sweden. In the proportions of people living at low income, all countries show greater disadvantages for lone parents, but the extent of

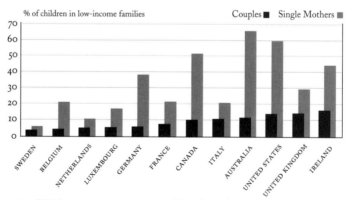

FIG 8.3 Child poverty rates, by type of family and country, mid-1980s

Source: Battle and Muszynski 1995: 7.

346

these relative disadvantages is noteworthy in the United States, Australia, Canada, Ireland, and Germany (Figure 8.3).

Table 8.7 shows the poverty rates for 17 countries, by family type, before and after taxes and transfers. For two-parent families with children, Canada is below the mean—it does better than the United States, Ireland, Israel, United Kingdom, Italy, and Australia, but worse than the other 10 countries. In Sweden the poverty rates for two-parent families are less than a third of the Canadian rate. For lone-parent families, the rates of poverty are significantly higher in the United States, Australia, and Canada. Other countries are more successful at reducing the disadvantage of lone-parent families through the tax and transfer systems. Transfers reduce the poverty levels of lone-mother families by more than half in several European countries. In Sweden lone-mother families have a poverty rate of 54.9 percent before transfers but 5.2 percent after transfers—a poverty rate that is even lower than the level for two-parent families in several countries.

The problems are compounded by the increased numbers: between 1975 and 1992, the proportion of children living with lone parents increased from 8.7 percent to 14.7 percent of all children, and they have come to represent 47.1 percent of all child poverty (Table 7.9). These figures are not that different from other countries. In 1990 lone parents represented 10 to 15 percent of all families in OECD countries, and 25 percent in the United States (OECD 1990).

In all countries, children living with one parent do less well on average than those living with both parents, but transfers reduce the gap more in some countries than in others (Smeeding, Danzinger, and Rainwater 1995). In most cases, earnings and social transfers play a larger role than private transfers in helping to reduce the poverty rates of children in lone-parent families. In Sweden private transfers from fathers play a very small role, but the labour-force participation of lone mothers is similar to that of married mothers, and the lone parents are more likely to be working full-time. In addition, the policy framework does not differentiate solo mothers from married mothers, and as a consequence the poverty rate for children in lone-parent families is close to 5 percent. In contrast, the rate is 50 percent in Canada and 60 percent in the United States (Table 8.7).

Phipps (1998) compared the situation of children with lone mothers in Canada, Norway, and the United States. In terms of mean adjusted disposable income, in the United States children with lone mothers have 52 percent of the income of all children, compared to 66 percent in Canada and 81 percent in Norway. The main differences observed for Norway are a more generous and universal family allowance (doubled for lone parents), an advance maintenance of payments for child support, and a higher labour-force participation of lone mothers.

It is difficult to apply the policy models used for two-parent households to the one-parent case. Eichler (1996) contrasted the three models called "patriarchal model," "individual responsibility model," and "social responsibility model." In particular, the individual responsibility model, which is dominant in Canada, assumes that parents are responsible for the economic well-being and care of dependent children. This approach presents problems for a lone parent, who cannot, at the same time, be both earner and

CHILD POVERTY RATES BEFORE AND AFTER GOVERNMENT TAXES AND TRANSFERS

	PRE-TRANSFER CHILD POVERTY RATES			POST-TRANSFER CHILD POVERTY RATES			% LONE
	ALL CHILDREN	TWO-PARENT HOUSE-HOLDS	LONE MOTHERS	ALL CHILDREN	TWO-PARENT HOUSE-HOLDS	LONE MOTHERS	MOTHERS IN TOTAL FAMILIES
Australia 1989	19.6	11.5	73.2	14.0	7.7	56.2	12.4
Belgium 1992	16.2	13.1	50.7	3.8	3.2	10.0	8.1
Canada 1991	22.5	14.9	68.2	13.5	7.4	50.2	13.4
Denmark 1992	16.0	10.6	45.0	3.3	2.5	7.3	14.3
Finland 1991	11.5	8.6	36.3	2.5	1.9	7.5	9.5
France 1984	25.4	22.8	56.4	6.5	5.4	22.6	6.5
Germany 1989	9.0	5.2	43.9	6.8	2.3	4.2	9.9
Ireland 1987	30.2	28.0	72.6	12.0	10.5	40.5	5.3
Israel 1986	23.9	21.6	61.3	11.1	10.3	27.5	5.1
Italy 1991	11.5	10.6	31.7	9.6	9.5	13.9	4.4
Luxembourg 1985	11.7	8.4	55.7	4.1	3.6	10.0	6.8
Netherlands 1991	13.7	7.7	79.7	6.2	3.1	39.5	8.4
Norway 1991	12.9	4.4	57.4	4.6	1.9	18.4	15.4
Sweden 1992	19.1	12.5	54.9	2.7	2.2	5.2	14.6
Switzerland 1982	5.1	1.9	33.7	3.3	1.0	25.6	6.9
United Kingdom 1982	29.6	22.1	76.2	9.9	8.4	18.7	13.0
United States 1991	25.9	13.9	69.9	21.5	11.1	59.5	21.2

Source: Smeeding, Danzinger, and Rainwater 1995.

TABLE 8.7

carer, especially for young children. As we've seen (chapter 4), lone mothers of young children are now less active in the paid labour force than are mothers in two-parent families. Eichler concludes that Canada has the right policies for health and primary and secondary education, but needs better provisions for day care, postsecondary education, and family days off. More generally, she argues for the social responsibility model, in which "the public is responsible for the cost of care of adults who cannot care for themselves, and shares the responsibility for the cost of care of dependent children," including "taking over the financial contributions of the unavailable parent" (p.320).

Child support payments

The law has evolved in a way that seeks to ensure that absent parents retain financial responsibility for their children. This approach has included the potential to garnishee wages, even for absent parents in another province. However, the rates of default on child payments remain high. In 1994-95 more than half of the children's parents had settled their custody arrangements out of court (Canadian Council on Social Development 1998: 14). Regular child support payments were being received for three-quarters of out-of-court agreements and half of court-ordered agreements. The state, then, has not been able to impose the "individual responsibility model" on absent parents. In some cases, an absent parent is unemployed or otherwise unable to pay. Given the significant numbers of lone-parenthood cases associated with early parenthood, some of the cases of default can be attributed to general difficulties in the economic integration of young adults.

The provisions in Sweden offer an important contrast. They have managed to significantly reduce levels of poverty for single parents, in spite of comparable rates of separation and divorce. An important element is the advance maintenance provisions wherein payments are set by the state and made directly to the lone parent, with the state subsequently seeking to obtain the child support funds from the absent parent. In addition, joint custody is the default condition; some 80 percent of cases involve joint custody. The payments are also relatively low, at about $215 per month per child in 1997. These can be perceived as fair, corresponding to the effective additional costs sustained by the parent with whom the child is living.

Not only does the Swedish state make the payments directly to the parent, but also the collection is taken only from absent parents who can afford to pay. For instance, absent parents can argue that they should be making only partial payments to the state because a full payment would not allow them to have the housing necessary to accommodate the child at certain times of the year. In effect, the state collects only 70 to 75 percent of the total advance maintenance payments (Kindlund 1997). Absent fathers are paying only 30 to 35 percent of what the state pays to lone mothers, under various provisions.

In Canada, only 21 percent of child custody arrangements established in 1995 involved joint custody, while 68 percent involved mothers and 11 percent fathers with sole custody. In 1996, the federal government initiated child support guidelines. This helps to ensure that child maintenance payments established by the courts follow comparable standards. For instance, with two children, a father with an income of $20,000 would pay $285 per month, and the amount increases to $700 per month for an income of $50,000 (Driedger 1998).

A Parliamentary committee recommended in 1998 that the Divorce Act be changed to replace the concepts of "custody" and "access" with "shared parenting" (McIlroy 1998). This would give absent parents more input and responsibility in how children are raised, but not necessarily change the amount of time spent with each parent. For cases in which parents cannot agree, the committee recommended that parents take a mandatory course on the impact of a bad break-up on children.

Employment of lone mothers

In addition to the method of obtaining payments from absent parents, public attitudes toward the employability of mothers are another important consideration. Baker (1996) contrasts a model in which low-income mothers with young children at home are considered to be employable with one in which governments are willing to use public money to support mothers caring for their children at home. Australia and the Netherlands are examples of countries in which mothers of young children are not considered to be employable, while in Sweden and the United States the orientation is to have mothers in the workforce.

Terrance Hunsley (1997: 81-82) demonstrates the conflicting public attitudes in Canada. The country's policies encourage mothers of young children to work, but the structure of programs offers little incentive to work full-time unless they can make well above the average wage earned by women. Given the limited human capital of lone parents on social assistance, Hunsley does not find it surprising that dependence on social assistance is increasing. In effect, the structure of benefits favours informal work in home production or other forms of activities in the underground economy. He proposes that the country encourage part-time employment, which would provide experience or the opportunity for continued education, plus time for children and less need for subsidized formal child care. In effect, his proposals are similar to the methods built into the Swedish model. Despite the rhetoric in other countries, Hunsley (1997: 98-99) observes that only Sweden and France effectively encourage lone mothers of young children to be employed. In Sweden, the encouragement is to work part-time, while in France it is to work after the child reaches age three. Gordon Cleveland and Douglas Hyatt (1996) observe that high child-care costs are much more likely to discourage lone mothers from participating in the labour force.

Supporting families with lone parents and two parents

While provisions for the employment of young mothers are important, Baker (1996: 486) concludes that family poverty is particularly "influenced by the generosity and scope of government benefits (including the level of cash benefits and tax concessions for families with children), the availability of jobs with statutory protection (such as pay equity, parental benefits, and leave for family responsibilities), the availability and affordability of child care, and the existence of universal social programs such as health insurance and unemployment insurance." These conclusions join those of Kim Clare and Robert Glossup (1993: 213), who argue that the policy challenges regarding economic well-being in lone-parent families "cut across several domains of public policy including family law, income security, education and training, employment and labour, and housing."

Similarly, from his analysis of ten countries, Hunsley (1997: 7) concludes that the "variance in the living standards of lone parents is largely a result of public policy." In particular, the countries such as Canada, United States, Australia, and the United Kingdom that target expenditures toward those in need have higher proportions of poverty among lone parents. Countries with more universal programs, such as Sweden, France, Netherlands, and Germany, have lower levels of poverty among lone-mother families (p.56). Canada, for instance, spends more than other countries on health and education but slightly less than the average on social security (p.37). The countries with lower taxation than Canada are the United States, United Kingdom, and Australia, while the other countries have higher taxation than Canada. Apparently, higher taxation and greater relative spending on social security, in comparison with health and education, particularly benefit lone-parent families.

Hunsley (1997) concludes that countries that have made gains in reducing lone-parent poverty have not focused on reducing poverty but on creating equality and supporting family life through the provisions of family allowance, housing, child care, and child support payments. His suggestions for Canada include improving both child benefits and child support payments, making rent subsidies available to all low-wage earners, supporting lone parents in training and education, and initiating mutual aid and strategic interventions in the area of day care (pp.102-8).

The provisions for lone parents do not mean neglecting the needs of children in two-parent families. Richards (1997a) suggests that social policy should unambiguously provide a fiscal advantage to child-rearing in the context of traditional families. He argues that this is because two-parent families are more successful at raising children, and policy should encourage this alternative. This joins the suggestion made by Paul Amato and Alan Booth (1997) that separating parents undergo counselling regarding the impact of divorce on children, and that couples with children should have incentives to work harder at keeping their marriages together. Anne-Marie Ambert (1989) found that a significant proportion of divorced couples came to regret the decision and that in a third of cases there were no serious grounds for divorce. With important exceptions in cases of abuse, fathers can be useful to their children when they are absent, but even more useful when they are present (Amato 1998). Consequently, policy can help children by discouraging separation.

Given the pressing financial needs of lone-parent families, it is admittedly difficult to follow the Richards (1997a) suggestion of providing a fiscal advantage to child-rearing by two-parent families. Nonetheless, the argument provides an important reminder that policy should first focus on the needs of children, regardless of whether they live with one or both parents. It is particularly important that there be some kind of accepted agreement regarding the involvement of separated parents with their children.

TOWARD NEW FAMILY MODELS FOR A BALANCE OF EARNING AND CARING

A crucial question, then, is the involvement of both men and women in earning and caring, along with the social supports for a more equal division of labour that would overcome the separation between the public and private spheres. For instance, if we look for the reason why women can seldom support themselves and their children outside of marriage, according to Baker (1996: 499), "The answer would lead us back to the gendered division of both paid and unpaid work." The problem may be even more fundamental: it is very difficult for one parent to be completely responsible for *both* earning and caring. Rare are the circumstances, in any society past or present, in which one parent could adequately handle the earning and caring needs of young children. As Eichler (1997) concludes, the "individual responsibility" model is largely not feasible.

Even with more equal opportunity in education and the labour market, if women and men continue to have different options and responsibilities in the family domain, this will continue to affect their economic independence. In Sweden, Nasman (1997) speaks of the mediation between "gender-symmetric public regulations and gender-typed family behaviour." Even in a society that promotes gender equality, when family behaviour remains unequal the opportunity structure of women and men will continue to be differentiated. Still, looking at "The Future of Fatherhood," Scott Coltrane (1995: 273) sees a potential for the "erosion of separate gender spheres within the family as potentially contributing to a fundamental reordering of relationships between men and women throughout society."

These perspectives clearly emphasize the importance of what is happening within families, and their consequences for either maintaining or reducing gender inequality. Other authors suggest that we should start by looking at the role of the broader society. Pupo (1997: 144) proposes that couples may negotiate their own division of unpaid work, "but they do so within the context of cultural assumptions and expectations regarding men's and women's roles and a social structure that may not easily accommodate their desire for change." For instance, Duffy and Pupo (1996) observe that most of women's employment possibilities are in the service sector, with its jobs that tend to have lower pay, fewer benefits, less security, and more part-time hours. This situation in turn leads to the continuation of inequality in the home. If men continue to be the primary breadwinners, patriarchal dynamics inside the home will probably be maintained.

Given more equal opportunities for education and jobs, though, the earning strategies of women and men will be largely based on what is happening within families. In particular, women may lean toward jobs that allow for flexibility in balancing family and work roles. Ultimately, the question as to whether the persistence of gender differences is due to family questions or to the broader society is answerable. Both spheres are the products of complex interactions.

There is a long way to go before men and women will be equal in families, but as Pamomba (1995: 195) puts it, "The state must stop seeing men and women as vastly different in terms of roles within the couple and the family." The state must not only encourage women's economic roles but also encourage men to find more of their identities in a fatherhood based on companionship rather than authority. To achieve this goal, the restructuring of the paid workplace is not sufficient. Already, opportunities in the workplace are being pushed in a gender-symmetric direction, mainly through equal opportunity legislation. The emphasis must instead be on creating a greater symmetry in the private domain.

My own policy suggestions would, therefore, emphasize a reduction in the division of labour within the home as a primary factor, along with encouraging further efforts to establish equal opportunity in the broader society. This approach is also in line with the Swedish experience that involved a "concerted effort by government, organized labor and other institutions to distribute the burden of parenting between men and women, and to facilitate the employment of all adults, including those caring for infants and children" (Moen 1989: 5). The Swedish approach, as we've seen, has involved various provisions, including the requirement that one parent take no more than 11 of the 12 months of leave. There are other explicit attempts to reduce spousal dependency, such as no provisions for pension splitting and, for couples who married after 1989, no widow's pensions. Those solutions still have their problems. While men's involvement in parental leaves has increased, there are reported cases in which a man's parenthood is not declared so that the mother can take the full 12 months. Also, while either parent can reduce time at work to 30 hours per week until a child is eight years old, it is overwhelmingly women who opt for these alternatives. Consequently, the gender differences in Swedish society are persistent. For instance, the gender division of part-time work is even more unequal than in Canada, and occupational segregation is probably higher.

Instead of seeking a better distribution of the burden of parenting between men and women, some analysts propose that the state should be more actively involved in the facilitation of child care. Addressing the policy needs to overcome the separation between public and private spheres, Pupo (1997: 151) starts with the priority of high-quality, accessible child care and also suggests improved respite and health-care programs, along with family-friendly workplace policies. While this approach would relieve women's burden, it does not necessarily increase men's involvement. For instance, couples who look after more of the child care themselves may be forced to involve fathers to a larger extent than if child care were to become a public responsibility.

To encourage co-parenting in two-parent situations, policy could establish *equal parental leave*. For instance, parental leave could be increased from six months to one year, with the requirement that neither parent may take more than 26 weeks. There is nothing magical about the current time frame of 15 weeks of maternal and 10 weeks of parental leave. There is no specific threshold associated with a child's 26th week—indeed, many infants are still not sleeping through the night by that age. When they have very young children, many parents consider it best to take prime responsibility for child care, which also necessitates a longer period of leave.

For similar reasons, policy could also allow for another two years in which one parent could *work part-time*—for instance, six hours per day—but again a given parent could only take one of the two years. The greater flexibility in parental time could be complemented with *community-based child care* involving volunteers, parent fees, and state subsidies. In effect, many parents of children under three currently arrange these combinations of part-time work, shift work, and parental care, along with some day care or informal care. As parents know very well, having children will always carry an opportunity cost. Adults who cannot shoulder some of these costs should not be having children. But essentially, each parent would have the right to reduce work hours for one year and return to full-time work after the child is three. In addition, part-time work amounting to 30 or more hours a week should be subject to the same benefits, pro-rated, as full-time work. This proposition is taken from the Swedish experience, in which one parent has the right to reduce work hours to six hours per day until the child is eight years old and to return to full-time work at any point.

When the child is age three, public nursery schools, kindergarten, or day care should become available, as in France. In effect, the Ontario Royal Commission on Learning (1994) proposed that children should start school as of age three. Their research convinced the Commission that this was the optimal arrangement from the point of view of the child's educational welfare. The approach is also in keeping with Johnson and Mathien's (1998) proposal for an integrated system of care and school for children aged four and five. It is also similar to a program proposed by Gordon Cleveland and Michael Krashinsky (1998) for children aged two to five, with full-time and part-time nursery schools and kindergartens.

While a public system that starts at age three necessitates more parental leave and part-time work, it reduces the child-care costs. The federal cost of a full system of child-care centres for all preschoolers would be in excess of $8 billion (Kent 1999). Parents who want to return to full-time work more quickly could use their higher income to pay for the costs of child care. The proposition is also based on a view that is prevalent among parents: that they would like to be primarily responsible for the care of young children, especially as babies and toddlers. Nonetheless, the country does need to enhance its budgets for child-care centres and for subsidizing the child-care costs of low-income parents.

In one-parent situations, policy should take as a first priority the establishment of *joint custody* as a default condition, except in cases in which one of the parents is incapable of looking after or is harmful to the child. Separated parents could still have the possibility of sharing leave time and part-time work, and consequently of being equally involved with their children. Alternatively, the parent with whom the child is residing could take all the leaves and part-time work. More important, *advance maintenance payments* would ensure that if a parent is not making the child support payments, the moneys would still flow to the lone parent. While provisions vary, some 12 European countries already have systems of advance maintenance payments (Hunsley 1997: 100), and Sweden uses the default condition of joint custody.

As for *child benefits*, Canada already has it about right. While the payments could clearly be higher, a system operating through taxes permits redistribution toward those with lower income and a type of guaranteed annual income for children. It is important that government seeks to have all social assistance to children operate through this system so that persons on low income receive the payments, regardless of the source of income, whether it is low wages or social assistance. There would then no longer be an incentive to remain on welfare just to have access to welfare provisions for children. To have all social assistance to children operate through the child tax benefit, the country would need to raise the benefit to $2,500 per child (Battle 1997c). There are already some plans in this direction: the total budget, which was $5.1 billion in 1997, was raised by $850 million in 1998 and by another $425 million in each of 1999 and 2000.

The child tax benefit has another advantage: it is easy to add funds and change the benefit levels. Battle (1997c) suggests that we aim at $4,000 per child by the year 2010 or sooner, to cover a low estimate of the cost of children. Still, although this approach would reduce the depth of poverty in poor families, it would not eliminate child poverty. To move all children above the low-income line would probably cost in excess of $15 billion, in addition to the $6 billion of current expenditures.

Once the level of $2,500 per child is reached, an alternative might be to use a slower sliding scale so that a less rapid reduction in benefits occurs at family incomes above $30,000. That way, taxpayers would not see the program as benefiting mostly low-income families, and lone-parent families in particular. This approach might even increase the willingness of middle-class families to pay the taxes for a system that brings them some benefit. At least for symbolic reasons, and also to provide some redistribution between those with and without children, some minimal payments at higher incomes would indicate the support of society to families with children. Most European countries have some form of family allowance, which is normally subject to taxation, as a means of supporting some of the costs of children, regardless of the income level of the family. Such payments help to equalize the standards of living of families with and without children. Nonetheless, especially for reasons of cost, the structure of the benefit should retain a sliding scale that works to the advantage of families with the lowest income.

Other *social benefits* should be tied less to work and more to basic citizenship in a welfare state. As others have argued, a universal program such as guaranteed annual income would permit greater efficiency in the delivery of benefits (Royal Commission on the Economic Union 1985; Beaujot 1991; Courchene 1994; Woolley 1998). In addition, such a universal system would remove the vestiges of the family wage model wherein dependants gain access to benefits through their family connection to an employed person. In effect, the income-tested guaranteed annual income that now exists for the elderly and for children would be extended to the adult population, regardless of the reason for lack of self-sufficiency. The difficulty with this particular proposition is that some categories of persons now receive considerably higher benefits than would be received under a guaranteed annual income system. Existing systems provide greater benefits for the elderly, for persons benefiting from the disability provisions of the Canada Pension Plan, and for those benefiting from unemployment insurance. Adults who cannot work, but who also cannot benefit from these particular plans, have much lower benefits. Equalizing the benefits would thus include some savings. However, this change would need to come slowly, so as not to suddenly disadvantage certain categories of recipients.

In all advanced industrial societies, gender differences have declined significantly in terms of education and opportunities in the labour force. These societies differ in the extent to which family models have evolved in a similar direction. In effect, fertility appears to be lowest in the industrial societies where the public sector operates under conditions of gender equity but where patriarchal dynamics apply to families (Chesnais 1996; McDonald 1997). Provisions like those discussed here would help achieve gender equity in families by viewing parents as *co-providers* and *co-parents*. State support for child benefits, for other basic social benefits, for sharing parental leaves, and education as of age three would undermine gender differences in families, and consequently in the broader society. In particular, it would undermine the potential for the exploitation of one spouse by another based on the inequality in earning capacities generated by family responsibilities.

The evolution of social policy seems to be facing two main roadblocks. One is the pressure for globalization, which is often interpreted as meaning a limited amount of space for a policy independent of the U.S. model. While we cannot ignore the economic context of globalization, instead of a "race to the bottom" in social policy we should be able to move our policies in the direction of the European provisions, encouraging societal support for families and the economic independence of adults. As Ursel (1992: 302) argues, the pressures of globalization need not mean a move to reprivatize the costs of reproduction.

The other major constraint on the discussions of family and social policy involves our disagreement regarding the relative roles of the provinces and the national government. Quebec has taken a much more pro-active stance in the family area, as one of the means through which it can take control of its future as a distinct society. Consequently other discussions, particularly those spanning the interests of the provinces, face the additional difficulty of federal-provincial agreement and disagreement. Following the establishment of block funding through the Canada Health and Social Transfer, interprovincial understandings were to evolve with regard to health, education, and welfare (Courchene 1994, 1995). In February 1999, all provinces but Quebec signed a social union understanding regarding national standards, opting-out provisions, and the roles of federal and provincial governments. If this asymmetry is accepted, it may allow Quebec to maintain more provincial control over social programs, and a social union of the rest of Canada with continuing federal roles to ensure national standards.

These dimensions of family policy consequently have extensive ramifications. They not only determine how we define ourselves as a society, including its opportunity structures for women and men, but also how we relate to other societies, both next door and in a globalizing world.

references

Achilles, Rona. 1986. "The Social Implications of Artificial Reproductive Technologies." Ottawa: Report for Review of Demography, Health and Welfare.

Adams, Owen B. 1988. "Divorce in Canada." *Canadian Social Trends* 11: 18-19.

Adams, Owen B. and D.N. Nagnur. 1988. *Marriage, Divorce and Mortality*. Ottawa: Statistics Canada, cat. no. 84-536.

Akyeampong, Ernest. 1993. "Flexible Work Arrangements." *Perspectives on Labour and Income* 5,3: 17-22.

— 1997. "Work Arrangements: 1995 Overview." *Perspectives on Labour and Income* 9,1: 48-52.

— 1998. "Work Absences: New Data, New Insights." *Perspectives on Labour and Income* 10,1: 16-22.

Albrecht, James W., Per-Anders Edin, Marianne Sundstrom, and Susan Vroman. 1997. "Career Interruptions and Subsequent Earnings: A Re-examination Using Swedish Data." Stockholm University: Research Reports in Demography, no. 111.

Alder, George. 1992. "Theories of Fertility Decline: A Non-Specialist's Guide to the Current Debate." In John R. Gillis, Louise A. Tilly, and David Levine, eds., *The European Experience of Fertility Decline, 1850-1970*. Cambridge: Blackwell.

Allahar, Anton and James Côté. 1998. *Richer and Poorer: The Structure of Inequality in Canada*. Toronto: Lorimer.

Amato, Paul R. 1998. "More than Money? Men's Contributions to Their Children's Lives." In A. Booth and A.C. Crouter, eds., *Men in Families: When Do They Get Involved? What Difference Does It Make?* Mahwah, N.J.: Lawrence Erlbaum.

Amato, Paul R. and Alan Booth. 1997. *A Generation at Risk: Growing up in an Era of Family Upheaval*. Cambridge, Mass.: Harvard University Press.

Ambert, Anne-Marie. 1989. *Ex-Spouses and New Spouses: A Study of Relationships*. Greenwich, Conn.: JAI Press.

— 1992. *The Effect of Children on Parents*. New York: Harworth Press.

Ambert, Anne-Marie and Maureen Baker. 1988. "Marriage Dissolution." In B. Fox, ed., *Family Bonds and Gender Divisions*. Toronto: Canadian Scholar's Press.

Anderson, David. 1997. "Men, Reproduction and Fertility." *Policy and Research Papers*, no. 12. Liège, Belgium: International Union for the Scientific Study of Population.

Andersson, Gunnar. 1996. "The Impact of Children on Divorce Risks of Swedish Women." Stockholm Research Reports in Demography, no. 102.

Arber, Sara and Jay Ginn. 1995. "The Mirage of Gender Equality: Occupational Success in the Labour Market and within Marriage." *British Journal of Sociology* 46,1: 21-43.

Ariès, Philippe. 1962. *Centuries of Childhood*. New York: Knopf.

— 1980. "Two Successive Motivations for the Declining Birth Rate in the West." *Population and Development Review* 6,4: 645-50.

Armstrong, Jane. 1998. "Home Alone: How a Toddler Ended Up on the Street at 2:00 A.M." *The Globe and Mail* 10 August 1998: A1, A5.

Armstrong, Pat and Hugh Armstrong. 1990. *Theorizing Women's Work*. Toronto: Garamond Press.

— 1994. *The Double Ghetto: Canadian Women and Their Segregated Work*. Toronto: McClelland and Stewart.

Arthur, W. Brian. 1988. "Intergenerational Relations." In R. Lee, ed., *Economics of Changing Age Distributions in Developed Countries*. Oxford: Clarendon Press.

Atkinson, T. 1980. "Public Perceptions on the Quality of Life." In *Perspectives Canada III*. Ottawa: Statistics Canada, cat. no. 11-511.

Avison, William and Terrance Wade. 1995. "Marital Transitions and Distress among Women: A Longitudinal Analysis." Presentation, Society for the Study of Social Problems Meetings, Washington, D.C., August 1995.

Axinn, William, Jennifer Barber, and Arland Thornton. 1998. "The Long-Term Impact of Parent's Childbearing Decisions on Children's Self-Esteem." *Demography* 35,4: 435-43.

Baines, Carol, Patricia Evans, and Sheila Neysmith. 1991. *Women's Caring: Feminist Perspectives on Social Welfare*. Toronto: McClelland and Stewart.

Baker, Maureen. 1991. "A Sociological Perspective on Child Care Research." In I. Kyle, Martha Friendly, and Lori Schmidt, eds., *Proceedings from the Child Care Policy and Research Symposium*. Toronto: University of Toronto Press.

— 1995a. *Canadian Family Policies: Cross-National Comparisons*. Toronto: University of Toronto Press.

— 1995b. "Eliminating Child Poverty: How Does Canada Compare?" *American Review of Canadian Studies* 25,1: 79-110.

— 1996. "Social Assistance and the Employability of Mothers: Two Models from Cross-National Research." *Canadian Journal of Sociology* 21,4: 483-503.

— 1997. "Parental Benefit Policies and the Gendered Division of Labour." *Social Service Review* 71,1: 51-74.

Baker, Maureen and Shelley Phipps. 1997. "Family Change and Family Policies: Canada." In S.B. Kamerman and A.J. Kahn, eds., *Family Change and Family Policies in Great Britain, Canada, New Zealand, and the United States.* Oxford: Clarendon Press.

Balakrishnan, T.R. 1987. "Therapeutic Abortions in Canada and Their Impact on Fertility." In *Contributions to Demography.* Edmonton: Population Research Laboratory.

— 1989. "Changing Nuptiality Patterns and Their Fertility Implications in Canada." In J. Légaré, T.R. Balakrishnan, and R. Beaujot, eds., *The Family in Crisis: A Population Crisis?* Ottawa: Royal Society of Canada.

Balakrishnan, T.R. and Jiajian Chen. 1990. "Religiosity, Nuptiality and Reproduction in Canada." *Canadian Review of Sociology and Anthropology* 27,3: 316-40.

Balakrishnan, T.R. and Carl Grindstaff. 1988. "Early Adulthood Behaviour and Later Life Course Paths." Ottawa: Report for Review of Demography, Health and Welfare.

Balakrishnan, T.R., K.J. Krotki, and E. Lapierre-Adamcyk. 1985. "Contraceptive Use in Canada, 1984." *Family Planning Perspectives* 17,5: 209-15.

Balakrishnan, T.R., Evelyne Lapierre-Adamcyk, and Karol J. Krotki. 1993. *Family and Childbearing in Canada.* Toronto: University of Toronto Press.

Balakrishnan, T.R., K. Vaninadha Rao, Karol J. Krotki, and Evelyne Lapierre-Adamcyk. 1988. "Age at First Birth and Lifetime Fertility." *Journal of Biosocial Science* 20: 167-74.

Barrère-Maurisson, Marie-Agnès. 1995. "Régulation familiale, marchande ou politique: les variations de la relation travail-famille." *Sociologie et Sociétés* 27,2: 69-85.

Basset, Penny. 1994. "Declining Female Labour Force Participation." *Perspectives on Labour and Income* 6,2: 36-39.

Battle, Ken. 1997a. "The 1997 Budget's Child Benefits Package." Ottawa: Caledon Institute of Social Policy.

— 1997b. "National Child Benefit: Renewing the Federation through Social Policy Reform." *Policy Options* 18, 1: 46-49.

— 1997c. "The National Child Benefit: Best Thing since Medicare or New Poor Law?" Ottawa: Caledon Institute of Social Policy.

— 1998. "No Taxation without Indexation." Ottawa: Caledon Institute of Social Policy.

Battle, Ken and Leon Muszynski. 1995. "One Way to Fight Child Poverty." Ottawa: Caledon Institute of Social Policy.

Battle, Ken and Michael Mendelson. 1997. "Child Benefit Reform in Canada: An Evaluative Framework and Future Directions." Ottawa: Caledon Institute of Social Policy.

Battle, Ken and Sherri Torjman. 1994. "Opening the Books on Social Spending." *Perception* 17,4: 12-16.

Beach, C.M. and G.A. Slotsve. 1996. *Are We Becoming Two Societies? Income Polarization and the Myth of the Declining Middle Class in Canada.* Toronto: C.D. Howe Institute.

Beaudry, Paul and David Green. 1997. "Cohort Patterns in Canadian Earnings." Toronto: Canadian Institute for Advanced Research Working Paper, no. 96.

Beaujot, Roderic. 1986. "Dwindling Families." *Policy Options* 7,7: 3-7.

— 1988. "Attitudes among Tunisians toward Family Formation." *International Family Planning Perspectives* 14,2: 54-61.

— 1991. *Population Change in Canada: The Challenges of Policy Adaptation.* Toronto: Oxford.

— 1992. "Rationales Used in Marriage and Childbearing Decisions." *The Peopling of the Americas*. Proceedings of International Union for the Scientific Study of Population Conference, Veracruz, 1992, vol. II: 137-54.

— 1995. "Family Patterns at Mid-Life (Marriage, Parenting and Working)." In R. Beaujot, Ellen M. Gee, Fernando Rajulton, and Zenaida Ravanera, *Family over the Life Course*. Ottawa: Statistics Canada, cat. no. 91-543.

— 1997. "Parental Preferences for Work and Child Care." *Canadian Public Policy* 23,3: 275-88.

— 1998. "Families." In J.J. Teevan and W.E. Hewitt, *Introduction to Sociology: A Canadian Focus*. Toronto: Prentice Hall.

Beaujot, Roderic and Elisabeth Beaujot. 1991. "Social and Economic Effects of Changing Family Patterns: The Case of Child Care." Ottawa: Report for Review of Demography and Its Implications for Economic and Social Policy, Health and Welfare Canada.

Beaujot, Roderic and Tony Haddad. 1999. "Productivity Patterns at Mid-Life: Family and Work." *Canadian Studies in Population* 26,2: forthcoming.

Beaujot, Roderic and Judy-Lynn Richards. 1997. "Intergenerational Equity in Reforming the CPP." *Policy Options* 17,9: 45-48.

Beaujot, Roderic and Kevin McQuillan. 1982. *Growth and Dualism: The Demographic Development of Canadian Society*. Toronto: Gage.

Beaujot, Roderic, Ellen Gee, Fernando Rajulton, and Zenaida R. Ravanera. 1995. *Family Over the Life Course*. Ottawa: Statistics Canada.

Beaulieu, Denise. 1998. "Discussion to Plenary on Capacity Development for Partnership." Hull: Fifth Canadian Conference on International Health, 15-18 November 1998.

Becker, Gary S. 1965. "A Theory of the Allocation of Time." *Economic Journal* 75: 484-517.

— 1981. *A Treatise on the Family*. Cambridge, Mass.: Harvard University Press.

Bélanger, Alain and Daniel Larrivée. 1992. "New Approach for Constructing Canadian Working Life Tables, 1986-1987." *Statistical Journal of the United Nations ECE* 9: 27-49.

Bélanger, Alain and Jean Dumas. 1998. *Report on the Demographic Situation in Canada 1997*. Ottawa: Statistics Canada, cat. no. 91-209.

Bélanger, Danièle. 1992. "Fécondité et politiques familiales en Scandinavie depuis 1960." Etudes et Analyses, Québec: Secrétariat à la famille.

Belkhodja, Alya. 1992. "Staying Put: Job Tenure and Paid Workers." *Perspectives on Labour and Income* 4,4: 20-26.

Bellamy, Lesley and Neil Guppy. 1991. "Opportunities and Obstacles for Women in Canadian Higher Education." In J. Gaskell and A. McLaren, eds., *Women in Education*. Calgary: Detselig.

Belle, Marilyn and Kevin McQuillan. 1994. "Births outside of Marriage." *Canadian Social Trends* 33: 14-17.

Berk, Sarah Fenstermaker. 1985. *The Gender Factory: The Apportionment of Work in American Households*. New York: Plenum.

Bernard, Paul, Douglas Bear, Johanne Boisjoly, James Curtis, and Maryanne Webber. 1996. "How Canada Works: Changes in the Makeup of the Labour Force in the 1970s and 1980s." Presentation, Canadian Population Society Meetings, St. Catherines, June 1996.

Bernhardt, Eva. 1987. "Labour Force Participation and Childbearing." Stockholm Research Reports in Demography, no. 41.

— 1988. "Changing Family Ties, Women's Position and Low Fertility." Stockholm Research Reports in Demography, no. 46.

— 1989. "Fertility and Employment." Stockholm Research Reports in Demography, no. 55.

— 1991. "Working Parents in Sweden: An Example for Europe?" In *Human Resources in Europe at the Dawn of the 21st Century*. Luxembourg: Eurostat Conference.

— 1993. "Fertility and Employment." *European Sociological Review* 9,1: 25-41.

Bernier, Christiane, Simon Laflamme, and Run-Min Zhou. 1996. "Le travail domestique: tendances à la désexisation et à la complexifaction." *Canadian Review of Sociology and Anthropology* 33,1: 1-21.

Best, Pamela. 1995. "Men, Women and Work." *Canadian Social Trends* 36: 30-33.

Betcherman, Gordon and Graham S. Lowe. 1997. *The Future of Work in Canada*. Ottawa: Renouf.

Betcherman, Gordon and René Morissette. 1994. "Recent Youth Labour Market Experiences in Canada." Statistics Canada: Analytic Studies Research Paper Series, no. 63.

Bianchi, Suzanne and Daphne Spain. 1996. "Women, Work and Family in America." *Population Bulletin* 51,3: 1-48.

Bibby, Reginald. 1995. *The Bibby Report: Social Trends Canadian Style*. Toronto: Stoddart.

Bibby, Reginald and D.C. Posterski. 1985. *The Emerging Generation*. Toronto: Irving Publishing.

Binder, Sarah. 1998. "Homosexual Couple Seek to Be Legally Married." *Globe and Mail* 15 September 1998: A7.

Blair, Sampson Lee and Daniel T. Lechter. 1991. "Measuring the Division of Household Labour." *Journal of Family Issues* 12,1: 91-113.

Blanchflower, David and Richard Freeman. 1998. "Why Youth Unemployment Will Be Hard to Reduce." *Policy Options* 19,3: 3-7.

Blood, Robert and Donald M. Wolfe. 1960. *Husbands and Wives: The Dynamics of Married Living*. Glencoe, IPP.: Free Press.

Bloss, Thierry, Alain Frickey, and Michel Novi. 1994. "Modes d'entrée dans la vie adulte et trajectoires sociales des femmes mariées." *Population* 49,3: 637-56.

Blumstein, P. and P. Schwartz. 1983. *American Couples: Money, Work and Sex.* New York: William Morrow and Co.

Boily, Nicole. 1987. "Dénatalité, immigration et politique familiale: la point de vue des femmes." Presentation, Association des Démographes du Québec Meetings, Ottawa, May 1987.

Bonvalet, Catherine and Eva Lelièvre. 1995. "Du concept de ménage à celui d'entourage." *Sociologie et Sociétés* 27,2: 177-90.

Booth, Alan and Ann C. Crouter. 1998. *Men in Families: When Do They Get Involved? What Difference Does It Make?* Mahwah, N.J.: Lawrence Erlbaum.

Boroditsky, Richard, William Fisher, and Michael Sand. 1996. "The 1995 Canadian Contraception Study." *Journal SOGC* December 1996: 1-31.

Boswell, John. 1988. *The Kindness of Strangers: The Abandonment of Children in Western Europe from Late Antiquity to the Renaissance.* New York: Pantheon.

Bourbeau, Robert and Jacques Légaré. 1982. *Evolution de la mortalité au Canada et au Québec, 1831-1931.* Montreal: Presses de l'Université de Montréal.

Boutilier, Marie. 1977. "Transformation of Ideology Surrounding the Sexual Division of Labour: Canadian Women during World War Two." Presentation, Second Conference on Blue-Collar Workers, London, Ont., May 1977.

Boyd, Monica. 1984. *Canadian Attitudes towards Women: Thirty Years of Change.* Ottawa: Supply and Services.

— 1997. "Feminizing Paid Work." *Current Sociology* 45,2: 49-73.

Boyd, Monica and Doug Norris. 1995. "Leaving the Nest? Impact of Family Structure." *Canadian Social Trends* 38: 14-17.

— 1998. "Changes in the Nest: Young Canadian Adults Living with Parents, 1981-1996." Presentation, Canadian Population Society Meetings, Ottawa, June 1998.

Bracher, Michael and Gigi Santow. 1998. "Economic Independence and Union Formation in Sweden." *Demography* 52,3: 275-94.

Bradshaw, Jonathan. 1997. "Le partage du coût de l'enfant." *Futuribles* 224: 69-83.

Brayfield, April. 1992. "Employment Resources and Housework in Canada." *Journal of Marriage and the Family* 54,1: 19-30.

Brigham, John. 1986. *Social Psychology.* Boston: Little, Brown and Company.

Brines, Julie. 1994. "Economic Dependency, Gender and the Division of Labor at Home." *American Journal of Sociology* 100,3: 652-88.

— 1995. "Review of Familiar Exploitation: A New Analysis of Marriage in Contemporary Western Societies." *Contemporary Sociology* 24,2: 237-38.

Broderick, Carlfred. 1979. *Marriage and the Family.* Englewood Cliffs, N.J.: Prentice-Hall.

Brook, Paula. 1997. "Every Mother Is a Working Mother." *The Globe and Mail* 25 October 1997: D1, D3.

Brooks, Stephen. 1993. *Public Policy in Canada: An Introduction*. Toronto: McClelland and Stewart.

Brouillette, Liliane, Claude Felteau, Pierre Lefebvre, and Alain Pelletier. 1990. "L'évolution de la situation économique des familles avec enfants au Canada et au Québec depuis 15 ans." *Cahiers Québécois de Démographie* 19,2: 241-71.

— 1991. "Les familles sans enfants ou avec enfants: aisance ou pauvreté?" *L'Actualité économique* 67,1: 80-102.

Bumpass, Larry L. 1991. "What's Happening to the Family? Interactions between Demographic and Institutional Change." *Demography* 27: 913-27.

— 1993. "Review of New Families, No Families?" *Population and Development Review* 19,1: 193-98.

— 1994. "L'enfant et les transformations du milieu familial aux Etats-Unis." *Cahier Québécois de Démographie* 23,1: 27-52.

Bumpass, Larry L. and James A. Sweet. 1995. "Cohabitation, Marriage and Union Stability: Contemporary Findings from NSFH2." University of Wisconsin: NSFH Working Paper, no. 65.

Bunge, Valerie Pottie and Andrea Levett. 1998. *Family Violence in Canada: A Statistical Profile, 1998*. Ottawa: Statistics Canada, cat. no. 85-224.

Burch, Thomas K. 1985. *Family History Survey: Preliminary Findings*. Ottawa: Statistics Canada, cat. no. 99-955.

— 1990. *Families in Canada*. Ottawa: Statistics Canada, cat. no. 98-127.

Burch, Thomas K. and Ashok Madan. 1986. *Union Formation and Dissolution*. Ottawa: Statistics Canada, cat. no. 99-963.

Burgess, E.W., H. Locke, and M. Thomas. 1963. *The Family: From Institution to Companionship*. New York: American.

Burggaf, Shirley. 1997. *The Feminine Economy and Economic Man: Revising the Role of Family in the Post-Industrial Age*. Reading, Mass.: Addison-Wesley.

Burke, M.A. and S. Crompton. 1991. "Caring for Children." *Canadian Social Trends* 22: 12-15.

Calastanti, Toni and Carol Bailey. 1991. "Gender Inequality and the Division of Household Labour in the United States and Sweden: A Socialist-Feminist Approach." *Social Problems* 38,1: 34-53.

Caldwell, John C. 1976. "Toward a Restatement of Demographic Transition Theory." *Population and Development Review* 2,3-4: 321-66.

— 1997. "The Global Fertility Transition: The Need for a Unifying Theory." *Population and Development Review* 23,4: 803-12.

Calot, Gérard. 1990. "La politique démographique d'autres pays." In R. Beaujot, ed., *Faire Face au Changement Démographique*. Ottawa: Royal Society of Canada.

Calzavara, Liviana. 1988. "Trends and Policy in Employment Opportunities for Women." In J. Curtis, E. Grabb, N. Guppy, and S. Gilbert, eds., *Social Inequality in Canada: Patterns, Problems, Policies*. Scarborough, Ont.: Prentice-Hall.

Canadian Council on Social Development. 1996. *The Progress of Canada's Children 1996.* Ottawa: Canadian Council on Social Development.

— 1997. *The Progress of Canada's Children 1997.* Ottawa: Canadian Council on Social Development.

— 1998. *The Progress of Canada's Children 1998.* Ottawa: Canadian Council on Social Development.

Canadian Social Trends. 1996. "Canadian Children in the 1990s." *Canadian Social Trends* 44: 2-9.

CARNET. 1993. "Work and Family: The Survey." CARNET: Canadian Aging Research Network.

Carrier, Patricia Jane. 1995. "The Division of Household Labour among Dual-Earner Couples." M.A. thesis, University of Western Ontario, London, Ont.

Cassidy, Gale. 1997. "Gender Differences in Perceived Control over Life." M.A. thesis, University of Western Ontario, London, Ont.

Chafetz, Janet Saltzman and Jacqueline Hagan. 1996. "The Gender Division of Labour and Family Change in Industrial Societies." *Journal of Comparative Family Studies* 27,2: 187-219.

Charette, Dan. 1995. "Hours of Working Couples." *Perspectives on Labour and Income* 7,2: 9-11.

Charles, Enid. 1936. *The Menace of Under-Population.* London: Watts.

Chaula, Raj K. 1992. "The Changing Profile of Dual-Earner Families." *Perspectives on Labour and Income* 4,2: 22-29.

Che-Alford, Janet, Catherine Allan, and George Butlin. 1994. *Families in Canada.* Statistics Canada, cat. no. 96-307.

Cheal, David. 1996. "Stories about Step-Families." In *Growing Up in Canada.* Statistics Canada, cat. no. 89-550, no. 1.

— 1997. "Hidden in the Household: Poverty and Dependence at Different Ages." Presentation, Intergenerational Equity in Canada Conference, Ottawa, February 1997.

Cherlin, Andrew. 1992. *Marriage, Divorce, Remarriage.* Cambridge, Mass.: Harvard University Press.

— 1998. "On the Flexibility of Fatherhood." In A. Booth and A.C. Crouter, eds., *Men in Families: When Do They Get Involved? What Difference Does It Make?* Mahwah, N.J.: Lawrence Erlbaum.

Cherlin, Andrew and Frank Furstenberg. 1994. "Step-Families in the United States: A Reconsideration." *Annual Review of Sociology* 20: 359-81.

Cherlin, Andrew, P. Lindsay Chase-Landale, and Christine McRae. 1997. "Effects of Divorce on Mental Health through the Life Course." *American Sociological Review* 63,2: 239-49.

Chesnais, Jean-Claude. 1987. "Population Trends in the European Community 1968-1986." *European Journal of Population* 3,3-4: 281-96.

— 1996. "Fertility, Family and Social Policy in Contemporary Western Europe." *Population and Development Review* 22,4: 729-39.

Child Care Human Resources Steering Committee. 1998. "Our Child Care Workforce: From Recognition to Remuneration." Ottawa.

Clare, Kim and Robert Glossop. 1993. "Canadian Public Policy Impacts." In J. Hudson and B. Galaway, eds., *Single Parent Families*. Toronto: Thompson.

Clark, S. and A. Harvey. 1976. "The Sexual Division of Labour: The Use of Time." *Atlantis* 2,1: 46-66.

Clark, Warren. 1997. "School Leavers Revisited." *Canadian Social Trends* 44: 10-12.

Cleveland, Gordon and Douglas Hyatt. 1991. "The Effect of Price on the Choice of Child Care Arrangements." In I. Kyle, Martha Friendly, and Lori Schmidt, eds., *Proceedings from the Child Care Policy and Research Symposium*, University of Toronto.

— 1996. "Child Care, Social Assistance and Work: Lone Mothers with Pre-School Children." Human Resources Development Canada: Applied Research Working Papers W-96-2E.

Cleveland, Gordon and Michael Krashinsky. 1998. "The Benefits and Costs of Good Child Care." Toronto: University of Toronto at Scarborough.

Coale, Ansley J. 1973. "The Demographic Transition." In *International Population Conference*. Liège: International Union for the Scientific Study of Population.

Cohen, Gary L. 1993. "Paid Overtime." *Perspectives on Labour and Income* 5,3: 11-16.

Coish, David and Alison Hale. 1995. "The Wage Gap between Men and Women: An Update." Statistics Canada: SLID Research Paper Series, no. 95-14.

Coleman, James S. 1988. "Social Capital in the Creation of Human Capital." *American Journal of Sociology* 94: S95-S120.

Coltrane, Scott, 1995. "The Future of Fatherhood." In William Marsiglio, ed., *Fatherhood*. Thousand Oaks, Cal.: Sage.

— 1996. *Family Men: Fatherhood, Housework and Gender Equality*. New York: Oxford.

— 1998a. "Gender, Power, and Emotional Expression: Social and Historical Contexts for a Process Model of Men in Marriages and Families." In A. Booth and A. C. Crouter, eds., *Men in Families: When Do They Get Involved? What Difference Does It Make?* Mahwah, N.J.: Lawrence Erlbaum.

— 1998b. *Gender and Families*. Thousand Oaks, Cal.: Pine Forge Press.

Connelly, M. Patricia and Martha MacDonald. 1990. *Women in the Labour Force*. Ottawa: Statistics Canada, cat. no. 98-125.

Connelly, Rachel. 1992. "Self-Employment and Providing Child Care." *Demography* 29,1: 17-29.

Connidis, Ingrid. 1989. "Contact between Siblings in Later Life." *Canadian Journal of Sociology* 14,4: 429-42.

Connor, Sarak and Lynn McIntyre. 1998. "How Tobacco and Alcohol Affect Newborn Children" Presentation, Investing in Children Conference, Ottawa, October 1998.

Conway, John F. 1997. *The Canadian Family in Crisis*. Toronto: James Lorimer.

Cook, Cynthia and Roderic Beaujot. 1996. "Labour Force Interruptions: The Influence of Marital Status and Presence of Young Children." *Canadian Journal of Sociology* 21,1: 25-41.

Cooksey, Elisabeth and Michelle Fondell. 1996. "Spending Time with the Kids: Effects of Family Structure on Father's and Children's Lives." *Journal of Marriage and the Family* 58,3: 693-707.

Corak, Miles and Andrew Heisz. 1998. "How to Get Ahead in Life: Some Correlates of Intergenerational Income Mobility in Canada." In M. Corak, ed., *Labour Markets, Social Institutions and the Future of Canada's Children*. Ottawa: Statistics Canada, cat. no. 89-553.

Cordell, Denis, Danielle Gauvreau, Raymond R. Gervais, and Céline Le Bourdais. 1993. *Population, Reproduction, Sociétés*. Montreal: Presses de l'Université de Montréal.

Côté, James E. and Anton L. Allahar. 1994. *Generation on Hold: Coming of Age in the Late Twentieth Century*. Toronto: Stoddart.

Courchene, Thomas J. 1994. *Social Canada in the Millennium*. Ottawa: C.D. Howe.

— 1995. *Redistributing Money and Power: A Guide to the Canada Health and Social Transfer*. Ottawa: C.D. Howe.

Coverman, Shelley. 1985. "Explaining Husbands' Participation in Domestic Labor." *The Sociological Quarterly* 26: 81-97.

Cranswick, Kelly. 1997. "Canada's Caregivers." *Canadian Social Trends* 47: 2-6.

Crompton, Rosemary and Fiona Harris. 1998. "Explaining Women's Employment Patterns: Orientation to Work Revisited." *British Journal of Sociology* 49,1: 118-36.

Crompton, Susan. 1994. "Left behind: Lone Mothers in the Labour Market." *Perspectives on Labour and Income* 6,2: 23-28.

— 1995. "Employment Prospects for High School Graduates." *Perspectives on Labour and Income* 7,3: 8-13.

— 1996. "Transfer Payments to Families with Children." *Perspectives on Labour and Income* 8,3: 42-48.

Crompton, Susan and Leslie Geran. 1995. "Women as Main Breadwinners." *Perspectives on Labour and Income* 7,4: 26-29.

Crouch, Mirn and Lenore Manderson. 1993. *New Motherhood*. Newark, N.J.: Gordon and Breach Science Publishers.

Crowley, Brian Lee. 1998. "Review of J. Richards, Retooling the Welfare State." *The Globe and Mail* 14 February 1998: D16.

Crysdale, Steward and Harry MacKay. 1994. *Youth's Passage through School to Work*. Toronto: Thompson.

Daly, Kerry and Michael Sobol. 1994. "Adoption." *Canadian Social Trends* 32: 2-5.

David, Paul A. 1986. "Comment." *Population and Development Review* 12, Suppl: 77-86.

Davies, Lorraine and Donna D. McAlpine. 1998. "The Significance of Family, Work, and Power Relations for Mothers' Mental Health." *Canadian Journal of Sociology* 23,4: 369-87.

Davies, Scott, Clayton Mosher, and Bill O'Grady. 1996. "Educating Women: Gender Inequalities among Canadian University Graduates." *Canadian Review of Sociology and Anthropology* 33,2: 126-42.

Davis, Kingsley. 1984. "Wives and Work: Consequences of the Sex Role Revolution." *Population and Development Review* 10,3: 397-417.

— 1986. "Low Fertility in Evolutionary Perspective." *Population and Development Review* 12, Suppl: 48-65.

De Broucker, Patrice and Laval Lavallée. 1998. "Intergenerational Aspects of Education and Literacy Skills Acquisition." In M. Corak, ed., *Labour Markets, Social Institutions and the Future of Canada's Children*. Ottawa: Statistics Canada, cat. no. 89-553.

Delphy, Christine and Diana Leonard. 1992. *Familiar Exploitation: A New Analysis of Marriage in Contemporary Western Societies*. Cambridge, Mass.: Polity Press.

Demeny, Paul. 1986. "Pronatalist Policies in Low-Fertility Countries: Patterns, Performance and Prospects." *Population and Development Review* 12, Suppl: 335-58.

Demo, D.H. and A.C. Acock. 1988. "The Impact of Divorce on Children." *Journal of Marriage and the Family* 50: 619-48.

Demos, John. 1977. "The American Family in Past Time." In A.S. Skolnick and J.H. Skolnick, eds., *Family in Transition*. Boston: Little, Brown.

Denis, Hubert. 1994. "Les enfants de la monoparentalité hier et aujourd'hui." *Cahiers Québécois de Démographie* 23,1: 53-74.

Desai, Sonalde and Linda J. Waite. 1991. "Women's Employment during Pregnancies and after the First Birth: Occupational Characteristics and Work Commitment." *American Sociological Review* 56: 551-66.

Desrosiers, Hélène and Céline Le Bourdais. 1991. "The Impact of Age at Marriage and Timing of First Birth on Marriage Dissolution in Canada." *Canadian Studies in Population* 18,1: 29-51.

— 1995. "New Forms of Male Family Life in Canada." In M.C.P. van Dogen, ed., *Changing Fatherhood*. Amsterdam: Thesis Publishers.

De Vault, Marjorie. 1991. *Feeding the Family: The Social Organization of Caring as Gendered Work*. Chicago: University of Chicago Press.

Devereau, Mary Sue. 1993. "Time Use of Canadians in 1992." *Canadian Social Trends* 30: 13-16.

Devereau, Mary Sue and Colin Lindsay. 1993. "Female Lone Parents and the Labour Market." *Perspectives on Labour and Income* 5,1: 9-15.

De Wit, David J., David R. Offord, and Kathy Braun. 1998. "What Does Moving Do to Your Children?" Presentation, Investing in Children Conference, Ottawa, October 1998.

De Wit, Margaret and Zenaida Ravanera. 1998. "The Changing Impact of Women's Educational Attainment and Employment on the Timing of Births in Canada." *Canadian Studies in Population* 25,1: 45-68.

Dickinson, James and Bob Russell. 1986. "The Structure of Reproduction in Capitalist Society." In J. Dickinson and B. Russell, eds., *Family, Economy and State*. Toronto: Garamond.

Dienhart, Anna. 1998. *Reshaping Fatherhood: The Social Construction of Shared Parenting*. London: Sage.

Dionne, Claude. 1989. "Le choix d'avoir un enfant." Presentation, A.S.D.E.Q. Conference, April 1989.

Dooley, Martin. 1988. "An Analysis of Changes in Family Income and Family Structure in Canada between 1973 and 1986 with an Emphasis on Poverty among Children." McMaster University, Hamilton: QSFP Research Report, no. 238.

— 1991. "The Demography of Child Poverty in Canada: 1973-86." *Canadian Studies in Population* 18,1: 53-74.

— 1993. "Recent Changes in the Economic Welfare of Lone Mother Families in Canada: The Roles of Market Work, Earnings and Transfers." In J. Hudson and B. Galaway, eds., *Single Parent Families*. Toronto: Thompson.

— 1994. "Women, Children and Poverty in Canada." *Canadian Public Policy* 20,4: 430-43

Dooley, Martin, Lori Curtis, Ellen L. Lipman, and David H. Feeney. 1998. "Child Psychiatric Disorders, Poor School Performance and Social Problems: The Roles of Family Structure and Low-Income." In M. Corak, ed., *Labour Markets, Social Institutions, and the Future of Canada's Children*. Ottawa: Statistics Canada, cat. no. 89-553.

Douthitt, Robin A. 1989. "The Division of Labor within the Home: Have Gender Roles Changed?" *Sex Roles* 20,11-12: 693-704.

Draper, Patricia. 1998. "Why Should Fathers Father?" In A. Booth and A.C. Crouter, eds., *Men in Families: When Do They Get Involved? What Difference Does It Make?* Mahwah, N.J.: Lawrence Erlbaum.

Driedger, Sharon Doyle. 1998. "Divorce." *Maclean's* 20 April 1998: 39-43.

Drolet, Marie and René Morissette. 1997. "Working More? Working Less? What Do Workers Prefer?" *Perspectives on Labour and Income* 9,4: 32-38.

Duchesne, Louis. 1997. "Naître au naturel: Les naissances hors mariage." *Statistiques* 1,3: 1-4.

Duffy, Ann. 1997. "The Part-time Solution: Toward Entrapment or Empowerment." In A. Duffy, D. Glenday, and N. Pupo, eds., *Good Jobs, Bad Jobs, No Jobs*. Toronto: Harcourt Brace.

Duffy, Ann and Norene Pupo. 1992. *Part-Time Paradox: Connecting Gender, Work and Family*. Toronto: McClelland and Stewart.

— 1996. "Family Friendly Organizations and Beyond: Proposals for Policy Directions with Women in Mind." In National Forum on Family Security, *Family Security in Insecure Times*, vol. II. Ottawa: Canadian Council on Social Development.

Duffy, Ann, D. Glenday, and N. Pupo. 1997b. "Introduction: Debating the Future of Work." In A. Duffy, D. Glenday, and N. Pupo, eds., *Good Jobs, Bad Jobs, No Jobs*. Toronto: Harcourt Brace.

Duffy, Ann, Nancy Mandell, and Norene Pupo. 1989. *Few Choices: Women, Work and Family*. Toronto: Garamond.

Dumas, Jean. 1990. *Report on the Demographic Situation in Canada 1988*. Ottawa: Statistics Canada, cat. no. 91-209.

Dumas, Jean and Alain Bélanger. 1996. *Report on the Demographic Situation in Canada 1995*. Ottawa: Statistics Canada, cat. no. 91-209.

— 1997. *Report on the Demographic Situation in Canada 1996*. Ottawa: Statistics Canada, cat. no. 91-209.

Dumas, Jean and Yves Péron. 1992. *Marriage and Conjugal Life in Canada*. Statistics Canada, cat. no. 91-534.

Dupuis, Dave. 1998. "What Influences People's Plans to Have Children? *Canadian Social Trends* 48: 2-5.

Durkheim, Emile. 1960 [1893]. *The Division of Labour in Society*. Glencoe, Ill.: The Free Press.

Duvander, Ann-Zofie. 1998. *Why Do Swedish Cohabitants Marry?* Stockholm University: Demographic Unit.

Duxbury, Linda and Christopher Higgins. 1994. "Families and the Economy." In M. Baker, ed., *Canada's Changing Families: Challenges to Public Policy*. Ottawa: Vanier Institute of the Family.

Easterlin, Richard. 1980. *Birth and Fortune: The Impact of Numbers on Personal Welfare*. New York: Basic Books.

Easterlin, Richard and Eileen Crimmins. 1985. *The Fertility Revolution: A Supply-Demand Analysis*. Chicago: University of Chicago Press.

Economic Council of Canada. 1990. *Good Jobs, Bad Jobs*. Ottawa.

— 1992. *The New Face of Poverty: Income Security Needs of Canadian Families*. Ottawa.

Eggebeen, David, Anastasia Snyder, and Wendy Manning. 1996. "Children in Single-Father Families in Demographic Perspective." *Journal of Family Issues* 17,4: 441-65.

Eichler, Margrit. 1988. *Families in Canada Today*. Toronto: Gage.

— 1996. "Lone Parent Families: An Instable Category in Search of Stable Policies." In C.J. Richardson, ed., *Family Life: Patterns and Perspectives*. Toronto: McGraw-Hill Ryerson.

— 1997. *Family Shifts: Families, Policies and Gender Equality*. Toronto: Oxford University Press.

Engels, Frederick. 1975. *The Origin of the Family, Private Property and the State*. E.B. Leacock, ed., New York: International Publishers.

Evans, Patricia. 1991. "The Sexual Division of Poverty: The Consequences of Gendered Caring." In C. Baines, Patricia M. Evans, and Sheila M. Neysmith, eds., *Women's Caring*. Toronto: McClelland and Stewart.

Farber, Bernard. 1964. *Family Organization and Interaction*. San Francisco: Chandler.

Fast, Janet and Judith A. Frederick. 1996. "Working Arrangements and Time Stress." *Canadian Social Trends* 43: 14-19.

Fast, Janet and Moreno Da Pont. 1997. "Changes in Women's Work Continuity." *Canadian Social Trends* 46: 2-7.

Federal, Provincial, and Territorial Family Law Committee. 1995. *Report and Recommendations on Child Support*. Ottawa: Department of Justice.

Fellegi, Ivan. 1998. "Release of the First Longitudinal Data from the NLSCY." Presentation, Conference on Investing in Children, Ottawa, October 1998.

Feree, Myra Marx. 1990. "Beyond Separate Spheres: Feminism and Family Research." *Journal of Marriage and the Family* 52,3: 866-84.

— 1991a. "The Gender Division of Labor in Two-Earner Marriages: Dimensions of Variability and Change." *Journal of Family Issues* 12: 158-80.

— 1991b. "Feminism and Family Research." In A. Booth, ed., *Contemporary Families*. Minneapolis: National Council on Family Relations.

Feree, Myra Marx and Elaine J. Hall. 1996. "Rethinking Stratification from a Feminist Perspective: Gender, Race and Class in Mainstream Textbooks." *American Sociological Review* 61,6: 929-50.

Festy, Patrick. 1994. "L'environment familial des enfants en France et au Canada." *Cahiers Québécois de Démographie* 23,1: 11-25.

Finnie, Ross. 1993. "Women, Men and the Economic Consequences of Divorce: Evidence from Canadian Longitudinal Data." *Canadian Review of Sociology and Anthropology* 30,2: 205-41.

Fisher, Berenice and Joan Tronto. 1990. "Toward a Feminist Theory of Caring." In E. Abel and M. Nelson, eds., *Circles of Care: Work and Identity in Women's Lives*. Albany: State University of New York Press.

Flood, Lennart and Urban Grasjo. 1995. "Changes in the Time Spent at Work and Leisure: The Swedish Experience, 1983-93." Manuscript, Department of Economics, University of Gothenburg.

Folbre, Nancy. 1994. *Who Pays for the Kids? Gender and the Structures of Constraint*. London: Routledge.

Folk, K.F. and A.H. Beller. 1993. "Part-Time Work and Child Care Choices for Mothers of Preschool Children." *Journal of Marriage and Family* 55,1: 146-57.

Foot, David and Daniel Stoffman. 1996. *Boom, Bust and Echo*. Toronto: Macfarlane Walter and Ross.

Ford, David and François Nault. 1996. "Changing Fertility Patterns, 1974 to 1994." *Health Reports* 8,3: 39-46.

Fortin, Nicole and Sophie Lefebvre. 1998. "Intergenerational Income Mobility in Canada." In M. Corak, ed., *Labour Markets, Social Institutions and the Future of Canada's Children*. Ottawa: Statistics Canada, cat. no. 89-553.

Fox, Bonnie. 1988. "Conceptualizing Patriarchy." *Canadian Review of Sociology and Anthropology* 25,2: 163-81.

— 1997. "Another View of Sociology of the Family in Canada: A Comment on Nett (1996)." *Canadian Review of Sociology and Anthropology* 34,1: 93-99.

Fox, Bonnie and John Fox. 1987. "Occupational Gender Segregation of the Canadian Labour Force, 1931-1981." *Canadian Review of Sociology and Anthropology* 24,3: 374-97.

Fox, Bonnie and Meg Luxton. 1991. "Conceptualizing 'Family'." Paper prepared for Review of Demography, Health and Welfare.

Fraser, Graham. 1998. "PQ Unveils Plan Giving Parents Generous Leave." *The Globe and Mail* 10 November 1998: A4.

Frederick, Judith. 1993. "Are You Time Crunched?" *Canadian Social Trends* 31: 6-9.

— 1995. *As Time Goes By*. Ottawa: Statistics Canada, cat. no. 89-544.

Frederick, Judith and Jason Hamel. 1998. "Canadian Attitudes to Divorce." *Canadian Social Trends* 48: 6-11.

Frederick, Judith and Monica Boyd. 1998. "The Impact of Family Structure on High School Completion." *Canadian Social Trends* 48: 12-14.

Freidan, Betty. 1963. *The Feminine Mystique.* New York: Norton.

Friedman, Debra, Michael Hechter, and Satoshi Kanazawa. 1994. "A Theory of the Value of Children." *Demography* 31,3: 375-401.

Friendly, Martha. 1994. *Child-Care Policy in Canada: Putting the Pieces Together.* Don Mills, Ont.: Addison-Wesley.

— 1997. "What Is the Public Interest in Child Care?" *Policy Options* 18,1: 3-6.

Furstenberg, Frank F. 1995. "Family Change and the Welfare of Children: What Do We Know and What Can We Do about It?" In K. Mason and A-M. Jensen, eds., *Gender and Family Change in Industrialized Countries.* Oxford: Clarendon.

— 1998. "Social Capital and the Role of Fathers in the Family." In A. Booth and A.C. Crouter, eds., *Men in Families: When Do They Get Involved? What Difference Does It Make?* Mahwah, N.J.: Lawrence Erlbaum.

Galambos, Nancy and Lauree Tilton-Weaver. 1998. "Multiple-Risk Behaviour in Adolescents and Young Adults." *Health Reports* 10,2: 9-20.

Galarneau, Diane. 1993. "Alimony and Child Support." *Canadian Social Trends* 28: 8-11.

— 1994. *Female Baby Boomers: A Generation at Work.* Ottawa: Statistics Canada, cat. no. 96-315.

— 1998. "Income after Separation: People without Children." *Perspectives on Labour and Income* 10,2: 32-37.

Galarneau, Diane and Cécile Dumas. 1993. "About Productivity." *Perspectives on Labour and Income* 5,1: 39-48.

Galarneau, Diane and Jim Sturrock. 1997. "Family Income after Separation." *Perspectives on Labour and Income* 9,2: 18-28.

Garfield, Chad. 1990. "The Social and Economic Origins of Contemporary Families." In M. Baker, ed., *Families: Changing Trends in Canada.* Toronto: McGraw-Hill Ryerson.

Gartley, John. 1994. *Employment of Canadians.* Ottawa: Statistics Canada, cat. no. 96-317.

Gaskell, Jane. 1983. "The Reproduction of Family Life: Perspectives of Male and Female Adolescents." *British Journal of Sociology of Education* 4: 19-38.

Gauthier, Anne Hélène. 1987. "Nouvelles estimations du coût de l'enfant au Canada." *Cahiers Québécois de Démographie* 16,2: 187-208.

— 1991. "The Economics of Childhood." In A.R. Pence, ed., *Childhood as a Social Phenomenon.* Vienna: European Centre for Social Welfare Policy and Research.

— 1993. "Toward Renewed Fears of Population Decline?" *European Journal of Population* 9: 143-67.

— 1996. *The State and the Family.* Oxford: Clarendon.

Gauthier, Hervé, Louis Duchesne, Sylvie Jean, Denis Laroche, and Yves Nobert. 1997. *D'une génération à l'autre: évolution des conditions de vie.* Québec: Bureau de la statistique du Québec.

Gauthier, Madeleine. 1990. "Valeurs et genres de vie des jeunes d'aujourd'hui." In R. Beaujot, ed., *Facing the Demographic Future.* Ottawa: Royal Society of Canada.

Gee, Ellen. 1986. "The Life Course of Canadian Women: An Historical and Demographic Analysis." *Social Indicators Research* 18,3: 263-83.

— 1993. "Adult Outcomes Associated with Childhood Family Structure: An Appraisal of Research and an Examination of Canadian Data." In J. Hudson, B. Galaway, eds., *Single Parent Families*. Toronto: Thompson.

— 1995. "Families in Later Life." In R. Beaujot, Ellen M. Gee, Fernando Rajulton, and Zenaida Ravanera, eds., *Family over the Life Course*. Ottawa: Statistics Canada, cat. no. 91-543.

Gee, Ellen, Barbara A. Mitchell, and Andrew Wister. 1995. "Returning to the Parental Nest: Exploring a Changing Canadian Life Course." *Canadian Studies in Population* 22,2: 121-44.

Gentleman, Jane and Evelyn Park. 1997. "Divorce in the 1990s." *Health Reports* 9,2: 53-58.

Gershuny, Jonathan and John Robinson. 1988. "Historical Changes in Household Division of Labour." *Demography* 25,4: 537-52.

Ghalam, Nancy Zukenwick. 1993. *Women in the Workplace*. Ottawa: Statistics Canada, cat. no. 71-534.

— 1997. "Attitudes toward Women, Work and Family." *Canadian Social Trends* 46: 13-17.

Gilbert, Lucia Albino. 1993. *Two Careers/One Family*. Newbury Park, Calif.: Sage Publications.

Gilbert, Sid. 1993. "Labour Market Outcomes for High School Leavers." *Perspectives on Labour and Income* 5,4: 12-16.

Gillis, John R., Louise A. Tilly, and David Levine. 1992. "The Quiet Revolution." In J.R. Gillis, L. Tilly, and D. Levine, eds., *The European Experience of Fertility Decline, 1850-1970*. Cambridge: Blackwell.

Glass, Jennifer and Sarah Estes. 1997. "The Family Responsive Workplace." *Annual Review of Sociology* 23: 289-313.

Glenn, Noval. 1997. "A Critique of Twenty Marriage and Family Textbooks." *Family Relations* 46,3: 197-208.

Globe and Mail. 1997. "Let's Give Parents a Big Break." Editorial, *The Globe and Mail* 30 October 1997: A22.

— 1998. "Toddler on Loose Highlights Problems Facing Many Families." *The Globe and Mail* 10 August 1998: A1, A5.

Glossop, Robert. 1994. "The Canadian Family." *Canadian Social Trends* 35: 2-10.

Goelman, Hillel, Alan R. Pence, Donna S. Lero, Lois M. Brockman, Ned Glick, and Jonathan Berkowitz. 1993. *Where Are the Children?* Ottawa: Statistics Canada, cat. no. 89-527.

Goldscheider, Frances and Calvin Goldscheider. 1994. "Composition familiale, soutien parental et départ du foyer des jeunes américains au XXe siècle." *Cahiers Québécois de Démographie* 23,1: 75-102.

Goldscheider, Frances and Gayle Kaufman. 1996. "Fertility and Commitment: Bringing Men Back In." *Population and Development Review* 22, Suppl: 87-99.

Goldscheider, Frances and Linda J. Waite. 1986. "Sex Differences in the Entry into Marriage." *American Journal of Sociology* 92,1: 91-109.

— 1991. *New Families, No Families?* Berkeley: University of California Press.

Goldscheider, Frances, Eva M. Bernhardt, and Gayle Kaufman. 1996. "Complex Paternal Roles in the United States and Sweden: Biological, Step- and Informal Fatherhood." Brown University: PSTC Working Paper, no. 96-06.

Goldscheider, Frances, Pamela Webster, and Gayle Kaufman. 1995. "Men, Parenthood and Divorce in the Era of the Second Demographic Transition." *Male Fertility in an Era of Fertility Decline.* Liège, Belgium: International Union for the Scientific Study of Population.

Goode, William J. 1963. *World Revolution and Family Patterns.* New York: The Free Press.

— 1977. "World Revolution and Family Patterns." In A.S. Skolnick and J.H. Skolnick, eds., *Family in Transition.* Boston: Little, Brown.

— 1981. "Why Men Resist." In B. Thorne and M. Yalom, eds., *Rethinking the Family: Some Feminist Questions.* New York: Longman.

Gower, Dave. 1995. "Men Are Retiring Early, How Are They Doing?" *Perspectives on Labour and Income* 7,4: 30-34.

Goyder, John C. 1981. "Income Differences between the Sexes: Findings from a National Canadian Survey." *Canadian Review of Sociology and Anthropology* 18,3: 321-42.

Green, David. 1991. "Joint Custody and the Emerging Two-Parent Family." In J. Veevers, ed., *Continuity and Change in Marriage and Family.* Toronto: Holt, Rinehart and Winston.

Greenstein, Theodore. 1996. "Husbands' Participation in Domestic Labour: Interaction Effects of Wives' and Husbands' Gender Ideologies." *Journal of Marriage and the Family* 58,3: 585-95.

Grenon, Lee and Barbara Chun. 1997. "Non-Permanent Paid Work." *Perspectives on Labour and Income* 9,3: 21-31.

Grindstaff, Carl F. 1986. "The High Cost of Childbearing: The Fertility of Women Age 30-44, Canada, 1981." Ottawa: Report for Review of Demography, Health and Welfare.

— 1989. "Socio-Economic Associations with Fertility: A Profile of Women at Age 30." *Canadian Studies in Population* 16,1: 43-60.

— 1990a. "Long-Term Consequences of Adolescent Marriage and Fertility." In *Report on the Demographic Situation in Canada, 1988.* Ottawa: Statistics Canada.

— 1990b. "Canada as a Pro-Natal Society." Manuscript, University of Western Ontario, London, Ont.

— 1991. "The Canadian Family in Transition." Ottawa: Report for Review of Demography, Health and Welfare.

— 1995. "Canadian Fertility, 1951 to 1993." *Canadian Social Trends* 39: 12-16.

— 1996. "The Costs of Having a First Child for Women Aged 33-38, Canada 1991." *Sex Roles* 35,3-4: 137-51.

Grindstaff, Carl F. and Frank Trovato. 1990. "Junior Partners: Women's Contribution to Family Income in Canada." *Social Indicators Research* 22,3: 229-53.

Grindstaff, Carl F., T.R. Balakrishnan, and Paul S. Maxim. 1989. "Life Course Alternatives: Factors Associated with Differential Timing Patterns in Fertility among Women Recently Completing Childbearing, Canada 1981." *Canadian Journal of Sociology* 14,4: 443-60.

Gunderson, Morley. 1989. "Male-Female Wage Differentials and Policy Responses." *Journal of Economic Literature* 27: 46-72.

— 1998. *Women and the Canadian Labour Market*. Toronto: ITP Nelson.

Haas, Linda. 1981. "Domestic Role Sharing in Sweden." *Journal of Marriage and the Family* 43,2: 957-67.

Haddad, Tony. 1996. "The Sexual Division of Household Labour: Pragmatic Strategies or Patriarchal Dynamics." Ph.D. thesis, York University, Toronto.

— 1998. "Custody Arrangements and the Development of Emotional and Behavioural Problems by Children." Presentation, Investing in Children Conference, Ottawa, October 1998.

Haddad, Tony and Lawrence Lam. 1988. "Canadian Families: Men's Involvement in Family Work: A Case Study of Immigrant Men in Toronto." *International Journal of Comparative Sociology* 29,3-4: 269-81.

Hall, David R. 1996. "Marriage as a Pure Relationship: Exploring the Links between Pre-Marital Cohabitation and Divorce in Canada." *Journal of Comparative Family Studies* 27,1: 1-12.

Hall, David R. and John Z. Zhao. 1995. "Cohabitation and Divorce in Canada: Testing the Selectivity Hypothesis." *Journal of Marriage and Family* 57,2: 421-27.

Halli, Shiva. 1991. "Origins of the Modern Family, Changing Sex Roles, and Division of Household Labour in Canada." Ottawa: Report for Review of Demography, Health and Welfare.

Halli, Shiva and Zachary Zimmer. 1991. "Common-Law Unions as a Differentiating Factor in the Failure of Marriage in Canada, 1984." *Social Indicators Research* 24,4: 329-45.

Hamilton, Roberta. 1978. *The Liberation of Women: A Study of Patriarchy and Capitalism*. London: Allen and Unwin.

— 1996. *Gendering the Vertical Mosaic: Feminist Perspectives in Canadian Society*. Toronto: Copp Clark.

Hammel, E.A. 1990. "A Theory of Culture for Demography." *Population and Development Review* 16,3: 455-86.

Hango, Darcy. 1998. "Childhood Residential Mobility and Educational Attainment." M.A. thesis, University of Western Ontario, London, Ont.

Hannan, Michael T., Klaus Schomann, and Hans-Peter Blossfeld. 1990. "Sex Differences in the Dynamics of Wage Growth in the Federal Republic of Germany." *American Sociological Review* 55,5: 694-713.

Hareven, Tamara K. 1977. "Family Time and Historical Time." *Daedalus* 106,2: 57-70.

— 1983. "American Families in Transition: Historical Perspective on Change." In A.S. Skolnick and J.H. Skolnick, eds., *Family in Transition*. Boston: Little, Brown and Co.

Harman, Leslie. 1992. "The Feminization of Poverty: An Old Problem with a New Name." *Canadian Women's Studies* 12,4, 6-9.

Harrell, W. Andrew. 1995. "Husband's Involvement in Housework: Effects of Relative Earning Power and Masculine Orientation." *Psychological Reports* 77,3: 1331-37.

Harris, C.C. 1983. *The Family and Industrial Society.* London: George Allen and Unwin.

Hartmann, Heidi. 1981. "The Family as the Locus of Gender, Class and Political Struggle: The Example of Work." *Signs* 6,3: 366-94.

— 1984. "The Family as the Locus of Gender, Class, and Political Struggle: The Example of Housework." In A. Juggar and P. Rothenberg, eds., *Feminist Frameworks.* New York: McGraw-Hill.

Harvey, Andrew S., Katherine Marshall, and Judith Frederick. 1991. *Where Does Time Go?* Ottawa: Statistics Canada, cat. no. 11-612, no. 4.

Heitlinger, Alena. 1991. "Overview Report on Direct and Indirect Provision of Childcare by Families." Report for Review of Demography and Its Implications for Economic and Social Policy, Health and Welfare Canada.

— 1993. *Women's Equality, Demography and Public Policies.* New York: St. Martin's Press.

Henripin, Jacques. 1957. "From Acceptance of Nature to Control: The Demography of the French Canadians since the Seventeenth Century." *Canadian Journal of Economics and Political Science* 23,1: 10-19.

— 1989. *Naître ou ne pas être.* Québec: Institut québécois de recherche sur la culture.

Henripin, Jacques and Evelyne Lapierre-Adamcyk. 1986. "Essai d'évaluation du coût de l'enfant." Report submitted to Bureau de la statistique du Québec.

Hernandez, Donald. 1993. *America's Children.* New York: Russell Sage.

Hertz, Rosanna. 1986. *More Equal than Others: Women and Men in Dual-Career Marriages.* Berkeley: University of California Press.

Hessing, Melody. 1993. "Mothers' Management of Their Combined Workloads: Clerical Work and Household Needs." *Canadian Review of Sociology and Anthropology* 30,1: 37-63.

Higgins, C., L. Duxbury, and C. Lee. 1993. *Balancing Work and Family: A Study of the Canadian Private Sector.* London: National Centre for Research, Management and Development, University of Western Ontario.

Hirdman, Yvonne. 1994. "Women in Families: Possibility to Problem?" Stockholm: The Swedish Centre for Working Life, Research Report Series, no. 3.

Hirschman, Charles. 1994. "Why Fertility Changes." *Annual Review of Sociology* 20: 203-33.

Hobart, Charles. 1991. "Interest in Parenting at the End of the Eighties." *Canadian Studies in Population* 18,1: 75-100.

Hobson, Barbara. 1993. "Feminist Strategies and Gendered Discourses in Welfare States: Married Women's Right to Work in the United States and Sweden." In S. Koven and S. Michel, eds., *Mothers of a New World: Maternalist Policies and the Origins of Welfare States.* New York: Routledge.

Hochschild, Arlie Russell. 1989. *The Second Shift*. New York: Viking.

— 1995. "Understanding the Future of Fatherhood." In M. van Dongen, Gerard Frinking, and Menno Jacobs, eds., *Changing Fatherhood*. Amsterdam: Thesis Publishers.

— 1997. *The Time Bind: When Work Becomes Home and Home Becomes Work*. New York: Holt.

Hoem, Britta. 1992. "The Way to the Gender Segregated Swedish Labour Market." Stockholm Research Reports in Demography, no. 68.

— 1997. Personal Communication. Statistics Sweden, June 1997.

Hoem, Britta and Jan Hoem. 1996. "Sweden's Family Policies and Roller-Coaster Fertility." *Journal of Population Problems* 52,3-4: 1-22.

Hoem, Jan. 1993. "Public Policy as the Fuel of Fertility: Effects of a Policy Reform on the Pace of Childbearing in Sweden in the 1980s." *Acta Sociologica* 36,1: 19-31.

— 1995. "Educational Capital and Divorce Risk in Sweden in the 1970s and 80s." Stockholm Research Reports in Demography, no. 95.

Hofferth, S. and A. Brayfield. 1991. "Making Time for Children: Family Decisions about Employment and Child Care." Presentation, Population Association of America Meetings, Washington, D.C., March 1991.

Horna, Jarmila and Eugene Lupri. 1987. "Fathers' Participation in Work, Family Life and Leisure: A Canadian Experience." In C. Lewis and M. O'Brien, eds., *Reassessing Fatherhood*. London: Sage Publications.

Hoult, T.F., L.F. Henze, and J.W. Hudson. 1978. *Courtship and Marriage in America*. Boston: Little, Brown.

Houseknecht, Sharon K. and Jaya Sastry. 1996. "Family 'Decline' and Child Well-Being: A Comparative Assessment." *Journal of Marriage and the Family* 58,3: 726-39.

Howe, R. Brian and Katherine Covell. 1997. "Children's Rights in Hard Times." In R. Blake, P. Bryden, and J. Strain, eds., *The Welfare State in Canada: Past, Present and Future*. Concord, Ont.: Irwin.

Huber, Joan and Glenna Spitze. 1983. *Sex Stratification: Children, Housework and Jobs*. New York: Academic Press.

Hughes, Karen. 1995. "Women in Non-Traditional Occupations." *Perspectives on Labour and Income* 7,3: 14-19.

Hum, Derek and Wayne Simpson. 1991. "Income Maintenance, Work Effort, and the Canadian MINCOME Experiment." Ottawa: Economic Council of Canada.

Human Resources Development Canada. 1996. "Labour Market Polarization: What's Going On?" *Applied Research Bulletin* 2,2: 5-6.

— 1997. "Flexible Work Arrangements: Gaining Ground." *Applied Research Bulletin* 3,1: 5-7.

— 1998. "Is High School Enough?" *Applied Research Bulletin* 4,3: 17-20.

Human Resources Development Canada and Statistics Canada. 1996. *Growing up in Canada: National Longitudinal Survey of Children and Youth*. Ottawa: Statistics Canada, cat. no. 89-550.

— 1997. *The National Longitudinal Survey of Children and Youth, 1994-95: Initial Results from the School Component*. Ottawa: Statistics Canada.

Hunsley, Terrance. 1997. *Lone Parent Incomes and Social Policy Outcomes: Canada in International Perspective*. Kingston, Ont.: School of Policy Studies, Queen's University.

Hutter, Mark. 1988. *The Changing Family: Comparative Perspectives*. New York: Wiley.

Insight Canada Research. 1993. "National Child Care Survey." Toronto: Ontario Coalition for Better Child Care.

Ishii-Kuntz, Masoko and Scott Coltrane. 1992. "Re-Marriage, Step-Parenting and Household Labor." *Journal of Family Issues* 13,2: 215-33.

Jackson, Chris. 1996. "Measuring and Valuing Household's Unpaid Work." *Canadian Social Trends* 42: 25-29.

Jansson, Jan and Michael Gahler. 1997. "Family Dissolution, Family Reconstruction, and Children's Educational Careers: Recent Evidence for Sweden." *Demography* 34,2: 277-93.

Jenkins, Eric and Jacques Légaré. 1995. "La vie en couple comme stratégie adaptive pour répondre aux besoins des persons âgées en perte d'autonomie." In *Towards the 21st Century: Emerging Socio-Demographic Trends and Policy Issues in Canada*. Ottawa: Federation of Canadian Demographers.

Jennings, Philip. 1997. "What Explains the Declining Youth Participation Rate." *Applied Research Bulletin* 3,2: 4-5.

— 1998. "School Enrolment and the Declining Youth Participation Rate." *Policy Options* 19,3: 10-14.

Jensen, An-Magritt. 1995. "Gender Gaps in Relationships with Children: Closing or Widening." In K. Mason and A-M. Jensen, eds., *Gender and Family Change in Industrialized Countries*. Oxford: Clarendon.

Jensen, An-Magritt and Angelo Sapariti. 1992. *Do Children Count? A Statistical Compendium*. Vienna: European Centre.

Johnson, Holly. 1994. "Work-Related Sexual Harassment." *Perspectives on Labour and Income* 6,4: 9-12.

Johnson, Laura and Julie Mathien. 1998. "Early Childhood Services for Kindergarten Age Children in Four Canadian Provinces: Scope, Nature and Models for the Future." Ottawa: Caledon Institute of Social Policy.

Jones, Charles L., Lorna Marsden, and Lorne Tepperman. 1990. *Lives of Their Own: The Individualization of Women's Lives*. Toronto: Oxford University Press.

Jones, Charles L., Lorne Tepperman, and Susannah J. Wilson. 1995. *The Future of the Family*. Englewood Cliffs, N.J.: Prentice-Hall.

Juby, Heather and Céline Le Bourdais. 1998. "The Changing Context of Fatherhood in Canada: A Life Course Analysis." *Population Studies* 52,2: 163-75.

Kalmijn, Matthijs. 1991. "Status Homogamy in the United States." *American Journal of Sociology* 97,2: 496-523.

Kamerman, Sheila B. and Alfred J. Kahn. 1991. *Child Care, Parental Leave and the Under Three's: Policy Innovation in Europe.* New York: Auburn.

Kano, Yoshinori. 1988. "Determinants of Household Division of Labor: Resources, Power, Ideology." *Journal of Marriage and Family Issues* 9,2: 177-200.

Kaplan, Hillard S., Jane B. Lancaster, and Kermyt G. Anderson. 1998. "Human Parental Investment and Fertility: The Life Histories of Men in Albuquerque." In A. Booth and A. C. Crouter, eds., *Men in Families: When Do They Get Involved? What Difference Does It Make?* Mahwah, N.J.: Lawrence Erlbaum.

Kempeneers, Marianne. 1987. "Questions sur les femmes et le travail: une lecture de la crise." *Sociologie et Sociétés* 19,1: 57-71.

— 1991. "La discontinuité professionelle des femmes au Canada: permanence et changement." *Population* 46,1: 9-28.

— 1992. *Le Travail au féminin.* Montreal: Presses de l'Université de Montréal.

Kempeneers, Marianne and Marie-Hélène Saint-Pierre. 1993. "Travail et famille: une relation à construire." In D. Cordell, Danielle Gauvreau, Raymond R. Gervais, and Céline Le Bourdais, eds., *Population, Reproduction, Sociétés.* Montreal: Presses de l'Université de Montréal.

Kent, Tom. 1999. "Social Policy 2000: An Agenda." Ottawa: Caledon Institute of Social Policy.

Kerr, Don. 1992. "Life-Cycle Demographic Effects and Economic Well-Being of Children." Ph.D. thesis, University of Western Ontario, London, Ont.

Kerr, Don, Daniel Larrivée, and Patricia Greenhalgh. 1994. *Children and Youth: An Overview.* Ottawa: Statistics Canada, cat. no. 96-320.

Kersten, Karen and Lawrence Kersten. 1991. "A Historical Perspective on Intimate Relationships." In J. Veevers, ed., *Continuity and Change in Marriage and Family.* Toronto: Holt, Rinehart and Winston.

Kettle, John. 1980. *The Big Generation.* Toronto: McClelland and Stewart.

Keyfitz, Nathan. 1986. "The Family That Does Not Reproduce Itself." *Population and Development Review* 12, Suppl: 139-54.

— 1989. "On Future Mortality." IIASA Working Paper 89-59.

— 1994. "Preface." *Cahiers Québécois de Démographie* 23,1: 3-10.

Kindlund, Soren. 1997. Personal Communication. National Social Insurance Board, Sweden, June 1997.

Kluwer, Esther, José Heesink, and Evart Van de Vliert. 1996. "Marital Conflict about the Division of Household Labor and Paid Work." *Journal of Marriage and the Family* 58,4: 958-69.

— 1997. "The Marital Dynamics of Conflict over the Division of Labor." *Journal of Marriage and the Family* 59,3: 635-53.

Knowles, Caroline. 1996. *Family Boundaries: The Invention of Normality and Dangerousness.* Peterborough, Ont.: Broadview.

Kohn, Dafna and Clyde Hertzman. 1998. "The Importance of Quality of Care." Presentation, Investing in Children Conference, Ottawa, October 1998.

Krahn, Harvey. 1995. "Non-Standardized Work on the Rise." *Perspectives on Labour and Income* 7,4: 35-42.

Krahn, Harvey and Graham Lowe. 1993. *Work, Industry and Canadian Society.* Scarborough, Ont.: Nelson.

Kravdal, Oystein. 1992. "The Emergence of a Positive Relationship between Education and Third Birth Rates in Norway with Supportive Evidence from the United States." *Population Studies* 46,3: 459-75.

Kyriazis, Natalie. 1982. "A Parity-Specific Analysis of Completed Fertility in Canada." *Canadian Review of Sociology and Anthropology* 19,1: 29-43.

Lam, Lawrence and Tony Haddad. 1992. "Men's Participation in Family Work: A Case Study." *International Journal of Sociology of the Family* 22: 67-104.

Lamb, Michael. 1995. "Paternal Influences on Child Development." In M. van Dogen, Gerard Frinking, and Menno Jacobs, eds., *Changing Fatherhood.* Amsterdam: Thesis Publishers.

Lapierre-Adamcyk, Evelyne. 1987. "Mariage et politique de la famille." Presentation, Association des Démographes du Québec Meetings, Ottawa, May 1987.

— 1989. "Le mariage et la famille: mentalités actuelles et comportements récents des femmes canadiennes." In J. Légaré, T.R. Balakrishnan, and R. Beaujot, eds., *The Family in Crisis: A Population Crisis?* Ottawa: Royal Society of Canada.

— 1990. "Faire face au changement démo-graphique: la nécessaire participation des femmes." In R. Beaujot, ed., *Faire Face au Changement Démographique.* Ottawa: Royal Society of Canada.

Lapierre-Adamcyk, Evelyne and Nicole Marcil-Gratton. 1995. "Prise en change des enfants: stratégies individuelles et organisation sociale." *Sociologie et Sociétés* 27,2: 121-42.

Lapierre-Adamcyk, Evelyne, Céline Le Bourdais, and Karen Lehrhaupt. 1995. "Les departs du foyer parental des jeunes Canadiens nés entre 1921 et 1960." *Population* 50,4-5: 1111-35.

Laroche, Mireille. 1998. "In and out of Low Income." *Canadian Social Trends* 50: 20-24.

Larson, Lyle, J. Walter Goltz, and Charles Hobart. 1994. *Families in Canada: Social Context, Continuities, and Changes.* Scarborough, Ont.: Prentice-Hall.

Lathe, Heather and Philip Giles. 1995. "Work experience." *Perspectives on Labour and Income* 7,2: 15-19.

Leach, Penelope. 1994. *Children First.* New York: Knopf.

Leacock, Eleanor. 1977. "On Engels' Origin of the Family, Private Property and the State." In P.J. Stein, J. Richman, and N. Hannon, eds., *The Family.* Reading, Mass.: Addison-Wesley.

Leblanc, Michel, Pierre Lefebvre, and Philip Merrigan. 1996. "Comment accroître le soutien public en faveur des enfants." *Choix* 2,6: 1-46.

Le Bourdais, Céline. 1989. "L'impact des transformations familiales sur l'activité professionelle des femmes au Canada." *Revue Suisse de Sociologie* 15,1: 57-74.

Le Bourdais, Céline and Annie Sauriol. 1994. "Transformations familiales et partage des tâches domestiques." In F. Descarries and C. Corbeil, eds., *Réconciliation famille-travail: les enjeux de recherche.* Québec: Université du Québec.

— 1998a. *La part des pères dans la division du travail domestique au sein des familles canadiennes.* Montreal: INRS-Urbanisation, Etudes et Documents, no. 69.

— 1998b. "The Effects of Changing Forms of Employment on the Division of Housework within Canadian Families." Presentation, Canadian Population Society Meetings, Ottawa, June 1998.

Le Bourdais, Céline and Hélène Desrosiers. 1988. "Trajectoires démographiques et professionelles: une analyse longitudinale des processus et des déterminants. Ottawa: Report for Review of Demography, Health and Welfare.

Le Bourdais, Céline and Nicole Marcil-Gratton. 1994. "Quebec's Pro-active Approach to Family Policy: Thinking and Acting Family." In M. Baker, ed., *Canada's Changing Families: Challenges to Public Policy.* Ottawa: Vanier Institute of the Family.

— 1996. "Family Transformations across the Canadian/American Border: When the Laggard Becomes the Leader." *Journal of Comparative Family Studies* 27,3: 415-36.

— 1998. "The Impact of Family Disruption in Childhood on Demographic Outcomes in Young Adulthood." In M. Corak, ed., *Labour Markets, Social Institutions and the Future of Canada's Children.* Ottawa: Statistics Canada, cat. no. 89-553.

Le Bourdais, Céline, Ghislaine Neill, and Pierre Turcotte. 1998. "Diversity of Conjugal Trajectories of Canadian Women." Presentation, Canadian Population Society Meetings, Ottawa, June 1998.

Le Bourdais, Céline, Hélène Desrosiers, and Benoît Laplante. 1995. "Factors Related to Union Formation among Single Mothers in Canada." *Journal of Marriage and Family* 57,2: 410-20.

Le Bourdais, Céline, Pierre Hamel, and Paul Bernard. 1987. "Le travail et l'ouvrage: change et partage des tâches domestiques chez les couples québécois." *Sociologie et Sociétés* 19,1: 37-55.

Leck, Joanne, Sylvie St. Onge, and Isabelle Lalancette. 1995. "Wage Gap Changes among the Organizations Subject to the Employment Equity Act." *Canadian Public Policy* 21,4: 387-400.

Lefebvre, Pierre and Philip Merrigan. 1998. "Working Mothers and Their Children." Presentation, Conference on Investing in Children, Ottawa, October 1998.

Lefebvre, Pierre, Liliane Brouillette, and Claude Felteau. 1994. "Les effets des impôts et des allocations familiales sur les comportements de fécondité et de travail des Canadiennes, 1975-1987: résultats d'un modèle de choix discrets." *Population* 54,2: 415-56.

Lefebvre, Pierre, Philip Merrigan, and Stéphane Gascon. 1996. "La pauvreté des enfants au Canada de 1973 à 1993." In Jacques Alary and Louise Ethier, eds., *Comprendre la famille.* Quebec: Presses de l'Université du Québec.

Lefebvre, Sophie and Nicole Fortin. 1997. "Intergenerational Income Mobility Using a Parsimonious Occupation Classification System." Presentation, Conference on Intergenerational Mobility, Statistics Canada, February 1997.

Leira, Arnlaug. 1992. *Welfare States and Working Mothers: The Scandinavian Response.* Oxford: Cambridge University Press.

LeMasters, E.E. and John DeFrain. 1983. *Parents in Contemporary America.* Homewood, Ill.: The Dorsey Press.

Lennon, Mary Clare and Sarah Rosenfield. 1994. "Relative Fairness and the Division of Housework: The Importance of Options." *American Journal of Sociology* 100,2: 506-31.

Lenton, R. 1992. "Home versus Career: Attitudes towards Women's Work among Canadian Women and Men, 1988." *Canadian Journal of Sociology* 17,1: 89-98.

Leridon, Henri and Catherine Villeneuve-Gokalp. 1994. *Constances et Inconstances de la Famille.* Paris: Presses Universitaires de la France.

Lerner, Gerda. 1986. *The Creation of Patriarchy.* New York: Oxford.

Lero, Donna and Lois Brockman. 1993. "Single Parent Families in Canada: A Closer Look." In J. Hudson and B. Galaway, eds., *Single Parent Families.* Toronto: Thompson.

Lero, Donna, Hillel Goelman, Alan R. Pence, Lois M. Brockman, and Sandra Nuttall. 1992a. *Parental Work Patterns and Child Care Needs.* Ottawa: Statistics Canada, cat. no. 89-529.

Lero, Donna, Alan R. Pence, Lois M. Brockman, Hillel Goelman, and Margot Shields. 1992b. *Introductory Report: National Child Care Study.* Ottawa: Statistics Canada, cat. no. 89-526.

Lero, Donna, Lois M. Brockman, Alan R. Pence, Hillel Goelman, and Karen L. Johnson. 1993. *Workplace Benefits and Flexibility: A Perspective on Parents' Experiences.* Ottawa: Statistics Canada, cat. no. 89-530.

Leslie, Leigh A., Elaine A. Anderson, and Meredith P. Branson. 1991. "Responsibility for Children: The Role of Gender and Employment." *Journal of Family Issues* 12,2: 197-210.

Lesthaeghe, Ron. 1983. "A Century of Demographic and Cultural Change in Western Europe." *Population and Development Review* 9,3: 411-35.

— 1995. "The Second Demographic Transition in Western Countries: An Interpretation." In K. Oppenheim Mason and A-M. Jensen, eds., *Gender and Family Change in Industrialized Countries.* Oxford: Clarendon.

Lesthaeghe, Ron and C. Vanderhoeft. 1997. "Ready, Willing and Able: A Conceptualization of Transitions to New Behavioral Forms." Brussels: Interuniversity Papers in Demography, no. 1997-8.

Lever, Janet. 1978. "Sex Differences in Complexity of Children's Play." *American Sociological Review* 43,4: 471-83.

Levi-Strauss, Claude. 1971. "The Family." In H. Shapiro, ed., *Man, Culture and Society.* London: Oxford University Press.

Levine, Beth. 1997. "How to Get Your Husband to Help at Home." *Reader's Digest* January 1997: 21-28.

Lévy, Michel Louis. 1998. "Politiques familiales en Europe." *Population et Sociétés* 340: 1-3.

Lewis, Jane and Kathleen Kiernam. 1996. "The Boundaries between Marriage, Non-marriage, and Parenthood: Changes in Behaviour and Policy in Postwar Britain." *Journal of Family History* 21,3: 372-87.

Li, Peter. 1996. *The Making of Post-War Canada*. Toronto: Oxford.

Lichter, Daniel. 1994. "Environment familial et bien-être économique des enfants américains." *Cahiers Québécois de Démographie* 23,2: 151-77.

Lindsay, Colin. 1992. *Lone-Parent Families in Canada*. Ottawa: Statistics Canada, cat. no. 89-522.

Lipman, Ellen, David Offord, and Martin Dooley. 1996. "What Do We Know about Children from Single-Mother Families?" In *Growing up in Canada*. Ottawa: Statistics Canada, cat. no. 89-550, no. 1.

Lipps, Garth and Jeffrey Frank. 1997. "The Social Context of School for Children." *Canadian Social Trends* 47: 22-26.

Little, Bruce. 1997. "Why the First Cuts Have Been the Deepest." *The Globe and Mail* August 1997: A6.

Livingstone, David and Elizabeth Asner. 1996. "Feet in Both Camps: Household Classes, Divisions of Labour, and Group Consciousness." In D. Livingstone and J.M. Mangan, eds., *Recast Dreams: Class and Gender Consciousness in Steeltown*. Toronto: Garamond Press.

Livingstone, David and Meg Luxton. 1989. "Gender Consciousness at Work: Modification of the Male Breadwinner Norm among Steelworkers and Their Spouses." *Canadian Review of Sociology and Anthropology* 26, 240-75.

— 1996. "Gender Consciousness at Work: Modification of the Male Breadwinner Norm." In D. Livingstone and J.M Mangan, eds., *Recast Dreams: Class and Gender Consciousness in Steeltown*. Toronto: Garamond Press.

Logan, Ron. 1994. "Voluntary Part-Time Workers." *Perspectives on Labour and Income* 6,3: 18-24.

Logan, Ron and Jo-Anne Belliveau. 1995. "Working Mothers." *Canadian Social Trends* 36: 24-28.

London Free Press. 1992. "Defining the Family: The New Cold War." *London Free Press* 5 September 1992: E1, E4.

Lundberg, Shelly and Elaine Rose. 1998. "Parenthood and the Earnings of Married Men and Women." University of Washington: Seattle Population Research Center Working Paper, no. 98-9.

Lupri, Eugen. 1991. "Fathers in Transition: The Case of Dual-Earner Families in Canada." In J.E. Veevers, ed., *Continuity and Change in Marriage and Family*. Toronto: Holt, Rinehart and Winston.

Lupri, Eugen and Donald L. Mills. 1987. "The Household Division of Labour in Young Dual-Earner Couples: The Case of Canada." *International Review of Sociology* Series 2: 33-53.

Lupri, Eugen and Gladys Symons. 1982. "The Emerging Symmetrical Family: Fact or Fiction?" *International Journal of Comparative Sociology* 23: 166-89.

Lupri, Eugen and James Frideres. 1981. "The Quality of Marriage and the Passage of Time: Marital Satisfaction over the Life Cycle." *Canadian Journal of Sociology* 6,3: 283-306.

Lupton, Deborah and Leslie Barklay. 1997. *Constructing Fatherhood: Discourses and Experiences*. London: Sage.

Luxton, Meg. 1980. *More than a Labour of Love*. Toronto: Women's Press.

— 1990. "Two Hands on the Clock: Changing Patterns in the Gendered Division of Labour in the Home." In M. Luxton, H. Rosenberg, and S. Arat Koc, eds., *Through the Kitchen Window: The Politics of Home and Family*. Toronto: Garamond.

— 1997a. "Nothing Natural about It: The Contradictions of Parenting." In M. Luxton, ed., *Feminism and Families: Critical Policies and Changing Practices*. Halifax: Fernwood Publishing.

— 1997b. "Feminism and Families: The Challenge of Neo-Conservatism." In M. Luxton, ed., *Feminism and Families: Critical Policies and Changing Practices*. Halifax: Fernwood Publishing.

Mackie, Marlene. 1991. *Gender Relations in Canada: Further Explorations*. Toronto: Harcourt Brace.

— 1995. "Gender in the Family: Changing Patterns." In N. Mandell and A. Duffy, eds., *Canadian Families: Diversity, Conflict and Change*. Toronto: Harcourt Brace.

Marcil-Gratton, Nicole. 1988. "Les modes de vie nouveaux des adultes et leur impact sur les enfants au Canada." Ottawa: Report for Review of Demography, Health and Welfare.

— 1993. "Growing up with a Single Parent: A Transitional Experience? Some Demographic Measurements from the Children's Point of View." In J. Hudson and B. Galaway, eds., *Single Parent Families: Perspectives on Research and Policy*. Toronto: Thompson.

— 1998. *Growing up with Mom and Dad? The Intricate Family Life Course of Canadian Children*. Ottawa: Statistics Canada, cat. no. 89-566.

Marcil-Gratton, Nicole and Jacques Légaré. 1987. "Being Old Today and Tomorrow: A Different Proposition." *Canadian Studies in Population* 14,2: 237-41.

Marcoux, Richard, Richard Morin, and Demarais Rose. 1990. "Jeunes et précarisation économique: analyse de la situation des couples." *Cahiers Québécois de Démographie* 19,2: 273-307.

Marleau, Jacques D. and Jean-François Saucier. 1993. "Préférence des femmes canadiens et québécoises non enceintes quant au sexe du premier enfant." *Cahiers Québécois de Démographie* 22,2: 363-72.

Marshall, Katherine. 1990. "Household Chores." *Canadian Social Trends* 16: 18-19.

— 1993a. "Dual Earners: Who's Responsible for Housework?" *Canadian Social Trends* 31: 11-14.

— 1993b. "Employed Parents and the Division of Housework." *Perspectives on Labour and Income* 5,3: 23-30.

— 1994. "Balancing Work and Family Responsibilities." *Perspectives on Labour and Income* 6,1: 26-30.

— 1998a. "Stay-at-Home Dads." *Perspectives on Labour and Income* 10,1: 9-15.

— 1998b. "Couples Working Shift."
Perspectives on Labour and Income 10,3:
9-14.

Marsiglio, William. 1998. "In Search of a
Theory: Men's Fertility and Parental
Investment in Modern Economies." In A.
Booth and A.C. Crouter, eds., *Men in
Families: When Do They Get Involved?
What Difference Does It Make?* Mahwah,
N.J.: Lawrence Erlbaum.

Marx, Karl. 1973 [1867]. *Le capital.* Livre premier, Tome III, Paris: Editions sociales.

Mason, Karen Oppenheim. 1995. *Gender and
Demographic Change: What Do We Know?*
Liège, Belgium: International Union for
the Scientific Study of Population.

Matthews, Beverly. 1994. "The Relationship
between Gender and Fertility Strategies."
Ph.D thesis, University of Western
Ontario, London, Ont.

Matthews, Beverly and Roderic Beaujot. 1997.
"Gender Orientations and Family Stra-
tegies." *Canadian Review of Sociology and
Anthropology* 34,4: 415-28.

Maxwell, Judith. 1990. "The Economic Role
of Women." *Au Courant* 10,4: 12-13.

McDaniel, Susan. 1989. "Reconceptualizing
the Nuptiality\Fertility Relationship in
Canada in a New Age." *Canadian Studies
in Population* 16,2: 163-85.

— 1991. "Feminist Scholarship in Sociology:
Transformations from Within." *Canadian
Journal of Sociology* 16: 303-12.

— 1994. *Family and Friends.* Ottawa: Statistics
Canada, cat. no. 11-612, no. 9.

McDonald, Peter. 1990. "The 1980s: Social
and Economic Change." *Family Matters*
26: 13-18.

— 1997. "Gender Equity, Social Institutions
and the Future of Fertility." Australian
National University, Working Papers in
Demography, no. 69.

McFarlane, Seth. 1997. "Work-Family Conflict and the Domestic Division of Labour." M.A. thesis, University of Western
Ontario, London, Ont.

McIlroy, Anne. 1998. "Recognize Both
Parents as Crucial for Children:
Parliamentary Committee Recommends
Changes to Divorce Act." *The Globe and
Mail* 10 December 1998: A8.

McLaren, Angus and Arlene Tiger McLaren.
1986. *The Bedroom and the State: The
Changing Practices and Politics of Contraception and Abortion in Canada, 1880-1980.*
Toronto: McClelland and Stewart.

McMahon, Martha. 1995. *Engendering
Motherhood: Identity and Self-Transfor-
mation in Women's Lives.* New York: The
Guilford Press.

McMullin, Julie Ann and Peri Ballantyne.
1995. "Employment Characteristics and
Income: Assessing Gender and Age Group
Effects for Canadians Aged 45 Years and
Over." *Canadian Journal of Sociology* 20,4:
529-55.

McQuillan, Julia and Myra Marx Feree. 1998.
"The Importance of Variation among Men
and the Benefits of Feminism for Fami-
lies." In A. Booth and A.C. Crouter, eds.,
*Men in Families: When Do They Get
Involved? What Difference Does It Make?*
Mahwah, N.J.: Lawrence Erlbaum.

McQuillan, Kevin. 1989. "Discussion." In J.
Légaré, T.R. Balakrishnan, and R.
Beaujot, eds., *The Family in Crisis: A
Population Crisis?* Ottawa: Royal Society of
Canada.

— 1991. "Family Change and Family Income in Ontario." In L.C. Johnson and D. Barnhorst, eds., *Children, Families and Public Policy in the 90s*. Toronto: Thompson Education Publishing.

McQuillan, Kevin and Marilyn Belle. 1997. "Who Does What? Gender and the Division of Labour in Canadian Households." University of Western Ontario: Population Studies Centre Discussion Paper, no. 97-16.

Meissner, Martin. 1985. "The Domestic Economy." In M. Safir, Martha T. Mednick, Daphne Israeli, and Jessie Berrard, eds., *Women's Worlds*. New York: Praeger.

Meissner, Martin, Elizabeth Humphreys, Scott Meis, and William Scheu. 1975. "No Exit for Wives: Sexual Division of Labour and The Cumulation of Household Demands." *Canadian Review of Sociology and Anthropology* 12,4: 424-39.

Meunier, Dominique, Paul Bernard, and Johanne Boisjoly. 1998. "Eternal Youth? Changes in the Living Arrangements of Young People." In M. Corak, ed., *Labour Markets, Social Institutions and the Future of Canada's Children*. Ottawa: Statistics Canada, cat. no. 89-553.

Michelson, William. 1985. *From Sun to Sun: Daily Obligations and Community Structure in the Lives of Employed Women and Their Families*. Totowa, N.J.: Rowman and Allanheld.

Mintz, Steven. 1998. "From Patriarchy to Androgyny and Other Myths: Placing Men's Roles in Historical Perspective." In A. Booth and A.C. Crouter, eds., *Men in Families: When Do They Get Involved? What Difference Does It Make?* Mahwah, N.J.: Lawrence Erlbaum.

Moen, Phyllis. 1989. *Working Parents: Transformation in Gender Roles and Public Policies in Sweden*. Madison: University of Wisconsin Press.

— 1992. *Women's Two Roles: A Contemporary Dilemma*. New York: Auburn House.

Moen, Phyllis and Yan Yu. 1997. "Does Success at Work Compete with Success at Home?" Cornell University: BLCC Working Papers 97-06.

Montgomery, Mark R. 1996. "Comments on Men, Women and Unintended Pregnancy." *Population and Development Review* 22, Suppl: 100-6.

Moore, Maureen. 1987. "Women Parenting Alone." *Canadian Social Trends* 7: 31-36.

— 1988. "Female Lone Parenthood: The Duration of Episodes." *Canadian Social Trends* 10: 40-42.

— 1989a. "Female Lone Parenting over the Life Course." *Canadian Journal of Sociology* 14,3: 335-52.

— 1989b. "Dual Earner Families: The New Norm." *Canadian Social Trends* 12: 24-26.

Morgan, Laurie. 1998. "Glass Ceiling or Cohort Effect? A Longitudinal Study of the Gender Earnings Gap for Engineers, 1982-1989." *American Sociological Review* 63,4: 479-83.

Morissette, René. 1997. "Declining Earnings of Young Men." *Canadian Social Trends* 46: 8-12.

— 1998. "The Declining Labour Market Status of Young Men." In M. Corak, ed., *Labour Markets, Social Institutions and the Future of Canada's Children*. Ottawa: Statistics Canada, cat. no. 89-553.

Morisette, René, J. Myles, and G. Picot. 1994. "What Is Happening to Employment Inequality." Statistics Canada: Survey of Consumer Finances, Research Paper, no. 60.

— 1996. "Earnings Polarization in Canada: 1969-1991." In K. Banting and C. Beach, eds., *Labour Market Polarization and Social Policy Reform*. Kingston, Ont.: Queen's University School of Policy Studies.

Morris, Lydia. 1990. *The Workings of the Household*. Cambridge: Polity Press.

Moss, Peter. 1997. "Early Childhood Services in Europe." *Policy Options* 18,1: 27-30.

Myles, John. 1981. "The Aged and the Welfare State." Presentation, International Sociological Association Meetings, Paris, July 1981.

— 1991. "Women, the Welfare State and Care-Givers." *Canadian Journal on Aging* 10,2: 82-85.

Myles, John, G. Picot, and T. Wannell. 1993. "Does Post-Industrialism Matter? The Canadian Experience." In G. Esping-Anderson, ed., *Changing Classes: Stratification and Mobility in Post-Industrial Societies*. London: Sage.

Nakhaie, M. Rela. 1995. "Housework in Canada: The National Picture." *Journal of Comparative Family Studies* 24,3: 409-25.

Nakhaie, M. Rela and James Curtis. 1998. "Effects of Class Position of Parents on Educational Attainment of Daughters and Sons." *Canadian Review of Sociology and Anthropology* 35,4: 483-515.

Nasman, Elisabeth. 1990. "The Importance of Family Policy for Father's Care of Their Children." Presentation, Men as Carers for Children Seminar, Glasgow, May 1990.

— 1992. "Parental Leave in Sweden: A Workplace Issue?" Stockholm Research Reports in Demography, no. 73.

— 1993. *Childhood as a Social Phenomenon: National Report, Sweden*. Vienna: Eurosocial Reports, vol. 36.

— 1995. "Childhood, Family and New Ways of Life: The Case of Sweden." In L. Chisholm, Peter Buechner, Hermann Heinz Kruger, and Manuela Reymond du-Bois, eds., *Growing up in Europe*. Berlin: Walter De Gruyter.

— 1997. Personal Communication. Uppsala University, Sweden: June 1997.

National Council of Welfare. 1998. *Poverty Profile 1996*. Ottawa: National Council of Welfare.

Nault, François and Alain Bélanger. 1996. *The Decline of Marriage in Canada 1981 to 1991*. Statistics Canada, cat. no. 84-536.

Neale, Deborah. 1993. "Women and Work: Changing Gender Role Attitudes in Alberta." University of Alberta: Population Research Laboratory, Survey Highlights, no. 12.

Nett, Emily. 1993. *Canadian Families: Past and Present*. Toronto: Butterworths.

Nevitte, Neil. 1996. *The Decline of Deference*. Peterborough, Ont.: Broadview.

Neysmith, Sheila. 1991. "From Community Care to a Social Model of Care." In C.T. Baines, P. Evans, and S. Neysmith, eds., *Women's Caring: Feminist Perspectives on Social Welfare*. Toronto: McClelland and Stewart.

Ng, Edward. 1992. "Children and Elderly People: Sharing Public Income Resources." *Canadian Social Trends* 15: 12-15.

Ng, Edward and François Nault. 1996. "Census Based Estimates of Fertility by Mother's Socio-Economic Characteristics in Canada, 1991." Presentation, Canadian Population Society Meetings, St. Catherines, Ont., June 1996.

Ni Bhrolchain, Maire. 1993. "Women's and Men's Life Strategies in Developed Societies." Presentation, International Union for the Scientific Study of Population Meetings, Montreal, August 1993.

Nock, Steven. 1998. "Marriages in Men's Lives." In A. Booth and A.C. Crouter, eds., *Men in Families: When Do They Get Involved? What Difference Does It Make?* Mahwah, N.J.: Lawrence Erlbaum.

Normand, Josée. 1995. "Education of Women in Canada." *Canadian Social Trends* 39: 17-21.

Novack, Lesley and David Novack. 1996. "Being Female in the Eighties and Nineties: Conflicts between New Opportunities and Traditional Expectations." *Sex Roles* 35,1-2: 57-77.

O'Connell, Martin. 1993. "Where's Papa? Father's Role in Child Care." *Population Trends and Public Policy*. Population Reference Bureau, no.20.

Oakley, Ann. 1974. *The Sociology of Housework.* New York: Pantheon Books.

Oderkirk, Jillian and Clarence Lockhead. 1992. "Lone Parenthood: Gender Differences." *Canadian Social Trends* 27: 16-19.

Oderkirk, Jillian, Cynthia Silver, and Mark Prud'homme. 1994. "Traditional Earner Families." *Canadian Social Trends* 34: 19-25.

Odynak, Dave. 1994. "Age at First Intercourse in Canada." *Canadian Studies in Population* 21,1: 51-70.

OECD (Organization for Economic Co-operation and Development). 1990. *Lone Parent Families: The Economic Challenge*. Paris: OECD.

O'Hara, Kathy. 1998. "Comparative Family Policy: Eight Countries' Stories." Toronto: Canadian Policy Research Network Study, no. F/04.

Olah, Livia. 1996. "The Impact of Public Policies on the Second-Birth Rates in Sweden: A Gender Perspective." Stockholm Research Reports in Demography, no. 98.

Oppenheimer, Valerie K. 1988. "A Theory of Marriage Timing." *American Journal of Sociology* 94,3: 563-91.

— 1994. "Women's Rising Employment and the Future of the Family in Industrial Societies." *Population and Development Review* 20,2: 293-342.

— 1997. "Women's Employment and the Gain to Marriage: The Specialization and Trading Model." *Annual Review of Sociology* 23: 431-53.

Ornstein, Michael and Perri Stewart. 1996. "Gender and Faculty Pay in Canada." *Canadian Journal of Sociology* 21,4: 461-81.

Ornstein, Michael and Tony Haddad. 1993. *About Time: Analysis from a 1986 Survey of Canadians*. York: Institute for Social Research.

Pal, Leslie. 1993. *Interests of State: The Politics of Language, Multiculturalism, and Feminism in Canada*. Montreal: McGill-Queen's University Press.

Pamomba, Rosella. 1995. "Changes in the Family and Emerging Policy Issues." In M. Van Dogen, Gerard Frinking, and Menno Jacobs, eds., *Changing Fatherhood*. Amsterdam: Thesis Publishers.

Parcel, Toby and Elizabeth Menaghan. 1994. *Parents' Jobs and Children's Lives*. New York: Aldine de Gruyter.

Park, N. 1991. "Child Care in Ontario." In R. Barnhorst and L. Johnson, eds., *The State of the Child in Ontario*. Toronto: Oxford University Press.

Parliament, Jo-Anne. 1989. "Women Employed outside the Home." *Canadian Social Trends* 13: 3-6.

Parsons, Talcott. 1949. "The Social Structure of the Family." In R. Anshen, ed., *The Family: Its Function and Destiny*. New York: Harper and Brothers.

Parsons, Talcott and Robert F. Bales. 1955. *Family, Socialization and Interaction Process*. New York: Free Press.

Peitchinis, Stephen. 1989. *Women at Work: Discrimination and Response*. Toronto: McClelland and Stewart.

Péron, Yves and Jacques Légaré. 1988. "L'histoire matrimoniale et parentale des générations atteignant le seuil de la vieillesse d'ici l'an 2000." Ottawa: Report for Review of Demography, Health and Welfare.

Péron, Yves, E. Lapierre-Adamcyk, and Denis Morissette. 1987. "Les répercussions des nouveaux comportements démographiques sur la vie familiale: la situation canadienne." *International Review of Community Development* 18,58: 57-66.

Péron, Yves, Hélène Desrosiers, Heather Juby, Evelyne Lapierre-Adamcyk, Céline Le Bourdais, Nicole Marcil-Gratton, and Jael Mongeau. 1999. *Canadian Families at the Approach of the Year 2000*. Ottawa: Statistics Canada cat. no. 96-321, no.4.

Pérusse, Dominique. 1998. "Working at Home." *Perspectives on Labour and Income* 10,2: 16-23.

Peters, Suzanne. 1995. "Public Policy Dimensions and Dynamics of Families." *Towards the XXIst Century: Socio-Demographic Trends and Policy Issues in Canada*. Ottawa: Federation of Canadian Demographers.

Peterson, Richard R. and Kathleen Gerson. 1992. "Determinants of Responsibility for Child Care Arrangements among Dual-Earner Couples." *Journal of Marriage and the Family* 54: 527-36.

Philip, Margaret. 1998. "Parental Leave: Men Taking Baby Steps." *The Globe and Mail* 19 October 1998: A16.

Phipps, Shelley. 1996. "Lessons from Europe: Policy Options to Enhance the Economic Security of Canadian Families." In National Forum on Family Security, *Family Security in Insecure Times*, vol. II. Ottawa: Canadian Council on Social Development.

— 1998. "Comparing the Economic Well-Being of Children in Lone-Mother Families in Canada, Norway and the United States." *Policy Options* 19,7: 10-13.

Phipps, Shelley and Peter Burton. 1996. "Collective Models of Family Behaviour." *Canadian Public Policy* 22,2: 129-43.

Picot, Garnett. 1980. *The Changing Education Profile of Canadians, 1961 to 2000*. Ottawa: Statistics Canada.

— 1989. "Modelling the Lifetime Employment Patterns of Canadians." In J. Légaré, T.R. Balakrishnan, and Roderic Beaujot, eds., *The Family in Crisis: A Population Crisis?* Ottawa: Royal Society of Canada.

— 1998. "What Is Happening to Earnings Inequality and Youth Wages in the 1990s." *Canadian Economic Observer* 11,9: 3.1-3.18.

Picot, Garnett and John Myles. 1996a. "Social Transfers and Changes in Family Structure and Low Income among Children." *Canadian Public Policy* 22,3: 244-67.

— 1996b. "Children in Low-Income Families." *Canadian Social Trends* 42: 15-19.

Picot, Garnett, John Myles, and Wendy Pyper. 1998. "Markets, Families and Social Transfers: Trends in Low-Income among the Young and Old, 1973-95." In M. Corak, ed., *Labour Markets, Social Institutions and the Future of Canada's Children*. Ottawa: Statistics Canada, cat. no. 89-553.

Pittman, Joe F. and David Blanchard. 1996. "The Effects of Work History and Timing of Marriage on the Division of Household Labour: A Life-Course Perspective." *Journal of Marriage and the Family* 58,1: 78-90.

Pollak, Robert A. and Susan Cotts Watkins. 1993. "Culture and Economic Approaches to Fertility: Proper Marriage or Mésalliance?" *Population and Development Review* 19,3: 467-96.

Pollard, June. 1991. "Ideology, Social Policy and Home-Based Child Care." In I. Kyle, Martha Friendly, and Lori Schmidt, eds., *Proceedings from the Child Care Policy and Research Symposium*, University of Toronto.

Popenoe, David. 1988. *Disturbing the Nest: Family Change and Decline in Modern Societies*. New York: Aldine de Gruyter.

Powell, Lisa. 1997. "Family Behaviour and Child Care Costs: Policy Implications." *Policy Options* 18,1: 11-15.

Prentice, Susan. 1992. "Workers, Mothers and Reds: Toronto's Postwar Daycare Fight." In M.P. Connelly and P. Armstrong, eds., *Feminism in Action*. Toronto: Canadian Scholar's Press.

Presser, Harriet B. 1994. "Employment Schedules among Dual-Earner Spouses and the Division of Household Labor by Gender." *American Sociological Review* 59,3: 348-64.

— 1995. "Are the Interests of Women Inherently at Odds with the Interests of Children and the Family? A Viewpoint". In K. Mason and A-M. Jensen, eds., *Gender and Family Change in Industrialized Countries*. Oxford: Clarendon.

— 1998. "Toward a 24 Hour Economy: The U.S. Experience and Implications for the Family." In D. Vannoy and P.J. Dubeck, eds., *Challenges for Work and Family in the Twenty-First Century*. New York: Aldine De Gruyter.

Pressland, Pauline and John K. Antill. 1987. "Household Division of Labour: The Impact of Hours Worked in Paid Employment." *Australian Journal of Psychology* 39: 273-91.

Preston, Samuel H. 1984. "Children and the Elderly: Divergent Paths for America's Dependents." *Demography* 21: 435-58.

— 1986. "Changing Values and Falling Birth Rates." *Population and Development Review* 12, Suppl: 176-95.

Prince, Michael J. 1985. "Startling Facts, Sobering Truths and Sacred Trust: Pension Policy and the Tories." In M. Marlove, ed., *How Ottawa Spends, 1985*. Toronto: Methuen.

Propper, Alice. 1984. "The Invisible Reality: Patterns and Power in Family Violence." In M. Baker, ed., *The Family: Changing Trends in Canada*. Toronto: McGraw-Hill Ryerson.

Pupo, Norene. 1997. "Always Working, Never Done: The Expansion of the Double Day." In A. Duffy, D. Glenday, and N. Pupo, eds., *Good Jobs, Bad Jobs, No Jobs*. Toronto: Harcourt Brace.

Rajulton, Fernando and T.R. Balakrishnan. 1990. "Interdependence of Transitions among Marital and Parity States in Canada." *Canadian Studies in Population* 17,1: 107-32.

Rajulton, Fernando and Zenaida Ravanera. 1998. "Gender and Cohort Experiences of Work Histories: Evidence from the GSS." Presentation, Canadian Population Society Meetings, Ottawa, June 1998.

Rajulton, Fernando, T.R. Balakrishnan, and Zenaida R. Ravanera. 1990. "Measuring Infertility in Contracepting Populations." Presentation, Canadian Population Society Meetings, Victoria, B.C., June 1990.

Ram, Bali. 1990. *New Trends in the Family*. Ottawa: Statistics Canada, cat. no. 91-535.

Ram, Bali and Abdur Rahim. 1993. "Enduring Effects of Women's Early Employment Experience on Child-Spacing: The Canadian Evidence." *Population Studies* 47,2: 307-17.

Ranson, Gillian. 1995. "Careers and\or Families: Choices and Dilemmas of Young Professional Women." In L.C. Johnson, ed., *Canadian Families*. Toronto: Thompson.

— 1998. "Education, Work and Family Decision Making: Finding the Right Time to Have a Baby." *Canadian Review of Sociology and Anthropology* 35,4: 517-33.

Rao, K.V. and T.R. Balakrishnan. 1988. "Age at First Birth in Canada: A Hazards Model Analysis." *Genus* 44,1-2: 53-72.

Rashid, Abdul. 1989. *Family Income*. Ottawa: Statistics Canada, cat. no. 98-128.

— 1993. "Several Decades of Wage Changes." *Perspectives on Labour and Income* 5,2: 9-21.

— 1994. *Family Income in Canada*. Ottawa: Statistics Canada, cat. no. 96-318.

— 1998. "Family Income Inequality, 1970-1995." *Perspectives on Labour and Income* 10,4: 12-17.

— 1999. "Family Income: 25 Years of Stability and Change." *Perspectives on Labour and Income* 11,1: 9-15.

Ravanera, Zenaida. 1995. "A Portrait of the Family Life of Young Adults." In R. Beaujot, Ellen M. Gee, Fernando Rajulton, and Zenaida R. Ravanera, eds., *Family over the Life Course*. Ottawa: Statistics Canada, cat. no. 91-543.

Ravanera, Zenaida and Fernando Rajulton. 1996. "Stability and Crisis in the Family Life Course: Findings from the 1990 General Social Survey, Canada." *Canadian Studies in Population* 23,2: 165-84.

Ravanera, Zenaida, Fernando Rajulton, and Thomas Burch. 1994. "Trends in the Life Course of Canadians." *Canadian Studies in Population* 21,1: 21-34.

— 1995. "A Cohort Analysis of Home Leaving in Canada, 1910-1975." *Journal of Comparative Family Studies* 26,2: 179-94.

— 1998a. "Trends and Variations in the Early Life Courses of Canadian Men." University of Western Ontario, London, Ont.: Discussion Paper, no. 98-7.

— 1998b. "Early Life Transitions of Canadian Women: A Cohort Analysis of Timing, Sequences, and Variations." *European Journal of Population* 14: 179-204.

Reskin, Barbara and Irene Padavic. 1994. *Women and Men at Work.*Thousand Oaks, Cal.: Pine Forge Press.

Rexroat, Cynthia. 1985. "Women's Work Expectations and Labour Market Experience in Early and Middle Family Life-Cycle Stages." *Journal of Marriage and the Family* 47,1: 131-42.

Richards, John. 1997a. *Retooling the Welfare State*. Toronto: C.D. Howe.

— 1997b. "Poor Families with Kids." *Inroads* 6: 39-54.

Rietschlin, John and Cathy Thorpe. 1997. "Family Structure, Social Networks and Social Support." Presentation, American Sociological Association Meetings, Toronto, August 1997.

Rifkin, Jeremy. 1995. *The End of Work*. New York: Putnam.

Riley, Nancy. 1997. "Gender, Power, and Population Change." *Population Bulletin* 52,1: 1-48.

Rindfuss, Ronald and Audrey VandenHeuvel. 1990. "Cohabitation: Precursor to Marriage or an Alternative to Being Single." *Population and Development Review* 16,4: 703-26.

Rindfuss, Ronald and Karin Brewster. 1996. "Childrearing and Fertility." *Population and Development Review* 22, Suppl: 258-89.

Rindfuss, Ronald, Karin Brewster, and Andrew Kovee. 1996. "Women, Work and Children: Behavioral and Attitudinal Change in the United States." *Population and Development Review* 22,3: 457-82.

Rinehart, James W. 1996. *The Tyranny of Work: Alienation and the Labour Process*. Toronto: Harcourt Brace.

Robertson, A.F. 1991. *Beyond the Family and the Social Organization of Human Reproduction*. Berkeley: University of California Press.

Robinson, Patricia. 1989. "Women's Work Interruptions and the Family: An Exploration of the Family History Survey." In J. Légaré, T.R. Balakrishnan, and R. Beaujot, eds., *The Family in Crisis: A Population Crisis?* Ottawa: Royal Society of Canada.

Rodgers, Karen. 1994. "Wife Assault in Canada." *Canadian Social Trends* 34: 2-8.

Romaniuc, Anatole. 1984. *Fertility in Canada: From Baby-Boom to Baby-Bust*. Ottawa: Statistics Canada.

— 1991. "Fertility in Canada: Retrospective and Prospective." *Canadian Studies in Population* 18,2: 56-77.

Ronsen, Marit and Marianne Sundstrom. 1997. "Women's Return to Work after a First Birth in the Nordic Countries: Full-Time or Part-Time." Stockholm University: Research Reports in Demography, no. 112.

Ross, Catherine E., John Mirowsky, and Joan Huber. 1983. "Dividing Work, Sharing Work, and In-Between: Marriage Patterns and Depression." *American Sociological Review* 48: 809-23.

Ross, David P. and Richard Shillington. 1989. *The Canadian Fact Book on Poverty, 1989.* Ottawa: Canadian Council on Social Development.

Ross, David P., Katherine Scott, and Mark Kelly. 1996. "Overview: Children in Canada in the 1990s." In *Growing up in Canada.* Statistics Canada, cat. no. 89-550, no. 1.

Ross, David P., Paul A. Roberts and Katherine Scott. 1998a."How Do Lone-Parent Children Differ from All Children?" Presentation, Conference on Investing in Children, Ottawa, October 1998.

— 1998b. "Comparing Children in Lone-Parent Families: Differences and Similarities." Presentation, Conference on Investing in Children, Ottawa, October 1998.

Rossi, Alice S. 1977. "A Biosocial Perspective on Parenting." *Daedalus* 106,2: 1-31.

— 1984. "Gender and Parenthood." *American Sociological Review* 49,1: 1-19.

— 1985. *Gender and the Life Course.* New York: Aldine de Gruyter.

— 1994. "Eros and Caritas: A Biopsychological Approach to Human Sexuality and Reproduction." In Alice S. Rossi, *Sexuality and the Life Course.* Chicago: University of Chicago Press.

Roussel, Louis. 1979. "Générations nouvelles et mariage traditionnel." *Population* 34,1: 141-62.

— 1987. "Deux decennies de mutations demographiques (1965-1985) dans les pays industrialisés." *Population* 42,3: 429-48.

— 1989. "*La famille incertaine.*" Paris: Editions Odile Jacob.

— 1992. "Fertility and Family." United Nations, Economic Commission for Europe: Presentation, European Population Conference, Geneva, March 1993.

Rowe, Geoff. 1989. "Union Dissolution in a Changing Social Context." In J. Légaré, T.R. Balakrishnan, and R. Beaujot, eds., *The Family in Crisis: A Population Crisis?* Ottawa: Royal Society of Canada.

Royal Commission on Learning, Ontario, 1994. *For the Love of Learning.* Toronto: Queen's Printer.

Royal Commission on New Reproductive Technologies. 1993. *Proceed with Care.* Ottawa: Minister of Government Services.

Royal Commission on the Economic Union and Development Prospects for Canada. 1985. *Report.* 3 vols. Ottawa: Supply and Services.

Russell, Bob. 1993. "Working Class Resistance and Collective Action." In J. Curtis, E. Grabb, and N. Guppy, eds., *Social Inequality in Canada.* Toronto: Prentice-Hall.

Rutledge, Margie. 1998. "Motherhood and the Muse." *The Globe and Mail* 7 November 1998: D1-D2.

Rydenstan, Klas. 1997. Personal Communication. Statistics Sweden, July 1997.

Sainsbury, Diane. 1996. *Gender, Equality and Welfare States.* Cambridge: Cambridge University Press.

Scanzoni, Letha and John Scanzoni. 1976. *Men, Women and Change: A Sociology of Marriage and the Family.* New York: McGraw-Hill.

Schellenberg, Grant. 1997. "The Changing Nature of Part-Ttime Work." *Perception* 21,2: 9-12.

Schembari, Patricia. 1998. "Estimates of Private Households and Economic Entities." Presentation, Statistics Canada Advisory Committee on Demographic Statistics and Studies Meetings, Ottawa, December 1998.

Scherer, Peter. 1997. "Socio-Economic Change and Social Policy." *Family, Market and Community: Equity and Efficiency in Social Policy.* Paris: Organization for Economic Co-operation and Development.

Schmid, Carol. 1991. "The Changing Status of Women in the United States and Canada: An Overview." In J. Veevers, ed., *Continuity and Change in Marriage and Family.* Toronto: Holt, Rinehart and Winston.

Schoen, Robert, Young J. Kim, Constance A. Nathanson, Jason Fields, and Nan Marie Astone. 1997. "Why Do Americans Want Children?" *Population and Development Review* 23,2: 333-58.

Scommegna, Paola. 1996. "Do Working Moms Anticipate the Trade-Offs?" *Population Today* 24,6-7: 3.

Scott, Katherine. 1996. "Investing in Canada's Children: Our Current Record." *Perception* 20,3: 5-7.

Seltzer, Judith A. 1994. "Consequences of Marital Dissolution for Children." *Annual Review of Sociology* 20: 235-66.

Sev'er, Aysan. 1996. "Mainstream Neglect of Sexual Harassment as a Social Problem." *Canadian Journal of Sociology* 21,2: 185-202.

Shamir, Boas. 1986. "Unemployment and Household Division of Labour." *Journal of Marriage and Family* 48: 195-206.

Shapiro, D.M. and M. Stelcner. 1987. "The Persistence of the Male-Female Earnings Gap in Canada, 1970-1980: The Impact of Equal Pay Laws and Language Policies." *Canadian Public Policy* 13,4: 462-76.

Sharif, Najma and Shelley Phipps. 1994. "The Challenge of Child Poverty: Which Policies Might Help." *Canadian Business Economics* 2,3: 17-30.

Shaw, Susan M. 1988. "Gender Differences in the Definition and Perception of Household Labor." *Family Relations* 37: 333-37.

Shea, Catherine. 1990. "Changes in Women's Occupations." *Canadian Social Trends* 18: 21-23.

Shehan, Constance and Karen Seccombe. 1996. "The Changing Circumstances of Children's Lives." *Journal of Family Issues* 17,4: 435-40.

Shelton, Beth Anne. 1990. "The Distribution of Household Tasks: Does Wife's Employment Status Make a Difference?" *Journal of Family Issues* 11,2: 115-35.

— 1992. *Women, Men and Time: Gender Differences in Paid Work, Housework and Leisure.* New York: Greenwood Press.

Shelton, Beth Anne and Daphne John. 1993. "Does Marital Status Make a Difference?" *Journal of Family Issues* 14,3: 401-20.

Sheridan, Mike, Deborah Sunter, and Brent Diverty. 1996. "The Changing Work Week: Trends in Weekly Hours of Work in Canada, 1976-1995." *The Labour Force, June 1996.* Ottawa: Statistics Canada, cat. no. 71-001.

Shorter, Edward. 1975. *The Making of the Modern Family.* New York: Basic Books.

Sinclair, Peter and Lawrence Felt. 1992. "Separate Worlds: Gender and Domestic Labour in an Isolated Fishing Region." *Canadian Review of Sociology and Anthropology* 29,1: 55-71.

Skolnick, Arlene. 1987. *The Intimate Environment.* Boston: Little, Brown.

— 1991. *Embattled Paradise: The American Family in an Age of Uncertainty.* New York: Basic.

Skrypnek, Berna and Janet Fast. 1996. "Work and Family Policy in Canada: Family Needs, Collective Solutions." *Journal of Family Issues* 17,6: 793-812.

Smeeding, Timothy, Sheldon Danzinger, and Lee Rainwater. 1995. "The Welfare State in the 1990s: Toward a New Model of Anti-Poverty Policy for Families with Children." Manuscript, Luxembourg Income Study.

Smith, Dorothy. 1997. "Sociology of Everyday Life." Presentation, Department of Sociology, University of Western Ontario, London, Ont., 17 January 1997.

Smith, Gordon and Jean Dumas. 1994. "The Sandwich Generation: Myths and Realities." In *Report on the Demographic Situation.* Ottawa: Statistics Canada.

Smock, Pamela and Wendy Manning. 1997. "Cohabitating Partners' Economic Circumstances and Marriage." *Demography* 34,3: 331-41.

Sorenson, A.M. and C. Grindstaff. 1995. "Adolescent Mothers: The Report of Living Arrangements on Long-Term Economic Outcomes." *Canadian Studies in Population* 22,2: 91-105.

South, Scott and Glenna Spitze. 1994. "Housework in Marital and Non-Marital Households." *American Sociological Review* 59,3: 327-47.

Spain, Daphne and Suzanne Bianchi. 1996. *Balancing Act: Motherhood, Marriage and Employment among American Women.* New York: Sage Foundation.

Stafford, James. 1987. "The Political Economic Context of Post-War Fertility Patterns in Canada." In *Contributions to Demography.* Edmonton: Population Research Laboratory.

Statistics Canada. 1992. *Lone-Parent Families in Canada.* Ottawa: Statistics Canada, cat. no. 89-522.

— 1995a. *Women in Canada: A Statistical Report.* Ottawa: Statistics Canada, cat. no. 89-503.

— 1995b. *Household's Unpaid Work: Measurement and Valuation.* Ottawa: Statistics Canada, cat. no. 13-603, no. 3.

— 1996. *Education in Canada, 1995.* Ottawa: Statistics Canada, cat. no. 81-229.

— 1997a. "1996 Census: Marital Status, Common-Law Unions and Families." *The Daily* 14 October 1997.

— 1997b. *Marriage and Divorce.* Ottawa: Statistics Canada, cat. no. 84-212.

— 1997c. "Youth and the Labour Market." *Labour Force Update.* Ottawa: Statistics Canada, cat. no. 71-005.

— 1998a. "1996 Census: Labour Force Activity." *The Daily* 17 March 1998.

— 1998b. "1996 Census: Private Households, Housing Costs and Social and Economic Characteristics of Families." *The Daily* 9 June 1998.

— 1998c. "1996 Census: Sources of Income, Earnings and Total Income and Family Income." *The Daily* 12 May 1998.

— 1998d. *Earnings of Men and Women, 1996.* Ottawa: Statistics Canada, cat. no. 13-217.

— 1998e. "Education, Mobility and Migration." *The Daily* 14 April 1998.

— 1998f. *Income after Tax, Distribution by Size.* Ottawa: Statistics Canada, cat. no. 13-210.

— 1998g. "Key Labour and Income Facts." *Perspectives on Labour and Income* 10,4: 55-69.

— 1998h. "Minimum Wage Workers." *Labour Force Update* 2,3: 26-33.

— 1998i. "National Longitudinal Survey of Children and Youth." *The Daily* 28 October 1998.

— 1998j. *Scan* Winter 1998.

— 1998k. "National Longitudinal Survey of Children and Youth." *The Daily* 2 June 1998.

— 1999. *Scan* Winter 1999.

Stephens, Linda. 1996. "Will Johnny See Daddy This Week?" *Journal of Family Issues* 17,4: 466-94.

Stone, Lawrence. 1977. *The Family, Sex and Marriage in England 1500-1800.* London: Weidenfeld and Nicolson.

Stone, Leroy O. 1988. *Family and Friendship Ties among Canada's Seniors.* Ottawa: Statistics Canada, cat. no. 89-508.

— 1994. *Dimensions of the Job-Family Tension.* Ottawa: Statistics Canada, cat. no. 89-540.

Stone, Leroy O., Carolyn Rosenthal, and Ingrid Connidis. 1998. *Parent-Child Exchanges of Supports and Intergenerational Equity.* Ottawa: Statistics Canada, cat. no. 89-557.

Stout, Cameron W. 1992. "A Degree of Change." *Perspectives on Labour and Income* 4,4: 14-19.

Strain, Laurel A. 1990. "Receiving and Providing Care: The Experiences of Never-Married Elderly Canadians." Presentation, XII World Congress of Sociology, Madrid, July 1990.

Strike, Carol. 1995. "Women Assaulted by Strangers." *Canadian Social Trends* 36: 2-6.

Sullerot, Evelyne. 1992. *Quels pères? quels fils.* Paris: Fayard.

Sullivan, Oriel. 1997. "The Division of Housework among Re-Married Couples." *Journal of Family Issues* 18,2: 205-23.

Sundstrom, Marianne. 1991a. "Sweden: Supporting Work, Family and Gender Equality." In S.B. Kamerman and A.J. Kahn, eds., *Child Care, Parental Leave and the Under Three's: Policy Innovation in Europe.* New York: Auburn House.

— 1991b. "Part-Time Work in Sweden: Trends and Equity Effects." *Journal of Economic Issues* 25,1: 167-78.

— 1994. "Managing Work and Children: Part Time Work and the Family Life Cycle of Swedish Women." Stockholm Research Reports in Demography, no. 81.

— 1997. Personal communication. Stockholm University, Sweden, June 1997.

Sundstrom, Marianne and Frank P. Stafford. 1992. "Female Labour Force Participation, Fertility and Public Policy in Sweden." *European Journal of Population* 8: 199-215.

Sunter, Deborah. 1993. "School, Work, and Dropping Out." *Perspectives on Labour and Income* 5,2: 44-52.

— 1994. "Youths: Waiting It Out." *Perspectives on Labour and Income* 6,1: 31-36.

Sunter, Deborah and Geoff Bowlby. 1998. "Labour Force Participation in the 1990s." *Perspectives on Labour and Income* 10,3: 15-21.

Sunter, Deborah and René Morissette. 1994. "The Hours People Work." *Perspectives on Labour and Income* 6,3: 8-13.

Sussman, Deborah. 1998. "Moonlighting: A Growing Way of Life." *Perspectives on Labour and Income* 10,2: 24-31.

Sweeney, Megan. 1997. "Women, Men and Changing Families: The Shifting Economic Foundations of Marriage. University of Wisconsin-Madison: Center for Demography and Ecology, Working Paper, no. 97-14.

Swift, Jamie. 1997. "From Cars to Casinos, from Work to Workfare: The Brave New World of Canadian Employment." In A. Duffy, D. Glenday, and N. Pupo, eds., *Good Jobs, Bad Jobs, No Jobs.* Toronto: Harcourt Brace.

Szreter, Simon. 1995. *Fertility, Class and Gender in Britain, 1860-1940.* Cambridge: Cambridge University Press.

— 1996. "Falling Fertilities and Changing Sexualities in Europe since circa 1850." Canberra: Australia National University Working Papers in Demography, no. 62.

Tam, Tony. 1997. "Sex Segregation and Occupational Gender Inequality in the United States: Devaluation or Specialized Training?" *American Journal of Sociology* 102,6: 1652-92.

Teevan, James and W.E. Hewitt. 1998. *Introduction to Sociology: A Canadian Focus.* Toronto: Prentice-Hall.

Thadani, Veena. 1978. "The Logic of Sentiment: The Family and Social Change." *Population and Development Review* 4,3: 457-99.

The Economist. 1996. "The Trouble with Men." *The Globe and Mail* 5 October 1996: D5.

Thomas, Derrick. 1996. "The Social Welfare Implications of Immigrant Family Sponsorship Default." Presentation, National Symposium on Immigration and Integration, Winnipeg, October 1996.

Thompson, Linda. 1991. "Family Work: Women's Sense of Fairness." *Journal of Family Issues* 12: 181-96.

Thompson, Linda and Alexis Walker. 1989. "Gender in Families: Women and Men in Marriage, Work, and Parenthood." *Journal of Marriage and the Family* 51: 845-71.

Thomson, Elizabeth. 1997. "Couple Child-bearing Desires, Intentions and Births." *Demography* 34,3: 343-54.

Thomson, Elizabeth and Jan Hoem. 1998. "Couple Childbearing Plans and Births in Sweden." *Demography* 35,3: 315-22.

Thornton, Arland. 1989. "Changing Attitudes toward Family Issues in the United States." *Journal of Marriage and Family* 51,4: 873-93.

Thornton, Arland and William Axia. 1989. "Changing Patterns of Marital Dissolution in the United States: Demographic Implications." *International Population Conference, New Delhi.* Liège, Belgium: International Union for the Scientific Study of Population, vol. 3: 149-61.

Tougas, J. 1993. "Child Care: Consensus Already Exists." *The Globe and Mail* 1 May 1993.

Touleman, Laurent and Evelyne Lapierre-Adamcyk. 1995. "Demographic Patterns of Motherhood and Fatherhood in France." *Male Fertility in an Era of Fertility Decline.* Liège, Belgium: International Union for the Scientific Study of Population.

Trost, Jan. 1986. "What Holds Marriage Together." In J. Veevers, ed., *Continuity and Change in Marriage and Family.* Toronto: Holt, Rinehart and Winston.

— 1996. "Family Structure and Relationships: The Dyadic Approach." *Journal of Comparative Family Studies* 27,2: 395-408.

Turcotte, Pierre and Alain Bélanger, 1997. "Moving in Together." *Canadian Social Trends* 47: 7-9.

Tuzlak, Aysan and David W. Hillock. 1991. "Single Mothers and Their Children after Divorce: A Study of Those Who Make It." In J.E. Veevers, ed., *Continuity and Change in Marriage and Family.* Toronto: Holt, Rinehart and Winston.

United Nations. 1994. *Population and Development: Program of Action Adopted at the International Conference on Population and Development, Cairo, 5-13, September 1994.* New York: United Nations.

— 1995. *The World's Women: Trends and Statistics.* New York: United Nations.

— 1998. *Human Development Report.* New York: United Nations.

Ursel, Jane. 1986. "The State and the Maintenance of Patriarchy: A Case Study of Family, Labour and Welfare Legislation in Canada." In James Dickinson and Bob Russell, eds., *Family, Economy and State.* Toronto, Garamond Press.

— 1992. *Private Lives, Public Policy.* Toronto: Women's Press.

Van de Kaa, Dirk. 1987. "Europe's Second Demographic Transition." *Population Bulletin* 42,1: 1-58.

Van de Walle, Etienne and John Knodel. 1980. "Europe's Fertility Transition: New Evidence and Lessons for Today's Developing World." *Population Bulletin* 34,6: 1-58.

Van Dongen, Mirjam. 1995. "Men's Aspirations Concerning Child Care: The Extent to Which They Are Realized." In M. van Dongen, Gerard Frinking, and Menno Jacobs, eds., *Changing Fatherhood*. Amsterdam: Thesis Publishers.

Van Leeuwen, Mary Stewart. 1998. "Postmodern Marriage and the Deconstruction of the Culture of Divorce." Presentation, Veritas Conference, University of Western Ontario, London, Ont., 4-5 November 1998.

Vandelac, Louise. 1985. *Du travail et de l'amour*. Montreal: Saint-Martin.

Veevers, Jean E. 1980. *Childless by Choice*. Toronto: Butterworths.

Verbrugge, Lois. 1993. "Marriage Matters: Young Women's Health." In Bonita Long and Sharon Kahn, *Women, Work and Coping: A Multidisciplinary Approach to Workplace Stress*. Montreal and Kingston: McGill-Queen's University Press.

Vienneau, D. 1991. "Most Preschoolers at Home, Tory Poll Finds." *Toronto Star* 6 June 1991.

Wadhera, Surinder. 1990. "Therapeutic Abortions, Canada." *Health Reports* 1,2: 229-45.

Wadhera, Surinder and Wayne Millar. 1997. "Teenage Pregnancies, 1974 to 1994." *Health Reports* 9,3: 9-17.

Waite, Linda J. 1995. "Does Marriage Matter?" *Demography* 32,4: 483-507.

Waite, Linda J. and Lee A. Lillard. 1991. "Children and Marital Disruption." *American Journal of Sociology* 96,4: 930-53.

Walker, J.R. 1995. "The Effects of Public Policies on Recent Swedish Fertility Behaviour." *Journal of Population Economics* 8,3: 223-52.

Wannell, T. and N. Caron. 1994. "The Gender Earnings Gap among Recent Postsecondary Graduates, 1984-92." Research Paper Series, no. 68. Ottawa: Analytical Studies Branch, Statistics Canada.

Wannemo, Irene. 1994. *Sharing the Costs of Children*. Stockholm University: Swedish Institute for Social Research, no. 25.

Ward, Russell and Glenna Spitze. 1996. "Will Children Ever Leave?" *Journal of Family Issues* 17,4: 514-39.

Watkins, Susan Cotts. 1990. "From Local to National Communities: The Transformation of Demographic Regimes in Western Europe, 1870-1960." *Population and Development Review* 16,2: 241-72.

Wente, Margaret. 1993. "Who Gets to Be a Feminist?" *The Globe and Mail* 9 October 1993: A2.

— 1994. "The Break That Families Don't Get." *The Globe and Mail* 29 January 1994: A2

West, Candace and Don Zimmerman. 1987. "Doing Gender." *Gender and Society* 1,2: 125-51.

Westoff, Charles F. 1986. "Perspective on Nuptiality and Fertility." *Population and Development Review* 12, Suppl: 155-70.

Whitehead, Barbara D. 1998. *Divorce Culture*. New York: Random House.

Willms, J. Douglas. 1996. "Indications of Mathematics Achievement in Canadian Elementary Schools." In *Growing up in Canada*. Statistics Canada, cat. no. 89-550, no. 1.

Wilson, Susannah. 1990. "Alternatives to Traditional Marriage." In M. Baker, *Families: Changing Trends in Canada*. Toronto: McGraw-Hill.

— 1991. *Women, Families and Work*. Toronto: McGraw-Hill Ryerson.

Wister, Andrew, Barbara A. Mitchell, and Ellen M. Gee. 1997. "Does Money Matter? Parental Income and Living Arrangement Satisfaction among 'Boomerang' Children during Coresidence." *Canadian Studies in Population* 24,2: 125-45.

Woolley, Frances. 1998. "For a Radical Redesign of Our Tax Treatment of the Family." *Policy Options* 19,7: 7-10.

Woolley, Frances, Arndt Vermaeten, and Judith Madill. 1996. "Ending Universality: The Case of Child Benefits." *Canadian Public Policy* 22,1: 24-39.

Wright, Robert. 1988. "The Impact of Income Redistribution on Fertility in Canada." *Genus* 44,1-2: 139-56.

Wright, Robert and Paul Maxim. 1987. "Canadian Fertility Trends: A Further Test of the Easterlin Hypothesis." *Canadian Review of Sociology and Anthropology* 24,3: 339-57.

Wrigley, E. Anthony. 1977. "Reflection on the History of the Family." *Daedalus* 106,2: 71-86.

Wu, Zheng. 1995. "Childbearing in Cohabiting Relationships." Presentation, Canadian Population Society Meetings, Victoria, June 1995.

— 1997. "Third Birth Intentions and Uncertainty in Canada." Presentation, Canadian Population Society Meetings, St. John's, Nfld., June 1997.

Wu, Zheng and Douglas E. Baer. 1996. "Attitudes toward Family Life and Gender Roles: A Comparison of English and French Canadian Women." *Journal of Comparative Family Studies* 27,3: 437-52.

Yalnizyan, Armine. 1998. *The Growing Gap: A Report on Growing Inequality between the Rich and Poor in Canada*. Toronto: Centre for Social Justice.

Yeung, Wei-Jun Jean. 1991. "Female Employment and Fertility in Canada: A Sequential Life-Cycle Analysis." Ph.D. thesis, University of Alberta, Edmonton, Alta.

Yogev, Sara and Jeanne Brett. 1985. "Perceptions of the Division of Housework and Child Care and Marital Satisfaction." *Journal of Marriage and the Family* 47: 609-18.

Yu, Yan and Phyllis Moen. 1997. "Working Couples: Work Context, Life Stage, and the Division of Labor." Cornell University: BLCC Working Paper, no. 97-10.

Zeck, Cathleen and Jane McCullough. 1991. "Trends in Married Couples' Time-Use: Evidence from 1977-78 and 1987-88." *Sex Roles* 24,7-8: 459-87.

Zhao, John. 1994. "Leaving Parental Homes in Canada." Ph.D. thesis, University of Western Ontario, London, Ont.

Zhao, John, Fernando Rajulton, and Zenaida Ravanera. 1995. "Leaving Parental Homes in Canada: Effects of Family Structure, Gender, and Culture." *Canadian Journal of Sociology* 20,1: 31-50.

Zyblock, Myles. 1996a. "Child Poverty Trends in Canada." Human Resources Development Canada, Working Paper W-96-1E.

— 1996b. "Individual Earnings Inequality and Polarization: An Explanation with Population Sub-Group Trends in Canada 1980-93." Manuscript, Human Resources Development Canada, Ottawa.

— 1996c. "Why Is Family Market Income Inequality Increasing in Canada?" Human Resources Development Canada, Ottawa: Applied Research, WP 96-11.

copyrights

The Statistics Canada information cited by catalogue number below is used with the permission of the Minister of Industry, as Minister responsible for Statistics Canada. Information on the availability of the wide range of data from Statistics Canada can be obtained from Statistics Canada's Regional Offices, its World Wide Web site at http://www.statcan.ca, and its toll-free access number 1-800-263-1136.

TABLE 2.1 is adapted from *Universities, Enrolment and Degrees*, cat. no. 81-204, and *Education in Canada, A Statistical Review*, cat. no. 81-229.

TABLE 2.2 is adapted from *The Changing Education Profile of Canadians, 1961 to 2000*, G. Picot, and *The Labour Force*, cat. no. 71-001.

TABLE 2.3 is adapted from *Income after Tax, Distributions by Size in Canada*, cat. no. 13-210.

TABLE 2.4 is adapted from *Income Distributions by Size in Canada, 1996*, cat. no. 13-207.

TABLE 2.5 is adapted from *Women in Canada: A Statistical Report*, cat. no. 89-503.

TABLE 2.6 is adapted with permission from *The Canadian Journal of Sociology*, vol. 17, no. 1.

TABLE 3.1 is adapted from *Selected Birth and Fertility Statistics, Canada, 1921-1990*, cat. no. 82-553, *Selected Marriage Statistics*, cat. no. 82-552, *Marriages*, cat. no. 84-212, *Births and Deaths, Vital Statistics*, cat. no. 84-204, *Report on the Demographic Situation in Canada, 1996*, cat. no. 91-209, *1941 Census of Canada*, vol. V, *1951 Census of Canada*, vol. III, and Statistics Canada, special tabulations.

TABLE 3.3 is adapted from *Report on the Demographic Situation in Canada, 1996*, cat. no. 91-209.

TABLE 3.4 is adapted from *Age, Sex and Marital Status*, cat. no. 92-901, *Age, Sex, Marital Status and Common-Law Status*, cat. no. 92-325, and *Family over the Life Course*, cat. no. 91-543.

TABLE 3.5 is adapted from *Marriage, Divorce and Mortality, 1988*, cat. no. 84-536, and *The Decline of Marriage in Canada 1981 to 1991, 1996*, cat. no. 84-536.

TABLE 3.6 is adapted from *Family over the Life Course*, cat. no. 91-543.

TABLE 3.7 is adapted from *Age, Sex, Marital Status and Common-Law Status*, cat. no. 92-325, and *The Daily*, cat. no. 11-001, October 14, 1997.

TABLE 3.8 is adapted from *Canadian Families at the Approach of the Year 2000*, cat. no. 96-321, no. 4.

TABLE 4.1 is adapted from *Canadian Social Trends*, cat. no. 11-008, no. 40 and no. 44, and *Historical Statistics of Canada*, cat. no. 11-516.

TABLE 4.2 is adapted from *The Daily*, cat. no. 11-001, May 12, 1998, *Perspectives on Labour and Income*, cat. no. 75-001, vol. 5, no. 2, and *Consumer Prices and Price Indexes*, cat. no. 62-010.

TABLE 4.3 is adapted from *Perspectives on Labour and Income*, cat. no. 75-001, vol. 7, no. 4.

TABLE 4.4 is adapted from *Income Distributions by Size in Canada 1996*, cat. no. 13-207.

TABLE 4.5 is adapted from *The Daily*, cat. no. 11-001, May 12, 1998.

TABLES 4.6 and 4.7 are adapted from *The Labour Force*, cat. no. 71-001.

TABLE 4.8 is adapted from *The Daily*, cat. no. 11-001, May 12, 1998.

TABLE 4.9 is adapted from *Earnings of Men and Women*, cat. no. 13-217.

TABLE 4.10 is adapted from *Family over the Life Course*, cat. no. 91-543.

TABLE 4.11 is adapted from *Family Income in Canada*, cat. no. 96-318.

TABLE 4.12 is adapted from *Income Distributions by Size in Canada 1996*, cat. no. 13-207.

TABLE 4.13 is adapted from *Dimensions of Job-Family Tensions*, cat. no. 89-540.

TABLE 4.14 is adapted from *Perspectives on Labour and Income*, cat. no. 75-001, vol. 7, no. 2.

TABLE 5.1 is adapted from *Households' Unpaid Work: Measurement and Valuation*, cat. no. 13-603, no. 3.

TABLE 5.2 is adapted from *Women in the Workplace*, cat. no. 71-534, *Canadian Social Trends*, cat. no. 11-008, no. 30, and *Where Does Time Go?* cat. no. 11-612, no. 4.

TABLE 5.3 is adapted from *As Time Goes By...: Time Use of Canadians*, cat. no. 89-544.

TABLE 5.5 is reproduced with permission from *La part des pères dans la division du travail domestique au sein des familles canadiennes*, by C. Le Bourdais and A. Sauriol, published by Institut National de la Recherche Scientifique — Urbanisation, Université du Québec.

TABLE 5.7 is adapted from *Women in the Workplace*, cat. no. 71-534.

TABLE 5.8 is adapted from *Parent-Child Exchanges of Supports and Intergenerational Equity*, cat. no. 89-557.

TABLE 6.1 is adapted from *Report on the Demographic Situation in Canada 1996*, cat. no. 91-209.

Table 6.2 is adapted from *Family over the Life Course*, cat. no. 91-543.

TABLE 6.3 is adapted from *Selected Birth and Fertility Statistics, 1921-1990*, cat. no. 82-553, and Statistics Canada, special tabulations.

TABLES 6.4 and 6.5 are adapted from *Family over the Life Course*, cat. no. 91-543.

TABLE 6.6 is adapted from *Family over the Life Course*, cat. no. 91-543, and 1996 Census.

FIGURE 7.1 is adapted from *Canadian Families at the Approach of the Year 2000*, cat. no. 96-321, no. 4.

FIGURE 8.1 is reproduced from *Applied Research Bulletin*, vol. 3, no. 2, with permission from the Minister of Human Resources Development Canada, 1999.

FIGURES 8.2 and 8.3 are reproduced with permission from "One Way to Fight Child Poverty," by K. Battle and L. Muszynski, The Caledon Institute of Social Policy.

BOX 2.2 is adapted with permission from *The Canadian Review of Sociology and Anthropology*, vol. 26, and *Recast Dreams: Class and Gender Consciousness in Steeltown*, edited by D. Livingstone and J.M. Mangan, Garamond Press.

BOX 5.2 is adapted from *Canadian Social Trends*, cat. no. 11-008, no. 42.

BOX 5.6 is adapted with permission from *The Canadian Review of Sociology and Anthropology*, vol. 12, no. 4.

BOX 5.7 is adapted with permission from *Through the Kitchen Window: The Politics of Home and Family*, by M. Luxton, H. Rosenberg, and S. Arat-Koc, Garamond Press.

BOX 6.3 is adapted with permission from M. Rutledge, "Motherhood and the Muse," *The Globe and Mail*, November 7, 1998.

BOX 7.3 is adapted with permission from *The Effect of Children on Parents*, by A.M. Ambert, The Harworth Press.

BOX 7.5 is adapted with permission from "Home Alone: How a Toddler Ended Up on the Street at 2:00 A.M.," *The Globe and Mail*, August 10, 1998.

BOX 8.2 is adapted from *Family Security in Insecure Times*, vol. II, Canadian Council on Social Development.

BOX 8.3 is adapted with permission from "Who Gets to Be a Feminist?" by M. Wente, *The Globe and Mail*, October 9, 1993.

CHAPTER 7 SECTION ON "CHILD CARE" is adapted from R. Beaujot, "Parental Preferences for Work and Child Care," *Canadian Public Policy* vol. 23, no. 3 (1997).

author index

subject index

corporate concentration, 132
couples with children, 238-39;
and income, 287
couples without children, 89,
236, 238-39; attitudes to,
249; and income, 287

day care. *See* child care;
policy; children
demographic transition,
240-42, 246; second
transition, 242
dependency. *See* policy
divorce, 107, 110-14, 125; and
age at marriage, 110, 112-13;
attitudes on, 112, 113; and
children, 111, 114, 120, 295-
96, 296-98; and cohabita-
tion, 100, 111; determinants,
110, 112; economic conse-
quences, 113-14; legislation,
113; rates, 89, 97, 105, 107,
114-15
domestic work. *See* unpaid
work
dual income, 163-64, 168,
222-24, 276

earnings. *See* income
Economic Council of
Canada, 130, 133, 140, 321
education. *See* gender; youth
egalitarian attitudes. *See*
attitudes on gender
elderly: families, 123; income,
170-71; living alone, 117;
and policy, 219, 317; elder
care, 217, 219-22
employment: and marital
status, 41-42, 149, 150-54,
261; non- standard, 44,
138-40; and parental status,
256-62, 276, 279- 80, 294;
and unpaid work, 207,
210-13; youth, 298-300,
302-04
expected fertility. *See* child-
bearing intended

families: attitudes to, 93, 94;
census families, 122; and
children, 118-21, 238-39,
270-76, 306-07; definitions
of, 84, 86-88; diversity
among, 84; income, 141-43,
149, 158, 162, 164; and individual welfare, 40-41; and
public sphere, 27-29, 37,
162- 63, 172-73; reconstituted, 124, 125; size, 235-36.
See also children; cohabitation; lone-parent fa-
milies; theory
family allowance, 336, 340-42,
354-55
family breakup. *See* divorce
family change, 85, 88-89, 92-
93, 95-96, 233-34; cultural
explanations, 91-96, 101-
02; structural explanations,
90-91, 101, 256-58
family policies. *See* policy
family structure, 121-23; and
paid work, 141-43, 158, 162,
164; tends, 85, 88-89. *See
also* lone parents
fathers, 22, 120-21, 126-27. *See
also* child custody; child
support; child care; step-
families
fecundity, 247
Federal, Provincial, and
Territorial Family Law
Committee, 159
femininity. *See* gender
feminism, 22-23, 324-25; and
policy, 328-30; and theory,
34-35
fertility. *See* child-bearing
flex-time, 139, 166

GDP per capita, 316, 319, 321
gender: attitudes, 69-72; and
biology, 54-55, 56; com-
plementarity, 68-69, 71, 91;
and cultural explanations,
66-73; definitions, 49-51;
and earning and caring,

74-80; and education, 56-
60; equality, 71-73; and
family, 17, 42, 77, 79, 80-81,
83; and income, 60-62, 79,
143-46, 148-49, 155-57, 302-
04, 316; and love, 53-54;
and material explanations,
64-66; and mortality, 54-
55; and paid work, 41-43,
53, 144-46, 261, 302-04,
325-26; and play, 56; and
poverty, 61-62; and psy-
chological traits, 55-56;
strategy, 51; system, 79-80;
theory, 52-53, 64-80; and
unpaid work, 76-77, 179-
80, 185, 186, 202-03, 351-56;
and work interruptions,
34, 74-75, 159-62. *See also*
occupations segregation;
policy; violence; theory

home leaving, 97, 98-99, 300-
02; consequences, 75-76,
98-99; explanations, 98
homosexuality. *See* same sex
households, 121-23
household tasks. *See* unpaid
work
housework. *See* unpaid work
Human Resources
Development Canada, 136,
138, 139, 294, 304

income: and child-bearing,
251-52; and children, 153-
54, 159, 166; distribution,
316; and elderly families,
170-71; family, 141; and
family type, 141-43, 158,
162, 164; individual, 141,
148, 153-54; inequality,
136-37, 140, 173; and intergenerational transfer, 291;
and marital status, 144,
159; of men, 136-37, 148-49,
164; of women, 136-37,
148-49, 164; and persons
not in families, 171-72;